Power Programming Techniques™

Excel 5 For Windows Power Programming Techniques is part of the *InfoWorld Techniques* series of books, brought to you by IDG Books Worldwide. The *Power Programming Techniques* books are designed and written for individuals who need to get the most out of their software environment. These titles provide the information you need to take contol of your program's performance. Authorities in their respective areas, the authors of the *Power Programming Techniques* books are professional consultants who share their knowledge of how to get the job done.

The formula for a book in the *Power Programming Techniques* series is simple: Give an expert author a forum to pass on his or her expertise to readers. A *Power Programming Techniques* author, rather than the publishing company, directs the organization, pace, and treatment of the subject matter and focuses the discussion on those items most important to the developer and consultant. Our authors are working consultants who use the knowledge they present in this book on a daily basis. The authors' close contact with the needs of computer professionals and the business world as well as their knowledge of the changes in the computer industry give the *Power Programming Techniques* books a strategic advantage over most computer books. Our authors do not distance themselves from the reality of daily computing; instead, they immerse themselves in the process of developing new computer applications and intergrating their knowledge into the business world.

We believe that the author has the experience to approach a topic in the most efficient manner, and we know that you, the reader, will benefit from a "one-to-one" relationship, through the text, with the author. The author's voice — and experience — is always evident in a *Power Programming Techniques* book.

And of course, the author is free to include or recommend useful software, both shareware and proprietary, in a *Power Programming Techniques* book. The software that accompanies a *Power Programming Techniques* book is not intended as casual filler. The software is strategically linked to the content, theme, or procedures of the book. In many of the *Power Programming Techniques* titles, the enclosed disk also includes all of the programming code presented in the text, giving you an immediate gain in productivity as you work your way through the material.

Whether you read it cover to cover, section to section, or simply a topic at a time, you deserve the comprehensive and informative resource of answers that *Excel 5 For Windows Power Programming Techniques* delivers.

Karen A. Bluestein
Publisher

INFO WORLD

Excel 5 For Windows Power Programming Techniques

INFO WORLD

Excel 5 For Windows Power Programming Techniques

by John Walkenbach

Forward by
Craig Stinson

IDG BOOKS

IDG Books Worldwide, Inc.
An International Data Group Company

Foster City, CA ♦ Chicago, IL ♦ Indianapolis, IN
Braintree, MA ♦ Dallas, TX

Excel 5 for Windows Power Programming Techniques

Published by
IDG Books Worldwide, Inc.
An International Data Group Company
919 E. Hillsdale Blvd.
Suite 400
Foster City, CA 94404

Library of Congress Catalog Card No.: 94-79828

ISBN: 1-56884-303-8

Printed in the United States of America

10 9 8 7 6 5 4 3 2 1

1B/RR/QR/ZU

Distributed in the United States by IDG Books Worldwide, Inc.

Distributed in Canada by Macmillan of Canada, a Division of Canada Publishing Corporation; by Computer and Technical Books in Miami, Florida, for South America and the Caribbean; by Longman Singapore in Singapore, Malaysia, Thailand, and Korea; by Toppan Co. Ltd. in Japan; by Asia Computerworld in Hong Kong; by Woodslane Pty. Ltd. in Australia and New Zealand; and by Transworld Publishers Ltd. in the U.K. and Europe.

For general information on IDG books in the U.S., including information on discounts and premiums, contact IDG Books 800-434-3422 or 415-312-0650.

For information on where to purchase IDG Books outside the U.S., contact Christina Turner at 415-312-0650.

For information on translations, contact Marc Jeffrey Mikulich, Director, Foreign & Subsidiary Rights, at IDG Books Worldwide, 415-312-0650.

For sales inquiries and special prices for bulk quantities, write to the address above or call IDG Books Worldwide at 415-312-0650.

For information on using IDG Books in the classroom, or ordering examination copies, contact Jim Kelly at 800-434-2086.

About the Author

John Walkenbach is one of the country's leading authorities on spreadsheet software. He's principal of JWalk and Associates Inc., a Southern California-based consulting firm that specializes in spreadsheet application development. John is also a shareware developer; his most recent product is the Power Utility Pak add-in for Excel. John has written more than 250 articles and reviews for publications such as *PC World, InfoWorld, Windows*, and *PC/Computing*. In addition, he's authored a dozen spreadsheet books, including *PC World Excel 5 for Windows Handbook*, and *Excel For Windows For Dummies Quick Reference*. When he's not banging away on his computer keyboard, he's probably banging away at a synthesizer keyboard, trying to compose decent music with the help of his MIDI software.

ABOUT IDG BOOKS WORLDWIDE

Welcome to the world of IDG Books Worldwide.

IDG Books Worldwide, Inc. is a subsidiary of International Data Group, the world's largest publisher of business and computer-related information and the leading global provider of information services on information technology. IDG was founded more than 25 years ago and now employs more than 7,000 people worldwide. IDG publishes more than 220 computer publications in 65 countries (see listing below). More than fifty million people read one or more IDG publications each month.

Launched in 1990, IDG Books Worldwide is today the fastest-growing publisher of computer and business books in the United States. We are proud to have received 3 awards from the Computer Press Association in recognition of editorial excellence, and our best-selling *...For Dummies*™ series has more than 12 million copies in print with translations in more than 24 languages. IDG Books, through a recent joint venture with IDG's Hi-Tech Beijing, became the first U.S. publisher to publish a computer book in the People's Republic of China. In record time, IDG Books has become the first choice for millions of readers around the world who want to learn how to better manage their businesses.

Our mission is simple: Every IDG book is designed to bring extra value and skill-building instructions to the reader. Our books are written by experts who understand and care about our readers. The knowledge base of our editorial staff comes from years of experience in publishing, education, and journalism — experience which we use to produce books for the '90s. In short, we care about books, so we attract the best people. We devote special attention to details such as audience, interior design, use of icons, and illustrations. And because we use an efficient process of authoring, editing, and desktop publishing our books electronically, we can spend more time ensuring superior content and spend less time on the technicalities of making books.

You can count on our commitment to deliver high-quality books at competitive prices on topics consumers want to read about. At IDG, we value quality, and we have been delivering quality for more than 25 years. You'll find no better book on a subject than an IDG book.

John Kilcullen
President and CEO
IDG Books Worldwide, Inc.

VIII
WINNER
Eighth Annual Computer Press Awards 1992

IX
WINNER
Ninth Annual Computer Press Awards 1993

IDG BOOKS

IDG Books Worldwide, Inc. is a subsidiary of International Data Group, the world's largest publisher of computer-related information and the leading global provider of information services on information technology. International Data Group publishes over 220 computer publications in 65 countries. More than fifty million people read one or more International Data Group publications each month. The officers are Patrick J. McGovern, Founder and Board Chairman; Kelly Conlin, President; Jim Casella, Chief Operating Officer. International Data Group's publications include: **ARGENTINA'S** Computerworld Argentina, Infoworld Argentina; **AUSTRALIA'S** Computerworld Australia, Computer Living, Australian PC World, Australian Macworld, Network World, Mobile Business Australia, Publish!, Reseller, IDG Sources; **AUSTRIA'S** Computerwelt Oesterreich, PC Test; **BELGIUM'S** Data News (CW); **BOLIVIA'S** Computerworld; **BRAZIL'S** Computerworld, Connections, Game Power, Mundo Unix, PC World, Publish, Super Game; **BULGARIA'S** Computerworld Bulgaria, PC & Mac World Bulgaria, Network World Bulgaria; **CANADA'S** CIO Canada, Computerworld Canada, InfoCanada, Network World Canada, Reseller; **CHILE'S** Computerworld Chile, Informatica; **COLOMBIA'S** Computerworld Colombia, PC World; **COSTA RICA'S** PC World; **CZECH REPUBLIC'S** Computerworld, Elektronika, PC World; **DENMARK'S** Communications World, Computerworld Danmark, Computerworld Focus, Macintosh Produktkatalog, Macworld Danmark, PC World Danmark, PC Produktguide, Tech World, Windows World; **ECUADOR'S** PC World Ecuador; **EGYPT'S** Computerworld (CW) Middle East, PC World Middle East; **FINLAND'S** MikroPC, Tietoviikko, Tietoverkko; **FRANCE'S** Distributique, GOLDEN MAC, InfoPC, Le Guide du Monde Informatique, Le Monde Informatique, Telecoms & Reseaux; **GERMANY'S** Computerwoche, Computerwoche Focus, Computerwoche Extra, Electronic Entertainment, Gamepro, Information Management, Macwelt, Netzwelt, PC Welt, Publish, Publish; **GREECE'S** Publish & Macworld; **HONG KONG'S** Computerworld Hong Kong, PC World Hong Kong; **HUNGARY'S** Computerworld SZT, PC World; **INDIA'S** Computers & Communications; **INDONESIA'S** Info Komputer; **IRELAND'S** ComputerScope; **ISRAEL'S** Beyond Windows, Computerworld Israel, Multimedia, PC World Israel; **ITALY'S** Computerworld Italia, Lotus Magazine, Macworld Italia, Networking Italia, PC Shopping Italy, PC World Italia; **JAPAN'S** Computerworld Today, Information Systems World, Macworld Japan, Nikkei Personal Computing, SunWorld Japan, Windows World; **KENYA'S** East African Computer News; **KOREA'S** Computerworld Korea, Macworld Korea, PC World Korea; **LATIN AMERICA'S** GamePro; **MALAYSIA'S** Computerworld Malaysia, PC World Malaysia; **MEXICO'S** Compu Edicion, Compu Manufactura, Computacion/Punto de Venta, Computerworld Mexico, MacWorld, Mundo Unix, PC World, Windows; **THE NETHERLANDS'** Computer! Totaal, Computable (CW), LAN Magazine, Lotus Magazine, MacWorld; **NEW ZEALAND'S** Computer Buyer, Computerworld New Zealand, Network World, New Zealand PC World; **NIGERIA'S** PC World Africa; **NORWAY'S** Computerworld Norge, Lotusworld Norge, Macworld Norge, Maxi Data, Networld, PC World Ekspress, PC World Nettverk, PC World Norge, PC World's Produktguide, Publish& Multimedia World, Student Data, Unix World, Windowsworld; **PAKISTAN'S** PC World Pakistan; **PANAMA'S** PC World Panama; **PERU'S** Computerworld Peru, PC World; **PEOPLE'S REPUBLIC OF CHINA'S** China Computerworld, China Infoworld, China PC Info Magazine, Computer Fan, PC World China, Electronics International, Electronics Today/Multimedia World, Electronic Product World, China Network World, Software World Magazine, Telecom Product World, **PHILIPPINES'** Computerworld Philippines, PC Digest (PCW); **POLAND'S** Computerworld Poland, Computerworld Special Report, Networld, PC World/Komputer, Sunworld; **PORTUGAL'S** Cerebro/PC World, Correio Informatico/Computerworld, MacIn; **ROMANIA'S** Computerworld, PC World, Telecom Romania; **RUSSIA'S** Computerworld-Moscow, Mir - PK (PCW), Sety (Networks); **SINGAPORE'S** Computerworld Southeast Asia, PC World Singapore; **SLOVENIA'S** Monitor Magazine; **SOUTH AFRICA'S** Computer Mail (CIO),Computing S.A.,Network World S.A., Software World; **SPAIN'S** Advanced Systems, Amiga World, Computerworld Espana, Communicaciones World, Macworld Espana, NeXTWORLD, Super Juegos Magazine (GamePro), PC World Espana, Publish; **SWEDEN'S** Attack, ComputerSweden, Corporate Computing, Macworld, Mikrodatorn, Natverk & Kommunikation, PC World, CAP & Design, Datalngenjoren, Maxi Data,Windows World; **SWITZERLAND'S** Computerworld Schweiz, Macworld Schweiz, PC Tip; **TAIWAN'S** Computerworld Taiwan, PC World Taiwan; **THAILAND'S** Thai Computerworld; **TURKEY'S** Computerworld Monitor, Macworld Turkiye, PC World Turkiye; **UKRAINE'S** Computerworld, Computers+Software Magazine; **UNITED KINGDOM'S** Computing /Computerworld, Connexion/Network World, Lotus Magazine, Macworld, Open Computing/ Sunworld; **URAGUAY'S** PC World Uraguay; **UNITED STATES'** Advanced Systems, AmigaWorld, Cable in the Classroom, CD Review, CIO, Computerworld, Computerworld Client/Server Journal, Digital Video, DOS World, Electronic Entertainment Magazine (E2), Federal Computer Week, Game Hits, GamePro, IDG Books, Infoworld, Laser Event, Macworld, Maximize, Multimedia World, Network World, PC Letter, PC World, Publish, SWATPro, Video Event; **VENEZUELA'S** Computerworld Venezuela, PC World; **VIETNAM'S** PC World Vietnam.

Dedication

For VaRene

Acknowledgments

I've written several books in the past few years, but this one is my favorite by far. I devoted several months, full time, to writing it, but the book is really based on knowledge that I've gleaned over the past decade using a variety of spreadsheet software. In my humble opinion, Excel 5 has taken spreadsheets to a new level. My thanks to the Redmond folks for developing such a fine product. A company the size of Microsoft is an easy target for the critics, but my experiences with the Excel group have been uniformly impressive. I can't wait for Excel 6.

This book is in your hands right now because of the talented people at IDG Books. I'm proud to be associated with this publisher, and I'm continually impressed with quality of their employees. Many thanks to Mary Corder and Shawn MacLaren, editors extraordinaire, for correcting the "grammatic mistakes and spelling erors, eliminating, removing and deleting lots of extra redundancy, and helping me write gooder than I did." Also, I'm indebted to Ellen Finkelstein for her thorough technical review of the manuscript. She caught quite a few errors, and made many good suggestions.

The ideas for many of the topics in this book came from two sources: The Excel VBA Forum on CompuServe, and the comp.apps.spreadsheets Usenet group on the Internet. Thanks to all who frequent these services. Your problems were the inspiration for more than a few of the examples I present in this book.

Several people read early drafts of the chapters and provided constructive feedback. My thanks to Jay Hardymon, a friend and client, for several good suggestions — and for leaving me alone during the final weeks of writing. I'd also like to acknowledge my Florida-based e-mail buddy, Glenn Daily. Although we've never met, Glenn and I have a long history of e-mail, and I feel at least partially responsible for turning him on to Excel. Thanks also to Keyuan Jiang of Vanderbilt University (another faceless e-mail pal) for his keen insights on the beta version of the Power Utility Pak (a product I developed in order to learn VBA).

I'd also like to acknowledge Nicholson Baker, an extraordinary novelist whose works I recently discovered. His books, which I recommend highly, provided a welcome diversion during the course of this project. Finally, special thanks to my best friend VaRene, who provided moral support and endured my 15-hour workdays without complaint — well, most of the time.

(The publisher would like to give special thanks to Patrick J. McGovern, without whom this book would not have been possible.)

Credits

Publisher
Karen A. Bluestein

Managing Editor
Mary Bednarek

Associate Acquisitions Editor
Megg Bonar

Production Director
Beth Jenkins

Senior Editors
Tracy L. Barr
Sandra Blackthorn
Diane Graves Steele

Production Coordinator
Cindy L. Phipps

Pre-Press Coordinator
Steve Peake

Associate Acquisitions Editor
Suki Gear

Assistant to the Managing Editor
Jodi Thorn

Project Editor
Mary C. Corder

Editors
Kezia Endsley
Shawn MacLaren

Editorial Assistant
Tamara S. Castleman

Technical Reviewer
Ellen Finkelstein

Production Staff
Tony Augsburger
Linda M. Boyer
Dwight Ramsey
Carla Radzikinas
Patricia R. Reynolds
Gina Scott
Kathie Schnorr

Proofreader
Alys Caviness-Brosius

Indexer
Liz Cunningham

Cover Design
Kavish + Kavish

Contents at a Glance

Table of Contents

Part III:Understanding Visual Basic for Applications ... 105

Chapter 6: Introducing Visual Basic for Applications 107

Chapter 15: Creating Custom Toolbars 441

Chapter 16: Providing Help for Your Applications 467

Foreword

Over the past decade, I've watched spreadsheet software evolve at a rapid clip. Microsoft Excel has contributed quite a bit to the spreadsheet gene pool, and continues to offer innovative features that are not found in other products. Many of these features relate to the process of application development. Excel's new Visual Basic for Applications (VBA) raises the standard for macro languages to a new level.

Excel 5 for Windows Power Programming Techniques will teach you how to use this new language — but it's not just another VBA tutorial. This book is filled with useful examples and creative techniques that you can apply to your own work. It emphasizes practical solutions to the real problems spreadsheet developers face. Even a quick browse through the book will almost certainly give you some new insights and help you hone your application development skills.

John Walkenbach has been involved with spreadsheets since the early days of VisiCalc, and has used Excel's VBA language since the initial betas of Excel 5. This experience comes through loud and clear in the pages of this book. John shares his knowledge of Excel and offers dozens of tips and techniques that will reduce your frustration level and help you get up to speed quickly.

Bottom line? If you want to create better spreadsheet applications using Excel, you're reading the right book. Enjoy.

Craig Stinson
Contributing Editor, *PC Magazine*

Introduction

Welcome to *Excel 5 For Windows Power Programming Techniques*. If your job involves developing spreadsheets that others will use —or if you simply want to get the most out of Excel 5 for Windows — you've come to the right place. By reading this book, you can expand your programming horizons and gain a new appreciation for this impressive product.

My experience tells me that many spreadsheet users spend much of their time creating spreadsheets that other people use. Increasingly, spreadsheets designed in applications like Excel, 1-2-3, and Quattro Pro are suitable for situations that once required a custom program written in a traditional programming language. Thanks to their macro and customization features, these products now can serve as development platforms for many types of applications. In this book, I cover every aspect of application development using Excel 5.

Why I Wrote This Book

As *InfoWorld*'s sole spreadsheet reviewer for the past eight years, I've seen spreadsheets evolve from simple accounting worksheets to incredibly powerful applications. During the summer of 1993, while I (along with David Maguiness) revised the *PC World Excel For Windows Handbook*, I began receiving prerelease copies of Excel 5 from Microsoft. As I explored the new version, I realized that it pushes the spreadsheet envelope to new levels. In other words, it goes well beyond what most people consider to be the realm of spreadsheet software. I was particularly impressed with the new capabilities in the area of application development, especially the new Visual Basic for Applications (VBA) macro language.

I've used Excel for Windows since it was first released in 1987. Although Excel has always been the premier Windows spreadsheet, it didn't become my favorite until Version 3 arrived. Despite some recent stiff competition from Quattro Pro and 1-2-3, Excel is still the sheet to beat; Version 5 offers many advantages over its competitors, especially for advanced users.

Quite a few VBA books exist, but this is the first book that deals with application development from a larger perspective — VBA is just one component, albeit a fairly large component. Excel is an extremely deep software product: It has many interesting features that lurk in the background — the typical user doesn't even know about them. And some of the well-known features can be used in novel ways.

Millions of people throughout the world use Excel. But as I monitored the Excel VBA Forum on CompuServe, as well as the comp.apps.spreadsheets Usenet group on the Internet, it became clear to me that people need (and want) help in the areas that this book covers. My guess is that five percent of Excel users really understand what the product is capable of. In this book, I attempt to nudge you into that elite company. Are you up to it?

What You Need to Know

This is not a book for beginning Excel users. If you have no experience with Excel, I recommend that you read either of the following books:

- *Excel For Dummies,* by Greg Harvey, written for users who want to know just enough to get by — and want to be entertained in the process.
- *PC World Excel 5 For Windows Handbook* (by yours truly, along with David Maguiness) covers all of the basic features of Excel. It is meant for beginning to intermediate users.

To get the most out of this book, you should be an experienced Excel for Windows user. I didn't write too many pages on basic how-to information. In fact, I assume that you know

- How to create workbooks, save files, and so on
- How to navigate through a workbook
- How to use the menus and shortcut menus
- How to manage Excel's toolbars
- How to enter formulas
- How to use Excel's worksheet functions
- How to name cells and ranges
- How to use basic Windows features, such as the Clipboard

If you don't pass the preceding test, you may find some of this material over your head, so consider yourself warned.

If you're an experienced spreadsheet user who hasn't used Excel 5, Chapter 2 presents a short overview of what this product offers.

What You Need to Have

To make the best use of this book, you obviously need a copy of Microsoft Excel 5 for Windows. To run Excel 5, you need a copy of Windows 3.1 (or later).

Any system that can run Windows will suffice, but you'll be much better off with a 486 or a Pentium-based machine with plenty of memory. (I recommend at least 16MB of RAM.) Excel is a large program and using it on a slower system can be extremely frustrating.

When you use multisheet workbooks, you often will want to view different sheets in separate windows. As a result, I recommend using a high-resolution video driver (800 x 600 is okay, but 1024 x 768 is ideal). A standard VGA resolution will do in a pinch, but it just doesn't let you see enough on-screen.

Conventions in This Book

Take a minute to skim this section and learn some of the typographic conventions used throughout this book.

Keyboard conventions

You need to use the keyboard to enter data. In addition, you can work with menus and dialog boxes directly from the keyboard — a method you may find easier if your hands are already positioned over the keys.

Input

Input that you type from the keyboard appears in boldface — for example, enter **=SUM(B2: B50)** into cell B51.

More lengthy input usually appears on a separate line in `monospace font`. For example, I may instruct you to enter the formula

```
=VLOOKUP(STOCKNUMBER,PRICELIST,2)
```

VBA code

This book contains many snippets of VBA code. Each listing appears in a `monospace font`; each line of code sits on a separate line. (I copied these listings directly from the VBA module and pasted them into my word processor.) To make the code easier to read, I often use a tab to create an indentation. Indentation is optional, but it does help to delineate statements that go together.

If a line of code doesn't fit on a single line in this book, I use the standard VBA line continuation sequence: at the end of the line, a space followed by an underscore character indicates that the line of code extends to the next line. For example, the following is actually a single line of code:

```
MsgBox "The bottom right corner is in cell " & _
 Worksheets(1).TextBoxes(1).BottomRightCell.Address
```

You can enter this code either exactly as shown on two lines or on a single line without the underscore character.

Key names

Names of keys on the keyboard appear in normal type. When you should press two keys simultaneously, the keys are connected with a plus sign: "Press Alt+E to select the Edit menu." Here's a list of the key names I refer to throughout the book:

Alt	Down arrow	Num Lock	Right arrow
Backspace	End	Pause	Scroll Lock
Caps Lock	Home	PgDn	Shift
Ctrl	Insert	PgUp	Tab
Del	Left arrow	Print Screen	Up arrow

Functions, filenames, and named ranges

Excel's worksheet functions appear in all uppercase, like so: "Enter a SUM formula in cell C20." Filenames (such as BUDGET.XLS) and named ranges (such as PRICELIST) appear as all capital letters, as well.

Macro and procedure names appear in normal type: "Execute the GetTotals procedure." I often used mixed upper- and lowercase to make these names easier to read.

Mouse conventions

I assume that you're using a mouse or some other pointing device. If you shun such tools, I leave it to you to translate my mouse-oriented commands into their keyboard equivalents. However, some actions in Excel require a mouse (using the toolbars and manipulating graphics objects, for example). The mouse terminology I use is all standard fare: pointing, clicking, dragging, and so on.

What the Icons Mean

Throughout the book, I've used *icons*, in the left margin to call your attention to points that are particularly important.

I use Note icons to tell you that something is important — perhaps a concept that may help you master the task at hand or something fundamental for understanding subsequent material.

Tip icons indicate a more efficient way of doing something, or a technique that may not be obvious.

These icons indicate that an example file is on the companion disk (see the "About the Companion Disk" section, later in the intro). This 3.5-inch disk holds many of the examples that I cover in the book, as well as other utilities you may find useful and instructive.

I use Caution icons when the operation that I'm describing can cause problems if you're not careful.

I use the Cross Reference icon to refer you to other chapters that have more to say on a subject.

How This Book Is Organized

There are hundreds of ways to organize this material, but I settled on a scheme that divides the book into four main parts plus, I've included a few appendices that provide supplemental information.

Part I: Some Essential Background

In this part, I set the stage for the rest of the book. Chapter 1 presents a brief history of spreadsheets so that you can see how Excel fits into the big picture. In Chapter 2, I offer a conceptual overview of Excel 5 — quite useful for experienced spreadsheet users who are switching to Excel. In Chapter 3, I detail the ins and outs of the various files used and generated by Excel.

Part II: Excel Application Development

This part consists of just two chapters. In Chapter 4, I broadly discuss the concept of a spreadsheet application. Chapter 5 goes into more detail and covers the steps typically involved in a spreadsheet application development project.

Part III: Understanding Visual Basic for Applications

Chapters 6 through 13 make up this part, and they include everything you need to know to learn VBA. In this part, I introduce you to VBA, provide programming fundamentals, and detail how to develop VBA subroutines and functions. In Chapter 10, I tell you how to create custom dialog boxes, while Chapter 11 describes interesting and useful VBA techniques, Chapter 12 talks about VBA utilities, and Chapter 13, which rounds out the part, discusses the creation and use of add-ins.

Part IV: Putting It All Together

The final part ties the previous information together. Chapters 14 through 16 cover custom menus, toolbars, and help files. In Chapter 17, I reveal methods for interacting with other applications. For those hungry for more, I list additional resources at your disposal and then conclude with a chapter full of common questions and answers about application development with Excel.

Part V: Appendixes

Six appendices round out the book. Appendix A summarizes the Excel 5 object model, and Appendix B is a comprehensive listing of all objects, methods, and properties. Appendix C contains a complete list of all constants defined in Excel and VBA, and Appendix D is a reference guide to all of VBA's statements and functions. I explain VBA error codes in Appendix E, and Appendix F is a handy ANSI code reference chart.

About the Companion Disk

The inside back cover of this book contains one 3½-inch high-density diskette. Whatever you do, don't ignore this disk; it holds many useful examples.

When I write about computer-related material, I emphasize learning by example. I know that I learn more from a well-thought-out example than from reading a dozen pages in a book. I assume that this is true for many other people. Consequently, I spent more time developing the examples on the companion disk than I did writing chapters.

The files on the companion disk are compressed, so you'll have to install them before you can use them. You'll find installation instructions on the last page of this book.

About the Power Utility Pak Offer

Towards the back of the book, you'll find a coupon that you can redeem for a free copy of my Power Utility Pak software — a collection of 17 useful Excel utilities, plus 17 new worksheet functions. I developed this package using VBA exclusively.

I think you'll find this product useful in your day-to-day work with Excel, and I urge you to take advantage of this free offer. Chapter 12 briefly describes the Power Utility Pak's features.

How to Use This Book

You can use this book any way you please. If you choose to read it cover to cover, be my guest. But because I'm dealing with intermediate-to-advanced subject matter, the chapter order is immaterial. I suspect that most readers will skip around, picking up useful tidbits here and there. If you're faced with a challenging task, you may try the index first to see whether your problem is specifically addressed.

Reach Out

The publisher and I want your feedback. After you have had a chance to use this book, please take a moment to complete the IDG Books Worldwide Registration Card (in the back of the book). Please be honest with your evaluation. If you thought a particular chapter didn't tell you enough, let me know. Of course, I would prefer to receive comments like "This is the best book I've ever read" or "Thanks to this book, I was promoted and now make $150,000 a year."

You can contact me care of IDG Books Worldwide with your comments, suggestions, or questions. If you prefer, you can reach me directly at any of the following e-mail locations:

- Internet (jwalk@crash.cts.com)
- CompuServe (70363,3014)
- MCI Mail (329-9078)
- America Online ("Walkenbach")

Feel free to send me specific questions regarding the material in this book (e-mail only, please). I'll do my best to help you out and answer your questions.

Part I

Some Essential Background

The three chapters in this section provide some useful background information about Excel 5 and spreadsheets in general. In Chapter 1, you get a brief history of spreadsheets, with insights as to why Excel is superior. Chapter 2 provides a quick-and-dirty overview of using Excel, complete with lots of tips and helpful suggestions. Chapter 3 cues you in on many details about the files used and generated by Excel — important information for application developers.

Chapter 1

Excel 5: Where It Came From

In This Chapter

- A historical digression about spreadsheets — where they came from, who makes them, and what differentiates them
- A discussion of Excel's various versions
- An analysis of why Excel is the best spreadsheet available for developers

A Brief History of Spreadsheets

To fully appreciate the application development features available in Excel 5, it's important to understand where this product came from and how it fits into the overall scheme of spreadsheets. You probably weren't planning on a history lesson when you bought this book, but bear with me. (Of course, if you've worked with personal computers over the past decade, this information may be old hat; you can safely skip it.)

And if you're a trivia buff, this chapter is a gold mine; you'll be the toast of your next spreadsheet-trivia party.

It all started with VisiCalc

Spreadsheets are a billion-dollar business, but most of us tend to take this software for granted. In fact, it may be hard to fathom, but there really was a time when spreadsheets were not available. People used clumsy mainframes or calculators and spent hours doing what now takes minutes.

The world's first electronic spreadsheet, VisiCalc, was conjured up by Dan Bricklin and Bob Frankston back in the late 1970s, when personal computers were unheard of in the office environment. VisiCalc was written for the Apple II computer, an interesting little machine that is something of a toy by today's standards. But in its day, the Apple II kept me mesmerized for days at a time. VisiCalc caught on quickly, and many forward-looking companies purchased the Apple II for the sole purpose of developing their budgets with VisiCalc. Consequently, VisiCalc is often credited for much of the Apple II's initial success.

In the meantime, another class of personal computers was evolving; these PCs ran the CP/M operating system. A company called Sorcim developed SuperCalc, a spreadsheet that also attracted a legion of followers.

When the IBM PC arrived on the scene in 1982, legitimizing personal computers, VisiCorp wasted no time porting VisiCalc to this new hardware environment. Sorcim soon followed with a PC version of SuperCalc.

By today's standards, both VisiCalc and SuperCalc were very crude. For example, text entered into a cell could not extend beyond the cell — a lengthy title had to be entered into multiple cells. Nevertheless, the capability to automate the budgeting tedium was enough to lure thousands of accountants from paper ledger sheets to floppy disks.

Lotus 1-2-3

Envious of VisiCalc's success, a small group of computer freaks at a start-up company in Cambridge, Massachusetts, refined the spreadsheet concept. Headed by Mitch Kapor and Jonathon Sachs, they designed a new product and launched the software industry's first full-fledged marketing blitz. Released in January 1983, Lotus Development Corporation's 1-2-3 was an instant success. Despite its $495 price tag, it quickly outsold VisiCalc, rocketing to the top of the sales charts, where it remained for many years — it was, perhaps, the most popular application ever.

Lotus 1-2-3 not only improved on all the basics embodied in VisiCalc and SuperCalc, but it was the first program to take advantage of the new and unique features found in the powerful 16-bit IBM PC. For example, 1-2-3 avoided the slower DOS calls and wrote text directly to display memory, giving it a snappy and responsive feel that was unusual for the time. The on-line help system was a breakthrough, and the ingenious "moving bar" menu style set the standard for many years. The one feature that really set 1-2-3 apart, though, was its macro capability, a powerful tool that allowed spreadsheet users to automate many procedures.

1-2-3 was not the first *integrated* package, but it was the first successful one. It combined (1) a powerful electronic spreadsheet with (2) elementary graphics and (3) some limited but handy database features. Easy as 1, 2, 3 — get it?

Lotus followed up the original 1-2-3 Release 1 with Release 1A in June of 1983. This product enjoyed tremendous success and put Lotus in the enviable position of virtually owning the spreadsheet market. In September 1985, Release 1A was replaced by Release 2, a major upgrade that was superseded by the bug-fixed Release 2.01 the following July. Release 2 introduced *add-ins*, special-purpose programs that can be attached to give an application new features and extend the application's useful life. Release 2 also had improved memory management, more @functions, four times as many rows as its predecessor, and added support for a math coprocessor. It also enhanced the macro language, whose popularity exceeded the developers' wildest dreams.

Not surprisingly, the success of 1-2-3 spawned many *clones* — work-alike products that usually offered a few additional features and at a much lower price. Among the more notable were Paperback Software's VP Planner series and Mosaic Software's Twin. Lotus eventually took legal action against Paperback software for copyright infringement (for copying the "look and feel" of 1-2-3); the successful suit essentially put Paperback out of business.

In the summer of 1989, Lotus shipped DOS and OS/2 versions of the long-delayed 1-2-3 Release 3. This product literally added a dimension to the familiar row-and-column-based spreadsheet; it extended the paradigm by adding multiple spreadsheet pages. The idea wasn't really new, however: a relatively obscure product called Boeing Calc originated the 3-D spreadsheet concept, and SuperCalc 5 and CubeCalc also incorporated it.

Release 3 offered features that users wanted, features that ultimately became standard fare: multilayered worksheets, the ability to work with multiple files simultaneously, file linking, improved graphics, and direct access to external database files. But it still lacked an important feature that users were begging for: a way to produce high-quality output.

Release 3 began life with a reduced market potential because it required an 80286-based PC and a minimum of 1 MB of RAM — fairly hefty requirements in 1989. But Lotus had an ace up its corporate sleeve. Concurrent with the shipping of Release 3, the company surprised nearly everyone by announcing an upgrade of Release 2.01 (the product materialized a few months later as 1-2-3 Release 2.2). Release 3 was *not* a replacement for Release 2, as most analysts had expected. Rather, Lotus made the brilliant move of splitting the spreadsheet market into two segments: those with high-end hardware and those with more mundane equipment.

Release 2.2 wasn't a panacea for spreadsheet buffs, but it was a significant improvement. The most important Release 2.2 feature was Allways, an add-in that gave users the ability to churn out attractive reports, complete with multiple typefaces, borders, and shading. In addition, users could view the results on-screen in a WYSIWYG (*what you see is what you get*) manner. However, Allways didn't let you issue any worksheet commands while you viewed and formatted your work in WYSIWYG mode. Despite this rather severe limitation, most 1-2-3 users were overjoyed with this new capability, for they could finally produce near-typeset-quality output.

Microsoft's release of Windows 3.0 in May 1990 changed the way people used personal computers. Lotus was slow getting out of the gate with its first Windows spreadsheet, 1-2-3 for Windows; it wasn't introduced until late 1991. Worse, this product was, in short, a dud. It didn't really capitalize on the

Windows environment and disappointed many users. Consequently, Excel became the overwhelming Windows spreadsheet market leader. Lotus came back with 1-2-3 Release 4 for Windows in June 1993 — a vast improvement over the original. Release 5 for Windows (see Figure 1-1) appeared in mid-1994.

In mid-1994, Lotus unveiled 1-2-3 Release 4.0 for DOS. Many analysts (including myself) expected a product more compatible with the Windows product. But we were wrong; DOS Release 4.0 is simply an upgraded version of Release 3.4. Because of the widespread acceptance of Windows, this should be the last DOS version of 1-2-3 to see the light of day.

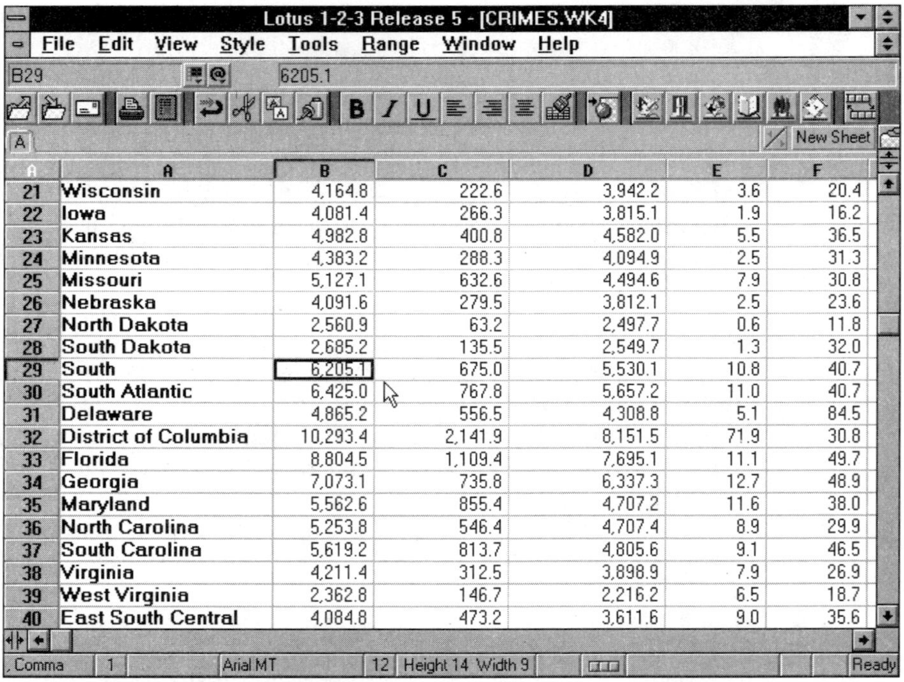

Figure 1-1: Lotus 1-2-3 Release 5 for Windows.

Borland's spreadsheets

The other major player in the spreadsheet world was Borland International. (When Novell recently purchased both WordPerfect International and Borland's entire spreadsheet business, Borland ceased to be a player in the spreadsheet game — although Quattro Pro for Windows remains a heavy hitter.) Borland started out in spreadsheets in 1987 with a product called Quattro. Essentially a clone of 1-2-3, Quattro offered a few additional features and an arguably better menu system. And it was also much cheaper. Importantly, users could opt for a 1-2-3-like menu system that let them use familiar commands and also ensured compatibility with 1-2-3 macros.

As a result of a recent lawsuit between Lotus and Borland, which Lotus won, none of the Quattro Pro series of spreadsheets include 1-2-3 macro compatibility or the 1-2-3 menu option.

In the fall of 1989, Borland began shipping Quattro Pro, a more powerful product that built upon the original Quattro and trumped 1-2-3 in just about every area. For example, the first Quattro Pro let you work with multiple worksheets in movable and resizable windows — although it did *not* have a graphical user interface (GUI). More trivia: Quattro Pro was based on an obscure product called Surpass, which Borland acquired.

Released in late 1990, Version 2.0 added 3-D graphs and a link to Borland's Paradox database. A mere six months later — much to the chagrin of Quattro Pro book authors — Version 3.0 appeared and featured an optional graphical user interface and a slide show feature. In the spring of 1992, Version 4 appeared with customizable SpeedBars and an innovative analytical graphics feature. Version 5, which came out in 1994, had only one significant new feature: worksheet notebooks (that is, 3-D worksheets).

Like Lotus, Borland was slow to jump on the Windows bandwagon. When Quattro Pro for Windows finally shipped in the fall of 1992, however, it provided some tough competition for the other two Windows spreadsheets, Excel 4.0 and 1-2-3 Release 1.1 for Windows. Importantly, Quattro Pro for Windows has an innovative feature, known as the UI Builder, that lets developers and advanced users easily create custom user interfaces.

Borland followed up the original Quattro Pro for Windows with Version 5, which was upgraded to Version 6 after Novell took over Borland's spreadsheet business (see Figure 1-2). For a while, Quattro Pro for Windows seemed the ultimate solution for spreadsheet developers. But then Excel 5 arrived.

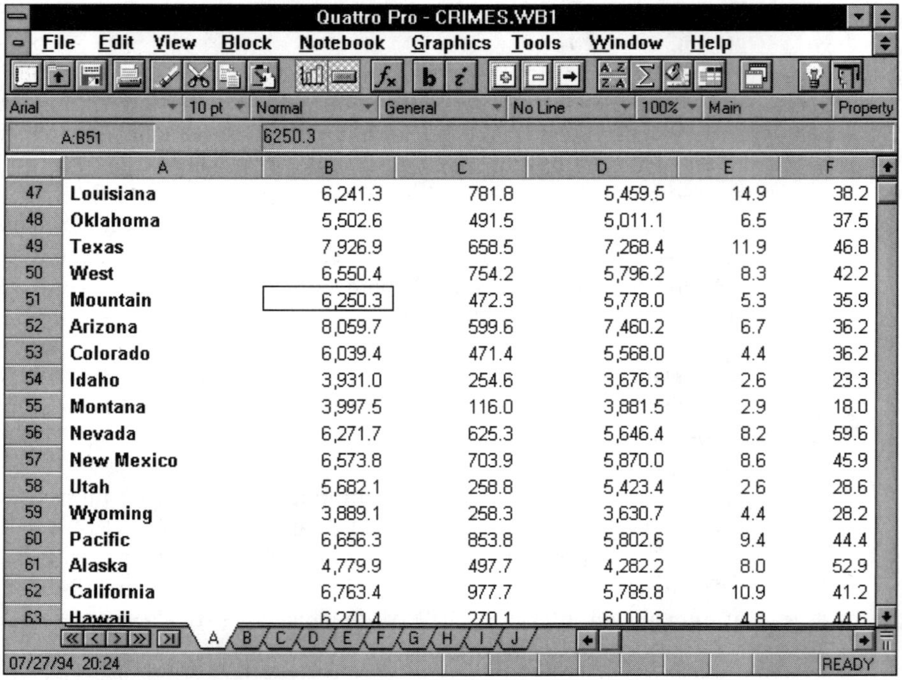

Figure 1-2: Quattro Pro for Windows.

Microsoft Excel

And now on to the good stuff.

Most people don't realize that Microsoft's experience with spreadsheets goes back more than a decade. Over the years, Microsoft's spreadsheet offerings have come a long way, from the barely adequate MultiPlan to the state-of-the-art Excel 5.

In 1982, the company released its first spreadsheet, MultiPlan. Designed for computers running the CP/M operating system, the product was subsequently ported to several other platforms, including Apple II, Apple III, Xenix, and MS-DOS.

MultiPlan essentially ignored existing software user-interface standards. A real bear to learn and use, it never earned much of a following in the U.S. Not surprisingly, Lotus 1-2-3 pretty much left MultiPlan in the dust.

Excel sort of evolved from MultiPlan, first surfacing in 1985 on the Macintosh. Like all Mac applications, Excel was a graphics-based program (unlike the character-based MultiPlan). In November 1987, Microsoft released the first version of Excel for Windows (labeled Excel 2.0 to correspond with the Macintosh version). Because Windows was not in widespread use at the time, this version included a *run-time* version of Windows — a special version that had just enough features to run Excel and nothing else. Less than a year later, the company released Version 2.1. In July 1990, Microsoft released a minor upgrade (2.1d) that was compatible with Windows 3.0. Although these 2.x versions were quite rudimentary by current standards (see Figure 1-3) and didn't have the attractive, sculpted look of later versions, they attracted a small but loyal group of supporters and provided an excellent foundation for future development.

Meanwhile, Microsoft developed a version of Excel (numbered 2.20) for OS/2 Presentation Manager, released in September 1989 and upgraded to Version 2.21 about ten months later. OS/2 never quite caught on, although IBM is still trying to make it viable with OS/2 2.1.

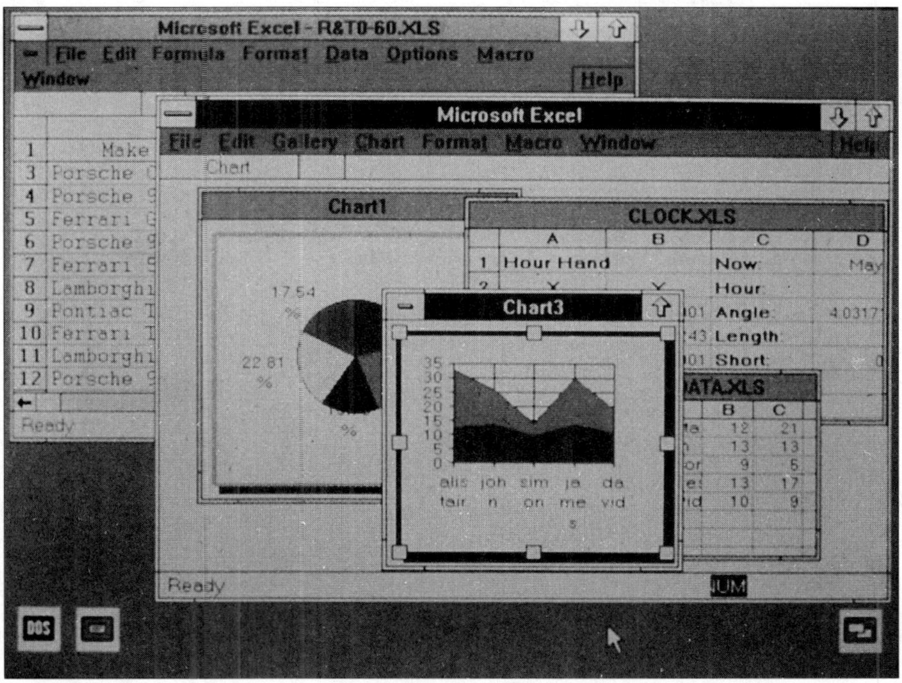

Figure 1-3: Excel 2.1, the original release for Windows. This product has come a long way, no? (Photo courtesy of Microsoft)

In December 1990, Microsoft released Excel 3 for Windows, a significant improvement in both appearance and features (see Figure 1-4). The upgrade included a toolbar, drawing capabilities, a powerful optimization feature (Solver), add-in support, embedded object (OLE) support, 3-D charts, macro buttons, simplified file consolidation, workgroup editing, and word-wrap text in a cell. Excel 3 also had the capability to work with external databases (via the Q+E program). The OS/2 version upgrade appeared five months later.

Version 4, released in the spring of 1992, was not only easier to use but it also had more power and sophistication for advanced users (see Figure 1-5). Excel 4 took top honors in virtually every spreadsheet product comparison published in the trade magazines. In the meantime, the relationship between Microsoft and IBM became increasingly strained; Excel 4 was never released for OS/2, and Microsoft has no plans to develop a version of Excel 5 for OS/2.

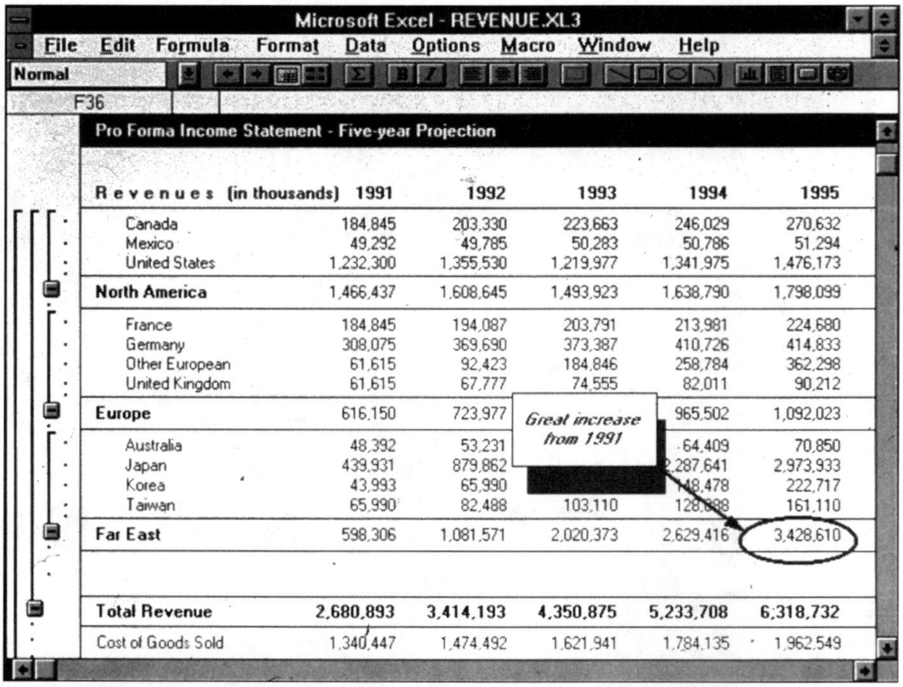

Figure 1-4: Excel 3 was a vast improvement over the original release. (Photo courtesy of Microsoft)

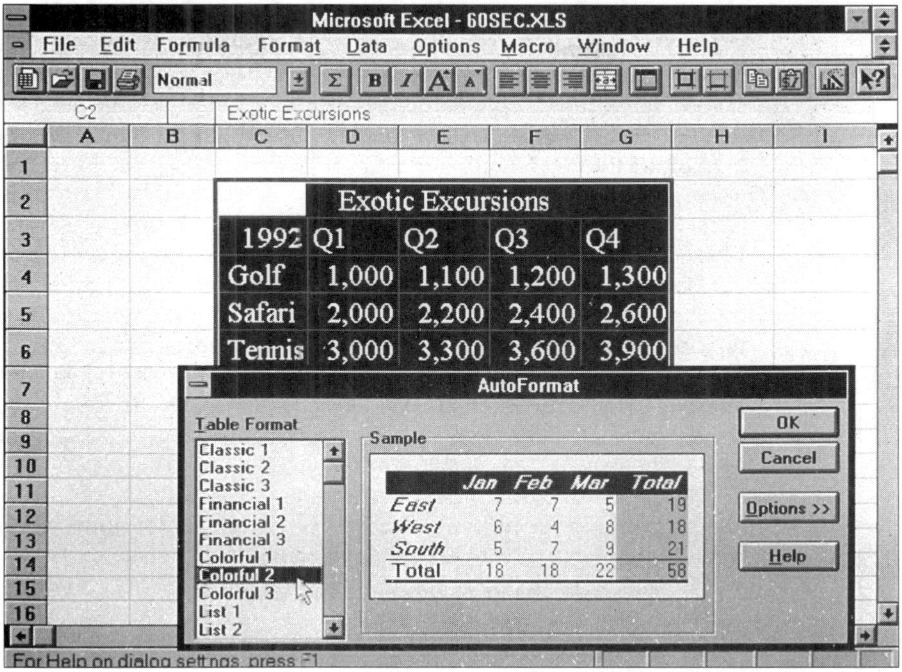

Figure 1-5: Excel 4 was another significant step forward, although still a long way from Excel 5. (Photo courtesy of Microsoft)

Excel 5 hit the streets in early 1994 and immediately earned rave reviews. Like its predecessor, it finished at the top of every spreadsheet comparison published in the leading trade magazines. Despite stiff competition from 1-2-3 Release 5 for Windows and Quattro Pro for Windows 5 — both are fine products that can handle just about any spreadsheet task thrown their way — Excel 5 should remain on top simply because it continues to provide the perfect blend of power and ease of use.

Different approaches

Anyone who has been around spreadsheets as long as I can't help but notice that Microsoft's approach to spreadsheets differs from that of Lotus and Borland.

As the first serious spreadsheet available for PCs, 1-2-3 grabbed a huge market share. While it has remained the best-selling DOS spreadsheet, Lotus also has developed versions of 1-2-3 for Windows and OS/2, as well as Macintosh and several other non-PC platforms. Consequently, with a huge user base to support, Lotus has focused more on compatibility with past versions rather than innovation.

Borland positioned Quattro Pro, on the other hand, as a better alternative to 1-2-3. Yet, despite a fair bit of innovation, Quattro Pro is clearly modeled after 1-2-3 (although Excel's influence is quite apparent in recent versions).

Windows's tremendous popularity seems to have surprised Lotus. The first version of 1-2-3 for Windows was rather poorly designed, filled with bugs, and offered virtually no new features (except SmartIcons). Borland's Quattro Pro for Windows was a much better product. Excel, meanwhile, virtually defined how spreadsheets work under Windows.

All four major versions of Excel have been available for both Windows and the Macintosh. The products are so similar that they even share the same documentation. Each version of Excel built upon the previous one, whereas Lotus's products have different menu systems and approach spreadsheet issues in a different manner.

When you develop Excel worksheets for others, it's critical that the end user has access to the same (or later) version of Excel that you used. Earlier versions of Excel cannot read files written by later versions. For example, you cannot load an Excel 5 file into Excel 4. I've seen far too many cases in which a file distributed to another Excel user was unusable because it was saved with a later version of the product. This word of caution is especially pertinent if you're working in an office where different versions are loaded on different machines (not an unusual situation).

Fortunately, Excel lets you save your work in a format that can be read by previous versions. Unfortunately, all versions of Excel produce files with the XLS extension, so you can't tell which version produced a file by looking at the extension (an idea that Microsoft should have borrowed from Lotus). Chapter 3 discusses issues relating to files in detail.

Microsoft's market research

Although most large software companies conduct market research, none approach the challenge like Microsoft. Besides using traditional research tools such as surveys and focus groups, the company devotes extensive resources to a laboratory that studies product usability.

Microsoft's programmers, for example, developed an *instrumented version* of Excel, which electronically records users' every keystroke and mouse click. The company then gives these instrumented versions to a representative sample of Excel users, who go about their normal spreadsheet business. The program automatically collects data on usage patterns. As a result, Microsoft knows which tasks users performed most often. More specifically, the company found that users spend about 95 percent of their time using only 5 percent of Excel's functionality.

After interpreting and analyzing its extensive studies, Microsoft changed the way it approaches product development and upgrades. The company now understands that innovation is required at the most basic levels. A primary goal of Microsoft's Excel 5 development team was to develop features based on the most commonly used spreadsheet tasks and make those tasks as easy as possible.

Microsoft also developed *Activity Based Planning,* which focuses product development on solving real-life user problems instead of just adding features. The research identifies what people really do, and Microsoft's researchers prioritize these activities and develop groups of features to support the most important. They also have a massive database compiled from hundreds of thousands of customer support calls and user suggestions. The usability lab, in turn, tests users' reactions to the new features so that they can be tweaked before they are incorporated into the final upgrade.

As a result, Excel — unlike many software products — is optimized for real use. Complex tasks are simplified, shortened, and even aided by interactive assistance in many cases. The bottom line: Users can accomplish more in less time.

I know that this whole research thing may sound like a bunch of hype, but I think that it works — and it clearly shows in Excel 5.

Spreadsheets Today

As I've watched the various spreadsheet products come and go over the years, I've seen even the best change dramatically. With each version of each product, the designers show a willingness to "borrow" their competitors' successful features. As a result, the three major spreadsheets are now, by and large, virtually identical.

How do you decide which product to use? Consider these factors:

- *Corporate policy*. Of course, most users end up using a particular spreadsheet because of corporate policy. Most companies choose a spreadsheet and stick with it. So most end users are stuck with a spreadsheet.

- *Inertia*. Users tend to stick with a product, upgrading when possible — even if a better product is available. The phrase *if it ain't broke, don't fix it* comes to mind.
- *Familiarity*. In the past, 1-2-3 users often found Excel difficult to adapt to — and vice versa. Although the user interfaces of the latest versions are strikingly similar, each product has its own distinct look and feel. Users tend to use products that just feel right.
- A *stand-out feature* or two can catch a user's fancy. Although today's spreadsheets possess similar features, not all implement these features equally well. For example, all three of the leading spreadsheets offer scenario management, but 1-2-3 for Windows far surpasses its competition in this area.
- Unless they're intimately involved with the spreadsheet industry, most people really don't have the foggiest idea where to start when evaluating spreadsheet products. Consequently, most rely heavily on *recommendations* from friends, associates, and the media.
- *Compatibility*. A broad term that covers an application's file formats and menu structures, as well as how it works with other software and operating environments (hardware and software). 1-2-3 long has been considered the industry standard, but that position is getting shakier by the moment.
- *Manufacturer stability*. Nobody wants to buy a spreadsheet from a company that may go out of business in six months. That means no support and no upgrades — a dead-end purchase.
- *Cost*. Unlike with most products, *price* is not usually a major issue. Until recently, all spreadsheets had a list price of $495, although large-volume buyers actually get huge discounts. When Microsoft realized that list prices were virtually meaningless, it stopped supplying a suggested retail price for its products. For individual users, Quattro Pro for Windows is an amazing bargain.

Given these factors, it's no wonder Excel remains the leading Windows spreadsheet. It was first on the scene, and I doubt that many original Excel users have switched. It has several standout features (outlining, data filtering, add-ins, and VBA, to name a few). It almost always comes out on top in head-to-head reviews. Its file format makes it quite compatible with other spreadsheets in terms, and it's also extremely compatible with other Microsoft applications. In addition, many individuals and corporations alike choose Excel because it and Windows come from the same company, Microsoft, which happens to be the world's most successful software company and isn't going to disappear any time in the near future. Finally, when you buy Excel as part of the Microsoft Office package, it's dirt cheap.

Why Excel Is Great for Developers

It's a safe bet that spreadsheet-based application development will become increasingly important over the next few years. Excel 5, a highly programmable program, is easily the best choice for developing spreadsheet-based applications now that it includes VBA and an easy way to create custom dialog boxes. Excel's key features include:

- *File structure*. The multisheet orientation makes it easy to organize elements of an application and store it in a single file. For example, a single workbook file can hold any number of worksheets, chart sheets, dialog box sheets, and VBA modules. Although Excel 4 had workbooks, these did not work very well in practice. Excel 5 got it right.
- *Visual Basic for Applications*. The new macro language lets you create structured programs directly in Excel — a *major* step forward. Excel isn't the first spreadsheet to include a structured language (Improv and Wingz, to name two others), but it's certainly the *best* implementation.
- *Dialog box controls directly on worksheets*. Excel makes it very easy to add controls such as buttons, list boxes, and option lists to a worksheet, often requiring little or no macro programming. Other spreadsheets limit you to simple macro buttons.
- *Custom dialog boxes*. You can easily create professional-looking dialog boxes. Other products allow this, but Excel does it best. (Although Quattro Pro for Windows does enable users to create custom dialog boxes, its macro language doesn't come close to Excel's. Lotus's implementation is, simply, clunky and obscure.)
- *Customizable menus*. You can change menu elements, add to existing menus, or create entirely new menus. Other products let you do this as well, but Excel makes it extremely easy.
- *Customizable shortcut menus*. Excel is the only spreadsheet that lets you customize the right-click, context-sensitive shortcut menus.
- *Customizable toolbars*. It's easy to create new toolbars as another user interface option. Again, other spreadsheets let you do this as well, but Excel outmuscles them all.
- *Slide shows*. Create self-running presentations using text, charts, pictures, and even sound. True, Quattro Pro for Windows beats Excel by a mile in this area. If you have a copy of Microsoft PowerPoint, however, you can embed an entire slide show in an Excel workbook by using OLE 2.
- *Microsoft Query*. You can access important data in standard database file formats directly from the spreadsheet environment. 1-2-3 for Windows may do this better.

- *Extensive protection options.* Your applications can be kept confidential and protected from changes. Again, pretty standard fare, but Excel has some advantages.
- *Ability to create "compiled" add-ins.* With a single command, you can create uneditable XLA add-in files that attach seamlessly. This feature is unique to Excel.
- *Custom worksheet functions.* Using VBA, you can create custom worksheet functions to simplify formulas and calculations. Another feature unique to Excel: The competitors allow custom functions, but you must be a C programmer and have lots of time on your hands.

Excel's Role in Microsoft's Strategy

Currently, most copies of Excel are sold as part of Microsoft Office — a *suite* of products that includes Excel (a spreadsheet), Word for Windows (a word processing program), and PowerPoint (a presentation graphics program). A more expensive version called Microsoft Office Professional also includes a copy of Access (a database program).

These days, the big topic is *interapplication operability*, or the use of two or more applications at a time. Obviously, it helps if the two or more programs can communicate well with each other. Microsoft is at the forefront of this trend. Currently, Excel, Word, PowerPoint, and Access all have extremely similar user interfaces.

As I write this book, only Excel and Microsoft Project include VBA, but eventually all Microsoft applications will feature VBA. So after you hone your VBA skills in Excel, you'll be able to put them to good use in other applications.

Summary

- In this chapter, I sketched the evolution of spreadsheets. I provided an overview of the various versions of the major spreadsheet product lines, and I explained why Excel is so successful and is an excellent choice for application development. I hope that you gained a new appreciation of Excel while preparing for your next spreadsheet trivia contest.
- In the next chapter, I provide a quick-and-dirty overview of Excel for newcomers. Pssst, I also reveal some of the program's secrets.

Chapter 2

Excel in a Nutshell

In This Chapter

- A conceptual overview of Excel 5, including a description of its major features
- Some tips and techniques that even advanced users may find helpful

In this chapter, I discuss the major components of Excel 5 and how its features work together — but I don't necessarily describe how to use these features. (Remember, this is not a beginner's book.) This chapter will prove especially useful for readers who have experience with another spreadsheet and are moving up to Excel. Hard-core 1-2-3 users, for example, usually need help thinking in Excel's terms. But even experienced Excel users still may learn a thing or two by skimming through this chapter.

Thinking About Objects

When developing applications with Excel (especially when dabbling with VBA), it's helpful to think in terms of *objects*, or Excel elements that you can manipulate manually or via a macro. Some Excel objects include

- Excel itself
- An Excel workbook
- A worksheet in a workbook
- A range in a worksheet
- A chart sheet
- A chart on a chart sheet
- A chart series on a chart

Notice that there's something of an *object hierarchy* here: the Excel object contains workbook objects, which contain worksheet objects, which contain range objects. This hierarchy is called Excel's *object model*.

Excel has 128 objects that you can control directly or by using VBA. For a sneak preview of Excel's objects, take a look at Appendix A.

Workbooks

One of the most common Excel objects is a *workbook* (sometimes referred to as a *document*). Everything you do in Excel takes place in a workbook, which is stored in a file with an XLS extension. The file format for Excel 5 is quite different from the file format used in previous versions (more on this in the next chapter).

A workbook can hold any number of sheets (limited only by memory). There are five types of sheets:

- Worksheets
- Chart sheets
- XLM macro sheets
- VBA modules
- Dialog sheets

You can open as many workbooks as you like (each in its own window), but at any given time only one workbook is the active workbook. Similarly, only one sheet in a workbook is the active sheet. To activate a sheet, click its tab at the bottom of the screen. To change a sheet's name, double-click the tab and enter the new text. Right-clicking a tab brings up a shortcut menu.

Worksheets

The most common type of sheet is a worksheet, which is what people normally think of when they think of a spreadsheet. Every Excel worksheet has 256 columns and 16,384 rows (twice as many rows as 1-2-3 for Windows and Quattro Pro for Windows).

Storing multiple worksheets in a workbook enables you not only to access more cells, but also, and more important, to better organize your work. Back in the old days, when a file comprised a single worksheet, developers wasted a lot of time trying to organize the worksheet to hold their information efficiently. Now you can store information on any number of worksheets and still be able to access it instantly. The workbook tabs make it very easy to activate a particular worksheet.

As you know, a worksheet cell can hold a value, formula, or text. Every worksheet also has an invisible draw layer, which lets you insert graphic objects, such as charts, drawing objects, pictures, and embedded OLE objects.

You have complete control over the column widths and row heights — in fact, you can even hide rows and columns. Text in a cell can be displayed vertically and even wrap around, as in any word processor.

Chart sheets

A chart sheet normally holds a single chart. Many users ignore chart sheets, preferring to store charts on the worksheet's draw layer. Using chart sheets is optional, but they make it a bit easier to print a chart on a page by itself, and are especially useful for presentations.

XLM macro sheets

An XLM macro sheet (also known as an MS Excel 4 macro sheet) is essentially a worksheet, but it has some different defaults. More specific, an XLM macro sheet displays formulas rather than the results of formulas. Also, the default column width is larger than in a normal worksheet.

As the name suggests, an XLM macro sheet is designed to hold XLM macros. As you may know, the XLM macro system is a holdover from previous versions of Excel. This book does not cover the XLM macro system, instead focusing on the more powerful VBA macro system.

VBA modules

A VBA module doesn't have rows and columns; in some ways, it looks like a word processing document. A VBA module, though, holds Visual Basic code, which is grouped into subroutines and functions. A single VBA module can hold approximately 4,000 lines of code. Part III of this book covers VBA in detail.

Dialog sheets

A dialog sheet holds a single custom dialog box, which is one of the user interface design components at your disposal. A workbook can hold as many as 256 dialog sheets. I describe the ins and outs of custom dialog boxes in Chapter 10.

User Interface (UI)

User interface is the means by which an end user and a developer communicate with a computer program. For the most part, Excel uses the standard Windows UI to accept commands, of course. Although it extends this UI in a few areas (most notably, drag-and-drop operations), it also deviates from it in at least one area — the method used to copy, cut, and paste ranges.

Menus

Excel's menu system is relatively straightforward. Five separate menu bars exist (the relevant one is displayed automatically): Worksheet, Chart, VBA Module, Info Window and No Document Open. In addition, there are four other menu bars for Excel 4 compatibilty.

Consistent with Windows conventions, inappropriate menu commands are dimmed and commands that open a dialog box are followed by an ellipsis.

When you highlight a menu item, Excel displays a brief description of the selected item in the status bar.

Where appropriate, the menus list any available shortcut key combinations (for example, the Edit menu lists Ctrl+Z as the shortcut key for Edit⇨Undo).

Several menu items are *cascading menus* — they lead to submenus that have additional commands (Edit⇨Fill is a cascading menu, for instance). Cascading menus are indicated by a small arrow.

The entire menu system can be customized by the end user or developer; to do so, choose the Tools⇨Menu Editor command from a VBA module.

Excel also features shortcut menus, which appear when the user right-clicks after selecting one or more objects. Importantly, each of the 25 different shortcut menus can be customized by the end user or developer — a feature unique to Excel. Following is a listing of the shortcut menus available in Excel 5:

Workspace: Workbook tab, Title bar, Desktop

Worksheets: Worksheet cell, Column, Row

Charts: Chart series, Chart text, Chart plot area, Entire chart, Chart axis, Chart grid line, Chart floor, Chart legend

VBA modules: Module, Watch pane, Immediate pane, Debug code pane

XLM macro sheets: Macrosheet cell

Dialog sheets: Dialog sheet

Toolbars: Toolbar, Toolbar button

Drawing objects: Drawing object, Button, Text box

Dialog boxes

Most of the menu commands in Excel display a dialog box. These dialog boxes are quite consistent in terms of how they operate, except for some subtle differences found in the dialog boxes produced by the Analysis ToolPak add-in (which was written by a third-party).

Some of Excel's dialog boxes use a notebook tab metaphor, which makes a single dialog box function as several different dialog boxes. The Options dialog box (choose Tools⇨Options) is an example of a tabbed dialog box (see Figure 2-1).

NOTE

A tabbed dialog box *cannot* be created with Excel's custom dialog box feature. Just about every other dialog box can be duplicated, however.

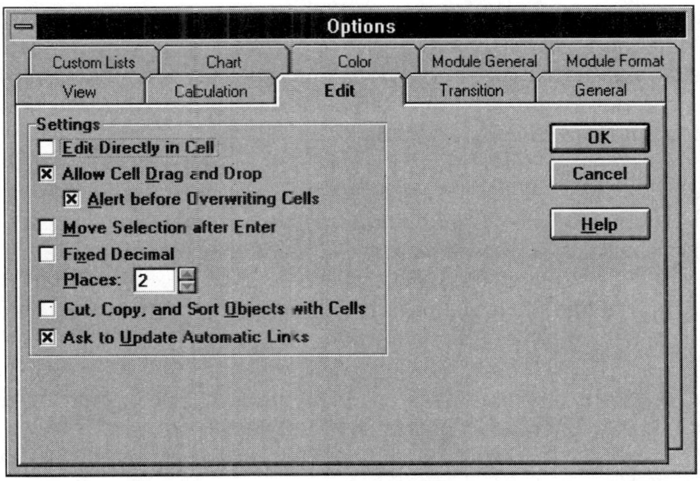

Figure 2-1: Tabbed dialog boxes provide lots of options without overwhelming the user.

Toolbars

Excel 5 ships with 13 predefined toolbars:

- Auditing toolbar
- Chart toolbar
- Drawing toolbar
- Formatting toolbar

- Forms toolbar
- Full Screen toolbar
- Microsoft toolbar
- Query and Pivot toolbar
- Standard toolbar
- Stop Recording toolbar
- TipWizard toolbar
- Visual Basic toolbar
- WorkGroup toolbar

You can *dock* toolbars (position them along any edge of the screen or make them *float*. By default, Excel displays the Standard and Formatting toolbars docked and stacked directly below the menu bar.

The prebuilt toolbars are completely customizable. And it's easy to create new toolbars: you can choose from the existing 209 toolbar buttons or any user-created icon that executes macros.

Some of the toolbar buttons are nonstandard. For example, the Font toolbar button is actually a drop-down list, and the Border button on the Formatting toolbar is actually a tear-off palette that can be moved to a convenient position.

NOTE

Toolbars that include nonstandard toolbar buttons cannot be docked at a window's left or right edge.

The toolbar buttons can be displayed in either of two different sizes. A crude but effective icon editor is built into Excel (see Figure 2-2). The existing toolbar buttons are so extensive that users can often bypass the menus to develop most simple worksheets.

Drag-and-drop

Thanks to Excel's drag-and-drop UI feature, you can freely drag objects that reside on the draw layer to change their position. Pressing Ctrl while dragging duplicates the selected object(s).

Excel also allows drag-and-drop actions on cells and ranges: You can easily drag a range to a different position. And pressing Ctrl while dragging copies the selected range.

Drag-and-drop is optional; it can be disabled in the Edit tab of the Options dialog box.

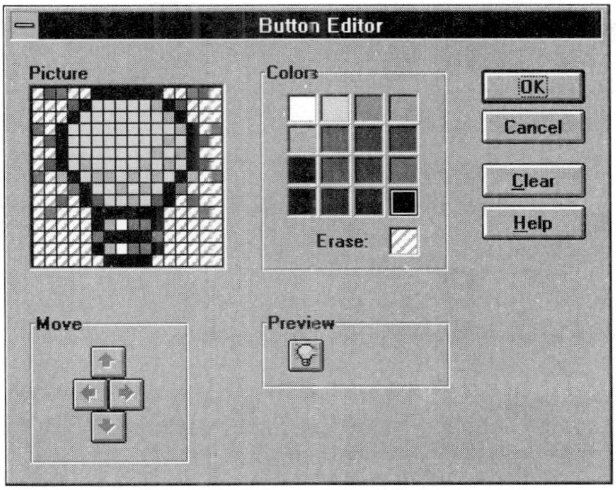

Figure 2-2: Excel's toolbar button editor is nothing to write home about, but it does the job.

Keyboard shortcuts

Excel has many keyboard shortcuts. For example, you can press Ctrl+C to copy a selection. If you're a newcomer to Excel — or you just want to improve your efficiency — I urge you to check out the on-line help (search for *Keyboard Guide* and go from there). The help file has tables that summarize useful keyboard commands and shortcuts.

Customizing the Display

Excel offers a great deal of flexibility regarding what is displayed on-screen (status bar, menus, toolbars, and so on). For example, by choosing View⇨Full Screen, you can get rid of everything except the menu bar, thereby maximizing the amount of information visible. In addition, by using the View tab in the Options dialog box, you can customize what gets displayed in a worksheet window (you can even hide scroll bars and grid lines).

In fact, Excel makes it possible to develop an application that doesn't even look like a spreadsheet.

Data Entry

Data entry in Excel is quite straightforward: Excel interprets each cell entry as a value, formula, or text.

Generally, formulas begin with an equal sign (=). And, unlike in most other spreadsheets, text in Excel that begins with a number is correctly interpreted as text.

The following list of data-entry tips are especially useful for those who are moving up to Excel from another spreadsheet.

- If you select a range of cells before entering data, you can press Enter to end a cell entry and move to the next cell, Shift+Enter to move up, Tab to move to the right, and Shift+Tab to move to the left.
- To enter data down a column without pressing the down-arrow key, enable the Move Selection after Enter option in the Edit tab of the Options dialog box (which is accessed from the Tools⇨Options command).
- Press Ctrl+; to insert the current date and Ctrl+Shift+; to enter the current time into a cell.
- Pressing Ctrl+Enter ends a cell entry and copies the contents of that cell to all other cells in a selected range.
- To copy the contents of the active cell to all other cells in a selected range, press F2 and then Ctrl+Enter.
- To fill a range with increments of a single value, press Ctrl while you drag the fill handle at the corner of the selection.
- To create a custom AutoFill list, use the Custom Lists tab of the Options dialog box.
- To copy a cell without incrementing, drag the fill handle at the corner of the selection. Or press Ctrl+D to copy down or Ctrl+R to copy to the right.
- You can enter tabs and carriage returns in a cell to make the text easier to read. To enter a tab, press Ctrl+Alt+Tab. To enter a carriage return, press Alt+Enter. Carriage returns cause a cell's contents to wrap within the cell.
- To enter a fraction, press 0, a space, and then the fraction.
- To automatically format a cell with the currency format, type a dollar sign before the value. To enter a value in percent format, type a percent sign after the value.

Selecting Objects

Generally, selecting objects conforms to standard Windows practices. Clicking an object that has been placed on the draw layer selects it. You can select a range of cells by clicking and dragging. To select multiple objects or noncontiguous cells, hold down Ctrl while you select. To select a large range, click a cell at any corner of the range, scroll to the opposite corner of the range, and press Shift while you click the opposite corner cell.

It's often more efficient to select a range by using the keyboard. If you're not familiar with Excel's many ways to do so, check the on-line help system.

Formatting

There are two types of formatting in Excel: numeric and stylistic.

Numeric formatting

Numeric formatting refers to how values appear. Of all the spreadsheets available, Excel provides the user with the most control over numeric formatting. In addition to choosing from an extensive list of predefined formats, you can create your own formats (see Figure 2-3) — the procedure is thoroughly explained in the on-line help system.

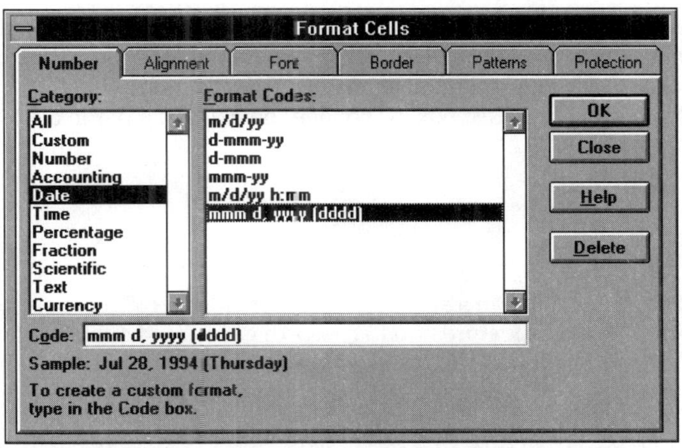

Figure 2-3: Excel's numeric formatting options are the best available.

Stylistic formatting

Stylistic formatting means making your work look good.

The easiest way to get to the correct dialog box and format an object is to select the object, right-click, and then choose Format *xxx* (where *xxx* is the selected object) from the shortcut menu. This action leads to a tabbed dialog box that holds all the formatting options for the selected object. Figure 2-4 shows the formatting dialog box for a range selection.

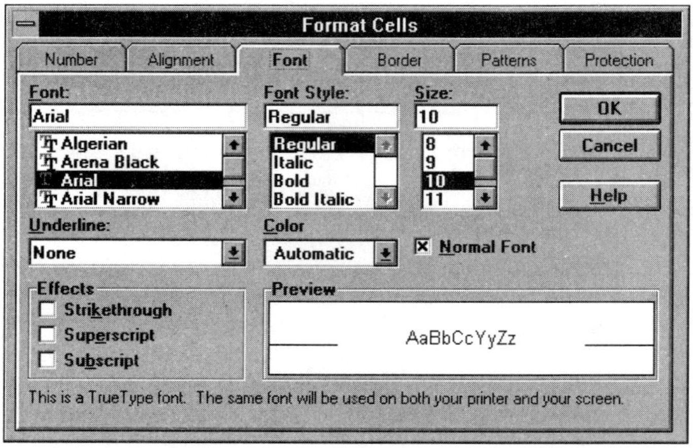

Figure 2-4: Excel's tabbed dialog boxes give you one-stop formatting shopping.

Many toolbar buttons offer direct access to common formatting options, regardless whether you're working with cells, drawn objects, or charts. For example, you can use the Color toolbar button to change the background color of a cell, change the fill color of a drawn text box, or change the color of a bar in a chart.

Formulas

Formulas are what make a spreadsheet a spreadsheet. Excel has some important formula-related features that are worth getting to know: they enable you to write array formulas, use an intersection operator, include links, and create megaformulas.

NOTE

By default, Excel cell references are relative; you can use the standard *$* symbol to specify absolute references.

Array formulas

Until Quattro Pro for Windows 5, Excel was the only spreadsheet that incorporated array formulas.

An *array* is simply a collection of cells or values that is operated on as a group. An *array formula* performs an operation on multiple inputs and produces multiple results — with each result displayed in a separate cell (because Excel can fit only one value in a cell). For example, when you multiply a 1 x 5 array by another 1 x 5 array, the result is a third 1 x 5 array. In other words, the results of this kind of operation occupies five cells; each element in the first array is multiplied by each corresponding element in the second array to create five new values, each getting its own cell.

To enter an array formula in Excel, write a formula and then press Ctrl+Shift+Enter.

NOTE

To remind you that a formula is an array formula, Excel surrounds it with brackets, { }. Don't enter the brackets yourself.

Some of the advantages of using array formulas rather than single-cell formulas include

- They use less memory.
- They can make your work much more efficient.
- They can eliminate the need for intermediate formulas.
- They can let you do things that would be difficult or impossible otherwise.

A few disadvantages of using array formulas are

- Some can slow your spreadsheet recalculation time to a crawl.
- They can make your worksheet more difficult for others to understand.
- You must remember to enter an array formula with a special key sequence (Ctrl+Shift+Enter).

Excel's array formulas let you perform individual operations on each cell in a range in much the same way as a program language's looping feature allows you to work with elements of an array. For example, an instructor's spreadsheet may contain a data range consisting of names and test grades. You can use array formulas to count the number of students earning each letter grade. The following array formula returns the number of cells in B1:B100 that contain "A":

```
{=SUM(IF(B1:B100="A",1,0))}
```

Intersection

Excel uses an intersection operator — a space — to determine the overlapping references in two ranges. Figure 2-5 shows a simple example. The formula in cell G5 is

```
=B1:B7  A4:E4
```

and returns 4, the value in cell B4 — that is, the value at the intersection of the two ranges.

You also can use the intersection operator with array formulas. In Figure 2-6, I used an array formula to obtain the intersection of the two ranges. G5:H6 contains the following formula:

```
{=B1:C7  A3:E4}
```

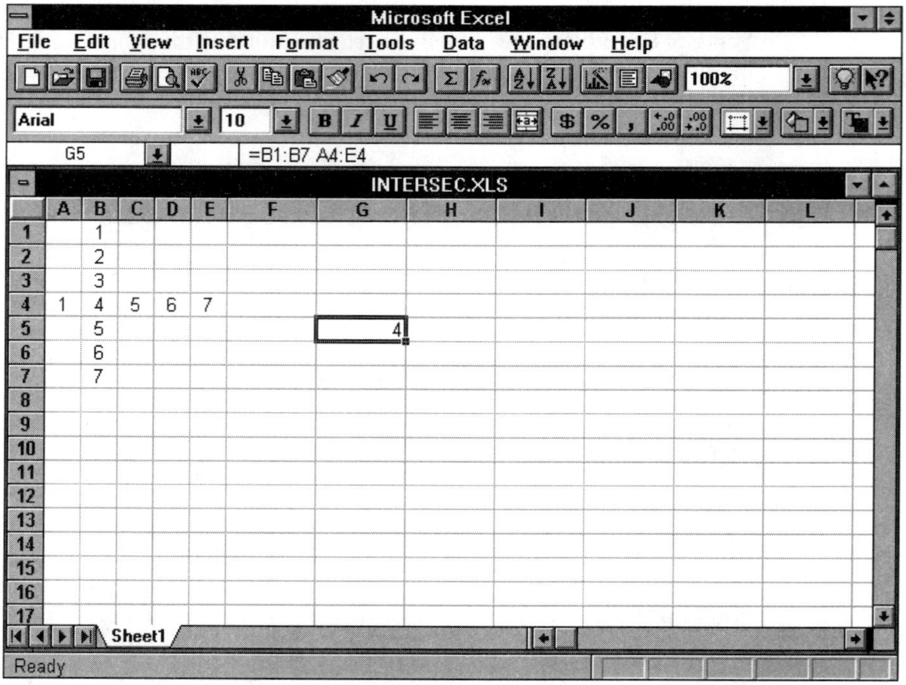

Figure 2-5: Using the intersection operator.

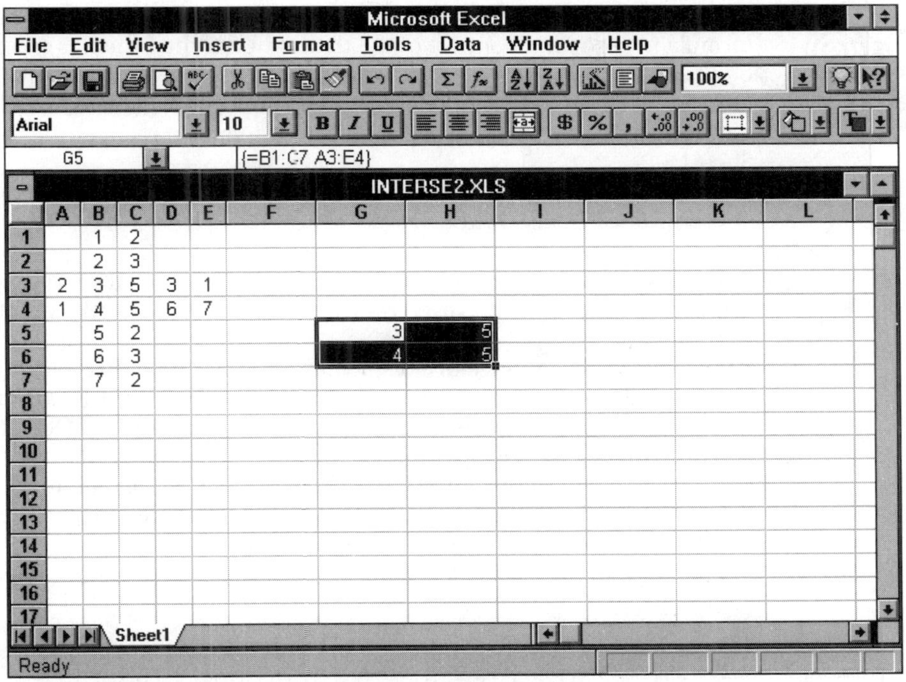

Figure 2-6: Using the intersection operator in an array formula.

Links

Like all modern spreadsheets, Excel lets you include links to other files in your formulas. The workbook that contains the original data is the *source* workbook, and the workbook that has the link formulas is the *dependent* workbook.

Here's a formula that includes a link to a different workbook:

```
=[TABLE.XLS]Sheet1!$A$3
```

In general, a link reference includes the source workbook name in square brackets, followed by the worksheet name, an exclamation point, and the cell reference. Although you can enter link formulas directly, you also can create the reference by using normal pointing methods: To do so, the source file must be open. When you do so, Excel creates absolute cell references (if you plan to copy the formula to other cells, make the references relative).

TIP

If you are unable to load a corrupted Excel workbook, you can write a link formula to recover all or part of the data (but not the formulas). You can do so because the source file in a link formula does not need to be open. If your corrupt file is named BADFILE.XLS, for example, open a blank workbook and enter the following formula into cell A1 to attempt to recover the data from Sheet1:

```
=[BADFILE.XLS]Sheet1!A1
```

Copy this formula down and to the right to recover as much information as you can. A better approach, however, is to maintain a backup of your important files.

If you need to link a range of cells, it may be easier to let Excel do the work. To create a link, for example, so that range A1:C3 in the MIRROR workbook always displays the same values as the corresponding range in the SOURCE workbook, copy the range A1:C3 in SOURCE, activate cell A1 in MIRROR, choose the Edit⇨Paste Special command, and then click the Paste Link button. Excel pastes the link formulas for you (refer to Figure 2-7). The formulas are actually an array formula.

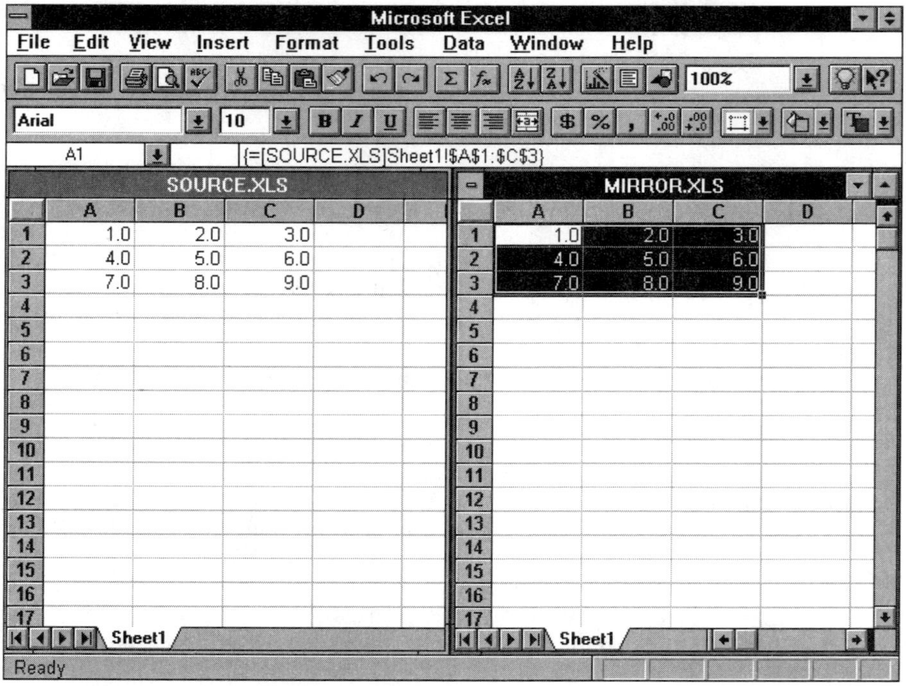

Figure 2-7: Pasting a link results in an array formula.

Working with links can be tricky. For example, if you use the File➪Save As command to make a backup copy of the source worksheet, you automatically change the link formulas to refer to the new file (not usually what you want). Another way to mess up your links is to rename the source workbook when the dependent workbook is not open.

Creating megaformulas

Often, spreadsheets require intermediate formulas to produce a desired result. After you get the formulas working correctly, it's often possible to eliminate the intermediate formulas and use a single *megaformula* instead. The advantages? You use fewer cells (less clutter), and recalculation take less time. Besides, people in the know will be impressed with your formula-building abilities. The disadvantage? The formula may be impossible to decipher or modify.

Here's an example: Imagine a worksheet with a column of people's names. And suppose that you've been asked to remove all of the middle names and middle initials from the names — but not all of the names have a middle name or initial. Editing the cells manually would take hours, so you opt for a formula-based solution. Although this is not a difficult task, it normally involves several intermediate formulas. Let's also assume that you want to use as few cells as possible in the solution.

Figure 2-8 shows the solution, which requires six intermediate formulas. The names are in column A; the end result goes in column H. Columns B through G hold the intermediate formulas.

Cell	*Intermediate Formula*	*What It Does*
B1	=TRIM(A1)	Removes excess spaces
C1	=FIND(" ",B1,1)	Locates first space
D1	=FIND(" ",B1,C1+1)	Locates second space
E1	=IF(ISERROR(D1),C1,D1)	Uses the first space if no second space
F1	=LEFT(B1,C1)	Extracts the first name
G1	=RIGHT(B1,LEN(B1)-E1)	Extracts the last name
H1	=F1&G1	Concatenates the two names

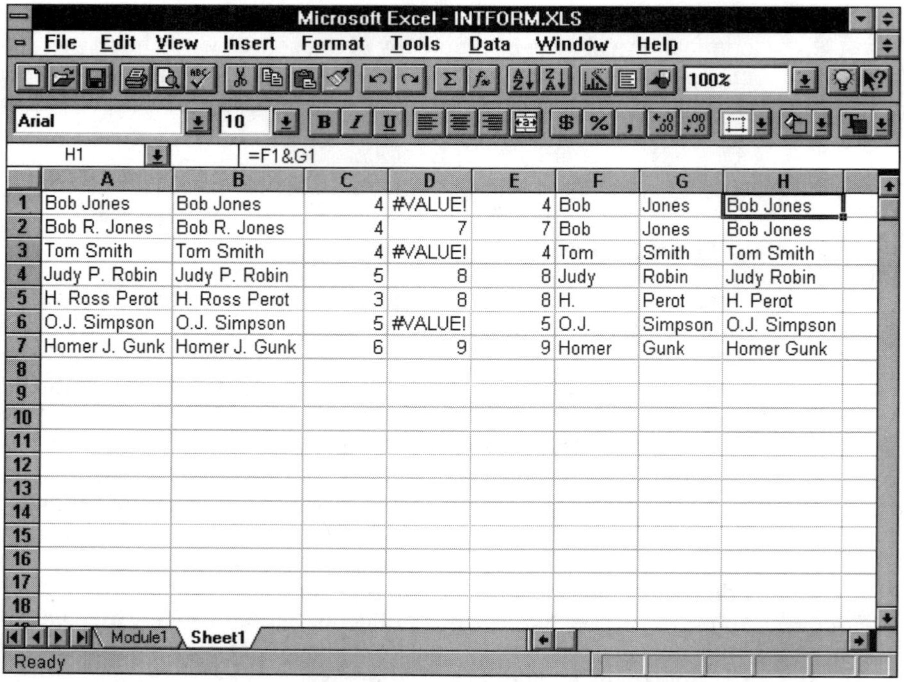

	A	B	C	D	E	F	G	H
1	Bob Jones	Bob Jones	4	#VALUE!	4	Bob	Jones	Bob Jones
2	Bob R. Jones	Bob R. Jones	4	7	7	Bob	Jones	Bob Jones
3	Tom Smith	Tom Smith	4	#VALUE!	4	Tom	Smith	Tom Smith
4	Judy P. Robin	Judy P. Robin	5	8	8	Judy	Robin	Judy Robin
5	H. Ross Perot	H. Ross Perot	3	8	8	H.	Perot	H. Perot
6	O.J. Simpson	O.J. Simpson	5	#VALUE!	5	O.J.	Simpson	O.J. Simpson
7	Homer J. Gunk	Homer J. Gunk	6	9	9	Homer	Gunk	Homer Gunk

Figure 2-8: Removing the middle names and initials requires six intermediate formulas.

You can eliminate all the intermediate formulas by creating a megaformula. You do so by starting with the end result and then replacing each cell reference with a copy of the formula in the cell referred to (but don't copy the equal sign). Fortunately, you can use the Clipboard to copy and paste. Keep repeating this process until cell H1 contains nothing but references to cell A1. You end up with the following megaformula in one cell:

```
=LEFT(TRIM(A1),FIND
(" ",TRIM(A1),1))&RIGHT(TRIM(A1),LEN(TRIM(A1))-
IF(ISERROR(FIND(" ",TRIM(A1),FIND(" ",TRIM(A1),1)+1)),FIND
(" ",TRIM(A1),1),FIND(" ",TRIM(A1),FIND(" ",TRIM(A1),1)+1)))
```

When you're satisfied that the megaformula is working, you can delete the columns that hold the intermediate formulas because they are no longer used.

The megaformula formula performs exactly as the same task as all the intermediate formulas — although it's virtually impossible for anyone to figure out. If you decide to use megaformulas, make sure that the intermediate formulas are performing correctly before you start building a megaformula. Even better, keep a copy of the intermediate formulas somewhere in case you discover an error or need to make a change.

NOTE

Your only limitation is that Excel's formulas can be no more than 1024 characters.

Because a megaformula is so complex, you may think that using one would slow down recalculation. Actually, the opposite is true. As a test, I created a worksheet that used a megaformula 16,384 times. Then I created another worksheet that used six intermediate formulas. The megaformula recalculated much quicker (see Table 2-1).

Table 2-1 Intermediate Formulas versus Megaformula

Method	*Recalc Time (Seconds)*	*File Size*
Intermediate formulas	138	5.63 MB
Megaformula	43	1.71 MB

As you can see, using the megaformula resulted in significantly faster recalculations as well as a much smaller file.

TIP

Another way to approach this problem is to create a custom worksheet function in VBA. Then you could replace the megaformula with a simple formula, such as

```
=NOMIDDLE(A1)
```

CROSS REFERENCE

I discuss custom functions in Chapter 9. But if you'd like to try this out, just insert a VBA module sheet and enter the following statements. Then you can use this function in worksheet formulas in the same workbook.

```
Function NOMIDDLE(FullName As String) As String
'   Get rid of extra spaces
    FullName = Trim(FullName)

'   Exit if no middle name
    If Not FullName Like "* * *" Then
        NOMIDDLE = FullName
        Exit Function
    End If

'   Determine first and second space positions
    Space1 = Application.Find(" ", FullName, 1)
    Space2 = Application.Find(" ", FullName, Space1 + 1)

'   Build result character by character
    NOMIDDLE = ""
    For i = 1 To Len(FullName)
        If i <= Space1 Or i > Space2 Then _
            NOMIDDLE = NOMIDDLE + Mid(FullName, i, 1)
    Next i
End Function
```

When I tested this code with 16,384 names, Excel took 260 seconds to recalculate — nearly twice as long as the intermediate formulas method, and about five times as long as the megaformula. The only advantage was the file size: 1.56 MB, or slightly smaller than the worksheet created by the megaformula.

Using Names

All spreadsheets let you use names for cells and ranges, but Excel handles names in some unique ways.

A *name* is an identifier that lets you refer to a cell, range, a value, formula, or graphic object. Formulas that use names are much easier to read and remember than formulas using cell references.

VBA users should definitely use cell and range names because VBA does not automatically update its references if you move a cell or range that's referred to in a VBA statement.

An advantage unique to Excel is that you can name values or formulas that don't even appear in cells in your worksheet (see the "Naming constants" section, later in this chapter).

You create names by using the Insert⇨Name⇨Define command (or pressing Ctrl+F3). An even faster way to create names is to use the Name Box (the drop-down list at the left side of the formula bar). You can choose the Insert⇨Name⇨Create command to create names automatically for cells or ranges based on row or column titles on your worksheet. In Figure 2-9, for example, B2:E2 is named *North*, C2:E2 is named *South*, and so on. Vertically, B2:B5 is named *Qtr1*, C2:C5 is named *Qtr2*, and so on.

Intersecting names

Using names with the intersection operator makes it very easy to create meaningful formulas. If, again referring to Figure 2-9, you enter the formula

```
=Qtr2  South
```

the result is 120 — the intersection of the *Qtr2* range and the *South* range. To get the total for the West region, you can use

```
=SUM(West)
```

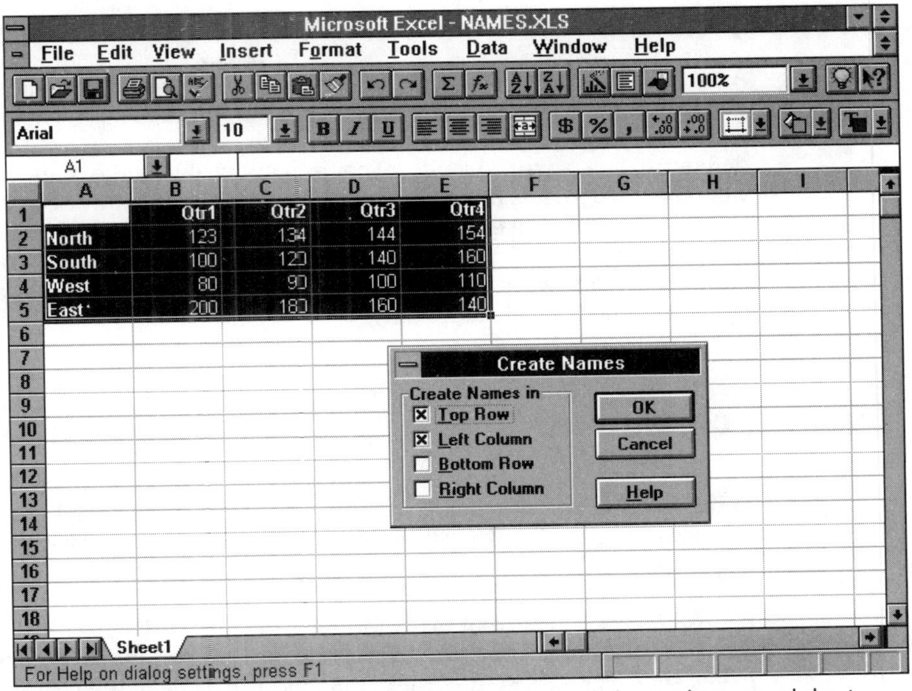

Figure 2-9: Excel makes it easy to create names that use descriptive text in your worksheet.

Naming columns and rows

With Excel, you also can name complete rows and columns. In the preceding example, the name *Qtr1* is assigned to the range B2:B5. Alternatively, *Qtr1* could be assigned to all of column B, *Qtr2* to column C, and so on. You also can do the same horizontally so that *North* refers to row 2, *South* to row 3, and so on.

The intersection operator works exactly as before. But now you can add additional regions or quarters without having to change the existing names.

When naming columns and rows, make sure that you don't store any extraneous information in named rows or columns. For example, remember that if you insert a value in cell B7, it is included in the *Qtr1* range.

Scoping names

A named cell or range normally has a workbook-level *scope* — in other words, you can use the name in any worksheet in the workbook. Names that have worksheet-level scope can be used only in the worksheet where they are defined; in fact, a worksheet-level name is not visible in the Name Box in a worksheet where it is not defined. You also cannot find a worksheet-level name in the Define Name dialog box from any sheet where it is not defined.

I think that using worksheet-level names is only asking for trouble, and so I tend to use workbook-level names only.

Naming constants

Virtually every Excel user knows how to create cell and range names (although not all Excel users actually do so). But most Excel users do not know that you can use names to refer to values that don't appear in your worksheet (that is, *constants*).

For example, suppose that many formulas in your worksheet need to use an interest rate. Most people would plug the interest rate into a cell and give it a name, such as RATE, so that they could use the name in their formulas. The other alternative is to call up the Define Name dialog box and enter the interest rate directly into the Refers to box (see Figure 2-10). Then you can use the name in your formulas just as if the value is stored in a cell. If the interest rate changes, just change the definition for RATE, and Excel updates all the cells that contain this name.

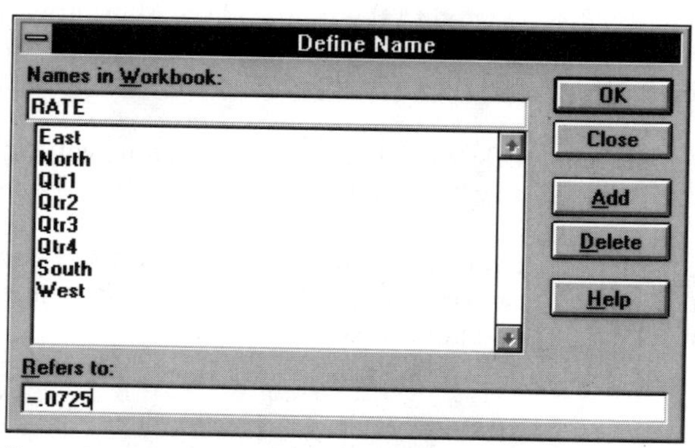

Figure 2-10: Excel lets you name constants that don't appear in worksheet cells.

By the way, this technique also works for text. If you define the name IDG to stand for *International Data Group*, when you enter =IDG into a cell, the cell displays the full name.

Naming formulas

You also can enter a formula directly into the Refers to box in the Define Name dialog box. The formula that you enter uses cell references relative to the active cell (if you use point method to build a formula, however, the references will be absolute).

Figure 2-11 shows a formula entered directly in the Refers to box in the Define Name dialog box. In this case, the active cell is C1, so the formula refers to the two cells to its left (notice that the cell references are relative). Once this name is defined, entering =POWER into a cell raises the value two cells to the left to the power represented by the cell directly to the left.

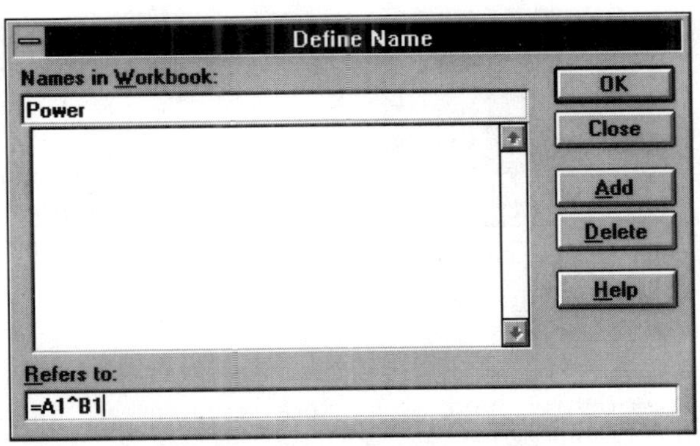

Figure 2-11: You can name a formula that doesn't appear in any worksheet cells

If you use this formula throughout a worksheet, you'll find that it's much easier to enter =POWER than to create the formula from scratch. Also, if you need to modify the formula, you can just change the definition in the Name Box, rather than edit each occurrence of the formula.

NOTE

In pre-Excel 5 days, defining a name for a formula that was used in many places throughout a worksheet actually reduced the worksheet's size because Excel stored the formula once, rather than in each cell. But Excel 5 uses a more efficient method of storing repeated formulas, so you won't see any decrease in file size by naming formulas.

Functions

Like all current spreadsheet products, Excel provides a huge number of built-in functions. You can access even more functions (many of them quite esoteric) by attaching the Analysis ToolPak add-in.

The easiest way to locate the function you need is to use the Function Wizard, shown in Figure 2-12. If you're not familiar with this feature, I encourage you to check it out. It's very handy.

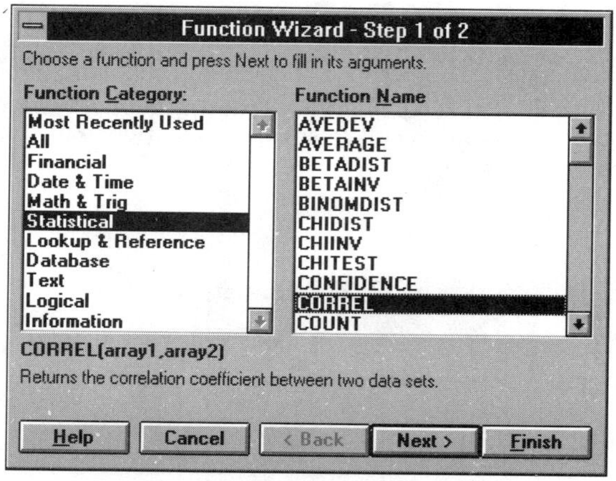

Figure 2-12: The Function Wizard is the best way to insert a worksheet function into a formula.

CROSS REFERENCE

Excel is the only spreadsheet that makes it very easy to create your own worksheet functions. You do so in VBA; for more information, see Chapter 9.

Drawing Objects

As I mentioned earlier in this chapter, each worksheet has an invisible draw layer, which holds charts, pictures, OLE objects, and drawing objects.

Excel enables you to draw some simple geometric shapes directly on your worksheet easily, thanks to buttons on the Drawing toolbar. In addition, you should be aware that you can group objects into a single object, which is easier to size or position.

Several drawing objects are worthy of additional discussion:

- The *text box* provides a way to display text that's independent of row and column boundaries — a good way to label rows in a table (see Figure 2-13). Although you can display text vertically in a cell, doing so changes the row height.

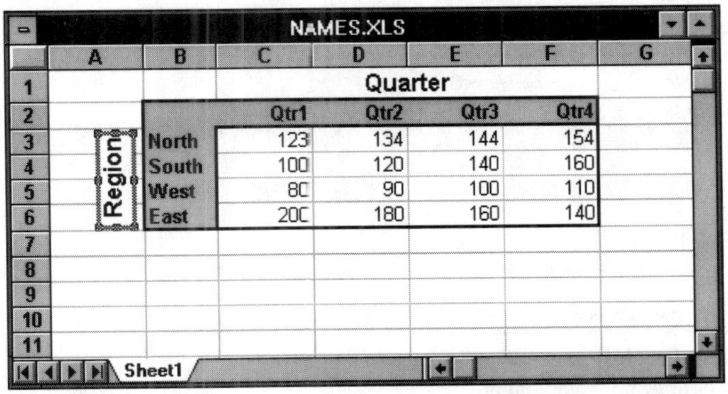

Figure 2-13: The text box drawing object is useful for displaying text vertically.

CROSS-REFERENCE

- The *linked picture object* is rather difficult to generate in Excel: you can use the Camera tool, which isn't on any of the predefined toolbars, or the Paste Picture Link command, which appears on the Edit menu only when you press Shift. I've heard that the Paste Picture Link command was originally designed to accommodate users who wanted to print a noncontiguous selection of ranges. Users could "take pictures" of the ranges and then paste the pictures together in a single area, which could then be printed. I've found an even better use for this command, however, in designing custom dialog boxes. As I describe in Chapter 10, a linked picture is the only way to display formatted text in a dialog box.
- Finally, many of the *custom dialog box controls* can be placed directly on a worksheet. Doing so can greatly enhance the usability of some worksheets and eliminate the need to create custom dialog boxes. Figure 2-14 shows a worksheet with some dialog box controls added to the draw layer.

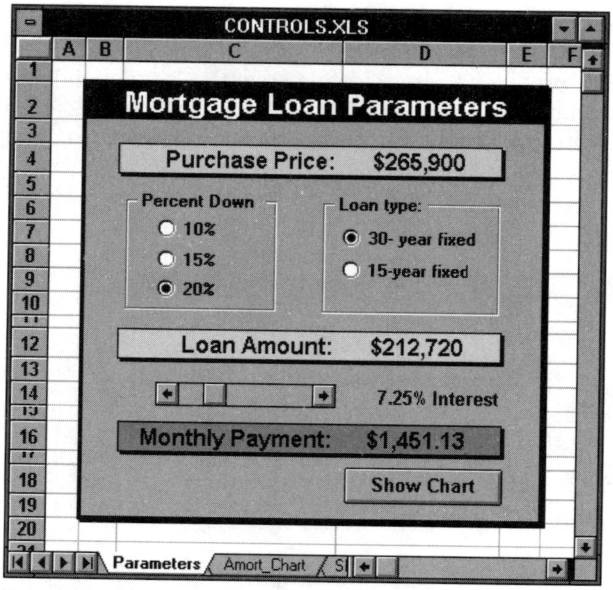

Figure 2-14: Excel lets you add most of its custom dialog box controls directly on a worksheet.

Charts

Excel, of course, has extensive charting capabilities. As I mentioned earlier in this chapter, you can store charts on a chart sheet or float them on a worksheet.

Excel offers extensive chart customization options. If a chart is free-floating, double-click it to edit it (a new menu bar will appear). Double-clicking a chart element brings up its formatting dialog box; right-clicking an element displays a shortcut menu.

The easiest way to create a chart is to select the data to be charted and then use the Chart Wizard (you can choose the corresponding button on the Standard toolbar). To create a chart on a separate chart sheet, select the data and use the Insert⇨Chart⇨As New Sheet command.

Excel uses a SERIES function to specify data for the chart (one SERIES formula for each data series). When you select a series in a chart, the SERIES function is displayed in the formula bar (see Figure 2-15).

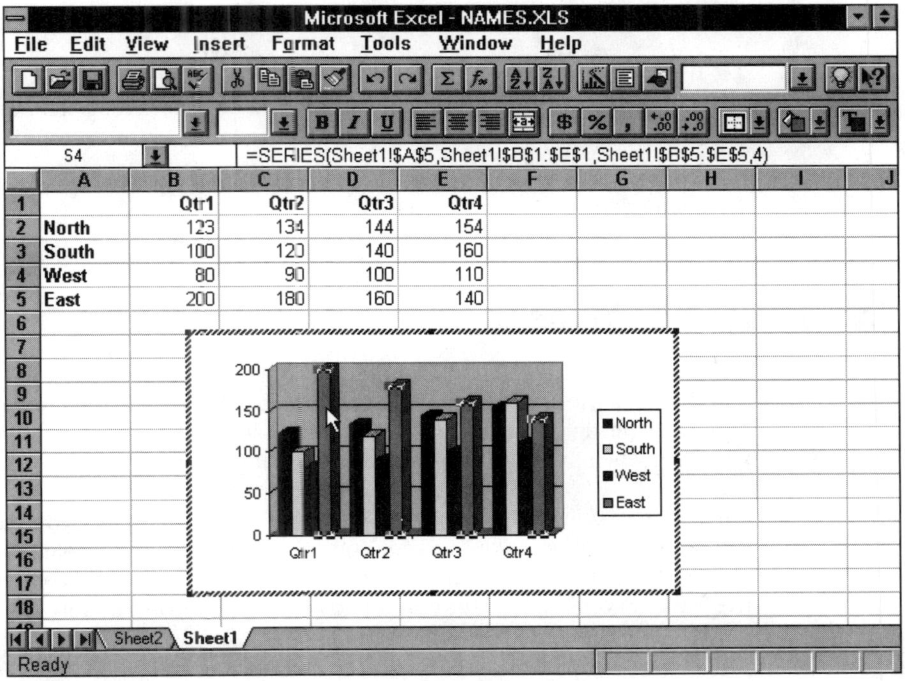

Figure 2-15: Data for a chart series is specified in a SERIES function.

Macros

All spreadsheets have a macro language. Excel has two: the original XLM macro language is being phased out in favor of VBA. Excel 5 still can execute any XLM macro you may run across, but you should use VBA to develop new macros.

Part III of this book is devoted to the VBA language.

Database Access

Over the years, all spreadsheets have allowed users to work with simple flat database tables (even the original version of 1-2-3 contained this feature). Excel has some slick tools.

Using databases from a spreadsheet falls into two categories:

- *Worksheet databases.* The entire database is stored in a worksheet, limiting the size of the database. In Excel, a worksheet database can have no more than 16,383 records and 256 fields.
- *External databases.* The data is stored in one or more disk files and accessed as needed.

Worksheet databases

Generally, when the cell pointer is located within a database, Excel recognizes it and displays the field names whenever possible. For example, if you move the cell pointer within a worksheet database and choose the Data⇨Sort command, Excel lets you select the sort keys by choosing field names from a drop-down list.

Particularly useful is Excel's data filtering feature, which lets you display only the records that you want to see. You can filter the data by selecting values from pull-down lists (which appear in place of the field names when you choose the Data⇨Filter⇨AutoFilter command). Rows that don't qualify are temporarily hidden. See Figure 2-16 for an example.

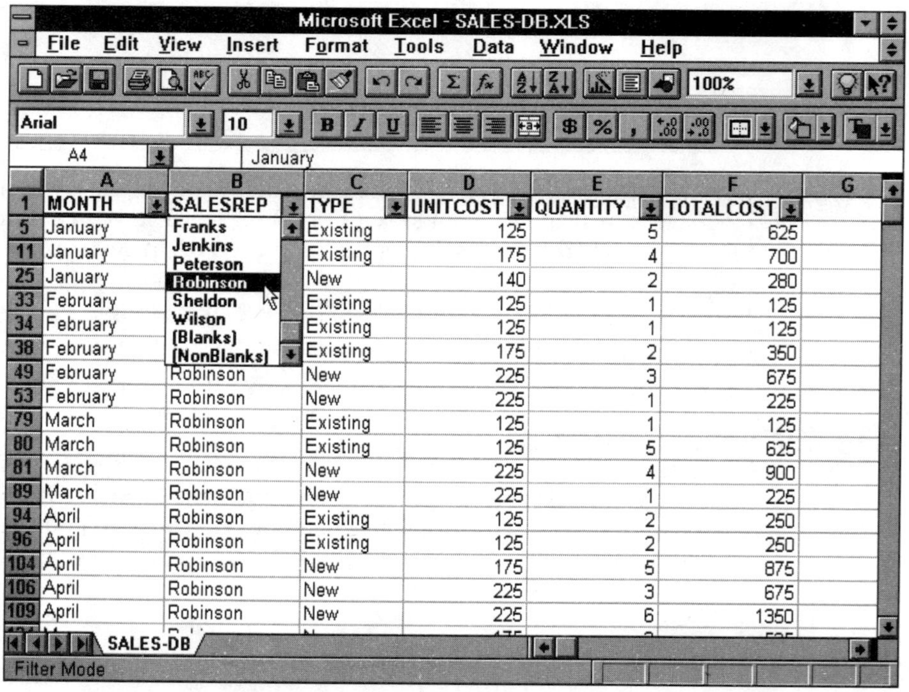

Figure 2-16: The data filtering feature makes it easy to view database records that qualify.

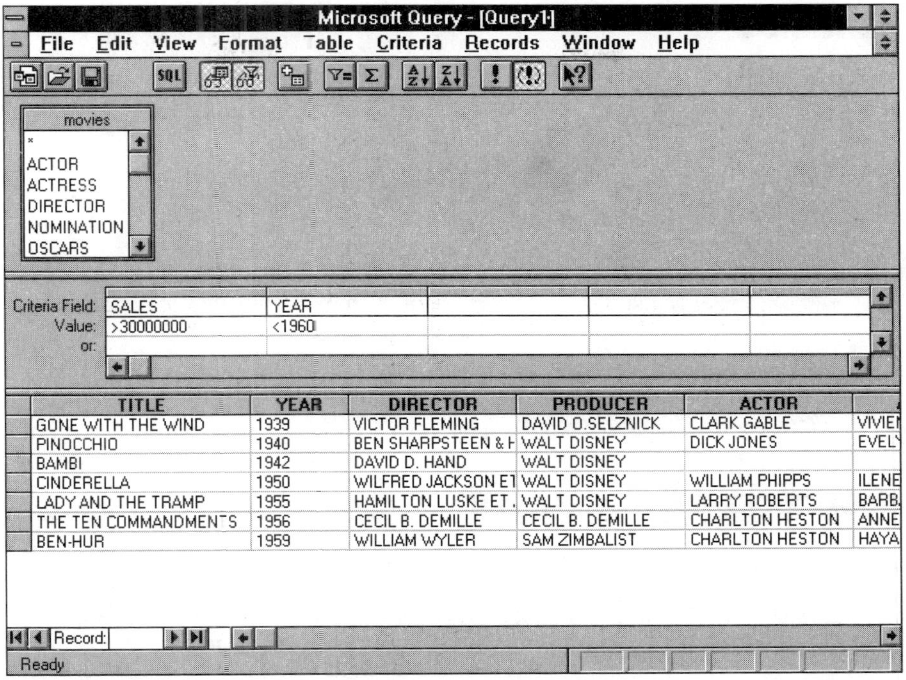

Figure 2-17: The Microsoft Query application lets you perform queries on external database files.

If you prefer to use the traditional database techniques that involve criteria ranges, choose the Data⇨Filter⇨Advanced Filter command.

External databases

To work with external database tables, you need to load the MS Query add-in. Doing so adds a new command, Data⇨Get External Data, which executes Microsoft Query (see Figure 2-17) and enables you to choose your databases and define queries. The results of a query can be directed back to your worksheet.

Analysis Tools

Excel is no slouch when it comes to analysis. After all, that's what most people use a spreadsheet for. Most analysis tasks can be handled with formulas, but Excel offers many other options.

Outlines

Excel introduced spreadsheet outlining in Version 3.0. Surprisingly, none of Excel's competitors has added this feature, which lets you quickly expand and collapse hierarchical data, such as budgets.

Automatic subtotals

Excel is also the only spreadsheet that can automatically insert (or remove) subtotal formulas in a table set up as a database. It also creates an outline from the data so that you can view only the subtotals or any level of detail you desire. Figure 2-18 shows some automatic subtotals and the accompanying outline.

Scenario management

If you're seeking flexible scenario management, 1-2-3's Version Manager is your best bet. Although Excel's scenario manager is quite weak in comparison, it takes care of simple scenario management tasks — and it's definitely easier than trying to keep track of different scenarios manually.

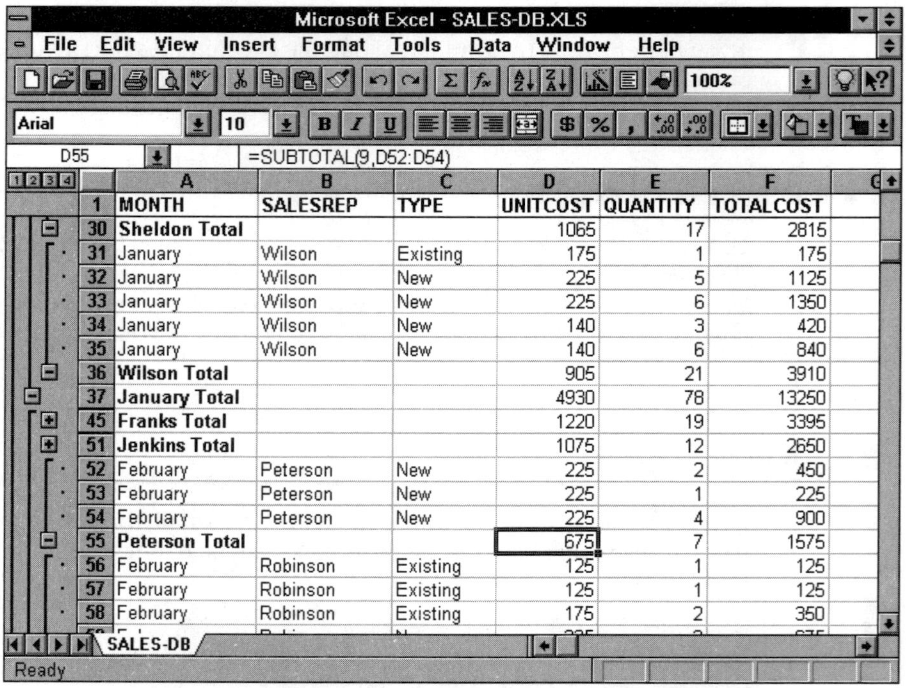

Figure 2-18: Excel can automatically insert subtotal formulas and create outlines.

Analysis ToolPak

The Analysis ToolPak add-in provides 19 special-purpose analysis tools (primarily statistical in nature) and many specialized worksheet functions. These tools make Excel suitable for small- to medium-scale statistical analysis.

Pivot tables

One of Excel 5's most innovative tools is its pivot tables, which gives Excel some Lotus Improv-like features. A *pivot table*, a special type of object, can be manipulated completely by using VBA. Data for a pivot table comes from a worksheet database or an external database and is stored in a special cache, which enables Excel to recalculate rapidly after a pivot table is altered. Figure 2-19 shows a pivot table.

Auditing

Excel also has some powerful and useful auditing capabilities that help you identify errors or track the logic in an unfamiliar spreadsheet.

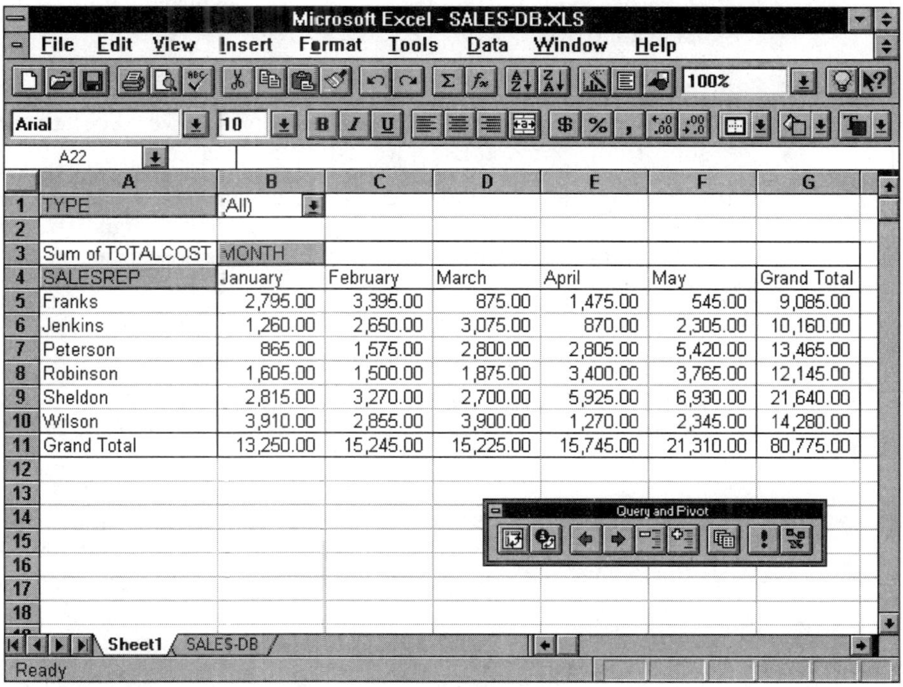

Figure 2-19: Excel's pivot table feature has many applications.

Solver

For specialized linear and nonlinear problems, Excel's Solver add-in calculates solutions to what-if scenarios based on adjustable cells, constraint cells, and, optionally, cells that must be maximized or minimized. Excel's Solver is very similar to the feature found in 1-2-3 for Windows and Quattro Pro for Windows. (This similarity is not surprising when you know that a single company, Frontline Systems, was largely responsible for the feature in all three products.)

Add-Ins

An *add-in* is a program that's attached to Excel to give it additional functionality. Excel 5 ships with the following add-ins:

- *Analysis ToolPak*, which adds financial and engineering functions, and provides tools to perform statistical and engineering analysis.
- *AutoSave* saves workbooks automatically as you work.
- *ODBC Function Add-in* adds worksheet and macro functions for retrieving data from external sources with Microsoft Open Database Connectivity (ODBC).
- *Microsoft Query Add-in* retrieves data from external database files and tables using Microsoft Query.
- *Report Manager* prints reports that consist of views and scenarios.
- *Slide Show* works with the Slide Show template workbook to create a slide show from Microsoft Excel worksheets and charts.
- *Solver* calculates solutions to what-if scenarios based on adjustable cells, constraint cells, and, optionally, cells that must be maximized or minimized. If you want to use Solver, you must select the Solver option during Setup.
- *Update Add-in Links*, used when converting Excel 4 worksheets to Excel 5, automatically updates links to Excel 4 add-ins that are no longer included because the features are built into Excel 5.
- *View Manager* saves the current window display as a view and lets you apply your saved views so that you can see your worksheet in different formats.

Besides these add-ins, there are many third-party add-ins that you can purchase. You can use the coupon in the back of the book to acquire a free copy of the Power Utility Pak add-in. And, as I detail in this book, it's *very* easy to create your own add-ins.

Compatibility

Excel 5 can import a variety of files generated by other spreadsheet and database products. I talk about this feature in the next chapter. If you're an experienced 1-2-3 user, Excel provides detailed on-line help that's designed to get you to think in terms of Excel. Check out the Help⇨Lotus 1-2-3 command for more information.

OLE Support

Excel 5 supports the OLE 2 specification as both a client and a server. Thus, you can insert Excel workbook objects into documents created by other OLE 2 applications, and you also can insert objects from other OLE 2 applications into an Excel worksheet. Figure 2-20 shows an example of an Excel workbook inserted into a Word for Windows document. Notice that Word displays Excel's menu and toolbars.

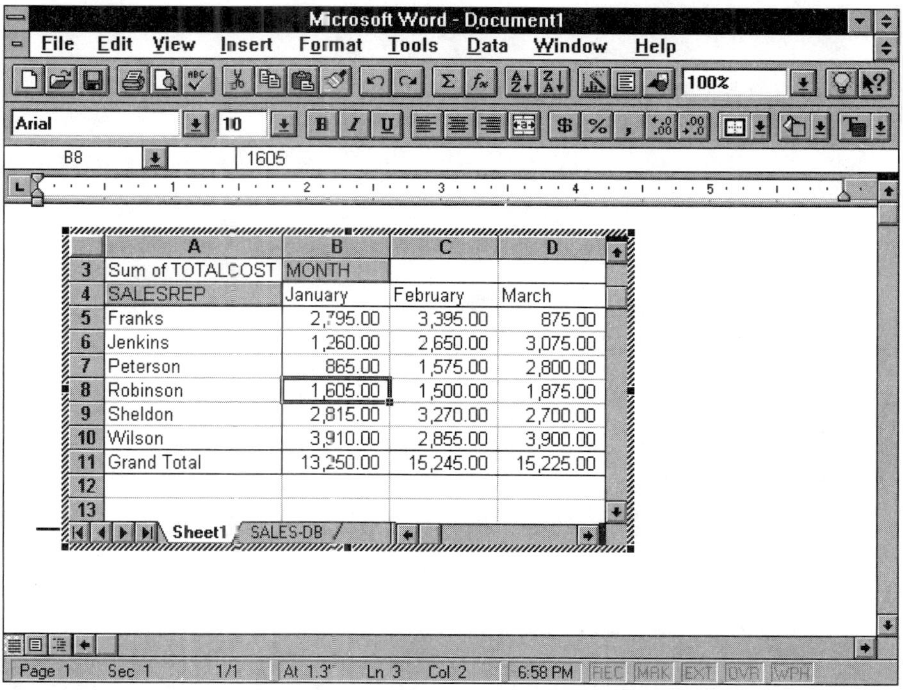

Figure 2-20: An Excel workbook inserted into a Word for Windows document.

Summary

- In this chapter, I provided a conceptual overview of Excel 5 for newcomers to the fold.
- Chapter 3 continues the saga, detailing the files used by Excel.

Chapter 3

Understanding Excel's Files

In This Chapter

- A discussion of the files used and produced by Excel
- Information about installing Excel
- Details about EXCEL5.INI

If you plan to do any advanced work with Excel, it's critical that you understand the ins and outs of the various files used and generated by Excel.

What Files Get Installed

Back in the early days of personal computers, you could run most applications from a floppy disk — *installation* was rarely necessary. However, you had to contend with complicated copy-protection schemes. PC software has come a long way in the past 12 years, and, fortunately, copy protection is generally a thing of the past.

But today's users must deal with bloated applications. I don't know of a single major Windows application that comes on a single disk. In fact, most programs come on multiple disks in compressed files. Luckily, most include an installation program that automatically expands and copies the files to their appropriate locations on your hard drive or network server. Nonetheless, within a few years, most applications will be distributed on CD-ROMs, eliminating the tedious floppy disk shuffle that characterizes today's software installations.

Installing a Windows application usually involves the following:

- Executing a setup program directly from a floppy disk
- Selecting various installation options
- Creating one or more directories on the target hard drive
- Expanding the compressed files stored on the distribution disks and copying them to the hard drive
- Adding library files to the WINDOWS and/or WINDOWS\SYSTEM directories
- Making changes to WIN.INI, AUTOEXEC.BAT, or CONFIG.SYS

- Adding a new INI file for the application
- Registering the program in the Windows registration database
- Creating a new Program Manager program group
- Adding one or more Program Manager icons to the new program group

Excel 5's installation follows this scenario: You run SETUP.EXE, which is located on the first distribution disk (labeled *Disk 1-Setup*). After you reply to SETUP's prompt for options, you need only insert the appropriate disks when prompted.

You can always run SETUP again to change options or add or delete components, such as add-ins or examples and demos. By the way, SETUP.EXE is copied to EXCEL\SETUP, so you don't have to reuse the original floppy disks.

When you install Excel, you choose among three setup options: complete, typical, or minimal. In addition, you can choose a custom installation, where you choose which components to install.

If you acquire Excel as part of the Microsoft Office suite, installation proceeds differently, because a single SETUP program installs all the products in the suite. But the basic process is the same.

Single-user installation

On a single-user system, a complete installation of Excel 5 uses 23,201,585 bytes of hard disk space and writes files to 17 directories. (This data applies to the initial release of Excel 5; it may vary slightly with interim updates.) The default directory structure created with a complete installation of Excel is

```
\EXCEL
 EXAMPLES
        SOLVER
 EXCELCBT
 LIBRARY
        ANALYSIS
        CROSSTAB
        MSQUERY
        SLIDES
        SOLVER
 SETUP
 XLSTART
```

A complete installation also writes files to the following subdirectories (which are created if they don't already exist):

```
\WINDOWS
 MSAPPS
        GRPHFLT
        MSINFO
        MSQUERY
        PROOF
 SYSTEM
```

The directory in which you install Excel contains a file called FILELIST.TXT. This file lists all the files installed for each installation option, their size, and where they are installed.

Network installation

Network installation is also straightforward. Typically, you start by installing Excel on a network server. Then users can run Excel from the server, or you can copy Excel from the server to each workstation.

If you do the latter, you can save quite a bit of work by creating a script (SETUP.STF) that lets you set which options are to be installed. This process is described in the NETWORK.TXT file, which is on the Disk 1-Setup disk.

Starting Excel

To start Excel is to execute EXCEL.EXE. The most common method is to click the Excel icon, located in Program Manager (or some other Windows shell).

When Excel starts, it begins with a blank workbook — the number of sheets in the workbook is determined by the DefSheets setting in the [Microsoft Excel] section of EXCEL5.INI. You can change this value by editing EXCEL5.INI or by changing the Sheets in New Workbook setting, in the General tab of the Options dialog box.

If your EXCEL\XLSTART directory contains any workbooks, they are opened automatically — no blank workbook appears. If EXCEL\XLSTART includes a workspace file, multiple workbooks are opened in a customized workspace. You also can define an alternate startup directory to hold other worksheet or workspace files you want opened automatically. You can set up this alternate startup directory by specifying a path in the Alternate Startup File Location setting, in the General tab of the Options dialog box.

If you want to change the default formats (or content) of blank workbooks that you create, simply create a default workbook and save it as a template with the name BOOK.XLT in your EXCEL\XLSTART directory.

Excel recognizes several command line switches. These are listed in Table 3-1.

Table 3-1 Excel Command Line Switches

Switch	*What It Does*
/e	Starts Excel without a blank workbook
filename	Opens the file specified
/r filename	Opens the file specified as read-only
/p directory	Specifies a default directory for the current session

You enter these switches in the Command Line box of the Program Item Properties dialog box in Program Manager. You can get to this dialog box by selecting the Excel icon and pressing Alt+Enter.

Excel's File Extensions

As Excel goes about its business, it uses many files in addition to EXCEL.EXE. Excel loads these other files, which usually have a DLL (Dynamic Link Library) extension, into memory as needed. Following is a summary of the file types that Excel may write to your hard disk during installation.

File Type	*Description*
CBT	A file used in the Excel tutorial (*CBT* stands for computer-based training).
DLL	A Dynamic Link Library file. DLLs are used by Windows applications to store program code.
EXE	An executable file. EXCEL.EXE is the executable file that runs Excel.
HLP	Standard Windows help file, produced by the Windows Help Compiler and read by WINHELP.EXE. Excel uses five HLP files.
INI	An initialization file (usually a plain ASCII text file). Excel's INI file is EXCEL5.INI, which is stored in the WINDOWS directory. Excel also installs (or updates) VBA.INI, which stores settings for Visual Basic for Applications.

File Type	*Description*
OLB	An object type library file. Two object type libraries installed by the English language version of Excel 5 are XLEN50.OLB and VBAEN.OLB.
REG	A text file that contains information that is merged into your Windows registration database.
TXT	A plain ASCII text file, readable from any text editor (such as NOTEPAD) or the DOS prompt. These files often contain late-breaking information not found in the manuals.
XLA	An Excel add-in file. Several are supplied with Excel, and you can also create your own add-ins by using the Tools⇨Make Add-In command from a VBA module.
XLB	An Excel toolbar configuration file. The current toolbar configuration is stored in EXCEL5.XLB.
XLC	An Excel 4 chart file (obsolete with Excel 5).
XLL	An Excel link library file.
XLM	An Excel 4 macro file (obsolete with Excel 5).
XLS	An Excel workbook file. Unfortunately, there is no way to tell from the extension which version of Excel produced the file.
XLT	An Excel template file.
XLW	An Excel 4 workbook file (obsolete in Excel 5 because all files are workbooks).

What About All Those DLLs?

Users are often confused by the many DLL files on their hard drives. Many of these are part of Windows, but others are installed by other applications.

TIP

You can find out which DLLs are loaded in memory at any time by using the Microsoft System Info application, which you can execute from Excel: choose Help⇨About Microsoft Excel, click the System Info button, and then choose the System DLLs category. The program lists the DLLs on your system and also indicates which are currently loaded into memory. Figure 3-1 shows an example.

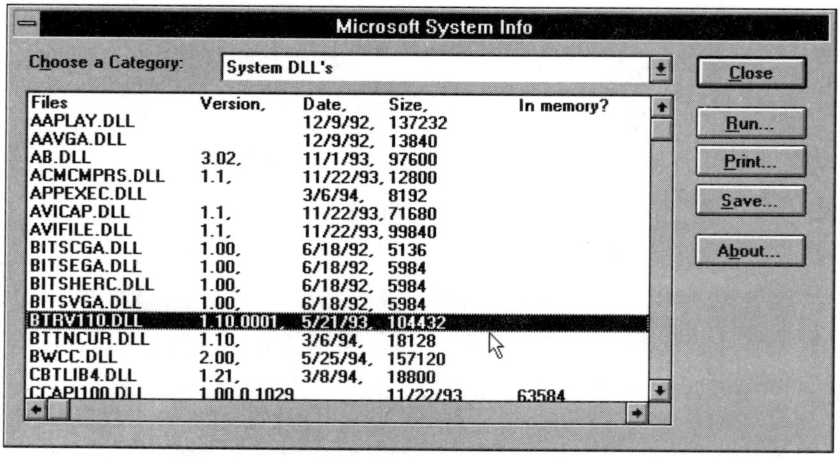

Figure 3-1: The Microsoft System Info program lists your system's DLL files and indicates which are loaded into memory.

Table 3-2 lists the DLL files included with Excel 5 (single-user installation). Which files are installed depends on the installation options selected.

Table 3-2 DLL Files Used by a Single-User Installation

DLL File	*Where It's Installed*	*Description*
CBTLIB4.DLL	\EXCEL\EXCELCBT	Used for help demos
CCAPI100.DLL	\WINDOWS\SYSTEM	Cue cards API
COMMTB.DLL	\WINDOWS\SYSTEM	Toolbar buttonface editor
COMPOBJ.DLL	\WINDOWS\SYSTEM	OLE 2 library
CTL3D.DLL	\WINDOWS\SYSTEM	3-D dialog box controls
CTL3DV2.DLL	\WINDOWS\SYSTEM	A later version of CTL3D.DLL
CUECARD2.DLL	\WINDOWS\MSAPPS\MSQUERY	Adds cue cards to MS Query
DBNMP3.DLL	\WINDOWS\SYSTEM	SQL server library
DDEML.DLL	\WINDOWS\SYSTEM	DDE management library
EXCEL_BB.DLL	\EXCEL\SETUP	Used by Setup
IFFPCX.DLL	\WINDOWS\MSAPPS\GRPHFLT	PCX file converter
IFFTIFF.DLL	\WINDOWS\MSAPPS\GRPHFLT	TIF file converter
MAPIVIM.DLL	\WINDOWS\SYSTEM	MAPI/VIM library
MSCPYDIS.DLL	\EXCEL\SETUP	Disk copier and expander used by Setup
MSFFILE.DLL	\WINDOWS\SYSTEM	Used by Find File command

DLL File	Where It's Installed	Description
MSJETDSP.DLL	\WINDOWS\SYSTEM	Jet engine library (for Access)
MSSETUP.DLL	\EXCEL\SETUP	Used by Setup
MSSPELL.DLL	\WINDOWS\MSAPPS\PROOF	Used by the spell-checker
MSTOOLBR.DLL	\WINDOWS\SYSTEM	Toolbar library
ODBC.DLL	\WINDOWS\SYSTEM	ODBC library
ODBCINST.DLL	\WINDOWS\SYSTEM	ODBC installation library
OLE2.DLL	\WINDOWS\SYSTEM	OLE 2 library
OLE2CONV.DLL	\WINDOWS\SYSTEM	Graphic filters library
OLE2DISP.DLL	\WINDOWS\SYSTEM	OLE Automation library
OLE2NLS.DLL	\WINDOWS\SYSTEM	OLE NLS library
OLE2PROX.DLL	\WINDOWS\SYSTEM	OLE 2 library
PDX110.DLL	\WINDOWS\SYSTEM	Paradox ISAM (for Access)
QEXLA.DLL	\EXCEL\LIBRARY\MSQUERY	Used by MS Query
QRYINTL.DLL	\WINDOWS\MSAPPS\MSQUERY	MS Query international library
RED110.DLL	\WINDOWS\SYSTEM	Red ISAM (for Access)
SCP.DLL	\WINDOWS\SYSTEM	Code page translation library
SDM.DLL	\WINDOWS\SYSTEM	Standard dialog manager library
SHARERES.DLL	\WINDOWS\SYSTEM	Shared resources library
SIMADMIN.DLL	\WINDOWS\SYSTEM	ODBC Simba administrator library
SIMBA.DLL	\WINDOWS\SYSTEM	ODBC Simba library
SOLVER.DLL	\EXCEL\LIBRARY\SOLVER	Used by Solver
SQLSRVR.DLL	\WINDOWS\SYSTEM	SQL server library
STORAGE.DLL	\WINDOWS\SYSTEM	OLE 2 library
TYPELIB.DLL	\WINDOWS\SYSTEM	OLE 2 type library
VBA.DLL	\WINDOWS\SYSTEM	VBA library
VBAEN.DLL	\WINDOWS\SYSTEM	VBA English language resources
XBS110.DLL	\WINDOWS\SYSTEM	dBASE ISAM (for Access)
XLCALL.DLL	\WINDOWS\SYSTEM	Excel callback library
XLCONVMP.DLL	\EXCEL	MultiPlan file converter
XLHELP.DLL	\EXCEL	Used for help demos
XLINTL.DLL	\EXCEL	Excel localized resource
XLODBC.DLL	\EXCEL\LIBRARY\MSQUERY	Used by MS Query
XLSLIDES.DLL	\EXCEL\LIBRARY\SLIDES	Used by slide show

File Types Supported

Although Excel's default file format is an XLS workbook file, it can also open and save files generated by several other applications.

Often you'll lose some information when you use a file format other than XLS.

In this section, I discuss the various types of files you can and cannot use with Excel.

Lotus 1-2-3 spreadsheet files

Lotus spreadsheets come in several flavors:

- *WKS files* are single-sheet files used by 1-2-3 Release 1.x for DOS. Excel can read and write these files.
- *WK1 files* are single-sheet files used by 1-2-3 Release 2.x for DOS. The formatting for these files is stored in ALL files (produced by the Allways add-in) or FM1 files (produced by the Wysiwyg add-in). Excel can read and write all these files. When you save a file to the WK1 format, you can choose which (if any) type of formatting file to generate.
- *WK3 files* are (potentially) multisheet files generated by 1-2-3 Release 3.x for DOS, 1-2-3 Release 4.x for DOS, and 1-2-3 Release 1.x for Windows. The formatting for these files are stored in FM3 files (produced by the Wysiwyg add-in). Excel can read and write WK3 files with or without the accompanying FM3 file.
- *WK4 files* are (potentially) multisheet files generated by 1-2-3 Release 4.x for Windows and 1-2-3 Release 5.x for Windows (Lotus finally got its act together and eliminated the separate formatting file). Excel can neither read nor write these files. If you need to read a WK4 file into Excel, your only option is to use 1-2-3 Release 4 for Windows (or later) and save the file in WK3 format, which Excel can read, from 1-2-3.

Quattro Pro spreadsheet files

Quattro Pro files also exist in several versions:

- *WQ1 files* are the single-sheet files generated by Quattro Pro for DOS Versions 1, 2, 3, and 4. Excel can read and write these files.
- *WQ2 files* are the (potentially) multisheet files generated by Quattro Pro for DOS Version 5. Excel can neither read nor write this file format.
- *WB1 files* are the (potentially) multisheet files generated by Quattro Pro for Windows Versions 1, 5, and 6 (there are no Versions 2 through 4). Excel can neither read nor write this file format.

Database file formats

DBF files are single-table database files generated by dBASE and several other database programs. Excel can read and write DBF files up to and including dBASE 4.

Excel cannot read or write any other database file formats directly. If you install the MS Query add-in, however, you can use Query to access many other database file formats and then copy or link the data into an Excel worksheet.

Text file formats

Text files simply contain data; there's no formatting. There are several relatively standard text file formats, but there are no standard file extensions.

- Each line in *tab-delimited files* consists of fields separated by tabs. Excel can read these files, converting each line to a row and each field to a column. Excel also can write these files, using TXT as the default extension.
- Each line in *comma-separated files* consists of fields separated by commas. Sometimes text is in quotes. Excel can read these files, converting each line to a row and each field to a column. Excel also can write these files, using CSV as the default extension.
- Each line in *space-delimited files* consists of fields separated by spaces. Excel can read these files, converting each line to a row and each field to a column. Excel also can write these files, using PRN as the default extension.

When you attempt to load a text file into Excel, the Text Import Wizard kicks in to help you specify how you want the file retrieved.

TIP

To bypass the Text Import Wizard, press Shift when you click OK in the Open dialog box.

Other file formats

- DIF (Data Interchange Format) file format was used by VisiCalc. I haven't seen a DIF file in ages. Excel can read and write these files.
- Sylk (Symbolic Link) file format was used by MultiPlan. Excel can read and write these files.

NOTE

Beginning with Excel 5, it is possible for developers to create custom file converters by using the C language. This topic is discussed in the *Microsoft Excel Developer's Kit Version 5* (Microsoft Press, 1994).

Importing files takes a bit longer than with previous versions because Excel 5 does some additional behind-the-scenes work — it finds and converts copied formulas to save space. Basically, Excel 5 keeps only one copy of a formula, which reduces file size and enhances performance.

Files Written by Excel

XLS files

The XLS files produced by Excel 5 are completely different from the XLS files generated by prior versions. The bad news is that earlier Excel versions cannot read these files. The good news is that this file format may become the standard for future versions of Excel — if so, Excel 5 will be able to read files produced by later versions.

Excel 5 XLS files are compound files, which is the OLE 2 of a standard known as the Structured Storage Model. An OLE 2 compound file can be thought of as a file system within a file. The XLS file format is described in detail in the *Microsoft Excel Developer's Kit Version 5*.

Workspace files

A workspace file is a special file that contains information about an Excel workspace. For example, if you have a project that uses two workbooks and you like to have the workbook windows arranged in a particular way, you can write an XLW file (use the File⇨Save Workspace command) to save this window configuration. Then whenever you open the XLW file, Excel restores the desired workspace.

The Personal Macro Workbook

Most custom macros are designed for a specific workbook. But if you want to use some macros in all your work, you can store them in the Personal Macro Workbook — a hidden workbook that's automatically loaded whenever Excel starts. (The file, PERSONAL.XLS, resides in your EXCEL\XLSTART directory.) The general-purpose macros stored in the Personal Macro Workbook are always available to you.

The Personal Macro Workbook is normally in a hidden window (to keep it out of the way). If you record a macro to this workbook, you need to unhide the window (choose the Window⇨Unhide command) before you can edit or view the macro. If you unhide the Personal Macro Workbook, though, make sure that you hide it before you exit Excel or it will not be hidden the next time you start Excel.

When you want to exit Excel, Excel asks whether you want to save changes to the Personal Macro Workbook.

NOTE

It's important to understand that a workspace file does *not* include the workbooks — only the configuration information. Also, the File⇨Save Workspace command does not save the workbooks themselves.

The XLW file format is described in detail in the *Microsoft Excel Developer's Kit Version 5.*

Template files

You can save any workbook as a template file (XLT extension). Doing so is useful if you tend to create similar files on a regular basis. For example, you may need to generate a monthly sales report. You can save some time by creating a template that holds the needed formulas. When you can start new files based on the template, you need only plug in the values.

When you open a template, you are working with a copy of the file. Therefore, if you choose the File⇨Save command, Excel prompts you for a filename and then saves the file as an XLS workbook file.

TIP

To make changes to a template file, press Shift when you click OK in the Open dialog box.

A related concept is *autotemplates*, or template files with special names that you store in your EXCEL\XLSTART directory. Autotemplates (see Table 3-3) are the basis for all new sheets that you insert into a workbook.

Table 3-3 Autotemplates

Name	***Sheet Type***
SHEET.XLT	Worksheet
CHART.XLT	Chart sheet
MACRO.XLT	MS Excel 4.0 macro
MODULE.XLT	VBA module
DIALOG.XLT	Dialog sheet

Because a template is created from a worksheet file, it's possible to save autotemplates with multiple sheets.

As I mentioned earlier, you can control how a new workbook looks by using a template named BOOK.XLT (it's in your EXCEL\XLSTART directory).

If you define a MODULE.XLT autotemplate, the Insert⇨Macro⇨Module command will not use it. To insert a module based on the autotemplate, right-click a sheet tab and choose the *second* instance of the word Module from the Insert dialog box. This appears to be a bug in Excel 5.

Toolbar files

Excel stores toolbar configurations in XLB files. Whenever you exit Excel, the current toolbar configuration is saved in EXCEL5.XLB, located in your WINDOWS directory.

Unfortunately, you cannot save custom toolbar configurations from Excel. But there is a way to create custom XLB toolbar configuration files; I discuss this technique in Chapter 15.

Add-in files

Excel 5 doesn't include as many add-ins as Excel 4 because many of the features that required an add-in are now built-in. For a list of the add-ins included with Excel 5, see Chapter 2.

You can easily create your own add-ins from XLS workbook files. These add-ins can add new features to Excel and also make it impossible for others to view your macros. In fact, creating add-ins is the preferred method of distributing your Excel applications. Chapter 13 covers this topic in detail.

Add-ins have an XLA extension.

Examining the INI Files

INI files are (usually) ASCII files that contain settings and options for a particular program. Installing Excel adds two more to your collection: EXCEL5.INI and VBA.INI. (INI files accumulate rapidly; I have more than 200 such files scattered across two hard drives, for example.)

About INI files

INI files for Windows programs usually adhere to a specific format: they are usually ASCII files and consist of sections and statements. Section names are enclosed in brackets, like

```
[DESKTOP]
```

Beneath each section header are statements that assign a value or setting. For example, the following are statements that may appear under the [DESKTOP] section of WIN.INI:

```
Pattern=(None)
TileWallPaper=1
GridGranularity=0
IconSpacing=70
Wallpaper=(None)
```

In this case, the [DESKTOP] section stores the user's preferences for wallpaper, icon spacing, and so on. When you make such changes by using the Windows Control Panel, the changes are written to your WIN.INI file. The next time you start Windows, these settings are retrieved.

You can edit INI files manually if you know what you're doing. Because INI files are plain text files, just about any text editor will do, including the Windows NOTEPAD. If you use a word processor to edit an INI file, just make sure that the file gets saved as a plain text file. If you edit an application's INI file while the application is running, the changes won't take effect until you restart the application.

The applications that you develop by using Excel and VBA can also read and write to INI files. This requires the use of a Windows API function call. This technique is discussed in Chapter 11.

EXCEL5.INI

The EXCEL5.INI file is located in your WINDOWS directory, not the EXCEL directory. Whenever you start Excel, it reads this file to get start-up settings. Whenever you exit Excel, it updates this file as needed. For example, it updates the [Recent File List] section and any changes you made in the Option dialog box.

It's important to understand that EXCEL5.INI is updated only when you exit Excel by normal methods. If Excel crashes your system (unfortunately, not all that uncommon an occurrence for developers), EXCEL5.INI is not updated.

If you install Excel on a network, the installation program creates an EXCEL5.INI file in the application's directory as well as an EXCEL5.INI file in the WINDOWS directory. Don't edit the EXCEL5.INI file in the network directory because this file is for network purposes only.

Table 3-4 lists the possible sections found in an EXCEL5.INI file. You may not find all these sections in your particular file.

Table 3-4 EXCEL5.INI File Sections

Section	Description
[Add-in Manager]	Lists add-ins that appear in the list box when you choose the Tools⇨Add-Ins command.
[AutoSave]	Holds the AutoSave option that you set.
[Delete Commands]	Lets you specify which menu commands you don't want to appear.
[Init Commands]	Holds information about custom commands.
[Init Menus]	Holds information about custom menus.
[Line Print]	Holds settings used in 1-2-3 macro printing. Excel updates this section whenever it executes a 1-2-3 macro that has /wgdu (Worksheet Global Default Update) in it.
[Microsoft Excel]	A catchall section; holds a wide variety of settings.
[Recent File List]	Stores the names of the last four files saved.
[Spell Checker]	Stores information about your spell-checking options.
[WK? Settings]	Contains settings for opening and saving 1-2-3 files (for example, whether to create an FMT or FM3 format file).

What good is EXCEL5.INI? Although most of the settings can be changed via Excel's Options dialog box, several other useful settings cannot be changed directly from Excel. I tell you about some of them in the following sections.

Earlier versions of Excel used the WIN.INI file to store start-up settings. With Excel 5, these settings are stored in the [Microsoft Excel] section of EXCEL5.INI. If you upgrade from a previous version, the SETUP program copies the current [Microsoft Excel] section settings from WIN.INI to EXCEL5.INI. However, the SETUP program does *not* get any settings from existing EXCEL.INI or EXCEL4.INI files. After upgrading, you can copy any settings from these files to your new EXCEL5.INI file. You also can safely delete EXCEL.INI, EXCEL4.INI, and the [Microsoft Excel] section of your WINI.INI file.

Here's a typical [Microsoft Excel] section of an EXCEL5.INI file:

```
[Microsoft Excel]
Comment=The open=/f lines load custom functions into the
Paste Function list.
Maximized=1
Basics=1
AutoFormat=18
AutoFormat Options=31
Options5=3585
CBTLOCATION=C:\EXCEL5\EXCELCBT
```

```
Options3=0
User=John Walkenbach
Font=Arial,10
AltStartup=
StickyPtX=539
StickyPtY=359
DefSheets=1
MRUFuncs=9,307,337,77,142,169,127,70,4,125
Pos=425,1,732,578
Options=87
Default Chart=MS Excel 4.0
PRTools001=6113
AutoFormat Options=31
OPEN=C:\LIBRARY\POWER\POWER.XLA
```

Opening files automatically

Files stored in the EXCEL\XLSTART directory are opened automatically whenever Excel starts. But there's another way to specify which files you want loaded automatically: the OPEN= statement in the [Microsoft Excel] section. This is useful if you don't want to (or can't) store the file in the \XLSTART directory.

Including the following statement in your EXCEL5.INI opens the file named SCHEDULE.XLS whenever Excel starts up.

```
OPEN=C:\EXCEL\WORK\SCHEDULE.XLS
```

You can have any number of OPEN= statements in your EXCEL5.INI file, but if you use more than one you must number them: OPEN1=, OPEN2=, and so on.

The OPEN= statement also can be used with the /r and /f switches. The /r switch opens the file as read-only. For example,

```
OPEN= /r C:\EXCEL\BUDGET.XLS
```

The /f switch works with XLT template files. Templates normally must be in the EXCEL\XLSTART directory, but the /f switch enables you to open a template from any directory. The following example causes the SALES.XLT template to be displayed in the dialog box that appears when you choose File⇨New:

```
OPEN= /f C:\EXCEL\SALES.XLT
```

XLM macro fans may have used the /f switch to specify an XLM macro file that contained custom functions. Doing so caused the functions to be listed in the Function Wizard, but the file itself was loaded only when needed. This technique still works in Excel 5, but for custom functions written in XLM only. I've had no luck getting this technique to work with custom functions written in VBA and saved as an XLA add-in.

The Tools⇨Add-Ins command reads and writes OPEN statements in EXCEL5.INI.

Other options

The Options=, Options3=, and Options5= statements in the [Microsoft Excel] section actually control 5, 6, and 15 options, respectively. To control these options, you total the values corresponding to the desired options (see Tables 3-5, 3-6, and 3-7) and place the sum in the appropriate Options= statement.

For example, the following line makes Excel hide the scroll bars, formula bar, and status bar:

```
Options=80
```

Meanwhile, the following line hides gridlines:

```
Options3=16384
```

Table 3-5 Options= Options

Value	*Indicates*
1	Show scroll bars
2	Show formula bar
4	Show status bar
16	Use A1-style references (as opposed to R1C1)
64	DDE is enabled

Table 3-6 Options3= Options

Value	*Indicates*
0	Alternate menu key on
2	Alternate navigation keys on
4	Lotus 1-2-3 help on
8	Cell note indicators off
32	Macro recording defaults to Personal Macro Sheet
16384	Gridlines in new sheets off

Table 3-7	Options5= Options
Value	*Indicates*
1	Tip Wizard is on
2	Prompt for Summary Info
4	In-cell editing is not allowed
8	Status bar is visible in full-screen mode
16	Formula bar is visible in full-screen mode
32	Full-screen mode
64	Most-recently used file list is not displayed
128	Cut, copy, and sort objects with cells
256	Tool tips off
512	Small toolbar buttons
1024	Toolbar auto-sensing
2048	Do not move to next cell after Enter key is pressed
4096	Do not warn before drag-drop copy or paste
8192	Use black and white toolbar buttons
16384	Ask to update automatic links

There's nothing secret about these options; most can be set from the Options dialog box. However, two Options3= settings (default macro recording and show/hide gridlines) and three Options5= settings (visibility of status bar, formula bar, and most-recently used file list) can be changed only by editing the EXCEL5.INI file.

Defining custom menus and commands

CROSS REFERENCE

Most users don't realize that they can use EXCEL5.INI to define custom menus and commands. This approach can be useful if you want a group of users to have new or changed menus: you can make the change in EXCEL5.INI and then distribute the file. I discuss this technique in Chapter 14.

Deleting built-in commands

You also can use EXCEL5.INI to delete one or more of Excel's built-in commands. You do so by inserting statements in the [Delete Commands] section of EXCEL5.INI.

The statements take the form

```
Keyword=MenubarNumber,MenuName,CommandPosition
```

where *Keyword* is a unique identifier that you supply, *MenubarNumber* is the number of the menubar you want to modify (see Table 3-8), *MenuName* is the name of the menu, and *CommandPosition* is the position or name of the command you want to delete. To delete the File⇨Send command, for example, use a statement such as:

```
DelSend=10,File,Send
```

Table 3-8 MenubarNumbers

Number	*Menubar*
1	Worksheet and macro sheet (Excel 4.0)
2	Chart (Excel 4.0)
3	Null (the menu displayed when no workbooks are open)
4	Info
5	Worksheet and macro sheet (short menus, Excel 3.0 and earlier)
6	Chart (short menus, Excel 3.0 and earlier)
7	Cell, toolbar, and workbook (shortcut menus)
8	Object (shortcut menus)
9	Chart (Excel 4.0 shortcut menus)
10	Worksheet and Macro sheet
11	Chart
12	Visual Basic

VBA.INI

Excel's installation program also creates VBA.INI. If the file already exists, Setup adds some information about Excel 5. The VBA.INI file, which is stored in the directory that holds your WIN.INI file, is accessed by all applications that use VBA. If you don't own any other VBA applications, this file has only one section: [EXCEL].

The statements in the [EXCEL] section of VBA.INI correspond to the options that appear when you choose the Tools⇨Options command and click on the Module General and Module Format tabs. Listing 3-1 is the complete contents of my VBA.INI file.

Listing 3-1 VBA.INI file

```
[Excel]
DefaultLCIDv5.0=9
BreakOnAllErrors=0
ForeColors=C 5 0 1 10 14 6 0
BackColors=C 0 9 6 0 0 0 0
RequireDeclaration=1
TabWidth=4
FontHeight5.0=9
FontFace5.0=Fixedsys
AutoIndent=1

[PROJECT]
DefaultLCIDv4.0=1033
```

If you don't have Microsoft Project installed, the last two lines will not appear in your VBA.INI. And if you've never changed any of the VBA settings in the Options dialog box, your VBA.INI file may have only one line.

The BreakOnAllErrors=0 setting is particularly important because it determines whether the error-handling features built into your application will work. If this setting is 1, VBA error messages are shown regardless of any On Error statements you have in your code. The BreakOnAllErrors=0 setting is based on the setting of the Break On All Errors check box in the Options dialog box (choose the Tools⇨Options command and click on the Module General tab).

Unfortunately, VBA does not have a command to determine what this setting is or to make sure that it's set to unchecked. So if you're distributing an application to a user, there's no way of knowing if the user has Break On All Errors set to on or off.

Fortunately, this becomes a moot point if your application is distributed as an add-in (XLA file). If your workbook is an XLA file, your error-handling procedures will work regardless of the setting of BreakOnAllErrors.

I discuss error-handling techniques in Chapter 8.

NOTE

Wait! There *is* a way to handle this situation — sort of. You can use a Windows API call to determine the setting of any INI file. See Chapter 11 for more details.

Summary

- In this chapter, I discussed the files used and created by Excel. I described Excel installation, various ways to load files automatically, Excel's file extensions, DLLs, and file formats supported by Excel. I also discussed some of the settings in EXCEL5.INI and outlined the various types of files Excel writes. Information in this chapter that's particularly relevant to application development and programming will appear in more detail in other chapters.
- This chapter concludes Part I. Part II provides information about developing user-oriented applications with Excel.

Part II

Excel Application Development

This part contains only two chapters, but they are important for readers who want to become effective Excel power programmers. In Chapter 4, I present my views on exactly what constitutes a spreadsheet application. Chapter 5 discusses the general steps involved in creating a spreadsheet application using Excel.

Chapter 4

What Is a Spreadsheet Application?

In This Chapter

- A working definition of a spreadsheet application
- The difference between a spreadsheet user and a spreadsheet developer
- A classification scheme for spreadsheet users, to help you conceptualize who is the audience for your applications
- Why people use spreadsheets
- A taxonomy of the basic types of spreadsheets

In this chapter I attempt to clarify how people use spreadsheets in the real world — a topic that's germane to this entire book because it may help you determine just how much effort you should devote to a particular development project. By the time you finish this chapter, you should have a pretty good idea of what I mean by a spreadsheet application. And after you've made it through the rest of the book, you'll be well on your way to developing your own spreadsheet applications with Excel. But first, I'll get down to the basics.

You've probably been working with spreadsheets for several years, but chances are good that your primary focus has been on simply generating spreadsheets to get the job done. You probably never really gave much thought to more global issues like those discussed in this chapter — the different types of spreadsheet users, how to classify various types of spreadsheets, and even basic questions such as why people use spreadsheets. If the title of this book attracted your attention, it's important for you to understand these issues so that you can become an effective "power programmer." I'll start with the concept of a *spreadsheet application*. This is, after all, the end result of your power programming efforts.

Spreadsheet Applications

Programming, as it relates to spreadsheet use, is essentially the process of building *applications* that use a spreadsheet rather than a traditional programming language such as C, Pascal, or BASIC. In most cases, these applications will be used by other people — not the developer of the application.

For purposes of this book, a spreadsheet application is

A spreadsheet file (or group of related files) that is designed such that someone other than the developer can perform useful work without extensive training.

Based on this definition, most of the spreadsheet files you've developed probably wouldn't qualify as spreadsheet applications. You may have dozens or hundreds of spreadsheet files on your hard drive. But it's a safe bet that most of them aren't designed for others to use.

More specifically, a good spreadsheet application is characterized by the following:

- It allows the end user to perform a task that he or she probably would not be able to do otherwise.
- It is the appropriate solution to the problem. Designing an application that works in a spreadsheet environment isn't always the optimal approach.
- It accomplishes what it is supposed to do. This may be an obvious prerequisite, but it's not at all uncommon for applications to fail to meet this test.
- It produces accurate results and is free of bugs.
- It uses appropriate and efficient methods and algorithms to accomplish its job.
- It traps errors before the user is forced to deal with them.
- It does not allow the user to accidentally (or intentionally) delete or modify important components.
- Its user interface is clear and consistent so the user always knows how to proceed.
- Its formulas, macros, and user interface elements are well documented.
- It is designed such that it can be modified in simple ways without making major changes.
- It has an easily accessible help system that provides useful information on at least the major procedures.
- It is designed so that it is portable and runs on any system that has the proper software (in this case, a copy of Excel 5).

It should come as no surprise that you can create spreadsheet applications at many different levels, ranging from simple fill-in-the-blanks templates to extremely complex applications that utilize custom menus and dialog boxes — and may not even look like a spreadsheet.

The Developer and the End User

I've already used the terms *developer* and *end user,* and you'll see these terms frequently throughout this book. Because you've gotten this far in the book, I think I can safely assume that you're either a spreadsheet application developer or you're a potential developer.

My definitions are simple. The person who creates the spreadsheet application is the developer. For joint projects, there are multiple developers (a development team). The person who uses the results of the developer's spreadsheet programming efforts is the *end user* (which I often shorten to simply *user*). In many cases, there will be multiple *end users* and often the developer is one of the users.

Who are developers? What do they do?

I've attended several conferences devoted to spreadsheet development, and I can only conclude that spreadsheet developers are a motley crew. I divide them into two primary groups:

- *Insiders* are developers who are intimately involved with the users and thoroughly understand their needs. In many cases, these developers are also users of the application. Often, they developed the application in response to a particular problem.
- *Outsiders* are developers who are hired to produce a solution to a problem. In most cases, developers in this category are familiar with the business in general, but not with the specifics of the application they are developing. In other cases, these developers are employed by the company that requests the application (but who normally work in a different department).

Some developers work full time as developers. They may be either insiders or outsiders. A fair number of consultants (outsiders) make a decent living developing spreadsheet applications on a freelance basis.

Other spreadsheet developers don't develop full time, and may not even realize they are developing spreadsheet applications. These developers are often the office computer gurus who seem to know everything about computers and software. These folks often create spreadsheet applications as a way to make their lives easier — the time spent developing a well-designed application for others will often save hours of training time and greatly reduce the time spent answering others' questions.

Spreadsheet developers are typically involved in the following activities, often performing most or all of each step on their own:

- Determining the needs of the user.
- Planning an application that meets these needs.
- Determining the most appropriate user interface.
- Creating the spreadsheet, formulas, macros, and user interface.
- Testing the application under all reasonable sets of conditions.
- Making the application bulletproof (often based on the previous step).
- Making the application aesthetically appealing and intuitive.
- Documenting the development effort.
- Distributing the application to users.
- Updating the application if and when it's necessary.

CROSS REFERENCE

I discuss these activities in more detail in Chapter 5.

Developers must understand their development environment thoroughly — in this case, Excel. And there's certainly a lot to know when it comes to Excel. By any standard, Excel is easy to use, but ease of use is defined in terms of the user. Developing nontrivial spreadsheet applications with Excel requires a thorough knowledge of formulas, functions, macros (VBA or Visual Basic for Applications), custom dialog boxes, custom toolbars, and add-ins. Most Excel users, of course, don't meet these qualifications and have no intention of learning these details — which brings me to the next topic: classifying spreadsheet users.

Classifying spreadsheet users

Over the years, I've found that it's often useful to classify people who use spreadsheets — this includes both developers and end users — along two dimensions: their *level of experience* with spreadsheets, and their *interest in learning* about spreadsheets (which roughly translates into motivation level).

Table 4-1 depicts this schema by showing the nine combinations across these two dimensions (assuming three levels of interest and experience). In reality, only seven segments are worth thinking about because moderately experienced and very experienced spreadsheet users generally have at least *some* interest in spreadsheets (that's how they got their experience). Any users who have a lot of spreadsheet experience and a low level of interest would make very bad developers.

Table 4-1 Classifying spreadsheet users by experience and interest in learning.

Interest & Experience	*No Interest*	*Moderately Interested*	*Very Interested*
Little Experience	User	User	User/Potential Developer
Moderately Experienced	NA	User	Developer
Very Experienced	NA	User	Developer

It should be clear that spreadsheet developers must have a great deal of *experience* with spreadsheets, as well as an uncommonly high *interest* in spreadsheets. Those with little spreadsheet experience — but with a great deal of interest — are potential developers. All they need is more experience. If you're reading this book, you probably fall into one of the boxes in the last column of the chart.

The audience for spreadsheet applications

The remaining segments in the preceding chart comprise spreadsheet end users — the consumers of spreadsheet applications. When you develop a spreadsheet application for use by others, you need to understand which of these groups of people will actually be using your application.

Users with little experience and no interest are a large percentage of all spreadsheet users — probably the largest segment of all. These are the folks who need to use a spreadsheet for their job, but view the spreadsheet as only a means to an end. Typically, they know very little about computers and software, and they usually have no interest in learning anything more than what's required to get their job done. They might even feel a bit intimidated by computers. Often, these users don't even know (much less care) which version of their spreadsheet they use, and they are largely unfamiliar with what it can do. Obviously, applications developed for this group *must* be friendly — that is, straightforward, unintimidating, easy to use, and completely bulletproof.

From the developer's point of view, a more interesting group of users are those who have little or moderate spreadsheet experience, but *are* interested in learning more. These users understand the concept of formulas, use built-in functions, and generally have a good idea of what the product is capable of. These users generally appreciate the work you put into an application and are often impressed by your efforts. Even better, they'll make excellent suggestions for improving your applications. Applications developed for this group should also be friendly (easy to use and bulletproof), but they can also be more complex and customizable than applications designed for the less experienced and less interested groups.

Why people use spreadsheets

If I asked you why people use spreadsheets, you would probably have to think about it before coming up with an answer. Interestingly, this question is rarely asked, but asking it and coming up with a meaningful answer can have a major impact on your development efforts. The real and not at all surprising answer is that it depends on the user.

A few years ago, I conducted an informal (and not very scientific) survey of spreadsheet users at a company I worked for. Most of them were using Excel, but there were also a few staunch 1-2-3 for DOS hold-outs in the group. The survey simply consisted of one question ("Why do you use a spreadsheet?") along with a series of check boxes. The survey respondents could choose as many reasons as they liked. After I received the completed survey I classified each user, based on my knowledge of them, into one of two categories: Inexperienced, or Moderately/Very Experienced. The results are shown in Table 4-2.

Table 4-2 "Why do you use a spreadsheet?"

Reason	*Inexperienced*	*Moderately or Very Experienced*
It makes my work look better	76%	82%
It helps prevent calculation errors	76%	82%
I know how to use it	68%	55%
It's the only way I know to perform a particular task	72%	36%
Making nice columns is easier than with a word processor	60%	18%
It saves time	20%	91%
It reduces the amount of work I have to do	12%	100%

Reason	*Inexperienced*	*Moderately or Very Experienced*
It can handle lots of different tasks	12%	82%
It was on my workstation when I came here	36%	18%
It's fun	12%	73%
It's the most appropriate tool for a particular task	8%	73%
It's all set up for me	28%	27%
It makes good graphs	12%	64%
Everybody else does	32%	0%
I like the macros	0%	9%

I certainly don't claim that this survey represents all spreadsheet users, but I find it interesting, and maybe you will, too. For what it's worth, I discuss my interpretations of this data in the following sections.

Inexperienced users

More than three-quarters of the inexperienced users claim to use a spreadsheet because it makes their work look better and helps prevent calculation errors. Other often-cited reasons among this group are it's the only way they know to perform a particular task, they know how to use it, and making nice columns is easier than with a word processor.

Only 12 percent claim that it reduces the amount of work they had to do, or that it can handle lots of different tasks — indicating perhaps that they're missing the point of spreadsheets. Another interpretation is that they perceive using a spreadsheet as being work, and they have no idea of what it can do.

This group often uses spreadsheet software because it's there. In many cases, users did not choose to have the software — it just happened to be installed on their workstation. Or the person who had the job before they took over used a spreadsheet, and it became a part of the job they inherited. When the time comes to produce the monthly sales report, these users fire up the spreadsheet and repeat the same procedures they've done for the past 12 months.

My experience with these users tells me that most of them learn only enough to perform basic operations, and they typically ignore about 90 percent of a product's features. The survey supported this perception. Most of these users did not use the graphics feature, and (not unexpectedly) none used a spreadsheet because of its macro capability. Only eight percent use a spreadsheet because it's the most appropriate tool. (They probably had no idea whether it was appropriate.)

As a side note, users in this group frequently use software inappropriately. For example, I've seen people attempt to summarize information from massive databases by importing huge files into a worksheet. Others write letters and memos using Lotus 1-2-3. Still others enter tables of numbers into a word processor and compute sums using a hand calculator.

Moderately experienced and very experienced users

The more experienced survey respondents clearly have a better appreciation for the potential uses of spreadsheet software, and generally checked off more reasons for using spreadsheets. The reasons most frequently cited by experienced users are generally those that were *not* checked by the inexperienced users, such as reduced workload (100 percent), time savings, most appropriate tool for a task, and so on. Interestingly, these users also frequently cited the top two reasons that inexperienced users gave, better looking work and reduced calculation errors.

Conclusions

This admittedly informal survey may shed some light on why people use spreadsheets. The bottom line is that people use spreadsheets:

- Because it makes them (and their work) look good
- Because the results are more accurate
- Because it saves time and eliminates manual effort

As a developer, you can translate these reasons into goals for your applications. Your application will be successful if it helps the user look good and generates attractive output, produces more accurate results, and saves time and effort.

Solving Problems with a Spreadsheet

I've covered the basic concept of a spreadsheet application, discussed the end users and developers of such applications, and even took a stab at figuring out why people use spreadsheets at all. It's time to take a look at the types of tasks that are appropriate for spreadsheet applications.

You may already have a pretty good idea of the types of tasks for which you can use a spreadsheet. Traditionally, spreadsheet software has been used for numerical applications that are largely *interactive* in nature. Corporate budgets are an excellent example of this. After the model has been set up (that is, formulas developed), working with the budget is simply a matter of plugging in amounts and observing the bottom-line totals. Often, budgeters simply need to allocate fixed resources among various activities and present the results in a reasonably attractive (or at least legible) format. A spreadsheet is ideal for this.

Budget-type problems, however, probably account for only a small percentage of your spreadsheeting time. If you're like me, you've learned that spreadsheet software (particularly in recent years) can often extend well beyond the types of tasks for which they were originally designed.

Here are just a few examples of nontraditional tasks that can be performed with a spreadsheet such as Excel:

- *As a presentation device.* For example, with minimal effort you create an attractive on-screen slide show using only Excel.
- *As a platform for simple games.* Clearly, Excel was not designed with this in mind. However, I've downloaded (and written) some interesting strategy games using the tools found in Excel and other spreadsheets.
- *As a data entry tool.* For repetitive data entry tasks, a spreadsheet is often the most efficient route to take. The data can then be exported to a variety of formats for use in other programs.
- *As a forms generator.* For creating attractive forms, many find it's easier to use Excel's formatting capabilities instead of learning a desktop publishing package such as PageMaker.
- *As an installation tool.* I developed an application that lets users install my Power Utility Pak software directly from Excel. (You can get the Power Utility Pak for only the cost of shipping and handling; see the coupon in the back of this book.)
- *As a text processor.* The text functions found in all spreadsheets let you manipulate text in ways that are impossible in a word processor.

You can probably think of many more examples for this list.

Ironically, the versatility of spreadsheets is a double-edged sword. On one hand, it's tempting to try to use a spreadsheet for every problem that crops up. On the other hand, you'll often be spinning your wheels by trying to use a spreadsheet for a problem that's better suited for a different solution.

Basic Spreadsheet Types

In this section, I classify spreadsheets into several basic types to provide a better perspective on how spreadsheet applications fit into the overall scheme of things. This is all quite arbitrary, of course, and is based solely on my experience. Also, there is quite a bit of overlap between the categories, but they cover most of the spreadsheets I've seen and developed.

My names for these categories are as follows:

- Quick and dirty
- For your eyes only
- Single-user applications
- Utility applications
- Single-block budgets
- What-if models
- Data storage and access
- Database front ends
- Turnkey applications.

I'll discuss each of these categories in the following sections.

Quick and dirty

This is probably the most common type of spreadsheet. Most of the spreadsheets in this category are fairly small and are developed to quickly solve a problem or answer a question. Here's an example: You're about to buy a new car, and you want to figure out your monthly payment for various loan amounts. Or perhaps you need to generate a chart that shows your company's sales by month, so you quickly enter twelve values and whip off a chart — which you paste into your word processor.

In this case, you don't care a whit what the spreadsheet looks like as long as it gives you the correct answer (or in the case of the second example, produces a nice-looking chart). You can probably input the entire model in a few minutes, and you certainly won't take the time to document your work. You won't even think of developing any macros or custom dialog boxes. In fact, you probably won't even deem these simple spreadsheets worthy of saving to disk. Obviously, spreadsheets in this category are not applications.

For your eyes only

As the name implies, no one except you — its creator — will ever see or use the spreadsheets that fall into this category. An example of this might be a file in which you keep information relevant to your income taxes. You open the file whenever a check comes in the mail, you incur an expense that can be justified as business, buy tax-deductible Girl Scout cookies, and so on. Another example is a spreadsheet that you use to keep track of your employees' time records (sick leave, vacation, and so on).

Spreadsheets in this category differ from *quick and dirty* spreadsheets in that you use them more than once, so you save these spreadsheets to files. But again, they're not worth spending a great deal of time on. You may apply some simple formatting, but that's about it (after all, you don't really need to impress yourself — or do you?). This type of spreadsheet also lacks any type of error detection because you understand how the formulas are set up; you know enough to avoid inputting data that will produce erroneous results. If an error does crop up, you immediately know what caused it.

Spreadsheets in this category don't qualify as applications, although they sometimes increase in sophistication over time. For example, I have an Excel workbook that I use to track my income by source. This workbook was simple when I first set it up, but I tend to add accouterments to it nearly every time I use it — more summary formulas, better formatting, and even a chart that displays income by month. My latest modification was to add a best fit line to the chart to project income based on past trends. I'll probably continue to add more to this file, and it may eventually qualify for the *single-user application* category.

Single-user application

This is a spreadsheet application that only the developer uses, but its complexity extends beyond the spreadsheets in the *for your eyes only* category. For example, I developed a workbook to keep track of registered users for my shareware applications. It started out as a simple worksheet database (for my eyes only), but then I realized that I could also use it to generate mailing labels and invoices. I spent an hour or so writing macros one day, and then realized that I had converted this to a *single-user application*.

No one else will ever use this spreadsheet, but it's a slick little application that's very easy to use. In this particular case, the time I spent modifying the spreadsheet from a "for your eyes only" spreadsheet to a "single-user application" was definitely time well spent because it has already saved me several hours of work. It now has buttons that execute macros, and has greatly reduced the amount of effort required to deal with the mechanics of mailing my products.

Creating single-user applications (for yourself, that is) is an excellent way to get practice with Excel's developer's tools. For example, you can learn to create custom dialog boxes, modify menus, create a custom toolbar, write VBA macros, and so on. You'll find that working on a meaningful project (even if it's meaningful only to you) is the best way to learn advanced features in Excel — or any other software, for that matter.

Utility applications

No one is ever completely satisfied with their spreadsheet. Great as it is, I find quite a bit lacking in Excel. Which brings me to the next category of spreadsheets, *utility applications*. Utilities are special tools designed to perform a single recurring task. For example, if you often import text into Excel, you may want some additional text-handling commands, such as the ability to convert selected text to uppercase (without using formulas). The solution? Develop a text-handling utility that does exactly what you want.

The Power Utility Pak, for which you will find a coupon in the back of this book, is a collection of utility applications. I developed these utilities to extend Excel's functionality. These utilities work just like normal Excel commands.

By their very nature, utility applications are very general in nature. Most macros are designed to perform a specific operation on a specific type of data found in a specific type of workbook. A good utility application essentially mimics a command normally found in Excel. In other words, the utility needs to recognize the context in which a command is executed and take appropriate action. This usually requires lots of error-handling code so that the utility can handle any situation that comes up.

CROSS REFERENCE

Utility applications always use macros and may or may not use custom dialog boxes. Fortunately, Excel makes it relatively easy to create such utilities, and they can be converted to add-ins and attached to Excel's user interface so that they look as if they are part of Excel. This topic is so important that I devoted an entire chapter to it. Chapter 12 discusses how to create custom Excel utilities using VBA.

Single-block budgets

By a *single-block budget*, I mean a spreadsheet — not necessarily a budget model — that essentially consists of one block of cells. The top row might have names that correspond to time (months, quarters, or years), and the left column usually has categories of some type. Typically, the bottom row and right column contain formulas that merely add the numbers together.

This is a very common type of spreadsheet. In fact, spreadsheet programs were originally developed with this in mind. In most cases, simple single-block budget models are not good candidates for applications because they are quite simple to begin with,but there are exceptions. For instance, you might consider converting such a spreadsheet into an application if the model is an unwieldy 3-D spreadsheet, needs to include consolidations from other files, or will be used by departmental managers who may not understand spreadsheets.

What-if models

Many consider the what-if model category to be the epitome of what spreadsheets are best at. The ability to quickly recalculate thousands of formulas makes spreadsheet software the ideal tool for financial modeling and other models that depend on the values of several variables. If you think about it, just about any spreadsheet that contains formulas is a what-if model. Changing the value of a cell used in a formula is akin to asking "what if...". My view of this category, however, is a bit more sophisticated. It includes spreadsheets designed exclusively for systematically analyzing the effects of various inputs.

What-if models are often good candidates for user-oriented applications — especially if the model will be used for some period of time. Creating a good user interface can make it very easy for anyone to use, including computer-illiterates. As an example, you might create an interface that lets the user provide names for various sets of assumptions, and then instantly see the results of a selected scenario and create a perfectly formatted summary chart with the click of a button.

Data storage and access

It's not surprising that spreadsheets are often used for keeping lists or modest database manipulations. Most people find that it's much easier to view and manipulate data in a spreadsheet than it is when using normal database software.

Spreadsheets in this category are often candidates for applications, especially if end users need to perform moderately sophisticated operations. However, Excel's built-in data form dialog box and its auto-filtering commands make working with databases so easy that even beginning users can master simple database operations quickly.

Database front ends

Increasingly, spreadsheet products are used to access external databases. Excel, as well as Quattro Pro for Windows and 1-2-3 for Windows, all provide tools to let the spreadsheet user access data stored in external files. When you create an application that does this, it's often referred to as an Executive Information System, or EIS. These systems combine data from several sources and summarize it for managers.

Executive Information Systems are ideal candidates for applications because the key element is usually ease of use. And besides, accessing external databases from a spreadsheet usually strikes fear in the heart of beginning users.

Turnkey applications

The final category of spreadsheet types is the most complex. By *turnkey,* I mean ready to go, with little or no preparation by the end user. For example, the user loads the file and is presented with a user interface that makes user choices perfectly clear. Turnkey applications may not even look like they are being powered by a spreadsheet, and often, the user interacts completely with dialog boxes rather than cells.

Actually, many of the categories described above can be converted into turnkey applications. The critical common element, as I'll discuss throughout the remainder of the book, is good planning, error handling, and user interface design.

Summary

This chapter introduced the concept of a spreadsheet application. I also discussed the distinction between a developer and an end user, and presented a two-way classification scheme that describes spreadsheet users. I also classified spreadsheets into several categories, some of which qualify as material for application developers.

Chapter 5 continues this discussion and goes into more detail about how spreadsheet developers typically go about their business.

Chapter 5

Essentials of Spreadsheet Application Development

In This Chapter

- A discussion of the basic steps involved in spreadsheet application development
- Determining end user needs and planning applications to meet those needs
- Developing and testing applications
- Documenting your development efforts and writing user documentation

There is no recipe for developing a spreadsheet application (and besides, this isn't a cookbook). Everyone develops his or her own style for creating spreadsheet applications; I don't know of a single best way that works for everyone. In addition to the variability of different developer styles, every project that you undertake is different and therefore requires its own approach. And finally, the demands and general attitude of the people you're working with (or for) also play a role in how the development process proceeds.

My goal in this chapter is to provide you with some *general* guidelines that I've found useful. At the very least, some of the information in this chapter might help you improve your own style. As I mentioned in the previous chapter, spreadsheet developers typically perform the following activities:

- Determining the needs of the user.
- Planning an application that meets these needs.
- Determining the most appropriate user interface.
- Creating the spreadsheet, formulas, macros, and user interface.
- Testing and debugging the application.
- Making the application bulletproof.
- Making the application aesthetically appealing and intuitive.
- Documenting the development effort.
- Developing user documentation and on-line help
- Distributing the application to the user.
- Updating the application when it's necessary.

Not all of these steps are required for each application, and the order in which these activities are performed varies from project to project. I describe each of these activities in the pages that follow, and in most cases I cover the technical details in subsequent chapters.

Determining User Needs

When you undertake a spreadsheet application development project, one of the first steps you need to take is identifying exactly what the end users require. Failure to thoroughly assess the end users' needs early on often results in additional work later when you have to adjust the application so it does what it was supposed to do in the first place.

In some cases, you'll be intimately familiar with the end users and may even be one yourself. In other cases (for example, a consultant developing projects for a client), you may know little or nothing about the users or their situation.

The following guidelines may make this phase easier.

- Don't assume that you know what the user needs. Second-guessing at this stage almost always causes problems later on.
- If possible, talk directly to the end users of the application, not just their supervisor or manager.
- Learn what, if anything, is currently being done to approach the problem. You may be able to save some work by adapting an existing application. At the very least, investigating will familiarize you with the operation.
- Identify the resources available at the user's site. For example, try to determine whether there are any hardware or software limitations that you must work around.
- Understand the skill levels of the end users. This information will help you design the application appropriately.
- Determine how long the application will be used. This may often influence the amount of effort you put into the project.

How do you determine the needs of the user? If you've been asked to develop a spreadsheet application, it's a good idea to meet with the end user and ask very specific questions. Better yet, put everything in writing, create flow diagrams, pay attention to minor details — and do anything else to ensure that the product you deliver is the product that's needed.

One final note: Don't be surprised if the project specifications change before you complete the application. This is quite common, and you'll be better off if you *expect* changes rather than be surprised by them. Just make sure your contract (if you have one) addresses the issue of changing specifications.

Planning an Application that Meets User Needs

After you determine the end users' needs, it's very tempting to jump right in and start fiddling around in Excel — take it from one who suffers from this problem. But try to restrain yourself. Builders don't construct a house without a set of blueprints, and you shouldn't develop a spreadsheet applications without a plan. The formality of your plan depends on the scope of the project and your general style of working, but you should at least spend *some* time thinking about what you're going to do and coming up with a plan of action.

Before rolling up your sleeves and settling down at your keyboard, you'll benefit by taking some time to consider the various ways that you can approach the problem. Here is where a thorough knowledge of Excel pays off. Avoiding blind alleys before you get to them is always a good idea.

If you ask a dozen Excel gurus to design an application based on very specific specifications, chances are you'll get twelve different implementations of the project that meet those specifications. And out of those, some will definitely be better than the others.

Excel often provides several different ways to accomplish a task. If you know Excel inside out, you'll have a pretty good idea of the potential methods at your disposal, and can choose the one most appropriate for the project at hand. Often, a bit of creative thinking yields an unusual approach that's vastly superior to other methods.

More specifically, at this stage you'll be considering some general options, such as:

- *File structure:* For example, should you use one workbook with multiple sheets, several single-sheet workbooks, or a template file?
- *Data structure.* If relevant, youl need to consider how your data will be structured. This includes the use of external database files versus storing everything in worksheets.
- *Formulas vs. VBA:* Should you use formulas to perform calculations, or write VBA procedures? Both have advantages and disadvantages.
- *Add-in or XLS file:* In most cases, you probably want your final product to be an XLA add-in, but in some cases, an XLS file is preferable.
- *How to handle errors:* Error-handling is a major issue with applications. You need to determine how your application will detect and deal with error conditions.
- *Use of special features:* For example, if your application needs to summarize a lot of data, you may want to consider using the built-in pivot table feature.

- *Performance issues:* Obviously, the approach you take will ultimately determine the overall performance of the application. The time to start thinking about increasing the speed and efficiency of your application is at this stage — not when the application is completed and users are complaining.
- *Level of security:* As you may know, Excel provides several protection options to restrict access to particular elements of a workbook. For example, you can lock cells so that formulas cannot be changed, and you can assign a password to prevent unauthorized users from viewing or accessing specific files. Determining up front exactly what you need to protect — and what level of protection is desired — will make your job easier.

You'll have to deal with many other project-dependent considerations in this phase. The important point is that you consider all options and don't settle on the first solution that comes to mind.

Another design consideration is remembering to plan for change. You'll do yourself a favor if you make your application as structured and generic as possible. When the inevitable changes are requested, such a design makes it easier for you to carry out the revisions. Also, you may find that the work you do for one project is similar to work you do for another. Planning your application with reusability in mind is always a good idea.

Learning while you develop

Now a few words about reality: Excel is a moving target. Excel's upgrade cycle is approximately 18 months, which means you have one and one-half years to get up to speed with its innovations before you have even *more* innovations to contend with.

Excel 5 was the most extensive upgrade to Excel yet — especially for developers. Thousands of people earned their living developing Excel applications that were largely based on the XLM macro language in Excel 2, 3, and 4. Although Excel 5 still supports XLM, every developer I know is firmly embracing VBA.

VBA is not difficult to learn, but it definitely takes time to become comfortable with it and even more time to master it. The VBA language is still evolving, and I expect that the implementation in Excel 6 will offer many additional enhancements. Consequently, it's not uncommon to be learning VBA while you're developing applications using it. In fact, I think it's impossible to learn VBA *without* developing applications. If you're like me, you'll find it much easier to learn VBA if you have a project that requires it. Learning VBA for the sake of learning VBA usually doesn't work.

One thing that I've learned from experience is to avoid letting the end user completely guide your approach to the problem. For example, suppose you meet with a manager who tells you the department needs an application that writes text files which will be imported into another application. Don't confuse the user's need with the solution. The user's real need is to share data. Using an intermediate text file to do it is one possible solution to the need. There may be other ways to approach the problem — such as direct transfer of information using DDE or OLE. In other words, don't let the users define their problem by stating it in terms of a solution approach. Determining the approach is your job.

Determining the Most Appropriate User Interface

When you develop spreadsheets that others will use, you need to pay special attention to the user interface. By *user interface,* I mean the method by which the user interacts with the application — clicking buttons, using menus, pressing keys, accessing toolbars, and so on.

One way to approach the user interface issue is to rely on Excel's built-in features: its menus, toolbars, scroll bars, and so on. In other words, you can simply set up the workbook and then let the user work with it however he or she wants. In many cases, this is fine — if the application will be used only by those who know Excel well. More often, however, you'll find that the audience for your application will consist of relatively inexperienced, disinterested users. This makes your job more difficult, and you'll need to pay particular attention to the user interface that drives your application.

Excel provides several features that are relevant to user interface design:

- Dialog box controls placed directly on a worksheet
- Custom dialog boxes
- Custom menus
- Custom toolbars
- Custom shortcut keys

I discuss these briefly in the following sections and cover them more thoroughly in later chapters.

Creating custom dialog boxes

Anyone who has used Windows for any length of time is undoubtedly familiar with dialog boxes. Consequently, custom dialog boxes play a major role in the user interfaces you design for your applications. Previous versions of Excel let you create custom dialog boxes, but the method for doing so left a lot to be desired. Fortunately, Excel 5 makes this a relatively painless task (actually, it can be rather fun).

Figure 5-1 shows a custom dialog box that I developed for an application.

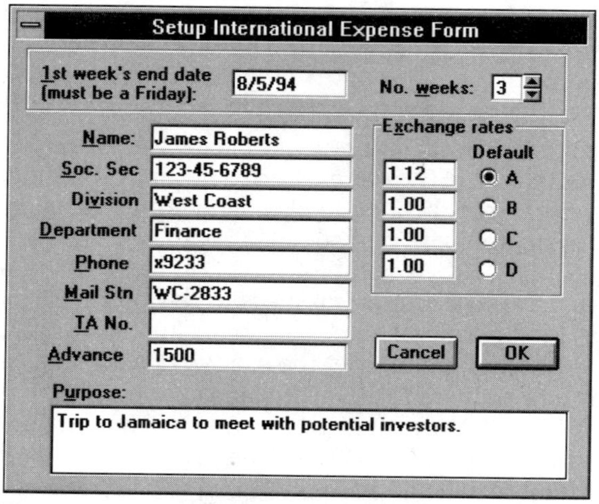

Figure 5-1: Creating custom dialog boxes is easy, and they are an important component in your applications' user interfaces.

You can use a custom dialog box to solicit user input, get a user's options or preferences, and direct the flow of your entire application. Excel dialog boxes are *modal*. This means that the dialog box must be dismissed before any action can take place. In other words, you can't use a dialog box as a separate window — to display the progress of a long task, for example. When a dialog box is displayed, the user cannot do anything with the workbook until the dialog box is dismissed.

Custom dialog boxes are stored in Dialog sheets (one dialog box per Dialog sheet). To add a custom dialog box to a workbook use the Insert⇨Macro⇨Dialog command. Excel inserts a new sheet with a dialog box on it and also displays the Forms toolbar. The elements that make up a dialog box — buttons, drop-down lists, check boxes, and so on — are called *controls.* All controls are available on the Forms toolbar.

After adding a control to a dialog box, you can link it to a worksheet cell by bringing up its Format dialog box (right-click and choose Format Object from the shortcut menu). Click the Control tab and enter a cell reference in the Cell Link edit box to establish a link to a cell. Linking a control to a cell is easy, but it's not always the best way to get user input from a dialog box. Most of the time, you'll want to develop macros that work with your custom dialog boxes.

CROSS REFERENCE

I cover custom dialog boxes in detail in Chapter 10.

Using dialog box controls on a worksheet

All Windows spreadsheet products let you insert buttons directly on a worksheet, but Excel 5 is unique in that it also lets you add other dialog box controls to a worksheet's draw layer. Figure 5-2 shows a simple workbook model with some dialog box controls inserted directly on the worksheet.

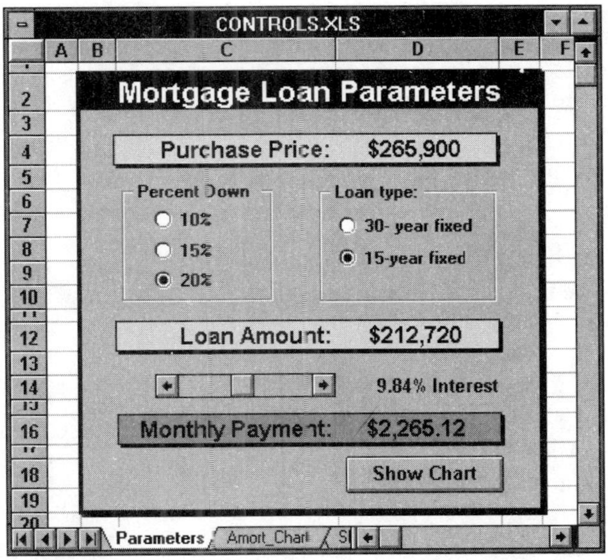

Figure 5-2: You can often make a model much easier to use by adding dialog box controls directly on the worksheet.

Perhaps the most common dialog box control is a button. Buttons by themselves don't do anything, so you have to attach a macro to each button.

Using dialog box controls directly in a worksheet often eliminates the need for custom dialog boxes. You can often greatly simplify the operation of a spreadsheet by adding a few dialog box controls. This lets the user make choices by operating familiar controls rather than making entries into cells. You need to display the Forms toolbar in order to place dialog box controls on a worksheet.

NOTE: You can use all the normal dialog box controls on a worksheet except the following: edit boxes, combination list-edit boxes, or combination drop-down edit boxes.

Customizing menus

Another way to control the user interface in spreadsheet applications is to modify Excel's menus or create your own menu system. Instead of creating buttons to execute macros, you can add one or more new menus or menu items to execute macros that you've created. An advantage to custom menus is that menus are always visible, whereas a button on a worksheet's draw layer can easily scroll out of view.

Figure 5-3 shows an example of a new menu bar — something that might be used in a specialized custom application. In such a case, the user would not have access to the normal menu system and could select only the commands in the custom menu bar. These commands would each trigger a macro.

There are three ways to customize Excel's menus:

- Attach a macro to a new command in the Tools menu.
- Use VBA code to make menu modifications.
- Use Excel's menu editor.

When you create a macro, you have the option of attaching the macro to a command under the Tools menu. You do this by selecting the Options button in the Record New Macro dialog box. To add an existing macro to the Tools menu, use the Tools⇨Macro command and click the Options button.

Adding a command to the Tools menu is easy enough, but most of the time you'll want to make other changes or additions to the menu system. One way is to use VBA commands to modify the menus. You have complete control over the menus.

An easier way is to use the Tools⇨Menu Editor command to change the menus and attach macros to commands (see Figure 5-4). The Tools⇨Menu Editor command is available only when a VBA module is the active sheet. After defining a menu, that menu appears as long as the workbook is loaded. When you close the workbook, the menus revert to normal.

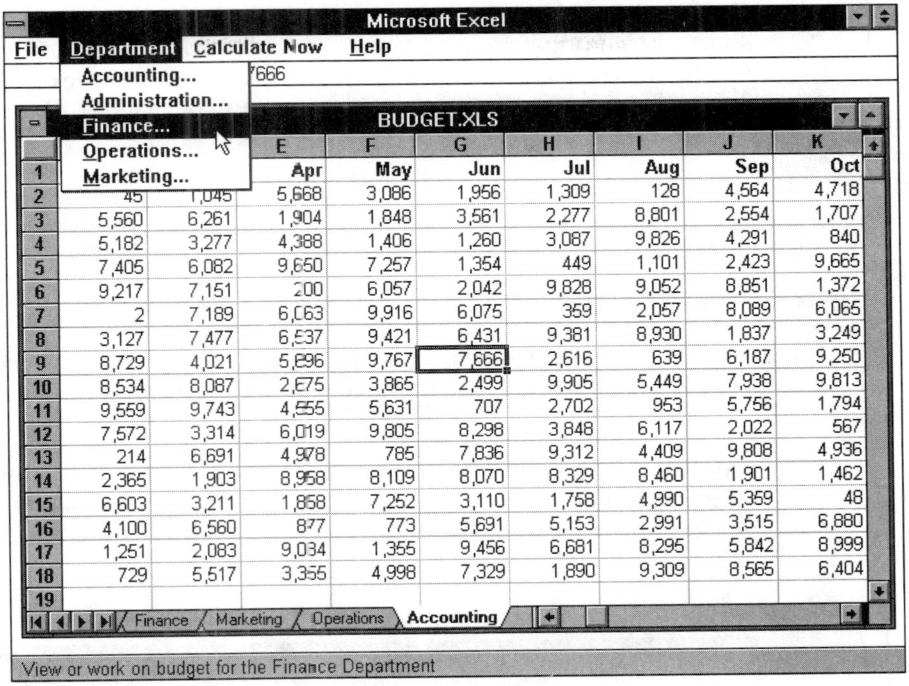

Figure 5-3: This worksheet uses a completely different menu system.

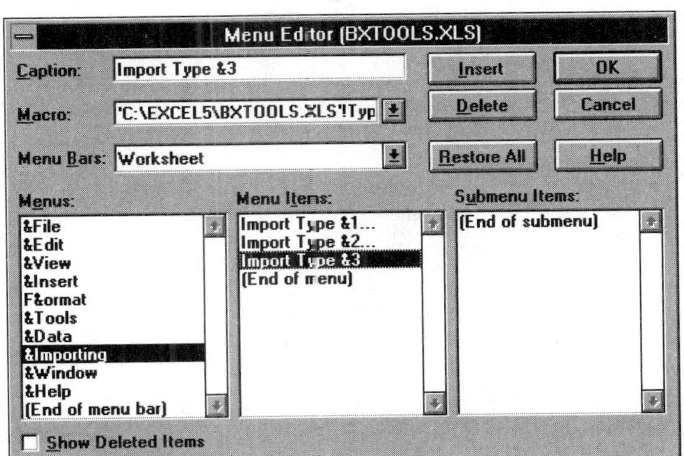

Figure 5-4: The Menu Editor dialog box makes it easy to modify the menus or create new menu systems.

You'll find that you can customize every menu that Excel displays — even the shortcut menus that appear when you right-click on an object. Figure 5-5 shows a customized shortcut menu that appears when you right-click a cell or range. Notice that this shortcut menu has several new commands that aren't normally available.

CROSS REFERENCE

I cover custom menus in detail in Chapter 14.

Customizing toolbars

Another user interface element is the toolbar. Toolbars are very common in Windows applications. Generally, toolbar buttons serve as shortcuts for commonly used menu commands, giving users a quicker way to issue commands. Because a mouse is required to click a toolbar button, a toolbar button generally isn't the *only* way to execute a particular operation. Excel's toolbars, for example, make it possible to do most of the common spreadsheet operations without even using the menus.

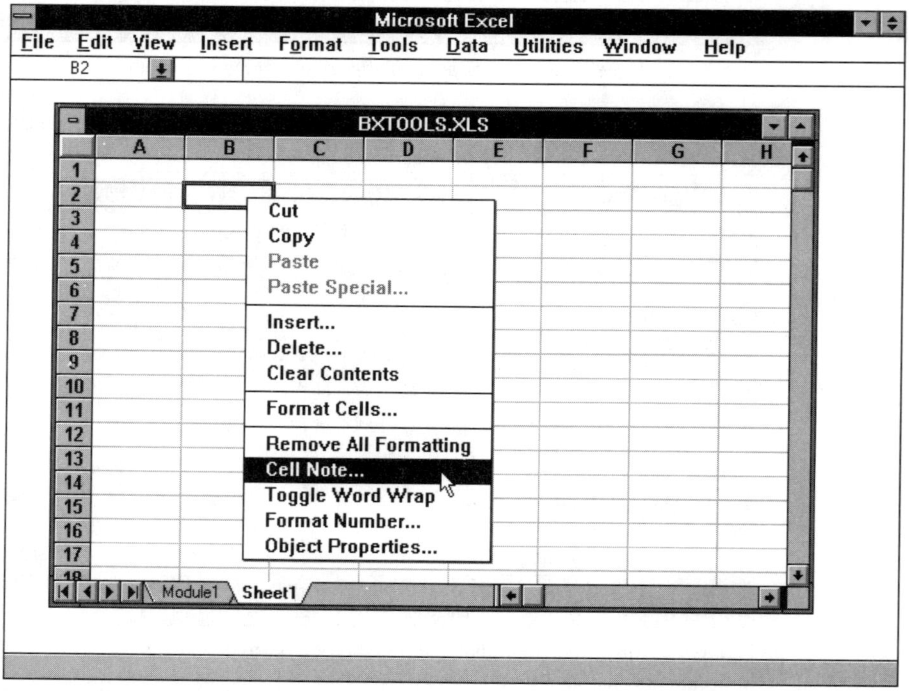

Figure 5-5: An example of a customized shortcut menu.

You can create a custom toolbar that contains only the tools you want users to be able to access. In fact, if you attach macros to these tools, a custom toolbar becomes the equivalent of a group of macro buttons. The advantage to using the toolbar in this way is that it is always visible, while buttons inserted on a worksheet may scroll off the screen.

You can set up your application so that the toolbar appears whenever your application is loaded. You do this by *attaching* a toolbar to a workbook that contains a VBA module. In a VBA module, use the Tools⇨Attach Toolbars command (see Figure 5-6). This lets you store individual toolbars with a workbook application so that you can distribute them to users of your application.

CROSS REFERENCE

Working with custom toolbars can be rather tricky. I discuss this subject in detail in Chapter 13.

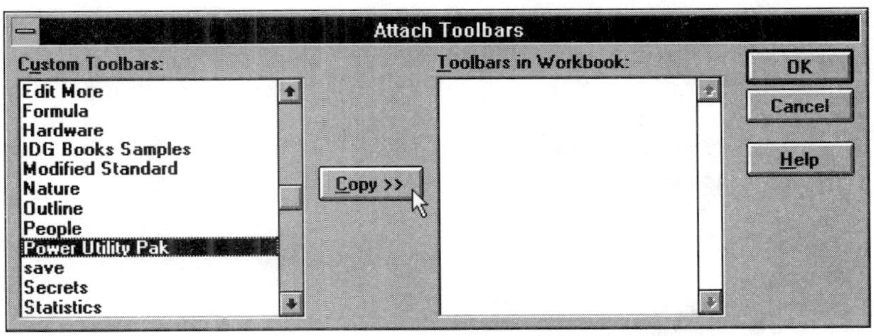

Figure 5-6: You can attach a custom toolbar to a worksheet with the Attach Toolbars dialog box.

Creating shortcut keys

The final user interface option at your disposal is custom shortcut keys. This is a rather crude approach, but it may useful in some situations. As you may know, you can assign a Ctrl key combination to a macro. When the user presses the key combination, the macro executes. Obviously, you have to make it clear to the user which keys are active and what they do. However, if speed is essential, pressing key combination is usually faster than issuing menu commands, using a toolbar, or working with a dialog box.

You need to be careful, however, to not assign a key combination that's already in use for something else. For example, Ctrl+S is a built-in shortcut key to save the current workbook. If you assign this key combination to a macro, you lose the ability to save the file with Ctrl+S. In other words, a key combination you assign to a macro takes precedence over the built-in shortcut keys. Shortcut keys are case-sensitive, so you can use a combination such as Ctrl+Shift+S.

Developing the Application

After you've identified user needs, determined the approach you'll take to meet those needs, and decided on the components you'll use for the user interface, it's time to get down to the nitty-gritty and start creating the application. This step, of course, comprises a great deal of the total time you spend on a particular project.

How you go about developing the application depends on your own personal style and the nature of the application. Except for simple template-type applications, your application will probably use macros. Developing the macros is the tough part. It's easy to create macros in Excel, but it's difficult to create *good* macros. Part III of this book is devoted to VBA, the language you'll use to write your macros.

Testing It Out

How many times have you used a commercial software application only to have it bomb out on you at a crucial moment? Probably far too many times; most likely, the problem was caused by insufficient testing that didn't catch all the bugs. All nontrivial software has bugs; in the best software, however, the bugs are simply more obscure. As you'll see, you sometimes have to work around the bugs in Excel to get your application to perform properly.

After you create your application, you need to test it. This is one of the most crucial steps; it's not uncommon to spend as much time testing and debugging an application as you did creating the application in the first place. Actually, you should be doing a great deal of testing during the development phase. After all, while you're writing a VBA routine or creating formulas in a worksheet, you'll want to make sure that the application is working the way it's supposed to work.

Bugs? In Excel?

You might think that a product like Excel — which is used by hundreds of thousands of people throughout the world — would be relatively free of bugs. Think again, pal. Excel is such a complex piece of software that it's only natural to expect some problems with it. And Excel *does* have some problems.

Getting a product like Excel out the door is not easy, even for a company like Microsoft with seemingly unlimited resources. Releasing a software product involves compromises and trade-offs. It's commonly acknowledged by industry insiders that Microsoft was aware of more than 1,000 bugs in Excel 5 when the product was released. (I've heard reports as high as 5,000.) Most of the bugs were considered insignificant enough to ignore. Sure, Microsoft could have postponed the release by a few months and fixed most of them, but software, like everything else, is ruled by economics. The benefits of delaying the product simply did not exceed the costs involved. My guess is that at least 95 percent of all Excel 5 users never encounter a bug in the program.

In this book, I point out the problems with Excel that I know about. You'll surely discover some more on your own. Some problems occur only under a specific configuration involving hardware and/or software. These are the worst of all bugs because they aren't easily reproducible.

So what's a developer to do? It's called a *workaround.* If something that you try to do doesn't work — and all indications say that it *should* work — it's time to move on to Plan B. Frustrating? Sure. Wasteful of your time? Absolutely. It's all part of being a developer.

Like standard compiled applications, spreadsheet applications are prone to bugs. A bug is usually defined as something that happens that shouldn't happen while a program (or application) is running. A bug can also be something that doesn't happen when it should happen. Both species of bugs are equally nasty, and you should plan on devoting a good portion of your development time to testing the application under all reasonable conditions and fixing any problems you find. In some cases, unfortunately, the problems aren't entirely your fault. Excel, too, has its problems (see "Bugs? In Excel?" sidebar).

I probably don't need to tell you to thoroughly test any spreadsheet development you do for others. And depending on the eventual audience, you might want to make your application *bulletproof.* In other words, try to anticipate all of the errors and screw-ups that could possibly occur, and make efforts to avoid them. This not only helps the end user, but also makes it easier on yourself and your reputation.

Although you can't possibly test for all possibilities, your macros should be able to handle common types of errors. For example, what if the user enters a text string instead of a value? What if he or she cancels a dialog box without making any selections? What happens if the user presses Ctrl+F6 and jumps to the next window? As you gain experience, issues like this become second nature, and you'll account for them without even thinking.

What about beta testing?

Software manufacturers typically have a rigorous testing cycle for new products. After extensive internal testing, the prerelease product is usually sent to a group of interested users for *beta testing.* This phase often uncovers additional problems that are usually corrected before the product's final release.

If you're developing an Excel application that more than a few people will use, you may want to consider a beta test. This allows your application to be used in its intended setting on different hardware (usually) and by the intended users.

The beta testing should occur after you've done all of your testing, and you feel the application is ready to distribute. You'll need to identify a group of users to help you. The process works best if you distribute everything that will ultimately be included in your application — user documentation, installation program, on-line help, and so on. You may evaluate the beta test in a number of ways, including face-to-face discussions, questionnaires, phone calls, and so on.

You will almost always become aware of problems you need to correct or improvements you need to make before widespread distribution of the application. Of course, a beta testing phase takes additional time and not all projects have that luxury.

CROSS REFERENCE

It's definitely in your best interest to thoroughly understand the VBA debugging tools built into Excel — they are very good. I discuss this topic in Chapter 7.

Making an Application Bulletproof

If you think about it, it's fairly easy to destroy a worksheet. Erasing one critical formula or value often causes errors throughout the entire worksheet — and perhaps other dependent worksheets. Even worse, if the damaged workbook is saved, it replaces the good copy on disk. Unless a backup procedure is in place, the user of your application could be in trouble — and you'll probably be blamed for it.

Obviously, it's easy to see why you need to add some protection when users — especially novices — will be using your worksheets. Excel provides several techniques for protecting worksheets and parts of worksheets:

- You can lock specific cells (using the Protection tab in the Format Cells dialog box) so that they cannot be changed. This takes effect only when the document is protected with the Tools➪Protection➪Protect Sheet command.
- You can protect an entire workbook — the structure of the workbook, and/or the window position and size. Use the Tools➪Protection➪Protect Workbook command for this.

- You can hide the formulas in specific cells (using the Protection tab in the Format Cells dialog box) so that others can't see them. Again, this takes effect only when the document is protected with Tools➪Protection➪Protect Sheet command.
- You can lock objects on the worksheet (using the Protection tab in the Format Object dialog box). This takes effect only when the document is protected with the Tools➪Protection➪Protect Sheet command.
- You can hide rows (Format ➪Row➪Hide), columns (Format ➪ Column➪Hide), sheets (Format ➪ Sheet➪ Hide) and documents (Window ➪ Hide). This helps prevent the worksheet from looking cluttered and also provides some protection against prying eyes.
- You can designate Excel workbooks as read-only to ensure that they cannot be overwritten with any changes. You do this by choosing the Options button in the Save As dialog box.
- You can assign a password to prevent unauthorized users from opening your file (using the Options button in the Save As dialog box).
- You can use an add-in, which doesn't allow the user to change *anything* on its worksheets.

The level of protection, and how you implement it, depends on the application and who will be using it.

Making the Application Aesthetically Appealing and Intuitive

If you've used many different software packages, you've undoubtedly seen examples of poorly designed user interfaces, difficult-to-use programs, and just plain ugly screens. If you're developing spreadsheets for other people, you should pay particular attention to how the application looks.

The way a computer program looks can make all the difference in the world to users, and so it goes with the applications you develop with Excel. The users of your applications will appreciate a good-looking user interface, and your applications will have a much more polished and professional look if you devote some additional time to design and aesthetic considerations. An application that looks good demonstrates that its developer cared enough about the product to invest some extra time and effort.

Strive for consistency: when designing dialog boxes, for example, try to emulate Excel's dialog box look and feel whenever possible. Be consistent with formatting, fonts, text size, and colors. A common mistake that developers make is trying to cram too much information into a single screen or dialog box.

A good rule of thumb is to present only one or two chunks of information at a time. If you use an input screen to solicit information from the user, consider breaking it up into several, less crowded screens.

Use color sparingly because it's very easy to overdo it and make the screen look gaudy. If your application will be used on laptops, make sure that you use color combinations that also look good in monochrome. Also pay attention to numeric formats, type faces and sizes, and borders. Do whatever you can to make individual parts of the worksheet appear to stay together. Evaluating aesthetic qualities is very subjective. When in doubt, keep your worksheets simple and generic looking.

Documenting the Development Effort

Putting a spreadsheet application together is one thing. Making it understandable by other people is another. As with traditional programming, it's important that you thoroughly document your work. Such documentation helps you if you need to go back to it (and you will), and it helps anyone else who you may pass it on to.

You may want to consider a couple of things when you document your project, however. For example, if you were hired to develop an Excel application, you may not want to share all your hard-earned secrets by thoroughly documenting everything. If this is the case, you should maintain two versions: one thoroughly documented and the other partially documented.

How do you document a workbook application? You can either store the information in a worksheet or use another file. You can even use a paper document if you prefer. Perhaps the easiest way is to use a separate worksheet to store your comments and key information for the project. For VBA code, use comments liberally (text preceded with an apostrophe is ignored). An elegant piece of VBA code may seem perfectly obvious to you today, but come back to it in a few months and your reasoning may be completely obscured. For dialog sheets, you can use the text box drawing tool to insert a box that holds your comments.

NOTE

Unfortunately, Excel does not eliminate the comments from your VBA module when you compile a workbook and make an XLA add-in. Consequently, your comments increase the size of the add-in file. Therefore, you may want to delete all of your comments before you create the add-in, but be sure you keep a copy of the XLS source file with the comments in it!

Developing User Documentation and On-Line Help

The other part of documentation is user documentation. You have basically two choices: paper-based documentation or electronic (on-line) documentation.

On-line help is standard fare in Windows applications. Fortunately, your Excel applications can also provide on-line help — even context-sensitive help — using the Windows standard Winhelp program. This takes quite a bit of additional effort, but for a large project it may be worth it.

CROSS REFERENCE

You can choose from many other ways to provide on-line help that don't use Winhelp. Chapter 16 discusses some options.

Distributing the Application to the User

You've completed your project, and you're ready to release it to the end users. How do you go about doing this? You can choose from many ways to distribute your application, and the method you choose depends on many factors.

You could just hand over a disk, scribble a few instructions, and be on your way. Or, you may want to install the application yourself (but this is not always feasible). Another option is to develop an official setup program that performs the task automatically. You can write such a program in a traditional programming language, purchase a generic setup program, or write your own in VBA. If you use the Power Utility Pak (see coupon in the back of this book), you'll see an example of an installation routine written entirely in VBA.

Updating the Application When Necessary

After you distribute your application, you're done with it, right? You can sit back, enjoy yourself, and try to forget about the problems you encountered (and solved) during the course of developing your application. In rare cases, yes, you may be finished. More often, however, the users of your application will not be completely satisfied. Sure, your application adheres to all of the *original* specifications, but things change. Seeing an application working frequently causes the user to think of other things that the application could be doing; we're talking updates.

When you need to update or revise your application, you'll appreciate that you designed it well in the first place and you fully documented your efforts. If not, well, we learn from our experiences.

Why no run-time version of Excel?

When you distribute your application, you need to be sure that each end user has a licensed copy of Excel 5. It's illegal to distribute a copy of Excel along with your application. Why, you might ask, doesn't Microsoft provide a run-time version of Excel? A run-time version is an executable program that can load files, but not create them; the end user doesn't need a copy of Excel to run your application (this is common with database programs).

I'm not sure why Microsoft does not have a run-time version of Excel — and no other spreadsheet manufacturer offers a run-time version of a product either. The most likely reason is that spreadsheet vendors fear that doing so would reduce sales of the software. Or, it could be that developing a run-time version would require a tremendous amount of programming that would never pay off.

Actually, there *is* a spreadsheet product that can generate executable files. Visual Baler, from Baler Software (708/506-9700), is a unique product that lets you create spreadsheet applications and distribute them, royalty-free, to any number of users. The end users need no additional software to run it.

Other Issues

You need to keep several other issues in mind when developing an application — especially if you don't know exactly who will be using the application. If you're developing an application that will have widespread use (a shareware application, for example), you have no way of knowing how the application will be used, what type of system it will be run on, what other software will be running concurrently, and so on. In other words, it's essential that you're mindful of some other details.

System Speed

You're probably a fairly advanced computer user and tend to keep your hardware reasonably up to date. In other words, you have a fairly powerful system — better than the average user. In some cases, you'll know exactly what hardware the end users of your applications are using. If so, it's vitally important that you test your application on that system. A procedure that executes almost instantaneously on your system may take several seconds on another system. In the world of computers, several seconds may be unacceptable.

As you gain more experience with VBA, you'll discover that there are ways to get the job done, and there are ways to get the job done *fast*. It's a good idea to get into the habit of coding for speed. Other chapters in this book will certainly help you out in this area.

System resources

One of the main limitations of Windows is limited system resources. When system resources are low, strange things happen, include general sluggishness, incorrect displays, “not enough memory” errors, and ultimately GPFs (general protection fault).

System resource requirements and whether an application releases all used resources when a program is exited varies from application to application. (Excel is something of a resource hog.) The only way to completely recover system resources is to restart Windows.

Using a function call to the Windows API, your application can monitor available system resources and warn the user if resources are getting too low (this technique is described in Chapter 11). Then the user can take action, such as exiting other programs or restarting Windows if necessary.

Hopefully, the next release of Windows will handle this problem better. Until then, grappling with limited system resources is a constant problem that developers (and users) must work with.

Video modes

As you may know, most Windows users use one of three standard video modes: VGA (640X480), Super VGA (800X600), and Hi-Resolution mode (1024X768). If you develop an application in anything but VGA mode, the application may look terrible when it runs on a VGA system.

This can be a big problem if your application relies on specific information being displayed on a single screen. For example, if you develop an input screen in SuperVGA mode, users with a standard VGA display may not be able to see all of the input screen without scrolling.

Although advanced users tend to use higher resolutions in Windows, using VGA is unavoidable in some cases — most laptops, for example, support only VGA for their built-in display. There’s no way to automatically scale things so they look the same regardless of the display resolution. Unless you’re certain of the video resolution that the users of your application will be using, it’s important that you test your application using the lowest common denominator — VGA mode.

As you’ll learn later, it’s possible to determine the user’s video resolution using Windows API calls from VBA. In some cases you may want to programatically adjust things depending on the video driver used.

Directory Structure

Another issue you need to think about is the directory structure of the user's hard drive. For example, don't assume that Excel is installed in a directory named EXCEL or that Excel is installed on drive C. You can't even assume that Windows is installed in a directory named WINDOWS. Although these are the default installation locations, many systems won't adhere to these. Fortunately, VBA has some built-in functions that will help you out.

Summary

- This chapter outlined the basic process for developing a spreadsheet application. Depending on the specific project, some of these steps may be irrelevant or unnecessary. Much of the information in this chapter is discussed in more detail later on in the book.
- This chapter concludes Part II. Part III discusses the ins and outs of Visual Basic for Applications — Excel's power programming language and a key element in application development. Chapter 6 begins with a general introduction to VBA.

Part III

Understanding Visual Basic for Applications

This section comprises the heart of the book, beginning with an introductory overview of Visual Basic for Applications (VBA) and continuing through key topics that get you started developing professional-looking Excel applications. You'll learn about VBA subroutines and functions, custom dialog boxes, and add-ins. In addition, you'll find many practical examples that you can adapt for your own use.

Chapter 6
Introducing Visual Basic for Applications

In This Chapter

- An introduction to VBA — a programming language built into Excel 5.
- How VBA differs from traditional spreadsheet macro languages, and how it differs from the Visual Basic language.
- Using VBA module sheets.
- An overview of methods, properties, and objects.
- Specific information and examples of working with Range objects.
- How to access lots of information about Excel objects, properties and methods.

Some BASIC Background

Many hard-core programmers scoff at the idea of programming in BASIC. The name itself (an acronym for **B**eginner's **A**ll-purpose **S**ymbolic **I**nstruction **C**ode) suggests that it's not a professional language. In fact, BASIC was first developed in the early 1960s as a way to teach programming techniques to college students. BASIC caught on quickly and is available in hundreds of dialects for many types of computers.

BASIC has evolved and been improved over the years. For example, BASIC was originally an interpreted language — each line was interpreted before it was executed, causing slow performance. Most modern dialects of BASIC allow the code to be compiled, resulting in much faster execution and improved program portability.

BASIC gained quite a bit of respectability in 1992 when Microsoft released Visual Basic for Windows. This product made it relatively easy to develop stand-alone applications for Windows. Visual Basic has very little in common with early versions of BASIC and is the foundation upon which VBA was built.

About VBA

Excel 5 was the first application on the market to feature Visual Basic for Applications. VBA is best thought of as Microsoft's common macro language which will eventually make its way into several more desktop applications. As I write this, the only other product that offers support for VBA is Microsoft Project. But eventually, all of Microsoft's office applications (Word for Windows, Access, PowerPoint, etc.) will incorporate VBA. Therefore, if you master VBA using Excel you'll be able to jump right in and write macros for other Microsoft products. Even better, you'll be able to create complete solutions that utilize features across various applications.

Perhaps the most important aspect of VBA is that it gives you easy access to the object models in Microsoft applications. For example, Excel provides several, very powerful data analysis objects, such as worksheets, charts, pivot tables, scenarios, and numerous mathematical, financial, engineering, and general business functions. With VBA, you can tie into these Excel objects and incorporate them into your own applications.

VBA uses a DLL (VBA.DLL) in the WINDOWS\SYSTEM directory that all Microsoft applications supporting VBA share.

VBA versus XLM

Earlier versions of Excel used a powerful macro language called XLM. That language is still available in Excel 5, but you probably don't need it. In fact, if you've never used XLM macros, you can ignore this feature. Excel 5 supports the old XLM language primarily for compatibility reasons — you can load Excel 3 or Excel 4 XLM macros files and they work just fine using Excel 5 (although they may require some minor tweaking). In addition, Excel 5's implementation of XLM supports all the new features in Excel 5. However, for all intents and purposes the XLM macro system is *frozen.* This means that future releases of Excel 5 will probably continue to support XLM, but the language will not be extended to incorporate features added to Excel 6 and later versions.

My point is you probably will want to use VBA for your development work and ignore the XLM language. Even if you're an experienced XLM programmer, you are still better off learning and using VBA.

Figures 6-1 and 6-2 show a simple procedure coded in both XLM and VBA. This macro works on the selected cells, and changes the the cell background color, text color, and makes the text bold. Most of you will agree that the VBA code is much easier to read. More important, however, the VBA code is also easier to modify when the need arises.

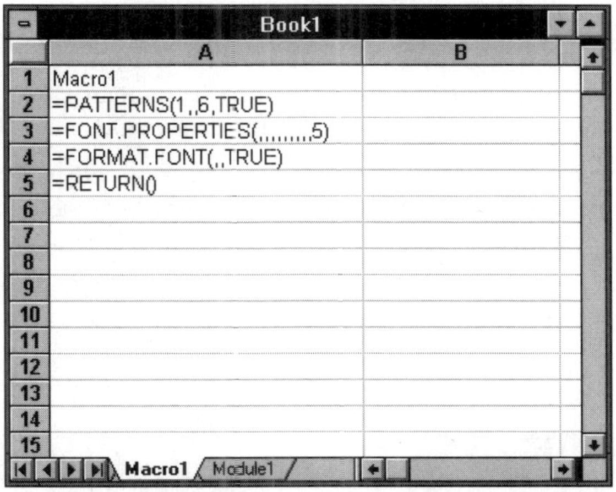

Figure 6-1: A simple macro coded in Excel's XLM language.

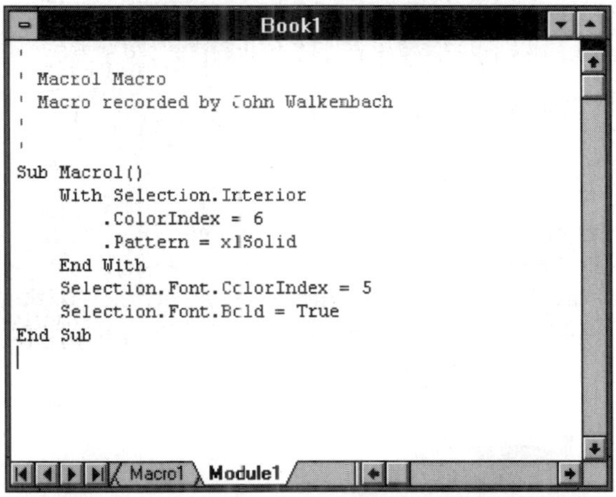

Figure 6-2: A simple macro coded in Excel's VBA language.

Following is a list of some key areas in which VBA differs from XLM.

- *Basic structural differences.* XLM commands are actually functions, which are evaluated and return a value. VBA commands are more in line with traditional programming languages and use concepts such as subroutines and functions. Compared to VBA, XLM macros are *very* difficult to read and modify.
- *Portability.* The XLM language is found only in Excel. VBA, on the other hand, will eventually be part of several major Microsoft applications — making it much more general-purpose.

- *Different sheet types.* XLM macros reside on a special XLM macro sheet (similar to a worksheet). VBA code is stored in a VBA module.
- *Variables.* VBA lets you use variables that aren't associated with a worksheet value. Any variable used in XLM must reside in a cell.
- *Using named cell references.* XLM macros can refer directly to named cells and ranges. With VBA, an additional step is required to use a named cell or range reference as a variable.
- *Strings.* In XLM, text strings are limited to 255 characters. VBA doesn't have this limit (unless you want to insert the text into a cell).

VBA versus Lotus macros

Lotus 1-2-3 was the first spreadsheet to incorporate macro capability. Although this feature was great in its day, it's quite crude by today's standards (even though it has continued to evolve). 1-2-3 macros are based on simple keystroke recording. For example, a 1-2-3 macro that names a range might look like this:

```
/WIR~
```

This represents the following command:

```
/Worksheet Insert Range (Enter)
```

The macro language in 1-2-3 for Windows has evolved beyond this and uses commands instead of actual keystrokes. You can create some powerful applications using 1-2-3's macro language, but there's really no comparison between 1-2-3 macros and VBA.

VBA versus Visual Basic 3

As I mentioned earlier, VBA is based on Microsoft's Visual Basic Programming System (VB) — a relatively easy to use programming language that lets the developer create stand-alone Windows applications. As I write this, the current version of VB is 3.0, but version 4.0 is expected to be available soon.

Figure 6-3 shows an example of the VB development environment. As you can see, it has virtually nothing in common with the VBA development environment.

Moving up from XLM

If you're an experienced XLM user and you've created lots of XLM macros, you're probably wondering if there's a utility that can automatically translate your XLM macros to VBA. You're out of luck; no such utility exists and it is unlikely that one will be developed. However, because Excel 5 still supports the XLM language, you don't really need to convert your macros.

But if you *really* want to convert your macros — or simply want to find the VBA equivalent for an XLM function — here's how to do it:

1. Choose the Help⇨Contents command from the menu.
2. Click Reference Information.
3. Under General Reference, select Microsoft Excel Macro Functions Contents.
4. Select Visual Basic Equivalents for Macro Functions and Commands.

   At this point, you might want to click the Bookmark command to define a bookmark that will bring you directly to this screen.
5. Click the first letter of the macro function and scroll through the list to find the macro function you're interested in.

The list contains each XLM macro function or command in alphabetical order and the adjacent column in the help window contains the equivalent Visual Basic command.

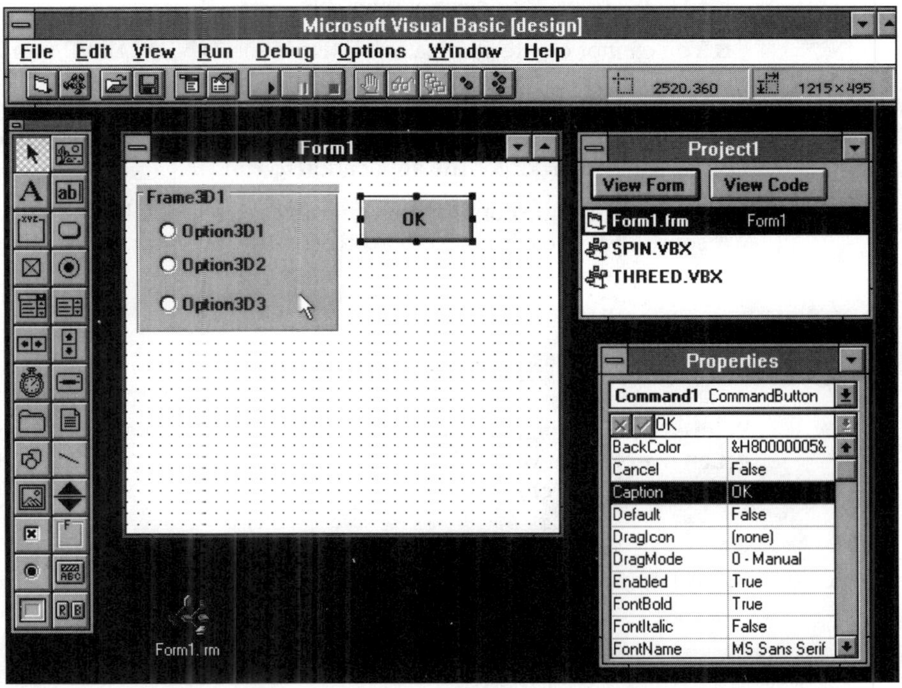

Figure 6-3: Microsoft's Visual Basic development environment.

Although you'll definitely have a head start if you're an experienced VB user, there are many differences between VBA and VB. However, VB 4.0 may eliminate some of these differences. Some of the most important differences include the following:

- VBA does not support custom controls, stored in VBX files. VB users thrive on these VBX files, which add lots of new features.
- Each VBA application has its own forms design capabilities. The way you design a form (dialog box) in Excel 5 is different from the method used in Project. And both methods are *very* different from the way it's done in VB.
- VBA doesn't support nearly as many events as VB. In VB, you can attach code to several events (button click, button double-click, button right-click, and so on.). VBA is much more limited.
- VBA offers two new syntax constructs. In VBA, you can use the For Each...Next control structure for looping through *collections* (which are essentially groups of like objects), and the With...End With construct for abbreviating object references. These aren't available in VB.
- VBA does not let you edit code while "stepping through" it in debug mode. This is a very useful debugging technique available in VB.
- VBA, as it is implemented in Excel 5 and Microsoft Project, provides access to collections. VB does not offer this.
- You cannot create stand-alone EXE files using VBA. All VBA applications require the host application. If you create a VBA application in Excel, the end user of the application must have a copy of Excel in order to use it. Excel, in such a case, serves as sort of an object library which must be available in order for the application to run.
- VBA offers a line continuation character (a space followed by an underscore). VB doesn't have this feature.

The Basics of VBA

Before I get into the meat of things, read through the material in this section to get an overview of where I'm heading. These are the topics that I cover in the remainder of this chapter.

VBA in a nutshell

Following is a quick-and-dirty summary of what VBA is all about:

- You perform actions in VBA by writing (or recording) code in a VBA module sheet.

  VBA modules are stored in an Excel workbook, and a workbook can hold any number of VBA modules.

- A VBA module consists of subroutine procedures.

  A subroutine procedure is basically computer code that performs some action on or with objects. Here's an example of a simple a subroutine called Test:

```
Sub Test()
    Sum = 1 + 1
    MsgBox "The answer is " & Sum
End Sub
```

- A VBA module can also have function procedures.

  A function procedure returns a single value. A function can be called from another VBA procedure, or even used in a worksheet formula. Here's an example of a function named AddTwo:

```
Function AddTwo(arg1, arg2)
    AddTwo = arg1 + arg2
End Function
```

- VBA manipulates objects.

  Excel provides you with 128 objects to manipulate. Examples of objects include a workbook, a worksheet, a range on a worksheet, a chart, and a drawn rectangle. Many, many more objects are at your disposal, and you can manipulate them using VBA code.

- Objects are arranged in a hierarchy.

  Object can act as containers for other objects. For example, Excel is an object called Application, and it contains other objects such as Workbook and Toolbar objects. The Workbook object can contain other objects such as Worksheet objects and Chart objects, A Worksheet object can contain objects such as Range objects, PivotTable objects, and so on. The arrangement of these objects is referred to as an object model. See Appendix A for a complete listing of Excel's object model.

- Like objects form a collection.

  For example, the Worksheets collection consists of all the worksheets in a particular workbook. The Toolbars collection consists of all Toolbar objects. Collections are objects in themselves.

- You refer to an object by specifying its position in the object hierarchy, using a period as a separator.

For example, you can refer to a workbook named BOOK1.XLS as

```
Application.Workbooks("Book1")
```

This refers to the BOOK1.XLS workbook in the Workbooks collection. The Workbooks collection is contained in the Application object (that is, Excel). Extending this to another level, you can refer to Sheet1 in Book1 as

```
Application.Workbooks("Book1").Worksheets("Sheet1")
```

You can take it to still another level and refer to a specific cell as follows:

```
Application.Workbooks("Book1").Worksheets("Sheet1").Range("A1")
```

- If you omit specific references, Excel uses the *active* objects.

  If Book1 is the active workook, the previous reference can be simplified as

  ```
  Worksheets("Sheet1").Range("A1")
  ```

  If you know that Sheet1 is the active sheet, you can simplify the reference even more:

  ```
  Range("A1")
  ```

- Objects have properties.

  A property can be thought of as a *setting* for an object. For example, a range object has properties such as *Value* and *Name.* A chart object has properties such as *HasTitle* and *Type.* You can use VBA to determine object properties and also change them.

- You refer to properties by combining the object with the property, separated by a period.

  For example, you can refer to the value in cell A1 on Sheet1 as

  ```
  Worksheets("Sheet1").Range("A1").Value
  ```

- You can assign values to variables.

  To assign the value in cell A1 on Sheet1 to a variable called *Interest*, use the following VBA statement.

  ```
  Interest = Worksheets("Sheet1").Range("A1").Value
  ```

- Objects have methods.

  A method is an action that is performed with the object. For example, one of the methods for a Range object is ClearContents. This method clears the contents of the range.

- You specify methods by combining the object with the method, separated by a period.

For example, to clear the contents of cell A1, use:

```
Worksheets("Sheet1").Range("A1").ClearContents
```

- VBA also includes all the constructs of modern programming languages, including arrays, looping, and so on.

Believe it or not, the preceding section pretty much describes VBA in a nutshell. Now you just have to learn the details, which is what I cover in the rest of this chapter.

An analogy

If you like analogies, here's one for you. It may help you understand the relationships between objects, properties, and methods in VBA (If you're not an analogy kind of person, feel free to skip right over this section.)

In this analogy I'm going to compare Excel with a fast-food restaurant chain.

The basic unit of Excel is a workbook object. In a fast-food chain the basic unit is an individual restaurant. With Excel, you can add workbooks and close workbooks, and all of the open workbooks are known as Workbooks (a collection of Workbook objects). Similarly, the management of a fast-food chain can add restaurants and close restaurants — and all of the restaurants in the chain can be viewed as a collection of Restaurant objects.

An Excel workbook is an object, but it also contains other objects such as worksheets, charts, VBA modules, and so on. Furthermore, each object in a workbook can contain its own objects. For example, a Worksheet can contain Range objects, PivotTable objects, Drawing objects, and so on.

Continuing with the analogy, a fast-food restaurant (like a workbook) contains objects such as the Kitchen, DiningArea, and ParkingLot. Furthermore, management can add or remove objects from the Restaurant object. For example, they may add a DriveupWindow object. Each of these objects can contain other objects. For example, the Kitchen object has a Stove object, VentilationFan object, a Chef object, Sink object, and so on.

So far so good—this analogy seems to work. Let's see if I can take it further.

Excel's object's have properties. For example, a Range object has properties such as Value and Name, and a Rectangle object has properties such as Width, Height, and so on. Not surprisingly, objects in a fast-food restaurant also have properties. The Stove object, for example, has properties such as Temperature and NumberofBurners. The VentilationFan has its own set of properties (TurnedOn, RPM, and so on).

Besides properties, Excel's objects also have methods, which perform an operation on an object. For example, the ClearContents method erases the contents of a Range object. An object in a fast-food restaurant also has methods. You can easily envision a ChangeThermostat method for a Stove object, or a SwitchOn method for a VentilationFan object.

With Excel, methods sometimes change an object's properties. The ClearContents method for a Range changes the Range's Value property. Similarly, the ChangeThermostat method on a Stove object affects its Temperature property.

With VBA, you can write subroutine procedures to manipulate Excel's objects. In a fast-food restaurant the management can give orders to manipulate the objects in the restaurants ("Turn the stove on and switch the ventilation fan to high."). Now is it clear?

With my obligatory analogy out of the way, I'll get down to the details.

Working in VBA Modules

An Excel workbook can hold any number of sheets, and these sheets come in four varieties: worksheets (including Excel 4 macro sheets), chart sheets, dialog sheets, and VBA module sheets. The work you do with VBA takes place in a VBA module sheet.

Inserting a new module sheet

When you open a new workbook, it starts out with a number of worksheets (the exact number depends on the setting in the General tab of the Options dialog box). You can add sheets of any type using the Insert menu. For example, to insert a VBA sheet before the current sheet use the Insert⇨Macro⇨Module command.

TIP

A slightly more efficient way to add a new VBA module is to right-click on any worksheet tab and use the shortcut menu. Select Insert and then click Module in the Insert dialog box.

Figure 6-4 shows an empty VBA module just begging for some code.

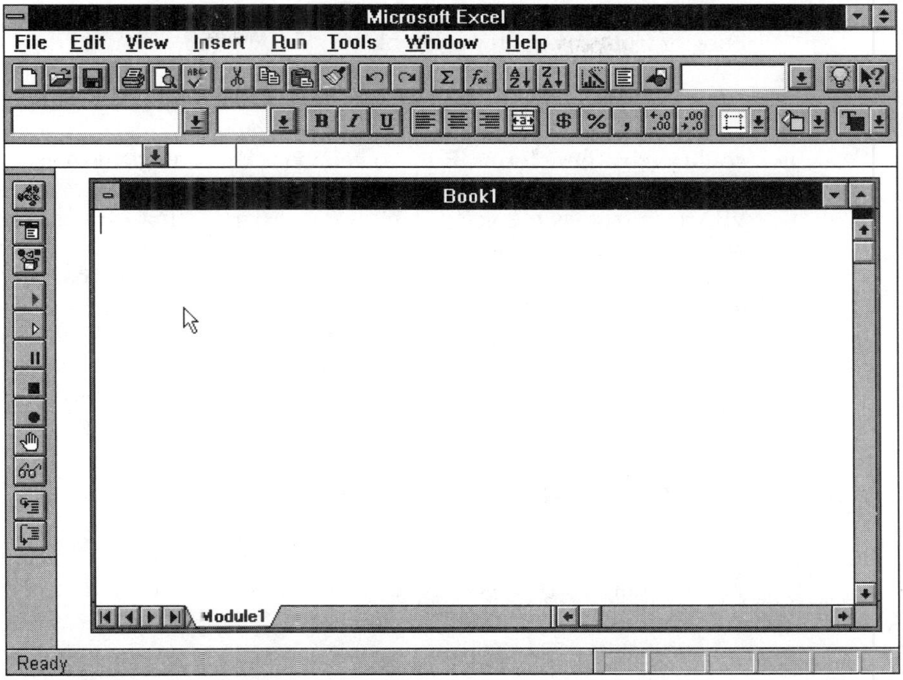

Figure 6-4: An empty VBA module.

What goes in a module sheet?

In general, a VBA module can holds three basic elements:

- *Subroutine Procedures:* A subroutine is a set of instructions that performs some action.
- *Function Procedures:* A function is a set of instructions that returns a single value (similar in concept to a worksheet function such as SUM).
- *Declarations:* A declaration is a statement of information that you provide to VBA. For example, you can declare the data type for variables you'll be using.

A single VBA module can store any number of subroutines, functions, and declarations. How you organize it is completely up to you. Some people prefer to keep all of their VBA code for an application on a single VBA module; others like to split the code up into several different modules.

You can access subroutines and functions from any other sheet in the workbook or from any open workbook.

I need to digress for a minute to discuss terminology. Throughout this book, I use terms such as *subroutine*, *routine*, *procedure*, and *macro*. You may be a bit confused by these terms. Prior to version 5, Excel users have used the term *macro* to describe an automated task performed from Excel. With the advent of VBA, terminology has gotten a bit fuzzy. Programming folks usually use the word *procedure* to describe an automated task (technically, a procedure can be a subroutine or a function — both of which are sometimes called *routines*). I use all of these terms pretty much interchangeably. However, there is an important difference between subroutines and functions, which will become quite clear in the coming chapters. For now, don't worry about the terminology. Just try to understand the concepts.

Entering VBA code

Before you can do anything meaningful, you must have some VBA code in the VBA module. You can get VBA code into a VBA module in three ways:

- Enter the code directly.
- Use Excel's macro recorder feature to record your actions.
- Copy the code from another module.

Entering code manually

Sometimes, the most direct route is the best. Entering code directly involves – well, entering the code directly. In other words, you type the code using your keyboard. You can use the Tab key to indent the lines. This isn't really necessary, but it makes the code easier to read, so it's a good habit to acquire.

Entering and editing text in a VBA module works just like you would expect. You can select text and copy it or cut it, paste it to another location, and so on.

Although it's completely undocumented, a VBA module has multiple levels of undo and redo. Therefore, if you find that you deleted a statement that you shouldn't have, you can press Ctrl+Z repeatedly until the statement comes back. After undoing, you can press F4 to redo changes that were previously undone. This is more complicated to describe than it is to use. I recommend that you play around with this feature until you understand how it works.

Try this. Enter the following statements into an empty VBA module:

```
Sub Hello()
    Msg = "Is your name " & Application.UserName & "?"
    Ans = MsgBox(Msg, vbYesNo)
    If Ans = vbNo Then MsgBox "Oh, never mind."
    If Ans = vbYes Then MsgBox "I must be clairvoyant!"
End Sub
```

Figure 6-5 shows how this looks in a VBA module.

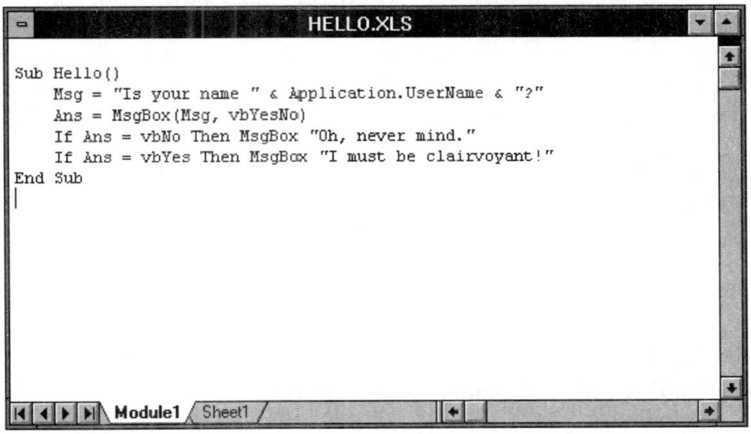

Figure 6-5: Your first VBA subroutine.

You might notice that Excel makes some adjustments to the text you enter. For example, if you omit the space before or after an equal sign (=), Excel inserts the space for you. Also, Excel changes the color of some of the text. This is all perfectly normal and you'll appreciate it later.

To execute this code, make sure the cursor is located anywhere within the text you typed, and press F5 (which is a shortcut for the Run⇨Start command). If you entered the code correctly, the macro will run and you can respond to a simple dialog box (See Figure 6-6).

At this point, it's not important that you understand how the code works; that becomes clear later in this chapter and in subsequent chapters.

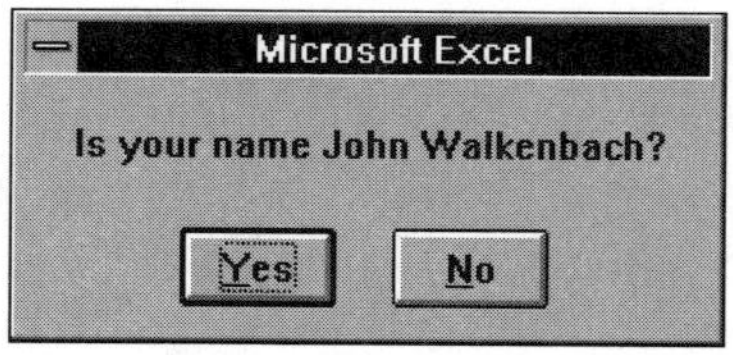

Figure 6-6: The result of running the procedure in Figure 6-5.

What you did was write a VBA subroutine (also known as a macro). When you pressed F5, Excel quickly compiled the code and executed it. In other words, each statement was evaluated and Excel simply did what it was told to do. You can execute this macro any number of times — although it tends to lose its appeal after a few times.

For the record, this simple subroutine uses the following concepts (all of which are covered later):

- Defining a subroutine procedure (the first line)
- Assigning a value to variables (Msg and Ans)
- String concatenation (using the & operator)
- Using a built-in VBA function (MsgBox)
- Using built-in VBA constants (vbYesNo, vbNo, and vbYes)
- Using an If-Then construct (two times)
- Ending a subroutine procedure (the last line)

Not bad for a first effort, eh?

Using the macro recorder

Another way to get code into a VBA module is to record your actions using Excel's macro recorder.

NOTE: There is absolutely no way to record the Hello macro shown previously. As you'll see recording macros is useful, but you usually need to enter some code manually.

This next example shows how to record a macro that simply changes the page setup to Landscape orientation.

If you want to try this, start with a blank workbook and follow these steps:

1. Activate a worksheet in the workbook (any worksheet will do).
2. Select the Tools➪Record Macro➪Record New Macro command.

   Excel displays its Record New Macro dialog box.
3. Just click OK to accept the defaults.

   Excel automatically inserts a new VBA module named Module1. From this point on, Excel converts your actions into VBA code. While recording, Excel displays the word *Recording* in the status bar, and also displays a miniature floating toolbar that contains a single toolbar button (Stop Macro).
4. Select the File➪Page Setup command.

   Excel displays its Page Setup dialog box.
5. Select the Landscape option and click OK to close the dialog box.
6. Click the Stop Macro button on the miniature toolbar.

   Excel stops recording your actions.

To take a look at the macro, activate the Module1 sheet. The code generated by this single command is shown in Listing 6-1.

Listing 6-1 Macro for changing page setup to landscape orientation.

```
Sub Macro1()
    With ActiveSheet.PageSetup
        .PrintTitleRows = ""
        .PrintTitleColumns = ""
    End With
    ActiveSheet.PageSetup.PrintArea = ""
    With ActiveSheet.PageSetup
        .LeftHeader = ""
        .CenterHeader = "&A"
        .RightHeader = ""
        .LeftFooter = ""
        .CenterFooter = "Page &P"
        .RightFooter = ""
        .LeftMargin = Application.InchesToPoints(0.75)
        .RightMargin = Application.InchesToPoints(0.75)
        .TopMargin = Application.InchesToPoints(1)
        .BottomMargin = Application.InchesToPoints(1)
        .HeaderMargin = Application.InchesToPoints(0.5)
        .FooterMargin = Application.InchesToPoints(0.5)
        .PrintHeadings = False
        .PrintGridlines = True
        .PrintNotes = False
```

(continued)

Listing 6-1 ***(continued)***

```
.CenterHorizontally = False
        .CenterVertically = False
        .Orientation = xlLandscape
        .Draft = False
        .PaperSize = xlPaperLetter
        .FirstPageNumber = xlAutomatic
        .Order = xlDownThenOver
        .BlackAndWhite = False
        .Zoom = 100
    End With
End Sub
```

You may be surprised by the amount of code generated by this single command (I know I was the first time I tried something like this). Although you only changed one setting in the Page Setup dialog box, Excel generates code that reproduces *all* of the settings in the dialog box.

This brings up an important concept. Often, the code produced when you record a macro is overkill. If you want your macro only to switch to landscape mode, you can simplify this macro considerably by deleting the extraneous code. This will make the macro easier to read — and the macro also runs faster because it doesn't do things that are not necessary. In fact, this macro can be simplified as

```
Sub Macro1()
    With ActiveSheet.PageSetup
        .Orientation = xlLandscape
    End With
End Sub
```

I deleted all of the code except for the line that sets the Orientation property. Actually, this macro can be simplified even more, since the With..End With construct isn't necessary:

```
Sub Macro1()
    ActiveSheet.PageSetup.Orientation = xlLandscape
End Sub
```

In this case, the macro changes the Orientation property of the PageSetup object on the active sheet. By the way, xlLandscape is a built-in constant that's provided to make things easier for you. A complete list of the built-in constants is provided in Appendix C, and you can also use the on-line help to learn the relevant constants for a particular command.

You could have entered this macro directly into a VBA module. To do so, you would have to know which objects, properties, and methods to use. Obviously, it's much faster to record the macro, and this example has a built-in bonus: You also learned that the PageSetup object has an Orientation property.

NOTE

A point I'll make throughout this book is that recording your actions is perhaps the *best* way to learn VBA. When in doubt, try recording. Although the result may not be exactly what you want, chances are it will steer you in the right direction.

I discuss the macro recorder in more detail later in this chapter.

Copying VBA code

The final method of getting code into a VBA module is to copy it from another module. For example, you may have written a subroutine or function for one project that would also be useful in your current project. Rather than reenter the code you can simply open the workbook, activate the module, and use the normal Clipboard copy and paste procedures to copy it into your current VBA module. After you've finished pasting, you can modify the code as necessary.

Customizing the VBA environment

Because you're going to be spending a lot of time with VBA modules on your screen, you may as well be as comfortable as possible. Excel provides a few customization options that you should be aware of.

When you choose the Tools⇨Options command, the Options dialog box appears. As you know, this dialog box has ten sections, which you access by clicking a tab. The two tabs VBA mavens need to know are Module General and Module Format.

Module General

The options available under the Module General tab are shown in Figure 6-7. Some of these settings can have a major effect on what happens when you write or execute VBA code. I'll discuss each of these options, and you can decide how you want to set them.

Auto Indent

This setting determines whether each new line of code is automatically indented by the same amount as the previous line. You can also use the spinner to set the number of spaces to indent for each Tab. I happen to be big on using indentations in my code, so I keep this option on.

CROSS REFERENCE

It's a good idea to set the indentation to an even number (2, 4, 6, and so on). This makes it easy to remove all excess spaces using the Edit⇨Replace command (search for two spaces and replace them with nothing). Why would you want to remove excess spaces in a module? As you'll learn in Chapter 13, Excel does *not* remove excess spaces when you compile a workbook into an XLA add-in — making your add-ins larger than they need be.

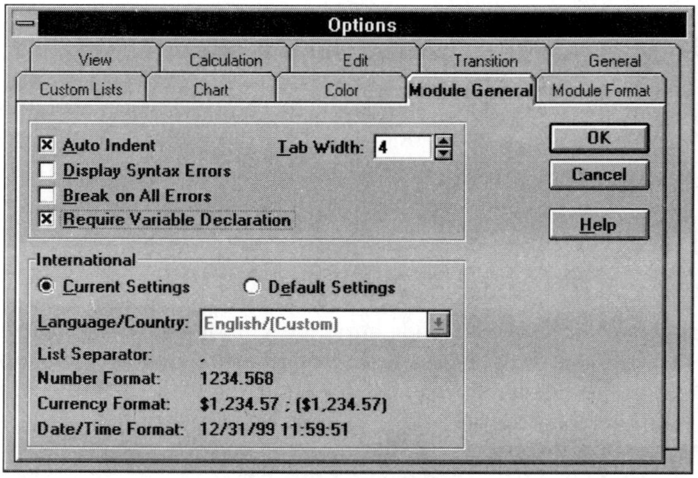

Figure 6-7: The Module General tab of the Options dialog box.

Display Syntax Errors

This setting determines whether Excel pops up a dialog box when it discovers a syntax error while you're entering your code. The dialog box tells roughly what the problem is. If this setting is not checked, syntax errors are flagged by appearing in a different color, but you won't have to deal with the dialog boxes that pop up. I usually keep this setting turned off because I find the dialog boxes annoying, and I can usually figure out the problem with a statement. But if you're new to VBA, you might find this assistance helpful.

Break on All Errors

If this is set, the procedure stops when an error is encountered. If you write any error-handling code, make sure that this option is not on because it causes the error-handling code to be ignored.

Require Variable Definition

If this option is set, Excel inserts the following statement at the beginning of each new VBA module you insert:

```
Option Explicit
```

Changing this setting affects only new modules, not existing modules. If this statement appears in your module, you must explicitly define each variable that you use. This is an excellent habit to get into. If you don't declare your variables, they will all be of the variant data type — which is flexible, but not efficient in terms of storage or speed. I'll discuss this in more depth later.

International

This setting lets you select international settings for procedures (this affects the default formats for numbers, currency, date and time, and list separator characters).

Module Format

Figure 6-8 shows the options you get when you click the Module Format tab of the Options dialog box. These options deal with how the text in a module looks. Again, I'll describe them and you decide how to proceed.

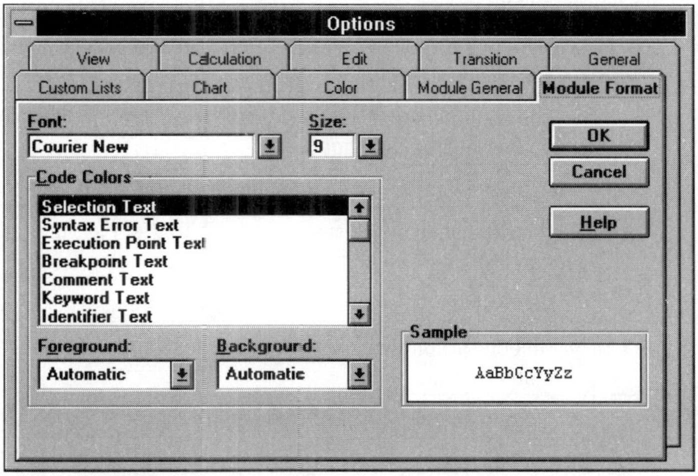

Figure 6-8: The Module Format tab of the Options dialog box.

Font

The fonts listed in this pull-down box are the fixed-width (that is, monospaced) fonts installed on your system. Unless you've installed other fonts on your system, you'll see only a few fonts listed. However, you can type any installed font name into this box and VBA will use it. However, it's a very good idea to stick with the fixed-width fonts for your coding— especially if you use the space character to make text line up vertically (this is virtually impossible with a variable-width font).

Size

This specifies the size of the font. Because you can't adjust the zoom factor of a VBA module or format the text itself, this setting will be a matter of personal preference determined by your video display resolution and your eyesight.

Code Colors

This is where you can set the text color (foreground and background) displayed for various elements of VBA code. Again, this is largely a matter of personal preference (personally, I find the default colors to be just fine).

The different types of code elements are described in Table 6-1.

Table 6-1 VBA Code Elements

VBA Element	*What it means*
Selection Text	This refers to how the text looks when you select it prior to copying or cutting it.
Syntax Error Text	When VBA spots a syntax error in your code, it displays the offending line in a different color.
Execution Point Text	The statement that will be executed next when stepping through your code using the debugger.
Breakpoint Text	A statement that you've identified as a breakpoint (used in debugging).
Comment Text	All text that follows a single quote character (') is ignored by VBA. You can display these comments in a different color.
Keyword Text	VBA keywords, such as Sub, With, and so on.
Identifier Text	Objects, properties, and methods. These are all displayed in the same color.
Normal Text	Everything else in your VBA module.

The Macro Recorder

Earlier in this chapter, I discussed Excel's macro recorder. You learned that this is just one way to get VBA code into a VBA module. This section covers the macro recorder in more detail.

TIP: The Visual Basic toolbar has several useful buttons for you. At this point, you may find the Record Macro, Stop Macro, and Run Macro buttons useful.

The macro recorder is an *extremely* useful tool, but it's important to remember the following points:

- The recorder is appropriate only for simple macros or for recording a small part of a more complex macro.
- The recorder cannot generate code that performs looping, assigns variables, displays dialog boxes, and so on.

- The code that is generated depends on certain settings that you specify.
- You'll often want to *clean up* the code to remove extraneous commands.

What is recorded

As you know, Excel's macro recorder translates your mouse and keyboard actions into (usually) valid VBA code. I could probably write several pages describing how this is done, but the best way to show you is by example. Follow these steps:

1. Start with a blank worksheet.
2. Activate the worksheet and start the macro recorder.

   Excel will insert a new module and start recording on that sheet.
3. Use the Window⇨New Window command to open a second window for your workbook.
4. Select the Window⇨Arrange command and choose the Horizontal option.
5. In the top windows, activate a worksheet, and in the bottom window activate the VBA module that Excel created (Module1)

   Your screen should look like Figure 6-9.

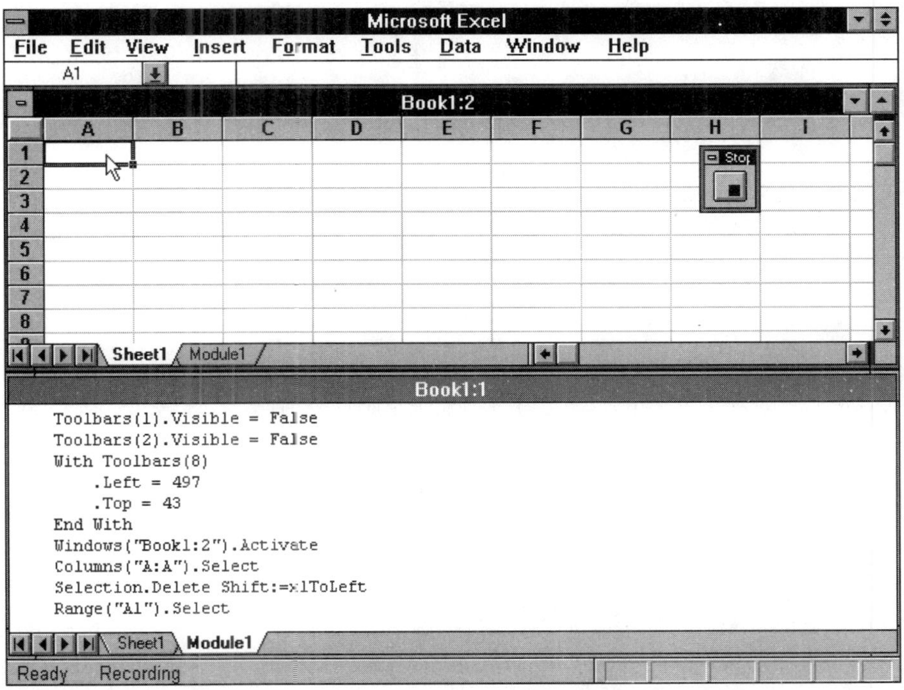

Figure 6-9: A convenient windows arrangement for watching the macro recorder do its thing.

Now, play around and select various Excel commands and watch as the code is generated in the window that displays the VBA module. Select cells, enter data, format cells, use the menus and toolbars, create a chart, manipulate graphic objects, and so on. I guarantee that you'll be enlightened as you watch the code being spit out before your very eyes.

NOTE

If you want to see an example in which Excel generates invalid code, try using drag-and-drop to move a range to another non-empty range (answer Yes in response to Excel's question about overwriting the range). The code that is generated has a syntax error and thus appears in a different color. This is a rare occurrence; in most cases the code produced by the macro recorder is valid (but not necessarily efficient).

Relative or absolute?

When recording your actions, Excel normally records absolute references to cells. For example, perform these steps and examine the code:

1. Activate a worksheet and start the macro recorder.
2. Activate cell B1.
3. Enter **Jan** into cell B1.
4. Move to cell C1 and enter **Feb**.
5. Continue this process until you've entered the first six months of the year in B1:G1.
6. Click cell B1 to activate it again.
7. Stop the macro recorder.

Excel generates the following code:

```
Sub Macro1()
    Range("B1").Select
    ActiveCell.FormulaR1C1 = "Jan"
    Range("C1").Select
    ActiveCell.FormulaR1C1 = "Feb"
    Range("D1").Select
    ActiveCell.FormulaR1C1 = "Mar"
    Range("E1").Select
    ActiveCell.FormulaR1C1 = "Apr"
    Range("F1").Select
    ActiveCell.FormulaR1C1 = "May"
    Range("G1").Select
    ActiveCell.FormulaR1C1 = "Jun"
    Range("B1").Select
End Sub
```

To execute this macro, a worksheet must be active (you can't execute it by pressing F5 from the module sheet). Choose the Tools⇨Macro command and select Macro1 (or whatever the macro is named) and click the Run button.

This is quite straightforward. The macro, when executed, selects cell B1 and inserts the month names in the cells to the left. Then, it activates cell B1. These same actions occur regardless of which cell is active when you execute the macro. Recording a macro using absolute references always produces the exact the same results.

In some cases, however, you'll want your recorded macro to work with cell locations in a *relative* manner. For example, you'd probably want such a macro to start entering the month names in the current cell. In such a case, you'll want to use relative recording.

You can change the manner in which your actions are recorded by choosing the Tools⇨Record Macro⇨Use Relative References command. This command is a toggle. When the command has a check mark next to it, recording is carried out using relative references. You can change the recording method at any time, even in the middle of recording.

To demonstrate how this works, perform the following steps:

1. Activate cell B1.
2. Choose the Tools⇨Record Macro⇨Use Relative References command (make sure this menu item is checked).
3. Start the macro recorder.
4. Enter the first six month names in B1:G1, as before.
5. Select cell B1.
6. Stop the macro recorder.

With the recording mode set to relative, the code that Excel generates is different:

```
Sub Macro2()
    ActiveCell.FormulaR1C1 = "Jan"
    ActiveCell.Offset(0, 1).Range("A1").Select
    ActiveCell.FormulaR1C1 = "Feb"
    ActiveCell.Offset(0, 1).Range("A1").Select
    ActiveCell.FormulaR1C1 = "Mar"
    ActiveCell.Offset(0, 1).Range("A1").Select
    ActiveCell.FormulaR1C1 = "Apr"
    ActiveCell.Offset(0, 1).Range("A1").Select
    ActiveCell.FormulaR1C1 = "May"
    ActiveCell.Offset(0, 1).Range("A1").Select
    ActiveCell.FormulaR1C1 = "Jun"
    ActiveCell.Offset(0, -5).Range("A1").Select
End Sub
```

You can execute this macro by activating a worksheet and then choosing the Tools⇨Macro command. Select the macro's name and click the Run button.

You'll also notice that I varied the procedure slightly in this example: I activated the beginning cell *before* I started recording. This is an important step when you record macros that use the active cell as a base.

Although it may look strange, this macro is actually quite simple. The first statement simply enters **Jan** into the active cell. (It uses the active cell because it's not preceded by a statement that selects a cell). The next statement moves the selection one cell to the right. The next inserts more text, and so on. Finally, the original cell gets selected. Unlike the previous macro, this one always starts entering text in the active cell.

You'll notice that this macro generates code that references cell A1 — which may seem strange, because cell A1 was not even involved in the macro. This is simply a by-product of the way the macro recorder works. (I discuss the Offset method later in this chapter.) At this point, all you need to know is that the macro works like it should.

By the way, the code generated by Excel is much more complex than it need be, and it's not the most efficient way to code the operation. The macro that follows, which I entered manually, is a simpler and faster way to perform this same operation. This example demonstrates that VBA doesn't have to select a cell before it puts information into it — an important concept that can also speed things up considerably.

```
Sub Macro3()
    ActiveCell.Offset(0, 0) = "Jan"
    ActiveCell.Offset(0, 1) = "Feb"
    ActiveCell.Offset(0, 2) = "Mar"
    ActiveCell.Offset(0, 3) = "Apr"
    ActiveCell.Offset(0, 4) = "May"
    ActiveCell.Offset(0, 5) = "Jun"
End Sub
```

The point here is that the recorder has two distinct modes, and you need to be aware of which mode you're recording in. Otherwise, the result will not be what you expected.

Recording options

When you record your actions to create VBA code, you have several options. Recall that the Tools⇨Record Macro⇨Record New Macro command displays the Record New Macro dialog box before recording begins. If you click the Options button, the dialog box expands as in Figure 6-10.

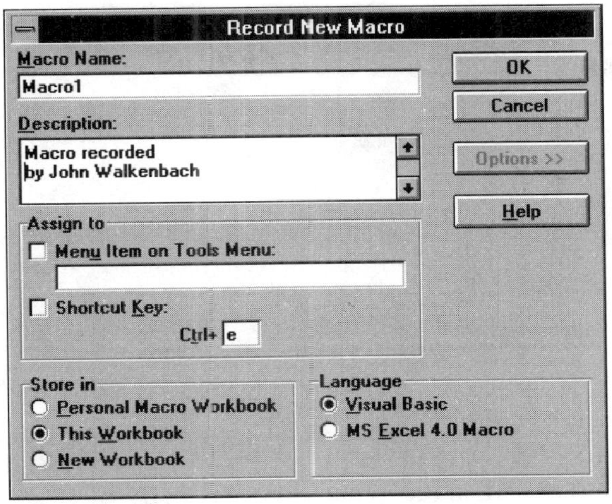

Figure 6-10: The Record New Macro dialog box, expanded to display some recording options.

This dialog box gives you quite a bit of control over your macro. The following paragraphs describe your options.

Macro Name

You can enter a name for the subroutine here. By default, Excel uses Macro1, Macro2, and so on for each macro you record. I usually accept the default name and change the name of the subroutine later.

Description

By default, Excel inserts five lines of comments (three of them blank) that list the macro name, the user's name, and the date. You can put anything you like here, or nothing at all. As far as I'm concerned, this is a waste of time because I always end up deleting this in the module.

Assign to

This option lets you assign the macro to a command on the Tools menu. For example, if you define a macro that changes the printer orientation to landscape, you could assign the macro to a command named Landscape Orientation. After doing so, the Tools menu would contain a new command. Use an ampersand (&) to specify a key to be underlined in the menu. For example, if you want the L in Landscape Orientation to be underlined, enter the menu item as &Landscape Orientation.

You can also assign shortcut keys to macros. For example, you could assign Ctrl+L to your landscape macro.

The Personal Macro Workbook

If you create some VBA macros that you find particularly useful, you may want to store these routines on your Personal Macro Workbook. This is a workbook (PERSONAL.XLS) that is stored in your EXCEL\STARTUP directory. Whenever you start Excel, this workbook is loaded. It's a hidden workbook, so it's out of your way. When you record a macro, one of your options is to record it to your Personal Macro Workbook.

To examine your Personal Macro Workbook or add existing macros to it, use the Window⇨Unhide command.

Both of these items — the Tools menu command and the shortcut key — can be added or changed at any time, so it's not critical that you take the time to respond to these items when recording a macro.

Store in

This tells Excel where to store the macro. By default, Excel stores the recorded macro in a module in the active workbook. It will insert a module for you if one doesn't exist. If you like, you can record the macro to a new workbook (Excel will open a blank workbook) or to your Personal Macro Workbook.

Language

You can choose either the Visual Basic option or the MS Excel 4.0 Macro option. If you choose the latter, this book won't do you any good.

Recording at a particular location

Normally, the Tools⇨Record Macro⇨Record New Macro command creates a new subroutine. But the macro recorder is also useful for adding new code to an existing subroutine.

Excel lets you specify the location in which you want to start recording. Here's how to do it:

1. In a VBA module, move the insertion point to the location in your code where you want recording to begin.
2. Choose the Tools⇨Record Macro⇨Mark Position for Recording command.
3. Choose the Tools⇨Record Macro⇨Record at Mark command.
4. Perform your actions.

   The generated code is inserted at the insertion point you specified.

Customizing the Visual Basic toolbar

Oddly, the Visual Basic toolbar doesn't include buttons to mark the position for recording, or to start recording at the mark. If you find yourself using these commands frequently, you'll find it useful to add a custom toolbar button that performs both of these actions in one step.

If you try recording the act of selecting these commands, you may be surprised to discover that the recorded macro is completely empty. This is an example of a case where your actions don't get recorded. Many of the commands you issue while a VBA module is active don't get recorded. However, there's a way around this: Using VBA's SendKeys statement. SendKeys simply sends keystrokes to the active window, and is often useful for performing actions that can't be recorded.

Following is a simple macro that executes the Tools⇨Record Macro⇨Mark Position for Recording command, followed immediately by the Tools⇨Record Macro⇨Record at Mark command. Your Personal Macro Workbook is a good place to store this macro.

The MarkandRecord subroutine uses the TypeName function to ensure that a module is active. Then, it simply sends the keystrokes that execute the two commands. In the macro, &trm represents Alt+TRM, and %tre represents Alt+TRE.

```
Sub MarkAndRecord()
    If  TypeName(ActiveSheet)  =
    "Module" Then
        SendKeys "%trm"
        SendKeys "%tre"
    End If
End Sub
```

To customize the Visual Basic toolbar, perform these steps:

1. Unhide your Personal Macro Workbook. Use the Window⇨Unhide command to do this.
2. Enter the MarkandRecord subroutine in a module in your Personal Macro Workbook.
3. Use the View⇨Toolbars command to display the Visual Basic toolbar if it's not already displayed.
4. Right-click any toolbar button and choose Customize from the shortcut menu.
5. Select the Custom category in the Categories list in the Customize dialog box.
6. Choose a button face that you like (the video camera is a good choice) and drag it to the Visual Basic toolbar.

   Excel responds with its Assign Macro dialog box.
7. Choose MarkAndRecord from the list and click OK.
8. Click Close to close the Customize dialog box. After performing these steps, clicking the new toolbar button when a VBA module is active immediately starts the macro recorder, and the code is placed at the current cursor position.

   When everything is working OK, use the Window⇨Hide command to hide the Personal Macro Workbook.

Another way to insert recorded code into an existing macro is to record your actions into a new subroutine and then cut and paste the results to the appropriate position in your existing subroutine.

Cleaning up recorded macros

Earlier in this section you saw how recording a single command (the File⇨Page Setup command) can produce an enormous amount of code. In many cases, the code includes extraneous commands that you can delete.

It's also important to understand that the macro recorder doesn't always generate the most efficient code. If you examine the generated code, you'll see that Excel generally records what is selected (that is, an object), and then uses the Selection object in subsequent statements. For example, here's what is recorded if you select a range of cells, change the numeric formatting, and apply bold and italic:

```
Range("A1:C5").Select
Selection.NumberFormat = "#,##0.00"
Selection.Font.Bold = True
Selection.Font.Italic = True
```

This is just *one* way to perform these actions. You can also use the more efficient With...End With construct, as follows:

```
Range("A1:C5").Select
With Selection
 .NumberFormat = "#,##0.00"
 .Font.Bold = True
 .Font.Italic = True
End With
```

Or you can avoid the Select method altogether and write the code even more efficiently like this:

```
With Range("A1:C5")
 .NumberFormat = "#,##0.00"
 .Font.Bold = True
 .Font.Italic = True
End With
```

If speed is essential in your application, you'll always want to examine any recorded VBA code closely to make sure it's as efficient as possible.

You will want to understand VBA thoroughly before you start cleaning up recorded macros (and you'll learn about this in subsequent chapters), but for now just be aware that recorded VBA code isn't always the best, most efficient code.

Understanding Objects and Collections

If you've worked through the first part of this chapter, you have an overview of VBA and you know how to work with VBA modules. You've also seen some VBA code and were exposed to concepts such as objects and properties. This section gives you some additional details about objects and collections of objects.

As you work with VBA, you must understand the concept of objects and Excel's object model. It helps to think of objects in terms of a hierarchy. At the top of this model is the Application object — in this case, Excel itself. But if you're programming in VBA using Microsoft's Project, the Application object is Project.

The object hierarchy

The Application object contains other objects. For example, Excel (the Application object we're interested in) contains these objects:

- Addin
- Debug
- Dialog
- Menubar
- Toolbar
- Window
- Workbook

Each of these objects can contain other objects. For example, a Workbook object can contain the following objects:

- Chart
- DialogSheet
- Mailer
- Module
- Name
- RoutingSlip
- Style
- Window
- Worksheet

Each of these objects, in turn, can contain other objects. A Worksheet object, for example, can contain the following objects:

- DrawingObject
- Outline
- PageSetup
- Pivot Table
- Range
- Scenario

If this seems confusing, trust me — it *will* make sense and you'll eventually realize that this whole object hierarchy thing is quite logical and well structured. By the way, the complete Excel object model is listed in Appendix A, so you might want to take a quick peek to see what you're in for.

Collections

Another key concept in VBA programming is *collections*. A collection is a group of same-type objects (and a collection is itself an object). For example, Workbooks is a collection of all Workbook objects currently open. Worksheets is a collection of all Worksheet objects contained in a particular Workbook object. You can work with an entire collection of objects or with an individual object in a collection. To reference a single object from a collection, you put the object's name or index number in parentheses after the name of the collection, like this:

```
Worksheets("Sheet1")
```

If Sheets1 is the first (or only) worksheet in the collection, you may also use the following method:

```
Worksheets(1)
```

There is also a collection called Sheets, which is made up of all sheets (regardlesss of their type) in a workbook. If Sheet1 is the first sheet in the workbook, you can reference it as:

```
Sheets(1)
```

Referring to objects

When you refer to an object using VBA, you often must qualify the object by connecting object names with the period (.) operator. What if you had two workbooks open and they both had a worksheet named Sheet1? The solution is to qualify the reference by adding the object's *container,* like this:

```
Workbooks("Book1").Worksheets("Sheet1")
```

To refer to a specific range (such as cell A1) on a worksheet named Sheet1 in a workbook named Book1, you can use the following expression:

```
Workbooks("Book1").Worksheets("Sheet1").Range("A1")
```

The fully-qualified reference for the previous example also includes the Application object, as follows:

```
Application.Workbooks("Book1").Worksheets("Sheet1").Range("A1")
```

Most of the time, however, you can omit the Application object in your references (it is assumed). If the Book1 object is the active workbook, you can even omit that object reference and use:

```
Worksheets("Sheet1").Range("A1")
```

And (I think you know where I'm going with this), if Sheet1 is the active worksheet, you can use an even simpler expression:

```
Range("A1")
```

NOTE

Contrary to what some may think, Excel does not have a Cell object. A cell is simply a Range object that happens to consist of just one element.

Simply referring to objects (as in these examples) doesn't do anything. To perform anything meaningful, you must read or modify an object's properties or specify a method to be used with an object.

Properties and Methods

It's easy to be overwhelmed with properties and methods — there are literally thousands available. Later in this chapter, I'll discuss some techniques that will make your job much easier.

Object properties

Every object has properties. For example, a Range object has a property called Value. You can write VBA code to display the Value property or write VBA code to set the Value property to a specific value. Here's a subroutine that uses the built-in MsgBox function to pop up a box that displays the value in cell A1 of on Sheet1:

```
Sub ShowValue()
    Answer = Worksheets("Sheet1").Range("A1").Value
    MsgBox Answer
End Sub
```

NOTE

MsgBox is a useful function that you'll use often to display results while your VBA code is executing.

The code in the previous example displays the current setting of the Value property of a cell. What if you want to change that property? The following subroutine changes the value displayed in cell A1 by changing the cell's Value property:

```
Sub ChangeValue()
    Worksheets("Sheet1").Range("A1").Value = 123
End Sub
```

After executing this routine, cell A1 on Sheet1 has the value 123.

Object methods

In addition to properties, objects also have methods. A *method* is an action that you perform with an object. Here's a simple example that uses the Calculate method on a range object to calculate the formula in cell A1 on Sheet1:

```
Sub CalcCell()
    Worksheets("Sheet1").Range("A1").Calculate
End Sub
```

Most methods also take arguments to define the action further. Arguments for a method are placed in parentheses. Here's an example that copies cell A1 to cell B1 using the Copy method of the Range object. In this example, the Copy method has one argument (the destination of the copy). Notice that I used the line continuation character (_) in this example.

```
Sub CopyOne()
    Worksheets("Sheet1").Range("A1").Copy _
        (Worksheets("Sheet1").Range("B1"))
End Sub
```

The Rectangle Object: A Case Study

To help you better understand the properties and methods available for an object, I randomly chose an object to examine closely. Okay, I did a random drawing and chose the Rectangle object — good thing, because a rectangle doesn't have too many properties and methods. A Rectangle object, by the way, is what you get when you use the Rectangle tool on the Drawing toolbar to draw a rectangle or square on a worksheet or a chart.

Before I delve into this list, be aware that objects share many properties. This means that once you know about the Name property of a Rectangle object, you know about the Name property for lots of other objects.

Properties of a Rectangle object

Table 6-2 contains a complete list of the properties for a Rectangle object, along with a brief description of each. If you've ever worked with rectangles drawn on a worksheet, most of these properties will be familiar to you (although you may not have thought of them as properties). Properties marked with an asterisk are read-only properties. This means that your VBA code can read the property but it can't change it.

The on-line help system lists all of the properties for each object. For example, you can search for "Rectangle Object" and see the help topic for this object. Then, click Properties to see a list of its properties.

Table 6-2 Properties for a Rectangle Object

Property	Description
Application*	Returns the application that created the Rectangle (that is, Excel).
Border	Returns or sets the border of the Rectangle.
BottomRightCell*	Returns the cell that lies under the bottom right corner of the Rectangle (applies only when the Rectangle object is on a worksheet).
Creator*	Returns a 32-bit integer that describes the application that created the Rectangle. Excel is assigned the number 5843454Ch (hexadecimal).
Enabled	True if the Rectangle is enabled, False otherwise.
Height	Returns or sets the height of the Rectangle in points (1/72 inch).
Index*	Returns the index number of the object within the collection of similar objects.
Interior	Returns or sets the interior of the object
Left	Returns or sets the position of the Rectangle, in points.
Locked	False if the Rectangle can be modified when the sheet is protected.
Name	Returns or sets the name of the object.
OnAction	Returns or sets the name of a macro that runs when the Rectangle is clicked.

(continued)

Table 6-2 *(continued)*

Property	*Description*
Parent*	Returns the parent object for the Rectangle.
Placement	Returns or sets how the Rectangle is attached to the cells below it. (applies only when the Rectangle object is on a worksheet).
PrintObject	True if the Rectangle is printed when the document is printed.
RoundedCorners	True if the Rectangle has rounded corners.
Shadow	True if the Rectangle has a shadow.
Top	Returns or sets the position of the Rectangle in points.
TopLeftCell*	Returns the cell that lies under the top left of the Rectangle (applies only when the Rectangle object is on a worksheet).
Visible	True if the Rectangle is visible.
Width	Returns or sets the Rectangle's width in points.
ZOrder*	Returns the Z-order (stacking) position of the Rectangle

To refer to a specific Rectangle object, you use the Rectangles collection. If a rectangle is named Rec1 and is located on Sheet1, the following statement returns the Rectangle object you're interested in:

```
Worksheets("Sheet1").Rectangles("Rec1")
```

Working with properties may be tricky at first because some of the properties actually return objects. For example, suppose you want to determine the color of a rectangle's border. You know that the rectangle is on Sheet1, and you named it Rec1.

If you look through the list of properties, however, you won't find a BorderColor property. Instead, you have to use the Border property to return the border of the rectangle, and then use the Color property of the Border object. Here's a statement that uses the MsgBox function to display the color value of the border of the rectangle named Rec1, which is located on Sheet1.

```
MsgBox Worksheets("Sheet1").Rectangles("Rec1").Border.Color
```

This type of referencing is certainly not intuitive, and can be difficult to get used to. If you were writing such a statement, you would need to know the properties for Rectangle objects as well as the properties for the Border object.

Similarly, to determine the interior color of the rectangle, you can use a statement like this:

```
MsgBox
Worksheets("Sheet1").Rectangles("Rec1").Interior.ColorMethods
of a Rectangle object
```

Table 6-3 shows the methods that you can use with a Rectangle object. Again, these methods perform common operations that you may have performed manually with a Rectangle at some point — but you probably never thought of these operations as methods. The methods for each object are also listed in the on-line help system.

Table 6-3 Methods for a Rectangle Object

Method	*Description*
BringToFront	Brings the Rectangle to the front of the Z-order (the stack).
Copy	Copies the Rectangle to the Clipboard.
CopyPicture	Creates a picture of the Rectangle on the Clipboard.
Cut	Cuts the Rectangle to the Clipboard.
Delete	Deletes the Rectangle.
Duplicate	Duplicates the Rectangle and returns a reference to the new copy.
Select	Selects the Rectangle.
SendToBack	Sends the Rectangle to the back of the Z-order (the stack).

These methods are all quite straightforward. For example, to delete a rectangle named Rec1 on Sheet1, use a statement like this:

```
Activesheet.Rectangles("Rec1").Delete
Worksheets("Sheet1").Rectangles("Rec1").Delete
```

So there you have it: A Rectangle object has 22 properties and eight methods. Armed with this information, you can manipulate Rectangles in more ways than you would ever want or need.

The Rectangles collection

The observant reader may have noticed that the preceding list doesn't include a method to add a new rectangle to a worksheet or chart. This is because the Add method is a method for a collection — in this case, you need to use the Rectangles collection. The following statement adds a rectangle to the Worksheet named Sheet1.

```
Worksheets("Sheet1").Rectangles.Add 100, 40, 50, 100
```

In this example, Sheet1 is the object, Rectangles is a collection of all Rectangle objects on the Sheet1 object, and Add is the method working on the collection. The Add method takes four arguments (left, top, width, and height), which are entered in order. The Rectangles collection also has a Delete method that erases Rectangle object.

If you'd like to see these Rectangle properties and methods in action, check out RECTANGL.XLS on the companion disk. This workbook contains several examples that manipulate Rectangle objects with VBA code. You probably won't understand all of the code, but you will get a feel for how you can use VBA to manipulate an object.

Working with Range Objects

Much of the work you will do in VBA involves cells and ranges in worksheets. After all, that's what spreadsheets are designed to do. The previous discussion on relative versus absolute macro recording exposed you to working with cells in VBA, but you need to know a lot more.

A Range object is a single cell or range of cells on a worksheet. A Range object is contained in a Worksheet object. Three methods are available for accessing Range objects:

- Range
- Cells
- Offset

I discuss each of these methods later in this section, but first you need to understand some important properties of the Application object that return a Range object.

Some useful Application properties

As you know, when you're working with Excel, only one workbook at a time can be activated. Furthermore, only one sheet in the workbook is the active sheet. And if the sheet is a worksheet, one cell is the active cell (even if a multi-cell range is selected).

VBA knows this and lets you refer to these active objects in a simplified manner. This is often useful because you won't always know the exact workbook, worksheet, or range that you want to operate on. VBA handles this by providing properties of the Application object. For example, the Application object has an ActiveCell property — which returns a reference to the active cell. The following statement assigns the value 1 to the active cell:

```
ActiveCell.Value = 1
```

Notice that I omitted the reference to the Application object in the preceding example, because it is assumed. It's important to understand that this statement will fail if a worksheet is not the active sheet. For example, if VBA executes this statement when a chart sheet or VBA module is the active sheet, the procedure halts and gives you an error message.

If a range is selected in a worksheet, the active cell is the upper-left cell in the range. In other words, the active cell is always a single cell. The Application object also has a Selection property that returns a reference to whatever is selected — which could be a single cell (the active cell) a range of cells, or an object such as a Rectangle.

Table 6-4 lists the other Application properties that are useful when working with cells and ranges.

Table 6-4 Some Useful Properties of the Application Object

Property	*Object It Returns*
ActiveCell	The active cell
ActiveSheet	The active sheet
ActiveWindow	The active window
ActiveWorkbook	The active workbook
Selection	The object selected (it could be a Range object, Drawing Object, and so on)
ThisWorkbook	The workbook that contains the procedure being executed

The advantage of using these properties to return an object is you don't need to know which cell, worksheet, or workbook is active, or provide a specific reference to it. The following statement clears the contents of the active cell:

```
ActiveCell.ClearContents
```

If a range on a worksheet is selected, you can fill the entire range with a value by using a single statement. In the following example, the Selection property of the Application object returns a Range object that corresponds to the selected cells. The statement simply modifies the Value property of this Range object and the result is a range filled with a single value.

```
Selection.Value = 12
```

The example that follows displays a message that tells you the name of the active sheet.

```
MsgBox ActiveSheet.Name
```

If you want to know the name of the active workbook, use a statement like this:

```
MsgBox ActiveWorkbook.Name
```

Getting help with VBA

It will pay off to get on familiar terms with VBA's on-line help system. The on-line help is very thorough, and provides lots of useful information about every object, property, and method.

The easiest way to access help is to move the cursor over a word in your code, and press F1. For example, if you want to find out about the MsgBox function, type the word "MsgBox," move the cursor anywhere within that word, and press F1. WinHelp will display the help topic for the MsgBox function.

Sometimes, when you press F1 for help you'll get a dialog box with two choices. For example, if you press F1 when the cursor is on the word "Range" you'll get the dialog box shown in the accompanying figure. This is because Range can be a method (the first choice) or an object (the second choice). Choose the option you want, and click OK.

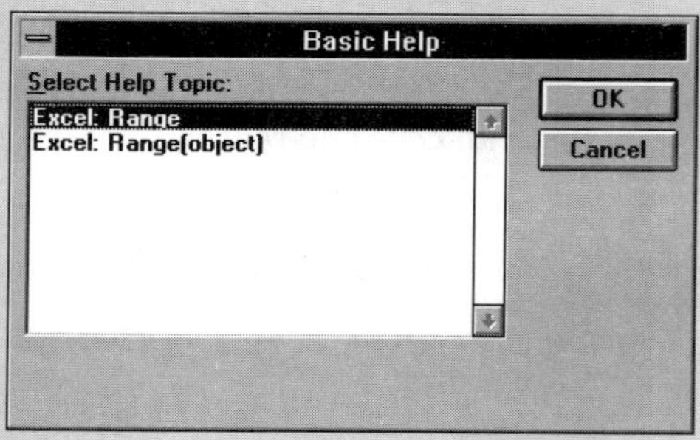

Once a topic is displayed, it will generally display underlined "jump words" that you can click for information on related topics. Many help topics have an example, which you can copy to your module and try out. You'll probably find yourself using the on-line help frequently, so it's worth the time to learn how to use it efficiently.

The Range method

The Range method returns a Range object that you specify. If you consult the on-line help for the Range method, you'll learn that this method has two syntaxes:

```
object.Range(cell1)
object.Range(cell1, cell2)
```

The Range method applies to two types of objects: a Worksheet object, or a Range object. The purpose of this method is to return a range. Following are a few examples for using the Range method.

You've already seen examples like the following one earlier in the chapter. The statement that follows simply enters a value into the specified cell. In this case, it puts a 1 into cell A1 on Sheet1 of the active workbook:

```
Worksheets("Sheet1").Range("A1").Value = 1
```

This method also knows about defined names in workbooks. Therefore, if a cell is named *Input*, you can use the following statement to enter the value into the cell:

```
Worksheets('Sheet1").Range("Input").Value = 1
```

The example that follows enters the same value into a range of 20 cells on the active sheet. If the active sheet is not a worksheet, this causes an error message.

```
ActiveSheet.Range('A1:B10").Value = 2
```

The next example produces exactly the same result as the previous example. However, the sheet reference is omitted, so the active sheet is assumed. Also, the value property is omitted, so the default property (which is Value) is assumed. This example also uses the second syntax of the Range method. With this syntax, the first argument is the cell at the top left of the range and the second argument is the cell at the lower right of the range.

```
Range("A1", "B10") = 2
```

The following example uses Excel's range intersection operator (a space) to return the intersection of two ranges. In this case, the intersection is a single cell, C6. Therefore, this statement enters 3 into a single cell.

```
Range("C1:C10 A6:E6") = 3
```

And finally, this next example enters the value 4 into five cells, that is, a noncontiguous range.

```
Range("A1,A3,A5,A7,A9") = 4
```

All of the examples so far have used the Range method on a worksheet object. As I mentioned, the Range method can also be used on a Range object. There aren't any real advantages in doing so, and it's rather confusing — but bear with me.

Following is an example of using the Range method on a Range object (in this case, the Range object is the active cell). This example treats the Range object as if it were the upper-left cell in the worksheet, and then enters a value of 5 into the cell that *would be* B2. In other words, the reference returned is relative to the upper-left corner of the Range object. Therefore, the statement that follows enters a value of 5 into the cell directly to the right and one row below the active cell:

```
ActiveCell.Range("B2") = 5
```

I said this is confusing. Fortunately, there is a clearer way to access a cell relative to a range, called the *Offset method.* I'll discuss this after the next section.

The Cells method

Another way to reference a range is to use the Cells method. Like the Range method, you can use the Cells method on Worksheet objects and Range objects. The Cells method has three syntaxes:

```
object.Cells(rowIndex, columnIndex)
object.Cells(rowindex)
object.Cells
```

I'll give you some examples that demonstrate how to use the Cells method. The first example enters the value 1 into cell A1 on Sheet1. In this case, I'm using the first syntax, which accepts the index number of the row (from 1 to 16384) and the index number of the column (from 1 to 256):

```
Worksheets("Sheet1").Cells(1, 1) = 1
```

Here's another example that enters the value 7 into cell D3 (that is, row 3, column 4) in the active worksheet:

```
ActiveSheet.Cells(3, 4) = 7
```

You can also use the Cells method on a Range object. When you do so, the Range object returned by the Cells method is relative to the upper-left cell of the referenced Range. Confusing? Probably. An example might help clear this up. The following statement enters the value 5 into the active cell. Remember, the active cell is treated as if it were cell A1 in the worksheet:

```
ActiveCell.Cells(1, 1) = 5
```

To enter a value of 5 into the cell directly below the active cell, you can use the following statement:

```
ActiveCell.Cells(2, 1) = 5
```

The second syntax of the Cells method uses a single argument that can range from 1 to 4,194,304. This number is equal to the number of cells in a worksheet (16,384 rows x 256 columns). The cells are numbered starting from A1 and continuing right and then down to the next row. The 256th cell is IV1, the 257th is A2.

The next example enters the value 2 into cell H3 (which is the 520th cell in the worksheet) of the active worksheet:

```
ActiveSheet.Cells(520) = 2
```

This syntax can also be used with a Range object. In this case, the cell returned is relative to the Range object referenced. For example, if the Range object is A1:D10 (50 cells) the Cells method can have an argument from 1 to 50 and return one of the cells in the Range object. In the following example, a value of 6 is entered into cell A2 because A2 is the fifth cell (counting from the top and to the right) in the referenced range:

```
Range("A1:D10").Cells(5) = 6
```

The third syntax for the Cells method isn't used very often; it simply returns a collection of all cells on the referenced worksheet. Unlike the other two syntaxes, this syntax does not return a single cell. This example uses the ClearContents method on the collection of cells returned by the using the Cells method on the active worksheet. The result is that the contents of every cell on the worksheet is cleared.

```
ActiveSheet.Cells.ClearContents
```

The Offset method

The Offset method (like the Range and Cells methods) also returns a Range object. But unlike these other two methods I discussed, the Offset method applies only to a Range object. Its syntax is

```
object.Offset(rowOffset, columnOffset)
```

The Offset method takes two arguments that correspond to the relative position from the upper-left cell of the specified Range object. The arguments can be positive (down or right), negative (up or left), or zero. The example that follows enters a value of 12 into the cell directly below the active cell:

```
ActiveCell.Offset(1,0).Value = 12
```

The next example enters a value of 15 into the cell directly above the active cell:

```
ActiveCell.Offset(-1,0).Value = 15
```

By the way, if the active cell is in row 1, the Offset property in the previous example generates an error because it can't return a Range object that doesn't exist.

The Offset method is quite useful, especially when you use looping procedures. Looping is discussed in the next chapter.

When you record a macro using the relative reference mode, Excel uses the Offset method to reference cells relative to the starting position. For example, I used the macro recorder to generate the following code. I started with the cell pointer in cell B1, entered values into B1:B3, and then returned to B1.

```
Sub Macro1()
    ActiveCell.FormulaR1C1 = "1"
    ActiveCell.Offset(1, 0).Range("A1").Select
    ActiveCell.FormulaR1C1 = "2"
    ActiveCell.Offset(1, 0).Range("A1").Select
    ActiveCell.FormulaR1C1 = "3"
    ActiveCell.Offset(-2, 0).Range("A1").Select
End Sub
```

You'll notice that the generated code references cell A1 — which may seem a bit odd because that cell was not even involved in the macro. This is a quirk in the macro recording procedure that makes the code more complex than necessary. You can delete all references to Range("A1") and the macro still works perfectly.

Things to Know About Objects

The preceding sections introduced you to objects, properties, and methods. But I've barely scratched the surface. In this section, I'll add some more concepts that are essential for would-be VBA gurus. These concepts become clearer as you work with VBA and read subsequent chapters.

- Objects have unique properties and methods.

  It's important to understand that each object has its own set of properties and methods. Although some similar objects may have identical properties and methods (for example, a Rectangle object and an Ellipse object), it is the exception, not the rule.

- You can manipulate objects without selecting them.

  This may be contrary to how you normally think about manipulating objects in Excel — especially if you've programmed XLM macros. Fact is, you can perform actions without selecting them first. When you record a macro, Excel generally selects the object first. This is not necessary and may actually make your macro run slower.

- It's important that you understand the concept of collections.

  Most of the time, you'll refer to an object indirectly by referring to the collection that it's in. For example, to access a Workbook object named Myfile, you do so by referencing the Workbooks collection as follows:

  ```
  Workbooks("Myfile")
  ```

  This reference returns an object — which is the workbook you are interested in.

- The Application object has methods that evaluate worksheet functions.

  The Application object has more than 400 properties and methods. This is not as overwhelming as you may think because half of these are actually methods that evaluate the built-in worksheet functions. You can use worksheet functions in your VBA code by preceding the function name with *Application*. For example, the following VBA statement uses the PMT functions:

  ```
  Payment = Application.Pmt(Rate, Periods, PresentVal,
            FutureVal)
  ```

- There can be many different ways to refer to the same object.

  Assume you have a workbook named Sales, and it's the only workbook open. Further assume that this workbook has one worksheet named Summary.

You can refer to the sheet in any of the following ways:

```
Workbooks("Sales.xls").Worksheets("Summary")
Workbooks(1).Worksheets(1)
Workbooks(1).Sheets(1)
Application.ActiveWorkbook.ActiveSheet
ActiveWorkbook.ActiveSheet
ActiveSheet
```

The method you use is determined by how much you know about the workspace. For example, if there is more than one workbook open, the second or third method is not reliable. If you want to work with the active sheet (whatever it may be), either of the last three methods would work. To be absolutely sure that you're referring to a specific sheet on a specific workbook, the first method is your best choice.

Learning More About Objects and Properties

If this is your first exposure to VBA, you're probably a bit overwhelmed about objects, properties, and methods. I don't blame you. If you try to access a property that an object doesn't have, you'll get a run-time error and your VBA code will grind to a screeching halt until you correct the problem.

Fortunately, there are several good ways to learn about objects, properties, and methods.

Read the rest of the book

Don't forget, the name of this chapter is *Introducing VBA*. The remainder of this book covers lots of additional details and provides many useful and informative examples.

Record your actions

The absolute best way — without question — to become familiar with VBA is to simply turn on the macro recorder and record some actions you make in Excel. It's even better if the VBA module in which the code is being recorded is visible while you're recording.

Use Appendix A and B

Appendix A of this book contains a list of Excel's objects arranged as an outline. This should give you a good idea of how the objects relate to each other. Appendix B is a complete list of each property and method for every Excel object.

Use the on-line help system

The main source of detailed information about Excel's objects, methods, and procedures is in the on-line help system. The VBA_XL.HLP file (located in your \EXCEL directory) is more than two megabytes.

Figure 6-11 shows the help topic for the ColorIndex property. This particular example displays jumps labeled See Also and Example. If you click See Also, you'll get a list of related topics. If you click Example, another window opens with one or more examples. You can copy the example text and paste it into a VBA module to try it out.

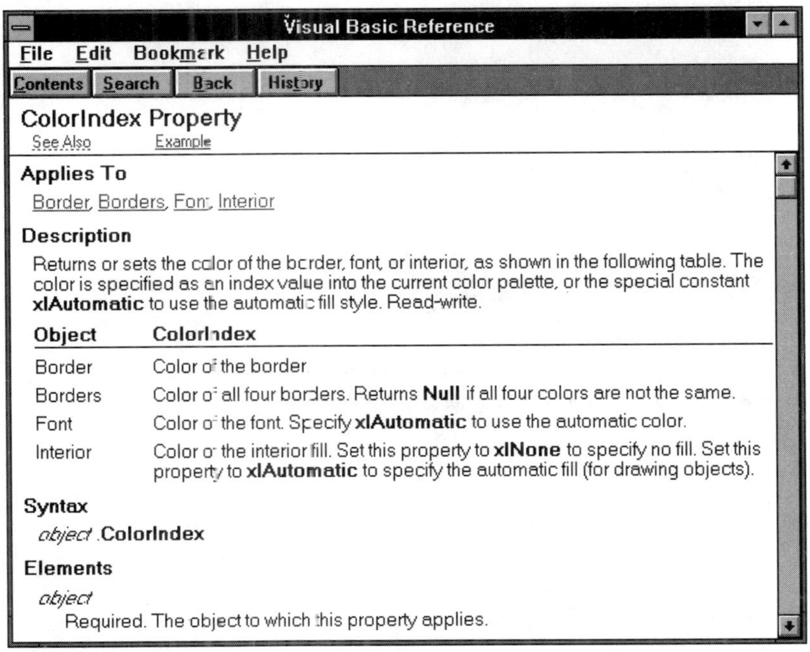

Figure 6-11: A typical VBA help screen.

Use the Object Browser

The Object Browser is a handy tool that lists every property and method for every object available. You can bring up the Object Browser in any of the following three ways, but you must be working in a VBA module:

- Choose the View⇨Object Browser command from the menu.
- Click the Object Browser tool on the Visual Basic toolbar.
- Press F2.

The Object Browser is shown in Figure 6-12.

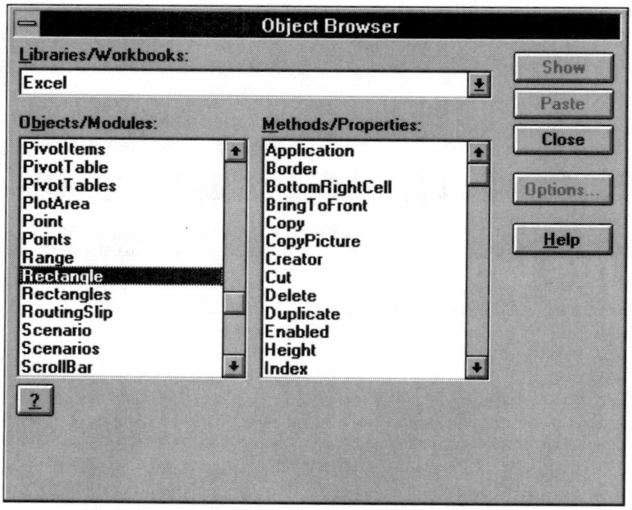

Figure 6-12: The Object Browser is a great reference source for learning about objects, properties, and methods.

The pull-down list labeled Libraries/Workbooks includes a list of all open workbooks, plus at least two additional type library entries: Excel and VBA. Your selection in this list determines what is displayed in the Objects/Modules portion of the dialog box. And, your selection in the Objects/Modules list determines what is displayed in the Methods/Properties section.

Choosing the VBA type library at the top lets you view VBA's built-in functions and constants. Choosing the Excel type library displays a list of Excel's objects and constants on the left, and the properties and methods for the selected object on the right. The question mark button is a direct link to on-line help; clicking it brings up the help topic for the selection object or property.

If you select a workbook in the Libraries/Workbooks list, the Object Browser displays a list of all modules in the Objects/Modules portion of the dialog box. When you select a module, the Methods/Properties section displays the procedures and functions in the module.

Experiment with the Immediate pane

VBA has some useful debugging tools built in. One of these is the Immediate pane of the Debug window. To display this window, activate a VBA module and choose View➪Debug Window (or press Ctrl+G). You'll see a window like the one shown in Figure 6-13.

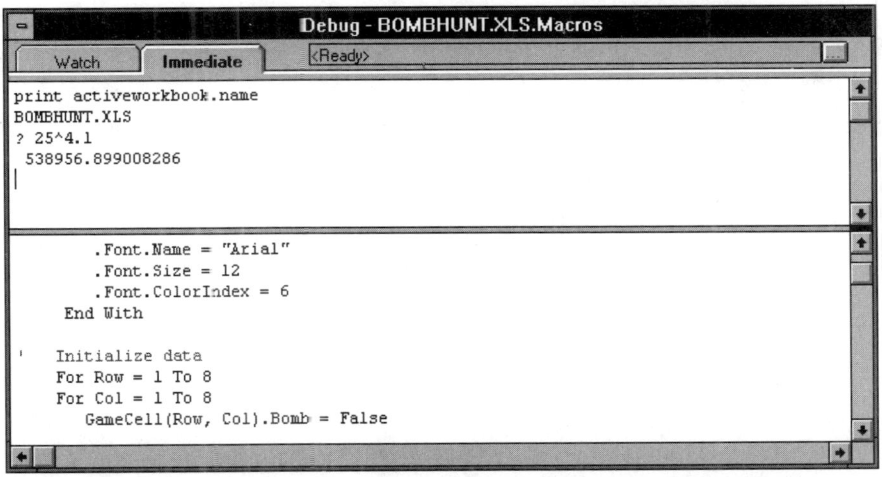

Figure 6-13: You can enter VBA code into the Immediate pane of the Debug window and see the results instantly.

The top part of this window has two tabs, Watch and Immediate. Make sure you click the Immediate tab to display the Immediate pane. You can enter VBA statements into the Immediate pane and display results. For example, you can enter the following statement:

```
Print ActiveWorkbook.Name
```

VBA evaluates the statement and enters the result in the next line. Although the Debug window is most useful for debugging VBA code, you can also use it to experiment with VBA and immediately see the results. You'll almost always want to use the Print command to see the results of what you type. A shortcut for Print is a question mark (?).

For example, if you enter the following line:

```
? Application.Name
```

VBA evaluates this expression and displays the result in the next line: Microsoft Excel.

CROSS REFERENCE

You'll learn more about debugging in Chapter 8.

Summary

- This chapter introduced VBA, including a discussion of how VBA compares to other languages. You learned that a VBA module can contain subroutine procedures and function procedures, and that VBA is based on objects, properties, and methods. You also learned how to use the macro recorder to translate your actions into VBA code.
- Chapter 7 discusses programming concepts that are necessary to get the most out of VBA.

Chapter 7

VBA Programming Fundamentals

In This Chapter

- Understanding VBA's language elements, including variables, data types, constants, and arrays
- Using built-in functions
- Manipulating objects and collections
- Controlling the execution of your procedures

In the preceding chapter, I introduced you to VBA; now it's time to get better acquainted. This chapter discusses some of the key language elements and programming concepts in VBA. If you've used other programming languages, much of this information may sound familiar. VBA has a few unique wrinkles, however, so even experienced programmers may find some new information.

VBA Language Elements: An Overview

In the preceding chapter, I introduced you to objects and discussed their properties and methods. But I didn't tell you much about how to manipulate objects so that they do meaningful things. This chapter gently nudges you in that direction by exploring VBA's *language elements*, or the keywords and control structures that you use to write VBA routines.

To get the ball rolling, I'll start by giving you a simple, but rather meaningless procedure. The following procedure adds 100 to a variable 10 times and then displays a message with the result:

```
Sub Demo()
'   This is a simple VBA Example
    Const MyNum As Integer = 100
    x = 0
    For i = 1 To 10
        x = x + MyNum
    Next i
    MsgBox x
End Sub
```

Entering VBA code

VBA code, which can reside in a VBA module sheet only, consists of lines, or statements. The accepted practice is to put one statement in each line. This standard is not a requirement, however: You can use a colon to separate statements on a single line. The following example combines four statements in one line:

```
Sub OneLine()
x= 1: y= 2: z= 3: MsgBox x + y + z
End Sub
```

Most programmers agree that code is easier to read if you use one statement per line:

```
Sub OneLine()
     x = 1
     y = 2
     z = 3
     MsgBox x + y + z
End Sub
```

Each line can be as long as you like; the VBA module scrolls to the left when you reach the right side of the window. For lengthy lines, you may want to use VBA's line continuation sequence: an underscore (_) preceded by a space. For example,

```
Sub LongLine()
SummedValue =
Workbooks("Book1").Worksheets("Sheet1").
Value_+Workbooks("Book2").Worksheets
("Sheet1").Value
End Sub
```

When you record macros, Excel often uses underscores to break long statements into multiple lines.

After you enter a line of code, VBA performs the following actions to improve readability:

- Inserts spaces between operators. If you enter Ans=1+2 (no spaces), for example, VBA converts it to

  ```
  Ans = 1 + 2
  ```

- Adjusts the case of the letters for keywords, properties, and methods. If you enter **Result=activesheet.range("a1").value=12**, VBA converts it to

  ```
  Result =
  ActiveSheet.Range("a1").Value = 12
  ```

  Notice that text within quotation marks is not changed.

- Adjusts previously used variables to correspond to your most recent case decision. For example, if you first specify a variable as **myvalue** (all lowercase) and then enter the variable as **MyValue** (mixed case), VBA changes all other occurrences of the variable to MyValue.

- Scans the statement for syntax errors. If VBA finds an error, it changes the color of the line and may display a message describing the problem. You control the color used and whether the error message is displayed in the Module Format and Module General tabs of the Options dialog box.

This procedure uses some common language elements, including a comment (the line preceded by the apostrophe), a constant (MyNum), a variable (x), two assignment statements (x = 0 and x = x + MyNum), a looping structure (For...Next), and a VBA function (MsgBox).

VBA procedures need not manipulate any objects. The preceding procedure does not do so, for example.

Comments

A *comment*, the simplest type of VBA statement, is for your use only; it is completely ignored by VBA. It's a good idea to use comments liberally to describe what you're doing (a code's purpose is not always obvious).

You can reserve a complete line for your comment. Or you can insert a comment after code on the same line.

A comment is indicated by an apostrophe: VBA ignores any text that follows an apostrophe — except when the apostrophe is contained within quotation marks. For example, the following statement does not contain a comment, even though it has an apostrophe:

```
Msg = "Can't continue"
```

The following example shows a VBA subroutine with three comments:

```
Sub Comments()
'   This subroutine does nothing of value
    x = 0   'x represents nothingness
    'Display the result
    MsgBox x
End Sub
```

Although the apostrophe is the preferred comment indicator, you also can use the Rem keyword to mark a line of code as a comment. For example,

```
Rem — The next statement prompts the user for a workbook
```

The Rem keyword is essentially a holdover from old versions of BASIC; it is included in Excel 5 for the sake of compatibility. Rem works only for complete lines of code.

Using comments is definitely a good idea, but not all comments are equally beneficial. To be useful, comments should convey information that's not immediately obvious from reading the code. Otherwise you're just wasting bytes. The following procedure, for example, contains many comments, but none really adds anything of value.

```
Sub BadComments()
'   Declare variables
    Dim x As Integer
    Dim y As Integer
    Dim z As Integer
'   Start the routine
    x = 100 ' Assign 100 to x
    y = 200 ' Assign 200 to y
'   Add x and y and store in z
    z = x + y
'   Show the result
    MsgBox z
End Sub
```

Following are a few general tips on making the best use of comments:

- Use comments to describe briefly the purpose of each subroutine or function you write.
- Use comments to track changes you make to a procedure.
- Use comments to indicate that you're using functions or constructs in an unusual or nonstandard manner.
- Use comments to describe variables, especially if the variables' names are not meaningful.
- Use comments to describe workarounds that you develop to overcome Excel bugs.
- Write comments as you code rather than after.

TIP

You may want to test a procedure without a particular statement or group of statements. Instead of deleting the statement, simply turn it into a comment by inserting an apostrophe. VBA then will ignore the statement(s) when the routine is executed. To convert the comment back to a statement, delete the apostrophe.

Removing comments

When you create an XLA add-in file from a workbook, the comments in your VBA modules are not removed; as a result, the add-in file is larger than it needs to be. To make the add-in as compact as possible, you should delete the comments from your VBA modules before you create an add-in. (I detail add-ins in Chapter 13.)

You can't remove comments automatically, but you can ease the task by taking advantage of the Use Pattern Matching feature in the Replace dialog box (see the accompanying figure). The trick is to issue the Edit⇨Replace command from a VBA module: search for an apostrophe followed by an asterisk ('*) and replace the characters with nothing. (The asterisk is a wild-card character that matches any other characters.) If the Use Pattern Matching option is enabled, Excel replaces all your comments with nothing — that is, it removes all the comment text.

Using this technique zaps important text if your code includes any apostrophes that don't indicate comments — for example, when you use a contraction within quotation marks (as in a string of text). A workaround: Develop a personal comment style. For example, you may want to get in the habit of using '/ (apostrophe followed by a slash) to indicate comments. Then you can search for '/* to remove comments only.

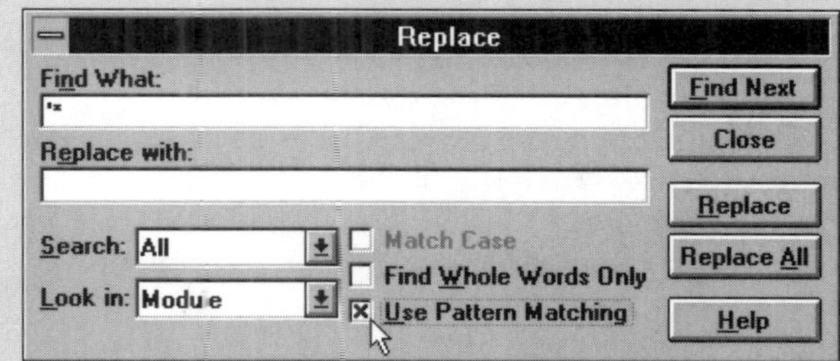

Variables, Data Types, and Constants

VBA's main purpose in life is to manipulate data. Some data resides in objects, such as worksheet ranges. Other data is stored in variables that you create.

A *variable* is simply a named storage location in your computer's memory. Variables can accommodate a wide variety of *data types* — from simple Boolean values (true or false) to large double-precision values (see the following section). You assign a value to a variable by using the equal sign operator (more about this later).

Go ahead and make your variable names as descriptive as possible.

However, VBA does have a few rules regarding variable names:

- You can use alphabetic characters, numbers, and some punctuation characters, but the first character must be alphabetic.
- VBA does not distinguish between case. To make variable names more readable, programmers often use mixed case (for example, InterestRate).
- You cannot use spaces or periods. To make variable names more readable, programmers often use the underscore character (Interest_Rate).
- Some characters — special type declaration characters — cannot be embedded in a variable name: #, $, %, &, or !.
- Variable names can comprise as many as 254 characters. But no one in their right mind would create a variable name that long.

The following list illustrates some examples of statements that use variables. The variable names are to the left of the equal sign.

```
x = 1
InterestRate = 0.075
LoanPayoffAmount = 243089
DataEntered = False
x = x + 1
MyNum = YourNum * 1.25
UserName = "Bob Johnson"
DateStarted = #3/14/94#
```

VBA has many *reserved words*, or words that you cannot use for variable or procedure names. If you attempt to use one of these words, you get an error message. For example, although the reserved word *Name* might make a very descriptive variable name, both of the following statements generate syntax errors:

```
Dim Name as String
Name = "Sally Jones"
```

Unfortunately, the errors aren't all that descriptive. `Dim Name as String` generates an *Expected: Shared or Identifier* error. The second statement produces an *Expected: Expression* error. So if a statement produces a strange error, check the list of taboo names (see Table 7-1).

Table 7-1 VBA Reserved Words

Abs	DefBool	Function	MidB	Select
And	DefCur	Get	Mod	Set
Any	DefDate	Global	Name	Sgn
As	DefDbl	GoSub	New	Shared
Boolean	DefInt	GoTo	Next	Single
ByRef	DefLng	If	Not	Spc
ByVal	DefObj	Imp	Nothing	Static
Call	DefSng	In	Null	Stop
Case	DefStr	Input	Object	StrComp
CBool	DefVar	InputB	On	String
CCur	Dim	Instr	Open	Sub
CDate	Dir	InstrB	Option	Tab
CDbl	Do	Int	Optional	Then
CDecl	Double	Integer	Or	To
CInt	Each	Is	Point	True
Circle	Else	LBound	Preserve	Type
CLng	ElseIf	Len	Print	TypeOf
Close	Empty	LenB	Private	UBound
Const	End	Let	Property	Unload
CSng	EndIf	Like	PSet	Unlock
CStr	Eqv	Line	Public	Until
CurDirrase	Erase	Load	Put	Variant
Currency	Error	Local	ReDim	Wend
CVar	Exit	Lock	Rem	While
CVDate	False	Long	Resume	Width
CVErr	Fix	Loop	Return	With
Date	For	LSet	RSet	Write
Debug	Format	Me	Scale	Xor
Declare	FreeFile	Mid	Seek	

Data types

VBA makes life easy for programmers because it can automatically handle all the details involved in dealing with data. Not all programming languages make it so easy. For example, some languages are *strictly typed*, which means that the programmer must explicitly define the data type for every variable used.

Data type is how data is stored in memory — as integers, real numbers, strings, and so on. Although VBA can take care of these details automatically, it does so at a cost (there's no such thing as a free lunch): slower execution and inefficient use of memory. As a result, letting VBA handle data typing may present problems when you're running large or complex applications, where you need to conserve every last byte of memory; then *you* need to be on familiar terms with data types.

Table 7-2 lists VBA's assortment of built-in data types (note that you can define custom data types).

Table 7-2 VBA's Built-In Data Types

Data Type	*Bytes Used*	*Range of Values*	*Significant Digits*
Boolean	2	True or False	1
Integer	2	–32,768 to 32,767	5
Long	4	–2,147,483,648 to 2,147,483,647	10
Single	4	–3.402823E38 to 1.401298E45	7
Double (negative)	8	–1.79769313486232E308 to –4.94065645841247E-324	15
Double (positive)	8	4.94065645841247E-324 to 1.79769313486232E308	15
Currency	8	–922,337,203,685,477.5808 to 922,337,203,685,477.5807	19
Date	8	1/1/100 to 12/31/9999	NA
String	1/char	Varies	NA
Object	16 + 1/char	Any defined object	NA
Variant	Varies	Any data type	NA
User-defined	Varies	Varies	NA

It's best to use the data type that uses the smallest number of bytes yet still can handle all the data assigned to it. When VBA works with data, execution speed is a function of the number of bytes VBA has at its disposal. In other words, the fewer bytes used by data, the faster VBA can access and manipulate the data.

Benchmarking variant data types

To test whether data-typing is important, I developed the accompanying routine, which performs some meaningless calculations in a loop and then displays the total time to execute the subroutine:

```
Sub TimeTest()
    Dim x As Integer, y As Integer
    Dim A As Integer, B As Integer,
C As Integer
    Dim i As Integer, j As Integer
    Dim StartTime, EndTime As Date
'   Store the starting time
    StartTime = Timer
'   Perform some calculations
    x = 0
    y = 0
    For i = 1 To 1000
        For j = 1 To 1000
            A = x + y + i
            B = y - x - i
            C = x - y - i
        Next j
    Next i
'   Get ending time
    EndTime = Timer
'   Display total time in seconds
        MsgBox  Format(EndTime  -
StartTime, "000")
End Sub
```

On my 486/66 system, this routine took 12 seconds to run. Then I *commented out* the Dim statements, which declare the data types. That is, I turned the Dim statements into comments by adding an apostrophe at the beginning of the lines. As a result, VBA used the default data type, variant. I reran the procedure: it took 39 seconds, more than three times as long as before.

The moral is simple: If you want your VBA applications to run as fast as possible, declare your variables!

Declaring and scoping variables

If you don't declare the data type for a variable that you use in a VBA routine, VBA uses the default data type, variant. Data stored as a variant acts like a chameleon: it changes type, depending on what you do with it. For example, if a variable is a variant data type and contains a text string that looks like a number (such as *143*), you can use this variable for numeric calculations as well as string manipulations. Thanks to VBA, the conversion is automatic. This process may seem like an easy way out, but remember that you sacrifice speed and memory.

Before you use variables in a procedure, you may want to *declare* your variables — that is, tell VBA the variable's name and data type. Declaring variables provides two main benefits:

- *Your programs run faster and use memory more efficiently.* The default data type, variant, causes VBA to repeatedly perform time-consuming checks and reserve more memory than necessary. If VBA knows the data type, it doesn't have to investigate and it can reserve just enough memory to store the data.
- *You avoid problems involving misspelled variable names.* Say that you use an undeclared variable named CurrentRate. At some point in your routine, however, you insert the statement `CurentRate = .07`This misspelled variable name, which is very difficult to spot, likely will cause your routine to give incorrect results.

To force yourself to declare all the variables that you use, include the following as the first statement in your VBA module:

```
Option  Explicit
```

This statement causes your program to stop whenever VBA encounters a variable name that has not been declared. VBA issues an error message, and you must declare the variable before you can proceed.

TIP

To ensure that the Option Explicit statement is inserted automatically whenever you insert a new VBA module, enable the Require Variable Declaration option in the Module General tab of the Options dialog box. I highly recommend doing so.

A variable's *scope* determines in which modules and procedures the variable can be used. A variable's scope can be any of the following:

Scope	***How Declared***
Procedure only	By using a Dim or Static statement within the procedure
Modulewide	By using a Dim or Static statement before the first Sub statement in a module
All	By using a Public statement before the first Sub statement in a module

I further discuss how to declare each scope in the following sections.

A note about the examples in this chapter

This chapter contains many examples of VBA code, usually presented in the form of a simple subroutine procedure. These examples demonstrate various concepts as simply as possible. Most of these examples do not perform any particularly useful task; in fact, the task can often be performed by using a different method. In other words, don't use these examples in your own work. Subsequent chapters provide many more code examples that *are* useful.

Procedure-only variables

Variables declared as procedure-only variables can be used only in the procedure in which they are declared. When the procedure ends, the variable no longer exists and Excel frees up its memory.

If you execute the procedure again, the variable comes back to life, but its previous value is lost.

The most common way to declare a procedure-only variable is with a Dim statement placed between a Sub statement and an End Sub statement (in fact, Dim statements usually are placed right after the Sub statement, before the procedure's code).

If you're curious about this word, Dim is a shortened form of *Dimension.* In old versions of BASIC, this statement was used exclusively to declare the dimensions for an array. In VBA, the Dim keyword is used to declare any variable, not just arrays.

The following are some examples of procedure-only variables declared by using Dim statements:

```
Sub MySub()
    Dim x As Integer
    Dim First As Long
    Dim InterestRate As Single
    Dim TodaysDate As Date
    Dim UserName As String * 20
    Dim MyValue
'   ... [The procedure's code goes here] ...
End Sub
```

Notice that the last Dim statement in the preceding example doesn't declare a data type; it just declares the variable itself. As a result, the variable is a variant.

By the way, you also can declare several variables with a single Dim statement. For example,

```
Dim x as Integer, y as Integer, z as Integer
Dim First as Long, Last as Double
```

CAUTION

Unlike in some languages, in VBA you cannot declare a group of variables to be a particular data type by separating the variables with commas. For example, the following statement, while valid, does not declare all the variables as integers:

```
Dim i, j, k as Integer
```

In VBA, only k is declared to be an integer; the other variables are declared variants.

If a variable is declared with procedure-only scope, other procedures in the same module can use the same variable name, but each instance of the variable is unique to its own procedure.

In general, variables declared at the procedure level are the most efficient because VBA frees up the memory they use when the procedure ends.

Another way of data-typing variables

Like most other dialects of BASIC, VBA lets you append a character to a variable's name to indicate the data type. For example, you can declare the MyVar variable as an integer by tacking % onto the name:

```
MyVar% = 189
```

Type-declaration characters exist for most of VBA's data types (data types not listed don't have type-declaration characters).

Data Type	*Type-Declaration Character*
Integer	%
Long	&
Single	!
Double	#
Currency	@
String	$

This method of data-typing variables is essentially a holdover from BASIC; it's better to declare your variables by using the procedures described in this chapter.

Modulewide variables

Sometimes, you'll want a variable to be available to all procedures in a module. If so, just declare the variable *before* the module's first Sub statement — outside of any subroutines.

In the following example, the Dim statement is the first statement in the module. Both MySub and YourSub have access to the CurrentValue variable.

```
Dim CurrentValue as Integer

Sub MySub()
'       ... [Code goes here] ...
End Sub

Sub YourSub()
'       ... [Code goes here] ...
End Sub
```

The value of a modulewide variable does not change when a procedure ends.

Public variables

If you need to make a variable available to all the procedures in all your VBA modules, declare it at the module level by using the Public keyword rather than Dim. Here's an example:

```
Public CurrentRate as Long
```

The Public keyword makes the CurrentRate variable available to any procedure in the workbook, even those in other VBA modules. You must insert this statement before the first Sub statement in a module.

Static variables

Static variables are a special case. Although they are declared at the procedure level, they retain their value when the procedure ends.

You declare static variables by using the Static keyword:

```
Sub MySub()
    Static Counter as Integer
 ... [Code goes here] ...
End Sub
```

Working with constants

A variable's value may, and often does, change while your procedure is executing. Sometimes, you need to refer to named values or strings that never change: *constants*.

You declare constants by using the Const statement. For example,

```
Const NumQuarters as Integer = 4
Const Rate = .0725, Period = 12
Private Const ModName as String = "Budget Macros"
Public Const AppName as String = "Budget Application"
```

Like variables, constants also have a scope: If you want a constant to be available within a single procedure only, declare it after the Sub statement. To make a constant available to all procedures in a module, use the Private keyword and declare it before the first Sub statement in the module. To make a constant available to all modules in the workbook, use the Public keyword and declare it before the first Sub statement in a module.

NOTE: If you attempt to change the value of a constant in a VBA routine, you get an error.

Using constants in place of hard-coded values or strings is an excellent programming practice. For example, if your procedure needs to refer to a specific value (such as an interest rate) several times, it's better to declare the value as a constant and refer to the constant's name rather than the value. This technique not only makes your code more readable, but it also makes it easier to change should the need arise — you only have to change one statement rather than several.

Excel and VBA contain many predefined constants, which you can use without declaring; in fact, you don't even need to know the value of these constants to use them. The macro recorder usually uses constants rather than actual values. The following procedure uses a built-in constant (xlManual) to change Calculation property of the Application object (that is, change Excel's recalculation mode to manual):

```
Sub CalcManual()
    Application.Calculation = xlManual
End Sub
```

In this case, I discovered the xlManual constant by recording a macro that changed the calculation mode. I also could have looked in the on-line help under Calculation Property; all the relevant constants for this property are listed there.

The actual value of xlManual is –4135. Obviously, it's easier to use the constant's name than look up the value.

By the way, the constant to change to automatic calculation mode is xlAutomatic, and its value is –4105. As you can see, there is no apparent system to these built-in constants.

TIP

The Object Browser contains a list of all Excel and VBA constants, but it doesn't include their values. To view the constants defined in Excel, activate a VBA module and press F2 to bring up the Object Browser. Select Excel in the Libraries/Workbooks pull-down list and then select Constants in the Objects/Modules list box. The Methods/Properties list box shows all the defined constants that you can use (see Figure 7-1). To view VBA's constants, choose VBA in the Libraries/Workbooks pull-down list. To get more information about a constant, select it and click the question mark icon: A help topic appears, describing where the selected constant can be used in your code.

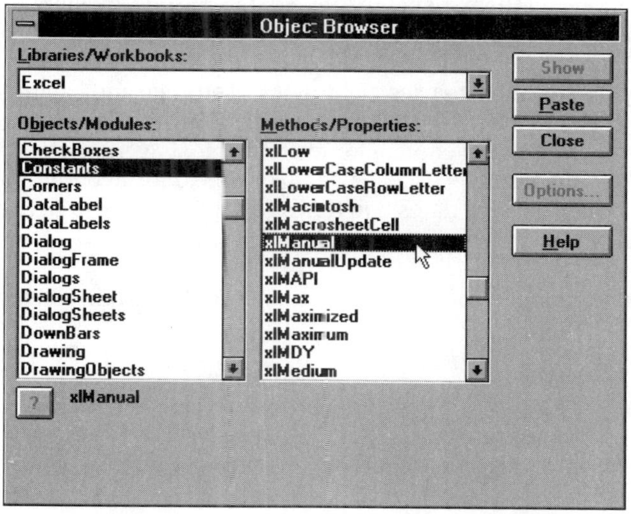

Figure 7-1: The Object Browser can display all the predefined constants in Excel and VBA.

CROSS REFERENCE

Appendix C contains a complete list of Excel's and VBA's constants.

Working with strings

Like Excel, VBA can manipulate both numbers and text. There are two types of strings (a data type) in VBA:

- *Fixed-length strings* are declared with a specified number of characters. The maximum length is 56,529 characters.
- *Variable-length strings* theoretically can hold up to 2 billion characters.

Each character in a string takes one byte of storage.

When you declare a string variable with a Dim statement, you can specify the maximum length if you know it (that is, a fixed-length string), or let VBA handle it dynamically (a variable-length string). In the following example, the MyString variable is declared to be a string with a maximum length of 50 characters. YourString is also declared as a string, but its length is unfixed.

```
Dim MyString as String * 50
Dim YourString as String
```

Working with dates

You can use a string variable to store dates, of course, but you can't perform date calculations on them. Using the date data type gives your routines much more flexibility.

A variable defined as a date uses eight bytes of storage and can hold dates ranging from January 1, 0100, to December 31, 9999. That's a span of nearly 10,000 years — more than enough for even the most aggressive financial forecast. The date data type is also useful for time data, accurate to whole seconds only.You refer to dates and times by enclosing them between two pound signs (#), as shown next.

Here are some examples of declaring variables and constants as a date data type:

```
Dim Today As Date
Dim StartTime As Date
Const FirstDay As Date = #1/1/95#
Const Noon = #12:00:00#
```

NOTE: Date variables display dates according to your system's short date format, and times appear according to your system's time format (either 12- or 24-hour). These system settings are stored in your WIN.INI file and can be modified by using the International option in the Windows Control Panel. Displaying a date or time by using VBA thus may vary, depending on the system's settings.

Assignment Statements, Expressions, and Operators

An *assignment statement* is a VBA statement that assigns the result of an expression to a variable or an object. Excel's on-line help defines *expression* as ". . . a combination of keywords, operators, variables, and constants that yield a string, number, or object. An expression can perform a calculation, manipulate characters, or test data." (Whew. I couldn't have said it better myself.) Much of the work done in VBA involves developing (and debugging) expressions.

If you know how to create formulas in Excel, you'll have no trouble creating expressions. The only difference is that an expression must have its result assigned to a variable.

The following are examples of assignment statements (the expressions are to the right of the equal sign):

```
x = 1
x = x + 1
x = (y * 2) / (z  * 2)
FileOpen = True
FileOpen = Not FileOpen
Range("TheYear").Value = 1995
```

NOTE: Expressions can be very complex; use the VBA code line continuation sequence (space followed by an underscore) to make lengthy expressions easier to read.

Often expressions use functions — VBA's built-in functions, Excel's worksheet functions, or custom functions that you develop in VBA. I discuss functions later in this chapter.

Operators play a major role in VBA. Familiar operators describe mathematical operations, including addition (+), multiplication (*), division (/), subtraction (-), exponentiation (^), and string concatenation (&). Less-familiar operators are the backslash (\), used in integer division, and the Mod operator, used in modulo arithmetic (the Mod operator returns the remainder of one number divided by another: 17 Mod 3 = 2).

VBA also provides a full set of logical operators, shown in Table 7-3. Consult the on-line help for complete details.

Table 7-3 VBA's Logical Operators

Operator	*What It Does*
Not	Performs a logical negation on an expression
And	Performs a logical conjunction on two expressions
Or	Performs a logical disjunction on two expressions
XoR	Performs a logical exclusion on two expressions
Eqv	Performs a logical equivalence on two expressions
Imp	Performs a logical implication on two expressions

The order of precedence for operators in VBA is exactly the same as in Excel. Of course, you can add parentheses to change the natural order of precedence.

Arrays

An *array* is a group of variables that have a common name; you refer to a specific variable in the array by using the array name and an index number. For example, you may define an array of 12 string variables so that each variable corresponds to the name of a different month. If you name the array *MonthNames*, you can refer to the first element of the array as MonthNames(1), the second element as MonthNames(2), and so on.

Declaring arrays

You declare an array with a Dim or Public statement, just like you declare a regular variable. But you also need to specify the number of elements in the array. You do so by specifying the first index number, the keyword *to*, and the last index number — all inside parentheses. For example, here's how to declare an array comprising 100 integers:

```
Dim MyArray(1 to 100) as Integer
```

TIP

When you declare an array, you need specify only the upper index (VBA assumes that 0 is the lower index). Therefore, the following statement declares the same array as `Dim MyArray(0 to 100) as Integer`

```
Dim MyArray(100) as Integer
```

If you want VBA to assume that 1 is the lower index for arrays that declare only the upper index, include the following statement before any Sub statements in your module:

```
Option Base 1
```

Multidimensional arrays

VBA arrays can have up to 60 dimensions, although it's rare to need more than three dimensions. The arrays in the preceding section were one-dimensional arrays. The following statement declares a 100-integer array with two dimensions:

```
Dim MyArray(1 to 10, 1 to 10) as Integer
```

You can think of the preceding array as occupying a 10 X 10 matrix. To refer to a specific element in a 2-D array, you need to specify two index numbers. For example, here's how you can assign a value to an element in the preceding array:

```
MyArray(3, 4) = 125
```

NOTE

Naturally, you can think of a 3-D array as a cube. But I can't tell you how to visualize the data layout of an array of more than three dimensions.

A *dynamic array* doesn't have a preset number of elements. You declare a dynamic array with a blank set of parentheses:

```
Dim MyArray() as Integer
```

Before you can use a dynamic array, however, you must use the ReDim statement to tell VBA how many elements are in the array. You can use the ReDim statement any number of times, changing the array's size as often as you need to.

Arrays crop up later in this chapter, as I discuss looping.

Object Variables

An *object variable* is a variable that holds an entire object, including its properties and methods. Object variables are important for two reasons:

- You can simplify your code significantly.
- Your code executes much faster.

Object variables, like other variables, are declared by using the Dim or Public statement. For example,

```
Dim Rate as Object
Public MyDialog as Object
```

To see how object variables simplify your code, examine the following simple procedure, which was written without using object variables:

```
Sub NoObjVar()
    ActiveWorkbook.Worksheets("Sheet1").Range("A1").
    Value = 124
    ActiveWorkbook.Worksheets("Sheet1").Range("A1").
    Font.Bold = True
    ActiveWorkbook.Worksheets("Sheet1").Range("A1").
    Font.Italic = True
End Sub
```

This routine enters a value into cell A1 of Sheet1 on the active workbook and then bolds and italicizes the cell's contents. That's a lot of typing. To save your fingers wear and tear, you can condense the routine by using an object variable:

```
Sub ObjVar()
    Dim MyCell As Object
    Set MyCell =
ActiveWorkbook.Worksheets("Sheet1").Range("A1")
    MyCell.Value = 124
    MyCell.Font.Bold = True
    MyCell.Font.Italic = True
End Sub
```

After the variable MyCell is declared as an object data type, the Set statement assigns an object to it. Subsequent statements then can use the simpler MyCell reference in place of the lengthy `ActiveWorkbook.Worksheets("Sheet1").Range("A1")` reference.

NOTE

The true value of object variables will become apparent when I discuss looping and dialog boxes.

Benchmarking object variables

To discover whether object variables really make code run faster, I developed the following procedure. This procedure, which doesn't use object variables, goes through a loop 5,000 times and assigns a value to the same cell. When the procedure finishes, it displays the elapsed time.

```
Sub TimeTest()
'    Store the starting time
     StartTime = Timer
'    Perform some calculations
     For i = 1 To 5000
ActiveWorkbook.Sheets("Sheet1").
Range("A1").Value = 123
     Next i
'    Get ending time
     EndTime = Timer
'    Display total time in seconds
      MsgBoxFormat(EndTime
      - StartTime, "000")
End Sub
```

On my 486/66 system, this routine took 63 seconds to run. Then I modified the procedure, defining an object variable:

```
Sub TimeTest()
'    Create object variable
     Dim TheCell As Object
Set TheCell = ActiveWorkbook.Sheets
("Sheet1").Range("A1")
'    Store the starting time
     StartTime = Timer
'    Perform some calculations
     For i = 1 To 5000
        TheCell.Value = 123
     Next i
'    Get ending time
     EndTime = Timer
'    Display total time in seconds
      MsgBoxFormat(EndTime
      - StartTime, "000")
End Sub
```

The modified procedure took 33 seconds — almost twice as fast. Fact: After an object is assigned to a variable, VBA can access it much faster than a normal lengthy reference. So when speed is critical, use object variables.

One way to think about this is in terms of "dot processing." Every time VBA encounters a dot, as in Sheets("Sheet1").Range("A1"), it takes time. In the first example above, there are three dots within the For...Next loop. In the second example there is only one dot. The fewer the dots, the faster the processing time.

User-Defined Data Types

VBA lets you create custom, or *user-defined*, data types (a concept much like much like Pascal records or C structures). A user-defined data type can ease your work with some types of data. For example, if your application deals with customer information, you may want to create a four-pronged user-defined data type (named CustomerInfo) as follows:

```
Type CustomerInfo
    Company As String * 25
    Contact As String * 15
    RegionCode As Integer
    Sales As Long
End Type
```

You define custom data types outside of procedures — usually at the top of your module.

After you create a user-defined data type, you can use a Dim statement to declare a variable as that type — usually, you define an array. For example:

```
Dim Customers(1 to 100) as CustomerInfo
```

Each of the 100 elements in this array consists of four components (as delineated by the user-defined data type, CustomerInfo). You can refer to a particular component of the record as follows:

```
Customers(1).Company = "Acme Tools"
Customers(1).Contact = "Tim Robertson"
Customers(1).RegionCode = 3
Customers(1).Sales = 150677
```

You also can work with an element in the array as a whole. For example, to copy the information from Customers(1) to Customers(2), use a statement like

```
Customers(2) = Customers(1)
```

The preceding statement is equivalent to the following block of statements:

```
Customers(2).Company = Customers(1).Company
Customers(2).Contact = Customers(1).Contact
Customers(2).RegionCode = Customers(1).RegionCode
Customers(2).Sales = Customers(1).Sales
```

Built-In Functions

Like all programming languages, VBA has a variety of built-in functions that simplify calculations and operations. Often, the functions allow you to easily perform operations that are otherwise difficult, or even impossible. Many of VBA's functions are similar (or identical) to Excel's worksheet functions; the functions have different names, though. For example, the VBA function UCase, which converts a string argument to uppercase, is equivalent to the Excel worksheet function UPPER.

CROSS REFERENCE

Appendix D contains a complete list of VBA's functions. And all are thoroughly described in the on-line help system.

You use functions in VBA expressions much like you use them in worksheet formulas. The main difference is that you assign the result of the function to a variable.

Here's a simple routine that calculates the square root of a variable by using the Sqr function, stores the result in another variable, and displays the result:

```
Sub ShowRoot()
    MyValue = 25
    SquareRoot = Sqr(MyValue)
    MsgBox SquareRoot
End Sub
```

NOTE

You can use many of Excel's worksheet functions in your VBA code because they are actually methods of the Application object. To use a worksheet function in a VBA statement, just precede the function name with the Application object. However, you cannot use worksheet functions that have an equivalent VBA function. For example, trying to calculate a square root in a VBA procedure by using the SQRT worksheet function produces an error message.

The following example demonstrates how to use an Excel worksheet function in a VBA procedure. (The ROMAN function converts a decimal number into a Roman numeral.)

```
Sub ShowRoman()
    DecValue = 1995
    RomanValue = Application.Roman(DecValue)
    MsgBox RomanValue
End Sub
```

When you execute this procedure, the MsgBox function displays the string MCMXCV. (Fans of old movies are usually dismayed when they learn that no function can convert a Roman numeral to its decimal equivalent.)

CROSS REFERENCE

As I describe in Chapter 9, you can use VBA to create custom worksheet functions that work just like Excel's built-in worksheet functions.

Manipulating Objects and Collections

Because VBA users spend a lot of time working with objects and collections, you'll want to know the most efficient ways to get the job done. VBA offers two important constructs that can simplify working with objects and collections:

- With...End With construct
- For Each...Next construct

The MsgBox function

The MsgBox function is one of the most useful VBA functions. Many of the examples in this chapter use this function to display the value of a variable.

This function often is a good substitute for a simple dialog box. It's also an excellent debugging tool, because you can insert MsgBox functions at any time to see the result of a calculation or assignment.

Most functions return a single value, which you assign to a variable. The MsgBox function not only returns a value, but it also displays a dialog box that the user can respond to. The value returned represents the user's response. You may use the MsgBox function even when you have no interest in the user's response but want to take advantage of the message display.

The official syntax of the MsgBox function has five arguments (those in square brackets are optional):

```
MsgBox(prompt[,buttons][,title]
      [,helpfile,context])
```

where *prompt* is the message that's displayed in the pop-up display. (Required.)

where *buttons* are value(s) that specify which buttons you want to appear in the message box, as well as an optional icon. Use built-in constants — for example, vbYesNo. (Optional.)

where *title* is text that appears in the message box's title bar. Default is *Microsoft Excel*. (Optional.)

where *helpfile* is the name of the help file associated with the message box. (Optional.)

and where *context* is the context ID of the help topic. (Optional.)

You can assign the value returned to a variable, or you can use the function by itself without an assignment statement. The example next assigns the result to the variable Ans. Notice that I used the sum of two constants (vbYesNo + vbQuestion) for the buttons argument. Using vbYesNo displays two buttons in the message box: one labeled Yes and one labeled No. Adding vbQuestion to the argument also displays a question mark icon (see the accompanying figure). When the first statement is executed, Ans contains one of two values, represented by the constants vbYes or vbNo. In this example, if the user clicks the No button, the subroutine ends.

```
Ans = MsgBox("Continue?", vbYesNo +
vbQuestion)

If Ans = vbNo Then Exit Sub
```

For more information, study the on-line help, which lists all of the constants you can use.

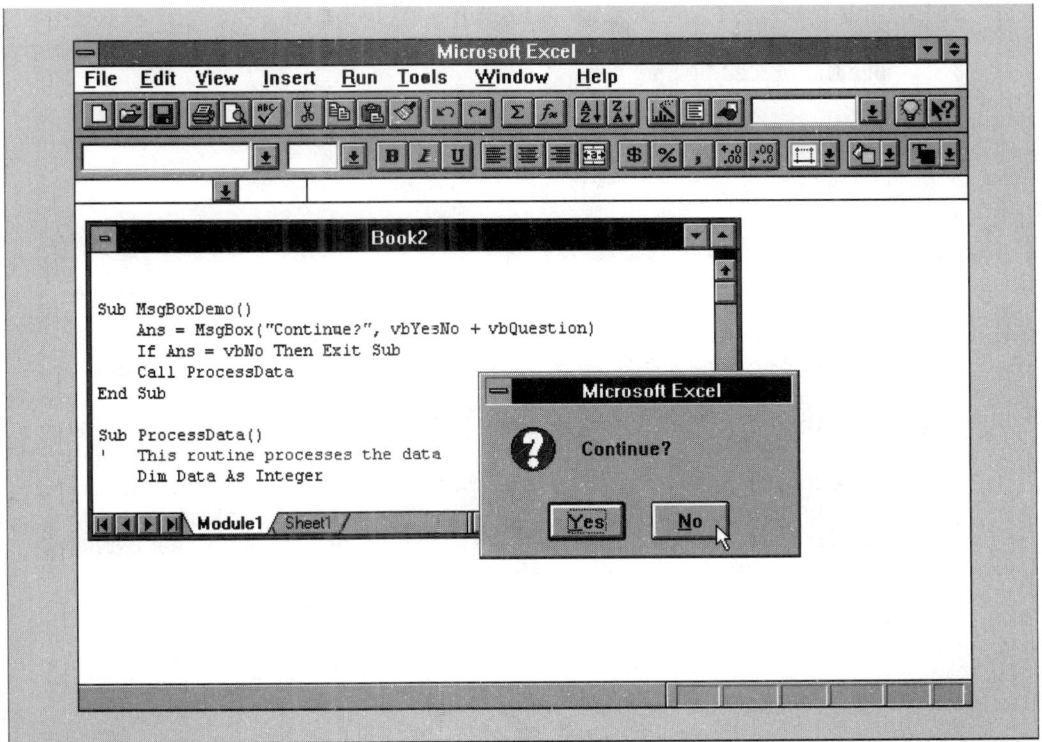

With...End With construct

The With...End With structure is unique to VBA; it isn't even available in Visual Basic 3.0. This construct lets you perform multiple operations on an object by using a shortcut syntax.

To start understanding how the With...End With construct works, examine the following procedure, which modifies five properties of the Range object's formatting:

```
Sub ChangeFont1()
    Selection.Font.Name = "Times New Roman"
    Selection.Font.FontStyle = "Bold Italic"
    Selection.Font.Size = 12
    Selection.Font.Underline = xlSingle
    Selection.Font.ColorIndex = 5
End Sub
```

This procedure, which acts on the current selection of cells, can be rewritten, using the With...End With structure. The following procedure performs exactly like the preceding one:

```
Sub ChangeFont2()
    With Selection.Font
        .Name = "Times New Roman"
        .FontStyle = "Bold Italic"
        .Size = 12
        .Underline = xlSingle
        .ColorIndex = 5
    End With
End Sub
```

Some think that the second incarnation of the routine is actually more difficult to read. Remember, though, that the objective is increased speed. Although I agree that the first version is more straightforward and easier to understand, the routine that uses the With...End With structure when changing several properties of an object is about twice as fast as the procedure that explicitly references the object in each statement.

When you record a VBA macro, Excel uses the With...End With structure every chance it gets. To see a good example of this construct, try recording your actions while you change the page setup by choosing the File⇨Page Setup command.

The For Each...Next construct

A *collection* is a group of related objects. For example, the Workbooks collection is a collection of all open Workbook objects. And the Sheets collection is a collection of all Sheet objects in a workbook. And the Toolbars collection is a collection of all Toolbar objects. And so on.

Suppose that you want to perform some action on all objects in a collection. Or suppose that you want to evaluate all objects in a collection and take action under certain conditions. These are perfect occasions for the For Each...Next construct. (This important construct is also unique to VBA.)

The syntax of the For Each...Next construct is

```
For Each element In group
 [statements]
 [Exit For]
 [statements]
Next [element]
```

NOTE The For Each...Next construct also works with array variables. This discussion, however, focuses entirely on collections.

The following procedure uses the For Each...Next construct with the Sheets collection in the active workbook. When you execute the procedure, the MsgBox function displays each sheet's name. (If there are five sheets in the active workbook, the MsgBox function is called five times.)

```
Sub CountSheets()
    For Each Item In ActiveWorkbook.Sheets
        MsgBox Item.Name
    Next Item
End Sub
```

NOTE In the preceding example, Item is an object variable. There's nothing special about the name Item; you can use any valid variable name in its place.

The Exit For statement is optional. It provides a way to exit the For Each...Next loop early. This is usually used in conjunction with an If...Then statement (described later in this chapter). The next example cycles through all objects in the Windows collection. If a Window is hidden, it changes the value of AllVisible to False and then exits the For Each...Next loop. The message box displays True if all windows are visible, and False if at least window one is hidden.

```
Sub HiddenWindows()
    AllVisible = True
    For Each Item In Windows
        If Item.Visible = False Then
            AllVisible = False
            Exit For
        End If
    Next Item
    MsgBox AllVisible
End Sub
```

Here's another example. This routine uses the If...Then construct to evaluate each workbook in the Workbooks collection. If the object's name is not the same as the active workbook's name, the workbook is closed. When this routine finishes executing, the only workbook left open is the active workbook.

```
Sub CloseInActive()
    For Each Book In Workbooks
        If Book.Name <> ActiveWorkbook.Name Then book.Close
    Next book
End Sub
```

You don't have to know how many elements are in a collection to use the For Each...Next construct.

I offer a final example. The following routine is designed to be executed after the user selects a range of cells. The Selection collection consists of Range objects (each cell in the selection is a Range object). The routine evaluates each cell and uses VBA's UCase function to convert its contents to uppercase (numeric cells are not affected).

```
Sub MakeUpperCase()
    For Each Cell In Selection
        Cell.Value = UCase(Cell.Value)
    Next Cell
End Sub
```

Controlling Execution

Some VBA procedures start at the top and progress line by line to the bottom. Macros that you record, for example, always work in this fashion. Often, however, you need to control the flow of your routines by skipping over some statements, executing some statements multiple times, and testing conditions to determine what the routine does next.

The previous section described the For Each...Next construct, which is a type of loop. This section discusses the additional ways of controlling the execution of your VBA procedures:

- The GoTo statement
- The If...Then structure
- The Select Case structure
- For...Next loops
- Do...While loops
- Do...Until loops

The GoTo statement

The most straightforward way to change the flow of a program is to use a GoTo statement. The GoTo statement simply transfers program control to a new statement; this new statement must be preceded by a label (a text string followed by a colon), however, for VBA to identify it.

VBA routines can contain any number of labels.

The following subroutine uses the InputBox function to get the user's name. If the user's name is not Julio, the procedure branches to the WrongName label and the subroutine ends. Otherwise, the procedure executes some additional code. The Exit Sub statement causes the subroutine to end.

```
Sub GoToDemo()
    UserName = InputBox("Enter Your Name:")
    If UserName <> "Julio" Then GoTo WrongName
    MsgBox ("Welcome Julio...")
'   ...[More code here] ...
    Exit Sub
WrongName:
    MsgBox ("Sorry. Only Julio can run this.")
End Sub
```

This simple routine works, but in general you should use the GoTo statement only when there's no other way to perform an action. In fact, a GoTo statement is really necessary in VBA only when you need to trap errors (refer to Chapter 8).

If...Then structure

The most important control structure in VBA is the If...Then structure. This common command gives your applications decision-making capability.

Good decision making is the key to writing successful programs. A successful Excel application boils down to making decisions and acting upon them.

The basic syntax of the If...Then structure is

```
If condition Then statements [Else elsestatements]
```

The If...Then structure is used to execute one or more statements conditionally. The Else part is optional. If included, it lets you execute one or more statements if the condition you're testing is not true.

The following routine demonstrates an If...Then structure without an Else clause. If the current system time is less than .5 (that is, before noon), a message is displayed. If the current system time is greater than or equal to .5, the routine ends and nothing happens.

```
Sub GreetMe()
    If Time < 0.5 Then MsgBox "Good Morning"
End Sub
```

If you want to display a different greeting if Time is greater than or equal to .5, add another If...Then statement, like so:

```
Sub GreetMe()
    If Time < 0.5 Then MsgBox "Good Morning"
    If Time >= 0.5 Then MsgBox "Good Afternoon"
End Sub
```

Another approach is to use an Else clause. For example,

```
Sub GreetMe()
    If Time < 0.5 Then MsgBox "Good Morning" else _
      MsgBox "Good Afternoon"
End Sub
```

Notice that I used the line continuation sequence; the If...Then...Else statement is actually a single statement.

If you need to expand a routine to handle three conditions (for example, morning, afternoon, and evening), you can use either three If...Then statements or a nested If...Then...Else structure. The first approach is the simpler:

```
Sub GreetMe()
 If Time < 0.5 Then MsgBox "Good Morning"
 If Time >= 0.5 And Time < 0.75 Then MsgBox "Good Afternoon"
 If Time >= 0.75 Then MsgBox "Good Evening"
End Sub
```

The following routine performs the same action, using the If...Then...Else structure:

```
Sub GreetMe()
 If Time < 0.5 Then MsgBox "Good Morning" Else
 If Time >= 0.5 And Time < 0.75 Then MsgBox "Good Afternoon"
 Else
 If Time >= 0.75 Then MsgBox "Good Evening"
End Sub
```

In both examples, every statement in the routine gets executed, even in the morning. A more efficient routine would include a structure that ends the routine when a condition is found to be true. For example, a more efficient routine displays the *Good Morning* message in the morning and then exits without evaluating the other, superfluous conditions. True, the difference in speed is inconsequential when you design a procedure as small as this routine. But for more complex applications, you need another syntax:

```
If condition Then
 [statements]
[ElseIf condition-n Then
 [elseifstatements]] . . .
[Else
 [elsestatements]]
End If
```

Here's how you can use this syntax to rewrite the GreetMe routine:

```
Sub GreetMe()
    If Time < 0.5 Then
        MsgBox "Good Morning"
        ElseIf Time >= 0.5 And Time < 0.75 Then
            MsgBox "Good Afternoon"
            ElseIf Time >= 0.75 Then MsgBox "Good Evening"
    End If
End Sub
```

With this syntax, when a condition is true, the conditional statements are executed and the If structure ends. In other words, the extraneous conditions are not evaluated. Although this syntax makes for a more efficient routine, the code is more difficult to understand. There's always a trade-off.

The following is another example that uses the simple form of the If...Then structure. This routine prompts the user for a Quantity and then displays the appropriate discount based on the quantity. Notice that each If...Then statement in this routine is always executed, and the value for Discount can change as the statements are executed. The final value, however, is the desired value.

```
Sub Discount1()
    Quantity = InputBox("Enter Quantity: ")
    If Quantity >= 0 Then Discount = 0.1
    If Quantity >= 25 Then Discount = 0.15
    If Quantity >= 50 Then Discount = 0.2
    If Quantity >= 75 Then Discount = 0.25
    MsgBox "Discount: " & Discount
End Sub
```

The following routine is the preceding routine recoded, using the alternate syntax. In this case, the routine ends after executing the statements for a true condition.

```
Sub Discount2()
    Quantity = InputBox("Enter Quantity: ")
    If Quantity >= 0 And Quantity < 25 Then
       Discount = 0.1
           ElseIf Quantity >= 25 And Quantity < 50 Then
               Discount = 0.15
                  ElseIf Quantity >= 50 And Quantity < 75 Then
                        Discount = 0.2
                            ElseIf Quantity > 75 Then
                                Discount = 0.25
    End If
    MsgBox "Discount: " & Discount
End Sub
```

I find nested If...Then structures rather cumbersome. As a result, I usually use the If...Then structure only for simple binary decisions. When you need to choose among three or more alternatives, the Select Case structure is usually a better alternative.

Select Case structure

The Select Case structure is useful for choosing among three or more options. (The Select Case structure also works with two options and is a good alternative to the If...Then...Else structure.) The syntax for the Select Case structure is

```
Select Case testexpression
[Case expressionlist-n
 [statements-n]] . . .
[Case Else
 [elsestatements]]
End Select
```

The following example of Select Case structure shows another way to code the examples presented in the preceding section:

```
Sub Discount3()
    Quantity = InputBox("Enter Quantity: ")
    Select Case Quantity
        Case 0 To 24
            Discount = 0.1
        Case 25 To 49
            Discount = 0.15
```

```
        Case 50 To 74
            Discount = 0.2
        Case Is >= 75
            Discount = 0.25
    End Select
    MsgBox "Discount: " & Discount
End Sub
```

Any number of statements can go below each Case statement, and they all get executed if the case is true. If you use only one statement, as in the preceding example, you may want to put the statement on the same line as the Case keyword (but don't forget VBA's statement separator character, the colon). This technique makes the code more compact. For example,

```
Sub Discount3()
    Quantity = InputBox("Enter Quantity: ")
    Select Case Quantity
        Case  0 To 24: Discount = 0.1
        Case 25 To 49: Discount = 0.15
        Case 50 To 74: Discount = 0.2
        Case Is >= 75: Discount = 0.25
    End Select
    MsgBox "Discount: " & Discount
End Sub
```

When VBA executes a Select Case structure, the structure is exited as soon as a True case is found.

Select Case structures also can be nested. The following routine, for example, tests for Excel's window state (maximized, minimized, or normal) and then displays a message describing the window state. If Excel's window state is normal, the routine tests for the window state of the active window and then displays another message.

```
Sub AppWindow()
    Select Case Application.WindowState
        Case xlMaximized: MsgBox ("App Maximized")
        Case xlMinimized: MsgBox ("App Minimized")
        Case xlNormal: MsgBox ("App Normal")
            Select Case ActiveWindow.WindowState
                Case xlMaximized: MsgBox ("Book Maximized")
                Case xlMinimized: MsgBox ("Book Minimized")
                Case xlNormal: MsgBox ("Book Normal")
            End Select
    End Select
```

```
End Sub
```

TIP

You can nest Select Case structures as deeply as you need, but make sure that each Select Case statement has a corresponding End Select statement.

Indents make this potentially confusing code easy to understand. For example, take a look at the same procedure — without indents:

```
Sub AppWindow()
Select Case Application.WindowState
Case xlMaximized: MsgBox ("App Maximized")
Case xlMinimized: MsgBox ("App Minimized")
Case xlNormal: MsgBox ("App Normal")
Select Case ActiveWindow.WindowState
Case xlMaximized: MsgBox ("Book Maximized")
Case xlMinimized: MsgBox ("Book Minimized")
Case xlNormal: MsgBox ("Book Normal")
End Select
End Select
End Sub
```

Fairly incomprehensible, eh?

Looping

Looping is the repeating of a block of commands. You may know the number of times to loop, or it may be determined by the values of variables in your program.

There are two types of loops: good loops and bad loops. The following code, which enters consecutive numbers into a range, demonstrates a bad loop. The procedure starts by prompting the user for two values: a starting value and the total number of cells to fill in (InputBox returns a string, so I converted the strings to integers with the Cint function). This loop uses the GoTo statement to control the flow. If the CellCount variable, which keeps track of how many cells are filled, is less than the number requested by the user, program control loops back to DoAnother.

```
Sub BadLoop()
    StartVal = Cint(InputBox("Enter the starting value: "))
    NumToFill = Cint(InputBox("How many cells? "))
    ActiveCell.Value = StartVal
    CellCount = 1
DoAnother:
    ActiveCell.Offset(CellCount, 0).Value = StartVal + CellCount
    CellCount = CellCount + 1
    If CellCount < NumToFill Then GoTo DoAnother Else Exit
Sub
End Sub
```

If you try this routine, make sure you execute it when a worksheet is active.

This routine works as intended, so why is it an example of bad looping? Programmers generally frown upon using a GoTo statement when not absolutely necessary. Using GoTo statements to loop is contrary to the concept of structured coding (see the "What is structured programming?" sidebar). In fact, a GoTo statement makes the code much more difficult to read because it's almost impossible to represent a loop by using line indents. And it makes the routine more open to error. Furthermore, using lots of labels results in *spaghetti code* — code that appears to have little or no structure and flows haphazardly.

VBA has enough structured looping commands that you almost never have to rely on GoTo statements for your decision making.

For...Next loops

The simplest type of good loop is a For...Next loop (which I've already used in a few previous examples). Its syntax is

```
For counter = start To end [Step stepval]
 [statements]
 [Exit For]
 [statements]
Next [counter]
```

What is structured programming?

Hang around with programmers and sooner or later you'll hear the term *structured programming*. You'll also discover that structured programs are considered superior to unstructured programs.

So what is structured programming? And can you do it with VBA?

The basic premise is that a routine or code segment should have only one entry point and one exit point. In other words, a block of code should be a stand-alone unit, and program control cannot jump into or exit from the middle of this unit. As a result, structured programming rules out the GoTo statement. When you write structured code, your program progresses in an orderly manner and is easy to follow — as opposed to spaghetti code, where a program jumps around.

A structured program is easier to read and understand. More important, it's also easier to modify.

VBA is a structured language. It offers standard structured constructs, such as the If...Then...Else and Select Case structures and the For...Next, Do...Until, and Do...While loops. Furthermore, VBA fully supports modular code construction.

If you're new to programming, it's a good idea to form good structured programming habits early.

Following is an example of a For...Next loop that doesn't use the optional Step value or the optional Exit For statement. This routine executes the Sum = Sum + Count statement 100 times and displays the result — that is, the sum of the first 100 integers.

```
Sub SumAll()
    Sum = 0
    For Count = 1 To 100
        Sum = Sum + Count
    Next Count
    MsgBox Sum
End Sub
```

In this example, Count (the loop counter variable) started out as 1 and increased by 1 each time through the loop. The Sum variable simply increases by the current value of Count.

When using For...Next loops, the loop counter is a normal variable. As a result, you can change its value within the block of code that is executed between the For and the Next statements. However, this is a *baaaaad* practice and can cause unpredictable results. In fact, you should take special precautions to ensure that the loop counter does not get changed by your code.

You also can use a Step value to skip some values in the loop. Here's the same procedure rewritten to sum just the odd numbers from 1 to 100:

```
Sub SumOdd()
    Sum = 0
    For Count = 1 To 100 Step 2
        Sum = Sum + Count
    Next Count
    MsgBox Sum
End Sub
```

In this procedure, Count starts out as 1 and then takes on values of 3, 5, 7, and so on. The final value of Count is 99.

The following routine does the same as the BadLoop example found at the beginning of the "Looping" section. However, I eliminated the GoTo statement, converting a bad loop into a good loop that uses the For...Next structure.

```
Sub GoodLoop()
    StartVal = Cint(InputBox("Enter the starting value: "))
    NumToFill = Cint(InputBox("How many cells? "))
    ActiveCell.Value = StartVal
```

```
    For CellCount = 1 To NumToFill
ActiveCell.Offset(CellCount, 0).Value = StartVal + CellCount
    Next CellCount
End Sub
```

For...Next loops also can include one or more Exit For statements within the loop. When this statement is encountered, the loop terminates immediately (see the following example).

The next routine identifies the cell in column A of the active worksheet that has the largest value. The maximum value in the column is calculated by using Excel's MAX function and then is assigned to the MaxVal variable. Then the For...Next loop checks each cell in the column. If the cell being checked is equal to MaxVal, the Exit For statement ends the routine. Before terminating the loop, though, the procedure informs the user of the location and activates the cell.

```
Sub ExitForDemo()
    MaxVal = Application.Max(Range("A:A"))
    For Row = 1 To 16384
        Set TheCell = Range("A1").Offset(Row - 1, 0)
        If TheCell.Value = MaxVal Then
            MsgBox "Max value is in Row " & Row
            TheCell.Activate
            Exit For
        End If
    Next Row
End Sub
```

The previous examples used relatively simple loops. But you can have any number of statements in the loop and even nest For...Next loops inside other For...Next loops. Here's an example that uses nested For...Next loops to initialize a 3-D array with all zeros:

```
Sub NestedLoops()
    Dim MyArray(1 to 10, 1 to 10, 1 to 10)
    For i = 1 To 10
        For j = 1 To 10
            For k = 1 To 10
                MyArray(i, j, k) = 0
            Next k
        Next j
    Next i
End Sub
```

Do...While loops

A Do...While loop is another type of looping structure available in VBA. Unlike a For...Next loop, a Do...While loop continues until a specified condition is met. A Do...While loop can have either of two syntaxes:

```
Do [While condition]
 [statements]
 [Exit Do]
 [statements]
Loop
```

or

```
Do
 [statements]
 [Exit Do]
 [statements]
Loop [While condition]
```

The following routine has a Do...While loop with the first syntax. This routine opens a text file (which is assumed to be located in the current directory), reads each line, and then stores it in Sheet1, beginning with cell A1 and continuing down the column. The routine uses VBA's EOF function, which returns True when the end of the file has been reached. The final statement closes the text file.

```
Sub DoWhileDemo1()
    Open "TEXTFILE.TXT" For Input As #1
    LineCt = 0
    Do While Not EOF(1)
     Input #1, LineOfText
 Sheets("Sheet1").Range("A1").Offset(LineCt, 0) =LineOfText
        LineCt = LineCt + 1
    Loop
    Close #1
End Sub
```

The following routine has a Do...While loop with the second syntax. It produces the same result. Which syntax you use is up to you.

```
Sub DoWhileDemo2()
    Open "TEXTFILE.TXT" For Input As #1
    LineCt = 0
    Do
        Input #1, LineOfText
 Sheets("Sheet1").Range("A1").Offset(LineCt, 0) = LineOfText
```

```
        LineCt = LineCt + 1
    Loop While Not EOF(1)
    Close #1
End Sub
```

Do...While loops also can contain one or more Exit Do statements. When an Exit Do statement is encountered, the loop ends immediately.

Do...Until loops

The Do...Until loop structure is very similar to the Do...While structure. The difference is when the condition is tested. In a Do...While loop, the loop executes *while* the condition is true. In a Do...Until loop, the loop executes *until* the condition is true.

Do...Until also has two syntaxes:

```
Do [Until condition]
  statements]
 [Exit Do]
 [statements]
Loop
```

or

```
Do
 [statements]
 [Exit Do]
 [statements]
Loop [Until condition]
```

The following example is the same as presented for the Do...While loop but recoded to use a Do...Until loop. The only difference is the line with the Do statement. This example makes the code a bit clearer because it avoids the negative required in the Do...While example.

```
Sub DoUntilDemo1()
    Open "TEXTFILE.TXT" For Input As #1
    LineCt = 0
    Do Until EOF(1)
        Input #1, LineOfText
 Sheets("Sheet1").Range("A1").Offset(LineCt, 0) = LineOfText
        LineCt = LineCt + 1
    Loop
    Close #1
End Sub
```

Summary

- In this chapter, I presented the fundamentals of programming in VBA. You read about variables, constants, data types, arrays, and VBA's built-in functions. You also learned some techniques for manipulating objects and controlling the execution of your procedures.
- Chapter 8 focuses on subroutines, one of the two types of procedures you can write in VBA.

Chapter 8
Working with VBA Subroutine Procedures

In This Chapter

- Declaring and creating VBA subroutines
- Executing subroutines
- Passing arguments to a subroutine
- Error handling techniques
- An example of developing a useful subroutine

A *procedure* holds a group of VBA statements that accomplishes a desired task. Most VBA code is contained in subroutine procedures — all of the examples so far have been subroutine procedures. VBA also supports function procedures, which I discuss in Chapter 9.

NOTE: Chapter 11 has many useful and practical examples of subroutine procedures that you can incorporate into your work.

About Subroutines

A *subroutine* is a series of VBA statements that resides in a VBA module sheet. A module can hold any number of subroutines.

There are a number of ways to *call*, or execute, subroutines. A subroutine is executed from beginning to end (it can be ended prematurely, however).

A subroutine can be any length, but it's good programming practice to avoid creating long subroutines that perform many operations. Rather, write small routines, each with a single purpose. Then design a main subroutine that calls the other subroutines.

Some subroutines are written to use arguments. Subroutine arguments work much like the arguments you use in Excel worksheet functions. An argument is simply information that is used by the subroutine that is "passed" to the subroutine when it is executed.

Declaring a subroutine

A subroutine procedure, which is declared with the Sub keyword, must adhere to the following syntax:

```
[Private | Public][Static] Sub name [(arglist)]
 [statements]
 [Exit Sub]
 [statements]
End Sub
```

where *Private* indicates that the subroutine is accessible only to other procedures in the same module. (Optional.)

where *Public* indicates that the subroutine is accessible to all other procedures in all other modules in the workbook. (Optional.)

where *Static* indicates that the subroutine's variables are preserved when the subroutine ends. (Optional.)

where *Sub* is a keyword that indicates the beginning of a subroutine. (Required.)

where *name* is any valid variable name. (Required.)

where *arglist* is a list of variables, enclosed in parentheses, that represent arguments passed to the subroutine. Use a comma to separate arguments. (Optional.)

where *statements* are valid VBA statements. (Optional.)

where *Exit Sub* is a statement that causes an immediate exit from the subroutine. (Optional.)

where *End Sub* is a keyword that indicates the end of the subroutine. (Required.)

TIP

With a few exceptions, all VBA statements in a module must be contained in subroutine procedures or function procedures. Exceptions include module-level declarations, user-defined data definitions, and a few other statements that specify module-level options (for example, Options Explicit).

> **Naming subroutines**
>
> Every subroutine must have a name. The rules governing subroutine names are generally the same as for variable names. The exception is that a subroutine name cannot be like a cell addresse. For example, you can't name a subroutine J34, because J34 is a cell address.
>
> Ideally, a subroutine's name should describe what the routine does. A good rule of thumb is to use a name that includes a verb and a noun (for example, ProcessDate, PrintReport, Sort_Array, or CheckFilename). Avoid meaningless names, such as DoIt, Update, and Fix.
>
> Some programmers use sentencelike names that describe the subroutine (for example, WriteReportToTextFile and Get_Print_Options_and_Print_Report). Although long names are very descriptive and unambiguous, they also are difficult to type.

Scoping a subroutine

In the preceding chapter, I noted that a variable's scope determines which modules and procedures it can be used in. Similarly, a subroutine's scope determines whether it can be called by subroutines in other modules.

Public subroutines

By default, subroutines are *public* — that is, they can be called by other subroutines in any module. It's not necessary to use the Public keyword, but programmers often include it for clarity. The following two subroutines are both public subroutines:

```
Sub First()
'      ... [code goes here] ...
End Sub

Public Sub Second()
'      ... [code goes here] ...
End Sub
```

NOTE

If your module contains an Option Private Module statement, all subroutines in the module are private, even if they're declared with the Public keyword.

Private subroutines

Private subroutines can be called by other subroutines in the same module, but not by subroutines in other modules.

When you choose the Tools⇨Macro command, the Macro dialog box displays only the public subroutines.

The following example declares a private subroutine, named *MySub*:

```
Private Sub MySub()
'       ... [code goes here] ...
End Sub
```

NOTE: You can force all procedures in a module to be private — even those declared with the Public keyword — by including the following statement before your first Sub statement:

```
Option Private Module
```

If you write this statement in a module, you can omit the Private keyword from your Sub declarations.

NOTE: Excel's macro recorder normally creates new subroutine procedures called *Macro1*, *Macro2*, and so on. These procedures are all public procedures with no arguments.

Executing Subroutines

A VBA subroutine is mere window dressing unless you execute it. There are many ways to execute, or call, a VBA subroutine:

- With the Run⇨Start command (or its equivalent, F5)
- From the Macro dialog box
- With a Ctrl shortcut key combination
- From an item on the Tools menu
- From a custom menu
- From another subroutine
- From a Toolbar button
- From a drawing object
- Automatically
- When an event occurs
- From the Debug window

I discuss these methods in the following sections.

NOTE: In many cases, a subroutine will not function properly unless you're in the appropriate context. For example, if a subroutine is designed to work with the active worksheet, it will fail if the active sheet is a module. A good subroutine incorporates code that checks for the appropriate context and exits gracefully if it can't proceed.

With the Run⇨Start command

When a VBA module is active, Excel's menu bar includes a Run menu. When you issue the Run⇨Start command, VBA executes the current subroutine (in other words, the subroutine that contains the cursor).

TIP: F5 is the shortcut key for Run⇨Start.

If the cursor is not located within a subroutine when you issue the Run⇨Start command, VBA displays its Macro dialog box so that you can select a subroutine to execute.

This method is used primarily to test a subroutine.

From the Macro dialog box

Choosing the Tools⇨Macro command displays the Macro dialog box, shown in Figure 8-1. This dialog box lists all subroutines in all open workbooks; subroutines not in the active workbook are preceded by the workbook name and an exclamation point.

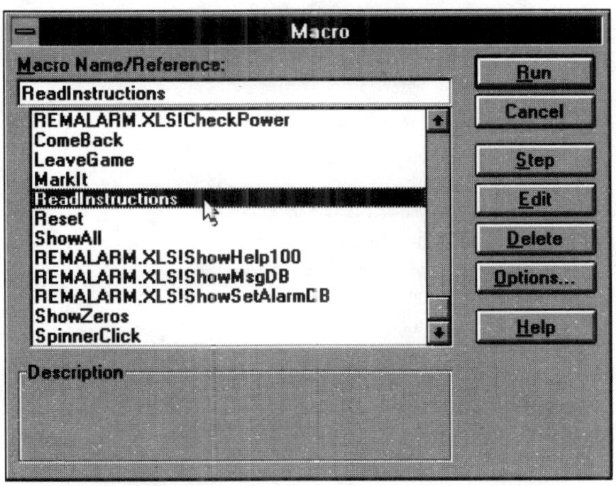

Figure 8-1: The Macro dialog box lists all subroutines in all open workbooks.

With a Ctrl shortcut key combination

You can assign a Ctrl shortcut key combination to every subroutine. If you assign the Ctrl+U key combo to a subroutine named *Update*, for example, pressing Ctrl+U calls Update.

To assign a Ctrl shortcut key combo to a subroutine, follow these steps:

1. Choose the Tools⇨Macro command.
2. Select the appropriate subroutine from the list box in the Macro dialog box.
3. Click the Options button to display the Macro Options dialog box (see Figure 8-2).
4. In the Assign to box, enter a character into the text box labeled Ctrl+.
5. Click OK to close the Macro Options dialog box.
6. Click Close to close the Macro dialog box.

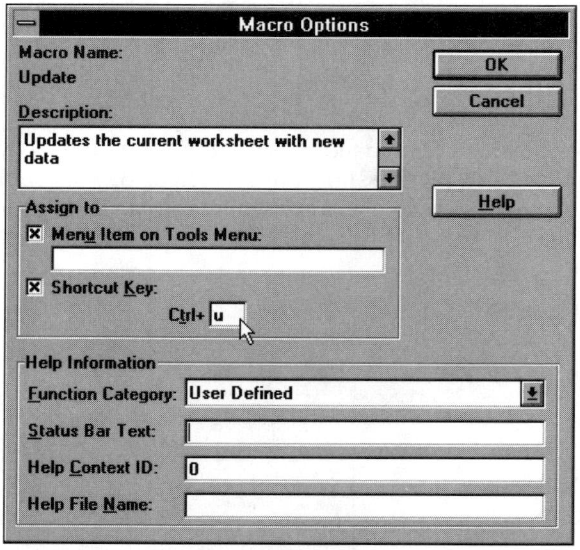

Figure 8-2: The Macro Options dialog box lets you assign a Ctrl key shortcut to a subroutine or to an item on the Tools menu.

NOTE: The character that you enter into the text box labeled Ctrl+ is case-sensitive. If you enter lowercase *s*, the shortcut key combo is Ctrl+S. If you enter uppercase *S*, the shortcut key combo is Ctrl+Shift+S.

If you assign one of Excel's predefined shortcut key combos to a subroutine, your key assignment takes precedence over the predefined key assignment. For example, Ctrl+S is Excel's predefined shortcut key for saving the active workbook. But if you assign Ctrl+S to a subroutine, pressing Ctrl+S no longer saves the active workbook.

From an item on the Tools menu

The Macro Options dialog box also enables you to create a new Tools menu item and then assign a subroutine to it. To do so, simply enter a descriptive name into the text box labeled Menu Item on Tools Menu.

You also can specify a hot key for the new menu item: when entering the command name into the Menu Item on Tools Menu text box, precede the desired hot key character with an ampersand (&).

While you're in the Macro Options dialog box to create a new Tools menu item, you also can describe the subroutine in the Status Bar Text text box. Then your text will appear in Excel's status bar when the menu item is selected (just like Excel's built-in commands). You also can assign a custom help topic to the new command (see Chapter 16 for details).

Figure 8-3 shows the Tools menu with a new menu item, Update List. Clicking this command executes the subroutine that is assigned to it.

The Tools menu displays the new command as long as the workbook that contains the macro is open. When you close the workbook, the command disappears from the Tools menu. You can add as many items as you want to the Tools menu.

From a custom menu

The Tools⇨Menu Editor command (available only when a VBA module is active) lets you modify Excel's menus; you even can add new menus and menu items. Then you can assign a subroutine to a custom menu item.

Following are the steps required to display a new command (Update List) at the bottom of a menu (Data). This new command, which appears only when the worksheet in question is active, executes a subroutine named *Update*.

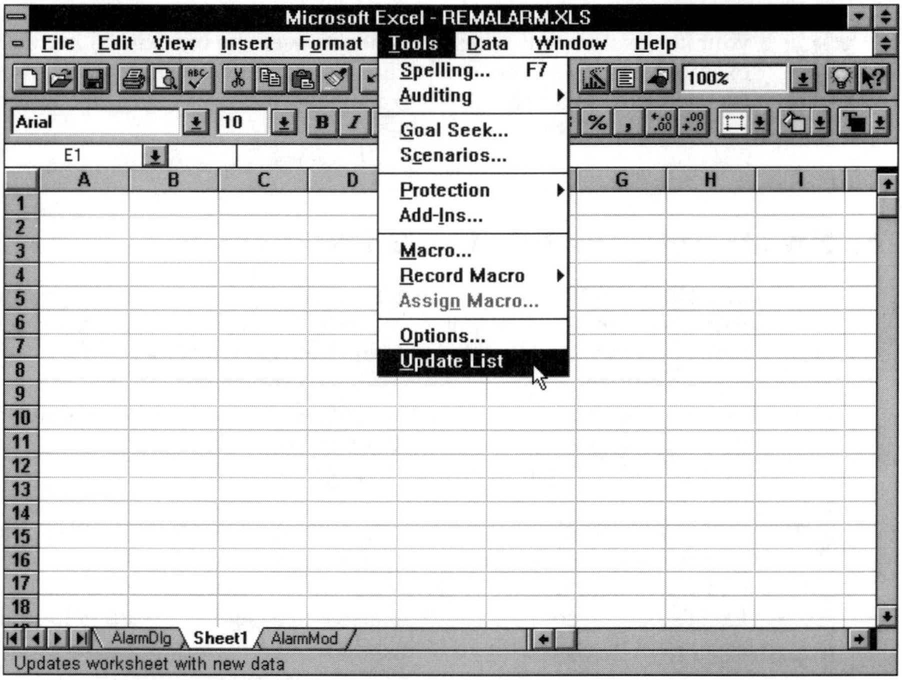

Figure 8-3: The Tools menu with a new menu item.

1. Choose the Tools➪Menu Editor command. Excel displays the Menu Editor dialog box.
2. Choose Worksheet from the Menu Bars drop-down list box.
3. Click &Data in the Menus list box.
4. Click (End of Menu) in the Menu Items list box.
5. Click the Insert button to add an empty menu item after the &Refresh Data item.
6. Enter **&Update List** in the text box labeled Caption.
7. Click the drop-down arrow to the right of the Macro text box. Excel lists all subroutines in all open workbooks.
8. Select Update.
9. Click OK to close the dialog box.

I discuss custom menus in detail in Chapter 14.

From another subroutine

One of the most common ways to execute a subroutine is from another subroutine. There are three ways to do so:

- Enter the subroutine's name followed by the subroutine's arguments (if any) separated by commas.
- Use the Call keyword followed by the subroutine's name and then its arguments (if any) enclosed in parentheses and separated by commas.
- Use the Run method of the Application object. This can be used to execute VBA procedures or XLM macros.

The following example demonstrates the first method. In this case, the MySub subroutine processes some statements (not shown), executes the Update subroutine, and then executes the rest of the statements.

```
Sub MySub()
'    ... [code goes here] ...
     Update
'    ... [code goes here] ...
End Sub

Sub Update()
'    ... [code goes here] ...
End Sub
```

The following example demonstrates the second method. The Call keyword executes the Update subroutine, which requires one argument; the calling subroutine passes the argument to the called subroutine. I discuss subroutine arguments later in this chapter.

```
Sub MySub()
     MonthNum = InputBox("Enter the month number: ")
     Call Update(MonthNum)
'    ... [code goes here] ...
End Sub

Sub Update(MonthSeq)
'    ... [code goes here] ...
End Sub
```

The next example uses the Run method to execute the Update routine, and passes MonthNum as the argument.

```
Sub MySub()
    MonthNum = InputBox("Enter the month number: ")
    Result = Application.Run("Update", MonthNum)
'   ... [code goes here] ...
End Sub

Sub Update(MonthSeq)
'   ... [code goes here] ...
End Sub
```

You can use either any of these methods to call subroutines. The Run method is generally not used to execute VBA subroutines. Rather, it is most useful for calling XLM macros from VBA. Some programmers always use the Call keyword to make it clear that another subroutine is being called.

Subroutines in the same module can always call each other.

Calling a subroutine in a different module

If VBA can't locate a called subroutine in the current module, it looks for Public subroutines in other modules in the same workbook.

If you want to call a Private subroutine from another subroutine, the subroutines must reside in the same module.

Subroutines in the same module cannot have the same name, but subroutines in different modules can. (I don't recommend this procedure, but VBA allows it.) You can persuade VBA to execute an *ambiguously named* subroutine — that is, another subroutine in a different module has the same name — by preceding the subroutine name with the module name in square brackets. For example, say that you define subroutines named *MySub* in Module1 and Module2. If you want to call the MySub in Module1, you can use either of the following statements:

```
[Module1].MySub
Call [Module1].MySub
```

If you do not differentiate between subroutines that have the same name, you get an *Ambiguous name detected* error message.

Calling a subroutine in a different workbook

If you want to execute a subroutine that's defined in a different workbook, you must establish a reference to the other workbook.

To add a reference to another workbook, choose the Tools⇨References command, which is available only when a VBA module is active. Excel displays its References dialog box (see Figure 8-4), which lists all available references, including all open workbooks. Simply check the box that corresponds to the workbook that you want to add as a reference and click OK. After you establish a reference, you can call subroutines in the workbook as if they were in the same workbook as the calling subroutine.

Don't try to create circular references between workbooks. For example, if BOOK1.XLS has a reference to BOOK2.XLS, Excel won't let you add a BOOK1.XLS reference to BOOK2.XLS; you get a *cyclic reference of projects* error message.

A referenced workbook does not have to be open; it is treated like a separate object library.

The list of references displayed in the References dialog box includes two object libraries: Visual Basic for Applications and Microsoft Excel 5.0 Object Library. Your workbooks always include references to both, and you can't unreference them because they are essential: the Microsoft Excel 5.0 Object Library contains information about all the objects exposed by Excel, while the Visual Basic for Applications library provides access to VBA's built-in functions and constants. In fact, the Object Browser gets its information from these libraries.

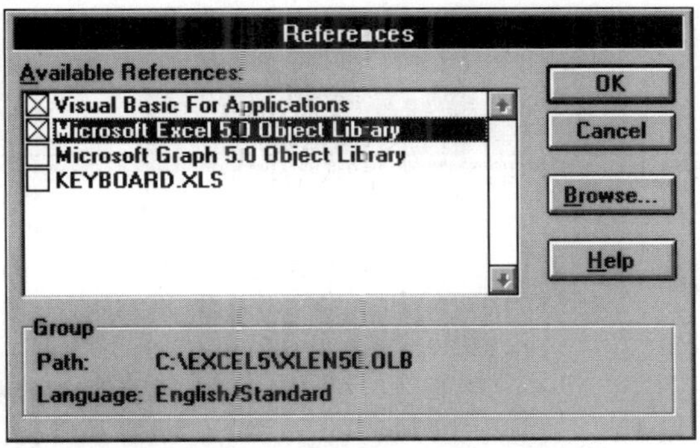

Figure 8-4: The Reference dialog box lets you establish a reference to another workbook, making it possible to execute subroutines in that workbook.

If you've established a reference to a workbook that contains the subroutine YourSub, you can use either of the following statements to call YourSub:

```
YourSub
Call YourSub
```

To precisely identify a subroutine in a different workbook, you can specify both the workbook and module name, using the following syntax:

```
[YOURBOOK.XLS].[YourModule].YourSub
```

Or you can use the Call keyword:

```
Call [YOURBOOK.XLS].[YourModule].YourSub
```

Why call other subroutines?

If you're new to programming, you may wonder why anyone would want to call a subroutine from another subroutine. You may ask, "Why not put the code from the called subroutine into the calling subroutine and keep things simple?"

One reason is to clarify your code. The simpler your code, the easier it is to modify it; smaller routines are easier to decipher and then debug. Examine the accompanying subroutine, which does nothing but call other subroutines. This subroutine is so easy to read, it acts like an outline.

```
Sub Main()
    Call GetUserOptions
    Call ProcessData
    Call CleanUp
    Call CloseItDown
End Sub
```

Calling other subroutines also eliminates redundancy. For example, suppose that you need to perform an operation at ten different places in your routine. Rather than enter the code ten times, you can write a subroutine to perform the operation and then simply call the subroutine ten times.

Remember, creating several small subroutines rather than a single large subroutine is simply a good programming practice. A modular approach not only makes your job easier, it makes life easier for the people who wind up working with your code.

From a toolbar button

Toolbars have become quite pervasive over the past few years. Now you can easily customize Excel's toolbars to include buttons that execute subroutines when clicked.

Assume that you want to assign a subroutine named *CleanUp* to a toolbar button on the Standard toolbar. Here are the steps required to do so:

1. Make sure that the Standard toolbar is displayed.
2. Choose the View➪Toolbars command. Excel displays the Toolbars dialog box.
3. Click the Customize button. Excel displays the Customize dialog box.
4. Click the Custom item in the Categories list box. Excel displays a variety of buttons (see Figure 8-5).
5. Drag an appropriate button to the Standard toolbar. Excel then displays the Assign Macro dialog box, which lists all available subroutines.
6. Select CleanUp from the list and click OK.
7. Click the Close button to dismiss the Customize dialog box. Clicking the new toolbar button executes the CleanUp subroutine.

I cover custom toolbars in Chapter 15.

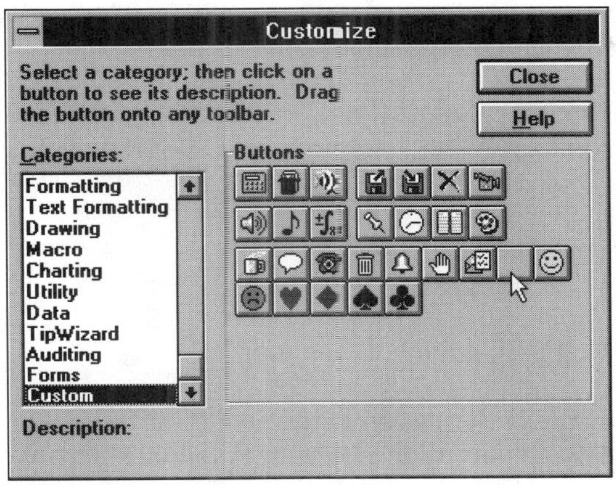

Figure 8-5: The Customize dialog box.

From a drawing object

Excel has a variety of objects that you can place on a worksheet, chart sheet, or dialog sheet. These objects, known as *drawing objects*, include buttons, check boxes, option buttons, rectangles, text boxes, lines, and so on. Drawing objects are available on the Drawing and Forms toolbars.

You can attach a subroutine to any drawing object (a button object is a good choice) so that the subroutine executes when the object is clicked.

To assign a subroutine to a drawing object, place the object, right-click it, and then choose Assign Macro from the shortcut menu. Choose a subroutine from the list in the familiar Assign Macro dialog box and click OK.

When you assign a subroutine to a drawing object, you're actually setting the object's OnAction property.

When you place a button object, the Assign Macro dialog box appears automatically.

Automatically

Subroutines with one of four special subroutine names (see Table 8-1) execute automatically.

If you write a subroutine that you want to run whenever its workbook is opened, for example, just name it *Auto_Open*. The following subroutine changes to Excel's drive and directory, opens a text file and inserts the current time and date. If this subroutine is in your Personal Macro Workbook, you can easily track every time Excel is started (remember, the Personal Macro Workbook is opened automatically whenever Excel is started).

```
Sub Auto_Open()
    ChDrive Left(Application.Path, 1)
    ChDir Application.Path
    Msg = Time & " on " & Date
    Open "XLTIME.TXT" For Append As #1
    Print #1, "Excel started at "; Msg
    Close
End Sub
```

The following macro writes information to the same text file whenever its workbook is closed. If this subroutine is in your Personal Macro Workbook, you can easily track every time Excel is closed.

```
 Sub Auto_Close()
    ChDrive Left(Application.Path, 1)
 ChDir Application.Path
    Msg = Time & " on " & Date
    Open "XLTIME.TXT" For Append As #1
    Print #1, "Excel ended at "; Msg
    Close
End Sub
```

Table 8-1 Special Subroutines That Are Executed Automatically

Subroutine	*When It's Executed*
Auto_Open	When the workbook is opened
Auto_Close	When the workbook is closed
Auto_Activate	When the workbook is activated
Auto_Deactivate	When the workbook is deactivated

CAUTION

The four Auto subroutines are not executed when a workbook is opened, closed, activated, or deactivated by a VBA statement. For example, a VBA statement can use the Open method of the Workbooks collection to open a workbook, but then the Auto_Open subroutine is not executed. To actually execute the Auto_Open macro, you must use the RunAutoMacros method. The following example illustrates how to open a workbook from VBA and execute its Auto_Open subroutine:

```
Sub OpenIt()
    Workbooks.Open "MYFILE.XLS"
ActiveWorkbook.RunAutoMacros xlAutoOpen
```

The RunAutoMacros method takes one argument. Besides xlAutoOpen, the other constants (used as arguments) are xlAutoClose, xlAutoActivate, and xlAutoDeactivate. See the on-line help for more details.

NOTE

Auto_Activate and Auto_Deactivate are included primarily for backward compatibility. VBA's OnSheetActivate and OnSheetDeactivate properties are more versatile.

When an event occurs

You also can tell VBA to execute a particular subroutine whenever a particular event occurs. For example, you can tell VBA call a particular subroutine whenever a user double-clicks a cell or enters data into a cell.

The following statement causes every double-click in any cell in the Sheets1 worksheet to execute the ShowWarning subroutine:

```
Sheets("Sheet1").OnDoubleClick = "ShowWarning"
```

This statement holds true until it is canceled. To cancel it, you need a command like the following:

```
Sheets("Sheet1").OnDoubleClick = ""
```

Table 8-2 lists the types of events that can trigger a subroutine execution and the property or method that you use to program it. For complete details, search the on-line help for the terms in the table's second column.

Table 8-2 Trappable Events That Can Execute a Subroutine

Event	*Property or Method*
Worksheet recalculation	OnCalculate
DDE or OLE data arrives	OnData
A cell is double-clicked	OnDoubleClick
Data is entered or edited in a cell	OnEntry
A specific key is pressed	OnKey
A sheet is activated	OnSheetActivate
A sheet is deactivated	OnSheetDeactivate
A specified time of day	OnTime
A window is activated	OnWindow

Using VBA Debugging Tools

You've probably discovered by now that it's fairly easy to make mistakes when writing VBA code. Syntax errors are identified before you can execute a procedure, but run-time errors are more difficult to track down. Even if you don't get any run-time errors, your procedure may not work like it should. Often, simply examining your code closely will help you spot the error. Other times, you'll need to use the built-in debugging tools to help you isolate the problem.

Debugging occurs in a separate Debug window that lets you step through your code line by line. You can use the Immediate pane of the Debug window to display the value of any variable at any time. To get into step mode, display a module and place the cursor in the procedure (anywhere, it doesn't matter). Press F8, and VBA will display the Debug window (see the accompanying figure). Every time you press F8, the next line of code is executed. To see the value of a variable, activate the Immediate pane and enter an expression such as **Print MyVar**. You can use a question mark (?) as a shortcut for the word Print.

There are several other debugging tools at your disposal. For example, you can set breakpoints in your code. When execution reaches a breakpoint, VBA pauses and displays the Debug window. You can then step through the code. Setting a breakpoint eliminates the need to step through your entire procedure. For example, you can set a breakpoint at a statement right before the problem area. Debugging techniques are thoroughly described in the on-line help, and I urge you to spend some time getting acquainted with them.

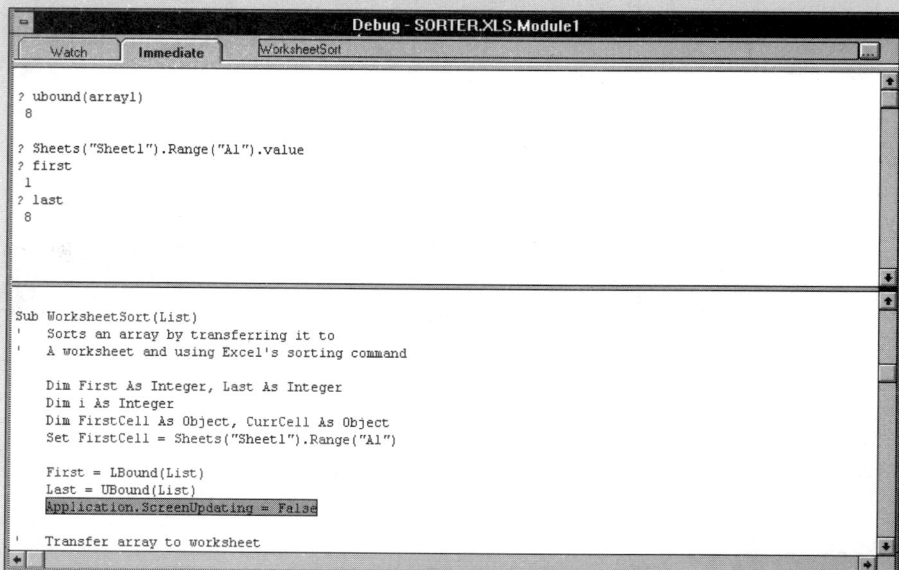

From the Debug window

You also can execute a subroutine by entering its name in the Immediate pane of the Debug window. To open the Debug window from a VBA module, choose the View⇨Debug Window command (or by press Ctrl+G). The window is divided into two panes; the top pane can display either the Watch pane or the Immediate pane.

The Immediate pane executes VBA statements as you enter them. To execute a subroutine, simply enter the name of the subroutine in the Immediate pane and press Enter.

This method can be quite useful when you're developing a subroutine because you can insert commands to display results in the Immediate pane. The following subroutine demonstrates this technique:

```
Sub ChangeCase()
    MyString = "This is a test"
    MyString = UCase(MyString)
    Debug.Print MyString
End Sub
```

Figure 8-6 shows what happens when you enter **ChangeCase** in the Immediate pane: the Debug.Print statement displays the result immediately. As you know, you can get immediate feedback on the value of a variable (without using the Debug window) by using a MsgBox function:

```
Sub ChangeCase()
    MyString = "This is a test"
    MyString = UCase(MyString)
    MsgBox MyString
End Sub
```

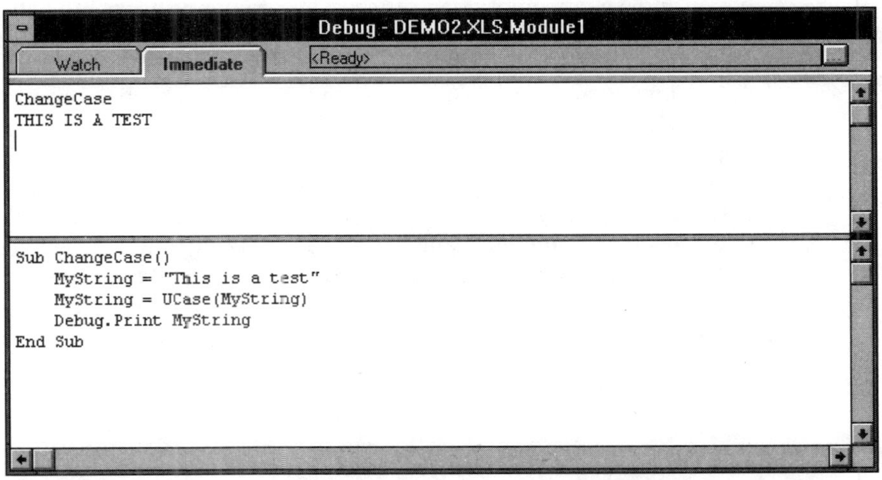

Figure 8-6: Executing a subroutine by entering its name in the Immediate pane of the Debug window.

Passing Arguments to Subroutines

A subroutine's *arguments* provide the subroutine with data that it uses in its statements. The data that's *passed* to an argument can be any of the following:

- A variable
- A constant, or *literal*
- An array
- An object

When it comes to arguments, subroutines are very similar to worksheet functions:

- A subroutine may not require any arguments.
- A subroutine may require a fixed number of arguments.
- A subroutine may accept an indefinite number of arguments.
- A subroutine may require some arguments, leaving others are optional.
- A subroutine may have all optional arguments.

For example, a few of Excel's worksheet functions, including RAND, use no arguments while COUNTIF requires two arguments. Other worksheet functions, such as SUM, have an indefinite number of arguments. Still other worksheet functions have optional arguments; the PMT function, for example, can have five arguments (three are required, two are optional).

Most of the subroutines that you've seen so far have been declared without any arguments; they were declared with just the Sub keyword, the subroutine's name, and a set of empty parentheses. Empty parentheses indicate that the subroutine does not accept arguments.

The following example shows two subroutines. The Main subroutine calls the ProcessFile subroutine three times (the Call statement is in a For...Next loop). Before calling ProcessFile, however, Main prompts the user for a filename. This filename becomes the argument for the subroutine call. (In this example, the variable passed to ProcessFile is named *NameOfFile*.) The ProcessFile subroutine takes one argument (named *TheFile*) — notice that the argument goes inside parentheses in the Sub statement. When ProcessFile finishes, program control continues with the statement after the Call statement.

```
Sub Main()
    For i = 1 To 3
        NameOfFile = InputBox("Enter File Name " & i)
        Call ProcessFile(NameOfFile)
    Next i
End Sub
```

```
Sub ProcessFile(TheFile)
    Workbooks.Open FileName:=TheFile
'   ...[more code here]...
End Sub
```

You can create subroutines that are independent of the subroutines that call them.

You also can pass literals (that is, not variables) to a subroutine. For example,

```
Sub Main()
    Call ProcessFile("BUDGET.XLS")
End Sub
```

When you pass an argument to a subroutine, you're not really passing the value. Rather, you are passing the memory address of the variable. Consequently, if the called subroutine changes the value that is passed to it, the variable in the calling subroutine also is changed.

The following example demonstrates this concept. After the Main subroutine assigns a value of 10 to MyValue, it calls the Process subroutine and passes MyValue as the argument. The Process subroutine multiplies the value of its argument (named *YourValue*) by 10. When Process ends and program control passes back to Main, the MsgBox function displays MyValue: 100.

```
Sub Main()
    MyValue = 10
    Call Process(MyValue)
    MsgBox MyValue
End Sub


Sub Process(YourValue)
    YourValue = YourValue * 10
End Sub
```

If you don't want the called subroutine to modify any variables passed as arguments, you can modify the called subroutine's argument list so that arguments are passed to it *by value* rather than *by reference*. To do so, precede the argument with the ByVal keyword. This technique causes the called routine to work with a copy of the passed variable's data, not the data itself. In the following subroutine, for example, the changes made to YourValue in the Process subroutine do not affect the MyValue variable in Main. As a result, the MsgBox function displays 10, not 100.

```
Sub Process(ByVal YourValue)
    YourValue = YourValue * 10
End Sub
```

NOTE: A subroutine's arguments can mix and match by value and by reference. Arguments preceded by ByVal are passed by value; all others are passed by reference.

NOTE: If you pass a user-defined data structure to a subroutine, it must be passed by reference. Attempting to pass it by value generates an error.

Because I didn't declare a data type for any of the arguments in the previous examples, all the arguments have been of variant data type. But a subroutine that uses arguments can define the data types directly in the argument list. The following is a Sub statement for a subroutine with two arguments of different data types. The first is declared as an integer, and the second is declared as a string.

```
Sub Process(Iterations As Integer, TheFile As String)
```

Public variables versus passing arguments to a subroutine

In Chapter 7, I pointed out how a variable declared as Public is available to all subroutines in the module. In some cases, you may want to access a Public variable rather than pass the variable as an argument when calling another subroutine.

For example, the subroutine that follows passes the value of MonthVal to the ProcessMonth subroutine:

```
Sub MySub()
    Dim MonthVal as Integer
'   ... [code goes here]
    MonthVal = 4
    Call ProcessMonth(MonthVal)
'   ... [code goes here]
End Sub
```

An alternative approach is

```
Public MonthVal as Integer
Sub MySub()
'   ... [code goes here]
    MonthVal = 4
    Call ProcessMonth
'   ... [code goes here]
End Sub
```

In the preceding example, because MonthVal is a public variable, the ProcessMonth subroutine can access it — eliminating the need for an argument for the ProcessMonth subroutine. However, the ProcessMonth routine must reference the variable by its name (MonthVal), making the subroutine much less general. Every routine that calls ProcessMonth then must set the value of the public MonthVal variable.

Using public variables rather than subroutine arguments may work in some cases, but it's usually a better idea to use arguments because you then can write more general-purpose code that function as stand-alone units.

When you pass arguments to a subroutine, it's important that the data types match. For example, if you call Process in the preceding example and pass a string variable for the first argument, you get a *type mismatch* error or, worse, unpredictable results.

NOTE

Arguments are relevant to both subroutine procedures and function procedures. In Chapter 9, where I focus on function procedures, I provide more examples of using arguments with your routines, including how to handle optional arguments.

Error Handling Techniques

When a VBA procedure is running, errors can occur (as you undoubtedly know). Errors are either syntax errors (which you must correct before you can execute a procedure) or run-time erors (which occur while the procedure is running). This section deals with run-time errors.

NOTE

In order for error handling procedures to work, the Break on All Errors setting *must* be turned off. Access the Options dialog box and click the Module General tab to check this setting. If Break on All Errors is checked, VBA will ignore your error handling code.

Normally, a run-time error causes VBA to stop, and the user sees the Macro Error dialog box that displays the error number and a description of the error. A good application doesn't make the user have to deal with these messages. Rather, it incorporates error handling code to trap errors and take appropriate actions. At the very least, your error handling code can display a more meaningful error message than the one popped up by VBA.

CROSS REFERENCE

Appendix E lists all of the VBA error codes and descriptions.

Trapping errors

You can use the On Error statement to specify what happens when an error occurs. Basically, you have two choices:

- Ignore the error, and let VBA continue. You can determine what the error was, and take action if necessary.
- Jump to a special error handling section of your code to take action.

To cause the VBA program to continue when an error occurs, insert the following statement in your code:

```
On Error Resume Next
```

Some errors are inconsequential, and can simply be ignored. But you may want to determine what the error was. When an error occurs you can use the Err function to determine the error number. VBA's Error function will display the text for the value of Err. For example, the following statement displays the same information as the Macro Error dialog box (the error number and the error description):

```
MsgBox Err & " " & Error(Err)
```

Figure 8-7 shows the VBA error message, and Figure 8-8 shows the same error displayed in a message box.

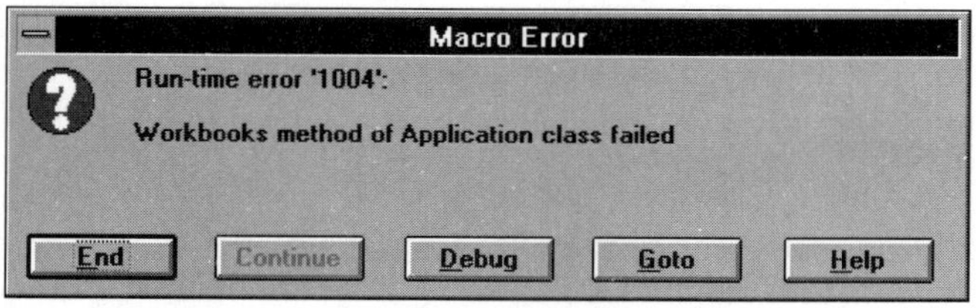

Figure 8-7: VBA's error messages aren't exactly user friendly.

Figure 8-8: You can create a message box to display the error code and description.

You also use the On Error statement to specify a location in your procedure to jump to when an error occurs. You use a label to mark the location.

Error handling examples

The first example demonstrates an error that can safely be ignored. The SpecialCells method selects cells that meet a certain criteria (this method is equivalent to selecting the Edit⇨Go To command and clicking the Special button to select, for example, cells that contain formulas). In the example that follows, the SpecialCells method will select the cells in the current range selection that contains a numeric formula. However, if no cells qualify VBA displays an error message. Using the On Error Resume Next statement simply prevents the error message from appearing.

```
Sub SelectFormulas()
    On Error Resume Next
    Selection.SpecialCells(xlFormulas, xlNumbers).Select
End Sub
```

The next example demonstrates error handling by jumping to a label. The procedure attempts to assign a value to the current selection. If a range is not selected, the assignment statement will result in an error. The On Error statement specifies a jump to the Handler label if an error occurs. Notice the use of the Exit Sub statement before the label. This prevents the error handling code from being executed if no error occurs.

```
Sub ErrorDemo()
    On Error GoTo Handler
    Selection.Value = 123
    Exit Sub

Handler:
    MsgBox "Cannot assign a value to the selection."
End Sub
```

The next example is a more sophisticated version of the preceding example. If an error occurs, program flow jumps to the Handler label, where one of four error messages is displayed based on the value of Err. For example, if the worksheet is protected, the value of Err is 1005.

```
Sub ErrorDemo()
    On Error GoTo Handler
    Selection.Value = 123
    Exit Sub
```

```
Handler:
    Select Case Err
        Case 91
            MsgBox "There is no active cell."
        Case 1000
            MsgBox "Cannot assign a value to the selection."
        Case 1005
            MsgBox "The worksheet is protected."
        Case Else
            MsgBox Error(Err)
    End Select
End Sub
```

Sometimes, you can take advantage of an error to get information. The example that follows simply checks to see whether a particular workbook is open. It uses a For Each...Next loop to cycle through all objects in the Workbooks collection. If the workbook is open, the FileExists variable is set to True. Finally, a message is displayed that tells the user whether the workbook is open.

```
Sub CheckForFile1()
    FileName = "BUDDGET.XLS"
    FileExists = False

'   Cycle through all workbooks
    For Each book In Workbooks
        If book.Name = FileName Then
            FileExists = True
        End If
    Next book

'   Display appropriate message
    If FileExists Then _
        MsgBox FileName & " is open." Else _
            MsgBox FileName & " is not open."
End Sub
```

The preceding routine can be rewritten to use error handling to determine whether the file is open. In the example that follows, the On Error statement points to the NotOpen label, so if an error occurs (i.e., referencing a workbook that is not open), program flow jumps to NotOpen and the message is displayed. If no error occurs, a different message is displayed and the Exit Sub statement ends the subroutine.

```
Sub CheckForFile()
    FileName = "BUDGET.XLS"
    On Error GoTo NotOpen
    x = Workbooks(FileName).Name
    MsgBox FileName & " is open."
    Exit Sub

NotOpen:
    MsgBox FileName & " is not open."
End Sub
```

Chapter 11 presents several additional examples that use error handling.

A Realistic Example

In this chapter, I have provided you with a foundation for creating subroutines. The previous examples, I must admit, have been rather wimpy. The remainder of this chapter is a real-life exercise that demonstrates many of the concepts covered in this and the previous two chapters.

This section describes the development of a useful utility that qualifies as an application as defined in Chapter 4. More important, I demonstrate the *process* of analyzing a problem and then solving it with VBA. A word of warning to old hands: I wrote this section with VBA newcomers in mind. As a result, I don't simply present the code, but I show how to find out what you need to know in order to develop the code.

The completed application can be found on the disk that accompanies this book. The file name is SHTSORT.XLS.

The goal

The goal of this exercise is to develop a utility that rearranges a workbook by alphabetizing its sheets.

If you tend to create workbooks that consist of many sheets, you know that it can be difficult to locate a sheet. If the sheets are ordered alphabetically, though, it's much easier to find a desired sheet.

Project requirements

Where to begin? I suggest listing the requirements for your application. As you develop your application, you can check your list to ensure that you're covering all the bases.

Here's the list I drew up for this example:

1. The application should sort the sheets in the active workbook in ascending order.
2. The application should be executed by choosing a command (Sort Sheets) from the Tools menu or a shortcut key (Ctrl+Shift+S).
3. The command should always be available — I shouldn't want to have to open a workbook to use this utility.
4. The application should work properly for any open workbook.
5. The application should not display any VBA error messages.

What you know

Chances are, you really won't have a clue where to begin. In this case, I started by listing things that I know about Excel that may be relevant to the project requirements:

- Excel doesn't have a command that sorts sheets.
- I can move a sheet easily by dragging its sheet tab.

  Mental note: Find out what kind of code this action generates. (To do so, turn on the macro recorder and then move a sheet to a new location in the workbook.)
- I'll need to know how many sheets are in the active workbook. I can get this information with VBA.
- I'll need to know the names of all the sheets. Again, I can get this information with VBA.
- Excel has a command that sorts data in worksheet cells.

  Mental note: Maybe I can transfer the sheet names to a range and use this feature.
- Thanks to the Macro Options dialog box, it's easy to assign a command to a menu item on the Tools menu.
- I need a way to test the application as I develop it. For certain, I don't want to be testing it by using the same workbook that I'm developing the code in.

  Mental note: Create a dummy workbook for testing purposes.
- If I develop the code properly, VBA won't display any errors.

  Mental note: Wishful thinking. . . .

The approach

Although I still didn't know how to proceed, I could devise a preliminary, skeleton plan:

1. Identify the active workbook.
2. Get a list of all the sheet names in the workbook.
3. Count the sheets.
4. Sort them (somehow).
5. Rearrange the sheets in the sorted order.

What you need to know

I saw a few holes in the plan: I knew that I had to determine the following:

- How to identify the active workbook
- How to count the sheets in the active workbook
- How to get a list of the sheet names
- How to sort the list
- How to rearrange the sheets according to the sorted list

When you lack information, you can consult this book, the VBA User's Guide, and the on-line help: you may eventually discover what you need to know. But your best bet is to turn on the macro recorder and see what it spits out when you perform some relevant actions.

Some preliminary recording

For example, I started with an empty workbook that contained one worksheet. Then I turned on the macro recorder, added two new worksheets, and dragged the third worksheet to the first sheet position. Here's what the macro recorder spat:

```
Sub Macro1()
    Sheets.Add
    Sheets.Add
    Sheets("Sheet1").Select
    Sheets("Sheet1").Move Sheets(1)
End Sub
```

I searched for *Add* in the on-line help and discovered that it's a method that adds a member to a collection — in this case, the Sheets collection. This information wasn't all that useful.

But I also searched for *Move* and discovered that it's a method that moves a sheet to a new location in the workbook. Very relevant.

Next I needed to find out how many sheets were in the active workbook. I searched for the word Count and found that it's a property of a collection. I created this quick-and-dirty subroutine to test it out:

```
Sub Test()
    MsgBox Sheets.Count
End Sub
```

I entered the routine and pressed F5 to run it. Sure enough, the message box displayed the correct number of sheets in the workbook. More useful information.

What about the sheet names? I modified my Test macro and — wow — it displayed the name of the first sheet in the workbook:

```
Sub Test()
    MsgBox Sheets(1).Name
End Sub
```

Then I remembered something about the For Each construct. After checking out the on-line help. I modified the macro as follows:

```
Sub Test()
    For Each Item In Sheets
        MsgBox Item.Name
    Next Item
End Sub
```

Another success. This macro kept popping up message boxes, each time with a different sheet name.

Finally, I focused on sorting options. From the on-line help, I learned that the Sort method applies to a range or a pivot table. So one option was to transfer the sheet names to a range and then sort the range, but that seemed like overkill for this application. I thought a better option was to dump the sheet names into an array of strings and then sort the array by using VBA code.

Setting up

Now I knew enough to get started. I revised my plan of action:

1. Create an empty workbook with five worksheets, named *Sheet1*, *Sheet2*, *Sheet3*, *Sheet4*, and *Sheet5*.
2. Move the sheets around randomly so that they aren't in any particular order.
3. Save the workbook as TEST.XLS.
4. Create another empty workbook to hold the VBA code for the application Insert a module sheet and save the workbook as SHTSORT.XLS.
5. Create an empty subroutine called *SortSheets* in Module1 of SHTSORT.XLS.
6. Use the Tools⇨Macro command (Options button) to assign this macro to a new menu item on the Tools menu (Sort Sheets). Also assign this macro to the Ctrl+Shift+S key combination.

Figure 8-9 shows how my screen looked at this point.

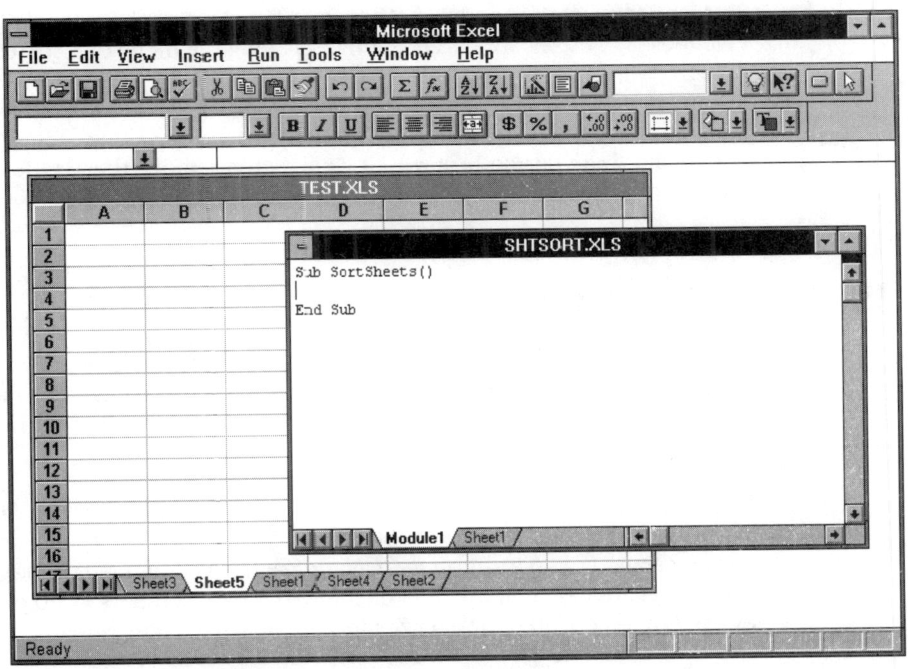

Figure 8-9: Preparing to create the Sheet Sorter application.

Writing some code

At this point, I was ready to write some code. I knew that I needed to put the sheet names into an array of strings. Because I won't usually know yet how many sheets are in the active workbook, I used a Dim statement with empty parentheses to declare the array. I knew that I could use ReDim afterward to redimension the array for the proper number of elements.

I entered the following code — which inserts the sheet names into the SheetNames array and displays each sheet name in a message box — into Module1 of SHTSORT.XLS:

```
Sub SortSheets()
    Dim SheetNames()
    SheetCount = ActiveWorkbook.Sheets.Count
    ReDim SheetNames(1 To SheetCount)
    For i = 1 To SheetCount
        SheetNames(i) = ActiveWorkbook.Sheets(i).Name
        MsgBox SheetNames(i)
    Next i
End Sub
```

To test the preceding code, I activated TEST.XLS and chose Tools⇨Sort Sheets. Five message boxes appeared, each displaying the name of a corresponding sheet.

It's a good idea to test various components as you go along. When you're convinced that your code is working correctly, remove the MsgBox statement — trust me, it gets annoying before long.

Writing a sort subroutine

It was time to sort the SheetNames array. I could have stuck the sorting code in the SortSheets subroutine, but I thought a better approach was to write a general-purpose sorting subroutine that I could reuse with other projects (sorting arrays is a common operation).

There are many ways to sort an array. I chose the bubble sort method; although it's not a particularly fast technique, it's easy to code. The *bubble sort* method uses a nested For...Next loop to evaluate each array element. If the array element is greater than the next element, the two elements swap positions. This evaluation is repeated for every pair of items (that is, n-1 times).

Here's the routine I developed:

```
Sub BubbleSort(List() As String)
'   Sorts the List array in ascending order
    Dim First As Integer, Last As Integer
    Dim i As Integer, j As Integer
    Dim Temp

    First = LBound(List)
    Last = UBound(List)
    For i = First To Last - 1
        For j = i + 1 To Last
            If List(i) > List(j) Then
                Temp = List(j)
                List(j) = List(i)
                List(i) = Temp
            End If
        Next j
    Next i
End Sub
```

I used the LBound and UBound functions to define the lower bound and upper bound of the array to the variables First and Last, respectively.

After I was satisfied that this routine worked reliably, I modified SortSheets by adding a call to the BubbleSort routine, passing the SheetNames array as an argument. At this point, my module looked like:

```
Sub SortSheets()
    Dim SheetNames()
    SheetCount = ActiveWorkbook.Sheets.Count
    ReDim SheetNames(1 To SheetCount)
    For i = 1 To SheetCount
        SheetNames(i) = ActiveWorkbook.Sheets(i).Name
    Next i
    Call BubbleSort(SheetNames)
End Sub

Sub BubbleSort(List() As String)
'   Sorts the List array in ascending order
    Dim First As Integer, Last As Integer
    Dim i As Integer, j As Integer
    Dim Temp
```

```
        First = LBound(List)
        Last = UBound(List)
        For i = First To Last - 1
            For j = i + 1 To Last
                If List(i) > List(j) Then
                    Temp = List(j)
                    List(j) = List(i)
                    List(i) = Temp
                End If
            Next j
        Next i
    End Sub
```

So far, so good. Now I merely had to rearrange the sheets to correspond to the sorted items in the SheetNames array.

The code that I recorded earlier again proved useful. Remember the statement that was recorded when I moved a sheet to the first position in the workbook?

```
Sheets("Sheet1").Move Sheets(1)
```

After a little thought, I decided to write a For...Next loop that would go through each element in SheetNames and move it to its corresponding sheet location in the workbook:

```
For i = 1 To SheetCount
    Sheets(SheetNames(i)).Move Sheets(i)
Next i
```

Time to clean things up. I declared all the variables used and then added a few comments and blank lines to make the code easier to read. The SortSheets routine now looked like the following:

```
Sub SortSheets()
'   This routine sorts the sheets of the
'   active workbook in ascending order.

    Dim SheetNames() As String
    Dim SheetCount As Integer
    Dim i As Integer

    SheetCount = ActiveWorkbook.Sheets.Count
    ReDim SheetNames(1 To SheetCount)
```

```
'   Fill array with sheet names
    For i = 1 To SheetCount
        SheetNames(i) = ActiveWorkbook.Sheets(i).Name
    Next i

'   Sort the array in ascending order
    Call BubbleSort(SheetNames)

'   Move the sheets
    For i = 1 To SheetCount
        Sheets(SheetNames(i)).Move Sheets(i)
    Next i
End Sub
```

Everything seemed to be working. To test the code further, I added a few more sheets to TEST.XLS and changed some of the names.

More testing

Just because the routine worked with the TEXT.XLS workbook didn't mean that it would work with all workbooks. To test it further, I loaded a few other workbooks and retried the routine. I soon discovered that the application was not perfect. In fact, I identified the following problems:

- Workbooks with many sheets took a long time to sort because the screen was continually updated during the move operations.
- The sorting didn't always work. For example, in one of my tests, a sheet named *SUMMARY* (all uppercase) appeared before a sheet named *Sheet1*. This problem was caused by the BubbleSort subroutine.
- If I interrupted the macro by pressing Ctrl+Break, VBA displayed an error message.
- If there were no workbooks open, pressing the Ctrl+Shift+S shortcut key combo caused the macro to fail. (Of course, I didn't have a similar problem with the Tools⇨Sort Sheets command because the Tools menu is not displayed unless a workbook is open.)
- If the workbook had one or more hidden sheets, the routine bombed — apparently, the Move method fails with hidden sheets.
- If the workbook's structure was protected, the Move method failed.
- After sorting, the last sheet in the workbook became the active sheet. Changing the active sheet is not a good practice, so I needed to redesign the routine so that the original active sheet was reactivated after the sorting.

Fixing the problems

Fixing the screen updating problem was a breeze. I inserted the following statement at the beginning of SortSheets to turn screen updating off:

```
Application.ScreenUpdating = False
```

It was also easy to fix the problem with the BubbleSort routine: I used VBA's UCase function to convert the sheet names to uppercase. The corrected line read

```
If UCase(List(i)) > UCase(List(j)) Then
```

Pressing Ctrl+Break normally halts a macro, and VBA usually displays an error message. But because one of my goals was to avoid VBA error messages, I needed to insert a command to prevent this situation. From the on-line help, I discovered that the Application object has a EnableCancelKey property that can disable Ctrl+Break. So I added the following statement at the top of the routine:

```
Application.EnableCancelKey = xlDisabled
```

To prevent the error message that appears when no worksheets are open, I added the following block of code at the top of the routine, which counts the number of visible windows. If none is visible, the Exit Sub statement causes a quick exit from the subroutine and nothing further happens.

```
VisibleWins = 0
For Each Item In Windows
    If Item.Visible Then VisibleWins = VisibleWins + 1
Next Item
If VisibleWins = 0 Then Exit Sub
```

It was also relatively easy to fix the problem caused by hidden sheets. The obvious solution: Unhide allsheets, can keep track of those that were hidden so they can be re-hidden after the sorting. I used a Boolean array named HiddenFlag to keep track of hidden sheets. Here is the code that unhide all sheets, moves the sheets to correspond to the sorted names, and then re-hides the hidden sheets.

```
I

'   Unhide all sheets
    For i = 1 To SheetCount
        HiddenFlag(i) = False
        If Sheets(i).Visible = False Then
            Sheets(i).Visible = True
            HiddenFlag(i) = True
        End If
```

```
    Next i

'   Sort the sheets
    For i = 1 To SheetCount
        Sheets(SheetNames(i)).Move Sheets(i)
    Next i

'   Hide previously hidden sheets
    For i = 1 To SheetCount
        If HiddenFlag(i) Then Sheets(i).Visible = False
    Next i
```

There's usually a good reason why a workbook's structure is protected. I decided that the best approach was to display a message box to that effect (with a stop sign icon generated by the vbcritical constant) and then exit the subroutine. (If desired, a user can unprotect the workbook and redo the sheet sorting.) Testing for a protected workbook structure was easy — the ProtectStructure property of a Workbook object returns True if a workbook is protected. I added the following block of code at the beginning of the routine:

```
'   Check for protected workbook structure
    If ActiveWorkbook.ProtectStructure Then
        MsgBox ActiveWorkbook.Name & " is protected.", _
           vbCritical, "Cannot Sort Sheets"
        Exit Sub
    End If
```

To reactivate the original active sheet, the code needed to store a reference to the original active sheet (as an object variable named OldActive).

After I made all these corrections, the SortSheets routine looked like Listing 8-1.

Listing 8-1 SortSheets routine.

```
Sub SortSheets()
'   This routine sorts the sheets of the
'   active workbook in ascending order.

    Dim SheetNames() As String
    Dim SheetCount As Integer
    Dim i As Integer
    Dim HiddenFlag As Boolean
    Dim VisibleWins As Integer
    Dim Item As Object
    Dim OldActive As Object
```

(continued)

Listing 8-1 *(continued)*

```
'   Check for protected workbook structure
    If ActiveWorkbook.ProtectStructure Then
        MsgBox ActiveWorkbook.Name & " is protected.", _
           vbCritical, "Cannot Sort Sheets"
        Exit Sub
    End If

'   Disable Ctrl+Break
    Application.EnableCancelKey = xlDisabled

'   Exit if no windows are visible
    VisibleWins = 0
    For Each Item In Windows
        If Item.Visible Then VisibleWins = VisibleWins + 1
    Next Item
    If VisibleWins = 0 Then Exit Sub

    SheetCount = ActiveWorkbook.Sheets.Count
    ReDim SheetNames(1 To SheetCount)

'   Store reference to the active sheet
    Set OldActive = ActiveSheet

'   Fill array with sheet names
    For i = 1 To SheetCount
        SheetNames(i) = ActiveWorkbook.Sheets(i).Name
    Next i

'   Sort the array in ascending order
    Call BubbleSort(SheetNames)

'   Turn off screen updating
    Application.ScreenUpdating = False

'   Unhide all sheets
    For i = 1 To SheetCount
        HiddenFlag(i) = False
        If Sheets(i).Visible = False Then
            Sheets(i).Visible = True
            HiddenFlag(i) = True
        End If
    Next i
```

```
'   Sort the sheets
    For i = 1 To SheetCount
        Sheets(SheetNames(i)).Move Sheets(i)
    Next i

'   Hide previously hidden sheets
    For i = 1 To SheetCount
        If HiddenFlag(i) Then Sheets(i).Visible = False
    Next i

'   Restore original active sheet
    OldActive.Activate
End Sub
```

Making the utility available

The easiest way to make a utility always be available is to copy the subroutines to a module in the Personal Macro Workbook: to do so, use the Window⇨Unhide command to unhide PERSONAL.XLS, copy the code from SHTSORT.XLS (both subroutines), and then paste it to a module in PERSONAL.XLS. Another option is to store the workbook in your EXCEL\XLSTART directory so it is loaded whenever Excel starts.

CAUTION

When you move code to a new module, you may have to make some changes. In this case, I needed to use the Tools⇨Macro command again and assigned the SortSheets subroutine to the Ctrl+Shift+S shortcut key and added the &Sort Sheets command to the Tools menu. Make sure you close the original workbook, or the Tools menu will have two Short Sheet commands.

Evaluating the project

There you have it. The utility works and meets all the original requirements: it sorts all sheets in the active workbook; it can be executed by selecting a command or a shortcut key; it's always available; it seems to work for any workbook; and I have yet to see it display a VBA error message.

NOTE

In retrospect, it may be more intuitive to make this new command available on the shortcut menu that appears when you right-click a sheet tab. You can do so by using the Tools⇨Menu Editor command from a VBA module (the menu to modify is the Workbook Tab menu in the Shortcut Menus 1 menu bar).

In this exercise, I tried to demonstrate the process of developing VBA subroutines — a valuable lesson even if you're not yet a VBA veteran. I imparted the following points:

- Developing a successful subroutine is not a linear process.
- It's a good idea to use short subroutines to test ideas or approaches before incorporating them into your routine.
- Even though a subroutine appears to work correctly, appearances can be deceiving. Therefore, it's important to test your work in a realistic situation.
- You can learn a lot by recording your actions and studying the code that gets recorded. Although I didn't actually use any of the recorded code, I learned several things.
- A project's original requirements aren't always complete. In this example, I didn't think to require that the original active sheet remain the active sheet after the sorting — but not doing so seemed like a bad idea.

Summary

- In this chapter, I detailed subroutines. I also gave an example of developing and debugging subroutines.
- In the next chapter, I focus on the other type of VBA procedure: function procedures.

Chapter 9

Creating Function Procedures

In This Chapter

- How to create custom functions
- How to call the Windows API to perform feats otherwise impossible
- An introduction to object libraries and custom properties
- Examples, examples, examples

VBA lets you create two types of procedures: subroutines and functions. I covered subroutines in the preceding chapter; in this chapter, I discuss functions. (Much of what you know about subroutines also applies to functions.)

CROSS REFERENCE

Chapter 11 has many useful and practical examples of function procedures. You can incorporate many of those techniques into your work.

Subroutines Versus Functions

You can think of a subroutine procedure as a command that can be executed by either the user or by another procedure. Function procedures, on the other hand, always return a single value — just as Excel's worksheet functions and VBA's built-in functions do. And like built-in functions, your function procedures can use arguments.

Function procedures are quite versatile and can be used in two situations:

- As part of an expression in a VBA procedure
- In formulas that you create in a worksheet

In fact, you can use a function procedure anywhere that you can use an Excel worksheet function or a VBA built-in function.

You are undoubtedly familiar with Excel's worksheet functions — even novices know how to use the most common worksheet functions, such as SUM, AVERAGE, and IF. By my count, Excel contains 319 predefined worksheet functions. If that's not enough, however, you can create custom functions by using VBA.

Why Create Custom Functions?

With all the functions available in Excel and VBA, you may wonder why you would ever need to create new functions. The answer: To simplify your work. With a bit of planning, custom functions are very useful in worksheet formulas and VBA procedures.

Often, for example, you can create a custom function that can significantly shorten your formulas. And shorter formulas are more readable and easier to work with.

As you create applications, you may notice that some subroutines repeat calculations. It's often possible to create a custom function that performs a calculation and then simply call the function from your subroutine. A custom function thus can eliminate the need for duplicated code, reducing errors.

Coworkers often can benefit from your specialized functions. And some may be willing to pay you for custom functions that can save them time and work.

Although many cringe at the thought of creating custom worksheet functions, the process is much easier with VBA than with Excel 4 or C. In fact, I enjoy creating custom functions. I especially like how my custom functions appear in the Function Wizard along with the built-in functions, as if I'm reengineering the software in some way.

In this chapter, I tell you what you need to know to get started, and I provide lots of examples.

An Introductory Example

Without further ado, here's an example of a VBA function procedure.

A custom function

The following is a custom function defined in a VBA module. This function, named *Reverse*, reverses an argument so that it reads backwards and returns the result as a string. (The function requires a single argument.)

```
Function Reverse(InString) As String
'   Returns its argument, reversed
    Reverse = ""
    StringLength = Len(InString)
    For i = StringLength To 1 Step -1
        Reverse = Reverse & Mid(InString, i, 1)
    Next i
End Function
```

I explain how this function works later, in the "Analyzing the custom function" section.

Using the function in a worksheet

When you enter a formula that uses Reverse, Excel executes the Reverse function to get the value (see Figure 9-1). Actually, the function works just like any built-in worksheet function. You can insert it in a formula by using the Function Wizard (custom functions are located in the User Defined category). You also can nest custom functions and combine them with other elements in your formulas.

The following worksheet formula shows the Reverse function nested with itself. In other words, this rather useless formula returns the same value displayed in cell A1 (talk about a waste of computing power!).

```
=Reverse(Reverse(A1))
```

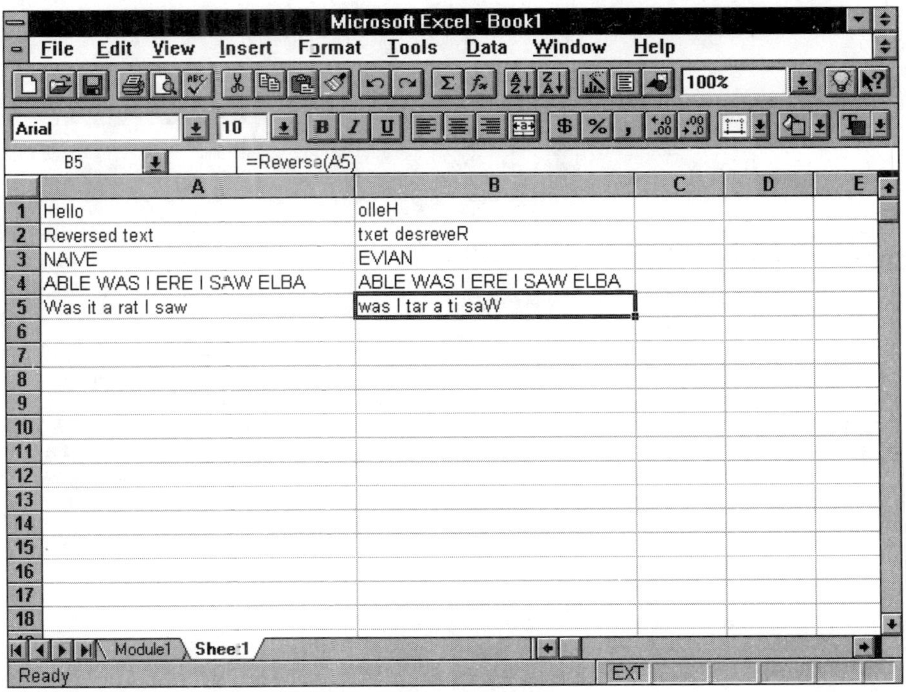

Figure 9-1: Using a custom function in a worksheet formula.

Using the function in a VBA subroutine

The following VBA subroutine procedure, which is defined in the same module as the custom Reverse function, first displays an input box to solicit some text from the user. Then the subroutine uses the built-in MsgBox function to display the user input (see Figure 9-2) after it's processed by the Reverse function.

```
Sub ReverseIt()
     UserInput = InputBox("Enter some text:")
     MsgBox(Reverse(UserInput))
End Sub
```

In the example shown in Figure 9-2, the string entered in response to the InputBox function was *Microsoft Excel*. The MsgBox function displays the reversed text.

Analyzing the custom function

Function procedures can be as complex as you need. Most of the time, they are more complex and much more useful than this sample procedure. Nonetheless, an analysis of this example may help you understand what is happening.

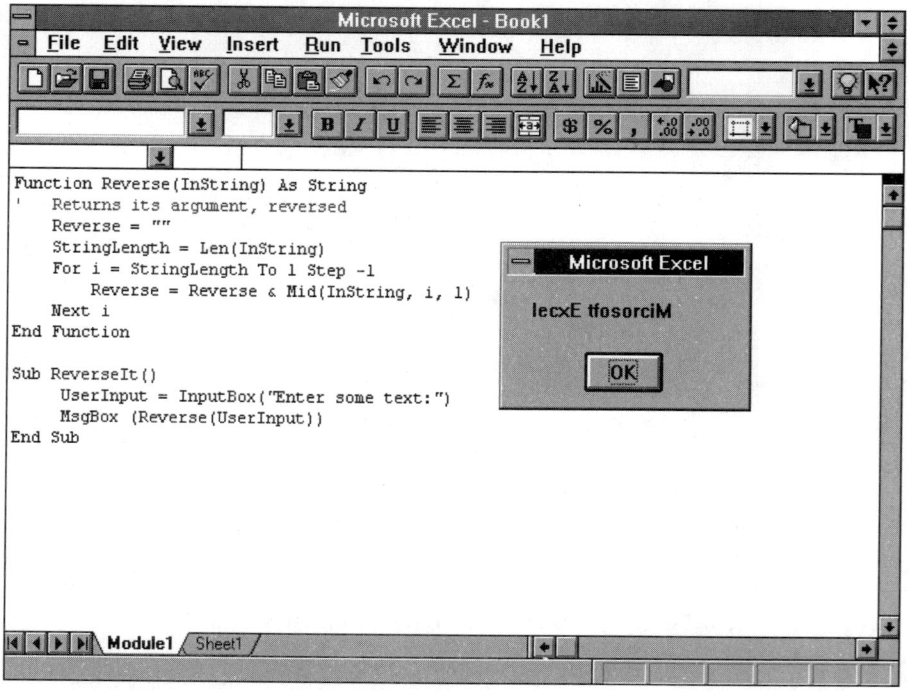

Figure 9-2: Using a custom function in a VBA subroutine.

Here's the code, again:

```
Function Reverse(InString) As String
'   Returns its argument, reversed
    Reverse = ""
    StringLength = Len(InString)
    For i = StringLength To 1 Step -1
        Reverse = Reverse & Mid(InString, i, 1)
    Next i
End Function
```

Notice that the procedure starts with the keyword *Function* rather than *Sub*, followed by the name of the function (*Reverse*). This custom function only uses one argument (*InString*); the argument's name is enclosed in parentheses. *As String* defines the data type of the function's return (Excel uses the variant data type if none is specified).

The second line is simply a comment that describes what the function does.

Then the procedure initializes the result as an empty string. Note that I use the function's name as a variable here. When the function ends, it returns the current value of the variable that corresponds to the function's name.

Next, the Len function determines the length of the input string and assigns this value to the StringLength variable.

The next three statements comprise a For...Next loop. The procedure loops through each character in the input (backwards) and builds the string. Notice that the Step value in the For...Next loop is a negative number, causing the looping in reverse. This function uses the Mid function to return a single character from the input string. When the loop is finished, Reverse consists of the input string, with the characters rearranged in reverse order. This string is the value that the function returns.

The procedure ends with an End Function statement.

About Function Procedures

A custom function procedure has a lot in common with a subroutine procedure. (For more information on subroutines, refer to Chapter 8.)

Declaring a function

The syntax for declaring a function is

```
[Public | Private][Static] Function name [(arglist)][As type]
 [statements]
 [name = expression]
 [Exit Function]
 [statements]
 [name = expression]
End Function
```

where *Public* indicates that the function is accessible to all other procedures in all other modules in the workbook. (Optional.)

where *Private* indicates that the function is accessible only to other procedures in the same module. (Optional.)

where *Static* indicates that the values of variables declared in the function are preserved between calls. (Optional.)

where *Function* is a keyword that indicates the beginning of a function procedure. (Required.)

where *name* can be any valid variable name. When the function finishes, the single-value result is assigned to the function's name. (Required.)

where *arglist* is a list (one or more) of variables that represent arguments passed to the function. The arguments are enclosed in parentheses. Use a comma to separate arguments. (Optional.)

where *type* is the data type returned by the function. (Optional.)

where *statements* are valid VBA statements. (Optional.)

where *Exit Function* is a statement that causes an immediate exit from the function. (Optional.)

where *End Function* is a keyword that indicates the end of the function. (Required.)

NOTE: The main thing to remember is that a value is assigned to the function's name when a function is finished executing.

To create a custom function, start by inserting a VBA module. (Or you can use an existing module.) Enter the keyword *Function*, followed by the function's name, and a list of the arguments (if any) in parentheses. Insert the VBA code that performs the work — and make sure that the variable corresponding to the function's name has the appropriate value (this is the value that the function returns). End the function with an End Function statement.

Function names must adhere to the same rules for variable names, and you cannot use a name that looks like a worksheet cells (for example a function named J21 won't be accepted). Refer to Chapter 9 for a detailed discussion and a list of forbidden words.

A function's scope

In Chapter 8, I discussed the concept of a subroutine's scope (public or private). The same discussion applies to functions: its scope determines whether it can be called by subroutines in other modules or in worksheets.

Here are a few things to keep in mind about a function's scope:

- If you don't declare a function's scope, the default is public.
- Functions declared as private do not appear in the Function Wizard. Therefore, when you create a function that should be used only in a VBA procedure, you should declare it to be private so that users don't try to use it in a formula.
- If you need to call a function that's defined in another worksheet, set up a reference to the other workbook by using the Tools⇨References command.

Executing function procedures

Although there are many ways to execute a subroutine procedure, you can execute a function procedure in just two ways: call it from another procedure or use it in a worksheet formula.

From a procedure

You can call custom functions from a procedure just like you call built-in functions. For example, after you define a function called *SumArray*, you can enter a statement like the following:

```
Total = SumArray(MyArray)
```

This statement executes the SumArray function with MyArray as its argument, returns the function's result, and assigns it to the Total variable.

In a worksheet formula

Using custom function in a worksheet formula is like using built-in functions, except that you must ensure that Excel can locate the function procedure. If the function procedure is in the same workbook, you don't have to do anything special. If it's in a different workbook, you may have to tell Excel where to find it.

You can do so in three ways:

- *Precede the function's name with a file reference.* For example, if you want to use a function called CountNames that's defined in a workbook named MYFUNCS.XLS, you can use a reference like

  ```
  =MYFUNC.XLS!CountNames(A1:A1000)
  ```

  If you insert the function with the Function Wizard, the workbook reference is inserted automatically.

- *Set up a reference to the workbook.* You do so with the Tools⇨References command (which is available only when a VBA module is active). If the function is defined in a referenced workbook, you don't need to use the worksheet name. Even when the dependent workbook is assigned as a reference, the Function Wizard continues to insert the workbook reference.

- *Create an add-in.* When you create an add-in from a workbook that has function procedures, you don't need to use the file reference when you use one of the functions in a formula; the add-in must be installed, however. I discuss add-ins in Chapter 13.

Notice that your function procedures don't appear in the Macros dialog box when you issue the Tools⇨Macro command. In addition, neither can you choose a function when you issue the Run⇨Start command (or press F5) if the cursor is located in a function procedure (you get the Macro dialog box that lets you choose a macro to run). As a result, you need to do a bit of extra up-front work to test your functions as you're developing them. One approach is to set up a simple subroutine that calls the function. If the function is designed to be used in worksheet formulas, you have to enter a simple formula to test it.

Function Arguments

Keep in mind the following about function procedure arguments:

- Arguments can be variables (including arrays), constants, literals, or expressions.
- Some functions do not have arguments.
- Some functions have a fixed number of required arguments (from 1 to 60).
- Some functions have a combination of required and optional arguments.

Function Examples

In this section, I present a series of examples, demonstrating how to use arguments effectively with functions.

This discussion of arguments also applies to subroutine procedures.

A function with no argument

Like subroutines, functions need not have arguments. Excel, for example, has a few built-in functions that don't use arguments, including RAND( ), TODAY( ), and NOW( ). You can create similar functions.

Here's a simple, almost trivial, example. The following function returns the UserName property of the Application object. This name appears in the Options dialog box (General tab) and is stored in EXCEL5.INI in the [Microsoft Excel] section.

```
Function User()
'   Returns the name of the current user
    User = Application.UserName
End Function
```

When you enter the following formula, the cell returns the name of the current user (as long as it's listed properly in the EXCEL5.INI file):

```
=User()
```

When you use a function with no arguments, you must include a set of empty parentheses.

To use this function in another procedure, you must assign it to a variable, use it in an expression, or use it as an argument for another function.

The following example uses this function as an argument for the MsgBox function: the concatenation operator (&) joins the literal string with the result of the User function.

```
Sub ShowUser()
    MsgBox ("The user is " & User())
End Sub
```

Another function with no argument

I used to use Excel's RAND( ) function to quickly fill a range of cells with values. But I didn't like the fact that the random numbers change whenever the worksheet is recalculated. So I wound up converting the formulas to values by using the Edit⇨Paste Special command (with the Values option).

Then I realized that I could create a custom function that returned random numbers that didn't change. I used VBA's Rnd function, which returns a random number between 0 and 1. The custom function is

```
Function StaticRand()
'   Returns a random number that doesn't change when
recalc'ed
    StaticRand = Rnd
End Function
```

If you want to generate a series of random integers between 0 and 1000, you can use a formula such as

```
=INT(StaticRand()*1000)
```

The values produced by this formula will never change, unlike those created by the built-in RAND() function.

Controlling function recalculation

When you use a custom function in a worksheet formula, when does it get recalculated?

Custom functions behave like Excel's built-in worksheet functions. Normally, a custom function gets recalculated only when it needs to be recalculated — that is, when any of a function's arguments are modified — but you can force functions to recalculate more frequently. Adding the following statement to a function procedure makes the function recalculate whenever any cell is changed:

```
Application.Volatile (True)
```

The Volatile method of the Application object has one argument (either True or False). Marking a function procedure as volatile forces the function to be calculated whenever calculation occurs in any cell in the worksheet.

For example, the custom StaticRand function can be changed to emulate Excel's RAND( ) function by using the Volatile method:

```
Function NonStaticRand()
'   Returns a random number that
'   doesn't change when recalc'ed
    Application.Volatile (True)
    StaticRand = Rnd
End Function
```

Using the False argument of the Volatile method causes the function to be recalculated only when one or more of its arguments change (if a function has no arguments, this method has no effect).

A function with one argument

Here's a function for sales managers that need to calculate the commissions earned by their sales forces. The calculations in this example are based on the following table:

Monthly Sales	***Commission Rate***
0 – $9,999	8.0%
$10,000 – $19,999	10.5%
$20,000 – $39,999	12.0%
$40,000+	14.0%

Note that the commission rate depends on the month's total sales: those who sell more earn a higher commission rate.

There are several ways to calculate commissions for various sales amounts entered into a worksheet. If you're not thinking too clearly, you might waste lots of time and come up with a formula such as

```
=IF(AND(A1>=0,A1<=9999.99),A1*0.08,IF(AND(A1>=10000,A1<=19999.99),A1*0.105,
IF(AND(A1>=20000,A1<=39999.99),A1*0.12,IF(A1>=40000,A1*0.14,0))))
```

This is a bad approach for a couple reasons. First, the formula is overly complex. Second, the values are hard-coded into the formula, making the formula difficult to modify.

A better approach is to use a lookup table function to compute the commissions. For example,

```
=VLOOKUP(A1,Table,2)*A1
```

An even better approach is to create a custom function such as the following:

```
Function Commission(Sales)
    Const Tier1 = 0.08
    Const Tier2 = 0.105
    Const Tier3 = 0.12
    Const Tier4 = 0.14
'   Calculates sales commissions
    Select Case Sales
         Case 0 To 9999.99: Commission = Sales * Tier1
         Case 1000 To 19999.99: Commission = Sales * Tier2
         Case 20000 To 39999.99: Commission = Sales * Tier3
         Case Is >= 40000: Commission = Sales * Tier4
    End Select
End Function
```

After you define this function in a VBA module, you can use it in a worksheet formula or call the function from other VBA procedures.

Entering the following formula into a cell produces a result of 3,000 (the amount, 25,000, qualifies for a commission rate of 12 percent):

```
=Commission(25000)
```

Even if you don't need custom functions in a worksheet, creating function procedures can make your VBA coding much simpler. If your VBA procedure calculates sales commissions, for example, you can use the exact same function and call it from a VBA subroutine. Here's a tiny subroutine that asks the user for a sales amount and then uses the Commission function to calculate the commission due:

```
Sub CalcComm()
     Sales = InputBox("Enter Sales:")
     MsgBox "The commission is " & Commission(Sales)
End Sub
```

The subroutine starts by displaying an input box that asks for the sales amount. Then the procedure displays a message box with the calculated sales commission for that amount.

The preceding procedure works, but it is rather crude. Following is an enhanced version that displays formatted values and keeps looping until the user clicks No (see Figure 9-3).

```
Sub CalcComm()
'   Prompt for sales amount
    Sales = Val(InputBox("Enter Sales:", "Sales Commission
Calculator"))

'   Build the message
    Message = "Sales Amount:" & Chr(9) & Format(Sales, "$#,##0")
    Message = Message & Chr(13) & "Commission:" & Chr(9)
    Message = Message & Format(Commission(Sales), "$#,##0")
    Message = Message & Chr(13) & Chr(13) & "Another?"

'   Display the result and prompt for another
    Ans = MsgBox(Message, 4, "Sales Commission Calculator")
    If Ans = vbYes Then CalcComm
End Sub
```

where *Chr(9)* represents a tab (to space the output) and *Chr(13)* is a carriage return (to skip to the next line). The Format function displays a value in a specified format (in this case, with a dollar sign and comma).

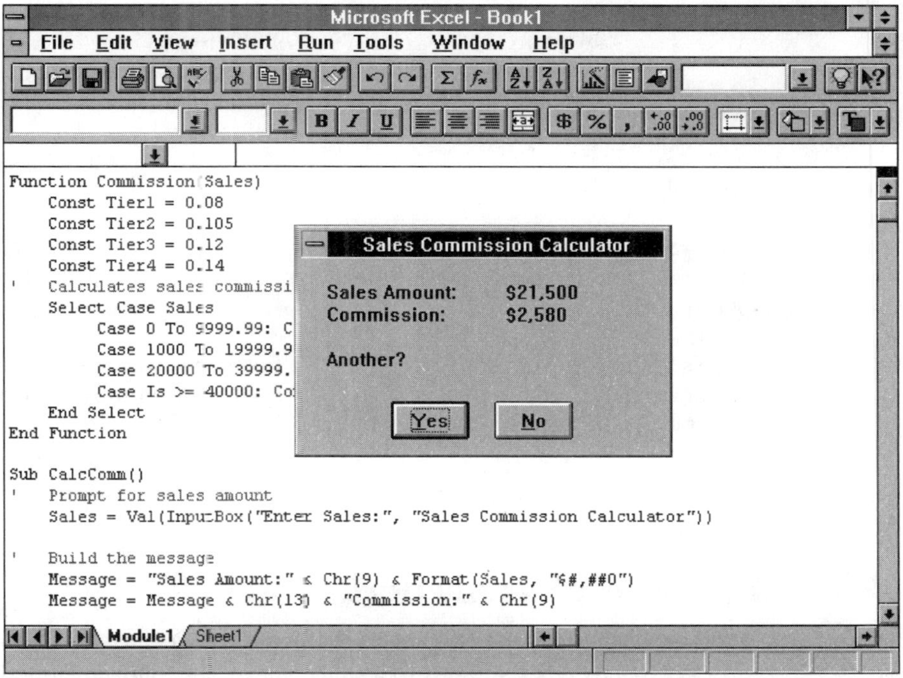

Figure 9-3: Using a function to display the result of a calculation.

In both of these examples, the Commission function must be available in the active workbook; otherwise, Excel displays a message saying that the function is not defined.

A function with two arguments

Imagine that the aforementioned hypothetical sales managers implement a new policy: the total commission paid is increased by 1 percent for every year that the salesperson has been with the company. I modified the custom Commission function (defined in the preceding section) so that it takes two arguments. Call this new function *Commission2*:

```
Function Commission2(Sales, Years) As Single
'    Calculates sales commissions based on years in service
     Const Tier1 = 0.08
     Const Tier2 = 0.105
     Const Tier3 = 0.12
     Const Tier4 = 0.14
     Select Case Sales
```

```
            Case 0 To 9999.99: Commission2 = Sales * Tier1
            Case 1000 To 19999.99: Commission2 = Sales * Tier2
            Case 20000 To 39999.99: Commission2 = Sales * Tier3
            Case Is >= 40000: Commission2 = Sales * Tier4
        End Select
        Commission2 = Commission2 + (Commission2 * Years / 100)
    End Function
```

Pretty simple, eh? I just added the second argument (Years) to the Function statement and included an additional computation that adjusts the commission before exiting.

Here's an example of how you can write a formula by using this function (it assumes that the sales amount is in cell A1 while the number of years the salesperson has worked is in cell B1):

```
=Commission2(A1,B1)
```

A function with an array argument

A function procedure also can accept one or more arrays as arguments, process the array(s), and return a single value. The following function accepts an array as its argument and returns the sum of its elements:

```
Function SumArray(List) As Double
    SumArray = 0
    For Each Item In List
        If Application.IsNumber(Item) Then _
            SumArray = SumArray + Item
    Next Item
End Function
```

TIP: The IsNumber function checks to see whether each element is a number before adding it to the total. Adding this simple error-checking statement eliminates the *Type Mismatch* error that occurs when you try to add a string to a value.

The following subroutine demonstrates how to call this function. The routine creates a 100-element array and assigns a random number to each element. Then the MsgBox function displays the sum of the values in the array by calling the SumArray function.

```
Sub MakeList()
    Dim Nums(1 To 100) As Double
    For i = 1 To 100
        Nums(i) = Rnd * 1000
    Next i
    MsgBox SumArray(Nums)
End Sub
```

Because the SumArray function doesn't declare its data type, it also works in your worksheet formulas. For example, the following formula returns the sum of the values in A1:C10:

```
=SumArray(A1:C10)
```

A function with optional arguments

Many of Excel's built-in worksheet functions use optional arguments. An example is the LEFT function, which returns characters from the left side of a string; its official syntax is

```
LEFT(text,num_chars)
```

The first argument is required, but the second is optional. If the optional argument is omitted, Excel assumes a value of 1. Therefore, the following two formulas return the same result:

```
=LEFT(A1,1)
=LEFT(A1)
```

Your custom functions also can have optional arguments. You specify an optional argument by preceding the argument's name with the keyword *Optional*.

The following is an example of a custom function that uses an optional argument. This function randomly chooses one cell from an input range. If the second argument is 1, the selected value changes whenever the worksheet is recalculated (the function is made volatile). If the second argument is 0 (or omitted), the function does not get recalculated unless one of the cells in the input range is modified. I used VBA's IsMissing function to determine whether the second argument was supplied.

```
Function DrawOne(InputRange as object, Optional Recalc)
'    Chooses one cell at random from a range
```

```
'     Assign default value if 2nd argument is missing
      If IsMissing(Recalc) Then Recalc = 0

'     Make function volatile if Recalc is 1
      If Recalc = 1 Then Application.Volatile (True)

'     Determine a random cell
      DrawOne = Rnd * (InputRange.Count - 1)
      DrawOne = Application.Round(DrawOne, 0) + 1
      DrawOne = InputRange(DrawOne)
End Function
```

NOTE: This function is actually very useful for choosing lottery numbers, picking a winner from a list of names, and so on.

A function that returns a VBA array

VBA includes a useful function called Array. The Array function returns a variant that contains an array. Importantly, the array returned is not the same as a normal array that's made up of elements of variant type. If you're familiar with Excel's worksheet arrays, you'll recognize that VBA's Array function implements this concept. You enter an array formula into a cell by pressing Ctrl+Shift+Enter. Excel inserts brackets around the formula to indicate that it's an array formula. See Chapter 3 for more details on array forumulas.

The MonthNames function (refer to the next code listing) is designed to be used in a worksheet formula. It has an optional argument that works as follows:

- If the argument is missing, the function returns a horizontal array of month names.
- If the argument is less than or equal to 0, the function returns a vertical array of month names. It uses the Transpose function to convert the array.
- If the argument is greater than or equal to 1, it returns the month name that corresponds to the argument value. (The following procedure adds a slight twist, using the Mod function to determine the month value. An argument of 13, for example, returns 1. An argument of 24 returns 12, and so on.)

```
Function MonthNames(Optional MIndex)
    Dim AllNames As Variant
    AllNames = Array("Jan", "Feb", "Mar", "Apr", "May", _
                     "Jun", "Jul", "Aug", "Sep", "Oct", _
                     "Nov", "Dec")
    Select Case IsMissing(MIndex)
        Case True
'           Horizontal array
            MonthNames = AllNames
        Case False
            Select Case MIndex
                Case Is >= 1
'                Determine month value (for example,, 13=1)
                   MonthVal = ((MIndex - 1) Mod 12)
MonthNames = AllNames(MonthVal)
                Case Else
'                   Vertical array
                   MonthNames = _
                   Application.Transpose(AllNames)
              End Select
    End Select
End Function
```

You can use this function in a number of ways, as illustrated in Figure 9-4. Range A1:L1 contains the following formula entered as an array. Start by selecting A1:L1, enter the formula, and then end it by pressing Ctrl+Shift+Enter.

```
=MonthNames()
```

Range E4:E15 contains the following formula entered as an array:

```
=MonthNames(-1)
```

Cell B4 contains the following (non-array) formula, which was copied to the 11 cells below it:

```
=MonthNames(A4)
```

NOTE

Remember, to enter an array formula, you must press Ctrl+Shift+Enter.

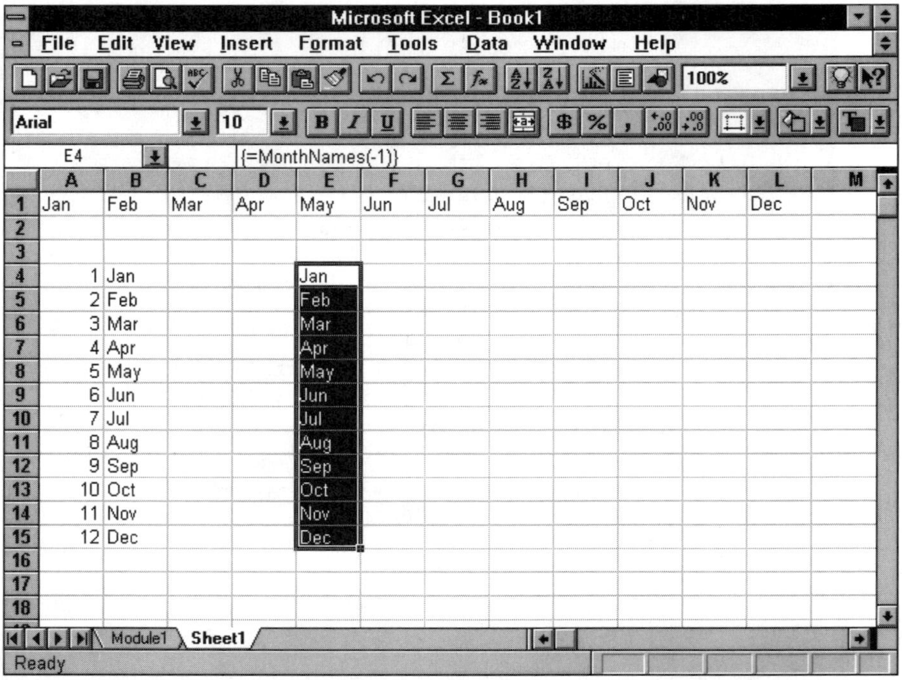

Figure 9-4: Different ways of using the MonthNames function to pass an array or a single value to a worksheet.

A function with an indefinite number of arguments

Some of Excel's worksheet functions take an indefinite number of arguments. A familiar example is the SUM function, whose syntax is

```
SUM(number1,number2...)
```

The first argument is required, but you can have as many as 30 additional arguments. Here's an example of a SUM function with four range arguments:

```
=SUM(A1:A5,C1:C5,E1:E5,G1:G5)
```

You can mix and match the argument types. For example, the following example uses three arguments: the first is a range, the second is a value, and the third is an expression.

```
=SUM(A1:A5,12,24*3)
```

Reinventing the wheel

Most of VBA's built-in functions are impossible to create in VBA. However, some *can* be duplicated.

Just for fun, I wrote my own version of the UCase function (which converts a string to all uppercase) and named it *UpperCase*.

```
Function UpperCase(InString As
String) As String

'   Converts its argument to all
'   uppercase.

    Dim StringLength As Integer
    Dim i As Integer

    StringLength = Len(InString)
    UpperCase = InString

    For i = 1 To StringLength
        ASCIIVal =
Asc(Mid(InString, i, 1))
        CharVal = 0
        If ASCIIVal >= 97 _
        And ASCIIVal <= 122 Then
        CharVal = -32
        Mid(UpperCase, i, 1) = _
        Chr(ASCIIVal + CharVal)
    Next i
End Function
```

I was curious to see how the custom function differed from the built-in function. So I created a subroutine that called the custom function 6,000 times, using an argument that was 24 characters long. The routine took 101.6 seconds to execute. Then I substituted VBA's UCase function and reran the test. Using the built-in function took 1.6 seconds — 64 times faster than my roll-your-own function.

I don't claim that my UpperCase function is the optimal algorithm for this task, but it's fairly obvious that a custom function won't match the speed of VBA's built-in function.

You can create function procedures that have an indefinite number of arguments. The trick is to use an array as the last argument preceded by the keyword *ParamArray*.

Here's a function that can have any number of single-value arguments (it doesn't work with ranges):

```
Function MySum(number1, ParamArray number2()) as Double
'   Demonstrates indefinite number of function arguments

'   Process the first argument
    MySum = number1
```

```
'    Process additional arguments (if any)
     If UBound(number2) <> 0 Then
         For args = 1 To UBound(number2)
             MySum = MySum + number2(args)
         Next args
     End If
End Function
```

The second argument, number2( ), is an array preceded by the ParamArray keyword. The UBound function determines how many elements are in the array. If the number of elements is not zero (that is, additional arguments exist), the For...Next loop processes each additional argument.

For obvious reasons, ParamArray can apply only to the *last* argument in the procedure. It is always a variant data type, and it is always an optional argument (although you don't use the Optional keyword).

Here are some examples of how to use this function in a worksheet formula:

- The following formula returns 1, the sum of its only argument:

  ```
  =MySum(1)
  ```

- The following formula returns 15, the sum of all its arguments:

  ```
  =MySum(1,2,3,4,5)
  ```

- The following formula returns the sum of the values in all its arguments:

  ```
  =MySum(A1,A3,A5,A7,A9,A11,A13,A14)
  ```

- The following formula does *not* return the sum of the values in A1:A10. Rather, it returns only the value in cell A1 because the MySum function was not written to work with range objects.

  ```
  =MySum(A1:A10)
  ```

Emulating the SUM function

The example in this section emulates Excel's SUM function. Although there is no reason to actually use this function, the code is instructive.

The SUM function is very versatile. It can have any number of arguments, and the arguments can be numerical values, cells, ranges, text representations of numbers, logical values, and even embedded functions. For example, the formula

```
=SUM(5,"6",TRUE,SQRT(4))
```

returns 14: 5 + 6 (the string converted to a value) + 1 (the value of TRUE) + 2 (the result of the SQRT function).

When creating a facsimile of the SUM function, a good starting point is the custom MySum function (defined in the preceding section). But I identified a few problems with MySum:

- *It doesn't handle ranges.* The following example returns only the value in A1:

  ```
  =MySum(A1:A20)
  ```

- *It doesn't handle text strings properly.* MySum can handle strings that look like values. The following example returns the #VALUE! error, not 0:

  ```
  =MySum("Hello")
  ```

- *It doesn't treat Boolean values (True or False) the way SUM does.* The SUM function returns a value: 1 for TRUE and 0 for FALSE. MySum returns –1 for TRUE and 0 for FALSE.
- *It doesn't handle missing arguments.* The following examples return the #VALUE! error (missing arguments don't cause such an error with the SUM function).

  ```
  =MySum(1,2,,3)
  =MySum(,A1)
  ```

The following sections describe how to create a function that counters these problems (well, most of them).

Making it work with ranges

To make this function work properly with a range argument, the procedure must determine the type of argument. If the argument is a range, the procedure needs to loop through each element and add its value to a running total.

Fortunately, VBA makes it easy to determine argument type. The TypeName function returns a string that describes its argument. For example, the following subroutine displays two message boxes. The first displays *Range* because the TypeName argument is a range object. The second message box displays *Integer*, the data type of MyVar.

```
Sub DemoTypeName()
    Set MyObject = Worksheets("Sheet1").Range("A1")
    MsgBox (TypeName(MyObject))
    MyVar = 123
    MsgBox (TypeName(MyVar))
End Sub
```

Armed with this knowledge, I modified MySum so that it checks the type of the arguments by using the TypeName function. If the argument is a range, the code loops through each element and increments MySum accordingly.

The modified function is

```
Function MySum(number1, ParamArray number2()) as Double
'   Emulates the SUM function

    MySum = 0

'   Process the first argument
    Select Case TypeName(number1)
        Case "Range"
            For Each item In number1
               MySum = MySum + item.Value
            Next item
        Case Else
               MySum = MySum + number1
    End Select

'   Process additional arguments (if any)
    If UBound(number2) <> 0 Then
        For args = 1 To UBound(number2)
            Select Case TypeName(number2(args))
                Case "Range"
                    For Each item In number2(args)
                        MySum = MySum + item.Value
                    Next item
                Case Else
                   MySum = MySum + number2(args)
            End Select
        Next args
    End If
End Function
```

Making it work with text strings

The SUM function considers text strings to have a value of 0 unless they appear as a literal argument (i.e., an actual value, not a variable). If you use a text string as a literal argument with SUM, the function returns an error. For example, the following formula returns an error:

```
=SUM("Hello")
```

The modified MySum returns an error when a cell in a range argument contains a string or when a string is used as a literal argument.

To correct MySum so that it behaves like SUM, the procedure needs to add the cell's value only if it can be evaluated as a number. You can make this so by modifying the statement within each of the For...Next loops as follows:

```
If Application.IsNumber(item.Value) Then MySum = MySum + _
     item.Value
```

This edited statement uses the IsNumber function to determine whether an element can be interpreted as a number. If so, the value is added to MySum. If not, nothing happens to MySum and no error is returned.

Making it work with Booleans

The modified MySum function still doesn't handle Booleans like SUM does.

SUM handles Boolean arguments as follows:

- =SUM(TRUE) returns 1
- =SUM(FALSE) returns 0

MySum, meanwhile, returns –1 for a literal TRUE and 0 for a literal FALSE.

If the argument refers to a cell, neither SUM nor MySum uses a logical value. For example, both =SUM(A1) and =MySum(A1) return 0 if cell A1 contains *either* TRUE or FALSE.

For MySum to emulate SUM exactly, it needs to test for a literal TRUE in the argument list and a way to compensate for the difference (that is, add 2 to –1 to get 1). So I added the following code after the first Case Else statement:

```
'     Check for literal TRUE and compensate
      If number1 = "True" Then MySum = MySum + 2
```

I also added the following code after the second Case Else statement to handle literal TRUE values in subsequent arguments:

```
'     Check for literal TRUE and compensate
      If number2(args) = "True" Then MySum = MySum + 2
```

Making it work with missing arguments

Tracking down the error that occurs when an argument is missing was difficult. Then I remembered that you can use the MsgBox function in a function.

To discover the data type of the missing argument, I inserted the following statement right before the second Select Case statement:

```
MsgBox TypeName(number2(args))
```

Then I entered the following formula into a cell:

```
=MySum(1,2,,3)
```

The message box told me the type name of each argument; the missing argument had a type name of *Error*. Armed with this knowledge, I circumvented the #VALUE! display by adding another Case that handled *Error*: that is, it did nothing.

The edited code could not handle a missing first argument, however. If the first argument is missing or the function has no arguments, I discovered, Excel doesn't even try to evaluate the function. I thus was unable to modify my code to handle such a case. The function cannot handle a case like

```
=MySum(,1,2,3)
```

The final MySum

DISK

The code for the MySum function can be found in MYSUM.XLS on the disk that accompanies this book.

The corrected code is shown in Listing 9-1.

Listing 9-1 MySum function

```
Function MySum(number1, ParamArray number2()) as Double
'   Emulates the SUM function

'   Initialize the variable
    MySum = 0

'   Process the first argument
    Select Case TypeName(number1)
        Case "Range"
            For Each item In number1
               If Application.IsNumber(item.Value) Then _
                  MySum = MySum + item.Value
            Next item
        Case Else
'           Check for literal TRUE and compensate
```

```
            If number1 = "True" Then MySum = MySum + 2
            MySum = MySum + number1
    End Select

'   Process additional arguments (if any)
    If UBound(number2) <> 0 Then
        For args = 1 To UBound(number2)
            Select Case TypeName(number2(args))
                Case "Error"
                Case "Range"
                    For Each item In number2(args)
                        If Application.IsNumber(item.Value) _
                          Then MySum = MySum + item.Value
                    Next item
                Case Else
'                  Check for literal TRUE and compensate
                   If number2(args) = "True" Then MySum = _
                     MySum + 2
                   MySum = MySum + number2(args)
            End Select
        Next args
    End If
End Function
```

NOTE: I could not fix one other MySum problem. If you enter a formula that uses one or more entire columns or rows, MySum laboriously cycles through every cell (even empty cells) — which seems to take forever. SUM, on the other hand, performs such a calculation in the blink of an eye. I've tried using the SpecialCells method to work with a subset of the Range object that contains only values and formulas, but this method does not work in function procedures that are used in a worksheet. SpecialCells works just fine, however, in function procedures that are called by other procedures. Go figure. To me, this is a serious flaw in VBA that makes it impossible to develop efficient worksheet functions.

I chose such nondescript argument names (number1 and number2) because these are the argument names that the Function Wizard uses. When you invoke the Function Wizard and select MySum from the list of User Defined functions, you'll see that it matches the SUM function closely.

NOTE: You may be curious about the relative speeds of SUM and MySum. It's not even close. A worksheet with 2,000 SUM formulas recalculated in about 1 second. I replaced the SUM functions with MySum functions and it then took 102 seconds. MySum may be improved a bit, but it can never come close to the SUM's speed.

The point of this example is not to create a new SUM function. Rather, it demonstrates how to create custom worksheet functions that look and work like those built into Excel.

Debugging Functions

When you're testing a function procedure by using a formula in a worksheet, run-time errors do not appear. If an error occurs, the formula simply returns an error value. Luckily, this does not present a problem for debugging functions; you have three possible approaches:

- *Place MsgBox functions at strategic locations to monitor the value of specific variables.* Fortunately, message boxes in function procedures do pop-up when the procedure is executed. But make sure that you only have one formula in the worksheet that uses your function, or the message boxes will appear for each formula that's evaluated.
- *Test the procedure by calling it from a subroutine procedure.* Run-time errors display as normal, and you can either fix the problem (if you know it) or jump right into the debugger.
- *Set a breakpoint in the function and then step through the function.* You then can access all the normal debugging tools.

Dealing with the Function Wizard

Excel's Function Wizard is a handy tool that lets you choose a worksheet function; you even can choose one of your custom worksheet functions. The Function Wizard also prompts you for the function's arguments.

NOTE: Function procedures defined with the Private keyword do not appear in the Function Wizard.

By default, custom functions are listed under the User Defined category, but you can change this organization. You also can add some text to describe the function (I highly recommend this step).

To force a custom function to appear under a different category in the Function Wizard or to add a description to your function, follow these steps:

1. Activate the VBA module that defines the custom function procedure.
2. Select the View➪Object Browser command (or press F2). The dialog box shown in Figure 9-5 appears.

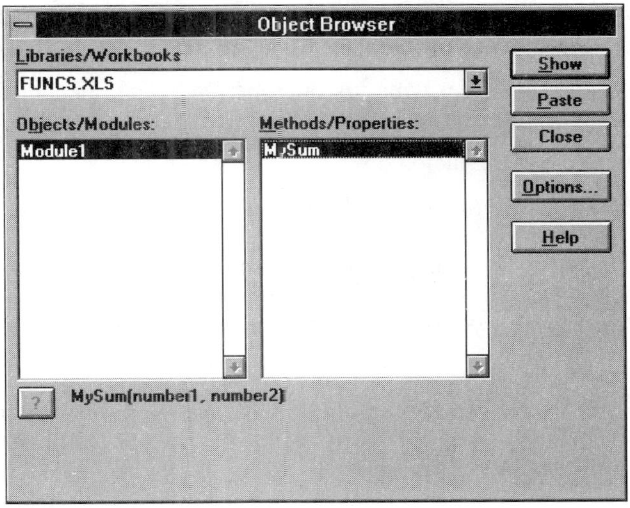

Figure 9-5: The Object Browser dialog box

3. Make sure that the module that contains your custom function is selected in the Objects/Modules list box.
4. Select the function's name in the Methods/Properties list box.
5. Click the Options button to get the Macro Options dialog box (see Figure 9-6).

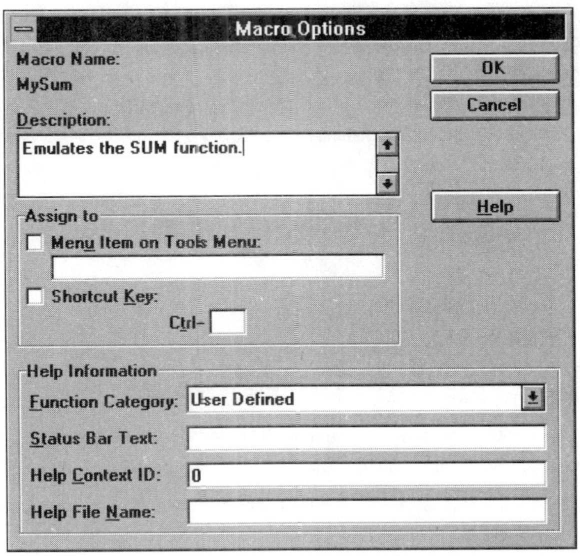

Figure 9-6: The Macro Options dialog box.

6. Enter a description of the function in the Description box. You can enter as long a description as you want.
7. Choose the category for your custom function from the Function Category pull-down list. Unfortunately, you cannot enter a new category name.
8. Click OK to close the dialog box.
9. Click Close to close the Object Browser dialog.

After performing the preceding steps, the Function Wizard displays your custom functions as if they were built-in functions. For information on creating a custom help topic for your function, accessible from the Function Wizard, refer to Chapter 16.

Figure 9-7 shows the second Function Wizard dialog box. Notice that the function is evaluated as you enter arguments and the result appears in the Value box in the upper-right corner.

When you access a built-in function from the Function Wizard, the second dialog box displays a description of each argument. Unfortunately, you cannot provide such descriptions for custom functions.

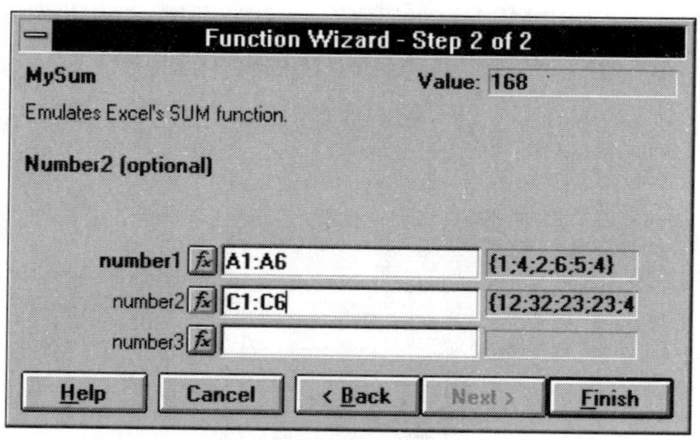

Figure 9-7: The Function Wizard at work.

Making Add-Ins from Custom Functions

It's a good idea to store custom functions that you use frequently in an add-in file (also known as an XLA file). The main advantage is that the functions can be used in formulas without a filename qualifier.

If you have a custom function named ZapSpaces, for example, and it's stored in MYFUNCS.XLS, you need to enter the following to use this function in any workbook except MYFUNCS.XLS:

```
=MYFUNCS.XLS!ZapSpaces(A1:C12)
```

If you create an add-in from MYFUNCS.XLS and the add-in is loaded, you can omit the file reference and enter a formula such as

```
= ZapSpaces(A1:C12)
```

CROSS REFERENCE

I discuss add-ins in Chapter 13.

Using DLL Functions

Amazingly, VBA can actually use code from other files that have nothing to do with Excel or VBA — for example, the DLL (Dynamic Link Library) files that Windows uses. As a result, you can do things with VBA that would otherwise be outside of the language's scope.

The Windows API (Application Programming Interface) is a set of functions available to Windows programmers. When you call a function in a DLL from VBA, you're accessing the Windows API. Many of the Windows resources used by Windows programmers are available in DLLs, which store programs and functions and are linked at run-time rather than compile-time.

Excel uses several DLLs, for example. The code in many of these DLLs could have been compiled right into EXCEL.EXE, but the designers chose to store it in DLLs, which are loaded when needed. This technique makes Excel's main executable file smaller; in addition, it is a more efficient use of memory because the library is loaded only when it's needed.

DLLs also are used to share code. For example, most Windows program use dialog boxes to open and save files. Windows comes with a DLL (COMMDLG.DLL) that has the code to generate several standard dialog boxes. Programmers thus can call this DLL rather than write their own routines.

If you're a C programmer, you can produce your own DLLs and use them from VBA. Most compilers can produce DLLs, but most likely you'll use existing DLLs to extend the capabilities of VBA.

Examples

Before you can use a function stored in a DLL, you must declare it at the top of a VBA module. The procedure for doing so is a bit tricky; it must be declared precisely.

The declaration statement tells VBA

- Which procedure you're using
- In which DLL the procedure is located
- The procedure's arguments

After you declare a procedure, you can use it in your code. Following is a function declaration:

```
Declare Function GetFreeSpace& Lib "KERNEL" (ByVal wFlags%)
```

This function, which has one argument, returns the amount of free memory by calling the GetFreeSpace function in the Windows Kernel DLL (unlike most DLLs Kernel is not a separate file)).

In almost all cases, the DLL function declarations that you use will be "lifted" from another source (it's very difficult to create such a declaration yourself). For example, Microsoft's Visual Basic language includes a file filled with DLL function declarations that can be copied into your code. This book also has several useful examples of DLL function, and this information is available from many other programming reference books.

When working with DLL functions, system crashes during testing are not uncommon, so save your work often.

After inserting the Declare statement at the top of your module, you can access the function by calling the GetFreeSpace functions. The following is an example of calling the function and displaying the result in a message box. I used the Format function to make the number more readable.

```
Sub ShowFreeMem()
    Dim BytesFree As Long
    BytesFree = GetFreeSpace&(0)
    MsgBox Format(BytesFree, "#,000") & " bytes free"
End Sub
```

The GetFreeSpace function isn't all that useful because the MemoryFree property of the Application object does exactly the same thing. In fact, when you execute the following statement, Excel itself calls GetFreeSpace to get the value of this property:

```
MsgBox Application.MemoryFree
```

The point of using API calls is to perform an action that is otherwise impossible. For example, if your program needs to find out the path of the Windows directory, you could search all day and not find a function in Excel or VBA to do the trick. In this case, you can use the GetWindowsDirectory function:

```
Declare Function GetWindowsDirectory% Lib "KERNEL" _
    (ByVal lpBuffer$, ByVal nSize%)
```

This function gets the name of the directory in which Windows is installed. The function itself returns a number that contains the length of the string. When the function is called, its two arguments contain a string buffer with the Windows directory in it (lpBuffer) and the size of the buffer (nSize).

The following subroutine demonstrates how to call GetWindowsDirectory. The Windows directory is contained in WinPath, and PathLength variable holds the length of the string that contains the Windows directory.

```
Sub WIN_DIR()
'   Returns the Windows directory by calling a Windows API
'   function
    Dim WinPath As String * 145
    Dim WindowsDir As String
    Dim PathLength As Integer
    PathLength = GetWindowsDirectory(WinPath, Len(WinPath))
    WindowsDir = Left(WinPath, PathLength)
    MsgBox WindowsDir
End Sub
```

The final example uses two API calls that deal with the colors displayed on your system. The declarations are

```
Declare Function GetSysColor& Lib "USER" (ByVal nIndex%)

Declare Sub SetSysColors Lib "USER" (ByVal nChanges%, _
    lpSysColor%, lpColorValues&)
```

GetSysColor is a function that returns a color value for a particular window element. For example, this function can tell you the current color for the title bar of the active window. The SetSysColors subroutine lets you change any of the colors. Retrieving and changing system colors is not normally possible in VBA, but these API calls give you the power to do so.

The preceding example demonstrates that you often need some additional information before you can use API calls. To retrieve and change system colors, you need to know the index values for the system colors.

By the way, you can modify the color of 21 Windows items. The settings for these items are stored in your WIN.INI file in the [colors] section.

The best way to work with these items is to define constants. I found the constants in a reference book for Windows programmer and changed their names to correspond to the entries in WIN.INI. They are

```
Global Const BACKGROUND = 1
Global Const APPWORKSPACE = 12
Global Const WINDOW = 5
Global Const WINDOWTEXT = 8
Global Const MENU = 4
Global Const MENUTEXT = 7
Global Const ACTIVETITLE = 2
Global Const INACTIVETITLE = 3
Global Const TITLETEXT = 9
Global Const ACTIVEBORDER = 10
Global Const INACTIVEBORDER = 11
Global Const WINDOWFRAME = 6
Global Const SCROLLBAR = 0
Global Const BUTTONFACE = 15
Global Const BUTTONSHADOW = 16
Global Const BUTTONTEXT = 18
Global Const GRAYTEXT = 17
Global Const HILIGHT = 13
Global Const HILIGHTTEXT = 14
Global Const INACTIVETITLETEXT = 19
Global Const BUTTONHILIGHT = 20
```

The following subroutine displays the color value of the active window's title bar. For this to work, the GetSysColor function and the constants must be declared in the same module.

```
Sub ShowColorValue()
    Dim CurrentColor as Long
    WinItem = ACTIVETITLE
    CurrentColor = GetSysColor(WinItem)
    MsgBox CurrentColor
End Sub
```

When you run the preceding subroutine, the message box displays a value that corresponds to your current system's color setting. This value is an RGB color value (see the accompanying sidebar for details).

Converting RGB colors

Here's the scoop on the strange RGB values returned by the GetSysColor function. The RGB color system defines colors in terms of its red, green, and blue components. Each component can range from 0 to 255. The value returned by GetSysColor is a Long data type, and it holds the value of each component color.

VBA's RGB function creates an RGB color value; it takes three arguments that correspond to the level of each color. For example, yellow is made up of maximum red, maximum green, and no blue. Therefore, the following assigns the RGB color for yellow to the font of the selected range:

```
Selection.Font.Color = RGB(255, 255, 0)
```

VBA doesn't have a function that converts an RGB color value to its component parts, but you can do so: Think of an RGB color value as a 6-digit hexadecimal value. The first two digits comprise the blue value, the second two digits comprise the green value, and the last two digits comprise the red value: BBGGRR. Therefore, performing "and" operations produce the desired components.

This method is demonstrated in the following routine, which displays the red, green, and blue components for 8421631. In hex, this number is 8080FF, which works out to 128 (blue), 128 (green), and 255 (red) — in other words, a fairly ugly pink.

```
Sub ShowColorValue()
    Dim RGBColor As Long
    Dim RedPart As Integer,
GreenPart As Integer, BluePart As
Integer
    RGBColor = 8421631
    RedPart = RGBColor And &hff&
    GreenPart = (RGBColor And
&hff00&) / 256
    BluePart = (RGBColor And
&hff0000) / 65536
    MsgBox "RGB: " & Chr(9) &
RGBColor & Chr(13) & _
           "Red:" & Chr(9) &
RedPart & Chr(13) & _
           "Green:" & Chr(9) &
GreenPart & Chr(13) & _
           "Blue:" & Chr(9) &
BluePart
End Sub
```

The following routine demonstrates how to change a color; it changes the color of the scroll bars to yellow. The SetSysColors subroutine and the constants must be declared in the same module.

```
Sub ChangeColor()
    Dim NumToChange As Integer
    Dim ToChange As Integer
    Dim NewColor As Long
    NumToChange = 1
    ToChange = SCROLLBAR
    NewColor = RGB(255, 255, 0)
    Call SetSysColors(NumToChange, ToChange, NewColor)
End Sub
```

The SetSysColors subroutine does not write the new color values to WIN.INI. To make the color changes permanent, use the Color icon in the Windows Control Panel.

Learning more about API calls

Working with DLL functions can be tricky. Many programming reference books list the declarations for common API calls and often provide examples. Often, you can simply copy the declarations and use the functions without really understanding the details.

Chapter 11 has several examples that are particularly useful for VBA programmers.

Creating Property Procedures

Subroutines and functions aren't the only procedures that you can write. In this section, I describe a third type: property procedures. I cover this topic in this chapter because property procedures often can be used in place of functions.

Excel and VBA as object libraries

Excel exposes many objects that you can control with your VBA procedures. From this perspective, Excel can be thought of as an object library. In fact, Excel appears as such in the Object Browser (press F2 while a VBA module is active). In addition, VBA is an object library; its objects are its built-in functions and its constants.

Workbooks as object libraries

A workbook also can be thought of as an object library; each open workbook appears as such in the Object Browser, which lists the custom functions and subroutines in each module. You can think of a VBA module as an object and the subroutines and functions contained in it as methods.

This concept is extremely important but not easily understood: I used VBA for about six months before I fully understood the implications. After you understand how VBA works, however, the door swings open to all sorts of interesting possibilities, giving you a better appreciation of the concept of objects.

Module = object, procedure = method

References to your subroutines follow the same syntax as references to objects and methods. For example, to execute the MySub subroutine in Module1, you can use the following:

```
Module1.MySub
```

The reference to Module1 isn't necessary unless the workbook contains another MySub subroutine, but the syntax works. To further qualify the reference, you can precede the reference with its "container" object's name, like this:

```
Book1.Module1.MySub
```

If the workbook has been saved, you need to include the workbook object's name in square brackets because the period would be confusing. For example, if Book1 was saved as MYBOOK.XLS, you would use the following fully qualified reference:

```
[mybook.xls].Module1.MySub
```

Remember that you can't execute a procedure in a different workbook unless you establish a reference to that workbook with the Tools⇨References command. A reference makes the objects in the object library (that is, the workbook) available.

Creating custom objects and properties

To recap: You can think of a workbook as an object library, a workbook's VBA modules as objects, and the procedures in a module as methods. The only missing element is properties, which is where property procedures enter the picture.

It's possible to create properties that you can manipulate by using standard VBA syntax. Like standard object properties, the properties that you create can be either read-write or read-only.

In this section, I examine the API calls that get and change system colors. After I create an object (that is, a module) named SystemColors, I create two properties for the object: ActiveTitleColor and InactiveTitleColor. Then I can use the new object in VBA code (as long as a reference is established).

For example, the following statement changes the active window's title bar color to red:

```
SystemColors.ActiveTitleColor = 255
```

A statement like the following returns the RGB color of the inactive window title bar:

```
MsgBox SystemColors.InactiveTitleColor
```

Although these custom objects work much like standard objects, VBA doesn't really consider them real objects. For example, you can't use the With...End With construct with these objects, and attempting to determine the type with the TypeName function generates an error.

Creating the object

Start with an empty workbook and insert a VBA module. Name the module SystemColors and save the workbook as LIBRARY.XLS. Insert the declaration for the API calls at the top of the module:

```
Declare Function GetSysColor& Lib "USER" (ByVal nIndex%)
Declare Sub SetSysColors Lib "USER" (ByVal nChanges%, _
    lpSysColor%, lpColorValues&)
```

The Property Get procedure

If a custom property can be read and modified, you need to create a Property Get procedure (for reading the property's value) and a Property Let procedure (for changing the property's value).

The procedure that I wrote follows. The property's name is the procedure's name. The procedure simply calls GetSysColor with an argument of 2 (which represents the active title bar). The last statement assigns the RGB color returned by GetSysColor to the procedure's name.

```
Property Get ActiveTitleColor() As Long
'   Retrieves color of active title bar
    Dim WindowItem As Integer
    WindowItem = 2
    ActiveTitleColor = GetSysColor(WindowItem)
End Property
```

Notice that the procedure ends with an End Property statement.

The Property Let procedure

Because the property also can be changed, I developed a Property Let procedure:

```
Property Let ActiveTitleColor(RGBColor As Long)
'   Changes color of active title bar
    Dim ColorsToChange As Integer
    Dim WindowItem As Integer
    ColorsToChange = 1
    WindowItem = 2
    Call SetSysColors(ColorsToChange, WindowItem, RGBColor)
End Property
```

This procedure has one argument, which corresponds to the value that this property will be set to. The procedure calls SetSysColors and changes the color of the active title bar.

Using the custom object

Creating a custom object makes it much easier to work with system colors. Once this object is created, it can be used by any other workbook; the programmer needs not be concerned with declaring API functions.

You can easily add more properties to SystemColors to handle the other 19 Windows items that can have their colors changed. All the procedures are essentially the same — you need to change only the names and a few constants. Actually, you don't need to do anything; I already did the work. SYSCOLOR.XLS (on the accompanying disk) contains an impressive demonstration. The file is an object library with one object (SystemColors) that has the following properties:

```
BackgroundColor
AppWorkspaceColor
WindowColor
WindowTextColor
MenuColor
MenutextColor
ActiveTitleColor
InactiveTitleColor
TitleTextColor
ActiveBorderColor
InactiveBorderColor
WindowFrameColor
ScrollBarColor
ButtonFaceColor
ButtonShadowColor
ButtonTextColor
```

```
GrayTextColor
HilightColor
HilightTextColor
InactiveTitleTextColor
ButtonHilightColor
```

Assume that you're working on a project and you want to change the active title bar's color to red while a certain operation is in progress. Activate a VBA module in your workbook and select the Tools⇨References command. Set up a reference to the workbook that contains the SystemColors object. This workbook does not have to be open to establish a reference. If it's not open, use the Browse button to specify its location (see Figure 9-8).

After creating the reference, use the Object Browser to identify the properties in the SystemColors object (see Figure 9-9).

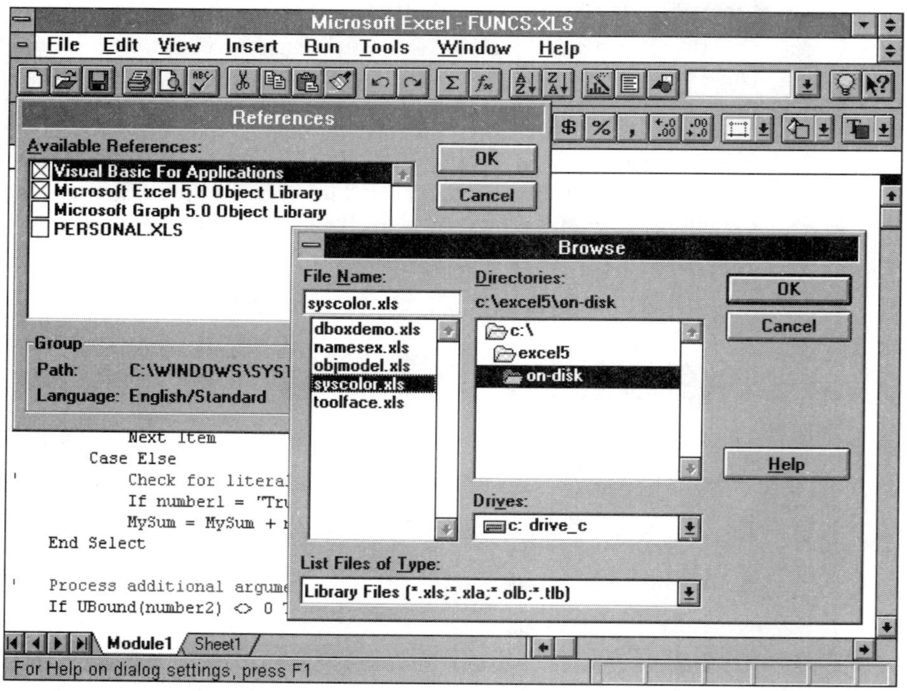

Figure 9-8: Browsing for a reference file.

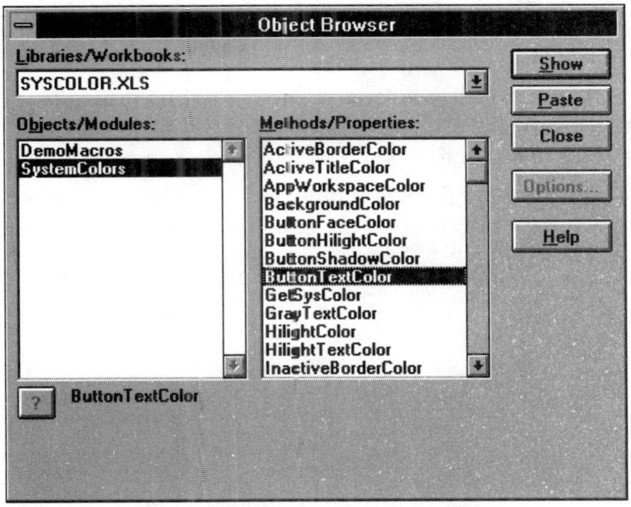

Figure 9-9: The new properties appear in the Object Browser.

The following is a simple routine that stores the current active title bar color, changes the title bar to red, and then displays a message box. When the message box is closed, it then changes the title bar back to its original color.

```
Sub ChangeTitleBar()
    Dim OldColor As Long
    OldColor = SystemColors.ActiveTitleColor
    SystemColors.ActiveTitleColor = RGB(255, 0, 0)
    MsgBox "Click  OK to restore the color"
    SystemColors.ActiveTitleColor = OldColor
End Sub
```

Notice that this example uses the RGB function to specify the color — this method is much easier than trying to figure out the actual RGB color.

DISK

The accompanying disk contains another file which demonstrates object libararies, KEYBOARD.XLS. This makes it easy to change the state of NumLock, CapsLock, and ScrollLock, and also determined if Shift, Ctrl, or Alt is pressed.

Summary

- In this chapter, you read how to create and use custom VBA functions. These functions can be used in worksheet formulas and in other VBA procedures. I also described how to call Windows API functions and create custom objects and properties.
- I switch gears in the next chapter and discuss how to put your knowledge of subroutines and procedures to work when creating custom dialog boxes.

Chapter 10

Creating Custom Dialog Boxes

In This Chapter

- An analysis of the alternatives to custom dialog boxes
- A discussion of the dialog box controls available to you
- Controlling custom dialog boxes with VBA procedures
- Examples, examples, examples

Dialog boxes are, perhaps, the most important user interface element in Windows programs. Virtually every Windows program uses them. And most users understand how they work (although they may not use them efficiently).

Excel makes it relatively easy to create custom dialog boxes for your applications. In fact, you can duplicate the look and feel of all Excel's dialog boxes except:

- Tabbed dialog boxes, such as the Options dialog box
- Checkbox list boxes, such as the Toolbars dialog box

CROSS REFERENCE

A spreadsheet application that you develop by using Excel can consist of any number of elements, or user interface controls, as discussed in Chapter 5. If your application depends on user input, you'll probably want to design custom dialog boxes.

Before I get into the nitty gritty, I discuss some other options that can take the place of custom dialog boxes.

Custom Dialog Box Alternatives

In some cases, you can save yourself the trouble of creating a custom dialog box by using one of five prebuilt dialog boxes. These are described in the following sections.

VBA's InputBox function

VBA's InputBox function always returns a string, so it may be necessary to convert the results to a value. The function's syntax is

```
InputBox(prompt[,title][,default][,xpos][,ypos][,helpfile,context])
```

The InputBox function prompts the user for a single bit of information, and always returns a string. The prompt can consist of about 1,024 characters (more or less, depending on the characters used). In addition, you can provide a title for the dialog box, a default value, and specify its position on the screen. And you can specify a custom help topic — if you do, the input box includes a Help button.

The following InputBox function asks for the user's full name. The procedure then attempts to extract the first name by searching for the first space character and using the Left function. Notice that the InputBox function is in a Do Until loop to ensure that something is entered. If the user clicks Cancel, UserName is an empty string and the input box reappears. The Find method searches for the first space character; if no space character exists, this method returns an error. The On Error statement causes execution to jump to the NoSpaces label if an error occurs. Figure 10-1 shows what the function creates.

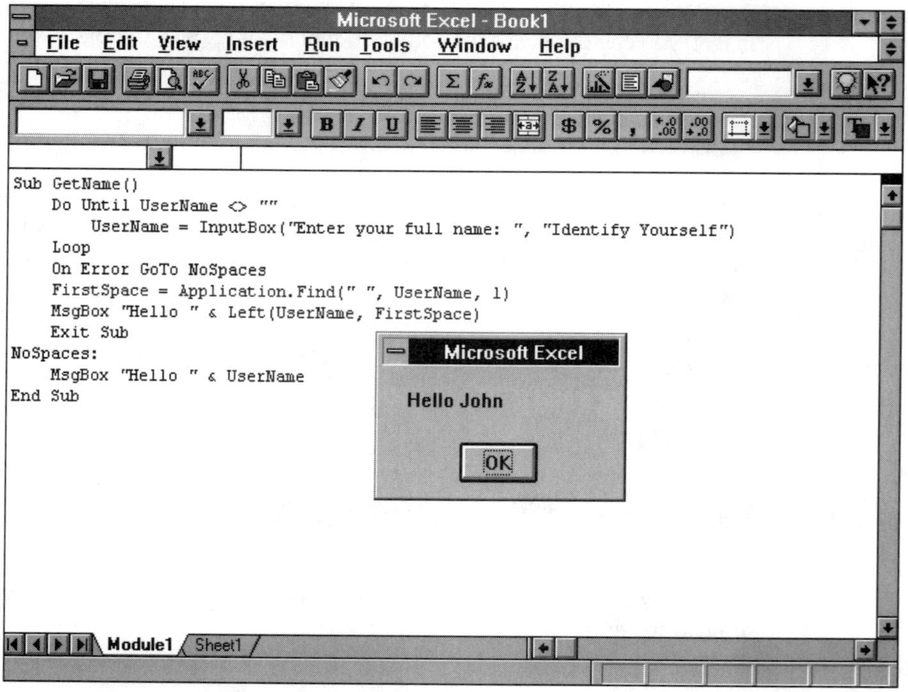

Figure 10-1: The InputBox function at work.

```
Sub GetName()
    Do Until UserName <> ""
        UserName = InputBox("Enter your full name: ", _
            "Identify Yourself")
    Loop
    On Error GoTo NoSpaces
    FirstSpace = Application.Find(" ", UserName, 1)
    MsgBox "Hello " & Left(UserName, FirstSpace)
    Exit Sub
NoSpaces:
    MsgBox "Hello " & UserName
End Sub
```

If the string returned by the InputBox function looks like a number, you can convert it to a value. However, a better approach is to use Excel's InputBox method.

Excel's InputBox method

The main advantage of Excel's InputBox method is that you can specify the data type returned. The method's syntax is

```
object.InputBox(prompt,title,default,left,top,helpFile,context,type)
```

The *prompt* argument is the text displayed; *title* is the caption, *default* is the default value to appear, *left* and *top* are its screen coordinates, *helpFile* and *context* specify the helpfile and help topic, and *type* is a code for the data type returned.

Table 10-1 shows the codes for the type argument.

Table 10-1 Codes to Determine the Data Type Returned by the InputBox Method

Code	*Meaning*
0	A formula
1	A number
2	A string (text)
4	A logical value (True or False)
8	A cell reference, as a range object
16	An error value, such as #N/A
64	An array of values

To specify more than one data type returned, use the sum of the pertinent codes. For example, for an input box that can accept text or numbers, set type equal to 3 (that is, 1 + 2 or number plus text).

The InputBox method is quite versatile. For example, if you use 8 for the type argument, the user can point to a range. In the following code, the InputBox method returns a range object (note the Set keyword) and then clears the values from the selected cells. The default value displayed in the input box is the current selection's address. The On Error statement ends the subroutine when the input box is canceled.

```
Sub GetRange()
    Dim UserRange As Object
    Default = Selection.Address
    On Error GoTo Canceled
    Set UserRange = Application.InputBox(prompt:="Range to
erase:", _
        Title:="Range Erase", Default:=Default,
Type:=8)UserRange.Clear
    UserRange.Select
Canceled:
End Sub
```

VBA's MsgBox function

I use VBA's MsgBox function in many of this book's examples as an easy way to display a variable's value. The official syntax for MsgBox is

```
MsgBox(prompt[,buttons][,title][,helpfile,context])
```

You can use the MsgBox function by itself or assign its result to a variable. The following example displays a message and does not return a result:

```
Sub MsgBoxDemo()
    MsgBox "Click OK to continue"
End Sub
```

To get a response from a message box, you can assign the results of the MsgBox function to a variable. In the following code, I use some built-in constants (described later) to make it easier to work with the values returned by MsgBox:

```
Sub GetAnswer()
    Ans = MsgBox("Continue?", vbYesNo)
    Select Case Ans
        Case vbYes
'           ...[code if Ans is Yes]...
        Case vbNo
'           ...[code if Ans is No]...
    End Select
End Sub
```

You can easily customize your message boxes because of the flexibility of the buttons argument. (Table 10-2 lists the many constants that you can use for this argument.) You can specify which buttons to display, whether an icon appears, and which button is the default. The following example uses a combination of constants to display a message box with a Yes button, a No button, and a question mark icon; the second button is designated as the default button (see Figure 10-2). For simplicity, I assigned these constants to the Config variable.

```
Sub GetAnswer()
    Config = vbYesNo + vbQuestion + vbDefaultButton2
    Ans = MsgBox("An error occurred. Continue?", Config)
    If Ans = vbNo Then End
    If Ans = vbYes Then Call TryAgain
End Sub
```

NOTE

If you use an invalid value for the buttons argument, the message box interprets it as 0 and displays only an OK button.

Figure 10-2: The buttons argument of the MsgBox function determines what appears in the message box.

Table 10-2 Constants Used in the MsgBox Function

Constant	*Value*	*Description*
vbOKOnly	0	Display OK button only
vbOKCancel	1	Display OK and Cancel buttons
vbAbortRetryIgnore	2	Display Abort, Retry, and Ignore buttons
vbYesNoCancel	3	Display Yes, No, and Cancel buttons
vbYesNo	4	Display Yes and No buttons
vbRetryCancel	5	Display Retry and Cancel buttons
vbCritical	16	Display Critical Message icon
vbQuestion	32	Display Warning Query icon
vbExclamation	48	Display Warning Message icon
vbInformation	64	Display Information Message icon
vbDefaultButton1	0	First button is default
vbDefaultButton2	256	Second button is default
vbDefaultButton3	512	Third button is default
vbSystemModal	4096	System modal; all applications are suspended until the user responds to the message box

Excel's GetOpenFilename method

If your application needs to get a filename from the user, you can use the InputBox function to ask the user to enter the filename. But this approach often leads to typographic errors. A better approach is to use the GetOpenFilename method of the Application object, which ensures that your application gets a valid filename (and its complete path).

This method displays the normal Open dialog box (displayed when you select the File⇨Open command) but does not actually open the file specified. Rather, the method returns the filename selected by the user. Then you can do whatever you want with the filename. The syntax for this method is

```
object.GetOpenFilename(fileFilter,filterIndex,title)
```

As you can see, you can specify the filter (for example, *.TXT), an index for the file filter, and even a different caption for the dialog box's title bar.

The fileFilter argument determines what appears in the dialog box's List Files of Type drop-down list. It consists of pairs of file filter strings followed by the wild-card file filter specification, with each part and each pair separated by commas. If omitted, this argument defaults to

```
" User (*.*),*.*"
```

Notice that the first part of this string (User (*.*)) is the text displayed in the List File of Type drop-down list. The second part (*.*) actually determines which files are displayed.

The following example prompts the user for a filename. It defines four file filters (an additional filter for *.* is always included as the last filter option). Notice that I used VBA's line continuation sequence to set up the Filter variable; doing so makes it much easier to work with this rather complicated argument.

```
Sub GetImportFileName()
'   Set up list of file filters
    Filter = "Text Files (*.txt),*.txt," & _
             "Lotus Files (*.prn),*.prn," & _
             "Comma Separated Files (*.csv),*.csv," & _
             "ASCII Files (*.asc),*.asc"

'   Display *.* by default
    FilterIndex = 5
'   Set the dialog box caption
    Title = "Select a File to Import"
'   Get the file name
    FileName = Application.GetOpenFilename(Filter, _
       FilterIndex, Title)
'   Exit if dialog box canceled
    If FileName = False Then
        MsgBox "No file was selected."
        Exit Sub
    End If

'   Display full path and name of the file
    MsgBox "You selected " & FileName
End Sub
```

Figure 10-3 shows this dialog box.

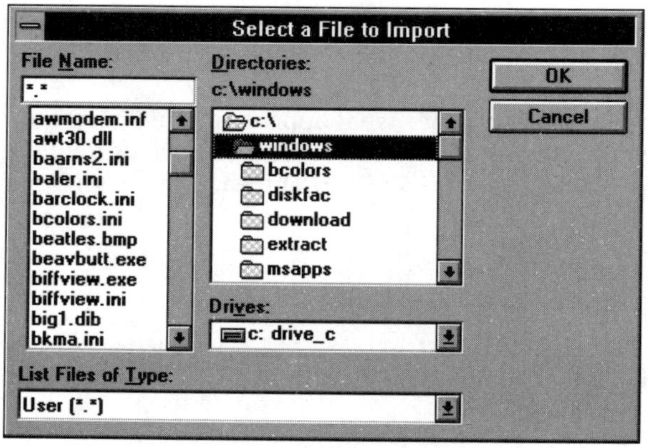

Figure 10-3: The GetOpenFilename method displays a customizable dialog box and returns the path and name of the selected file, but it does not open the file.

Excel's GetSaveAsFilename method

Excel's GetSaveAsFilename method, which works like the GetOpenFilename method, returns a filename and path but doesn't take any action. The syntax for this method is

```
object.GetSaveAsFilename(initialFilename, fileFilter, _
    filterIndex, title)
```

This method has an additional (and optional) argument that lets you specify a default name that appears in the File Name box.

How Excel Handles Dialog Boxes

A dialog sheet is one of five types of sheets that can be inserted into a workbook. Each dialog sheet holds one custom dialog box, and a workbook can have as many as 256 custom dialog boxes (if you need more, you're probably doing something wrong).

You can insert a new dialog sheet by using the Insert⇨Macro⇨Dialog command. Or right-click a workbook tab, choose Insert, and then select Dialog from the Insert dialog box.

Dialog sheets have names like Dialog1, Dialog2, and so on. I suggest changing the generic name so that it better describes your dialog box's function.

When you insert a new dialog sheet, Excel displays a dialog box with OK and Cancel buttons and the Forms toolbar (see Figure 10-4).

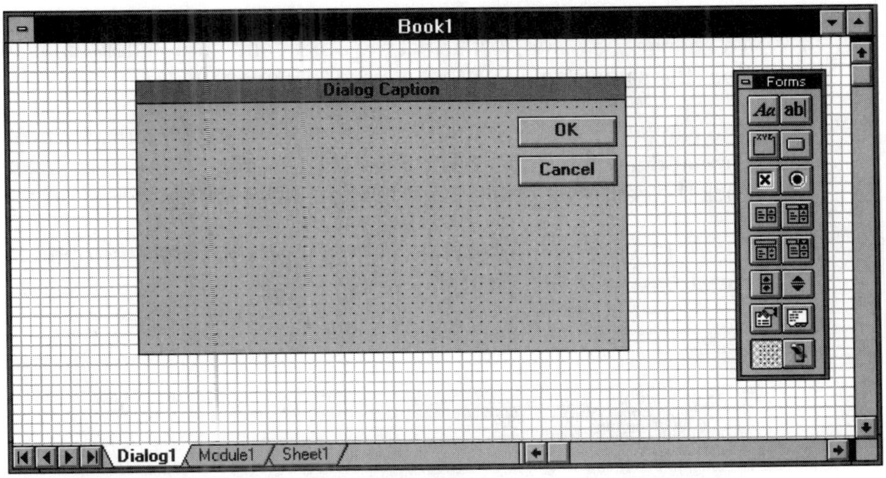

Figure 10-4: An empty dialog box and the Forms toolbar.

An Overview of Dialog Box Controls

In this section, I describe the elements, or *controls*, in Excel's dialog boxes.

Adding controls

To add controls to a dialog box, you must use the Forms toolbar; oddly, there are no pertinent menu commands. Just click the button that corresponds to the control you want to add; then drag it into the dialog box.

Every object on a dialog sheet has a name, which appears in the Name Box on the edit line. When you insert a new dialog sheet, the sheet already has three objects:

- The dialog box's frame, named Dialog Frame 1
- The OK button, named Button 2
- The Cancel button, named Button 3

When you add a new control, it is assigned a name that combines the control type with the sequence. For example, if you add a button to an empty dialog box, it is named Button 4. If you then add an edit box, it is named Edit Box 5.

TIP

It's a good idea to rename all the controls that you add; the new names make the controls easier to work with and you avoid causing any confusion with the numbers used in the default names. For example, a button named "Button 12" is the 12th object added to the dialog box. It is *not* the 12th object in the Buttons collection.

To change the name, just select the object and enter a new name in the Name Box (the same Name Box that is used to name ranges).

You can adjust some properties of these controls from the Control tab of the Format dialog box. (The easiest way to display the Format dialog box is to right-click the control and then choose Format Object from the shortcut menu.)

Figure 10-5 shows the Control tab for a button control (the options in this tab vary from control to control).

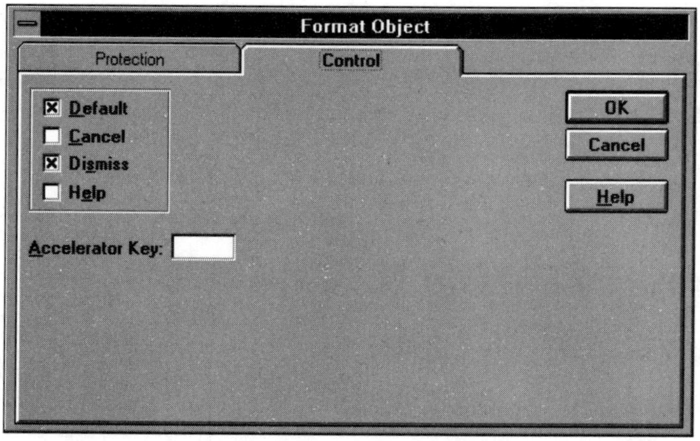

Figure 10-5: The Control tab of the Format Object dialog box.

Buttons

Every dialog box starts out with two button controls. Depending on how the box is set up, clicking a button can execute a procedure, close the dialog box (OK or Cancel), or display a custom help topic.

Figure 10-6 shows some buttons in a dialog box.

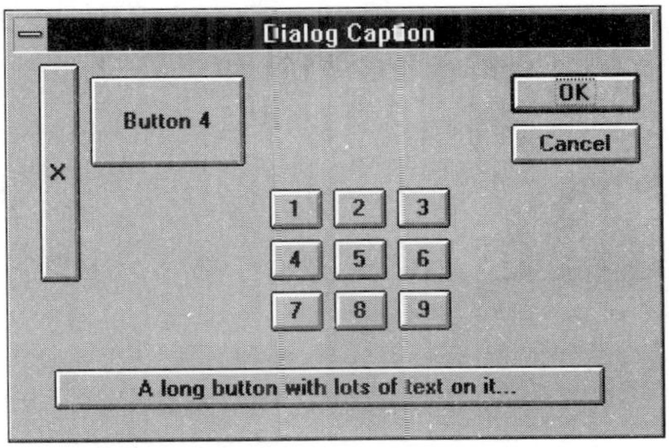

Figure 10-6: Button controls.

Buttons in a dialog box can display one line only of text. Although the text may appear to wrap around when you enter it, Excel will display it in a single line. As a result, when the dialog box is actually used, some text may be cut off.

To see how a dialog box will look, right-click anywhere in the dialog sheet (except on a control) and then select Run Dialog from the shortcut menu. Or, you can use the Run Dialog button on the Forms toolbar. This is a good way to test the hot key assignments because the underlines appear only when the dialog box is running.

The Control tab of the Format Object dialog box for a button control lets you adjust the following properties:

- Default: If checked, the button is the default button for the dialog box. In other words, the button is activated when the user presses Enter or double-clicks certain other controls. Only one button at a time can be the default button.
- *Cancel*: If checked, activating the button aborts the dialog box.
- *Dismiss*: If checked, activating the button dismisses the dialog box. Usually, OK and Cancel buttons both have this setting.
- *Help*: If checked, activating the button displays a help topic of your choice.
- *Accelerator Key*: Lets you specify a hot key. The corresponding letter in the button's text is underlined.

Labels

A label control, which is as simple as a control gets, holds up to 255 characters of text. You can resize labels, but the words rewrap when you do so. You have no control over a label's font or size.

NOTE

You can enter more than 255 characters into a label, but only the first 255 will appear when the dialog box is displayed.

Figure 10-7 shows some labels in a dialog box.

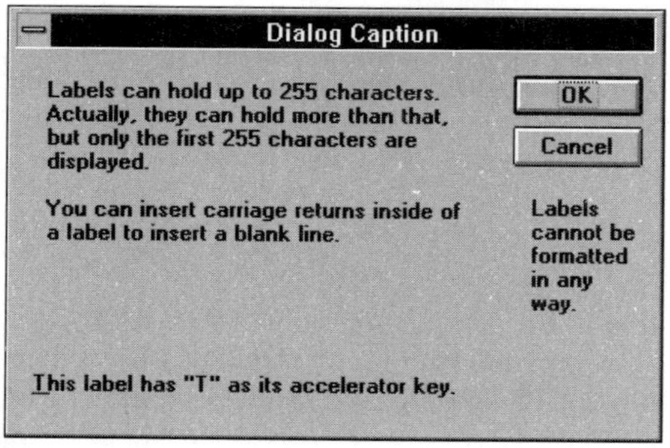

Figure 10-7: Label controls.

By the way, you also can specify an accelerator key for a label. Doing so enables users to access objects that don't have accelerator keys, such as edit boxes. If the label appears directly before an edit box in the dialog box's tab order, for example, pressing the label's hot key activates the edit box. I discuss tab order later in this chapter.

Edit boxes

An edit box accepts user input. The Format Object dialog box for an edit box control lets you adjust the following properties:

- *Edit Validation*: Determines which data type the edit box can hold.
- *Multiline Edit*: Specifies whether the text wraps if it exceeds the width of the edit box.
- *Vertical Scrollbar*: Specifies whether the edit box has a vertical scroll bar.

Figure 10-8 shows edit boxes in a dialog box.

Edit box controls are actually quite flexible because users can also enter formulas and cell references in an edit box.

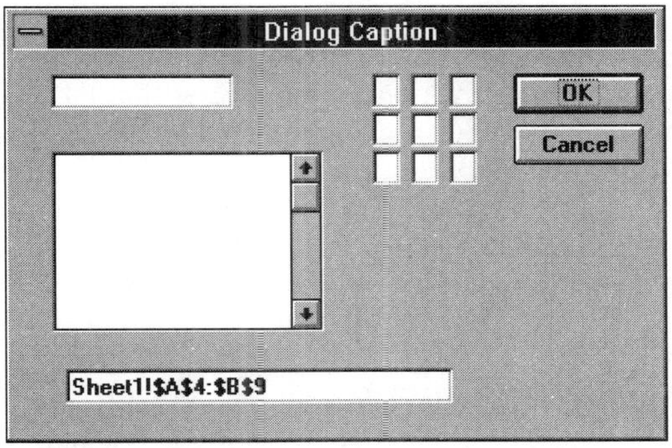

Figure 10-8: Edit box controls.

Group boxes

A group box doesn't really do anything, except visually (and functionally) combine a group of related controls, such as option buttons. You may add a descriptive label for the group box, but it isn't necessary.

Figure 10-9 shows two group boxes in a dialog box. One has a label and one doesn't.

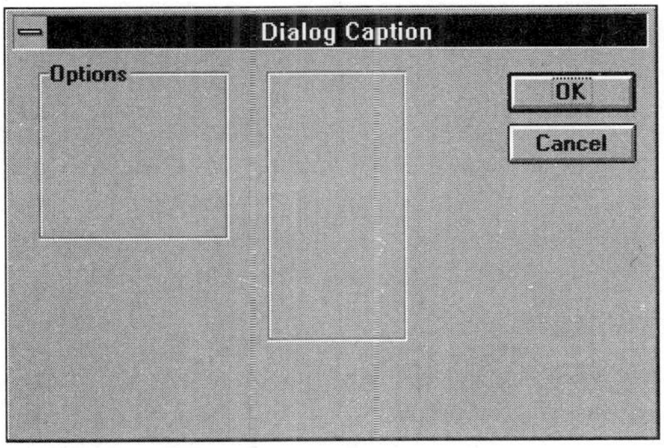

Figure 10-9: Group box controls.

When you have more than one set of option buttons, you must use a group box to enclose at least one set — otherwise, all the option buttons in the dialog box will work together and only one then can be selected.

Check boxes

Check boxes enable users to specify a binary choice — that is, a check box is either checked or not checked. When a check box is checked, it has a value that corresponds to the constant xlOn. When it's not checked, the check box's value is xlOff.

A check box can have a value of xlMixed, which is useful when the value is not consistent.

To see an example of a mixed check box, format cell A1 with wrapped text and cell B1 without wrapped text. Then select A1:B1, choose Format⇨Cells, and click the Alignment tab. The Wrap Text check box has a gray square, indicating that the selection is mixed.

A check box can be linked to a cell in a worksheet. If it has such a link, the cell displays TRUE when the check box is checked, FALSE when it's not checked, and #N/A when it's mixed.

Figure 10-10 shows three check boxes enclosed in a group box. The group box is not required.

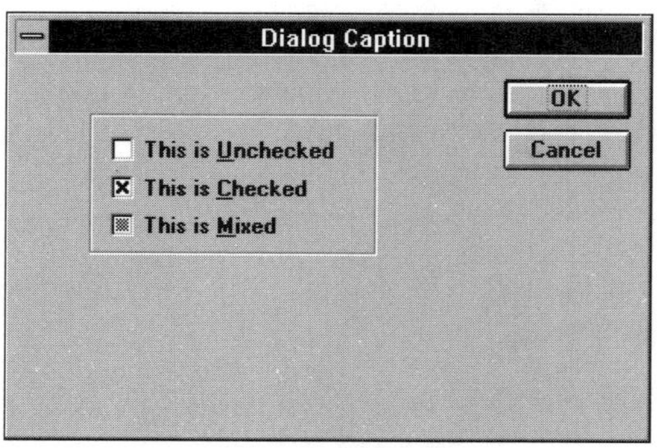

Figure 10-10: Check box controls.

Activating a check box's accelerator key toggles its value between xlOn and xlOff. If the check box had a value of xlMixed when it was displayed, however, pressing the hot key cycles through all three options.

Option buttons

Option buttons (sometimes called radio buttons) enable users to select one option from several possibilities. When one option button is selected, the other buttons in its group are deselected. As a result, option buttons are useful only when there are two or more in a group; an option button by itself is useless. When an option button is selected, it has a value of xlOn; otherwise, its value is xlOff.

You can link an option button to a cell: the cell displays an integer that corresponds to the selected option button in its group. If you have more than one set of option buttons in a dialog box, you need to enclose at least one group in a group box.

Figure 10-11 shows two sets of option buttons in a dialog box.

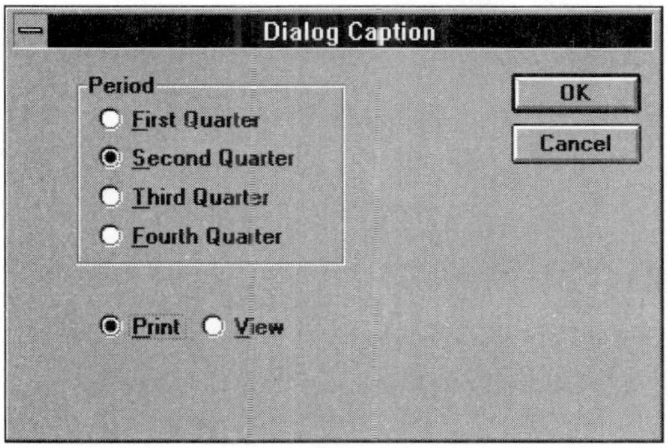

Figure 10-11: Option button controls.

When an option button is selected, you can press the arrow keys to select another option button in the same group. Or you can press an accelerator key to select one option button and deselect the others in its group.

List boxes

List boxes let the user choose one or more items from a list. The Format Object dialog box lets you control the following:

- *Input Range*: A vertical range of cells that contains the options to be displayed in the list box.

- *Cell Link*: A cell to store the selected item (an integer that corresponds to the selected item's position in the list).
- *Selection Type*: Single means that only one item can be selected. Multi lets the user select more than one item by holding down Ctrl while selecting. Extend, similar to Multi, also lets the user select a range of options by holding down Shift.

NOTE: When the selection type is Multi or Extend, the Cell Link option is ignored. To determine which items were selected, you need to write VBA code.

Figure 10-12 shows list boxes in a dialog box.

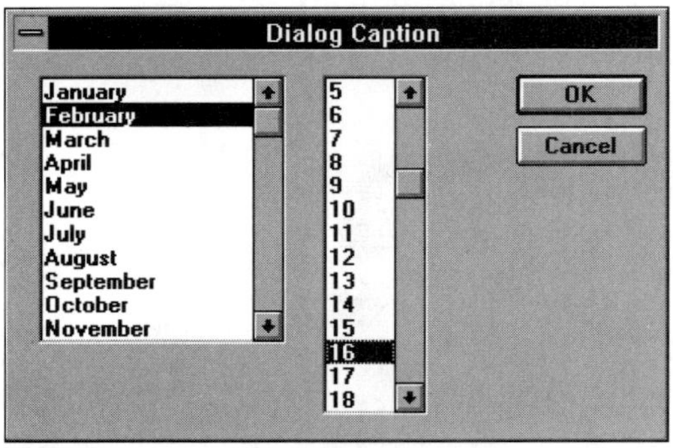

Figure 10-12: Two list box controls.

Although you can use a worksheet range to store the list box's options, you also can set the options with VBA code. In addition, you can change the selection type with VBA. So a single dialog box can be set for a single selection in some circumstances and a multiple selection in others.

Drop-down list box

Drop-down list boxes can substitute for list boxes if you don't need to allow for a multiple selection. The advantage is that this control is saves space — only one item appears initially. When the drop-down list is activated, it opens up to display other items.

The Format Object dialog box lets you control the following:

- *Input Range*: A vertical range of cells that contains the options to be displayed in the drop-down list.
- *Cell Link*: A cell to store the selected item (an integer that corresponds to the selected item's position in the list).

- *Drop-down Lines*: The number of lines that drop-down when the control is activated. If the number of items exceeds the number of drop-down lines, scroll bars appear.

Figure 10-13 shows drop-down list boxes in a dialog box.

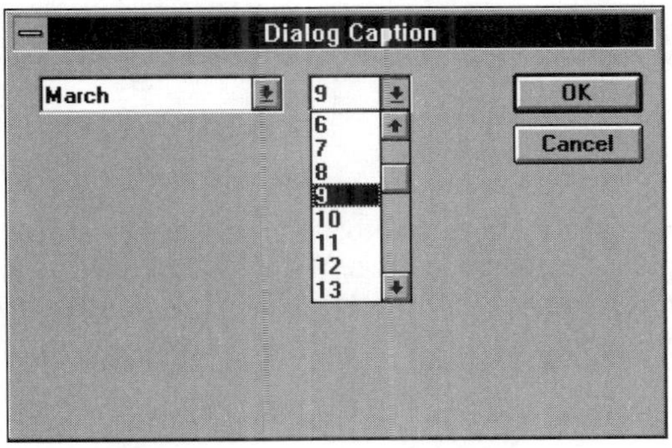

Figure 10-13: Drop-down list box controls.

Generally, the methods and properties for a list box can also be used in a drop-down box. However, those that deal with multiple selections do not apply.

Combination list-edit box

When you add a combination list-edit control, you're actually adding two controls: a drop-down list box and an edit box. These controls are independent of each other; you need to write VBA code to use them together.

Figure 10-14 shows a combination list-edit box in a dialog box.

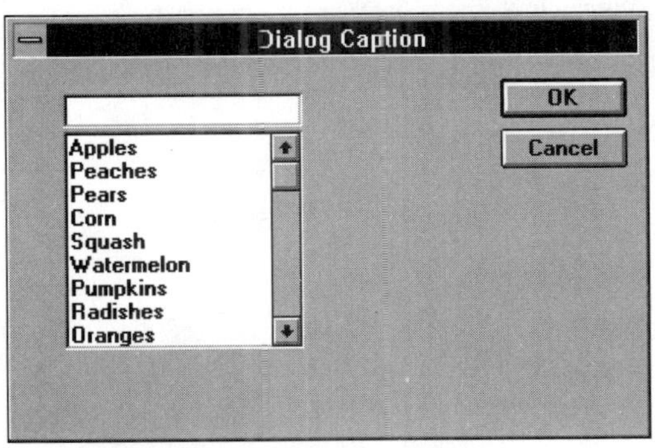

Figure 10-14: A combination list-edit box.

Combination drop-down edit boxes

This control is similar to a drop-down list box, but it also lets the user type an option into the list. In other words, this control is useful when all possible options may not appear in the list.

The Format Object dialog box has the same options as a drop-down list box. If the user enters an option that's not on the list, the linked cell has a value of 0. To determine what the entry was, you need to use VBA code.

Scroll bars

A scroll bar is a convenient way of changing a value. These controls work just like the scroll bars used in Excel's windows. When you place a scroll bar, it can either be vertically or horizontally oriented. A scroll bar doesn't display its value, so these are often teamed with a label or edit box control.

The Format Object dialog box lets you control the following:

- *Current Value*: The value of the scroll bar.
- *Minimum Value*: The minimum allowable value.
- *Maximum Value*: The maximum allowable value (up to 30,000).
- *Incremental Change*: The change in value when either of the arrows is clicked.
- *Page Change*: The change in value when the scroll bar button is clicked.
- *Cell Link*: A cell to store the scroll bar's value (an integer that corresponds to the selected item's position in the list).

Figure 10-15 shows some scroll bars in a dialog box.

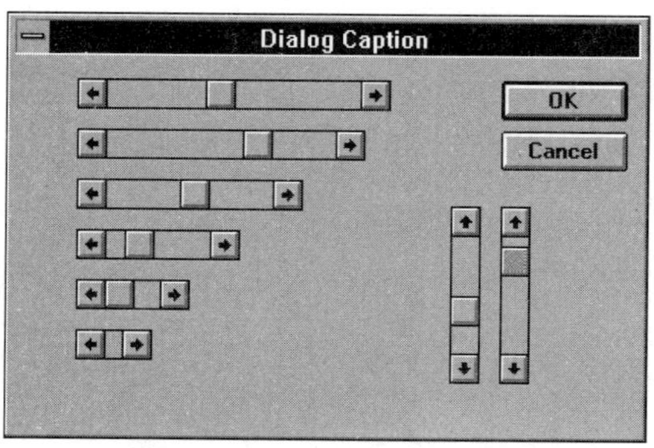

Figure 10-15: Scroll bar controls.

Spinners

A spinner is similar to a scroll bar except that it's smaller, it only displays the arrows, and it can only be placed vertically. A spinner's Format Object dialog box has the same options as a scroll bar except for the Page Change option. Like a scroll bar, a spinner doesn't display its value, so you may want to use an edit box or label control to provide feedback to the user.

Figure 10-16 shows some spinner controls in a dialog box.

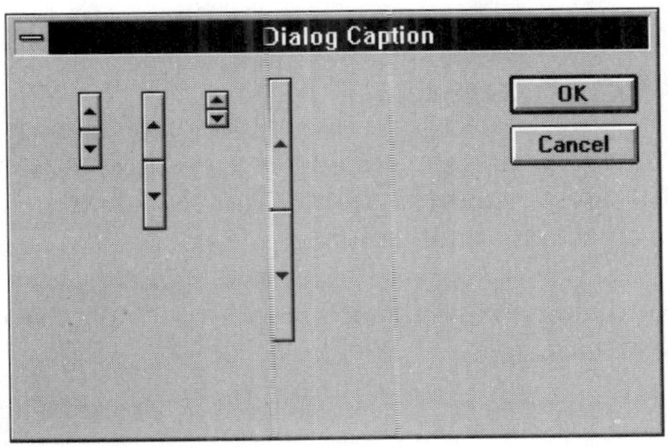

Figure 10-16: Spinner controls.

Working with Dialog Box Controls

In this section, I discuss how to work with dialog box controls in a dialog sheet.

Moving and resizing controls

After a control is placed in a dialog box, you can move and resize it by using standard mouse techniques. Some controls can't be completely resized — for example, a check box can't be made taller.

TIP: You can select multiple controls by Ctrl-clicking or click-and-dragging to lasso a group.

NOTE: A control may hide another control; in other words, controls can be stacked. You can move a control up or down in a stack by using the Format⇨Placement command, or the shortcut menu that appears when you right-click the control.

Aligning controls

Dialog boxes normally display a grid. Controls that you're moving or resizing automatically snap to the grid lines. If you want more precise control over a control's size or location, turn off the grid (clicking the Toggle Grid button, on the Forms toolbar, is the fastest way to do so).

TIP

Excel doesn't have any commands to help you align or resize your controls, but you may find the Object Size and Align utility, included with the Power Utility Pak, particularly useful (you can order a free copy of this package using the coupon in the back of the book).

Accommodating keyboard users

Many users prefer to navigate through a dialog box by using the keyboard: pressing Tab and Shift+Tab cycles through the controls, while pressing a hot key instantly activates a particular control.

To make sure that your dialog box works properly for keyboard users, you must be mindful of two areas:

- Tab order
- Accelerator keys

Changing the tab order

The tab order determines the order in which the controls are activated when the user presses Tab or Shift+Tab. It also determines which control has the initial *focus*, or which is the active control. If a user is entering text into an edit box, for example, the edit box has the focus. If the user clicks an option button, the option button has the focus. The control that's first in the tab order has the focus when a dialog box is first displayed.

To set the tab order of your controls, choose the Tools⇨Tab Order command while the dialog sheet is active. Or right-click the dialog box and choose Tab Order from the shortcut menu. In either case, you get the Tab Order dialog box, shown in Figure 10-17.

The Tab Order dialog box lists all the controls. The tab order in the dialog box corresponds to the order of the items in the list. To move a control, select it and click the arrow keys up or down. You can choose more than one control (click while pressing Shift or Ctrl) and move them all at once.

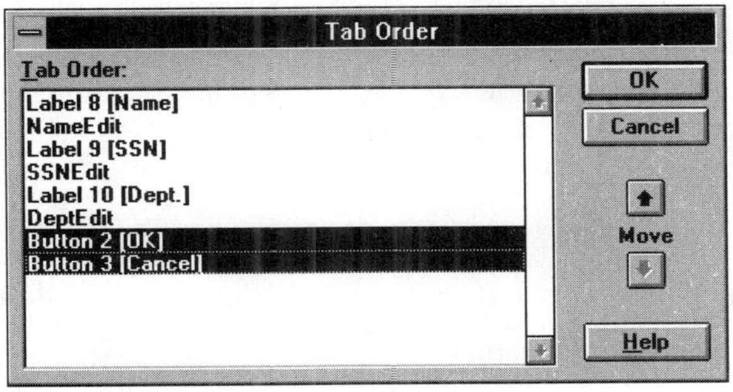

Figure 10-17: The Tab Order dialog box.

Setting hot keys

As I mentioned in the previous section, you can assign an accelerator key, or hot key, to some dialog box controls:

- Buttons
- Labels
- Group boxes
- Check boxes
- Option buttons

If a control doesn't have an accelerator key, you still can allow direct keyboard access to it by using a label control. That is, assign an accelerator key to the label and put the label directly before the control in the tab order.

Figure 10-18 shows several edit boxes. The labels that describe the edit boxes have accelerator keys, and each label precedes its corresponding edit box in the tab order. Pressing Alt+N, therefore, activates the edit box next to the Name label.

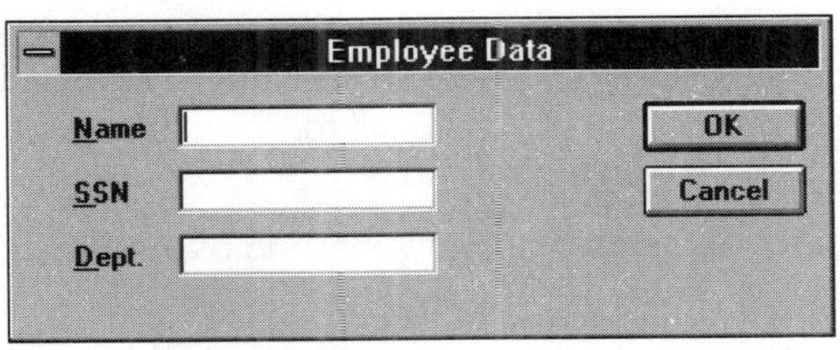

Figure 10-18: Using labels to provide direct access to controls that don't have accelerator keys.

Testing a dialog box

Accelerator key assignments don't appear in the dialog box until the dialog box is displayed. However, there are three ways that you can test a dialog box without actually calling it from a VBA procedure:

- Use the Tools⇨Run Dialog command.
- Right-click the dialog box and choose Run Dialog from the shortcut menu.
- Choose the Run Dialog tool on the Forms toolbar.

When a dialog box is displayed in this test mode, you can try out the tab order and accelerator keys.

Manipulating Dialog Boxes with VBA

To display a dialog box from VBA, you use the Show method of the DialogSheets object. You cannot execute a dialog box without using at least one line of VBA code. If your dialog sheet is named MyDialog, the following subroutine displays the dialog box on that sheet:

```
Sub ShowIt
    DialogSheets("MyDialog").Show
End Sub
```

The dialog box always appears in the center of the screen; you can't change its position with VBA code. However, if the user moves a dialog box to a new location, the upper-left corner of the next dialog box will appear in the same location as the upper-left corner of the previously displayed dialog box.

Most of the time, you need to write additional code or procedures to control your custom dialog boxes. This code manipulates the dialog box controls.

The general sequence of your VBA code is as follows:

1. Set the dialog box controls to the desired (or default) values. For example, you may want to set the Text property of an edit box to an empty string. Or perhaps set a check box to unchecked (xlOff).
2. Display the dialog box (by using the Show method of the DialogSheets object).
3. When the dialog box is dismissed, determine whether it was closed from the OK button or the Cancel button.
4. Take appropriate action. For example, if the dialog box was canceled, nothing usually happens. If the dialog box was closed because the user pressed the OK button, the controls' settings usually change.

You may need to write other procedures that can be executed while a dialog box is displayed. For example, if the dialog box has a button control, clicking the button may execute a subroutine.

NOTE Excel limits what can occur when a dialog box is displayed. For example, clicking a button on a dialog box may display another dialog box. But the user cannot call a third-level dialog box. Trying to do so generates a stack overflow error, and the procedure will grind to a halt. In addition, it's not possible to print while a dialog box is displayed. If you need to print, you must first dismiss the dialog box.

Your VBA code can change the properties of the controls while the dialog box is displayed. For example, you may assign to a list box control a subroutine that changes the text in a label object when an item is selected. This type of manipulation will become clearer later in this chapter.

An Example

In this example, I show how to create a simple dialog box. I also develop a VBA subroutine that displays the dialog box and enters information into a worksheet. If you want to follow along, start with a new workbook.

Creating the dialog box

Figure 10-19 shows a simple dialog box that is designed to get a person's name (by using an edit box) and their sex (by using option buttons).

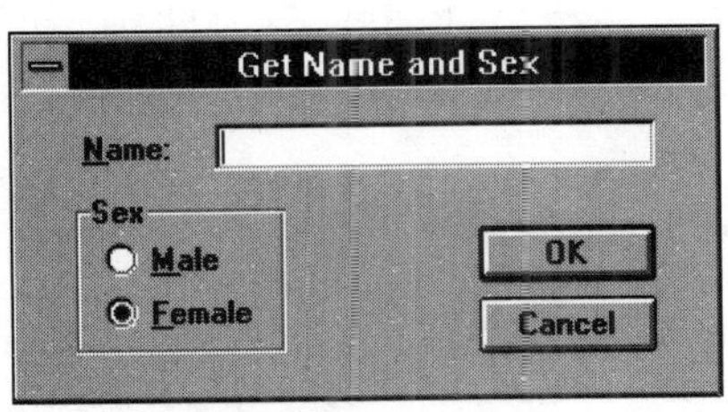

Figure 10-19: A simple dialog box.

To create this dialog box, follow these steps:

1. Insert a new dialog sheet and name it *GetInfo*.
2. Add a label control and use the Name Box to change its text to *Name*. Make its accelerator key *N*.

3. Add an edit box control and change its name to *EditName*.
4. Add two option buttons and change their text to display *Male* (with *M* as the accelerator key) and *Female* (with *F* as the accelerator key). Name one *OptionMale* and the other *OptionFemale*.
5. Add a group box control to surround the two option buttons.
6. Change the dialog box frame's caption to *Get Name and Sex*.
7. Move and size the controls and dialog box frame so that the dialog box resembles Figure 10-19.

Displaying the dialog box

Insert a VBA module and enter the following subroutine:

```
Sub GetData()
    DialogSheets("GetInfo").Show
End Sub
```

The preceding statement uses the Show method on an object (GetInfo) in the DialogSheets collection of the active workbook. In other words, the code displays the dialog box.

Execute the subroutine to display the dialog box. Then enter some text into the edit box. Click OK or Cancel to dismiss the dialog box. Execute the subroutine again, and the text that you entered will still be there.

Now modify the subroutine so that it clears out any text in the edit box before displaying the dialog box:

```
Sub GetData()
    DialogSheets("GetInfo").EditBoxes("EditName").Text = ""
    DialogSheets("GetInfo").Show
End Sub
```

The new statement changes the Text property of the edit box object. Notice that this new statement refers to an object (EditName) in the EditBoxes collection, which is contained in the GetInfo DialogSheets object. It's necessary to fully qualify the reference because the GetInfo sheet will not be the active sheet when the subroutine is executed. In fact, references to objects in dialog boxes can get very lengthy (although there is a solution, which I describe later).

Getting information from the dialog box

So far, the subroutine simply displays the dialog box but doesn't do anything with the information entered in the edit box. It's important to understand that the GetData subroutine continues to execute until the user presses OK or Cancel. When either of these events occurs, the End Sub statement is encountered and the subroutine ends.

To do something, anything, with the information in the dialog box, you need to insert some code before the End Sub statement. The modified routine is

```
Sub GetData()
'   Prepare and display dialog box
    DialogSheets("GetInfo").EditBoxes("EditName").Text = ""
    DialogSheets("GetInfo").Show
'   Insert the name into the worksheet
    Sheets("Sheet1").Range("A1").Value = _
        DialogSheets("GetInfo").EditBoxes("EditName").Text
'   Insert the sex into the worksheet
    Select Case
DialogSheets("GetInfo").OptionButtons("OptionMale")
        Case xlOn
            Sheets("Sheet1").Range("B1").Value = "Male"
        Case xlOff
            Sheets("Sheet1").Range("B1").Value = "Female"
    End Select
End Sub
```

Now when the dialog box is dismissed, the statements following the Show statement are executed. The code assigns the text in the edit box to cell A1 on Sheet1. The next few statements determine whether the OptionMale option button was selected. If so, it inserts *Male* into cell B1; otherwise, it inserts *Female*.

Try running this subroutine again but click Cancel rather than OK. No difference: The information in the dialog box is still transferred to the worksheet (normally, Cancel causes the dialog box to close with no action taken). In other words, you need to add a step that determines whether the dialog box is canceled.

The Show method returns either True — if OK is clicked — or False — if Cancel is clicked or Esc is pressed. Therefore you can assign the value of the dialog box to a variable, check that variable, and take appropriate action.

The modified subroutine is

```
Sub GetData()
'   Prepare and display dialog box
    DialogSheets("GetInfo").EditBoxes("EditName").Text = ""
    DBoxOK = DialogSheets("GetInfo").Show
    If Not DBoxOK Then Exit Sub
'   Insert name into worksheet
    Sheets("Sheet1").Range("A1").Value = _
        DialogSheets("GetInfo").EditBoxes("EditName").Text
'   Insert sex into the worksheet
    Select Case
DialogSheets("GetInfo").OptionButtons("OptionMale")
        Case xlOn
            Sheets("Sheet1").Range("B1").Value = "Male"
        Case xlOff
            Sheets("Sheet1").Range("B1").Value = "Female"
    End Select
End Sub
```

The If statement checks the value of DBoxOK and exits the subroutine if it's False. If DBoxOK is True, everything continues.

Referencing dialog sheet objects

When working with dialog box objects, you must fully qualify your object references because the dialog sheet that contains the object will not be the active sheet. For example, a statement like the following causes an error unless the active sheet has an EditBoxes collection and has an edit box named EditName:

```
EditBoxes("EditName").Text = ""
```

Normally, when a dialog box is displayed, its dialog sheet is not the active sheet. Therefore the reference must be fully qualified with a reference to the dialog sheet object.

TIP

If you execute a dialog box that's in a different workbook, you also need to qualify your references with the workbook object's name. Rather than use the actual name, it's much better to use ThisWorkbook, which returns a reference to the workbook that contains the dialog box. In fact, it's a good idea to always precede a dialog sheet reference with ThisWorkbook, as in

```
ThisWorkbook.DialogSheets("MyDialog").Show
```

The reason for this will become clear when you create add-ins.

Using object variables

An object variable is a variable that holds an object. You can use a Dim statement to declare an object variable and a Set statement to assign an object to it. For example, the following code assigns an object variable to a range object:

```
Dim InputArea as Object
Set InputArea = Worksheets("Sheet1").Range("A1:D4")
```

Thereafter you can use InputArea whenever you need to refer to cells A1:D4 on Sheet1.

The Dim statement isn't really necessary. If you omit it, VBA uses a variant data type. However, it's a good practice to declare your variables.

As you may expect, you can use object variables for objects in a dialog sheet. Here is the example from the preceding section rewritten to use object variables:

```
Sub GetData()
    Dim GetInfo As Object
    Dim EditName As Object
    Dim OptionMale As Object
    Dim NameCell As Object
    Dim SexCell As Object

'   Set object variables
    Set GetInfo = ThisWorkbook.DialogSheets("GetInfo")
    Set EditName = GetInfo.EditBoxes("EditName")
    Set OptionMale = GetInfo.OptionButtons("OptionMale")
    Set NameCell = Sheets("Sheet1").Range("A1")
    Set SexCell = Sheets("Sheet1").Range("B1")
'   Prepare and display dialog box
    EditName.Text = ""
    DBoxOK = GetInfo.Show
    If Not DBoxOK Then Exit Sub
'   Insert name into worksheet
    NameCell.Value = EditName.Text
'   Insert sex into worksheet
    Select Case OptionMale.Value
        Case xlOn:  SexCell.Value = "Male"
        Case xlOff: SexCell.Value = "Female"
    End Select
End Sub
```

The routine is quite a bit longer. However, the code is much easier to read. In addition, using object variable also speeds things up significantly — especially in more complicated applications.

By the way, the variable name for an object variable does not have to correspond to the object's name. But I find that doing so makes it easier to keep things straight.

Finishing touches

The GetInfo subroutine has a serious flaw: every time that it's used, it puts the data in the same cells, overwriting what's already there. Ideally, the routine should find the next empty row in the worksheet and insert the data there.

For the sake of closure, here's a version of this routine that does just that. In addition, I added a loop so that the dialog box keeps reappearing until the user cancels it. These changes make it a good model for creating a user-friendly data entry application.

DISK

This workbook, NAMESEX.XLS, is available on the disk that accompanies this book.

Listing 10-1 NAMESEX.XLS Workbook

```
Sub GetData()
    Dim GetInfo As Object
    Dim EditName As Object
    Dim OptionMale As Object
    Dim NameCell As Object
    Dim SexCell As Object
    Dim ColumnA As Object

'   Set object variables
    Set GetInfo = ThisWorkbook.DialogSheets("GetInfo")
    Set EditName = GetInfo.EditBoxes("EditName")
    Set OptionMale = GetInfo.OptionButtons("OptionMale")
    Set ColumnA = Sheets("Sheet1").Range("A:A")
    DBoxOK = True
    Do While DBoxOK
'       Prepare and display dialog box
        EditName.Text = ""
        DBoxOK = GetInfo.Show
        If Not DBoxOK Then Exit Sub
```

```
'       Determine the first empty row
        FirstBlank = Application.CountA(ColumnA)

'       Set references to next available cells
        Set NameCell = _
            Sheets("Sheet1").Range("A1").Offset(FirstBlank, 0)
        Set SexCell = _
           _Sheets("Sheet1").Range("B1").Offset(FirstBlank, 0)
'       Insert name into worksheet
        NameCell.Value = EditName.Text
'       Insert sex into worksheet
        Select Case OptionMale.Value
            Case xlOn:  SexCell.Value = "Male"
            Case xlOff: SexCell.Value = "Female"
        End Select
    Loop
End Sub
```

The routine uses Excel's COUNTA function to count the number of nonblank cells in column A. I then use this value with the Offset method to insert the values into the appropriate cells. The Do While...Loop structure repeats the instructions until DBoxOK is False (that is, the dialog box is canceled).

Emulating Excel's dialog boxes

The look and feel of Windows dialog boxes differ from program to program. When developing applications for Excel, it's best to try to mimic the Excel's dialog box style whenever possible.

In fact, a good way to learn how to create effective dialog boxes is to try to copy one of Excel's dialog boxes — down to the smallest detail. For example, make sure that you get all the hot keys defined and be sure that the tab order is the same. To re-create one of Excel's dialog boxes, you need to test it under various circumstances and see how it behaves. I guarantee that your analysis of Excel's dialog boxes will improve your own dialog boxes.

If you're really ambitious, you also can write VBA code to duplicate the workings of a dialog box. In Chapter 12, I demonstrate how to re-create the Move or Copy dialog box and write code to mimic its actions.

A few of Excel's dialog boxes are impossible to duplicate. For example, you cannot copy the Options dialog box because there is no way to duplicate the notebook-like tabs. Another example is the dialog box that appears when you select the Data⇨Subtotals command: it uses check boxes within a list box.

A List Box Example

List boxes are useful controls, but they can be a bit tricky to work with. Before displaying a dialog box that uses a list box, you need to fill the list box with items. And then you need to determine which item(s) was selected.

You need to know about the following properties and methods:

- *AddItem*: Method to add an item to a list box.
- *RemoveItem*: Method to remove an item from a list box.
- *ListCount*: Property that returns the number of items in the list.
- *ListIndex*: Property that returns the index number of the selected item or sets the item that's selected (single selections only).
- *List*: Property that returns or sets the text in an item in a list.
- *Selected*: Property that returns an array indicating selected items (multiple selections only).

Filling a list box

The example in this section assumes that

- You have a dialog box on a sheet named *ListBoxDlg*.
- This dialog box contains a list box control named *TheList*.

The procedure fills the list box with the names of the months. It starts by assigning the list box to an object variable. It then clears the list (if it's not empty) by using the RemoveItem method. Finally, the AddItem method is used to add 12 items to the list box. For complete details on these methods, consult the on-line help.

```
Sub ShowMonthNames()
    Dim ListBoxDlg As Object
    Dim TheList As Object

    Set ListBoxDlg = ThisWorkbook.DialogSheets("ListBoxDlg")
    Set TheList = ListBoxDlg.ListBoxes("TheList")
'   Clear list box if not empty
    If TheList.ListCount <> 0 Then _
        TheList.RemoveItem Index:=1,
Count:=TheList.ListCount
'   Fill the list box
    TheList.AddItem Index:=1, Text:="January"
    TheList.AddItem Index:=2, Text:="February"
    TheList.AddItem Index:=3, Text:="March"
```

```
    TheList.AddItem Index:=4, Text:="April"
    TheList.AddItem Index:=5, Text:="May"
    TheList.AddItem Index:=6, Text:="June"
    TheList.AddItem Index:=7, Text:="July"
    TheList.AddItem Index:=8, Text:="August"
    TheList.AddItem Index:=9, Text:="September"
    TheList.AddItem Index:=10, Text:="October"
    TheList.AddItem Index:=11, Text:="November"
    TheList.AddItem Index:=12, Text:="December"
'   Show the dialog
    ListBoxDlg.Show
End Sub
```

Figure 10-20 shows the dialog box with the list box filled with month names.

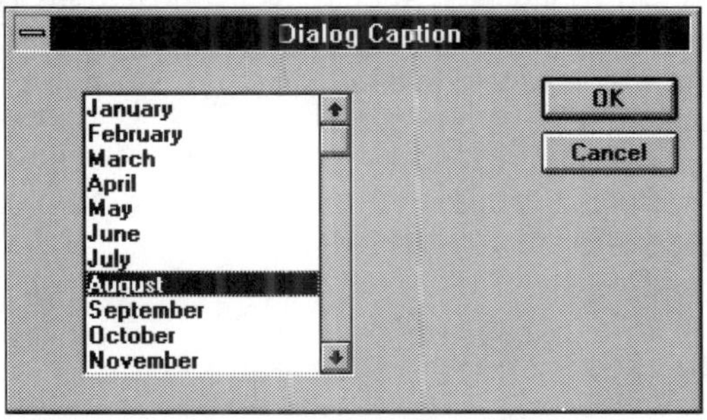

Figure 10-20: A list box filled with month names.

Determining the selected item

The preceding code merely displays a dialog box with a list box filled with month names. The procedure doesn't determine which item was selected.

The following statement accesses the ListIndex property, and displays a message box with the index number of the selected item:

```
MsgBox TheList.ListIndex
```

You also can use the Value property, which returns the selected item's index number:

```
MsgBox TheList.Value
```

If you need to know the text of the selected item, use the List property along with the ListIndex property:

```
MsgBox TheList.List(TheList.ListIndex)
```

Determining multiple selections

If the list box allows multiple selections (that is, its MultiSelect property is either 2 or 3), trying to access the ListIndex, Value, or List properties will generate an error. Instead, you need to use the Selected property, which returns an array. For example, the following statement displays True if the first item in the list is selected:

```
MsgBox TheList.Selected(1)
```

The following code loops through each item in the list box. If the item was selected, it appends the item's text to a variable called *Msg*. Finally, the names of all the selected items are displayed in a message box.

```
Msg = ""
For i = 1 To TheList.ListCount
    If TheList.Selected(i) Then Msg = Msg & TheList.List(i)
& " "
Next i
MsgBox "You selected: " & Msg
```

If you try to use the For Each...Next construct with items in a list box, you'll receive an error message. But there's an easy workaround: set an object variable equal to the list. For example,

```
Set TempList = DialogSheets("MyDialog").ListBoxes("MyList")
For Each element in TempList
'  ... [code goes here] ...
Next element
```

More Dialog Box Examples

The disk that accompanies this book has a file named DBOXDEMO.XLS that contains 16 sample dialog boxes, illustrating a variety of common (and some not-so-common) techniques.

Figure 10-21 shows the opening screen from DBOXDEMO.XLS. Clicking any of the 16 buttons displays a working dialog box. You may be able to adapt these techniques to your own work.

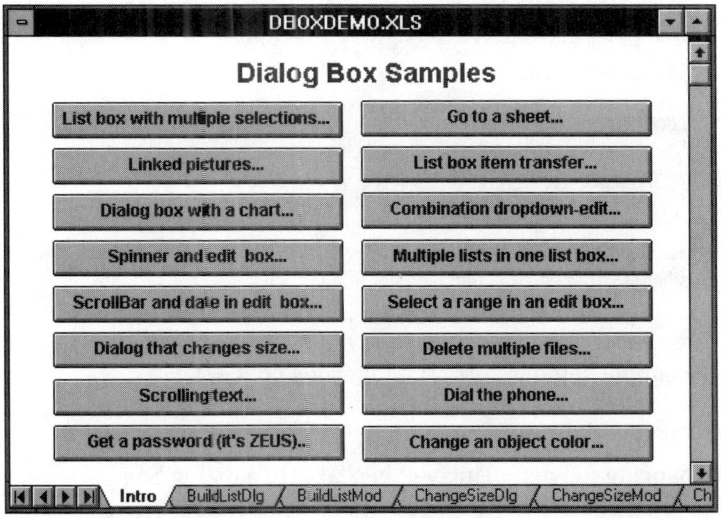

Figure 10-21: DBOXDEMO:XLS contains 16 informative dialog box examples.

The following sections describe the dialog box examples.

List box with multiple selections

This example demonstrates how to set up a list box that allows either a single selection or multiple selections.

When you start, a message box asks which list box style to use. Then it sets up the list box based on your response. When you click OK, a message box displays the selected item or items.

This example uses the following sheets:

- ListBoxDlg (dialog sheet)
- ListBoxMod (VBA module)

Figure 10-22 shows this dialog box in multiple selection mode.

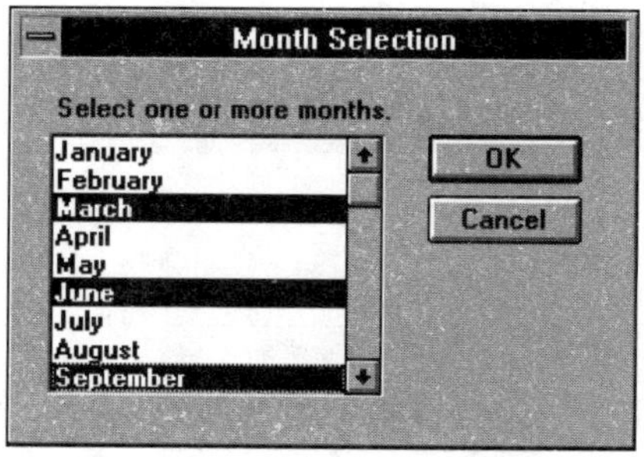

Figure 10-22: This sample demonstrates how to use a list box that allows multiple selections.

This example demonstrates the following concepts:

- Object variables
- Changing the text displayed in a label in a dialog box
- Inserting carriage return characters in a MsgBox function

Linked pictures

This example demonstrates how to use linked pictures in a dialog box.

Linked pictures are created through the Paste Picture Link command, which appears on the Edit menu only when you press Shift.

Figure 10-23 shows a dialog box that displays images of five dice. Each die is a picture linked to a worksheet range. The procedure "rolls" the dice and changes the link formula to display different images. The images were created in a worksheet by using a Wingding font.

The Click Me button is a picture object that I created in a worksheet cell. I then copied the cell and used the Edit⇨Paste Picture command to create the picture.

This example also demonstrates how to change the text in a label. In this case, the label displays the sum of the five dice.

Figure 10-23: The dice are linked pictures of worksheet ranges.

This example uses the following sheets:

- LinkedPicDlg (dialog sheet)
- LinkedPicMod (VBA module)
- LinkedPicSheet (worksheet)

Dialog box with a chart

Figure 10-24 shows a dialog box with a chart object on it. The chart was created in a worksheet and then pasted to the dialog box.

When the dialog box is displayed, the user can use the scroll bar to change the number of data points displayed in the chart (between 1 and 12). Two option buttons determine the type of chart to be displayed. The chart plots random numbers, and the New Data button simply recalculates the worksheet so that the chart uses different values.

This example also demonstrates

- How to modify a chart object by using VBA code
- A method that changes the SERIES formula used in the chart

This example uses the following sheets:

- ChartDlg (dialog sheet)
- ChartMod (VBA module)
- ChartSheet (worksheet)

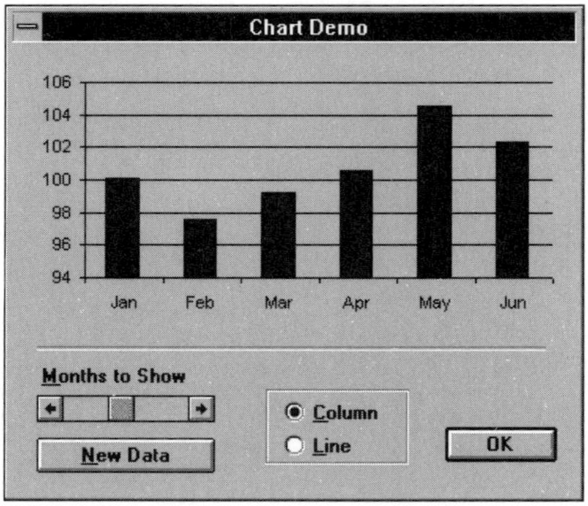

Figure 10-24: Dialog boxes can display charts and allow easy customization.

Spinner and edit box

A spinner control does not display its current value. In most cases, however, you will want the user to see the spinner's value; in some cases, you will want the user to change the spinner's value directly instead of clicking the spinner repeatedly.

This example demonstrates how to link a spinner and an edit box (see Figure 10-25). The edit box displays the spinner's current. In addition, the user can enter a new spinner value into the edit box. Some additional code is included to ensure that the value entered fits into the range of values allowed for the spinner. To test this code, try entering invalid data into the edit box and see how it adjusts automatically. The labels in this dialog box display the current upper and lower limits for the spinner control. If you change the limits, the labels will change.

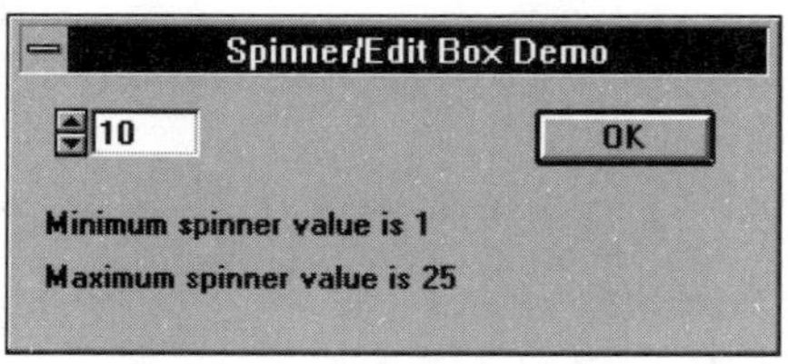

Figure 10-25: Linking a spinner and an edit box.

This example uses the following sheets:

- SpinnerDlg (dialog sheet)
- SpinnerMod (VBA module)

Scroll bar and date in text box

An edit box can display formatted values — in the case shown in Figure 10-26, a date. I used VBA's Format function to display the date in this custom format. Clicking the ends of the scroll bar changes the date by one day. Clicking inside the scroll bar changes the date by a week. In addition, you can drag the scroll bar to change the date displayed.

When the dialog box is displayed, it shows the current date (clicking the Today button also resets the display to the current date). A scroll bar can have values from 0 to 30,000. I assigned the current date to the mid-point (15,000). Therefore, the dialog box can display the current date plus or minus 15,000 days. If you're younger than 15,000 days old, you can use this example to determine on which day of the week you were born.

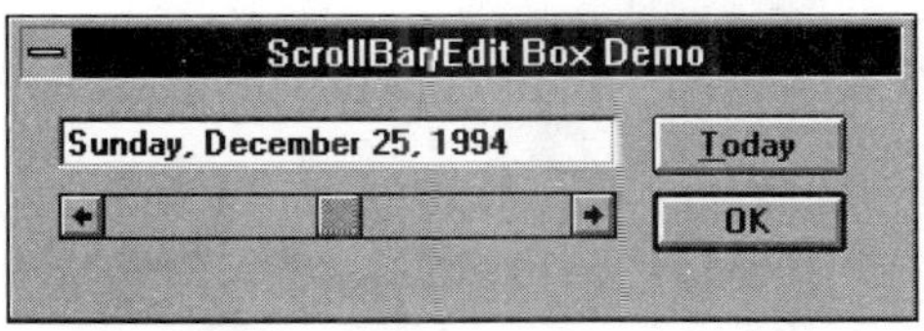

Figure 10-26: A scroll bar linked to an edit box.

This example uses the following sheets:

- ScrollerDlg (dialog sheet)
- ScrollerMod (VBA module)

Dialog that changes size

Many applications use dialog boxes that change their size. For example, Excel's Record New Macro dialog box increases its height when the user clicks the Options button.

This example demonstrates how to get a custom dialog box to change its size: changing a dialog box's size is done by altering the Width or Height property of the DialogFrame object.

Figure 10-27 shows the dialog box as it is first displayed, and Figure 10-28 shows it after the Options button is clicked.

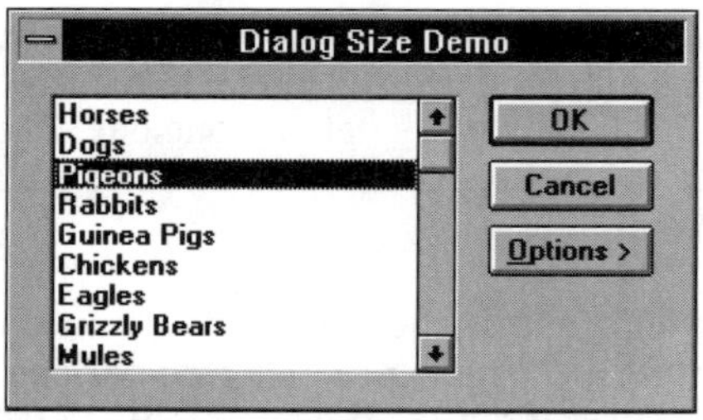

Figure 10-27: A sample dialog box in its standard mode.

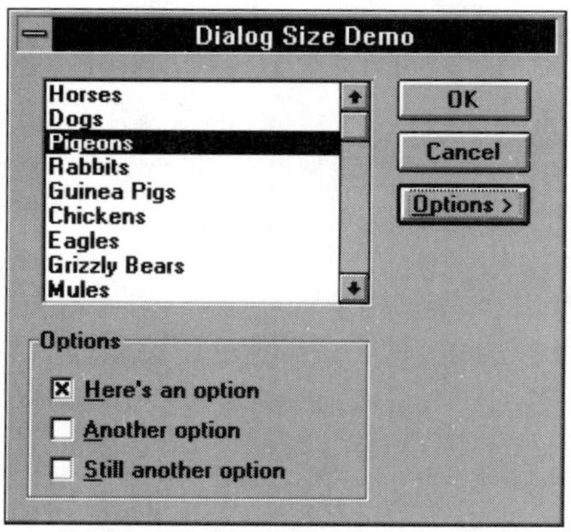

Figure 10-28: The same dialog box enlarged.

This example uses the following sheets:

- ChangeSizeDlg (dialog sheet)
- ChangeSizeMod (VBA module)

Scrolling text

Like the example in Figure 10-23, the dialog box shown in Figure 10-29 also uses a linked picture. In this case, the picture shows a worksheet range. When the user uses the scroll bar to scroll the text up or down, the link formula is changed for the picture object.

This example shows a relatively easy way to provide help text for an application. (By the way, the text displayed in this sample is something I discovered on the Internet.)

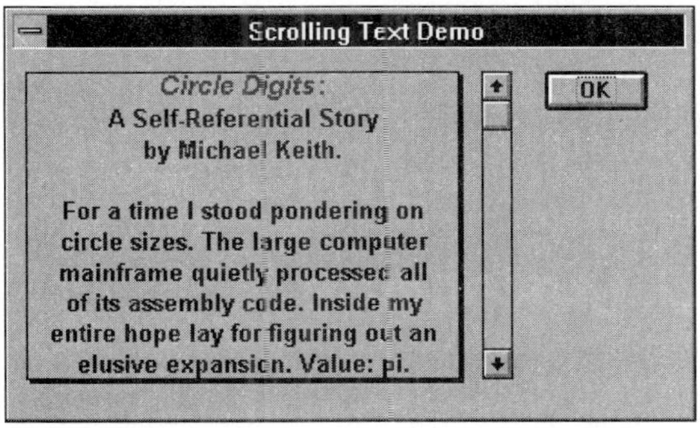

Figure 10-29: Displaying text by using a linked picture.

This example uses the following sheets:

- ScrollTextDlg (dialog sheet)
- ScrollTextMod (VBA module)
- ScrollTextSheet (worksheet)

Get a password

Sometimes you may want to limit access to your applications; one way of doing so is to require a password. Although Excel has password protection features, you may want to add your own security check.

The only problem: how to hide the text that's entered by the users. The example in Figure 10-30 demonstrates a trick, where every keystroke generates an asterisk. This sleight of hand works when you use an almost hidden edit box to receive the characters and then you write some VBA code to place asterisks in an exposed edit box. The users see their keystrokes produce asterisks.

This dialog box also demonstrates how to change the focus in a dialog box. The focus is the control that is currently receiving input from the user.

Figure 10-30: Entering text in the edit box displays asterisks.

If you use a technique like this, make sure that you take precautions to prevent the user from examining your code to discover the password.

This example uses the following sheets:

- PasswordDlg (dialog sheet)
- PasswordtMod (VBA module)

Go To a sheet

Figure 10-31 shows a dialog box that lists all the sheets in the active workbook. Select a sheet name and click the Go To button to activate the selected sheet. Because the Go To button is the default button in the dialog box, you can just double-click the sheet name to activate the sheet. An added feature displays the type of sheet as a label below the list box.

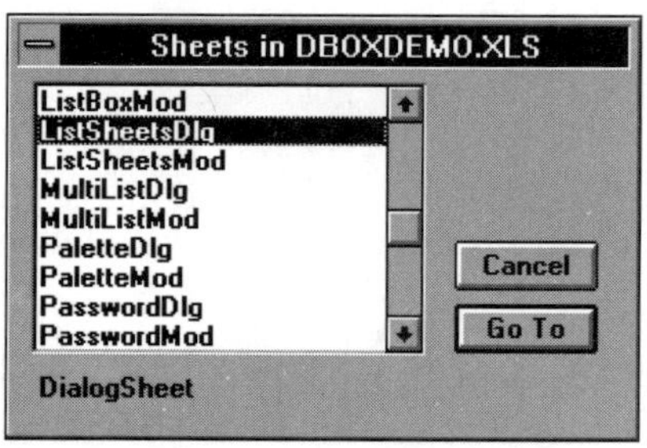

Figure 10-31: Displaying all sheet names in a list box.

This example uses the following sheets:

- ListSheetsDlg (dialog sheet)
- ListSheetsMod (VBA module)

TIP: This example is useful if you want to examine a particular dialog sheet or module in the DBOXDMO.XLS workbook.

List box item transfer

Some applications require a user to select several items from a list. It's often useful to create a new list of the selected items. (For an example of this situation, check out the dialog box that appears when you choose the Tools⇨Attach Toolbars command in a VBA module.)

Figure 10-32 shows a dialog box with two lists. Notice that the Add button is enabled only when an item is selected from the list on the left. The Delete button is enabled only when an item is selected from the list on the right.

A check box determines the behavior when a duplicate item is added to the list. If Allow Duplicates is not checked, a message box appears if the user attempts to add an item that's already on the list.

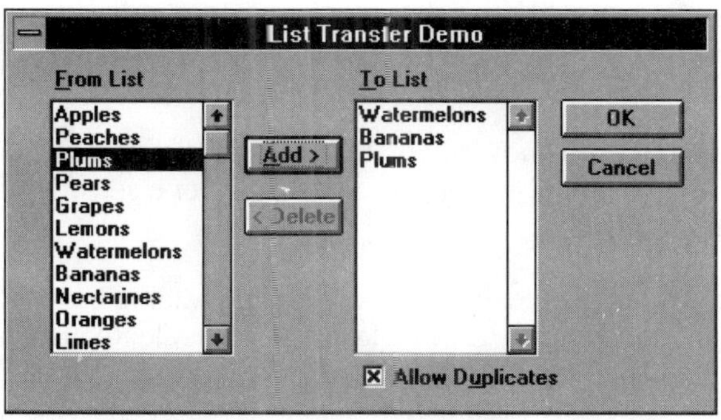

Figure 10-32: Building a list from another list.

This example uses the following sheets:

- BuildListDlg (dialog sheet)
- BuildListMod (VBA module)

Combination drop-down edit box

Figure 10-33 shows a combination drop-down edit control used in a dialog box. This control allows the user to enter text that's not in the drop-down list. When the dialog box is exited, a message box displays the appropriate text.

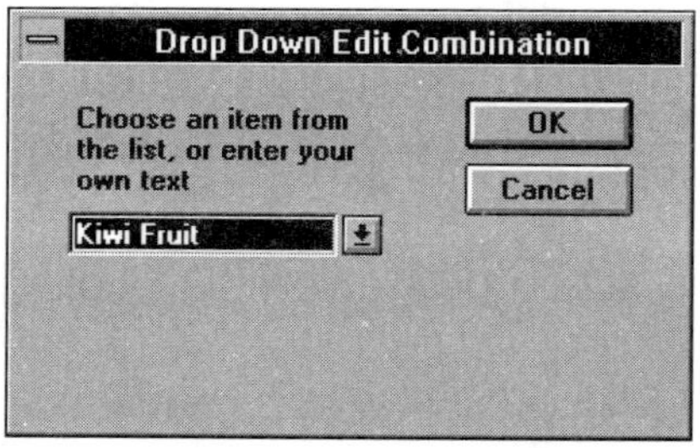

Figure 10-33: Using a combination drop-down edit control.

This example uses the following sheets:

- ComboDlg (dialog sheet)
- ComboMod (VBA module)

Multiple lists in a list box

This example demonstrates how to create a *dynamic* list box — that is, the contents of the list box changes depending on the user's selection from a group of option buttons.

Figure 10-34 shows the sample dialog box. When the dialog box is dismissed with the OK button, a message box displays the item selected for each option.

This example uses the following sheets:

- MultiListDlg (dialog sheet)
- MultiListMod (VBA module)

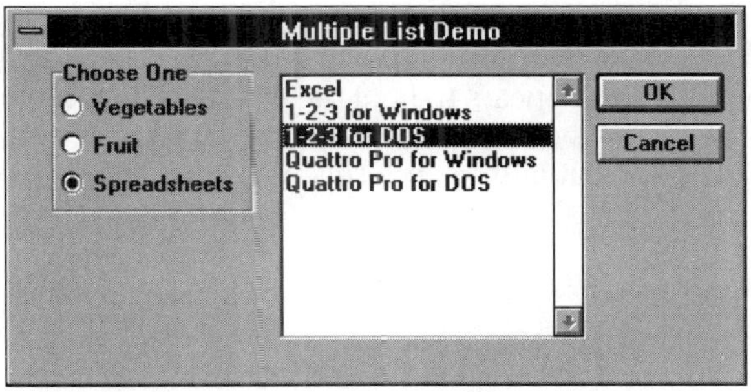

Figure 10-34: A dynamic list box.

Select a range in an edit box

Edit boxes can accept several different types of information. Figure 10-35 shows an edit box designed to accept a range. When the edit box is activated, the user can choose a range by dragging in the worksheet.

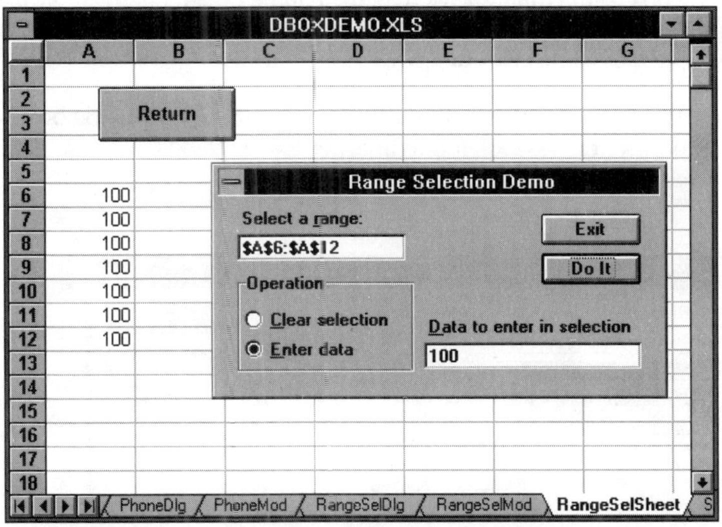

Figure 10-35: Using an edit box to select a worksheet range.

The option buttons determine what happens with the selected range: the range can be cleared or data can be entered into it. When the Enter data option is selected, another edit box appears to hold the data that the user wants to enter into the range selection. When the Clear selection option is selected, the data edit box is hidden. The Do It button performs the action but does not dismiss the edit box.

This example uses the following sheets:

- RangeSelDlg (dialog sheet)
- RangeSelMod (VBA module)
- RangeSelSheet (worksheet)

Delete multiple files

This example demonstrates how to use a Windows API call to display a common dialog box — in this case, a file dialog that lets you choose files that you want to delete from your disk.

You may recall that you can use the GetOpenFilename method to display a file dialog box. Unfortunately, GetOpenFilename doesn't allow multiple selections. Using a common dialog box gets around this limitation and lets the user select multiple files to be erased.

Figure 10-36 shows the dialog box. Unfortunately, this dialog box doesn't incorporate the 3-D look found in other Excel dialogs.

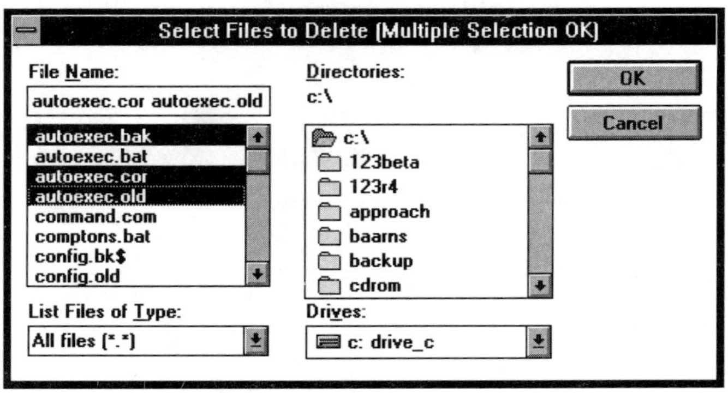

Figure 10-36: This dialog box, which was called from a DLL, lets the user select multiple files to be erased.

This example uses the DelFilesMod (VBA module) sheet.

Dial the phone

This example lets the user enter a phone number and then dials the number (see Figure 10-37). To test this example, you need a modem.

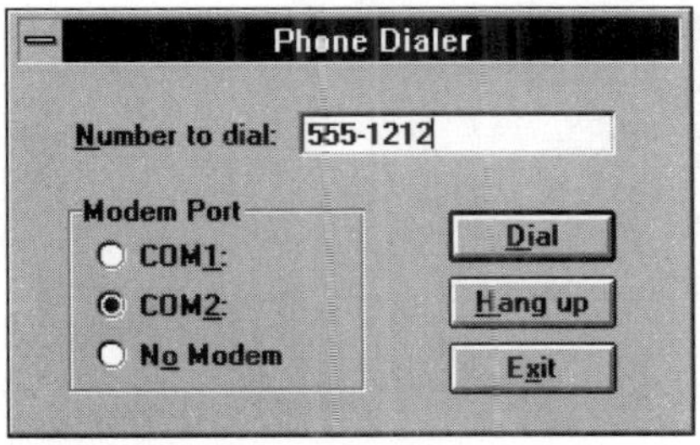

Figure 10-37: A dialog box that accepts a phone number. The accompanying code dials the number.

This example uses the following sheets:

- PhoneDlg (dialog sheet)
- PhoneMod (VBA module)

Change an object's color

The final example demonstrates how to dynamically change an object's color.

Figure 10-38 shows a dialog box containing a picture object and a list box. The list box contains 56 entries — one for each color in Excel's color palette. Selecting a color changes the picture's color and also displays the RGB color in the edit boxes below. The edit boxes are disabled.

This example uses the following sheets:

- PaletteDlg (dialog sheet)
- PaletteMod (VBA module)

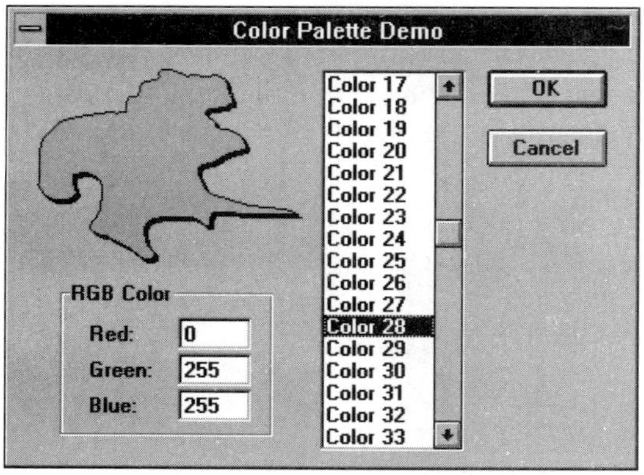

Figure 10-38: Changing an object's color.

A dialog box checklist

Before you unleash a custom dialog box on end users, be sure that everything is working correctly. The following checklist should help you identify potential problems.

- Are the controls aligned with each other?
- Are similar controls the same size?
- Can every control be accessed with a hot key?
- Is the tab order set correctly?
- Will VBA code take appropriate action if the dialog box is canceled or the user presses Esc?
- Are there any misspellings in the text?
- Does the dialog box have an appropriate caption?
- Will the dialog box display properly at all video resolutions?
- Are the controls grouped logically (by function)?
- Do all edit boxes have the appropriate validation setting?
- Do scroll bars and spinner controls allow valid values only?
- Are list boxes set properly (Single, Multi, or Extend)?
- Is the help topic correct? And does it explain all the controls?

Summary

- In this chapter, I introduced you to custom dialog boxes. And I presented many examples, illustrating how to create custom dialog boxes and use them with VBA.
- In the next chapter, I offer many more examples of VBA procedures and dialog boxes.

Chapter 11

VBA Programming Examples and Techniques

In This Chapter

- Examples of VBA subroutines and functions
- Examples of everyday VBA techniques
- Examples of uncommon but useful VBA tricks and techniques

I believe that all learning is accelerated by a heavy emphasis on examples. But VBA programmers especially benefit from a hands-on approach; a well-thought-out example usually communicates a concept much better than a description of the underlying theory. I decided, therefore, not to write a reference book; I chose not to painstakingly describe every nuance of VBA. Rather, I prepared numerous examples to better demonstrate important techniques.

The previous chapters in this section provide enough information to get you started. And, the on-line help system provides the details I left out. In this chapter, I pick up the pace and present examples that solve practical problems while furthering your knowledge of VBA.

I've categorized the examples in this chapter into four groups:

- Working with ranges
- VBA techniques
- Windows API calls
- Miscellaneous techniques

DISK

These examples are not stand-alone programs, although they are set up as executable subroutines that you can adapt for your own applications. Most of these examples are on the disk that accompanies this book.

I urge you to follow along on your computer as you read this chapter (in fact, feel free to modify the examples and see what happens). I guarantee that this hands-on experience will help more than reading a reference book.

Working with Ranges

The examples in this section demonstrate how to manipulate worksheet ranges with VBA.

Copying a range

Excel's macro recorder is a useful tool — not so much for generating usable code, but for discovering the names of relevant objects, methods, and procedures. The code that's generated by the macro recorder, however, isn't always the most efficient possible.

For example, recording a simple copy-and-paste operation generates five lines of VBA code:

```
Sub Macro1()
    Range("A1").Select
    Selection.Copy
    Range("B1").Select
    ActiveSheet.Paste
    Application.CutCopyMode = False
End Sub
```

But in VBA, you do not have to select an object to work with it. You would never learn this important point by mimicking the preceding recorded macro code, where two lines incorporate the Select method. This subroutine, in fact, can be replaced with a much simpler routine:

```
Sub Macro1()
    Range("A1").Copy(Range("B1"))
End Sub
```

Both of these macros assume that a worksheet is active and the operation takes place on the active worksheet.

Prompting for a cell value

If you want your routine to ask the user for a value that's in turn inserted into a cell, use the InputBox function because it returns the user's entry.

The following subroutine demonstrates how to solicit the user for a value and insert it into cell A1 of the active worksheet:

```
Sub GetValue()
    Range("A1").Value = InputBox("Enter the value")
End Sub
```

Selecting to the end of a range

VBA newcomers (especially former 1-2-3 users) often are surprised how keystroke combinations such as Ctrl+Shift+Right Arrow and Ctrl+Shift+Down Arrow are recorded by the macro recorder. When used in a worksheet, these key combinations extend the selected range to the right or down. When recorded in a macro, the address of the actual range selected is what gets recorded into the macro.

Well, you can't *record* a macro that simulates these key combinations, but you can *write* one. The trick is to use the End method of the range object. The End method takes one argument, which determines the direction.

DISK

The example in Listing 11-1 can be found in the file DEMO_01.XLS on the disk that accompanies this book. When the sheet is open, you can execute the subroutine by choosing the Tools⇨Select to End command.

This command selects a range beginning with the active cell and extending to the last filled cell in the column or the first empty cell in the column. Pressing Shift while you execute the command extends the selection to the right.

Listing 11-1 **DEMO_01.XLS**

```
Declare Function GetKeyState Lib "USER" (ByVal nVirtKey As _
    Integer) As Integer

Sub SelectToEnd()
    Const SHIFTKEY = 16
    Select Case GetKeyState(SHIFTKEY)
        Case Is < 0 'Shift key down
            Range(ActiveCell, ActiveCell.End(xlToRight))
            .Select Case Else 'Shift key not down
            Range(ActiveCell, ActiveCell.End(xlDown)).Select
    End Select
End Sub
```

This procedure uses a Windows API function, GetKeyState, to determine whether the Shift key is pressed (I discuss GetKeyState later in this chapter). If Shift is pressed, the routine simulates Ctrl+Right Arrow. Otherwise, it simulates pressing Ctrl+Down Arrow.

As you may expect, there are two other constants to simulate key combinations in the other directions: xlToLeft and xlUp.

Enter an AutoSum-like formula

When you click the AutoSum toolbar button, Excel analyzes the context of the active cell and attempts to determine which cells you want to sum in your formula.

Listing 11-2 enters a formula that averages the contents of the cells above the active cell. The code, which inserts a formula that uses Excel's AVERAGE function, only works when there are at least two cells directly above the active cell. Like the preceding example, this example uses the End method to determine the range to use for the AVERAGE function's argument.

DISK

This example can be found in DEMO_02.XLS. When this sheet is open, you can execute the subroutine with the Tools⇨Enter Average Formula command.

Listing 11-2 **DEMO_02.XLS file**

```
Sub EnterAvg()
'   Check for invalid conditions
    If TypeName(Selection) <> "Range" Then Exit Sub
    If ActiveCell.Row = 1 Then Exit Sub
    If ActiveCell.Offset(-1, 0).Value = "" Then Exit Sub
    If ActiveCell.Offset(-2, 0).Value = "" Then Exit Sub

'   Determine address of first and last cell in the range
    FirstCell = ActiveCell.Offset(-1, 0).End(xlUp).Address _
        (rowabsolute:=False, columnabsolute:=False)
    LastCell = ActiveCell.Offset(-1, 0).Address( _
        rowabsolute:=False, columnabsolute:=False)

'   Build the formula
    TheFormula = "=AVERAGE(" & FirstCell & ":" & LastCell & ")"

'   Assign the formula
    ActiveCell.Formula = TheFormula
End Sub
```

The formula is constructed as a string; the ampersand is the concatenation operator.

NOTE

Although the formula is constructed by using the A1 reference style, the routine will work correctly if the user uses the R1C1 reference style: Excel converts the formula automatically before inserting it into the cell.

Looping through a selected range efficiently

A common task is to create a macro that evaluates each cell in a range and performs an operation if the cell meets a certain criterion.

In Listing 11-3, which applies red text color to all cells in the selection that have a negative value, I create such a macro.

DISK

This example can be found in DEMO_03.XLS. When this sheet is open, you can execute the subroutine with the Tools⇨Color Negative Values command.

Listing 11-3 DEMO_03.XLS file

```
Sub SelectiveColor()
'   Makes each cell in the selection Red if it's negative

    Dim FormulaCells As Object
    Dim ConstantCells As Object

    Const REDINDEX = 3

'   Ignore errors
    On Error Resume Next

    Application.ScreenUpdating = False

'   Create subsets of original selection
    Set FormulaCells = Selection.SpecialCells(xlFormulas, _
    xlNumbers)
    Set ConstantCells = Selection.SpecialCells(xlConstants, _
    xlNumbers)

'   Process the formula cells
    For Each Cell In FormulaCells
        If Cell.Value < 0 Then Cell.Font.ColorIndex = _
        REDINDEX
```

(continued)

Listing 11-3 ***(continued)***

```
        Next Cell

'       Process the constant cells
        For Each Cell In ConstantCells
            If Cell.Value < 0 Then Cell.Font.ColorIndex = _
            REDINDEX
        Next Cell
    End Sub
```

This code performs some extra steps, which involve the SpecialCells method, because looping through the selection can take a very long time. For example, what if the selection consists of an entire column? Or 10 columns? Or the entire worksheet? The user would probably give up before all the cells were evaluated. Therefore I used the SelectSpecial method to generate two subsets of the selection: one subset includes only the cells with numeric constants, the other subset includes only the cells with numeric formulas. Then I processed the cells in these subsets by using two For Each...Next constructs. The net effect: Only nonblank cells are evaluated, speeding up the macro considerably.

NOTE

The On Error statement is necessary because the SpecialCells method generates an error if no cells qualify. This statement also handles situations in which a range is not selected when the subroutine is executed.

I set the ScreenUpdating property to False (the screen is not updated each time it changes) to speed up the macro. When the routine ends, ScreenUpdating is automatically set back to True.

Deleting empty rows

Listing 11-4 deletes all empty rows in the current selection. The selection can consist of any valid Excel selection, including columns, noncontiguous ranges, or even the entire worksheet.

DISK

This example can be found in DEMO_04.XLS. When this sheet is open, you can execute the subroutine with the Tools⇨Delete Empty Rows command.

Listing 11-4 **DEMO_04.XLS file**

```
Sub DeleteEmptyRows()
    Dim NewSel As Object, area As Object, row As Object
    Dim LastRow As Integer, LastCol As Integer

    Set NewSel = Selection

'   Exit if a range is not selected
    If TypeName(Selection) <> "Range" Then Exit Sub

'   If entire column is selected, use a subset
'   consisting of A1 thru last used cell
    If Selection.Rows.Count Mod 16384 = 0 Then

        LastRow = Selection.SpecialCells(xlLastCell).Row
        LastCol = Selection.SpecialCells(xlLastCell).Column
Set NewSel = Range(Cells(1, 1), Cells(LastRow, LastCol))
    End If

    Application.ScreenUpdating = False

'   Check each area (for noncontiguous selection)
    For Each area In NewSel.Areas
        For Each row In area.Rows
'       Check each row, delete if empty
            If Application.CountA(row.EntireRow) = 0 Then _
                row.EntireRow.Delete
            End If
        Next row
    Next area
End Sub
```

This routine starts by assigning the selection to a new object, NewSel. As a result, the original selection remains intact.

Then the routine determines whether one or more columns is selected. It does this by using the Mod operator. If the remainder of the the total number of cells divided by 16,384 equals 0, one or more complete columns is selected. If so, the routine uses the SpecialCells method to determine the last used cell in the worksheet. This step limits the processing to just the active area (that is, cell A1 through the last used cell); processing all 16,384 rows would take too long.

Because this routine also can work with a noncontiguous selection of cells, the code must step through each area of the selection — witness the two nested For Each...Next constructs. The code uses Excel's COUNTA function to count the number of nonblank cells in each row in NewSel. If COUNTA returns zero, the row is deleted.

Filling a range with values

Many spreadsheet tasks involve filling a range of cells. Listing 11-5 illustrates the most obvious way to do so: loop through each cell in the range and insert its value. This routine also includes code to compute the elapsed time.

DISK

The examples in this section can be found in DEMO_05.XLS. When this sheet is open, you can execute the subroutines with the Tools⇨Loop-Fill Range command and the Tools⇨Array-Fill Range command.

Listing 11-5 DEMO_05.XLS file

```
Sub LoopFillRange()
'   Fill a range by looping through cells

    Dim CurrRow As Integer, CurrCol As Integer, CurrVal As _
        Integer

'   Get the dimensions
    CellsDown = Val(InputBox("How many cells down?"))
    CellsAcross = Val(InputBox("How many cells across?"))

'   Record starting time
    StartTime = Timer

'   Loop through cells and insert values
    CurrVal = 1
    Application.ScreenUpdating = False
    For CurrRow = 1 To CellsDown
        For CurrCol = 1 To CellsAcross
            ActiveCell.Offset(CurrRow - 1, _
            CurrCol - 1).Value = CurrVal
            CurrVal = CurrVal + 1
        Next CurrCol
    Next CurrRow

'   Display elapsed time
    Application.ScreenUpdating = True
    MsgBox Format(Timer - StartTime, "00.00") & " seconds"
End Sub
```

The following example demonstrates another way to produce the same result by inserting the values into an array and then transferring the contents of an array to the range:

```
Sub ArrayFillRange()
'   Fill a range by transferring an array

    Dim TempArray() As Integer
    Dim TheRange As Object

'   Get the dimensions
    CellsDown = Val(InputBox("How many cells down?"))
    CellsAcross = Val(InputBox("How many cells across?"))

'   Record starting time
    StartTime = Timer

'   Redimension temporary array
    ReDim TempArray(1 To CellsDown, 1 To CellsAcross)

'   Set worksheet range
    Set TheRange = ActiveCell.Range(Cells(1, 1), _
        Cells(CellsDown, CellsAcross))

'   Fill the temporary array
    CurrVal = 0
    Application.ScreenUpdating = False
    For i = 1 To CellsDown
        For j = 1 To CellsAcross
            TempArray(i, j) = CurrVal + 1
            CurrVal = CurrVal + 1
        Next j
    Next i

'   Transfer temporary array to worksheet
    TheRange.Value = TempArray

'   Display elapsed time
    Application.ScreenUpdating = True
    MsgBox Format(Timer - StartTime, "00.00") & " seconds"
End Sub
```

NOTE

There's a limit to the size of the array that can be transferred to a range (about 6500 elements). If you get the *Unable to set the Value property of the Range class* message, you've reached the limit.

On my system, filling a 60 x 60 cell range (3,600 cells) took 36.47 seconds, using the loop method. The array transfer method took about half the time (18.59 seconds) to generate the same results.

Determining the type of range selection

There are many types of range selections. A range selection may be a single cell, a contiguous range of cells, an entire column, a column and a row, the entire worksheet, or dozens of other combinations. As a result, when your routine processes the selected range, you shouldn't make any assumptions about the range selected.

In the case of a multiple selection (to make a multiple selection, press Ctrl as you select ranges), the range object is made up of areas, and you must often process each area separately. The Areas collection is a collection of all the areas in a range object. The Areas method returns an Area object.

The example in this section identifies the range selection and displays the results in a message box (see Figure 11-1). Understanding how this routine works will give you a good foundation for working with range objects.

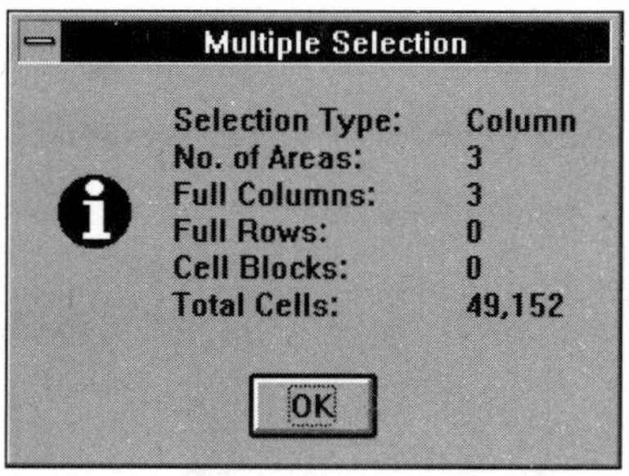

Figure 11-1: The AboutRangeSelection routine analyzes the current range selection and reports its findings.

DISK

This example can be found in DEMO_06.XLS. When this sheet is open, you can execute the subroutine with the Tools⇨About the Selected Range command.

The AboutRangeSelection subroutine uses the following custom function, AreaType:

```
Function AreaType(RangeArea As Object) As String
'   Returns the type of a range in an area
    If RangeArea.Count = 4194304 Then
        AreaType = "Worksheet"
        ElseIf RangeArea.Rows.Count = 16384 Then
            AreaType = "Column"
            ElseIf RangeArea.Columns.Count = 256 Then
                AreaType = "Row"
                Else AreaType = "Range"
    End If
End Function
```

This function accepts an area of a range object as its argument and returns one of four strings that describe the area: *Worksheet*, *Column*, *Row*, *Block*. The function works by counting the number of elements in the area. For example, if the area has 16384 rows, AreaType returns *Column*.

The AboutRangeSelection routine starts by ensuring that the selection is a range. If not, it makes a quick exit. If a range is selected, the routine initializes the counter variables that store the statistics, and it determines the number of areas in the selection.

As I developed this routine, I was surprised to find that Excel allows multiple selections to be identical. (For example, if you hold down Ctrl and click five times in cell A1, the selection will have five identical areas.) The tricky part about writing this routine was to avoid counting cells, rows, or columns more than once when a multiple selection consists of the same area selected more than once. So I used the Union function to create an object (UnionRange) comprising the union of all the areas. Then the routine analyzes the statistics by using the UnionRange object. Finally, the message is displayed (MsgBox function). I used Chr(13) to insert a carriage return to make the subsequent text appear on a new line.

The AboutRangeSelection routine is shown in Listing 11-6.

Listing 11-6 AboutRangeSelection routine.

```
Sub AboutRangeSelection()
    Dim Area As Object

'   Quit if a range is not selected
    If TypeName(Selection) <> "Range" Then Exit Sub
```

(continued)

Listing 11-6 *(continued)*

```
'   Initialize counters
    NumCols = 0
    NumRows = 0
    NumBlocks = 0
    NumCells = 0

'   Determine number of areas in selection
    NumAreas = Selection.Areas.Count
    If NumAreas = 1 Then
        SelType = "Single Selection"
            Else SelType = "Multiple Selection"
    End If

    FirstAreaType = AreaType(Selection.Areas(1))
    WhatSelected = FirstAreaType

'   Build the union of all areas
'   to avoid double-counting overlaps
    Set UnionRange = Selection.Areas(1)
    For Each Area In Selection.Areas
    CurrentType = AreaType(Area)
'   Count blocks before they're combined in the union
    If CurrentType = "Block" Then NumBlocks = NumBlocks + 1
    Set UnionRange = Union(UnionRange, Area)
'   Change label if multiple selection is "mixed"
If CurrentType <> FirstAreaType Then WhatSelected = "Mixed"
    Next Area

'   Loop through each area in the Union range
    For Each Area In UnionRange.Areas
        Select Case AreaType(Area)
            Case "Row"
                NumRows = NumRows + Area.Rows.Count
            Case "Column"
                NumCols = NumCols + Area.Columns.Count
            Case "Worksheet"
                NumCols = NumCols + Area.Columns.Count
                NumRows = NumRows + Area.Rows.Count
            Case "Block"
'             Blocks already counted in original selection above
        End Select
     Next Area
```

```
'   Count number of non-overlapping cells
    NumCells = UnionRange.Count

Msg = "Selection Type:" & Chr(9) & WhatSelected & _ Chr(13)
Msg = Msg & "No. of Areas:" & Chr(9) & NumAreas & _ Chr(13)
Msg = Msg & "Full Columns: " & Chr(9) & NumCols & _ Chr(13)
Msg = Msg & "Full Rows: " & Chr(9) & NumRows & Chr(13)
Msg = Msg & "Cell Blocks:" & Chr(9) & NumBlocks & _ Chr(13)
Msg = Msg & "Total Cells: " & Chr(9) & Format(NumCells, "#,###")
    MsgBox Msg, vbInformation, SelType
End Sub
```

VBA Techniques

The examples in this section illustrate common VBA techniques.

Toggling a Boolean property

The easiest way to toggle a Boolean property is to use the Not operator, as shown in the following example, which toggles the WrapText property of a selection.

This example can be found in DEMO_07.XLS. When this sheet is open, you can execute the subroutine with the Tools⇨Toggle Wrap Text command.

```
Sub ToggleWrapText()
'   Toggles text wrap alignment for selected cells
    If TypeName(Selection) <> "Range" Then Exit Sub
    Selection.WrapText = Not ActiveCell.WrapText
End Sub
```

Note that the active cell is the basis for toggling. When a range is selected and some cells hold a certain Boolean property (for example, bold), it is considered *mixed*, and Excel uses the active cell to determine how to toggle. If the active cell is bold, for example, everything in the selection is made unbold when you click the Bold toolbar button.

Notice also that this preceding subroutine uses the TypeName function to check whether the selection is a range. If not, it makes a quick exit.

You can use the Not operator to toggle many other properties. For example, to toggle the display of row and column borders in a worksheet, use the following code:

```
ActiveWindow.DisplayHeadings = Not
ActiveWindow.DisplayHeadings
```

To toggle the display of gridlines in the active worksheet, use the following code:

```
ActiveWindow.DisplayGridlines = Not
ActiveWindow.DisplayGridlines
```

Displaying the date and time

If you understand the serial number system that Excel uses to store dates and times, you won't have any problems using dates and times in your procedures.

Listing 11-7 displays a message box with the current date and time displayed. This example also displays a personalized message in the message box's title bar (see Figure 11-2).

This example can be found in DEMO_08.XLS. When this sheet is open, you can execute the subroutine with the Tools⇨Show Date and Time command.

Listing 11-7 **DEMO_08.XLS file**

```
Sub DateAndTime()
'   Displays the current date and time

    TheDate = Format(Date, "Long Date")
    TheTime = Format(Time, "Medium Time")

'   Determine greeting based on time
    Select Case Time
        Case Is < 0.5:     Greeting = "Good Morning, "
        Case Is >= 0.7083: Greeting = "Good Evening, "
        Case Else:         Greeting = "Good Afternoon, "
    End Select
```

```
'   Append user's first name to greeting
    FullName = Application.UserName
    SpaceInName = Application.Find(" ", FullName, 1)

'   Handle situation when name has no space
        If Application.IsErr(SpaceInName) Then SpaceInName = _
        Len(FullName)
    FirstName = Left(FullName, SpaceInName)
    Greeting = Greeting & FirstName

'   Show the message
    MsgBox TheDate & Chr(13) & TheTime, vbOKOnly, Greeting
End Sub
```

Figure 11-2: A message box displaying the current date and time.

This subroutine uses the Date function as an argument to the Format function. The result is a string with a nicely formatted date. I used the same technique to get a nicely formatted time.

In the preceding example, I used named formats ("Long Date" and "Medium Time"), but you can use other formats. For example, to display the date in mm/dd/yy format, you can use a statement like the following:

```
TheDate = Format(Date, "mm/dd/yy")
```

I used a Select Case construct to base the greeting displayed in the message box's title bar on the time of day. VBA time values work just like they do in Excel. If the time is less than .5 (noon), it's morning. If it's greater than .7083 (5 p.m.), it's evening. Otherwise, it's afternoon.

The next series of statements determines the user's first name, as determined by the information in the user's EXCEL5.INI file (and displayed in the General tab in the Options dialog box).

NOTE

I used Excel's FIND function to determine the first space in the user's name as an error check. When I first wrote this subroutine, I didn't consider how Excel would react to a user name that has no space. And when I ran this procedure on a machine with a user's name of *Nobody*, the code failed. Just goes to show you, I can't think of everything, and even the simplest procedures can run aground. (By the way, if the user's name is left blank, Excel always substitutes the name *User*.)

The MsgBox function concatenates the date and time but puts a Chr(13) — a carriage return — between them. vbOKOnly is a predefined constant that returns 0, causing the message box to appear with only an OK button. The final argument is the Greeting, constructed earlier.

Sorting an array

Although Excel has a built-in command to sort worksheet ranges, VBA doesn't offer a method to sort arrays. One viable but slow workaround is to transfer your array to a worksheet range, sort it by using Excel's commands, and then return the result to your array. But if speed is essential, it's better to write a sorting routine in VBA. The examples in this section demonstrate both methods.

DISK

These examples can be found in DEMO_09.XLS. The file includes a routine that demonstrates three different sorting techniques. You can use the these sorting subroutines with your own work.

The following example demonstrates how to transfer an array to a worksheet range, sort it, and transfer it back to the array. This subroutine accepts an array as its only argument.

```
Sub WorksheetSort(List() as Integer)
'   Sorts an array by transferring it to
'   A worksheet and using Excel's sorting command

    Dim First As Integer, Last As Integer
    Dim i As Integer
    Dim FirstCell As Object, CurrCell As Object
    Set FirstCell = Sheets("Sheet1").Range("A1")

    First = LBound(List)
    Last = UBound(List)
    Application.ScreenUpdating = False

'   Transfer array to worksheet
    For i = First To Last
        FirstCell.Offset(i - 1, 0).Value = List(i)
    Next i
```

```
'   Sort the worksheet range
    FirstCell.CurrentRegion.Sort _
        Key1:=FirstCell, _
        Order1:=xlAscending, _
        Orientation:=xlTopToBottom

'   Transfer range back to the array and clear range
    For i = First To Last
        Set CurrCell = FirstCell.Offset(i - 1, 0)
        List(i) = CurrCell.Value
        CurrCell.Clear
    Next i
End Sub
```

The WorksheetSort routine is limited to arrays with no more than 16,384 elements — the number of rows in a worksheet.

The following VBA routine, a simple bubble sort routine (also used in the Chapter 8 sheet sorting example), also sorts the array:

```
Sub BubbleSort(List() As Integer)
'   Sorts an array using bubble sort algorithm

    Dim First As Integer, Last As Integer
    Dim i As Integer, j As Integer
    Dim Temp As Integer

    First = LBound(List)
    Last = UBound(List)
    For i = First To Last - 1
        For j = i + 1 To Last
            If List(i) > List(j) Then
                Temp = List(j)
                List(j) = List(i)
                List(i) = Temp
            End If
        Next j
    Next i
End Sub
```

DISK

Although easy to program, the bubble sorting algorithm is not the fastest sorting technique. The *quick sort* algorithm is much faster, but it is also more difficult to understand. The DEMO_09.XLS file also includes a subroutine called QuickSort (not listed here) that is extremely fast.

I developed the following routine, which is in DEMO_09.XLS, to compare these three sorting techniques. To execute this procedure, choose the Tools➪Compare Sort Procedures command. This procedure prompts the user for the number of elements in the array, performs the sorting using all three methods, and displays the elapsed time for each method:

```
Sub DoThreeSorts()
'   Sorts an array using three different techniques

    Dim Array1() As Integer
    Dim Array2() As Integer
    Dim Array3() As Integer
    Dim i As Integer
    Dim Elements As Integer

    Elements = Val(InputBox("Number of array elements?"))
    If Elements = False Then Exit Sub
    ReDim Array1(1 To Elements)
    ReDim Array2(1 To Elements)
    ReDim Array3(1 To Elements)

'   Build three identical arrays
    For i = 1 To Elements
        Array1(i) = Int(Rnd * 1000)
        Array2(i) = Array1(i)
        Array3(i) = Array1(i)
    Next i

'   Do worksheet sort and save times
    Time1 = Timer
    Application.StatusBar = "Performing Worksheet Sort..."
    Call WorksheetSort(Array1)
    Time2 = Timer

'   Do VBA Bubble Sort and save times
    Time3 = Timer
    Application.StatusBar = "Performing VBA Bubble Sort..."
    Call BubbleSort(Array2)
    Time4 = Timer

'   Do VBA Quick Sort and save times
    Time5 = Timer
    Application.StatusBar = "Performing VBA Quick Sort..."
    Call QuickSort(Array3)
    Time6 = Timer

    Application.StatusBar = False

'   Display elapsed time
```

```
        Msg = "Worksheet Sort:" & Chr(9) & Format(Time2 - Time1, _
            "00.00") & _
            "00.00") & _
            " sec." & Chr(13)
        Msg = Msg & "VBA Bubble Sort:" & Chr(9) & Format(Time4 - _
            Time3, "00.00") & _
            " sec." & Chr(13)
        Msg = Msg & 'VBA Quick Sort:" & Chr(9) & Format(Time6 - _
            Time5, "00.00") & _
            " sec."
        MsgBox Msg, vbInformation, "Sorting Times for " & _
            Elements & " Items"
    End Sub
```

Figure 11-3 shows the result of running this routine.

Figure 11-3: The message box displayed at the end of the DoThreeSorts routine.

I executed this routine with seven different array sizes, ranging from 50 to 5,000 elements (random numbers). Table 11-1 shows the results of my tests. The bubble sort method is reasonably fast with small arrays, but the worksheet transfer method is faster with larger arrays. The quick sort method, however, is blazingly fast even for large arrays.

NOTE

These tests were done with random numbers. If the array is almost sorted, the Quick Sort method may actually be slower than the others.

Table 11-1 Sorting Times (in Seconds) of Three Array Sorting Techniques

Array Elements	*Worksheet Sort*	*VBA Bubble Sort*	*VBA Quick Sort*
50	0.93	0.05	0.05
100	1.49	0.17	0.06
500	7.14	3.24	0.44
1,000	14.22	12.03	0.88

(continued)

Table 11-1 *(continued)*

Array Elements	*Worksheet Sort*	*VBA Bubble Sort*	*VBA Quick Sort*
2,500	35.60	66.63	2.63
4,000	64.38	157.58	4.18
5,000	80.68	237.06	6.15

Determining the current selection

Many subroutines work with the user's current selection. But if you design a routine to work with a selected range object, you can't assume that the user has selected a range. Even if the active sheet is a worksheet, the user may select something other than a range — for example, an embedded chart, a button, or some other drawing object.

The following subroutine demonstrates how to determine the active sheet type (worksheet, chart, module, or dialog sheet) and the type of object that's currently selected. This information can be extremely useful when you create error-handling code for your macros. For example, if you create a macro that's appropriate only when a worksheet is the active sheet, you can write code that exits the macro if anything but a worksheet is the active sheet.

This example can be found in DEMO_10.XLS. When this sheet is open, you can execute the subroutine with the Tools⇨Info on Selection command.

```
Sub WhatIsSelected()
'   Determine the type of the active sheet and
'   Object type of selection
    Msg = "The current sheet is " & TypeName(ActiveSheet)
    Msg = Msg & Chr(13)
    Msg = Msg & "The selected object is a " & _
       TypeName(Selection)
    MsgBox Msg, vbInformation, ActiveWorkbook.Name
End Sub
```

This example uses the TypeName function to determine the object types of the ActiveSheet object and the selection. This info is displayed in a message box.

Figure 11-4 shows an example of message box that appears (the actual contents vary, of course, depending on the active sheet and the current selection). Notice how the routine also displays the Name property of the ActiveWorkbook object in the message box's title bar.

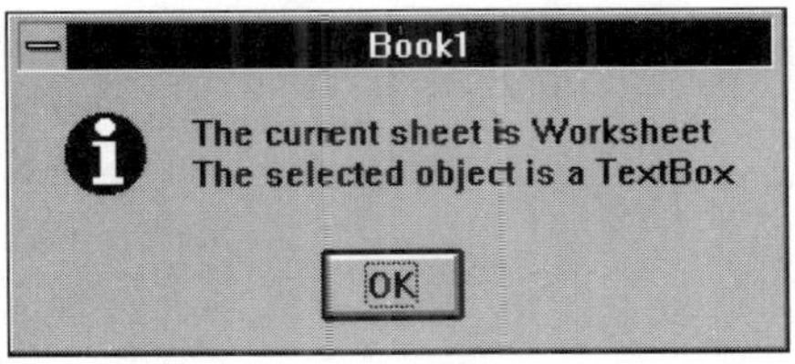

Figure 11-4: The What Is Selected macro tells you about the active sheet and the object that's currently selected. The active workbook name is displayed in the title bar.

NOTE

This routine is quite useful for VBA beginners because it identifies the names of objects selected. This information can be very useful when creating and debugging VBA macros. For example, create a chart object on a worksheet and double-click the chart to edit it. Then select a part of the chart and execute the WhatIsSelected routine to see the official name of the selected object. Or select some text in a VBA module and run the procedure.

Processing a series of files

This example demonstrates how to process a series of files stored on disk. This example, which may help you set up your own routine for this common task, prompts the user for a file specification and processes all files that match. In this case, processing consists of importing the file and entering summary formulas.

DISK

This example can be found in DEMO_11.XLS. When this sheet is open, you can execute the subroutine with the Tools⇨Batch Process Files command. This example uses three additional files, which are provided on the disk: TEXT01.TXT, TEXT02.TXT, and TEXT03.TXT.

NOTE

The example is designed to import the three text files supplied. You'll need to modify the routine to import other text files.

The routine is

```
Sub BatchProcess()
    Dim Files() As String
    Dim FileSpec As String

'   Get file spec
    DefaultPath = ThisWorkbook.Path & "\TEXT??.TXT"
FileSpec = InputBox("Enter path and file spec:", _
      "File Import", DefaultPath)
```

```
'   Extract the path and change directory
    NewPath = ExtractPath(FileSpec)
    If NewPath <> "" Then _
        ChDir NewPath _
            Else Exit Sub


'   See if any files exist
    FoundFile = Dir(FileSpec)
    If FoundFile = "" Then
        MsgBox "Cannot find file:" & Chr(13) & FileSpec
        Exit Sub
    End If

'   Get first file name
    FileCount = 1
    ReDim Preserve Files(FileCount)
    Files(FileCount) = FoundFile

'   Get other file names, if any
    Do While FoundFile <> ""
        FoundFile = Dir()
        If FoundFile <> "" Then
            FileCount = FileCount + 1
            ReDim Preserve Files(FileCount)
            Files(FileCount) = FoundFile
        End If
    Loop

'   Loop through all files and process them
    For i = 1 To FileCount
        Application.StatusBar = "Processing " & Files(i)
        Call ProcessFiles(Files(i))
    Next i
    Application.StatusBar = False
End Sub
```

The BatchProcess subroutine uses a custom function, ExtractPath, to extract the path from the file specification:

```
Function ExtractPath(Spec As String) As String
    SpecLen = Len(Spec)
    For i = SpecLen To 1 Step -1
```

```
        If Mid(Spec, i, 1) = "\" Then
            ExtractPath = Left(Spec, i - 1)
            Exit Function
        End If
    Next i
    ExtractPath = ""
End Function
```

The BatchProcess subroutine uses a For...Next loop to process the files. Within the loop, the status bar text is changed to display the file being processed, and the actual processing is done by calling the following subroutine, ProcessFiles. This is essentially a dummy routine for the example. You will, of course, substitute your own routine in place of this.

```
Sub ProcessFiles(FileName As String)
'   Import the file
    Workbooks.OpenText FileName:=FileName, _
        Origin:=xlWindows, _
        StartRow:=1, _
        DataType:=xlFixedWidth, _
        FieldInfo:= _
        Array(Array(0, 1), Array(3, 1), Array(12, 1))
'   Enter summary formulas
    Range("D1").Value = "A"
    Range("D2").Value = "B"
    Range("D3").Value = "C"
    Range("E1:E3").Formula = "=COUNTIF(B:B,D1)"
    Range("F1:F3").Formula = "=SUMIF(B:B,D1,C:C)"
End Sub
```

Creating a dialog box on the fly

The last example in this section is a rather clever and useful bit of code that creates a dialog box on the fly. (The MsgBox function, for example, is a dialog box that VBA creates on the fly: it uses the arguments provided to create a simple dialog box with the specified text, buttons, icon, and title bar caption.)

The function shown in Listing 11-8, called *OptionBox*, creates a dialog box that presents the user with a set of option buttons. The index of the selected option button is returned by the function. If the user clicks Cancel, the function returns False. The OptionBox function also demonstrates how to access dialog box objects directly with VBA code.

Listing 11-8 OptionBox function

```
Function OptionBox(OpList() As String, Optional Caption As _
    Variant)
    Dim i As Integer
    Dim OptionDlg As Object
    Dim CurrentSheet As Object

    Application.ScreenUpdating = False

'   Add a temporary dialog sheet
    ThisWorkbook.DialogSheets.Add
Set OptionDlg = ThisWorkbook.DialogSheets(1)

'   Add the option buttons
    TopPos = 40
    For i = 1 To UBound(OpList)
        OptionDlg.OptionButtons.Add
        OptionDlg.OptionButtons(i).
        TopPos = TopPos + 14
    Next i

'   Move the OK and Cancel buttons
    OptionDlg.Buttons.Left = 240

'   Set dialog height, width, and caption
    If IsMissing(Caption) Then Caption = "Choose an Option"
    With OptionDlg.DialogFrame
        .Height = Application.Max(68, _
      OptionDlg.DialogFrame.Top + TopPos - 34)
        .Width = 230
        .Caption = Caption
    End With

'   Make first item the default
    OptionDlg.OptionButtons(1).Value = xlOn

'   Change tab order of OK and Cancel buttons
'   so the 1st option button will have the focus
    OptionDlg.Buttons("Button 2").BringToFront
    OptionDlg.Buttons("Button 3").BringToFront

'   Display the dialog box
    DBoxOK = OptionDlg.Show

'   Assign False if canceled, or...
    If Not DBoxOK Then
```

May not be 1 !

Better:

.DialogSheets

(DialogSheets.Count)

```
            OptionBox = False
        Else
'           ... return the index of selected option
            For i = 1 To UBound(OpList)
                If OptionDlg.OptionButtons(i).Value = xlOn Then _
                OptionBox = i
            Next i
        End If

'   Delete temporary dialog sheet (without a warning)
    Application.DisplayAlerts = False
    OptionDlg.Delete
End Function
```

Note how the dialog sheet is created, set up with the appropriate number of option buttons, and then deleted just before the function ends. To better understand how this works, use the step mode in the Debugger (but make sure screen updating is turned on).

The following procedure is in the DEMO_12.XLS file. Execute the procedure by choosing the Tools⇨Create Option Box command. The procedure creates an array with 10 elements and then calls OptionBox with the array as the first argument and the dialog's caption as the second argument. The variable Ans contains the function's value: either False (if canceled) or the index of the selected option button. The dialog box created by the following procedure is shown in Figure 11-5.

```
Sub TestOptionBox()
    Dim Ops(10) As String
    Ops(1) = "California"
    Ops(2) = "Oregon"
    Ops(3) = "Montana"
    Ops(4) = "Wyoming"
    Ops(5) = "New Mexico"
    Ops(6) = "Nevada"
    Ops(7) = "Washington"
    Ops(8) = "Utah"
    Ops(9) = "Idaho"
    Ops(10) = "Texas"
    Ans = OptionBox(Ops, "Select a State")
    If Ans <> False Then MsgBox Ops(Ans)
End Sub
```

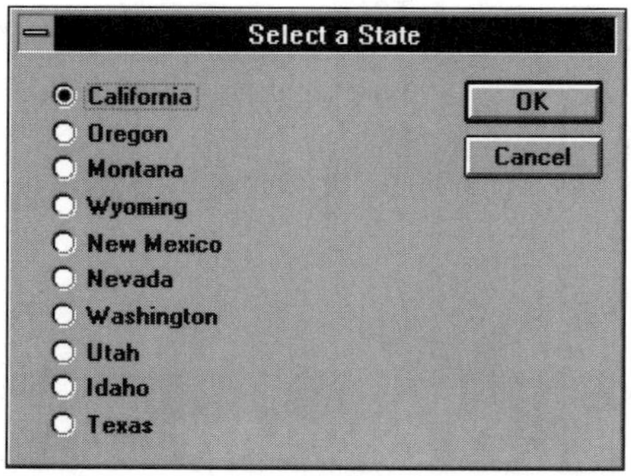

Figure 11-5: The OptionBox function creates a dialog box on the fly with a set of option buttons.

Windows API Calls

One of VBA's most important features is the capability to use functions that are stored in Dynamic Link Libraries (DLLs). The examples in this section use common Windows API calls. I introduced this topic in Chapter 9.

Getting the Windows and system directories

The following example demonstrates how to determine the directory in which Windows is installed (you can't just assume that it's in C:\WINDOWS) by using a Windows API call. Note that the strings returned do *not* have a final backslash (\).

DISK

This example can be found in DEMO_13.XLS. When this sheet is open, you can execute the subroutine with the Tools➪Windows Directory command.

```
Declare Function GetWindowsDirectory Lib "KERNEL" _
    (ByVal lpBuffer As String, ByVal nSize As Integer) As _
    Integer
Declare Function GetSystemDirectory Lib "KERNEL" _
    (ByVal lpBuffer As String, ByVal nSize As Integer) As _
    Integer

Sub GetWinDir()
    Dim WinDir As String * 144
    Dim SysDir As String * 144

    WLen = GetWindowsDirectory(WinDir, Len(WinDir))
    SLen = GetSystemDirectory(SysDir, Len(WinDir))
```

```
        WindowsDirectory = Left(WinDir, WLen)
        SystemDirectory = Left(SysDir, SLen)

'       Display the directory names
        MsgBox WindowsDirectory & Chr(13) & SystemDirectory
    End Sub
```

Figure 11-6 shows a sample message box that appears when this routine is executed. Your message may vary.

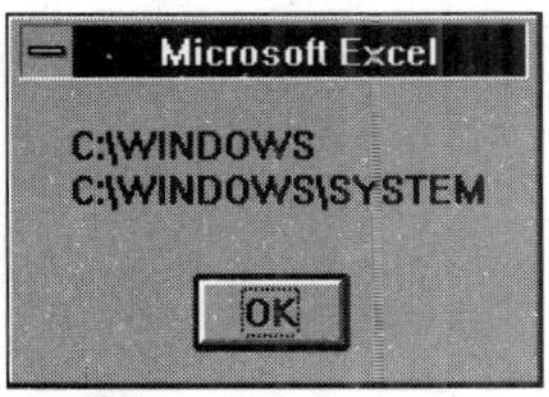

Figure 11-6: Determining the Windows and system directories by using a Windows API call.

Getting the DOS and Windows versions

This example uses an API call to determine the versions of DOS and Windows currently in use.

NOTE: If you're using Windows 3.11, the function returns 3.1.

DISK: This example can be found in DEMO_14.XLS. When this sheet is open, you can execute the subroutine with the Tools⇨Versions command.

```
Declare Function GetVersion Lib "KERNEL" () As Long

Sub GetVersionNumbers()
'   Returns the DOS and Windows version number
'   by calling a Windows API function

    Dim Ver As Long
    Dim DosVer As Long
    Dim WinVer As Long
```

```
        Ver = GetVersion()
        DosVer = Ver \ &h10000
        WinVer = Ver And &hffff&
    DOSVERSION = Format((DosVer \ 256) + _
            ((DosVer Mod 256) / 100), "Fixed")
        WINDOWSVERSION = Format((WInVer Mod 256) + _
            ((WInVer \ 256) / 100), "Fixed")

        MsgBox "DOS Version " & DOSVERSION & Chr(13) & _
            "Windows Version " & WINDOWSVERSION
    End Sub
```

Figure 11-7 shows a sample message box that appears when this routine is executed.

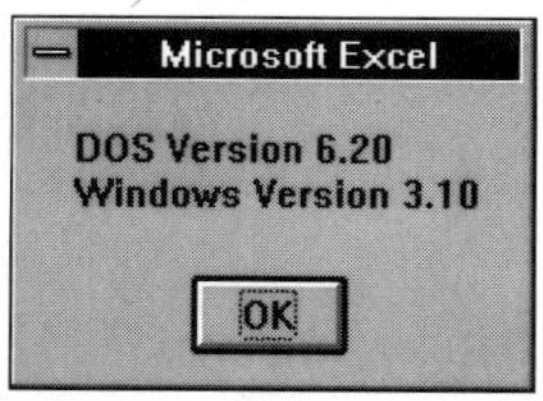

Figure 11-7: Determining the Windows and the DOS versions by using a Windows API call.

Getting a DOS environmental setting

The following function uses a Windows API call to get a DOS environment variable. For example, if you want to get the system path, you can call this function with "path" as its argument. Other arguments you can use with this function include "comspec," "prompt," and "windir."

This example can be found inDEMO_15.XLS. When this sheet is open, you can execute the subroutine with the Tools⇨Show Path command.

```
Option Compare Text

Declare Function GetDOSEnvironment Lib "KERNEL" () As Long
Declare Function Lstrcpy Lib "KERNEL" (ByVal ToStr As _
    String, _
```

```
        ByVal FromStr As Long) As Long

    Function GetEnvir(EnvVar As String)
        Dim Buffer As String * 256
        Dim CurrVarLen As Long
        Dim PTR As Long
    Dim EnvVarLen As Integer
        GetEnvir = ""
        EnvVarLen = Len(EnvVar) + 1
        PTR = GetDOSEnvironment
        Do
            CurrVarLen = Lstrcpy(Buffer, PTR)
            CurrVarLen = InStr(1, Buffer, Chr(0), 0)
            If Left(Buffer, EnvVarLen) = EnvVar & "=" Then
                GetEnvir = Mid(Buffer, EnvVarLen + 1, CurrVarLen _
                   - EnvVarLen)
                Exit Function
            End If
            PTR = PTR + CurrVarLen
        Loop Until Left(Buffer, 1) = Chr(0)
    End Function
```

The following subroutine calls GetEnvir with "path" as the argument, parses the resulting string into the directory names in the DOS path, and then displays each directory name in a series of message boxes. Figure 11-8 shows one of the message boxes.

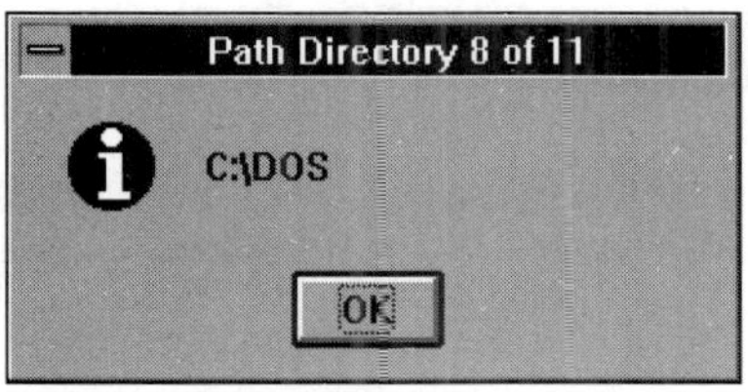

Figure 11-8: Using an API function to get the DOS path.

```
    Sub GetPathDirs()
        Dim PathDir() As String

    '   Call Windows API function to get the path
        ThePath = GetEnvir("Path")

        TempString = ""
        Found = 0
```

```
    For i = 1 To Len(ThePath)
        CurrChar = Mid(ThePath, i, 1)
        Select Case CurrChar
            Case ";"
                Found = Found + 1
                ReDim Preserve PathDir(Found)
                PathDir(Found) = TempString
                TempString = ""
            Case Else
                TempString = TempString & CurrChar
        End Select
    Next i

'   Display the directories in the path
    For i = 1 To Found
        MsgBox PathDir(i), vbInformation, "Path Directory " _
           & i & " of " & Found
    Next i
End Sub
```

Determining default printer information

The following example uses a Windows API function to return information about the active printer. The information is contained in a single text string. The example parses the string and displays the information in a more readable format.

NOTE: The ActivePrinter property of the Application object returns the name of the active printer (and lets you change it), but there's no direct way to determine what printer driver or port is being used.

DISK: The example in this section can be found in DEMO_16.XLS. When this sheet is open, you can execute the subroutine with the Tools➪About the Default Printer command.

```
Declare Function GetProfileString Lib "KERNEL" (ByVal
lpAppName As String, _
    ByVal lpKeyName As String, ByVal lpDefault As String, _
    ByVal lpReturnedString As String, ByVal nSize As _
        Integer) As Integer

Sub DefaultPrinterInfo()
    Dim Result As String * 255
    Call GetProfileString("Windows", "Device", "", Result, _
        254)
    ResultLength = Len(Result)
```

```
    FirstComma = Application.Find(",", Result, 1)
    SecondComma = Application.Find(",", Result, FirstComma + 1)

'   Gets printer's name
    Printer = Left(Result, FirstComma - 1)

'   Gets driver

    Driver = Mid(Result, FirstComma + 1, SecondComma - _
        FirstComma - 1)

'   Gets last part of device line
    Port = Right(Result, ResultLength - SecondComma)

'   Build message
    Msg = "Printer:" & Chr(9) & Printer & Chr(13)
    Msg = Msg & "Driver:" & Chr(9) & Driver & Chr(13)
    Msg = Msg & "Port:" & Chr(9) & Port

'   Display message
    MsgBox Msg, vbInformation, "Default Printer Information"
End Sub
```

Figure 11-9 shows a sample message box returned by this routine.

Figure 11-9: Getting information about the active printer by using a Windows API call.

Determining the current video mode

This example uses Windows API calls to determine a system's video mode. If your application needs to display a certain amount of information on one screen, knowing the display size can help you scale the text accordingly.

This example can be found inDEMO_17.XLS. When this sheet is open, you can execute the subroutine with the Tools➪Video Mode command.

```
Declare Function GetActiveWindow Lib "USER" () As Integer
Declare Function GetDeviceCaps Lib "GDI" (ByVal hDC As
Integer, ByVal _
    nIndex As Integer) As Integer
Declare Function GetDC Lib "USER" (ByVal hWnd As Integer) As _
   Integer

Sub DisplayVideoInfo()
    Const HorzRes = 8
    Const VertRes = 10
    Const BitsPixel = 12

    ActiveWin = GetActiveWindow()
    DevCon = GetDC(Act_Win)
    Horiz = GetDeviceCaps(DevCon, HorzRes)
    Vert = GetDeviceCaps(DevCon, VertRes)
    BitsPer = GetDeviceCaps(DevCon, BitsPixel)
MsgBox Horiz & " X " & Vert & " X " & BitsPer & " Bits per _
   pixel"
End Sub
```

Figure 11-10 shows the message box returned by this routine when running in standard VGA mode.

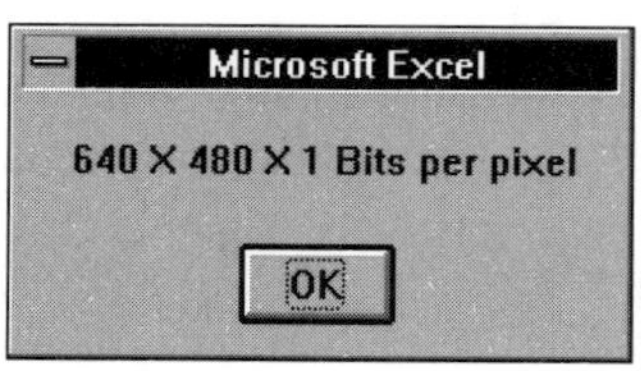

Figure 11-10: Determining the video display mode using a Windows API call.

Display system resources

The biggest problem with Windows 3.x is its limited system resources. If you usually run other applications while working in Excel, you've probably faced this problem. This example demonstrates how to determine free system resources.

DISK

This example can be found inDEMO_18.XLS. When this sheet is open, you can execute the subroutine with the Tools⇨System Resources command.

```
Declare Function GetFreeSystemResources Lib "USER" _
    (ByVal fuSysResource As Integer) As Integer

Sub Get_Resource()
    Const GDIRESOURCES = 1
    Const USERRESOURCES = 2
    Static LN As String * 1
    Dim Msg As String

'   Get information
    User = GetFreeSystemResources(USERRESOURCES)
    GDI = GetFreeSystemResources(GDIRESOURCES)

'   Build message and display it
    Msg = "System Resources:  " & Application.Min(GDI, User) _
      & "% Free"
    MsgBox Msg
End Sub
```

Figure 11-11 is an example of a message box that appears when you execute this procedure.

Figure 11-11: Displaying system resources available by using a Windows API call.

System resources refers to the amount of memory that Windows sets aside to store resources as they are created; these resources are managed by two DLLs: GDI.EXE and USER.EXE. When these resources are depleted, Windows starts to fall apart.

Common symptoms are:

- Incomplete displays
- *Out of memory* errors
- The inability to start an application

In most cases, applications free up system resources when they are no longer needed. At times, however, it may be necessary to restart Windows to regain lost resources.

The preceding example displays the smaller of GDI and User resources (this is the same method used in Program Manager's Help⇨About display).

Determining Whether Ctrl, Shift, or Alt Is Pressed

The following routine which uses the GetKeyState DLL function, demonstrates how to determine whether the Ctrl, Shift, or Alt keys are pressed.

This information can add functionality to a routine that's attached to a button. In other words, a routine can perform differently depending on whether the button is clicked or Shift-clicked. (Several of Excel's toolbar buttons perform differently if they're clicked while the Shift key is pressed; for example, the Sort Ascending toolbar button acts like Sort Descending if it is Shift-clicked.)

This example can be found inDEMO_19.XLS. When this sheet is open, you can execute the subroutine with the Tools⇨Show Shift State command.

```
Declare Function GetKeyState Lib "USER" (ByVal nVirtKey As _
    Integer) _
    As Integer

Sub GetStates()
    Const SHIFTKEY = 16
    Const CTRLKEY = 17
    Const ALTKEY = 18
    Dim Alt As Boolean, Ctrl As Boolean, Shift As Boolean

    If GetKeyState(ALTKEY) < 0 Then Alt = True: Msg = "Alt"
    If GetKeyState(CTRLKEY) < 0 Then Ctrl = True: Msg = _
        "Ctrl"
    If GetKeyState(SHIFTKEY) < 0 Then Shift = True: Msg = _
        "Shift"
    If Alt And Shift Then Msg = "Alt+Shift"
    If Alt And Ctrl Then Msg = "Alt+Ctrl"
    If Ctrl And Shift Then Msg = "Ctrl+Shift"
    If Ctrl And Alt Then Msg = "Ctrl+Alt"
    If Ctrl And Alt And Shift Then Msg = "Ctrl+Alt+Shift"
    If Not Ctrl And Not Alt And Not Shift Then Msg = "no _
        keys"
    MsgBox "You're holding down " & Msg
End Sub
```

Figure 11-12 shows this procedure in use.

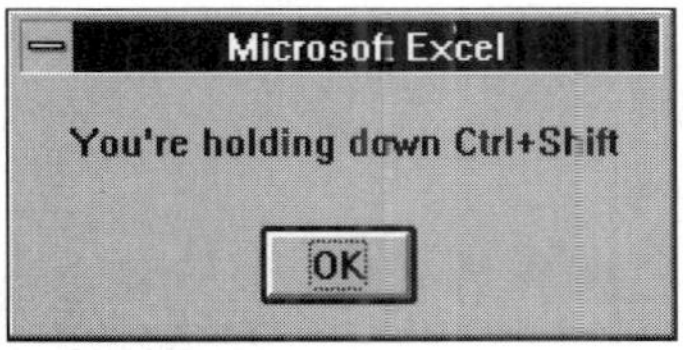

Figure 11-12: Determining whether Ctrl, Shift, or Alt is pressed.

Reading and writing INI files

Most Windows applications use INI files to store settings. Excel's INI file is EXCEL5.INI, which is stored in the WINDOWS directory.

The following example returns the value of the SPOOLER setting in the [Windows] section of the WIN.INI file. It also uses the GetWindowsDirectory DLL function to determine the location of the Windows directory (where WIN.INI is stored).

DISK

The examples in this section, which demonstrate how you can use DLL functions to read and write INI file settings directly from VBA, can be found in DEMO_20.XLS. When this sheet is open, you can execute the subroutines with the Tools⇨Read INI File command and the Tools⇨Write INI File command.

```
Declare Function GetWindowsDirectory Lib "KERNEL" _
    (ByVal lpBuffer As String, ByVal nSize As Integer) As _
        Integer

Declare Function GetPrivateProfileString Lib "KERNEL" (ByVal _
        section$, _
    ByVal entry$, ByVal default$, ByVal buffer$, ByVal _
        buffersize%, _
    ByVal FILENAME$) As Integer

Sub GetINIDemo()
    Dim buffer As String * 100
    Dim WinDir As String * 144
    Dim i As Integer
```

```
'   Get Windows directory
    WLen = GetWindowsDirectory(WinDir, Len(WinDir))
    WindowsDirectory = Left(WinDir, WLen)

'   Set up parameters
    INIFile = WindowsDirectory & "\WIN.INI"
    INISection = "Windows"
    INIEntry = "SPOOLER"
    ErrMsg = "<Not Found>"

    Res = GetPrivateProfileString(INISection, INIEntry, _
        ErrMsg, buffer, Len(buffer), INIFile)
TheSetting = buffer

'   Strip out extra characters from the right
    For i = 100 To 1 Step -1
        If Mid(TheSetting, i, 1) <> Chr(0) Then
            TheSetting = Left(TheSetting, i)
            Exit For
        End If
    Next i

'   Display the result
    MsgBox INIEntry & " = " & TheSetting, vbInformation,
INIfile
End Sub
```

Figure 11-13 shows the results of running the GetINIDemo routine.

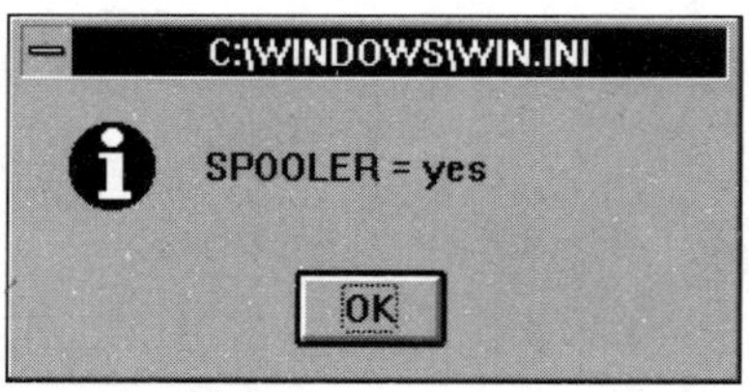

Figure 11-13: Displaying a setting from WIN.INI by using a Windows API call.

You also can change or add a setting to an INI file. The following example uses the WritePrivateProfileString DLL function to add a new entry to the [Microsoft Excel] section of EXCEL5.INI file. The new entry, called *LAST USED*, inserts the current date as its setting.

```
Declare Function GetWindowsDirectory Lib "KERNEL" _
    (ByVal lpBuffer As String, ByVal nSize As Integer) As _
        Integer

Declare Function WritePrivateProfileString% Lib "KERNEL" _
    (ByVal section$, _
    ByVal entry$, ByVal TheSetting$, ByVal FILENAME$)

Sub WriteINIDemo()
    Dim buffer As String * 100
    Dim WinDir As String * 144

'   Get Windows directory
    WLen = GetWindowsDirectory(WinDir, Len(WinDir))
    WindowsDirectory = Left(WinDir, WLen)

'   Set up parameters
    INIFile = WindowsDirectory & "\EXCEL5.INI"
INISection = "Microsoft Excel"
    INIEntry = "LAST USED"
    INIValue = Format(Now, "mm-dd-yy")

    x = WritePrivateProfileString(INISection, INIEntry, _
        INIValue, INIFile)
MsgBox INIEntry & "=" & INIValue & Chr(13) & Chr(13) & _
        "Written to the " & "[" & INISection & "] section _
        of" & Chr(13) & INIFile
End Sub
```

Figure 11-14 shows the results of running the WriteINIDemo routine.

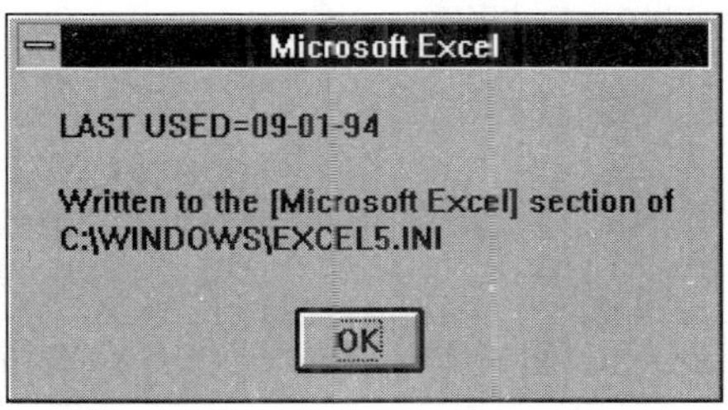

Figure 11-14: Using a Windows API call to add information to an INI file.

Be careful with the WritePrivateProfileString function because it doesn't return any error values. For example, if you specify a nonexistent INI file (such as XL5.INI), it creates the file and inserts the setting you specified.

Miscellaneous Techniques

The examples in this section cover uncommon but useful techniques.

Playing a sound file

Sound is playing an increasingly important role in computer applications. Although you can generate sound from Excel, you can't play a sound file by using pure VBA commands. The XLM macro language, however, has an appropriate function.

The example in this section demonstrates how to use the XLM SOUND.PLAY function in VBA to play a sound file in the WAV format.

This example can be found inDEMO_21.XLS. When this sheet is open, you can execute the subroutine with the Tools⇨Play WAV File command. This routine assumes that you have a sound card installed and requires one or more WAV files to do anything useful.

```
Sub PlayWaveFiles()
'   Prompts user for sound files and plays them

    WaveFile = True
    Filter = "Wave Files (*.wav), *.wav"
    Caption = "Choose a Sound File to Play"

'   Loop until dialog box is canceled
    Do Until WaveFile = False
        WaveFile = Application.GetOpenFilename(Filter, ,
Caption)
        XL4Macro = "SOUND.PLAY(, " & """" & WaveFile & """)"
        ExecuteExcel4Macro XL4Macro
    Loop
End Sub
```

The PlayWaveFiles procedure uses the GetOpenFilename method to prompt the user for a WAV file. When a file is selected, the SOUND.PLAY function is executed, using the ExcecuteExcel4Macro method. This procedure consists of a loop that is executed until the user selects Cancel from the GetOpenFilename dialog box.

Preventing exiting Excel

In some cases, you may require *complete* control over what the user can do while running your application. If you want to ensure that the user doesn't quit Excel or switch out of it, you must do four things:

- Remove the Exit choice from the File menu.
- Disable the Control menu on Excel's title bar.
- Trap the Alt+F4 key sequence and redirect it.
- Trap Alt+Tab, to prevent switching out of Excel.
- Disable the Task Manager that appears when you press Ctrl+Esc.

DISK

This example can be found in DEMO_22.XLS. When this sheet is open, you can execute the subroutines with the Tools⇨Prevent Excel Exit and the Tools⇨Allow Excel Exit commands.

NOTE

Although the following routine prevents most users from quitting Excel, it isn't foolproof. The savvy user can still activate a VBA module, display the Debug window, and type **Application.Quit**.

```
Declare Function GetActiveWindow Lib "USER" () As Integer
Declare Function GetSystemMenu Lib "USER" (ByVal hWnd As _
    Integer, _
    ByVal bRevert As Integer) As Integer
Declare Function DeleteMenu Lib "USER" (ByVal hMenu As _
    Integer, _
    ByVal nPosition As Integer, ByVal wFlags As Integer) As _
    Integer
Declare Function GetWindowsDirectory Lib "KERNEL" _
    (ByVal P$, ByVal S%) As Integer

Sub PreventExit()
'   Remove Exit from all File menus (it is always last)
    On Error Resume Next
    For Each Mbar In Application.MenuBars
        MenuPos = Mbar.Menus("File").MenuItems.Count
'       MsgBox MenuPos
        Mbar.Menus("File").MenuItems(MenuPos).Delete
    Next Mbar

'   Disable the Control menu (using Windows API call)
    For Item = 1 To 9
        Call DeleteMenu(GetSystemMenu(GetActiveWindow, _
           False), 0, 1024)
Next Item
```

```
'   Trap Alt+F4 and Alt+Tab
    Application.OnKey "%{F4}", ""
    Application.OnKey "%{Tab}", ""

'   Rename TASKMAN.EXE
    Dim WinPath As String
    WinPath = String(145, Chr(0))
    WINDIR = Left(WinPath, GetWindowsDirectory(WinPath, _
        Len(WinPath)))
    Name WINDIR & "\taskman.exe" As WINDIR & "\taskman.e_e"
End Sub

Sub DoNothing()
End Sub
```

The PreventExit routine removes all the obvious ways of quitting Excel, using several Windows API calls in the process. The DeleteMenu DLL function deletes a single item (the first item is always 0). Because there are nine items on Excel's Control menu (including the separators bars), this function is called nine times. To delete only the Close item, use the following statement:

```
Call DeleteMenu(GetSystemMenu(GetActiveWindow, True), 6, _
        1024)
```

Because Ctrl+Esc cannot be trapped with the OnKey method, I renamed TASKMAN.EXE so that pressing Ctrl+Esc has no effect.

The following routine restores the settings changed by the PreventExit subroutine. It requires the same API declarations listed in the preceding code.

```
Sub AllowExit()
'   Restore all File menus
    On Error Resume Next
    For Each Mbar In Application.MenuBars
        Mbar.Menus("File").MenuItems.Add Caption:="E&xit", _
                restore:=True
Next Mbar

'   Enable the Control menu (using Windows API call)
    For Item = 1 To 9
        Call DeleteMenu(GetSystemMenu(GetActiveWindow, _
                True), 0, 1024)
    Next Item

'   Remove Alt+F4 and Alt+Tab trap
    Application.OnKey "%{F4}"
    Application.OnKey "%{Tab}"
```

```
    Rename TASKMAN.EXE to its original
    Dim WinPath As String
    WinPath = String(145, Chr(0))
    WINDIR = Left(WinPath, GetWindowsDirectory(WinPath, _
        Len(WinPath)))
    Name WINDIR & "\taskman.e_e" As WINDIR & "\taskman.exe"
End Sub
```

Running a DOS program

The examples in this section demonstrate how to execute DOS programs from Excel.

The examples in this section can be found in DEMO_23.XLS. When this sheet is open, you can execute the subroutines with the Tools⇨Open DOS Window and Tools⇨Get DOS Help commands.

The following routine uses the Shell function to execute another program (COMMAND.COM in this case). If you have a file named DOSPRMPT.PIF, you can assign that name to the Program variable. To exit the window, type **Exit** at the DOS prompt.

```
Sub DOSWindow()
    Program = "COMMAND.COM"
    x = Shell(Program, 1)
End Sub
```

The Shell function can be tricky because you can't be sure that the program started with Shell will be finished before the next VBA statement gets executed. In other words, if you use Shell to run a program that creates a file, you can't be sure that the file will be created before VBA executes the next statement. In still other words, the Shell function does not cause Excel to pause; as a result, after Shell is executed, the macro continues running.

The following example uses a Windows API call to suspend Excel until the Shelled program is finished:

```
Declare Function GetModuleUsage% Lib "KERNEL" (ByVal _
     hModule%)

Sub GetDOSHelp()
    ProgName = "HELP"
```

```
x% = Shell(ProgName, 1)
    Do While GetModuleUsage(x%) > 0
        y% = DoEvents()
    Loop
    MsgBox "Resuming Excel Program"
End Sub
```

This example uses Shell to run the DOS HELP.COM program. Depending on your DOS version, you may need to change the file name to HELP.EXE. While the program is running, Excel continually calls the GetModuleUsage function within a Do While...Loop structure. When the program is finished, GetModuleUsage returns a nonpositive value of zero and the loop ends.

Sending keystrokes to a Windows application

This example demonstrates how to run a Windows program from Excel.

This example can be found in DEMO_24.XLS. When this sheet is open, you can execute the subroutines with the Tools⇨Start Solitaire command. This routine assumes that you have a copy of SOL.EXE (the Solitaire game that comes with Windows) in the current path.

The following routine starts the Windows Solitaire game and uses SendKeys to send keystrokes to it. These keystrokes issue commands to make sure that the “robot” card back is chosen and that the game being played is Draw One with standard scoring.

```
Private Declare Function GetModuleUsage% Lib "KERNEL" (ByVal _
   hModule%)

Sub StartSolitaire()
    ProgName = "SOL.EXE"
    x% = Shell(ProgName, 1)
    SendKeys "%gc{Tab 3}{Right 6}{Enter}"
    SendKeys "%go%o%a{Enter}", True
    Do While GetModuleUsage(x%) > 0
        y% = DoEvents()
    Loop
    MsgBox ("Resuming Excel Program")
End Sub
```

As described in the preceding section, the Shell function runs an executable program — in this case, the Solitaire game that comes with Windows. If Solitaire is already running, this procedure simply activates it. The second argument specifies how the application is to be run (see the on-line help for details). The remainder of the subroutine feeds keystrokes (see Table 11-2) to Solitaire, setting the game up with some specific options.

Table 11-2 Keystrokes Sent to Solitaire

Keystroke	*What It Is*	*What It Does*
%gc	Alt+G,C	Chooses Game⇨Deck command, bringing up the Select Card Back dialog box.
{Tab 3}	Tab three times	Chooses the first deck option.
{Right 6}	Right arrow six times	Chooses the "robot" card face.
{Enter}	Enter	Closes the Select Card Back dialog box.
%go	Alt+G,O	Chooses Game⇨Options command, bringing up the Options dialog box.
%o	Alt+O	Selects the Draw One option.
%a	Alt+A	Selects the Standard option.
{Enter}	Enter	Closes the Options dialog box.

The GetModuleUsage function suspends Excel. If you don't suspend the program, Excel's title bar flashes, signifying that it requires user input in response to the MsgBox function. (To see for yourself, remove the three statements preceding the MsgBox function.)

Activating or opening an application

The following example shows how to start or activate another Windows application.

If Minesweeper is running, the following routine activates it by using the AppActivate method. If Minesweeper is not running, the routine asks whether the user wants to start it. If so, the Shell function executes the file.

DISK

This example can be found inDEMO_25.XLS. When this sheet is open, you can execute the subroutine with the Tools⇨Go To MineSweeper command. This routine assumes that you have a copy of WINMINE.EXE (the Minesweeper game that comes with Windows) in the current path.

```
Sub GoToMineSweeper()
    AppName = "Minesweeper"
    AppFile = "WINMINE.EXE"
    On Error GoTo NotRunning
    AppActivate (AppName)
    Exit Sub
NotRunning:
    Ans = MsgBox(AppName & " is not running. Start it?", _
          vbYesNo)
    If Ans = vbYes Then x = Shell(AppFile, 1)
End Sub
```

NOTE

AppActivate, unlike Shell, does not let you change the window's state (maximized or minimized).

Summary

- In this chapter, I presented dozens of examples to help you better understand the capabilities of VBA.
- The next chapter focuses on one class of Excel applications: utility programs. They help you make Excel work like you want it to.

Chapter 12

Developing Excel Utilities with VBA

In This Chapter

- What is an Excel utility
- Why develop utilities
- What you need to know when developing utilities
- How to develop a utility
- Examples, examples, examples

What Is a Utility?

A *utility* is something that enhances software, adding useful features or making existing features more accessible.

The most popular collection of utilities is probably Symantec's Norton Utilities. This package, which has been around for a long time, adds useful features to DOS and Windows that aren't otherwise available (e.g, extensive disk diagnostics), and also improves upon existing features (e.g., better disk caching).

Although you can get by without utilities, those who use them often wonder how they survived without them.

In other words, a utility isn't an end product like a quarterly report. Rather, it's a tool that helps you produce end products.

I believe that Excel is an extraordinary program that gets better with every release. But as good as the Excel is, every user soon develops a wish list of features that she or he would like to see added to the software. For example, users who usually turn off the grid line display want a feature that toggles this attribute so that they no longer have to go through the tedious Tools⇨Options command. Users who work with dates hope to see a pop-up calendar feature. And some users desire an easier way to access cell notes.

Utilities need not be complicated. Some of the most useful ones are actually very simple. For example, the following VBA procedure is a utility that toggles the worksheet grid line display:

```
Sub ToggleGridDisplay()
    ActiveWindow.DisplayGridlines = _
        Not ActiveWindow.DisplayGridlines
End Sub
```

You can assign this macro to a toolbar button, a right-click shortcut menu, or a keystroke combination.

CROSS REFERENCE

Several of the examples in Chapter 11 are utilities. Or at least they easily can be turned into utilities.

Using VBA to Develop Utilities

When I first started reviewing Excel 5, I was blown away by VBA's potential. VBA was light years ahead of the already powerful XLM macro language.

To learn VBA, I wrote a collection of Excel utilities, using only VBA. (I figured that I would learn the language quicker if I shot for a tangible goal.) The result was the Power Utility Pak, which is available as shareware and described later in this chapter.

I learned several things from this project:

- VBA can be very difficult to grasp at first, but it gets easier with practice.
- Experimentation is the key to mastering VBA. Every project usually involves dozens of small experiments in coding that eventually lead to a finished product.
- VBA lets you extend Excel in a way that is entirely consistent with Excel's look and feel.
- Excel can do almost anything. When you reach a dead end, chances are there's another path that leads to a solution.

The bottom line: Few other software packages include as extensive a set of tools that lets the end user extend the software.

What Makes a Good Utility?

At its most basic, a utility should help *you* get a job done. But if you're developing utilities for other users, what really distinguishes the best Excel utilities?

In other words, what makes an Excel utility valuable?

- *It adds something to Excel.* Perhaps a new feature, a way to combine existing features, or just a way to make an existing feature easier to work with.
- *It's general in nature.* Ideally, a utility should be useful under a wide variety of conditions. Of course, it's more difficult to write a general-purpose utility than one that works in a highly defined environment.
- *It looks, works, and feels like an Excel command.* Although it's tempting to add your own special touch to utilities, other users will find them easier to use if they look and act like familiar Excel commands.
- *It traps errors.* An end user should never see a VBA error message. Any error messages that appear should be ones that you write.
- *Its effects are undoable.* Users who don't like the results caused by your utility should be able to reverse their path.

The Anatomy of a Utility

In this section, I describe a custom Excel utility that makes it easy to manipulate text in cells.

CROSS REFERENCE

The utility in this section is part of my Power Utility Pak shareware. To get the full Power Utility Pak (it's free to those who buy this book), see the ordering information at the back of this book for details.

Background

Excel has many text functions that enable you to manipulate text strings in useful ways. For example, you can make the text in a cell uppercase, concatenate it with other text, delete parts of it, and so on. But to do any of these things, you have to write formulas — thus using twice as many cells as before.

Of course, you can return to the original number of cells by copying the formula cells, pasting the formula results back to the original cells (use the Edit⇨Paste Special command), and then deleting the formula cells. But wouldn't it be nice if Excel had some text manipulation tools that didn't require formulas?

So I set out to create a utility that lets the user manipulate text in cells without using formulas. I call it the Text Tools utility.

By the way, lots of good utility ideas come from statements that begin, "Wouldn't it be nice if. . . ."

Project goals for Text Tools

The first step in designing a utility is to envision exactly how you want the utility to work. Here's my original plan, stated in the form of nine goals:

- It will have the same look and feel of other Excel commands. In other words, it will have a dialog box that looks like Excel's dialog boxes.
- It will operate with the current selection of cells. It will also respond appropriately when the selection is not a range.
- It will allow the user to
    - Change the text in each cell to uppercase.
    - Change the text in each cell to lowercase.
    - Change the text in each cell to proper case (that is, the first letter of each word is capitalized and the others are lowercase).
    - Concatenate another string to the text in each cell.
    - Delete a fixed number of characters from the text in each cell.
    - Remove all excess spaces from the text in each cell.
- It will allow the user to request the preceding types of changes on nontext cells.
- It will have no effect on cells that contain formulas.
- It will count the number of words and characters in all the selected cells.
- It will enable the user to undo the changes.
- It will have on-line help available.

The workbook

The Text Tools utility is in a separate workbook, which consists of a dialog sheet and a VBA module. TEXTOOLS.XLS is available on the disk that accompanies this book.

The dialog box

Figure 12-1 shows the dialog sheet for this utility.

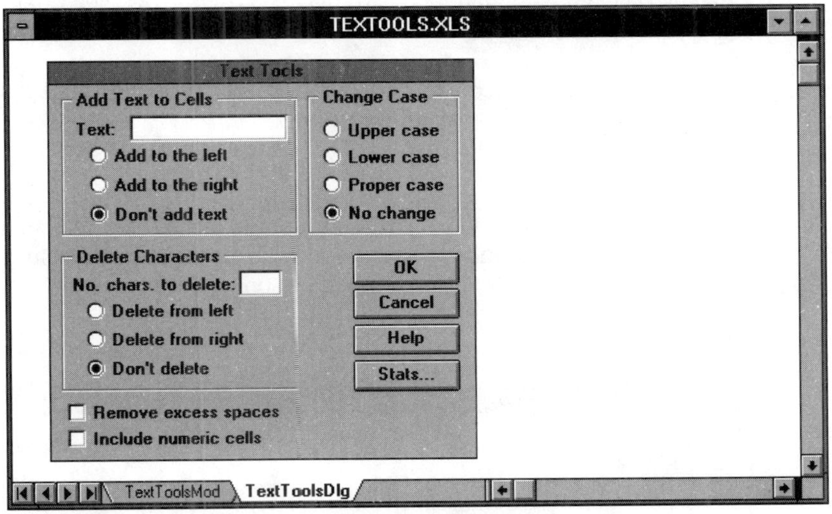

Figure 12-1: The dialog sheet used by the Text Tools utility.

The parts of the Text Tools dialog box correspond to the utility's features:

- *Change the case of the text.* The user can select the type of case change: uppercase, lowercase, proper case, and no change.
- *Add characters to the text.* The user can select where to add text: to the left, to the right, and neither (don't add any characters). The user types the characters to be added in the edit box.
- *Remove characters from the text.* The user can select how characters are removed from the text: from the left, from the right, and neither (don't remove any characters). The user types the number of characters to be deleted in the edit box. (I thought about using a different control — for example, a spinner — but I thought this was the most straightforward method).
- *Remove excess spaces.* The user can choose whether to remove excess spaces.
- *Include numeric cells.* The user can choose whether to include numeric cells.
- *Display word and character count.* I considered displaying this information automatically; I decided not to because the utility slowed slightly. For the user who wants this information, however, I inserted a button that executes a subroutine to perform the calculations and displays the result in a message box without dismissing the dialog box.

- *Display on-line help.* A Help button is standard for Excel dialog boxes.
- *OK and Cancel buttons.* These buttons also are standard fare.

I always assign meaningful names to dialog box controls (see Chapter 10 for more information).

I often like to start projects by designing the dialog box because doing so forces me to think through the project one more time.

The VBA module

Figure 12-2 shows a portion of the VBA module. Excluding blank lines, the module consists of about 200 lines of code — about 20 percent are comments. There are nine subroutine procedures and one function procedure.

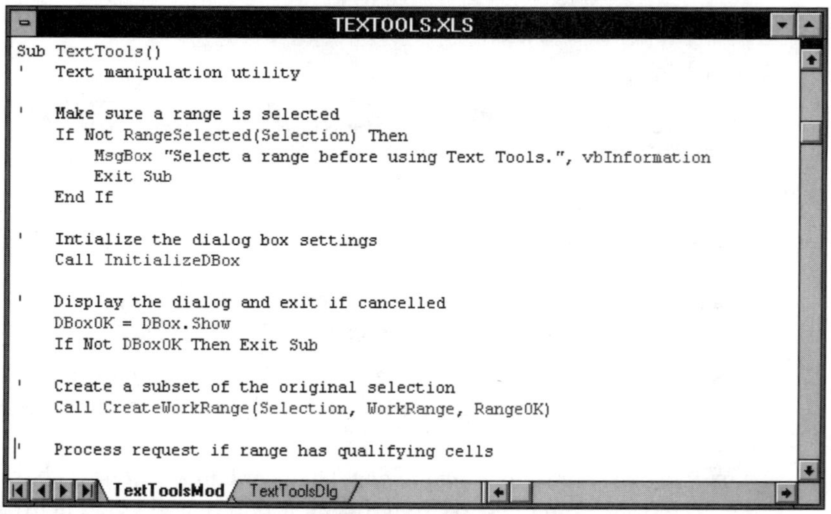

Figure 12-2: A portion of the VBA module for the Text Tools utility.

The VBA code

In this section, I explain how the utility works by listing and describing its procedures.

The main procedure

Listing 12-1 is the main routine for the Text Tools utilities, called *TextTools*.

Listing 12-1 Main Routine for the Text Tools Utilities

```
Sub TextTools()
'   Text manipulation utility

'   Make sure a range is selected
    If Not RangeSelected(Selection) Then
        MsgBox "Select a range before using Text Tools.", _
           vbInformation
        Exit Sub
    End If

'   Intialize the dialog box settings
    Call InitializeDBox

'   Display the dialog and exit if canceled
    DBoxOK = DBox.Show
    If Not DBoxOK Then Exit Sub

'   Create a subset of the original selection
    Call CreateWorkRange(Selection, WorkRange, RangeOK)

'   Process request if range has qualifying cells
    Select Case RangeOK
        Case False
            MsgBox "No cells contain text.", vbInformation
        Case True
'           Save original values so operation can be undone
            For i = 1 To WorkRange.Count
                ReDim Preserve SaveForUndo(i)
            SaveForUndo(i) = WorkRange(i).Value
            Next i
            Call ProcessRequests
            Application.OnUndo "&Undo Text Modification ",
"UndoTextTools"
    End Select
End Sub
```

This routine is very simple and easy to follow — mainly because most of the work is done by other routines. The TextTools subroutine basically calls other routines.

The TextTools subroutine starts by calling the custom function RangeSelected, which returns False if a range is not selected. If RangeSelected returns False, a message box appears and the routine ends.

Next, this subroutine calls the InitializeDBox routine, which creates object variables for most of the dialog box controls and sets the initial values.

Then the dialog box is displayed (the Show method). At this point, the user can change the dialog box settings. If the dialog box is canceled, the routine ends. If the dialog box is not canceled, the routine calls the CreateWorkRange subroutine, which takes three arguments:

- Selection, a range object, is the input range (that is, the current worksheet selection).
- WorkRange, another range object, holds a subset of the original selection. This subset consists of only the cells that contain text.
- RangeOK, a Boolean variable, is True when WorkRange doesn't have any cells that contain text.

What happens next depends on the value of RangeOK. If WorkRange doesn't contain any cells with text, a message box informs the user and the routine ends. If RangeOK is True, an array named SaveForUndo is filled with the values of the cells in WorkRange (these will be restored if the user chooses Edit⇨Undo after using the utility). Then the ProcessRequests routine is called (this subroutine does all the work). Finally, the OnUndo property of the Application object is set to the name of the subroutine to execute if the user chooses Edit⇨Undo.

Public variables

Because the dialog box is referred to by several subroutines, I made the object variables Public. The following statements go at the top of the module, before the TextTools subroutine:

```
Option Explicit
'   Declare public variables
    Dim OptionProper As Object
    Dim OptionUpper As Object
    Dim OptionLower As Object
    Dim OptionNoChange As Object

    Dim TextToAdd As Object
    Dim OptionAddToLeft As Object
    Dim OptionAddToRight As Object
    Dim OptionAddNone As Object
```

```
    Dim CharsToDelete As Object
    Dim OptionDeleteFromLeft As Object
    Dim OptionDeleteFromRight As Object
    Dim OptionDeleteNone As Object

    Dim CheckTrim As Object
    Dim IncludeNumeric As Object

    Dim DBox As Object
    Dim SaveForUndo() As Variant
    Dim WorkRange As Object
    Dim Cell As Object
    Dim DBoxOK As Boolean
    Dim NewText As String
    Dim NumToDelete As Integer

    Dim RangeOK As Boolean
    Dim i As Integer
```

NOTE: When the statement Option Explicit is present, all variables must be declared before they are used. This statement is not required, but I highly recommend adding it.

The RangeSelected function

The module has only one custom function, RangeSelected. It returns True if its argument is a range.

```
Private Function RangeSelected(InRange) As Boolean
'   False if argument is not a Range object
    If TypeName(InRange) = "Range" Then
        RangeSelected = True
        Else RangeSelected = False
    End If
End Function
```

Notice that this function is declared with the Private keyword. As a result, it will not be displayed in the Function Wizard.

The InitializeDBox subroutine

The Initialize DBox subroutine (shown in Listing 12-1) takes care of some initial housekeeping chores. More specific, it performs three tasks:

- Creates object variables for the dialog box controls.
- Initializes the dialog box controls with their default settings.
- Sets the OnAction property for the two dialog box buttons (HelpButton and StatsButton).

Listing 12-2 **InitializeDBox Subroutine**

```
Sub InitializeDBox()
'   Set object variables
    Set DBox = ThisWorkbook.DialogSheets("TextToolsDlg")

    Set OptionUpper = DBox.OptionButtons("OptionUpper")
    Set OptionLower = DBox.OptionButtons("OptionLower")
    Set OptionProper = DBox.OptionButtons("OptionProper")
    Set OptionNoChange = _
        DBox.OptionButtons("OptionNoChange")

    Set TextToAdd = DBox.EditBoxes("TextToAdd")
    Set OptionAddToLeft = _
        DBox.OptionButtons("OptionAddToLeft")
    Set OptionAddToRight = _
        DBox.OptionButtons("OptionAddToRight")
    Set OptionAddNone = DBox.OptionButtons("OptionAddNone")

    Set CharsToDelete = DBox.EditBoxes("CharsToDelete")
    Set OptionDeleteFromLeft = _
        DBox.OptionButtons("OptionDeleteFromLeft")
    Set OptionDeleteFromRight = _
        DBox.OptionButtons("OptionDeleteFromRight")
    Set OptionDeleteNone = _
        DBox.OptionButtons("OptionDeleteNone")
    Set CheckTrim = DBox.CheckBoxes("CheckTrim")
    Set IncludeNumeric = DBox.CheckBoxes("IncludeNumeric")

'   Initialize data for dialog box
    TextToAdd.Text = ""
    CharsToDelete.Text = ""
    OptionNoChange.Value = xlOn
    OptionAddNone.Value = xlOn
    OptionDeleteNone.Value = xlOn
    CheckTrim.Value = xlOff
    IncludeNumeric.Value = xlOff

'   Set subs for buttons
    DBox.Buttons("HelpButton").OnAction = "ShowHelp"
    DBox.Buttons("StatsButton").OnAction = "ShowStats"
End Sub
```

The CreateWorkRange subroutine

This subroutine (shown in Listing 12-3) creates a range object that consists of a subset of another range object. More specific, the range object created consists of the cells that contain text. If the Include numeric cells option is checked, the subset consists of the cells that contain text and the cells that contain values. In either case, the subset excludes blank cells and cells that contain formulas.

CreateWorkRange uses the SpecialCells method of the range object to quickly create a subset. This step is necessary if the original selection is large (for example, a complete column) because it eliminates the need to process empty cells.

Listing 12-3 CreateWorkRange Subroutine

```
Sub CreateWorkRange(InRange As Object, OutRange As Object, _
    RangeOK As Boolean)
'   Creates a working range - a subset with non-formula text
'       cells

    RangeOK = True
    Select Case InRange.Count
        Case 1 'Single cell selected
            If Not Application.IsText(ActiveCell) Or _
                ActiveCell.HasFormula Then
                RangeOK = False
                Exit Sub
            End If
            Set OutRange = ActiveCell

        Case Else 'Multiple cells selected
            On Error Resume Next 'To trap SpecialCells error
            If IncludeNumeric.Value = xlOn Then
                Set OutRange = _
                    InRange.SpecialCells(xlConstants, _
                        xlTextValues + xlNumbers)
                    Else Set OutRange = _
                       InRange.SpecialCells(xlConstants, _
                        xlTextValues)
            End If
            If Err = 1004 Then
                'SpecialCells error (none qualify)
                RangeOK = False
                Exit Sub
            End If
    End Select
End Sub
```

To understand how this code works, you need to understand the SpecialCells method. This method is very useful, but it can be rather tricky because:

- It generates an error (error 1004) when no cells qualify. I therefore had to build in some error-trapping code.
- If the range that it's working on consists of only one cell, it uses the entire worksheet as its range. So I added a Select Case structure to perform a different action if the input range is only one cell.

The ProcessRequests

The ProcessRequests subroutine modifies the cells in the selection according to the instructions entered into the dialog box.

This subroutine — which works with the subset (WorkRange), not the original selection — uses If...Then structures:

```
Sub ProcessRequests()
'   Performs requested text manipulations

    Application.ScreenUpdating = False

    For Each Cell In WorkRange

'       Remove excess spaces?
        If CheckTrim.Value = xlOn Then Cell.Value = _
            Application.Trim(Cell.Value)

'       Add text?
        If OptionAddNone.Value = xlOff Then
            NewText = TextToAdd.Text
            If OptionAddToLeft.Value = xlOn Then
                Cell.Value = NewText & Cell.Value
                Else Cell.Value = Cell.Value & NewText
            End If
        End If

'       Remove text?
        If OptionDeleteNone.Value = xlOff Then
            NumToDelete = CharsToDelete.Text
            If Len(Cell.Value) <= NumToDelete Then _
                 NumToDelete = _
                 Len(Cell.Value)
            If OptionDeleteFromLeft.Value = xlOn Then
               Cell.Value = Right(Cell.Value, _
                    Len(Cell.Value) - NumToDelete)
```

```
                Else Cell.Value = Left(Cell.Value, _
                   Len(Cell.Value) - NumToDelete)
            End If
        End If

'       Change case?
        If OptionProper.Value = xlOn Then
            Cell.Value = Application.Proper(Cell.Value)
            ElseIf OptionUpper.Value = xlOn Then
                Cell.Value = UCase(Cell.Value)
                ElseIf OptionLower.Value = xlOn Then
                    Cell.Value = LCase(Cell.Value)
        End If
    Next Cell
End Sub
```

Notice that the events occur in a particular (though arbitrary) order. This order can affect the end result. For example, text is added before the case is changed. So if instructions call for adding a text string to the cells *and* changing the case, the case of the added text also may be changed.

The ShowStats subroutine

ShowStats is executed when the Stats button is clicked. The dialog box remains while the statistics are calculated and displayed in a message box.

```
Sub ShowStats()
'   Displays word count and character count
'   Executed when Stats button is clicked

    Dim NumWords As Integer, NumChars As Integer
    Dim CellLength As Integer
    Dim Msg As String
    Dim Words As Integer
    Dim Contents As String

'   Create a subset of the original selection
    Call CreateWorkRange(Selection, WorkRange, RangeOK)

'   Exit if no cells qualify
    If Not RangeOK Then
        MsgBox "Nothing to count...", vbInformation
        Exit Sub
    End If

'   Count words and characters
    NumWords = 0
    NumChars = 0
```

```
        For Each Cell In WorkRange
            CellLength = Len(Cell.Value)
            NumChars = NumChars + CellLength
            Contents = Application.Trim(Cell)
            Words = 1
            For i = 1 To Len(Contents)
                If Mid(Contents, i, 1) = " " Then Words = Words + 1
            Next i
            NumWords = NumWords + Words
        Next Cell

'   Display the result
    Msg = "Words:" & Chr(9) & Chr(9) & NumWords
    Msg = Msg & Chr(13) & "Characters:" & Chr(9) & NumChars
    MsgBox Msg, vbInformation, "Current Selection"
End Sub
```

Other subroutines

The module has three other small subroutines. ShowHelp is executed when the Help button is clicked. It looks for the help file in the same directory as the application's workbook. The help file has only one topic, and its context ID is 0. I discuss accessing help files in Chapter 16.

```
Sub ShowHelp()
'   Executed when Help button clicked
    Application.Help ThisWorkbook.Path & "\TEXTOOLS.HLP", 0

End Sub
```

The AddBoxChange routine is executed whenever text in the TextToAdd edit box is modified. This routine sets the OptionAddLeft option button to xlOn (the default) — but only when the OptionAddNone button is on.

```
Sub AddBoxChange()
'   Executed when text is entered into TextToAdd edit box
    If OptionAddNone = xlOn Then OptionAddToLeft = xlOn
End Sub
```

The DelBoxChange routine is executed whenever text in the CharToDel edit box is modified. This routine sets the OptionDeleteFromLeft option button to xlOn (the default) — but only when the OptionDeleteNone button is on.

```
Sub DelBoxChange()
'   Executed when text is entered into CharsToDel edit box
    If OptionDeleteNone = xlOn Then OptionDeleteFromLeft = _
        xlOn
End Sub
```

Using the Text Tools utility

You can call the TextTools subroutine by choosing the Tools⇨Text Tools command or pressing Ctrl+T.

I used the Options button in the Object Browser to make these assignments.

If you still don't understand how this utility works, I urge you to load the file and then use the Debugger to step through it. Try it out with different types of selections, including an entire worksheet. You will see that regardless of the size of the original selection only the appropriate cells are processed and empty cells are completely ignored. If a worksheet only has one cell with text in it, the utility operates just as quickly whether you select that cell or the entire worksheet.

The Power Utility Pak

In this section, I briefly describe the utilities in the Power Utility Pak. The Power Utility Pak is a collection of utilities and custom worksheet functions, accessible from a custom Utilities menu or a custom toolbar. A complete on-line help file is included.

Text Tools

Manipulates text in cells. This utility not only enables you to change the case of text, it also lets you add specific text to each cell or delete a fixed number of characters from each cell. If you want, the utility counts the number of words and characters in the selected text.

I describe how I developed this utility in the preceding section.

Select By Value

Selects a group of cells based on its value. For example, this utility can flag cells that have a negative value. After this utility selects these cells, the user can apply formatting to make the values stand out. This utility also works with dates.

Figure 12-3 shows the dialog box for the Select By Value utility.

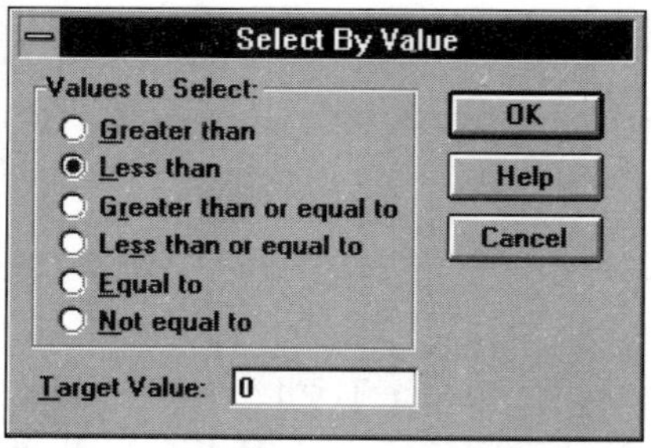

Figure 12-3: The Select By Value utility.

Interactive Zooming

Magnifies or reduces a worksheet or chart interactively. A handy scroller and preview button lets the users see the results before they commit to the new view. If the users choose auto-preview mode, the zooming changes automatically.

Figure 12-4 shows the dialog box for the Interactive Zooming utility.

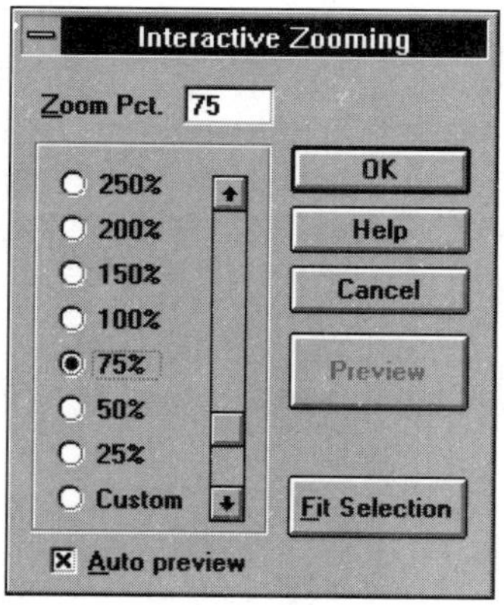

Figure 12-4: The Interactive Zooming utility.

Reminder Note

Adds a reminder note to a worksheet, chart, or dialog sheet. The user can choose the color, text style, and determine whether it will print.

Figure 12-5 shows the dialog box for the Reminder Note utility.

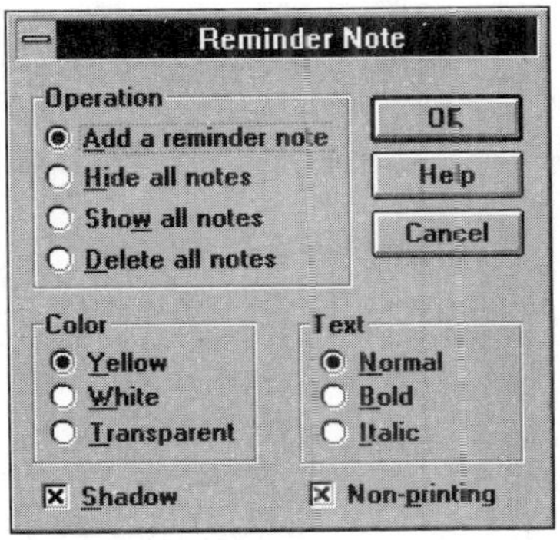

Figure 12-5: The Reminder Note utility.

Object Align, Size and Space

A fast, easy, and reliable way to align and resize drawn objects on a worksheet, chart, or in a custom dialog box. Another option adjusts the objects so that they are evenly spaced.

Figure 12-6 shows the dialog box for the Object Align, Size and Space utility.

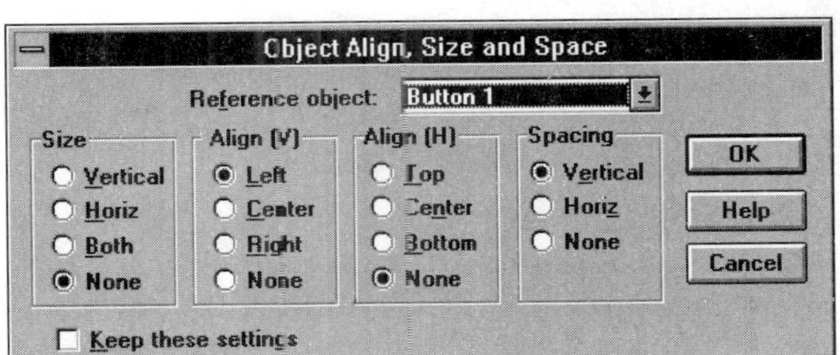

Figure 12-6: The Object Align, Size and Space utility.

Calculator

Displays a mouseable calculator (it also accepts input from the keyboard). Any result can be pasted into a cell.

Figure 12-7 shows the dialog box for the Calculator utility.

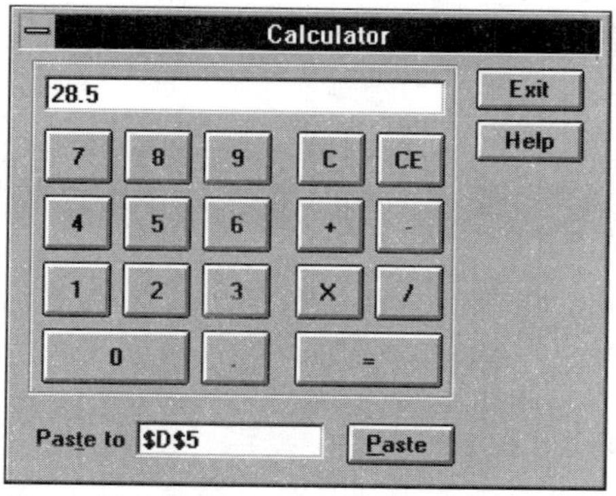

Figure 12-7: The Calculator utility.

3D Cell Shading

Adds an attractive three-dimensional look to a worksheet. The user can choose a raised or depressed look, designate the color, and specify the line thickness.

Figure 12-8 shows the dialog box for the 3D Cell Shading utility.

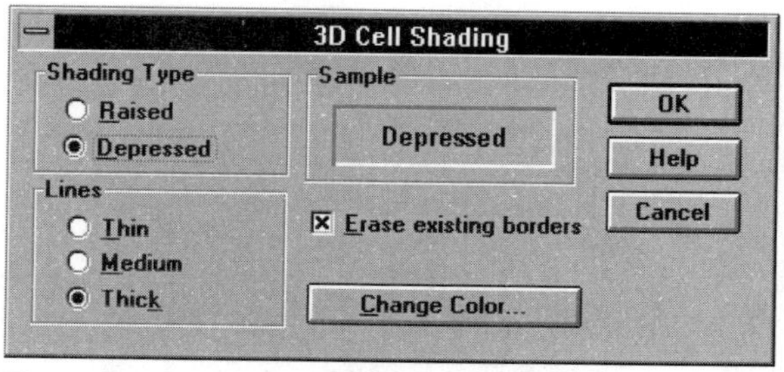

Figure 12-8: The 3D Cell Shading utility.

Date and Time

Displays the current date, time, and day of the week. This utility also lets the user adjust the system time and date.

Figure 12-9 shows the dialog box for the Date and Time utility.

Figure 12-9: The Date and Time utility.

Insert a Formatted Date

Inserts a formatted date into a cell. The user can choose the date from a calendar display; then the user can choose from a variety of date formats. The column width can be automatically adjusted to accommodate the pasted date.

Figure 12-10 shows the dialog box for the Insert a Formatted Date utility.

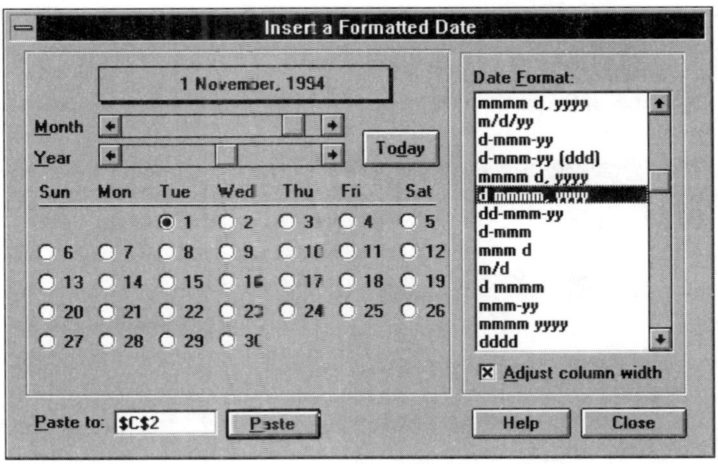

Figure 12-10: The Insert a Formatted Date utility.

Perpetual Calendar

Displays a handy and attractive pop-up calendar (for any month between 1900 and 2078). The calendar picture can be pasted into a worksheet or chart.

Figure 12-11 shows the dialog box for the Perpetual Calendar utility.

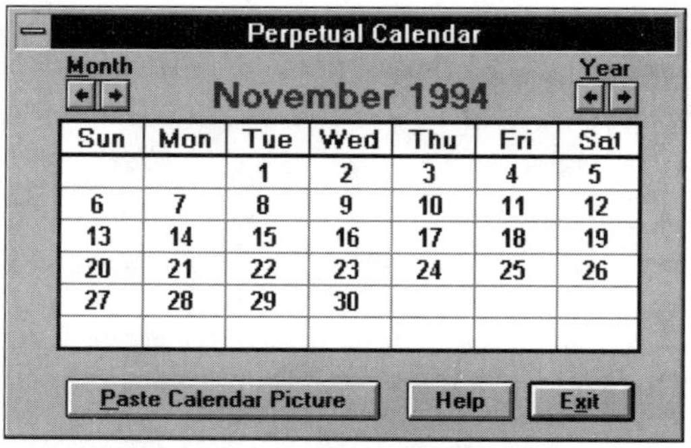

Figure 12-11: The Perpetual Calendar utility.

Set Reminder Alarm

Displays a reminder message at a specified time. After the user sets the alarm, Excel's title bar displays the time that the alarm is set for. Three beeps accompany the reminder message so that the reminder is effective even if the user is not working in Excel.

Figure 12-12 shows the dialog box for the Set Reminder Alarm utility.

Figure 12-12: The Set Reminder Alarm utility.

Time Tracker

Keeps track of the amount of time spent working on various projects (the projects need not be Excel projects). The user can track the time spent on up to four projects — the user can customize the project or client names used.

Figure 12-13 shows the dialog box for the Time Tracker utility.

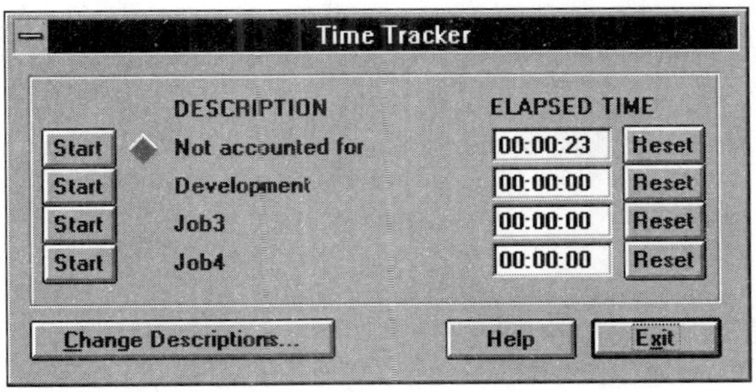

Figure 12-13: The Time Tracker utility.

Object Properties

Displays the dimensions and position of graphic objects. The user can enter new dimensions or reposition the object by specifying coordinates. This utility, which also allows hiding and unhiding objects, gives the user much more precise control than a mouse. (In fact, this utility enables the user to manipulate graphic objects even if a mouse is not installed.)

Figure 12-14 shows the dialog box for the Object Properties utility.

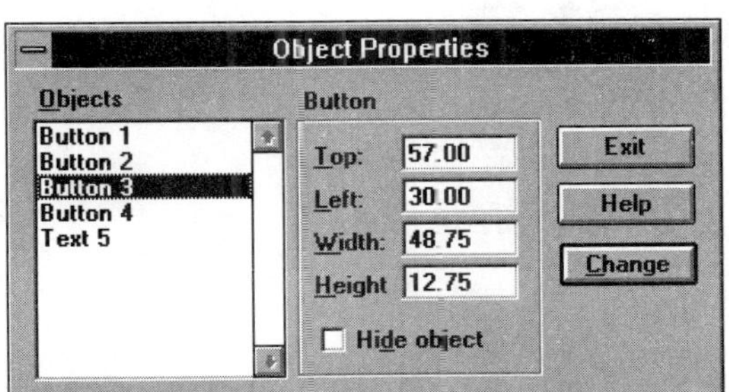

Figure 12-14: The Object Properties utility.

Super Go To

Allows easy navigation through multiple workbooks and worksheets. The user can select the workbook, sheet, or range to activate. A handy preview mode displays the selection (even if it's in a hidden or minimized workbook). The dialog box can be used in two sizes (smaller if ranges names are not used).

Figure 12-15 shows the dialog box for the Super Go To utility.

Figure 12-15: The Super Go To utility.

Workbook Table of Contents

Displays a handy table of contents that lists all sheets in the workbook. This utility also displays the type of sheet (worksheet, macro sheet, chart, and so on). Double-clicking activates the selected sheet.

Figure 12-16 shows the dialog box for the Workbook Table of Contents utility.

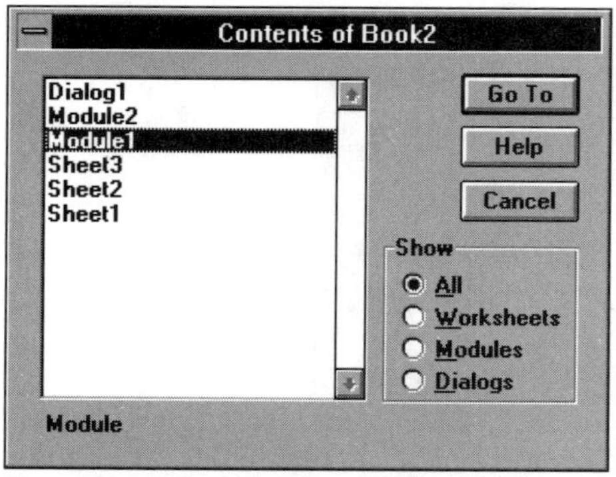

Figure 12-16: The Workbook Table of Contents utility.

Save With Backup

Saves the active workbook with a backup copy. Normally, saving a workbook to a floppy disk to make a backup is a cumbersome procedure because Excel remembers the floppy drive as the workbook's location. When the file is saved again, it is saved to the floppy disk, unless the user remembers to use the File⇨Save As command to redirect the save back to the hard drive. This utility saves a workbook to the selected floppy disk (or another directory) and then saves it back to the hard drive in one step.

Figure 12-17 shows the dialog box for the Save With Backup utility.

Figure 12-17: The Save With Backup utility.

Batch Printing

Prints a group of workbooks unattended. The user, who can designate any number of files to print, chooses exactly what gets printed — worksheets, chart sheets, VBA modules, or dialog sheets.

Figure 12-18 shows the dialog box for the Batch Printing utility.

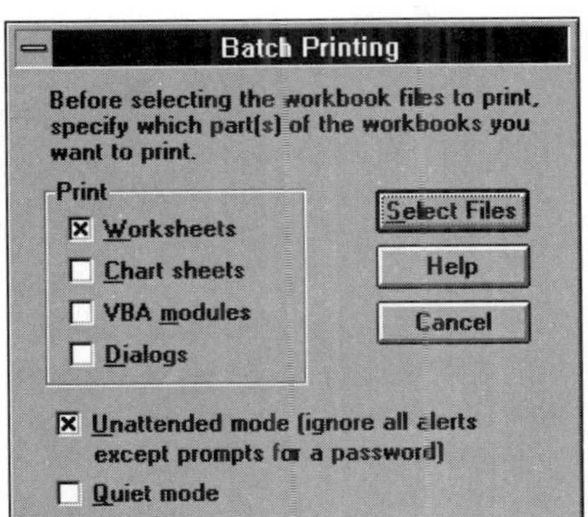

Figure 12-18: The Batch Printing utility.

Summary

- In this chapter, I discussed why it's a good idea to write your own Excel utilities with VBA. I also presented and explained the VBA code for the Text Tools utility.
- In the next chapter, I explain how to convert any Excel application — including a utility — into an add-in.

Chapter 13

Creating and Using Add-Ins

In This Chapter

- What is an add-in, and why you need to understand the concept thoroughly.
- Advantages of creating your own add-ins.
- Debunking some of the myths about add-ins.
- How to create an add-in.
- How XLA files differ from XLS files.
- Examples of VBA code that manipulates add-ins.

One of the ways Excel differs from other spreadsheets on the market is the way it handles add-ins. Other spreadsheet products support add-ins, but Excel is the only one that doesn't require an external compiler to create add-ins. This chapter discusses the ins and outs of Excel add-ins — an important topic for Excel developers.

What Is an Add-in?

Generally speaking, a spreadsheet add-in is something added to a spreadsheet to give it additional functionality. For example, many add-ins are available for 1-2-3 for DOS that add new features to the program. These new features can be industry-specific features (for example, the third-party financial forecasting add-ins) or very general features such as on-screen formatting (such as the WYSIWYG add-in that's included with 1-2-3). Some add-ins provide new worksheet functions that can be used in formulas. The new features usually blend in well with the original interface, so they appear to be part of the program (this is referred to as seamless integration). Lotus originated the concept of spreadsheet add-ins, and dozens of third-party developers market add-in products for 1-2-3.

Excel's approach to add-ins is a bit different because any Excel user can create add-ins from XLS workbooks. An Excel add-in is basically a different form of an XLS workbook file — although Excel add-ins can also be written entirely in C, and compiled. Any XLS file can be converted into an add-in, but not all XLS files are appropriate for an add-ins. For example, add-ins are always hidden so you can't display worksheets or chart sheets that are contained in an add-in. But you can access an add-in's VBA subroutines and functions, and display dialog boxes contained on dialog sheets.

Some typical uses for Excel add-ins include the following:

- *Storing one or more custom worksheet functions.* When the add-in is loaded, the functions can be used just like any of the built-in worksheet functions.
- *Storing Excel utilities.* As you read in Chapter 12, VBA is ideal for creating general-purpose utilities that extend the power of Excel.
- *Storing applications.* For example, you might create an add-in application that generates a custom budget template. The XLA file can store custom menu definition, custom dialog boxes, custom toolbars, and — of course — the VBA code that ties it all together.
- *Simplify using templates.* You can create an add-in from a template (XLT) file that creates a new workbook based on the template when the add-in is loaded. Excel's slide show feature is an example of a template add-in. This feature uses SLIDES.XLT.

Add-ins supplied with Excel 5

You may have used one or more of the add-ins supplied with Excel (maybe without even realizing it). The table below describes the add-ins included with Excel 5. Depending on how you installed Excel, not all of these may be available. You can re-run the Setup program to install add-ins that were omitted during the original installation.

Interestingly, all the add-ins supplied with Excel 5 were developed using the XLM macro language. A few of the add-ins do have VBA sheets, but the procedures simply call XLM macros. All of the dialog boxes are created with XLM code rather than with the custom dialog box feature. Does this mean that Microsoft trusts its XLM macro language more than VBA? I doubt it. My guess is that they just didn't see any need to redevelop add-ins that were already working.

Add-In	*File(s)*	*What It Does*
Analysis ToolPak – VBA	ATPVBAEN.XLA	VBA functions for Analysis ToolPak.
AutoSave	AUTOSAVE.XLA	Automatically saves your workbook at a time interval you specify.
MS Excel 4.0 Add-in Functions	ADDINFNS.XLA	Provides backward compatibility for Microsoft Excel 4.0 Add-in Functions.
MS Excel 4.0 Analysis Functions	ANALYSF.XLA	Provides backward compatibility for Microsoft Excel 4.0 Analysis Functions.
MS Excel 4.0 Analysis Tools	ANALYSIS.XLA	Provides backward compatibility for Microsoft Excel 4.0 Analysis Tools.
MS Query Add-In	XLQUERY.XLA	Works with Microsoft Query to gather external data.
ODBC Add-In	XLODBC.XLA XLODBC.DLL	Lets you use ODBC functions to connect to external data sources directly.
Report Manager	REPORTS.XLA	Prints reports that consist of a set sequence of views and scenarios.
Slideshow Template	SLIDES.XLT SLIDES.XLA XLSLIDES.DLL	Use this to create a slide show from worksheets and charts.
Solver Add-In	SOLVER.XLA SOLVER.DLL	A tool that helps you use a variety of numeric methods for equation solving and optimization.
Update Add-in Links	UPDTLINK.XLA	Updates links to MS Excel 4.0 add-ins to directly access the new built-in functionality.
View Manager	VIEWS.XLA	Creates, stores, and displays different views of a worksheet.

Why Create Add-ins?

Most Excel *users* have no need to create add-ins. But as a *developer,* you need to thoroughly understand what add-ins can do. The following list includes just some of the reasons you would want to convert your XLS application to an add-in:

- *Prevent access to your code.* When you distribute an application as an add-in, end users cannot view the sheets in the workbook. If you use proprietary techniques in your VBA code, you can prevent anyone from copying the code.
- *Avoid confusing users.* If an end user loads your application as an add-in, the file is not visible and is therefore less likely to confuse novice users or get in the way. Unlike a hidden XLS workbook, an add-in cannot be unhidden.
- *Simplify access to worksheet functions.* Custom worksheet functions that are stored in an add-in don't require the workbook name qualifier. For example, if you have a custom function named MOVAVG stored in NEWFUNCS.XLS, you need to use syntax like the following to use this function in a different workbook:

  ```
  =NEWFUNC.XLS!MOVAVG(A1:A50)
  ```

  But if this function is stored in an add-in file that's open, the syntax is much simpler because you don't need to include the file reference:

  ```
  =MOVAVG(A1:A50)
  ```

- *Easier access for users.* After you add your add-in to Excel's AddIns collection, it appears in the Add-Ins dialog box, with a friendly name and a description of what it does.
- *Gain better control over loading.* Add-ins can be opened automatically when Excel starts, regardless of the directory in which they are stored.
- *No prompts when unloading.* When an add-in is closed, the user never sees the "Save change in...?" prompt.

The rest of this chapter helps clarify these issues.

Myths about XLA files

According to the *Visual Basic User's Guide:*

"When you save a workbook in the add-in format, Microsoft Excel converts its code into a compressed form that cannot be read by anyone, and cannot be converted back into a workbook. This is called compiling. Compiling speeds execution of the resulting code and protects your work from being read or modified by anyone else."

As good as it sounds, the preceding statement is simply filled with untruths. I'll do my best to clear up these add-in myths.

- An add-in is not compressed in any way. For example, the comments in your VBA code are not even removed. Usually, the XLA version of an XLS file is exactly the same size as the original.
- Add-ins are not compiled — at least not according to the normal meaning of this term. When you execute a VBA routine, the VBA code is converted to *p-code* before it is executed. This same conversion occurs whether the code is run from an XLS file or from an XLA file.
- The code in an add-in does not run noticeably faster than the same code in a plain XLS file. This is easy enough to test, and my tests don't show any significant difference at all. In fact, some operations — those that access worksheets stored in an XLA — may be a bit slower.
- Despite claims to the contrary, XLA files *can* be converted back to their original XLS source. This requires a bit of trickery, but it is possible. As long as the XLA file can be loaded without a password, it is possible to recover all the original sheets in the XLA, including the VBA modules.

No doubt about it, add-ins are a great concept. But if you plan to use them, you should know the truth about them.

Creating an Add-in

Creating an add-in is amazingly simple. This section describes how to create an add-in from a normal workbook file.

1. Develop your application, and make sure that everything works properly.
2. Test the application by executing it when a different workbook is active.

   This simulates the applications's behavior when it's used as an add-in because an add-in is never the active workbook. You might find that some references no longer work. For example, the following statement works fine when the code resides in the active workbook, but fails when a different workbook is active:

   ```
   Dialogsheets("MyDialog").Show
   ```

You could qualify the reference with the name of the workbook object, like this:

```
Workbooks("MYBOOK.XLS").Dialogsheets("MyDialog").Show
```

I don't recommend this method because the name of the workbook changes when it's converted to an add-in. The solution is to use the ThisWorkbook qualifier, as follows:

```
ThisWorkbook.Dialogsheets("MyDialog").Show
```

3. Be sure that you remove any debugging code that you may have left behind, including MsgBox statements or Debug.Print statements (statements that print to the Debug window) that you may have used during the debugging stage.

4. Select the File➪Summary Info command, and enter a brief descriptive title in the Title field, and a longer description in the Comments field.

   This step is not required, but it makes it easier to use the add-in.

5. Activate any VBA module or any dialog sheet in the workbook and select the Tools➪Make Add-In command.

   Excel responds with the dialog box shown in Figure 13-1. It suggests the current workbook name, with an XLA extension. Click OK and the add-in is created. An add-in file can have any extension you want. But unless you have a good reason to do otherwise (and there *are* some good reasons), you should use the standard XLA extension.

NOTE

If Excel discovers any syntax errors in your VBA code, the add-in is not created. Correct the error, save your file, and try again to create the add-in. Also, Excel will not let you create an add-in if an add-in with the same name is already installed. Use the Tools➪Add-Ins command to uninstall the add-in; then try again.

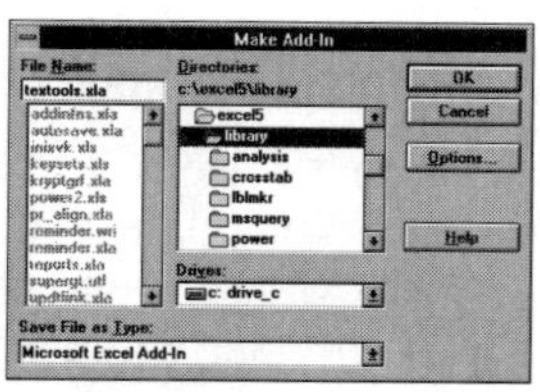

Figure 13-1: Creating an add-in is a simple process.

Strange as it may seem, there is no way to create an add-in from an XLS workbook using pure VBA code. The XLM macro language *does* have a function to create an add-in (it's the VBA.MAKE.ADDIN function). Therefore, you can use the following VBA statement to create an add-in from the active workbook:

```
ExecuteExcel4Macro "VBA.MAKE.ADDIN(""MYADDIN.XLA"")"
```

CAUTION

In the preceding example, if MYADDIN.XLA is open when the statement is executed, the add-in is not created — and you'll get no warning to that effect. Therefore, it's a good idea to check to see if an add-in that name is already installed.

Using Add-ins

Before you can use an add-in, it must be loaded into memory (this book is just filled with insights, no?). There's an important distinction between *opening* an add-in and *installing* an add-in.

About Excel's Add-In Manager

You access Excel's Add-In Manager by selecting the Tools⇨Add-Ins command, which displays the Add-Ins dialog box. This dialog box lists the names of all of the available add-ins (in VBA terms, the Add-In dialog box lists the Title property of each AddIn object in the AddIns collection). Of the listed add-ins, those that are checked are currently open (in VBA parlance, an open add-in has its Installed property set to True).

You can install an add-in by checking its box. You can close an open add-in by removing the checkmark from its box. To add an add-in to the list, use the Browse button to locate its file. The Add-In dialog box lists files of the following types:

XLA files	An add-in created from an XLS file.
XLL files	Stand-alone DLL files, written in C and compiled.
XLT files	Excel template files. When an XLT is opened by the Add-In Manager, it creates a new workbook based on the template.

You can add add-in files to the AddIns collection using VBA code (by using the Add method of the AddIns collection), but you can't remove them using VBA. You can also open an add-in from VBA by setting the AddIn object's Installed property to True. Setting it to False closes the add-in.

The Add-In manager stores the installed status of the add-ins in EXCEL5.INI when you exit Excel. Therefore, all add-ins that are installed when you close Excel are opened automatically the next time you start Excel.

Installing an add-in

To install an add-in file, use the Tools➪Add-Ins command. If the add-in is in the official AddIns collection, it appears in the list of add-ins. If it's not in the list, you can use the Browse button in the Add-Ins dialog box to locate the add-in file.

As you'll see, the Add-Ins dialog box lists all add-ins in the AddIns collection. Those with a checkmark next to them are *installed*, that is, loaded into memory and available for use. Add-ins, installed or not, are not part of the Workbooks collection.

To remove an installed add-in from memory, select the Tools➪Add-In command and remove the checkmark from the add-in.

Opening an add-in

You can also use the standard File➪Open command to load an add-in file into memory, but this does *not* install it. If the add-in is not part of the AddIns collection, Excel will not add the add-in to the collection. Even if the add-in *is* a member of the AddIns collection, Excel does not consider it to be installed. Furthermore, Excel doesn't add it to the Workbooks collection. In other words, an add-in that's opened using File➪Open command is in limbo — there is no direct way to unload an add-in opened with the File➪Open command.

As you may have surmised, using the Tools➪Add-Ins command is the preferred way to load an add-in into memory. In previous versions of Excel, the File➪Open command was the standard way to use an add-in. Consequently, many long-time Excel users continue to use this method.

Comparing XLA and XLS Files

This section describes exactly how an add-in version of a file differs from its XLS source file.

File size and structure

Most of the time an add-in created from an XLS is exactly the same size as the XLS source file. Occasionally, they may differ by a small amount (and I'm not sure why). When I made my first add-in using Excel 5, I was surprised to discover this. I assumed that the VBA code in XLA files would be compressed, or at least optimized in some way. I was wrong. Creating an add-in doesn't even strip out the comments in a VBA module.

TIP

If you need to keep the size of your VBA module as small as possible, save the XLS file, delete all the comments and blank lines, and then create the add-in. Then, *don't* save the XLS file again (despite Excel's warning), or you'll lose all of your comments. The size reduction depends on the amount of commenting you do, but I've been able to reduce the size of my XLA files by as much as 35 percent by removing the comments.

Windows

XLS workbooks are displayed in one or more windows. The following statement will display the number of windows for the active workbook:

```
MsgBox ThisWorkbook.Windows.Count
```

You can manipulate the visibility of each window for an XLS workbook by using the Window⇨Hide command, or by changing the Visible property. For example, the following code hides all windows for the active workbook:

```
For Each Win In ActiveWorkbook.Windows
      Win.Visible = False
Next Win
```

Add-in files are never visible, and they don't even have windows. They don't appear in the menu when you select the Window command. If MYADDIN.XLA is open, the following statement returns 0.

```
MsgBox Workbooks("MYADDIN.XLA").Windows.Count
```

Sheets

XLA files — like XLS files — can have any number of sheets. An XLA file must have at least one VBA module, however, or at least one dialog sheet. Actually, this isn't a strict requirement, but the command to create an add-in is available on the menu only when a module or dialog sheet is active. If you really insist, you can use the XLM function VBA.MAKE.ADDIN to create an add-in that consists only of worksheets.

When an add-in is open, your VBA code can access the sheets in the add-in just as if it were any other workbook. Because add-in files aren't part of the Workbooks collection, though, you must reference the workbook by its name. The following example displays the value in cell A1 of the first worksheet in MYADDIN.XLA (which is assumed to be open):

```
MsgBox
Workbooks("MYADDIN.XLA").Worksheets(1).Range("A1").Value
```

Accessing VBA procedures

Accessing VBA subroutines and functions in add-ins is a bit different than accessing procedures in a normal XLS workbook.

First of all, when you issue the Tools➪Macro command, the Macro dialog box does not display the macro names in the add-ins that are open (it's almost as if Excel is trying to prevent you from accessing them). This means that you normally have to provide other means to access the procedures in an add-in. Your choices include direct methods such as shortcut keys, custom menus, custom toolbars, as well as indirect methods — event handlers (for example, the OnTime method, which executes a procedure at a specific time of day).

If you know the name of the macro in the add-in, you can execute it in a number of different ways (as long as the procedure wasn't declared with the Private keyword).

TIP

You can use the Object Browser to determine the names of the macros in an open add-in (press F2 in a VBA module to display the Object Browser). The Methods/Properties listbox displays all subroutine and function names in the selected module of the selected add-in.

If you know the procedure's name, you can enter the name (preceded by its workbook name) into the Macro dialog box, and the procedure executes. For example, if MYADDIN.XLA is open and it has a subroutine named DisplayNames, you can enter the following text into the Macro Name/Reference edit box in the Macro dialog box:

```
MYADDIN.XLA!DisplayNames
```

Similarly, you can execute that subroutine by using the Run method of the Application object, like this:

```
Application.Run "MYADDIN.XLA!DisplayNames"
```

If you add the add-in as a reference (using the Tools➪References command), you can refer to it in your VBA code directly, without the filename qualifier. In fact, after you establish a reference to the add-in, you don't need to use the Run method. The following statement does the trick:

```
DisplayNames
```

Even with a reference to the add-in established, the add-in's macro names does not appear in the Macros dialog box.

Functions defined in an add-in work just like functions defined in an XLS workbook. They are easy to access because Excel displays their names in the Function Wizard dialog box under the User Defined category. The only exception is if the function was declared with the Private keyword, the function does not appear in the Function Wizard.

As I discussed earlier, you can use worksheet functions contained in add-ins without the workbook name qualifier. For example, if you have a custom function named MOVAVG stored in NEWFUNCS.XLS, you have to use a syntax like the following to use this function in a different workbook:

```
=NEWFUNCS.XLS!MOVAVG(A1:A50)
```

But if this function is stored in an add-in file that's open, you can omit the file reference and use something like:

```
=MOVAVG(A1:A50)
```

Manipulating Add-ins with VBA

The AddIns collection consists of all add-ins that Excel knows about. These add-ins can either be installed or not. The Tools⇨Add-Ins command displays the Add-Ins dialog box, which lists all add-ins in the AddIns collection (see Figure 13-2). Those with a checkmark next to them are currently installed.

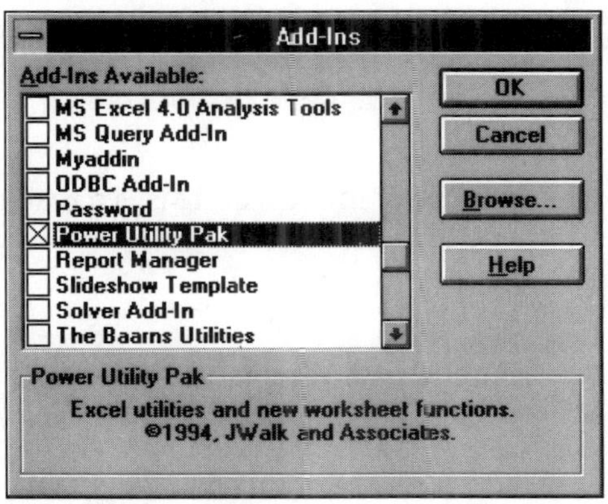

Figure 13-2: The Add-Ins dialog box lists all add-ins in the AddIns collection.

An AddIn object is a single add-in in the AddIns collection. For example, to display the filename of the first add-in in the AddIns collection, use the following:

```
Msgbox AddIns(1).Name
```

You can use the Add method to add an add-in to the AddIns collection, but — oddly — there is no direct way to remove an add-in from the AddIns collection (the AddIns collection doesn't have a Delete method). To remove an add-in from the Add-Ins dialog box, delete the reference to it in the [Add-In Manager] section of the EXCEL5.INI file. The add-in will not appear in the Add-Ins dialog box the next time you start Excel. Or, if you delete or move the add-in file, you'll get a warning the next time you try to install or uninstall the add-in — along with an opportunity to remove it from the AddIns collection (see Figure 13-3).

Figure 13-3: Trying to install an add-in that can't be found is one way to remove an add-in from the AddIns collection.

AddIn object properties

An AddIn object has 12 properties, which you can read about in the on-line help. Some of the terminology is a bit confusing, so I'll discuss a few of the more important properties.

Name

The Name property holds the filename of the add-in. This is a read-only property, so you can't change the name of the file by changing the Name property.

Path

The Path property holds the drive and path where the add-in file is stored. It does not include a final backslash, or the filename.

FullName

The FullName property holds the drive, path, and filename. This property is a bit redundant because this information is also available from the Name and Path properties. The following statements produce exactly the same message.

```
MsgBox AddIns(1).Path & "\" & AddIns(1).Name
MsgBox AddIns(1).FullName
```

Title

The Title property holds a descriptive name for the add-in. The Title property is what appears in the Add-Ins dialog box. This property is read-only, and the only way to add or change the Title property of an add-in is to use the File⇨Summary Info command (you must use this command with the XLS version, before converting it to an add-in). The Summary Info dialog box is shown in Figure 13-4.

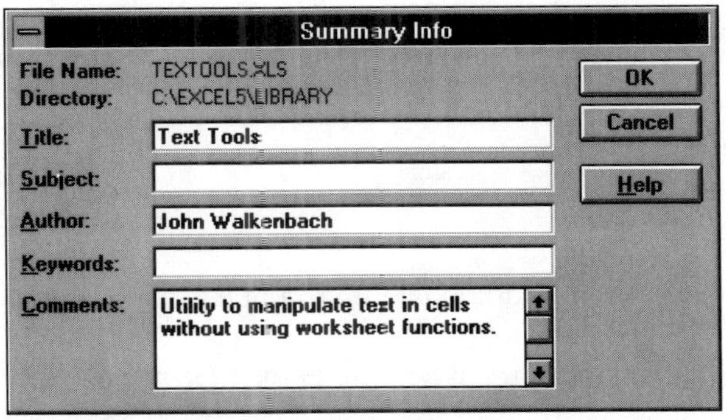

Figure 13-4: The Summary Info dialog box lets you change five properties for an add-in.

Most collections use the object's Name property to reference individual items in the collection. The AddIns collection is different — it uses the AddIn object's Title property. The following example displays the filename for the View Manager add-in (that is, VIEWS.XLA). The View Manager add-in's Title property is "View Manager".

```
Sub ShowName()
       MsgBox AddIns("View Manager").Name
End Sub
```

Installed

The Installed property is True if the add-in is currently in memory. When you examine the Add-Ins dialog box, the add-ins that are checked are currently installed. Setting the Installed property to True opens the add-in. Setting it to False unloads it. Here's an example of how to install (that is, open) the MS Query add-in using VBA.

```
Sub InstallQuery()
    AddIns("MS Query Add-In").Installed = True
End Sub
```

After this subroutine is executed, the Add-Ins dialog box displays an X next to MS Query Add-In. If the add-in is already installed, it has no effect. To remove this add-in (uninstall it), simply set the Installed property to False.

Comments

The Comments property stores text that is displayed in the Add-Ins dialog box when a particular add-in is selected. As with the Title property, Comments is a read-only property, and the only way to change it is to use the Summary Info dialog box before you create the add-in. Comments can be as long as 255 characters, but the Add-Ins dialog box can display only about 100 characters.

More VBA techniques

This section presents some additional VBA examples that deal with add-ins.

Adding an add-in to the AddIns collection

To add a new member to the AddIns collection, use the Add method. The following example adds MYADDIN.XLA to the AddIns collection.

```
Sub AddToCollection()
    AddIns.Add "MYADDIN.XLA"
End Sub
```

If the add-in you're adding is on a removable disk (for example, a floppy disk or CD-ROM), you can also copy the file to Excel's library directory with the Add method. The following example copies MYADDIN.XLA from drive B and adds it to the AddIns collection. The second argument (True, in this case) specifies whether the add-in should be copied. If the add-in is on a hard drive, the second argument is ignored.

```
Sub AddToCollection()
    AddIns.Add "B:\MYADDIN.XLA", True
End Sub
```

NOTE

Adding an add-in to the AddIns collection does not install it. Set the Installed property to True to load the add-in.

Determining if a file is an add-in

You can access a Workbook object's FileFormat property to determine if a particular workbook is an add-in. This may seem rather useless, but there are some good uses for this property. For example, if you're working on an application that you will convert to an add-in, you may not want the Auto_Open procedure to run while you're testing the application. In other words, you only want Auto_Open to execute in the XLA version of the file. You *could* press the Shift key when you open the file (this prevents Auto_Open from executing), but a better approach is to use the following code. This simply exits the subroutine if the FileFormat property is not equal to the xlAddIn constant:

```
Sub Auto_Open()
    If ThisWorkbook.FileFormat <> xlAddIn Then Exit Sub
'   [... code goes here ...]
End Sub
```

Accessing an add-in as a workbook

As I mentioned earlier, there are two ways to open an add-in file: using the File⇨Open command, and using the Tools⇨Add-Ins command. The latter method is the preferred method for the following reason: When you open an add-in with the File⇨Open command, its Installed property is *not* set to True. Therefore, you cannot close the file using the Add-Ins dialog box. In fact, the only way to close such an add-in is to use a VBA statement such as:

```
Workbooks("MYADDIN.XLA").Close
```

This suggests that an open add-in is part of the Workbooks collection, but it's not. Add-ins can be referenced as a Workbook object, even though they are not part of the Workbooks collection. To demonstrate, take a look at the following code. It opens an add-in file, installs an add-in, and then displays the Count property of the Workbooks collection.

```
Sub CountWorkbooks()
    Workbooks.Open filename:=Application.LibraryPath _
        & "\" & "VIEWS.XLA"
    AddIns("MS Query Add-In").Installed = True
    MsgBox Workbooks.Count
End Sub
```

The message box displays only the number of workbooks open (the two add-ins are not counted). However, you'll find that you can access the add-ins just as you can access a workbook in the Workbooks collection. For example, the following statement displays the number of sheets in the XLQUERY.XLA add-in:

```
MsgBox Workbooks("XLQUERY.XLA").Sheets.Count
```

Using the Close method on an installed add-in removes the add-in from memory, but it does *not* set its Installed property to False. Therefore, the Add-Ins dialog box still lists the add-in as installed — which can be very confusing. The proper way to remove an installed add-in is to set its Installed property to False.

If you use the File➪Open command to open an add-in that's currently installed or has already been opened with the File➪Open command, the command has no effect.

Counting installed add-ins

The following procedure displays the number of add-ins in the AddIns collection and the number of those that are installed. You'll find that the count does not include add-ins that were opened with the File➪Open command.

```
Sub CountInstalledAddIns()
    Count = 0
    For Each Item In AddIns
        If Item.Installed Then Count = Count + 1
    Next Item
    Msg = "Add-ins: " & AddIns.Count & Chr(13)
    Msg = Msg & "Installed: " & Count
    MsgBox Msg
End Sub
```

Accessing an add-in by its filename

There are only two ways to directly reference a specific add-in: using the index number for its position in the AddIns collection (which you usually won't know), or using the Title property as described earlier. Referencing the add-in by its filename does not work. For example, the following statement generates an error:

```
AddIns("VIEWS.XLA").Installed = True
```

This might lead you to believe that you can install an add-in with VBA only if you know the index number of the add-in, or if the add-in has its Title property set (and you know what it is). Normally this is true, but the following procedure presents a workaround. This subroutine either uninstalls VIEWS.XLA if it is installed; or reports that it isn't installed. Note that this routine does not use the Title property of the AddIn.

```
Sub UninstallFile()
    AddInFile = "VIEWS.XLA"
    Action = " was not installed."
    For Each Item In AddIns
        If Item.Name = AddInFile Then
            If Item.Installed Then
                Item.Installed = False
                Action = " uninstalled."
            End If
        End If
    Next Item
    MsgBox AddInFile & Action
End Sub
```

Uninstalling all add-ins

The next procedure loops through all add-ins in the AddIns collection and uninstalls any add-in that's installed. This procedure does not affect add-ins that were opened with the File⇨Open command.

```
Sub UninstallAll()
    Count = 0
    For Each Item In AddIns
        If Item.Installed Then
            Item.Installed = False
            Count = Count + 1
        End If
    Next Item
    MsgBox Count & " Add-Ins Uninstalled."
End Sub
```

Ensuring that an add-in is installed

If you want to make sure that your add-in is installed properly (that is, opened using the Tools⇨Add-Ins command, not the File⇨Open command), you can use the CheckInstall subroutine that follows. In this example, CheckInstall is executed from the workbook's Auto_Open subroutine only if the file is an add-in, which means that when you're developing the workbook, CheckInstall does not execute.

Here's a listing of the Auto_Open subroutine:

```
Sub Auto_Open()
    If ThisWorkbook.FileFormat = xlAddIn Then CheckInstall
End Sub
```

The CheckInstall subroutine (shown in Listing 13-1) starts by checking to see if the add-in is in the AddIns collection. If it's not, it displays a warning message and the file is closed. The message tells the user how to use the Tools⇨Add-Ins command to open the file properly. If the file is in the AddIns collection, its Installed property is set to True. The net effect is that using File⇨Open to open the add-in actually installs it properly.

Listing 13-1 CheckInstall Subroutine

```
Sub CheckInstall()
    Dim Msg As String
    Dim item As Object
    Dim InCollection As Boolean

'   See if add-in is in the AddIns collection
    InCollection = False
    For Each item In AddIns
         If item.Name = ThisWorkbook.Name Then InCollection = _
           True
    Next item

'   If not in collection, display warning and close the file
    If Not InCollection Then
        Msg = "This add-in cannot be opened with the "
        Msg = Msg & "File Open command. Select the Tools "
        Msg = Msg & "Add-Ins command, and then use the "
        Msg = Msg & "Browse button to locate the file."
        MsgBox Msg, vbCritical, ThisWorkbook.Name
        ThisWorkbook.Close
        Exit Sub
    End If

'   Otherwise, install it as an add-in
    AddIns(ThisWorkbook.Title).Installed = True
End Sub
```

Prompting to uninstall add-ins before exit

As I discussed earlier, add-ins that are installed when you exit Excel are automatically installed the next time you start Excel. I use a lot of add-ins, and I usually forget to uninstall them when I'm finished with them. Then, the next time I start Excel the unwanted add-ins increase the start-up time and take up extra memory so that I have to use Tools⇨Add-Ins command to remove the unwanted add-ins.

To prevent having to take this unnecessary step, I wrote a subroutine that prompts me to close any installed add-ins when I exit Excel. I named the routine Auto_Close so it is executed when I exit Excel. I made an add-in from the file (of course), but it can also be stored in your Personal Macro Workbook.

CROSS REFERENCE

The procedure is based on the OptionBox function I presented in Chapter 8. If you recall, OptionBox creates a dialog box on the fly that presents a list of option buttons. I modified the function and turned it into a subroutine that lists all installed add-ins as a series of check box controls. Unchecking the check box uninstalls the add-in so it isn't loaded the next time Excel starts.

Figure 13-5 shows an example of how it looks. The size of the dialog box adjusts automatically to accommodate the actual number of add-ins installed.

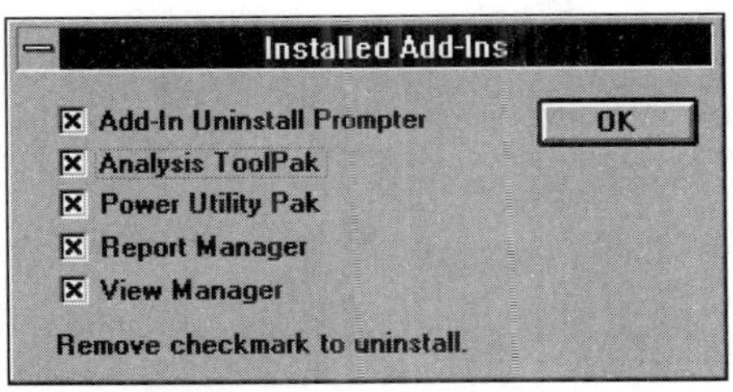

Figure 13-5: Excel creates this dialog box on the fly and prompts the user to uninstall add-ins before leaving Excel.

DISK

Listing 13-2 shows the Auto_Close routine. This code is available in AIPROMPT.XLS on the disk that accompanies this book.

Listing 13-2 **Auto_Close routine.Option Explicit**

```
Sub Auto_Close()
'   Prompts to uninstall add-ins before exiting Excel

    Dim i As Integer, Count As Integer
    Dim TopPos As Integer
    Dim AddInDlg As Object
    Dim CurrentSheet As Object
    Dim Item As Object
    Dim AddInList() As String
    Dim VisWin As Boolean
```

(continues)

Listing 13-2 *(continued)*

```
        Application.ScreenUpdating = False

'       Get add-in status
        Count = 0
        For Each Item In AddIns
            If Item.Installed Then
                Count = Count + 1
                ReDim Preserve AddInList(Count)
                AddInList(Count) = Item.Title
            End If
        Next Item

'       Exit if no add-ins installed
        If Count = 0 Then Exit Sub

'       The following is a work-around for a bug that
'       causes Add method to fail if there are no
'       unhidden worksheets open...
        VisWin = False
        For Each Item In Windows
            If Item.Visible = False Then VisWin = True
        Next Item
        If Not VisWin Then Workbooks.Add 'Not really added!

'       Add a temporary dialog sheet
        ThisWorkbook.DialogSheets.Add
        Set AddInDlg = ThisWorkbook.DialogSheets(1)

'       Add the checkboxes
        TopPos = 40
        For i = 1 To Count
            AddInDlg.CheckBoxes.Add 78, TopPos, 150, 16.5
            With AddInDlg.CheckBoxes(i)
                .Text = AddInList(i)
                .Value = xlOn
            End With
            TopPos = TopPos + 14
        Next i

'       Add a label
        AddInDlg.Labels.Add 78, TopPos + 6, 164, 13.5
        AddInDlg.Labels(1).Text = "Remove checkmark to _
           uninstall."
        TopPos = TopPos + 14
```

```
'   Delete the Cancel button
    AddInDlg.Buttons("Button 3").Delete

'   Move OK  button and make it last in tab order
    With AddInDlg.Buttons("Button 2")
        .Left = 240
        .BringToFront
    End With

'   Set dialog height, width, and caption
    With AddInDlg.DialogFrame
        .Height = Application.Max(50, _
              AddInDlg.DialogFrame.Top _
           + TopPos - 34)
        .Width = 230
        .Caption = "Installed Add-Ins"
    End With

'   Display the dialog box
    AddInDlg.Show

'   Uninstall add-ins
    For i = 1 To Count
        If AddInDlg.CheckBoxes(i).Value = xlOff Then _
            AddIns(AddInList(i)).Installed = False
    Next i

'   Delete temporary sheet if not an add-in
    If ThisWorkbook.FileFormat <> xlAddIn Then
        Application.DisplayAlerts = False
        ThisWorkbook.DialogSheets(1).Delete
    End If
End Sub
```

Special Problems with Add-ins

Add-ins are great, but you should realize by now that there's no free lunch. Add-ins also present their share of problems — or should I say challenges? In this section, I discuss some issues that you need to know about if you'll be developing add-ins for widespread user distribution.

Improper opening

The typical Excel user has no understanding of the concept of add-ins. Therefore, you can't count on the fact that they will use the Tools⇨Add-Ins command to open the add-in. Despite large-print instructions, when given an XLA file, many users still use the File⇨Open command to open add-ins. In some cases, this won't cause any problems. But if your application relies on the fact that your add-in is part of the AddIns collection, you need to ensure that the add-in is properly installed. The CheckInstall subroutine, presented earlier in this chapter, provides an easy way to make sure your add-in is installed properly.

Referencing other files

If your add-in uses other files, you need to be especially careful when distributing the application. You can't assume anything about the storage structure of the system that users will run the application on. The easiest approach is to insist that all files for the application be copied to a single directory. Then you can use the Path property of your application's workbook to build path references to all other files.

For example, if your application uses a custom help file, be sure that the help file is copied to the same directory as the application itself. Then you can use a procedure like the following to make sure the help file can be located.

```
Sub GetHelp()
    Path = ThisWorkbook.Path
    Application.Help Path & "\" & "USER.HLP"
End Sub
```

If your application uses API calls to standard Windows DLLs, you can assume that these can be found by Windows. But if you use custom DLLs, the best practice is to make sure that they are installed in the WINDOWS\SYSTEM directory (which may or may not be named WINDOWS\SYSTEM).

Toolbars

CAUTION

If you develop an application with a custom toolbar, at some point you'll probably be ready to tear your hair out. Why? Because you'll discover that clicking the toolbar buttons when the add-in is installed opens the XLS version of the file. Although this isn't supposed to happen, it does. It's a common problem, but you can avoid it. Chapter 15 discusses custom toolbars in detail, and tells you how to avoid this problem — or at least how to deal with it without losing your hair.

System resources

Finally, you need to be aware of system resource usage. It's great to have a dozen add-ins installed, ready when you need them. However, these files use up valuable system resources, which can slow your system down and even result in system crashes. Therefore, keep an eye on available system resources and avoid installing add-ins that you don't need.

Summary

- This chapter covered add-ins, and described what they are, how to create them, and how to manipulate them using VBA.
- This concludes Part III. The chapters in Part IV cover additional topics that are essential to creating effective applications in Excel.

Part IV

Putting It All Together

This part ties all the other parts together. Chapters 14 through 16 cover custom menus, toolbars, and help files. Chapter 17 covers methods for interacting with other applications. And finally, I discuss additional resources and common questions about Excel.

Chapter 14

Creating Custom Menus

In This Chapter

- An overview of Excel's menu system
- Types of menu modifications you can make
- Using the menu edit (and when it's appropriate)
- Manipulating menus with VBA
- Pointers for adhering to standard menu conventions
- Working around problems with Excel's implementation of shortcut menus

Every Windows program has a menu system, which is usually the primary user interface element. The Windows standard places the menu directly beneath the application's title bar. In addition, many programs now implement shortcut menus — which are usually displayed when the user right-clicks a selection.

Excel uses both type of menus. This gives developers almost complete control over Excel's entire menu system — although a few areas leave a bit to be desired in the current release. This chapter tells you everything you need to know about working with Excel's menus.

What You Can Do with Excel's Menus

Typical Excel users get by just fine with the standard menus. Because you're reading this book, however, you're probably not the typical Excel user. You may want to modify menus to make your life easier and to make your applications' users lives easier as well.

Modifying Excel's menus consists of removing elements, adding elements, and changing elements. I discuss each of these topics in the following sections.

Menu terminology

Menu terminology is often a bit confusing at first because many of the terms are similar. The following list is official Excel menu terminology — and that which I use in this chapter.

Menu Bar: The row of words that appears directly below the application's title bar. Excel has nine different menu bars that will appear automatically, depending on the context. For example, the menu bar displayed when a worksheet is active is different from the menu bar displayed when a VBA module is active.

Menu: A single, top-level element of a menu bar. For example, each of Excel's menu bars has a menu called File.

Menu Item: An element that appears in the drop-down list when a menu is selected. For example, the first menu item under the File menu is New. Menu items also appear in submenus and shortcut menus.

Submenu: A second-level menu (also known as a cascading menu) that is under some menus. For example, the Edit menu has a submenu called Clear.

Submenu Item: A menu item that appears in the list when a submenu is selected.

Shortcut Menu: The floating list of menu items that appears when the user right-clicks a selection or an object. Excel has 25 different shortcut menus.

Enabled: A menu item that can be used. If a menu item is not enabled, its text is grayed and it cannot be used.

Statusbar Text: Text that appears in Excel's status bar when a menu or menu item is selected. For custom menu items, the status bar text is associated with the macro that is executed by the menu item.

OnAction: The macro that is executed when a custom menu item command is executed.

Removing menu elements

You can remove just about any part of Excel's menu system, menus, menu items, and entire menu bars.

For example, if you don't want the end users of your application fiddling with the display, you can remove the View menu from the Worksheet menu bar. You can also remove one or more menu items from a menu. If you remove the New menu item from the File menu, for example, users can't use the menu to create a new workbook. Finally, you can eliminate an entire menu bar. You might do this if you want your application to be completely under the control of your macros.

NOTE

It's important to remember that simply removing menu bars, menus, or menu items doesn't affect the alternate method of accomplishing some actions. Specifically, if there are corresponding shortcut keys, toolbar buttons, or shortcut menus that perform the same action as a menu command, those alternate methods still work. For example, if you remove the New menu item from the File menu, the user can still use the New Workbook toolbar button, the Ctrl+N shortcut key, or the Desktop shortcut menu to create a new workbook.

Adding menu elements

You can also add your own custom menus to built-in menu bars, and add custom menu items to a built-in menu. In fact, you can create an entirely new menu bar if you like. For example, you might develop an application that doesn't require any of Excel's built-in menus. A simple solution is to create a new menu bar that consists of custom menus and custom menu items that execute your macros.

Changing menu elements

The final type of menu modification involves changing built-in elements. You can change the text displayed for the built-in menus and menu items. For example, you could change the Object menu item on the Insert menu to "OLE Object." You can also assign your own macros to built-in menu items — although this is a bit more complicated, two-step process that requires deleting the built-in menu item and replacing it with your own. You have many other options for changing menu elements, including rearranging the order of the menus on a menu bar (make the Help menu appear first, for example).

There are two way to change Excel's menus:

- Use the built-in menu editor
- Write VBA code to manipulate the menus

NOTE

Technically, there is a third way — but it affects only the Tools menu. As you know, the Tools⇨Macro command brings up the Macro dialog box. Clicking the Options button lets you assign a macro to a new menu item on the Tools menu. You can also accomplish this with a VBA statement such as the following:

```
Application.MacroOptions Macro:="MyMacro", _
          HasMenu:=True, _
          MenuText:="&Run my Macro"
```

The remainder of this chapter focuses on the menu editor and writing VBA code to modify menus.

The menu editor, although easy to use, doesn't enable you to do all of the modifications I listed in the preceding section. To make certain menu changes, you must write VBA code.

Interesting facts about menus

- There doesn't seem to be any limit to the number of menus on a menu bar. If you keep adding menus, they "wrap around" when the horizontal window limit is exceeded. In fact, you can fill up Excel's entire workspace with menus!
- You can't execute a macro by clicking a menu. In other words, every menu must have at least one menu item in order to do anything useful. If you want single-click action, you have to use a toolbar button.
- Normally, menu items drop down in a list that's flush left with the first letter of the menu's caption. However, you can make the menus drop down flush right for all of your Windows applications by adding the following line to the [Windows] section of the WIN.INI file:

  ```
  MenuDropAlignment=1
  ```

- Excel is somewhat inconsistent in how it deals with menus. For example, you can change the text (Caption property) of all menu items, but some of them are reset to their original text automatically when you access the menu. An example is the New command on the File menu; you can change its caption, but it is always reset when you select the File menu so you'll never see your change.

Using the Menu Editor

Using the menu editor for manipulating Excel's menus is easier than writing VBA code. However, the menu editor doesn't offer you the flexibility you get by using VBA to work with menus. If your menu changes are simple — just adding a menu item or two — the menu editor may be the best approach. If you want to do anything fancy, such as change menus on the fly, add checkmarks to menu items, or disable menu items under certain conditions, you need to write VBA code to do so.

NOTE

The menu modifications made with the menu editor are stored in the workbook that is active when you invoke the editor. When the workbook is opened, the customized menus are in effect until the workbook is closed. This can cause some strange things to happen if several workbooks are open, each of which has its own customized menu. For reliable results, it's best to have only one workbook open that has customized menus.

The menu editor is available only when a VBA module is active. However, you can also use the Menu Editor toolbar button (located on the Visual Basic toolbar), which lets you access the menu editor from any type of sheet. The Tools⇨Menu Editor command (or the Menu Editor toolbar button) brings up the dialog box shown in Figure 14-1.

By the way, if you've thought about using the macro recorder to record your actions while using the menu editor, forget it. Recording stops when the Menu Editor dialog box is displayed because the menus are stored in the workbook. When using VBA to modify menus, the modified menus aren't stored anywhere.

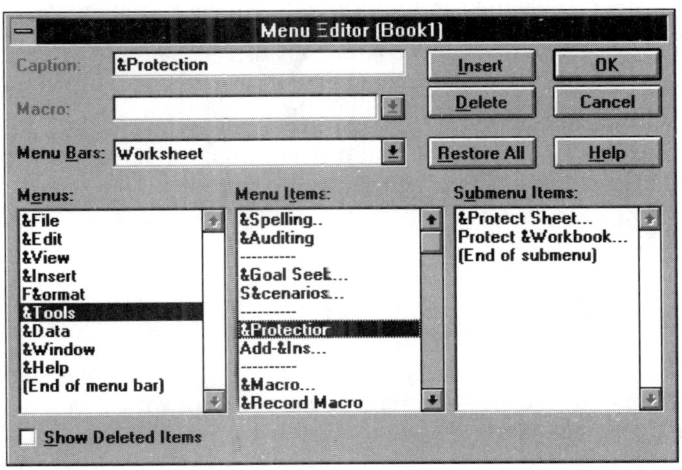

Figure 14-1: The menu editor is the easy way to modify Excel's menus.

The Menu Editor dialog box is divided into several parts. To modify a menu, start by choosing the appropriate menu bar from the Menu Bars drop-down list. Oddly, this control doesn't display all of the menu bars available (for example, the Excel 4 menus are missing).

When you select a menu bar, its menus are displayed in the Menus list box. Select a menu from the Menus list box, and its menu items appear in the Menu Items list box. Select a menu item from the list box and, if there are submenu items, they appear in the Submenu Items list box.

To modify a shortcut menu, choose one of the three Shortcut Menu listings in the Menu Bars drop-down list. The Menu Items list box will display shortcut menus to choose from.

The Insert button lets you insert a new menu, menu item, or submenu item. The item will be inserted above the currently selected item.

The Delete button removes the selected item (menu, menu item, or submenu item). The Restore All button resets the selected item to its built-in state.

When you insert a new item, you can enter the caption and specify a macro by choosing from a drop-down list of all available macros. To insert a separator bar, just enter a single hyphen as the caption.

You'll find that the menu editor is quite straightforward and easy to use. However, it has some limitations:

- You can't use the menu editor to create a new menu bar (despite what the on-line help claims).
- You can't change the captions for built-in menus or menu items.
- The menu editor doesn't recognize any menu changes you've made using VBA statements. Therefore, the menu structure displayed in the menu editor may not even correspond to the actual menu structure.
- If more than one workbook that has a customized menu is open, the actual results of using the menu editor can be unpredictable.

Menu Conventions

Menus in Windows programs typically adhere to established conventions. When you modify menus — with the menu editor or with VBA — keep the following points in mind:

- The File menu is always first, and the Help menu is always last.
- Menu item text is always proper case — the first letter of words are uppercase, except for minor words such as *the*, *a*, and *and*.
- Menu items are usually limited to three or fewer words.
- Every menu item should have a hot key that's unique to the menu.
- Menu items that display a dialog box are followed by ellipses (…).
- Avoid having a long list of menu items. If you must, it's a good idea to use a separator bar (a menu item whose Caption property is set to "-") to group items into logical groups.
- Menu items that are not appropriate in the current context are *grayed*. In VBA terminology, the menu item's Enabled property is set to False.
- Some menu items serve as a toggle. When the option is on, the menu item is preceded by a checkmark. In VBA terminology, the menu item's Checked property is True.

Manipulating Menus with VBA

Now that you know the limitations of the menu editor, you're probably all set to learn the ins and outs of how to change menus with VBA. As I mentioned, the macro recorder takes a mini-vacation when you issue the Tools⇨Menu Editor command, so you won't learn about VBA menu commands by examining recorded code.

After writing many VBA routines to manipulate menus, I can only conclude that this feature still needs some work. For example, you can easily write code to delete menu items in any of the shortcut menus, but there is no method available to restore the original shortcut menus (although such methods exist for menu bar menus). And, contrary to what you might expect, there is no ShortcutMenus collection — each shortcut menu must be addressed individually by name. I'm not sure why this is so, but it's a definite inconsistency in Excel's object model. But despite a few shortcomings, there is a lot you can do with VBA when it comes to menus.

NOTE: Unlike the menu editor, you can work with every menu bar when using VBA — with one exception. The menu bar that's active when the Debug window is active cannot be changed.

Before you jump into writing VBA code to work with menus, you must understand the object hierarchy, which is as follows.

```
Application
    MenuBar
      Menu
          MenuItem
             MenuItem
```

The Application object contains the MenuBars collection. A MenuBar object contains Menu objects, and Menu objects contain MenuItem objects. MenuItem objects may contain other MenuItem objects, as in the case of submenus. To reference the New menu item on the worksheet's File menu, use the following syntax:

```
MenuBars(xlWorksheet).Menus("File").MenuItems("New...")
```

xlWorksheet is a constant that represents the displayed menu bar when a worksheet is active. *"File"* is the caption of the first Menu object of the menu bar, and *"New..."* is the caption for the first menu item of the menu. This may be a bit confusing at first, but it becomes clear with practice.

The MenuBars collection

The MenuBars collection consists of nine menu bars. As you know, Excel automatically changes menu bars depending on the context. When a VBA module is active, for example, the menu bar is different than when a worksheet or dialog sheet is active. Table 14-1 lists the predefined constants for each menu bar, along with a description of the context in which it's shown.

Table 14-1 Built-In Constants for MenuBar Objects

Constant	*MenuBar Caption*	*Context*
xlWorksheet	Worksheet	Worksheet, XLM macro sheet, or dialog sheet is active
xlChart	Chart	Chart sheet is active
xlModule	Visual Basic Module	VBA module sheet is active
xlNoDocuments	No Documents Open	No documents are visible
xlInfo	Info	Info Window is active
xlWorksheet4	Worksheet (XL4)	NA*
xlChart4	Chart (XL4)	NA*
xlWorksheetShort	Worksheet (XL4, Short)	NA*
xlChartShort	Chart (XL4, Short)	NA*

* These menu bars are included for compatibility with Excel 4. The Options dialog box includes an option to use Excel 4 menus, and if this option is set, Excel uses the Excel 4 menu bars.

MenuBar objects have a Caption property (listed in Table 14-1), which you can access. The following subroutine displays the name of the current menu bar by using the ActiveMenuBar property of the Application object:

```
Sub GetCurrentMenuBar()
    MsgBox ActiveMenuBar.Caption
End Sub
```

You can use the Add method to add a new custom menu bar to the MenuBars collection. For example, to add a menu bar with "Custom MenuBar" as its caption, use the following statement:

```
MenuBars.Add "Custom MenuBar"
```

The following subroutine adds a new custom menu bar, and then counts and displays the number of built-in and custom menu bars in the MenuBars collection. It uses the BuiltIn property to determine if each menu bar is a built-in menu bar.

```
Sub CountMenuBars()
'   Add a new menu bar
    MenuBars.Add "Custom MenuBar"

'   Initialize counters
    CustomCnt = 0
    BuiltInCnt = 0

'   Cycle through MenuBars collection
    For Each Bar In MenuBars
        If Bar.BuiltIn Then BuiltInCnt = BuiltInCnt + 1 Else _
            CustomCnt = CustomCnt + 1
    Next Bar

'   Display message
    Msg = "Built-in: " & BuiltInCnt & Chr(10)
    Msg = Msg & "Custom: " & CustomCnt
    MsgBox Msg
End Sub
```

NOTE: If you run the preceding routine twice, the Add method will give an error message. This is because you cannot add a menu bar with a name that already exists.

As you'll see, you can add or remove menus from the built-in menu bars. To restore a built-in menu bar to its original state, use the Reset method. The following statement restores the worksheet menu bar to its default settings:

```
MenuBars(xlWorksheet).Reset
```

You can display a particular menu bar (including a custom menu bar) by using the Activate method of the MenuBars collection. For example, if you've created a menu bar named MyBar, you can display it with the following statement:

```
MenuBars("MyBar").Activate
```

After a custom menu bar is displayed, Excel no longer displays its own menus when you change context. For example, if a custom menu bar is in use, switching to a VBA module will *not* change to the VBA module menu bar.

The Activate method generates an error if you attempt to display a menu bar that's inappropriate for the current context — for example, trying to display the worksheet menu bar when a VBA module is active. The next example demonstrates a good way to return to the proper menu after displaying a custom menu bar. The On Error statement ignores the errors generated when an inappropriate menu bar is activated. The net effect is that the appropriate menu bar is the one that's activated.

```
Sub ReturnToNormalMenus()
    On Error Resume Next
    MenuBars(xlWorksheet).Activate
    MenuBars(xlModule).Activate
    MenuBars(xlChart).Activate
    MenuBars(xlWorksheet).Activate
    MenuBars(xlNoDocuments).Activate
    MenuBars(xlInfo).Activate
End Sub
```

The Menus collection

The Menus collection is a collection of Menu objects contained in a particular MenuBar object. You can refer to an individual Menu object by its index number or by its caption. For example, the following references refer to the same object, because "File" is the caption for the first Menu object on the menu bar.

```
MenuBars(xlWorksheet).Menus("File")
MenuBars(xlWorksheet).Menus(1)
```

The caption for a Menu object usually includes an ampersand (&) to indicate its hot key. For example, the caption for the first Menu object on the Worksheet menu bar is "&File". You can omit the ampersand in your code, so either Menus("File") or Menus("&File") is acceptable.

Counting menus

The following procedure simply counts the number of menus in the active menubar.

```
Sub CountMenus()
    MsgBox ActiveMenuBar.Menus.Count
End Sub
```

Pretty straightforward, eh? Well, not really. There's a slight anomoly involved here. It seems this procedure returns a different count (one additional menu) depending on whether the active workbook is maximized. It seems that the Count property includes the Control menu, which also appears on the menu bar when a workbook is maximized. This is not a big deal because cycling through the menus with a For Next loop doesn't include the extra menu.

If you want an accurate count of the menus, use a procedure like the following, which always returns the correct number of menus:

```
Sub CountMenus()
    MenuCount = 0
    For Each Menu In ActiveMenuBar.Menus
        MenuCount = MenuCount + 1
    Next Menu
    MsgBox MenuCount
End Sub
```

Adding menus

To add a new menu to a menu bar, you use the Add method of the Menus collection. The following subroutine adds a menu called Utilities before the Window menu on the worksheet menu bar:

```
Sub AddMenu()
    MenuBars(xlWorksheet).Menus.Add "&Utilities", "Window"
End Sub
```

By default, new menus are added before the Help menu, so if you want your new menu to be placed there, you can omit the second argument for the Add method. If there is no Help menu, new menus are added as the last menu. To add a new menu *after* the Help menu, you must go through three steps: delete the Help menu, add your new menu, and then restore the Help menu (using the Restore argument for the Add method). The following procedure demonstrates this by adding a new Utilities menu after the Help menu.

```
Sub AddMenuAfterHelp()
    MenuBars(xlWorksheet).Menus("&Help").Delete
    MenuBars(xlWorksheet).Menus.Add "&Utilities"
    MenuBars(xlWorksheet).Menus.Add "&Help", _
        Before:="Utilities", Restore:=True
End Sub
```

The next example creates a new menu bar and then adds three menus to it. Before creating the new menu bar, it stores the current menu bar (ActiveMenuBar) in an object variable so that it can be restored.

```
Sub CreateNewMenuBar()
    Set OldBar = ActiveMenuBar
    MenuBars.Add "New MenuBar"
MenuBars("New MenuBar").Menus.Add Caption:="&First"
    MenuBars("New MenuBar").Menus.Add Caption:="&Second"
    MenuBars("New MenuBar").Menus.Add Caption:="&Third"
    MenuBars("New MenuBar").Activate
    MsgBox "Click OK to restore the original menu bar"
    OldBar.Activate
    MenuBars("New MenuBar").Delete
End Sub
```

Deleting menus

The Delete method of the Menus collection deletes a menu (either custom or built-in) from a menu bar. The following example deletes the Help menu from all of the built-in menu bars. Notice that it uses an On Error statement to ignore errors that occur if the menu bar does not have a Help menu.

```
Sub RemoveHelpMenus()
    On Error Resume Next
    For Each Bar In MenuBars
        If Bar.BuiltIn Then Bar.Menus("Help").Delete
    Next Bar
End Sub
```

The following subroutine uses the Add method to restore all of the Help menus in the built-in menu bars.

```
Sub RestoreHelpMenus()
    On Error Resume Next
    For Each Bar In MenuBars
        If Bar.BuiltIn Then _
            Bar.Menus.Add "Help", Restore:=True
    Next Bar
End Sub
```

Changing menu text

You can also change the text displayed for menu items (both custom and built-in). You do so by changing the Caption property. This example changes the Help menu in the worksheet menu bar to display Assistance.

```
Sub ChangeHelp()
        MenuBars(xlWorksheet).Menus("Help").Caption = _
        "&Assistance"
End Sub
```

Here's another example that changes the text of all of the menus in all of the menu bars to uppercase — probably not something you'd want to do, but it *does* add a new look to Excel.

```
Sub UpperCaseMenus()
    For Each Bar In MenuBars
        For Each Menu In Bar.Menus
            Menu.Caption = UCase(Menu.Caption)
        Next Menu
    Next Bar
End Sub
```

To return the menus to normal, remove the code within the For Each...Next loop and replace it with:

```
Bar.Reset
```

Resetting a built-in menu

Sometimes, it may be necessary to restore a built-in menu to its original state. For example, if you added some custom menu items (described next), you may want to remove them all. You could use the Reset method of the MenuBar object, but this affects all menus in the menu bar.

Oddly, a Menu object does not have a Reset method. As I discussed, the Add method is used to restore a deleted Menu object, but the method generates an error if the Menu exists. Therefore, the only way to restore a Menu object to its original state is to delete it and then add it back with the restore option. The following subroutine demonstrates this with the File menu on the worksheet menu bar:

```
Sub ResetFileMenu()
    MenuBars(xlWorksheet).Menus("&File").Delete
    MenuBars(xlWorksheet).Menus.Add _
        "&File", Restore:=True, Before:=1
End Sub
```

The MenuItems collection

So far, I have discussed menu bars and menus in this chapter. Now it's time to move on to menu items. The MenuItems collection is a collection of all MenuItem objects contained in a Menu object.

Menu items are the words that drop down when a menu is selected. The separator bars are also included in the MenuItems collection. For example, the View menu on the worksheet menu bar has seven menu items — two of which are separator bars.

Adding menu items

To add a new menu item, use the Add method. The Add method has four arguments (only the caption argument is required):

caption	The text that appears in the menu
onAction	The macro to execute when the menu item is selected
before	The menu item before which the new item will be added (it can be an index number or a caption)
restore	If True, the deleted built-in menu item is restored

The next example demonstrates how to add a new menu item. The item becomes the fourth menu item on the File menu of the worksheet menu bar. The new menu item is Close All, and it executes a macro named CloseAllBooks. The routine starts by examining each menu item on the File menu. If the new item is already on the menu, the menu item is deleted first (otherwise, there would be multiple menu items with the same caption).

```
Sub AddItem()
'   Exit if item already exists
    For Each Item In _
        MenuBars(xlWorksheet).Menus("File").MenuItems
        If Item.Caption = "&Close All" Then Item.Delete
    Next Item

    MenuBars(xlWorksheet).Menus("File").MenuItems.Add _
        Caption:="&Close All", _
        Before:=4, _
        OnAction:="CloseAllBooks"
End Sub

Sub CloseAllBooks()
    For Each Book In Workbooks
        Book.Close
    Next Book
End Sub
```

Displaying a shortcut key with a menu item

You'll notice that some of Excel's built-in menu items also display a shortcut key combination that has the same effect as the menu command. For example, the Edit menu lists several shortcut keys.

Your custom menu items can also display a shortcut key. You set this up using the Add method. The trick is to use the Backspace character, that is, *Chr(8),* between the menu item's caption and a text string that contains the shortcut key. For example, the following variation of the command in the previous example displays a shortcut key (Ctrl+Shift+C) along with the menu item.

```
MenuBars(xlWorksheet).Menus("File").MenuItems.Add _
    Caption:="&Close All" & Chr(8) & "Ctrl+Shift+C", _
    Before:=4, _
    OnAction:="CloseAllBooks"
```

NOTE

This technique for displaying a shortcut key is not documented, and I discovered it by trial and error. As with all undocumented techniques, nothing guarantees that this will work with future versions of Excel.

When you use this technique, you make sure that the macro (in this case, CloseAllBooks) can in fact be executed by the key combination. You can use the Object Browser to set up a shortcut key for a macro, but another approach is to assign the shortcut key using the MacroOptions method of the Applications object. This method essentially automates the process of setting options for a macro using the Object Browser.

The following code uses the MacroOptions method to assign the Ctrl+Shift+C shortcut key to CloseAllBooks. It also sets the status bar text for the macro — which has a side benefit of displaying when the menu item is selected.

```
Application.MacroOptions _
   Macro:="CloseAllBooks", _
HasShortcutKey:=True, _
   ShortcutKey:="C", _
   StatusBar:="Closes all open workbooks"
```

The following example is a modified version of the example presented in the previous section:

```
Sub AddItem2()
'   Exit if item already exists
    For Each Item In
MenuBars(xlWorksheet).Menus("File").MenuItems
        If Item.Caption = "&Close All" Then Item.Delete
    Next Item
```

```
'   Add the menu item
    MenuBars(xlWorksheet).Menus("File").MenuItems.Add _
        Caption:="&Close All" & Chr(8) & "Ctrl+Shift+C", _
        Before:=4, _
        OnAction:="CloseAllBooks"

'   Make sure macro options are set properly
    Application.MacroOptions _
        Macro:="CloseAllBooks", _
        HasShortcutKey:=True, _
        ShortcutKey:="C", _
        StatusBar:="Closes all open workbooks"
End Sub
```

These changes produce a menu item whose appearance is identical to Excel's built-in commands, including a shortcut key displayed and status bar text that describes the menu choice (see Figure 14-2).

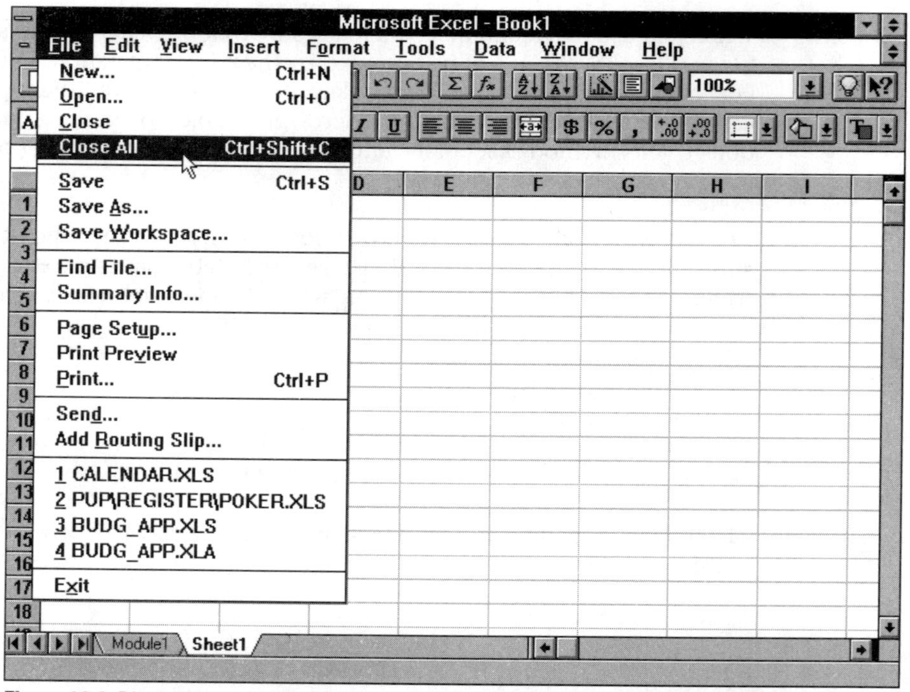

Figure 14-2: Displaying a shortcut key and status bar text along with a custom menu item.

Deleting menu items

Use the Delete method to delete custom or built-in menu items. The following statement deletes the Exit menu item from the File menu on the worksheet menu bar.

```
MenuBars(xlWorksheet).Menus("File").MenuItems("Exit").Delete
```

To get the menu item back, use the Add method, with the Restore option. For example:

```
MenuBars(xlWorksheet).Menus("File").MenuItems.Add "Exit", _
    Restore:=True
```

Changing menu item properties

MenuItem objects have a few properties that you can read or modify:

- *Caption:* The text that's displayed in the menu.
- *Checked:* Whether a checkmark appears to the left of the caption. Excel's View menu has several examples of this.
- *Enabled:* Whether the menu item can be used. If it's not enabled, it is grayed.

DISK

The following example demonstrates some useful techniques using menu item properties. The file, GRIDTOGL.XLS, is available on the disk that accompanies this book.

The AddGridItem subroutine adds a new menu item (Grid Display) to the View menu on the worksheet and VBA module menu bars. This new item is a toggle, like the Formula Bar and Status Bar menu items. When grid lines are displayed in the active sheet, the menu item is displayed with a checkmark. Selecting the Grid Display menu item removes the checkmark and the grid lines. This works for both worksheets and dialog sheets. Notice that the new menu item is added to the View menu in the VBA module menu bar, but it is permanently disabled because modules don't have grid lines. This is just to make the menus consistent (and demonstrate the use of the Enabled property).

Listing 14-1 is the AddGridItem routine. When this is executed, the View menu has a new menu item, as seen in Figure 14-3.

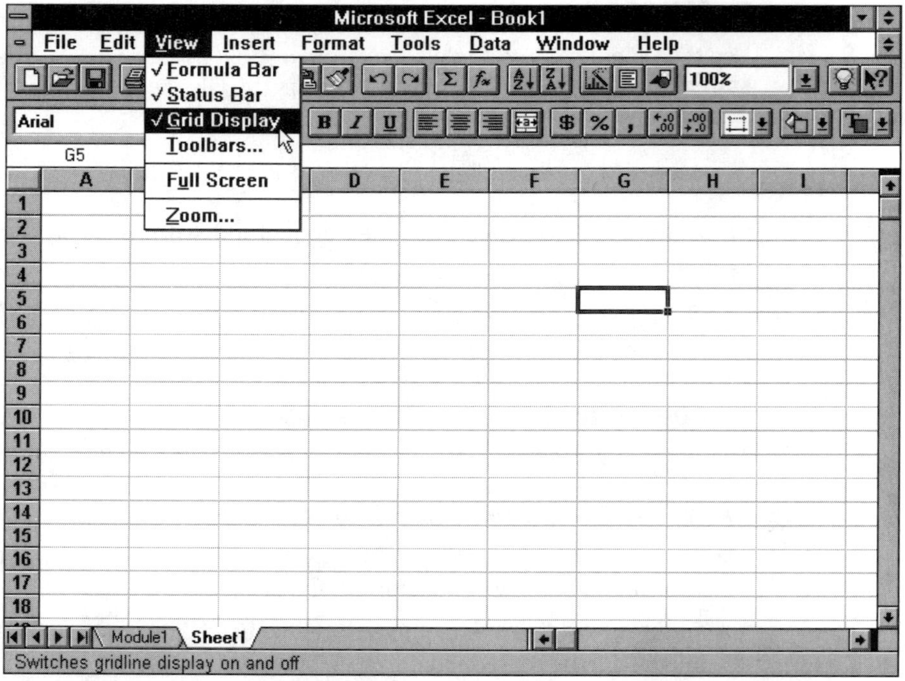

Figure 14-3: Adding a new menu item (Grid Display) that acts as a toggle.

Listing 14-1 The AddGridItem Routine

```
Sub AddGridItem()
'   Adds a new item to View menus

'   Reset menu bars
    MenuBars(xlWorksheet).Reset
    MenuBars(xlModule).Reset

'   Name of menu item to be added
    ItemName = "&Grid Display"

'   Add item to Worksheet menu
    MenuBars(xlWorksheet).Menus("View").MenuItems.Add _
        ItemName, _
        before:="&Toolbars…", _
        OnAction:="ToggleGrids"
```

```
'   Add item to Module menu for consistency
'   (always disabled)
    MenuBars(xlModule).Menus("View").MenuItems.Add _
        ItemName, _
        before:="&Toolbars..."
    MenuBars(xlModule).Menus("View").MenuItems(ItemName).Enabled _
    = False

'   Set status bar text for macro
    Application.MacroOptions _
        Macro ="ToggleGrids", _
        StatusBar:="Switches gridline display on and off"

'   Procedure to run when a sheet is activated
    Application.OnSheetActivate = "UpdateViewMenu"
    UpdateViewMenu
End Sub
```

When the Grid Display menu item is selected, the ToggleGrids routine is executed. Listing 14-2 shows this procedure. It simply changes the Checked property, and then adjusts the DisplayGridlines property of the Application object.

Listing 14-2 The ToggleGrids Routine

```
Sub ToggleGrids()
'   Toggles gridline display depending on menu

    Set GridItem = _
        MenuBars(xlWorksheet).Menus("View").MenuItems("Grid _
            Display')

'   Toggle checkmark display
    GridItem.Checked = Not GridItem.Checked

  ' Display or hide gridlines
    If GridItem.Checked Then _
        ActiveWindow.DisplayGridlines = True _
            Else ActiveWindow.DisplayGridlines = False
End Sub
```

The AddGridItem subroutine sets the OnSheetActivate property to UpdateViewMenu. That means UpdateViewMenu will be executed whenever a different sheet is activated. This is necessary to make sure the checked status of the Grid Display is in synch with the active sheet. Listing 14-3 is the UpdateViewMenu routine. It simply checks the active sheet. If grid lines are displayed, it sets the Checked property of the menu item to True, otherwise it's set to False.

Listing 14-3 UpdateViewMenu Routine

```
Sub UpdateViewMenu()
'   Executed when a different sheet is activated
    On Error Resume Next
    Set GridItem = _
        MenuBars(xlWorksheet).Menus("View").MenuItems("Grid _
           Display")

'   Update menu checkmark based on active sheet
    If ActiveWindow.DisplayGridlines Then _
        GridItem.Checked = True _
           Else GridItem.Checked = False
End Sub
```

NOTE

The OnSheetActivate remains in effect until it is explicitly canceled with a statement such as the following:

```
Application.OnSheetActivate = ""
```

Working with submenus

Submenus, sometimes known as cascading menus, are useful because they can make a complex menu system appear less complicated. They can also eliminate the need for a dialog box. Submenus are new to Excel 5, and if you've moved up from Excel 4 you've undoubtedly noticed that the new menus are much easier to use.

To add a submenu, use the AddMenu method of the MenuItems collection. The following example creates a new menu called First, and then uses the AddMenu method to create a submenu named Second. It then adds a menu item named Third to the submenu.

```
Sub SubMenuDemo()
    Set NewMenu = MenuBars(xlWorksheet)
    NewMenu.Menus.Add "First"
    NewMenu.Menus("First").MenuItems.AddMenu "Second"
    NewMenu.Menus("First").MenuItems("Second").MenuItems.Add _
      "Third"
End Sub
```

It's important to understand that Second, in the preceding example, is not a "real" menu item, although it's part of the MenuItems collection. For example, the following statement produces an error:

```
NewMenu.Menus("First").MenuItems("Second").Caption = "Level 2"
```

To change the caption of a submenu, you need to access the parent object of the "menu item." I discovered through trial and error that a statement like the following allows you to change the text displayed for a submenu.

```
NewMenu.Menus("First").MenuItems("Second").Parent.Caption = _
   "Level 2"
```

I don't really understand why this works, but it does.

The following routine is another example of creating submenus. This routine adds a new menu to the worksheet menu bar, adds four submenus, and then adds four submenu items to each submenu.

```
Sub MakeSubMenus()
    Set Bar = MenuBars(xlWorksheet)

'   Reset the MenuBar
    Bar.Reset

'   Create a new menu
    Bar.Menus.Add Caption:="&Reports"
    Set ReportsMenu = Bar.Menus("&Reports")

'   Create four menu items
    ReportsMenu.MenuItems.AddMenu "&Western Region"
    ReportsMenu.MenuItems.AddMenu "&Eastern Region"
    ReportsMenu.MenuItems.AddMenu "&Southern Region"
    ReportsMenu.MenuItems.AddMenu "&Northern Region"
```

```
'   Create submenus for each menu item
    For Each Item In ReportsMenu.MenuItems
        Item.MenuItems.Add "&1st Quarter…"
        Item.MenuItems.Add "&2nd Quarter…"
        Item.MenuItems.Add "&3rd Quarter…"
        Item.MenuItems.Add "&4th Quarter…"
     Next Item
End Sub
```

The MakeSubMenus routine generates a menu like the one shown in Figure 14-4.

NOTE

The placement of the submenus may depend on the video mode. For example, Figure 14-4 was captured in VGA mode. Because there's not enough room to display the submenus on the right, they are displayed to the left.

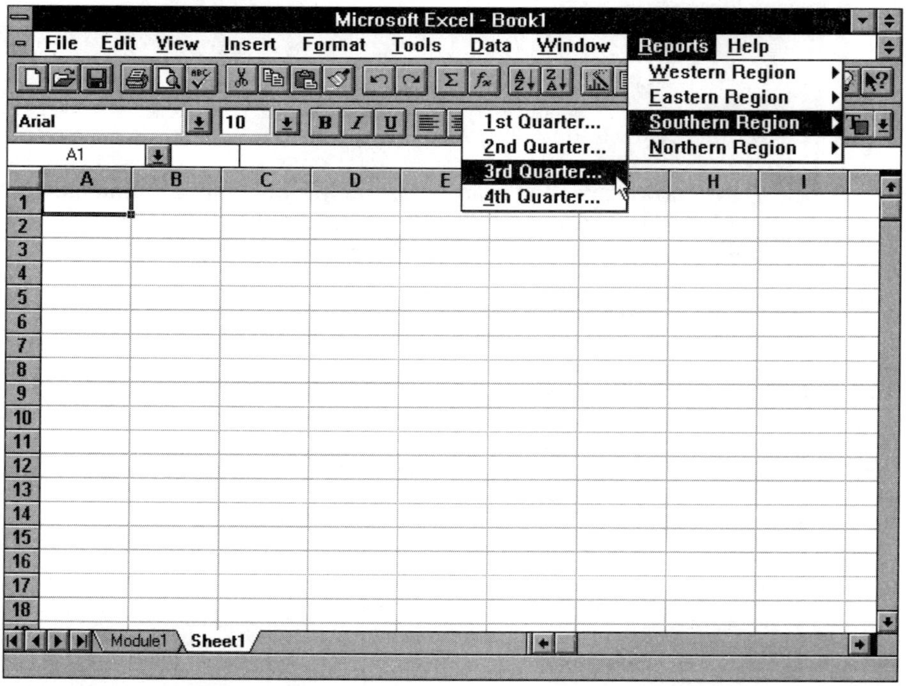

Figure 14-4: A menu with four submenus.

Menu shenanigans

Here's a good April Fool's trick to play on an office-mate (hopefully, one with a sense of humor). Create a routine that cycles through all of the menus, menu items, and submenu items, and changes their captions to be *backwards*. Name the routine Auto_Open and save the workbook in the victim's XLSTART directory. The next time Excel is started, the menus look like they're in a strange language.

For lazy pranksters, the file MENUSHEN.XLS is available on the disk that accompanies this book. This workbook is hidden, so you must use the Wodniw⇨Edihnu command (that is, the Window⇨Unhide command) if you want to examine the code. The routine performs its mischief by calling a custom function that reverses the text in the captions (except for the ellipses), converts the new text to proper case, and maintains the original hot keys. The net effect, as you can see in the accompanying figure, is a worksheet menu system that works exactly like the original (and is even keystroke compatible), but it looks very odd.

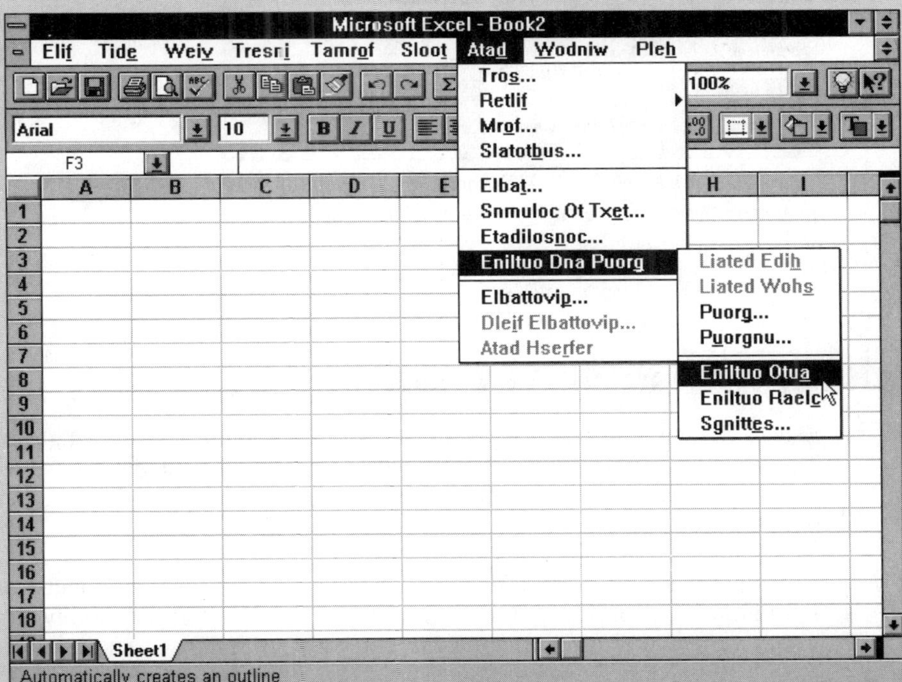

Before exiting, the routine adds an escape route: A new (legible) menu item to the Pleh menu (formerly the Help menu). This new item calls a routine that returns the menus to normal.

Actually, this trick can be rather instructive. For example, I found out that Excel automatically resets some of the menu items when a menu is accessed — for example, the New, Save, and Save As menu items on the File menu appear as they normally do. Go figure.

MENUDEMO.XLS, included on the disk that accompanies this book, demonstrates how to access all of the built-in menu bars, menus, menu items, and submenu items. It uses a dialog box to let you choose a menu bar, and then it displays the menus, menu items, and submenu items (see Figure 14-5). Studying the code in this application will give you a good understanding of menus. In fact, it would be a useful exercise to create a new menu editor, using MENUDEMO.XLS as the basis.

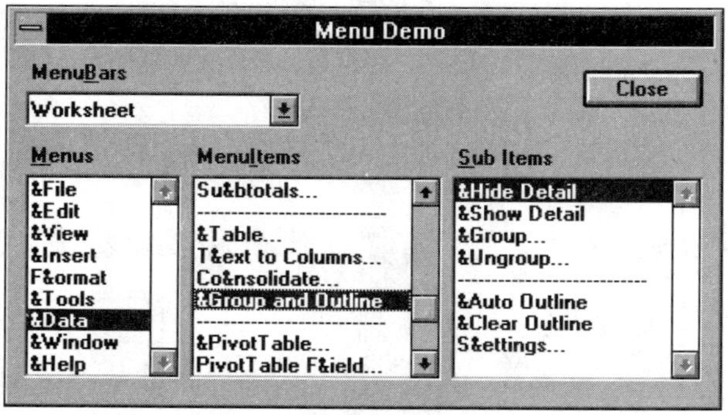

Figure 14-5: The MENUDEMO.XLS workbook demonstrates how to access menu bars, menus, menu items, and submenu items.

Working with Shortcut Menus

Excel's documentation for working with shortcut menus is exceedingly sparse. The lack of documentation, coupled with some other problems, leads me to suspect that this feature was added at the last minute — or at least not thought out very well.

Shortcut menus are a great idea that finally provide some functionality for the right mouse button. Excel has 25 shortcut menus that you can modify. You can't create new shortcut menus, but you can modify those that already exist.

A shortcut menu doesn't require a mouse. To display an object's shortcut menu using only the keyboard, select the object and then press Shift+F10.

You access a shortcut menu by referring to its constant value. For example, to work with the shortcut menu that appears when you right-click a Button object, use the following syntax:

```
ShortcutMenus(xlButton)
```

Table 14-2 describes the Shortcut menus, along with the constant for each.

Table 14-2 Shortcut menu Constants

Shortcut Menu	*Constant*
Button	xlButton
Chart Axis	xlAxis
Chart Floor	xlFloor
Chart Gridline	xlGridline
Chart Legend	xlLegend
Chart Plot Area	xlPlotArea
Chart Series	xlChartSeries
Chart Titles	xlChartTitles
Column	xlColumnHeader
Debug Code Pane	xlDebugCodePane
Desktop	xlDesktop
Dialog Sheet	xlDialogSheet
Drawing Object	xlDrawingObject
Entire Chart	xlEntireChart
Immediate Pane	xlImmediatePane
Macro Sheet Cell	xlMacrosheetCell
Module	xlModule
Row	xlRowHeader
Text Box	xlTextBox
Title Bar	xlTitleBar
Toolbar	xlToolbar
Toolbar Button	xlToolbarButton
Watch Pane	xlWatchPane
Workbook Tab	xlWorkbookTab
Worksheet Cell	xlWorksheetCell

Shortcut menus are unusual objects. Actually, they seem to be Menu objects, because the following statement displays "Menu".

```
MsgBox TypeName(ShortcutMenus(xlButton))
```

However, they are not part of the Menus collection, and there is no such thing as a collection of shortcut menus — which is completely inconsistent with Excel's object model. In fact, shortcut menu objects are not part of any collection. The following statement generates an error:

```
MsgBox TypeName(ShortcutMenus(xlButton).Parent)
```

Therefore, you can't use a construct such as:

```
For Each Item In ShortcutMenus.Menus
    Item.Delete
Next Item
```

What this all means is that working with shortcut menus is more difficult than it should be. Hopefully, Microsoft will correct these shortcut shortcomings in the next release of Excel. But for now, you'll just have to change your thinking a bit when you deal with shortcut menus.

Deleting a shortcut menu

You may want to disable one or more shortcut menus while your application is running. For example, you may not want the user to access the commands when a cell is right-clicked. You'll find that you can't use the menu editor to remove shortcut menus. It allows you to add or remove shortcut menu items, but not entire menus.

Therefore, you'll have to use VBA code to delete a shortcut menu. The statement that follows *should* work because ShortcutMenus(xlTextBox) returns a Menu object — but it generates an error.

```
ShortcutMenus(xlTextBox).Delete
```

Plan B: Use a For Each loop to delete each menu item in the menu. The procedure that follows *should* work, but it consistently generates an error. I'm not sure why, but only half of the menu items are deleted when using this procedure.

```
Sub DeleteShortcutMenu()
    For Each Item In ShortcutMenus(xlTextBox).MenuItems
        Item.Delete
    Next Item
End Sub
```

I've discovered that the only way to delete all menu items in a shortcut menu is to use code like the following:

```
Sub DeleteShortcutMenu()
    Set SCMenu = ShortcutMenus(xlTextBox)
    Do While SCMenu.MenuItems.Count > 0
        SCMenu.MenuItems(1).Delete
    Loop
End Sub
```

After a shortcut menu is deleted, you can't restore it using VBA. The only way to restore a deleted shortcut menu is to use the menu editor and select the Restore All button when a shortcut menu is selected. This restores *all* the shortcut menus, not just the one selected. Even then, you have to right-click an object *twice* before the menu appears again (I told you shortcut menus were weird!).

Unfortunately, there is no easy way to delete all the shortcut menus. The best I could do is the subroutine that follows. Notice that this routine skips over the 20th shortcut menu, which is xlToolbar. For some reason, the menu items on that shortcut menu cannot be deleted.

```
Sub DeleteAllShortcuts()
    SC = Array(xlAxis, xlButton, xlChartSeries, _
      xlChartTitles, _
        xlColumnHeader, xlDebugCodePane, xlDesktop, _
        xlDialogSheet, xlDrawingObject, xlEntireChart, _
        xlFloor, xlGridline, xlImmediatePane, xlLegend, _
        xlMacrosheetCell, xlModule, xlPlotArea, xlRowHeader, _
        xlTextBox, xlTitleBar, xlToolbar, xlToolbarButton, _
        xlWatchPane, xlWorkbookTab, xlWorksheetCell)

    For i = LBound(SC) To UBound(SC)
        If i <> 20 Then 'Skip xlToolbar
            Set SCMenu = ShortcutMenus(SC(i))
            Do While SCMenu.MenuItems.Count > 0
                SCMenu.MenuItems(1).Delete
            Loop
        End If
    Next i
End Sub
```

After running this routine the only way to restore the shortcut menus is to use the menu editor.

Adding menu items to a shortcut menu

Adding a menu item to a shortcut menu works just like a regular menu. The following example demonstrates how to add two menu items to the shortcut menu that appears when you right-click a cell. The first menu item is a separator bar added to the end of the menu, and the second is a new command, Toggle Word Wrap. Selecting the new menu item executes the ToggleWordWrap subroutine.

```
Sub AddItem()
    ShortcutMenus(xlWorksheetCell).MenuItems.Add "-"
    ShortcutMenus(xlWorksheetCell).MenuItems.Add _
        Caption:="Toggle Word Wrap", _
        OnAction:="ToggleWordWrap"
End Sub
```

Removing menu items from a shortcut menu

The following procedure demonstrates how to remove the two menu items added in the preceding example. Actually, it removes the last two items from the menu.

```
Sub RemoveItem()
    For i = 1 To 2
        Last =
ShortcutMenus(xlWorksheetCell).MenuItems.Count
       ShortcutMenus(xlWorksheetCell).MenuItems(Last).Delete
    Next i
End Sub
```

Summary

- This chapter covered the topic of custom menus. You learned that you can use the menu editor for simple menu modifications, and the modifications are stored with a worksheet. For more complete control over menus, you need to use the VBA techniques discussed here.
- The next chapter continues the discussion of customization, and covers custom toolbars.

Chapter 15

Creating Custom Toolbars

In This Chapter

- An overview of toolbars and toolbar buttons
- Understanding how Excel keeps track of toolbars
- Customizing toolbars and toolbar buttons
- Distributing toolbars
- Using VBA to manipulate toolbars

Toolbars have become increasingly common in Windows programs. In fact, software manufacturers use toolbars to create a common interface among products. For example, many of Excel's toolbar buttons also appear in other Microsoft products.

In this chapter, I discuss toolbars, including how to customize them for the end users of your applications.

About Toolbars and Buttons

All told, Excel comes with more than 200 toolbar buttons and 13 built-in toolbars. By the way, not all of the available toolbar buttons are on the prebuilt toolbars.

Some users like to create custom toolbars that conveniently contain the toolbar buttons that they use most often. Application developers also create custom toolbars and store them in their applications' worksheets; adding a toolbar with custom tools is a professional touch that improves the user interface, making the application more appealing for end users.

Buttons

A toolbar is made up of one or more toolbar buttons. (Well, technically, a toolbar can have no buttons, but empty toolbars aren't all that useful.)

Toolbar buttons come in four types:

- Built-in buttons have built-in functionalities.
- *Built-in controls* have built-in functionalities. The Zoom Control on the Standard toolbar is an example of a toolbar control (or *nonbutton*).
- *Custom buttons* have your own macros attached to them.
- *Gaps*, or spaces between buttons, make toolbars look a bit more organized.

You can customize toolbars in several ways (see the following section). In fact, toolbars can consist of any number of toolbar buttons, and you can mix and match the built-in buttons and controls with your custom toolbar buttons. You also can modify the image on any toolbar button (except the nonstandard buttons) by using a variety of techniques. You also can modify the width of drop-down list buttons, such as the Font or Zoom Control.

Toolbar buttons have a sculpted, 3-D look: when a toolbar button is clicked, it looks like it has been pressed (its Pushed property is set to True). For example, the Bold toolbar button on the Standard toolbar looks pushed in when the current range selection is formatted as bold.

Customizing toolbars

The following list summarizes how you can customize toolbars:

- *Remove buttons from built-in toolbars.* You can get rid of buttons that you never use. Or you can remove buttons that you don't want end users to use.
- *Add buttons to built-in toolbars.* You can add as many buttons as you want to any toolbar. The buttons can be custom buttons, come from other toolbars, or come from the stock of toolbar buttons contained in the 14 categories in the Customize dialog box.
- *Delete prebuilt toolbars.* If you never use some of the prebuilt toolbars, you can delete them to get them out of the way, reducing the size of your EXCEL5.XLB file.
- *Create new toolbars.* You can create as many new toolbars as you like; the buttons can come from any source.

- *Change the functionality of built-in buttons.* You do so by attaching your own macro to a built-in toolbar button.
- *Change the icon, or toolface, that appears on any button.* A rudimentary but functional toolbar button editor is included with Excel.

Don't be afraid to experiment with toolbars. If you screw up royally, it's very easy to reset a built-in toolbar to its default state.

Positioning toolbars

A toolbar is either floating or docked. *Floating* toolbars appear in an active window, whose size can be adjusted. A *docked* toolbar sits fixed in place at the top, bottom, left, or right edge of Excel's workspace.

Excel toolbars that contain nonstandard buttons (for example, the Zoom Control) cannot be docked on the left or right edges because the larger control would cause the toolbar to be too wide. By the way, not all Microsoft applications limit a docked toolbar's location, however. For example, Word for Windows allow toolbars that contain nonstandard controls to be docked in any position; it simply hides the nonstandard controls when the toolbar is at the left or right edge.

How Excel Handles Toolbars

Before you start working with custom toolbars, it's important to understand how Excel deals with toolbars. You may be surprised.

Storing toolbars

Toolbars can be attached to XLS or XLA files, which makes it easy to distribute custom toolbars with your applications. When the user opens your file, the toolbars appear automatically. You can attach any number of toolbars to a workbook.

Excel stores all of the toolbars that have ever been used in EXCEL5.XLB, which resides in the WINDOWS directory. Why is this fact important? Read on.

Assume that a colleague gives you an Excel workbook that has a custom toolbar stored in it. When you open the workbook, the toolbar appears. You examine the workbook but decide that you're not interested in it. Nonetheless, when you exit Excel, the custom toolbar is added to your EXCEL5.XLB file.

If you make *any* toolbar changes — from a minor adjustment of a built-in toolbar to an introduction of a custom toolbar — EXCEL5.XLB is resaved when you exit Excel. As a result, because the entire EXCEL5.XLB file is loaded every time you start Excel, the time Excel takes to start and exit Excel increase significantly as EXCEL5.XLB gets larger. Besides, all those toolbars eat up memory and — more important — system resources. Therefore, it's in your best interest to delete toolbars that you never use. (I describe how to do so later in this chapter.)

The EXCEL5.XLB file contains the master list of toolbars, as well as the toolbars themselves. When you open a workbook that contains a toolbar, Excel checks to see whether a toolbar by that name already exists. If not, the toolbar in the workbook is displayed, added to the collection, and saved in EXCEL5.XLB upon your exit. If a toolbar with the same name already exists, the toolbar in the workbook is not displayed, and it does not replace the toolbar of the same name that's already stored in EXCEL5.XLB.

This approach to storing toolbars can cause problems. Suppose that you have developed an application that uses a custom toolbar and you have stored the toolbar in the workbook. The first time an end user opens the workbook, the toolbar is displayed and saved in the user's EXCEL5.XLB file. If the user alters the toolbar — for example, accidentally removes a button — the next time your application is opened, the correct toolbar does not appear. Rather, the user sees the altered toolbar, which lacks an important button.

Fortunately, you can write VBA code to prevent this scenario. The trick is to never allow your custom toolbar to be added to the users' toolbar collection. (In other words, you trick Excel into thinking that your custom toolbar is a new toolbar every time the workbook is opened.) You can do so by writing an Auto_Close procedure that deletes the toolbar before the workbook is closed. That way, the toolbar never gets stored in the user's EXCEL5.XLB file, yet it remains attached to your workbook and is displayed whenever the workbook is opened.

TIP

Actually, with a bit of work, you can create your own XLB file that consists of a certain configuration of toolbars. Start by reconfiguring the toolbars as desired. This step includes hiding toolbars that you don't want to see, deleting toolbars that you don't want at all, and positioning those that you do want. Then quit Excel: the program updates the EXCEL5.XLB file according to your toolbar setup. Next, copy EXCEL5.XLB and give it a name, such as PREFERED.XLB. Then whenever you want to return to that toolbar setup, just open PREFERED.XLB. ***Note:*** The button size, however, is not maintained, because it is a property of the Application object, not the Toolbar objects. This setting, along with a few other toolbar-related settings, is stored in EXCEL5.INI.

Toolbars autosensing

Excel displays a particular toolbar automatically when you change contexts. When you activate a dialog sheet, for example, the Forms toolbar appears.

You can easily override this feature, called *autosensing*, by hiding the toolbar (to do so, click its control menu or use the View⇨Toolbars command). Excel then will not display that toolbar when you switch to its former context. However, you can restore autosensing by displaying the appropriate toolbar when you're in the appropriate context. Thereafter, Excel will display the toolbar automatically when you switch to that context. (Table 15-1 lists when Excel automatically displays a toolbar.)

Table 15-1 Autosensing

User Action	*Toolbar Displayed*
Activates a VBA module	Visual Basic
Activates a chart sheet	Chart
Activates embedded chart	Chart
Activates a dialog sheet	Forms
Starts recording a macro	Stop Recording
Enters full-screen mode	Full Screen
Activates a sheet with a pivot table	Query and Pivot

It's possible to program this automatic behavior in applications by using VBA. For example, you can use the OnSheetActivate and OnSheetDeactivate properties to specify that a macro be run when a particular sheet is activated or deactivated.

The following SetupAutoMenu subroutine sets Excel up so that activating the Budget worksheet executes the ShowToolbar routine (which shows the Budget Tools toolbar) and deactivating the Budget worksheet executes the HideToolbar routine (which hides the Budget Tools toolbar):

```
Sub SetupAutoMenu()
    With ThisWorkbook.Worksheets("Budget")
        .OnSheetActivate = "ShowToolbar"
        .OnSheetDeactivate = "HideToolbar"
    End With
End Sub
```

```
Sub ShowToolbar()
    Toolbars("Budget Tools").Visible = True
End Sub

Sub HideToolbar()
    Toolbars("Budget Tools").Visible = False
End Sub
```

NOTE

OnSheetActivate and OnSheetDeactivate remain in effect until canceled or until the current Excel session ends. To cancel, assign an empty string to the properties. For example,

```
With ThisWorkbook.Worksheets("Budget")
    .OnSheetActivate = ""
    .OnSheetDeactivate = ""
End With
```

Storing toolbar settings

When you exit, Excel updates two files: EXCEL5.XLB and EXCEL5.INI. These files are how Excel remembers your preferences from one session to another. As I discussed, EXCEL5.XLB stores all of the toolbars in the Toolbars collection, as well as the exact configuration.

EXCEL5.INI stores a variety of settings, including a few that deal with toolbars. The [Microsoft Excel] section of EXCEL5.INI has a setting called Options5. It may look something like

```
Options5=3073
```

The Options5 value actually controls 15 different settings for Excel. To translate the value, you need to convert it to a 15-bit binary number; then check a few bits to see whether certain toolbar-related options are on or off:

- The 1st bit is set when the Tip Wizard is on.
- The 9th bit is set when Tooltips are off.
- The 10th bit is set when the toolbar buttons are regular size.
- The 11th bit is set when toolbar autosensing is on.
- The 14th bit is set when the toolbar buttons are black and white.

Actually, you never need to check these bits because you can easily get or change these settings (except for autosensing) by accessing the Application object with VBA.

Modifying and Creating Toolbars

In the last chapter, I related how Excel's menus can be modified manually (by using the menu editor) or by using VBA code. Well, you also have two choices when working with toolbars:

- Manually — by using the toolbar customization commands
- By using VBA code

I discuss both methods in this chapter.

Manipulating Toolbars and Buttons Manually

Although Excel has no toolbar editor per se, you easily can create new toolbars and modify existing toolbars. In fact, you may not even have to use VBA to work with toolbars because you can do just about all your toolbar customization without it.

Customizing toolbars

To make changes to a toolbar, you must enter what I call *toolbar customization mode*. To do so, choose the View⇨Toolbars command. Excel displays its Toolbars dialog box, shown in Figure 15-1. When this dialog box is on-screen, you can do any of the following:

- *Hide or display any toolbar in the list.* Add a checkmark to display a toolbar; remove a checkmark to hide a toolbar.
- *Create a new toolbar.* Enter a name in the Toolbar Name edit box and click the New button. Excel creates and displays an empty toolbar.
- *Reset a built-in toolbar.* Select a built-in toolbar from the Toolbars list and click the Reset button (when you select a custom toolbar, this button says Delete).
- *Delete an existing toolbar.* Select a custom toolbar from the list and click the Delete button (when you select a built-in toolbar, this button says Reset).
- *Toggle toolbar button color.* Check or uncheck the Color Toolbars check box.
- *Toggle the toolbar button size.* Check or uncheck the Large Buttons check box.
- *Toggle the Tooltips display.* Tooltips are the yellow pop-up messages that display the button names when you pause the mouse pointer over a button. Check or uncheck the Show Tooltips check box.

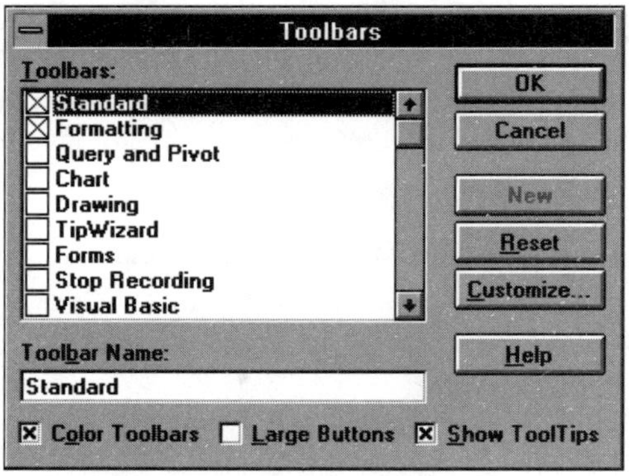

Figure 15-1: The Toolbars dialog box.

The changes described in the preceding list do not take effect until you close the Toolbars dialog box.

In addition, you can make the following changes while the Toolbars dialog box is displayed:

- *Move a toolbar button from any displayed toolbar to any other displayed toolbar.* Click a button and drag it to its new location.
- *Copy a toolbar button from any displayed toolbar to any other displayed toolbar.* Ctrl-click a button and drag it to another location.
- *Copy the image on a toolbar button to the Clipboard.* Right-click a button and choose Copy Button Image from the shortcut menu.
- *Paste the contents of the Clipboard to a toolbar button face.* Right-click a button and choose Paste Button Image from the shortcut menu.

For additional customization options, click the Customize button in the Toolbars dialog box. Excel displays the Customize dialog box, shown in Figure 15-2.

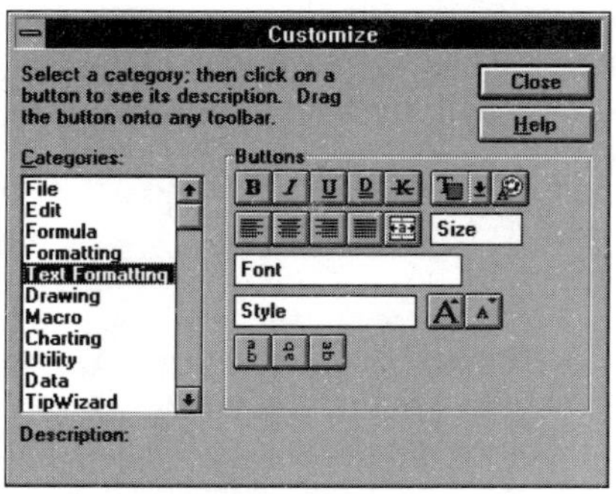

Figure 15-2: The Customize dialog box.

The Customize dialog box contains Excel's built-in toolbar buttons arranged in 13 categories. To find out what a button does, click it; you then can read a description of the button at the bottom of the dialog box. The 14th category, Custom, contains 28 additional buttons that do nothing; you can use them for your macros.

When the Customize dialog box is displayed, you can copy and move buttons freely among any visible toolbars

TIP

A slightly faster way to get to the Customize dialog box is to right-click any toolbar button and choose Customize from the shortcut menu.

Attaching macros

When you use a toolbar button that's not a built-in button, you need to assign a macro to it.

So when you add a button from the Custom category, Excel automatically prompts you for the macro (see Figure 15-3). Just select the appropriate macro from the list and click OK.

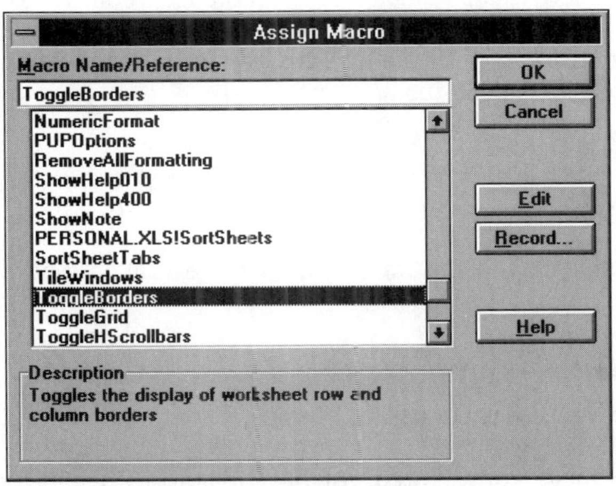

Figure 15-3: Assigning a macro to a toolbar button.

To change the macro assignment, first get into toolbar customization mode. Right-click the toolbar button and choose Assign Macro from the shortcut menu. The Assign Macro dialog box appears. Select the appropriate macro from the list and click OK.

Changing the Tooltip

One of the most frequently asked questions on the Excel/VBA Forum on CompuServe is, "My custom toolbar button's Tooltip always says *Custom*. How can I change it?" To edit the Tooltip, you must use VBA; the Tooltip is actually the Name property of the toolbar button. (By default, all the toolbar buttons in the Custom category are named *Custom*.)

For example, the following procedure changes the Tooltip (that is, Name property) of the first toolbar button on the Budget Tools toolbar to *Show Chart*.

```
Sub ChangeToolTip()
     Toolbars("Budget Tools").ToolbarButtons(1).Name = "Show _
       Chart"
End Sub
```

Changing the status bar text

When you hold the mouse pointer over a built-in button, Excel displays the Tooltip and a longer description of the button's function in the status bar.

The status bar display has nothing to do with the toolbar button. Rather, it's a property of the macro that's assigned to the toolbar button. To add status bar text to a macro, use the Tools⇨Macro command, select the macro, and click the Options button. Then enter the text that you want to appear in the status bar in the edit box labeled Status Bar Text.

Changing the look

To change the look of a toolbar button, you have several options, described in the following sections.

Creating images from scratch

Excel's button editor is easy to use, but basic.

To create a new image from scratch, you have to start with some button. You may want to use the blank toolbar button (in the Custom category of the Customize dialog box). Or you can start with any button and then clear (erase) the image in the button editor.

To edit a button image, you must be in toolbar customization mode (that is, either the Toolbars or Customize dialog box must be visible). To begin editing, right-click the button you want to edit and then choose Edit Button Image from the shortcut menu. The image appears in the Button Editor dialog box, where you can change individual pixels and shift the entire image up, down, left, or right.

If you've never worked with icons before, you may be surprised at how difficult it is to create attractive images in such a small area.

This dialog box is straightforward. Just click a color and then click a pixel (or drag across pixels). The Preview box displays the edited image in its normal size. When you like what you see, click OK.

If at any time you don't like what you're doing or have done, click Cancel and the button retains its original image.

How to avoid distorted button images

If you're going to create or modify toolbar button images, you need to be aware that toolbar buttons can be displayed in two sizes: regular or large. Users with high-resolution video drivers often choose to display the large buttons because the buttons are more legible.

By the way, Excel's built-in toolbar buttons look good at both sizes because each of built-in button is actually stored as two different bitmaps, one for each size. Button images that you create are stored as only one bitmap.

Button Image Rule #1: If your toolbar button images will be displayed in both sizes, you should create them while the buttons are displayed at regular size. If you create them in large-button mode and then switch to normal size, Excel scales the images to fit the smaller space but they never look good.

Button Image Rule #2: Don't use the button editor when you are in large-button mode. If you do, even good-looking buttons developed in regular-button mode will get messed up.

The bottom line: Never create or edit your buttons while in large-button mode. Use the regular-button mode exclusively. The normal size of toolbar buttons is 16 x 15 pixels. When you choose the large-button mode, the buttons are displayed 24 x 23 pixels. When switching from regular to large buttons, the actual image remains the same size, but Excel pads it with a gray border that's four pixels wide.

Copying and modifying other buttons

Another way to get a button image on a custom toolbar is to copy it from another toolbar button. In toolbar customization mode, right-clicking a toolbar button displays a shortcut menu that enables you to copy a button image to the Clipboard or paste the Clipboard contents to the selected button.

The disk that accompanies this book includes TOOLFACE.XLS, a workbook that has a custom toolbar attached with 100 new button images. To use any of these button faces, load the TOOLFACE.XLS workbook before you start customizing your toolbar. You then can drag the desired button faces to your new toolbar and attach your macros.

TOOLFACE.XLS includes an Auto_Close subroutine that deletes the custom toolbar from Excel's workspace when the workbook is closed. This procedure prevents the large toolbar from being added to and thus considerably increasing the size of your EXCEL5.XLB file.

Copying from the Clipboard

You can copy any image from the Clipboard to a toolbar button. This method works best when the copied image is exactly the right size. An incorrectly sized image will be scaled to fit — and usually won't look good.

For example, you can create picture objects in Excel and copy them to toolbar buttons. For optimal results, the dimensions of the picture object should be exactly 11.25 x 10.50 points, with no border. An image of this size will paste precisely onto a toolbar button face.

Figure 15-4 shows an example of a character in a cell copied to a toolbar button.

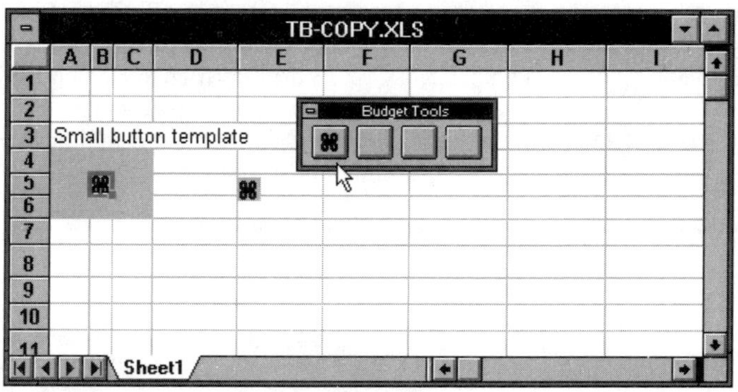

Figure 15-4: The contents of the cell was converted to a picture and copied to a toolbar button.

Here's how to create an image of the correct size in Excel and the paste it to a toolbar button. Make sure that you don't have the Large Buttons option set.

1. Choose a cell and make its column exactly 1.43 characters wide (11.25 points) and its row height 10.5 points.
2. Make the cell's background color gray.
3. Enter a character or two into the cell and format it as you like, adjusting the font size so that it fits in the cell. Center the contents vertically and horizontally in the cell.
4. Copy the cell to the Clipboard.
5. Activate a different cell and choose the Edit⇨Paste Picture command (you have to press Shift to use this command).
6. Select the pasted image and remove the border in the Format Object dialog box.
7. Copy the pasted image to the Clipboard.
8. Get into toolbar customization mode, right-click a toolbar button, and choose Paste Button Image. You may need to edit the image slightly, using the button editor.

NOTE

For large-button images, make the picture object 17.25 x 16.5 points (column width = 2.57 characters). Note that images copied to a large button, however, usually do not look good when the buttons are displayed in regular size.

Distributing Toolbars

In this section, I describe how to distribute custom toolbars to others, and I outline what you need to be aware of to prevent problems.

Attaching a toolbar to a workbook

To store a toolbar in a workbook file, activate a VBA module and choose the Tools⇨Attach Toolbars command. Excel brings up the Attach Toolbars dialog box, shown in Figure 15-5. This dialog box lists all the custom toolbars in the Toolbars collection in the list box on the left. Toolbars already stored in the workbook are listed in the list box on the right.

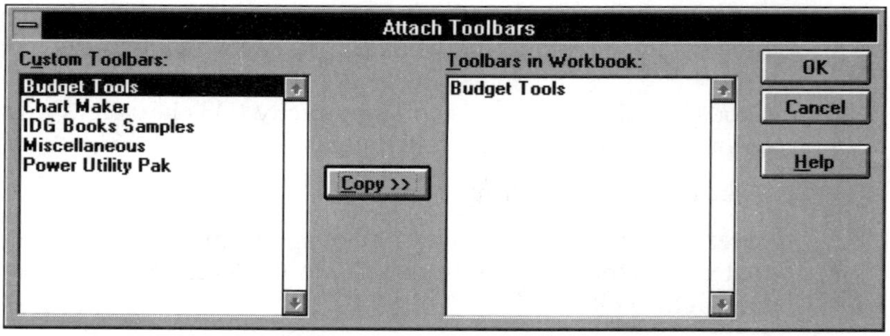

Figure 15-5: The Attach Toolbars dialog box.

To attach a toolbar, select it and then click the Copy button. When a toolbar in the right list box is selected, the Copy button says Delete; you can click it to remove a selected toolbar from a workbook.

The toolbar that's stored in the workbook is an exact copy of the toolbar at the time you attach it. If you modify the toolbar after attaching it, the changed version is not stored in the workbook automatically. You must manually remove the old toolbar and then add the edited toolbar.

A toolbar that's attached to a workbook appears automatically when the workbook is opened unless the workspace already has a toolbar by the same name. See the "How Excel Handles Toolbars" section for more information.

Distributing a toolbar with an add-in

As I wrote about in Chapter 13, add-ins are the preferred way of distributing applications to end users. Not surprisingly, an add-in also can include one or more custom toolbars.

Here's a typical scenario: You create an application that uses a custom toolbar. The buttons on the toolbar execute VBA routines in the application's workbook. You attach the toolbar to the workbook and save the workbook. You create an add-in from the workbook. You close the XLS version of the application. You install the add-in. You click a button on the custom toolbar *and the XLS file opens*!

The intent, of course, is to have the toolbar buttons execute procedures in the add-in, *not* the XLS file. But when you attach the toolbar to the workbook, the toolbar is saved in its current state — which includes references to the macros in the XLS file. Consequently, clicking a button opens the XLS file so that the macro can be executed.

As far as I can determine, the only workaround involves several more steps:

1. After creating the toolbar — but before you attach it to the workbook — you need to *modify the references*. To do so, get into toolbar customization mode, right-click the toolbar button, and choose Assign Macro. Remove the file reference from the Macro Name/Reference edit box. For example, if it reads BUDGETS.XLS!MACRO1, remove the file reference so that it reads MACRO1. Do so for each toolbar button in your custom toolbar.
2. *Attach the toolbar.* If the toolbar has already been attached, remove the old version first.
3. *Add an Auto_Open procedure*, which displays the toolbar stored in the workbook. Here's an example for a toolbar named *Budget Tools*:

```
Sub Auto_Open
    Toolbars("Budget Tools").Visible = True
End Sub
```

4. *Add an Auto_Close procedure,* which deletes the toolbar so that it isn't added to the user's EXCEL5.XLB file. Here's an example for a toolbar named Budget Tools:

```
Sub Auto_Close
    Toolbars("Budget Tools").Delete
End Sub
```

5. *Save the workbook* (and the attached toolbar along with it). The references in the toolbar do not refer to the XLS file.
6. *Create an add-in from the workbook* to create an XLA version of the file, which also includes the custom toolbar.

After performing the preceding steps, you can install the add-in. Because the toolbar stored in it does not exist in the Toolbars collection, the toolbar is displayed. Clicking the toolbar buttons executes the macros in the XLA version. When you uninstall the add-in, the toolbar is deleted and will not be stored in the user's EXCEL5.XLB file.

Using VBA to Manipulate Toolbars and Buttons

While performing any of the operations described in the preceding section, you can turn on the macro recorder to see what VBA code is generated. The steps you take while customizing toolbars, unless you're editing buttons, generates code. If you examine this code, you will discover how the object model for toolbars is arranged. The model actually is pretty simple:

```
Application
               Toolbars
      ToolbarButtons
```

The Toolbars collection, which is contained in the Application object, is a collection of all Toolbar objects, and each Toolbar object has a collection of ToolbarButtons. These objects have properties and methods that allow you to control toolbars by using VBA procedures.

The Toolbars collection

The Toolbars collection consists of all toolbars, built-in as well as custom. These toolbars are stored in EXCEL5.XLB.

The Toolbars collection only has a few properties and methods. Perhaps the most useful methods are Add and Delete. The following procedure uses the Add method to add a new, empty toolbar named *Budget Tools* to the collection. This subroutine only adds the toolbar to the collection; it does not display it.

```
Sub AddToolbar()
    Toolbars.Add "Budget Tools"
End Sub
```

To delete this toolbar, use a procedure like the following:

```
Sub DeleteToolbar()
    Toolbars("Budget Tools").Delete
End Sub
```

You get an error message if you try to delete a toolbar that doesn't exist. If you try to delete a built-in toolbar, it doesn't generate an error message, but nothing happens because built-in toolbars cannot be deleted.

Toolbar objects

You can refer to toolbar objects by name or index. The names and indices of the built-in toolbars are shown in Table 15-2.

Table 15-2 Names and Indices of Excel's Built-In Toolbars

Name	*Index*
Standard	1
Formatting	2
Query and Pivot	3
Chart	4
Drawing	5
Tip Wizard	6
Forms	7
Stop Recording	8
Visual Basic	9
Auditing	10
Workgroup	11
Microsoft	12
Full Screen	13

Toolbars have quite a few properties and methods, which are thoroughly described in the on-line help. In the following sections, I present a few simple VBA procedures to help you get the hang of working with Toolbar objects.

Resetting all built-in toolbars

The following procedure resets all built-in toolbars to their virgin state:

```
Sub ResetAll()
    For Each Bar In Toolbars
        Bar.Reset
    Next Bar
End Sub
```

Using the Reset method on a custom toolbar has no effect (and does not generate an error).

CAUTION

Be careful with the preceding routine. Calling it erases all customizations to all built-in toolbars.

Counting toolbars

The following procedure cycles through each toolbar in the Toolbars collection and counts the number that are built-in and custom. Figure 15-6 shows some typical output from this procedure.

```
Sub CountToolbars()
    BuiltInCnt = 0
    CustomCnt = 0
    For Each Bar In Toolbars
        If Bar.BuiltIn Then _
            BuiltInCnt = BuiltInCnt + 1 _
                Else CustomCnt = CustomCnt + 1
    Next Bar
    Msg = "Built-in: " & BuiltInCnt & Chr(13)
    Msg = Msg & "Custom: " & CustomCnt
    MsgBox Msg, vbInformation, "Toolbars"
End Sub
```

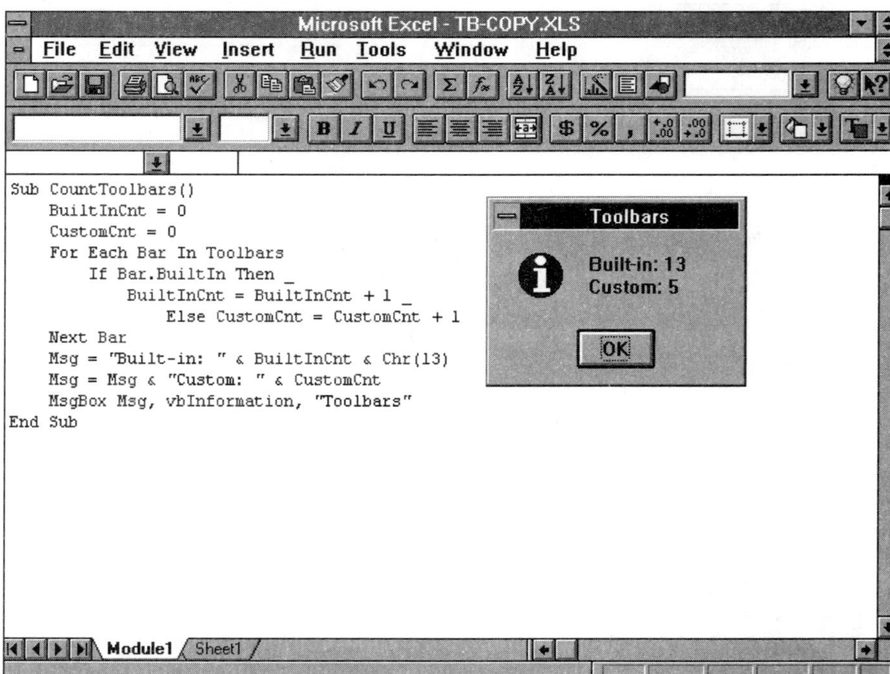

Figure 15-6: Counting the number of built-in and custom toolbars.

The number of built-in toolbars is always 13 because it's impossible to delete a built-in toolbar.

Toggling the display of all toolbars

The following procedure, which causes lots of on-screen action, simply reverses the Visible property of each toolbar. Hidden toolbars are displayed, and visible toolbars are hidden. To return to normal, rerun this routine.

```
Sub ToggleDisplay()
    For Each Bar In Toolbars
        Bar.Visible = Not Bar.Visible
    Next Bar
End Sub
```

The ToolbarButton collection

The ToolbarButtons collection only has a few methods and properties. The most useful are the Add and Delete methods.

Adding a toolbar button

To add a button to a toolbar, use the Add method of the ToolbarButtons collection.

The following procedure starts by determining the position of the last button on the toolbar and then uses the Add method twice to add buttons 98 (the Record Macro button) and 0 (a gap button):

```
Sub AddButton()
'   Determine last position on Standard toolbar
    LastPos = Toolbars(1).ToolbarButtons.Count

'   Add Record Macro button
    Toolbars(1).ToolbarButtons.Add _
        Button:=98, _
        Before:=LastPos + 1

'   Add a gap before the new button
    Toolbars(1).ToolbarButtons.Add _
        Button:=0, _
        Before:=LastPos + 1
End Sub
```

In this example, I add the button and then I insert a gap before the button. This order may seem backward, but you get an error if you try to add a gap to the end of a toolbar. Therefore, you must add the button and then insert the gap before it.

NOTE: By the way, you can reference toolbar buttons by either their name or ID number. I discovered the button ID number for Record Macro by recording my actions. All built-in toolbar buttons have unique ID numbers; they are listed in Appendix D of the *Visual Basic User's Guide*.

Adding a toolbar button (with all the frills)

The following code adds a toolbar button, changes its Tooltip, assigns a macro, and ensures that the toolbar button displays a description in the status bar when the mouse pointer is moved over the button:

```
Sub AddButton()
'   Add the button, first on the toolbar
    Toolbars("Budget Tools").ToolbarButtons.Add _
        Button:=211, _
        Before:=1

'   Assign macro and Tooltip
    With Toolbars("Budget Tools").ToolbarButtons(1)
        .OnAction = "ShowChart"
        .Name = "Show Chart"
    End With

'   Set up status bar text for macro
    Application.MacroOptions Macro:="ShowChart", _
        StatusBar:="Display the pie chart"
End Sub
```

ToolbarButton objects

ToolbarButton objects have several useful properties and methods. The examples in this section demonstrate some of them.

Deleting a toolbar button

The following code, which removes the button and the gap, uses the ToolbarButton object's Delete method:

```
Sub RemoveButton()
    For i = 1 To 2
        LastPos = Toolbars(1).ToolbarButtons.Count
        Toolbars(1).ToolbarButtons(LastPos).Delete
    Next i
End Sub
```

This procedure goes through a loop. Each time through, it determines the past button position and then uses this value as the index for the toolbar button to delete.

Manipulating gaps

The following example automatically spaces the buttons in a toolbar by first removing all gaps (using the IsGap property to determine whether a button is a gap) and then inserting a gap before each remaining button except the first:

```
Sub SpaceOutButtons()
    BarName = "Sample Toolbar"
    On Error Resume Next

'   Remove all gaps
    For Each Button In Toolbars(BarName).ToolbarButtons
        If Button.IsGap Then Button.Delete
    Next Button

'   Insert a gap after each button
    EndNumber = (Toolbars(BarName).ToolbarButtons.Count * 2) - 1
    For i = 2 To EndNumber Step 2
        Toolbars(BarName).ToolbarButtons.Add _
            Button:=0, _
            before:=i
    Next i
End Sub
```

Notice that I use an On Error statement to ignore errors. For some reason, the first part of the routine (removing the gaps) always generates an error when it reaches the end.

More Examples

I wrap up this chapter with two more examples. The first demonstrates how to remove all toolbars when an application is loaded and then restore all of them when the application ends. The second example is a subroutine that lets you change a toolbar's name — an action that's otherwise impossible.

Hiding and restoring toolbars

If as an application developer, you want the user's undivided attention, you may want to remove all the toolbars when the application is loaded. It's only polite, however, to restore the toolbars when your application is closed.

The following subroutine, SaveToolbars, saves the names of all visible toolbars in column A of Sheet1 and then hides all the toolbars. Notice that the routine saves the toolbar names in a worksheet range rather than an array, ensuring that the toolbar names are still available when the RestoreToolbars routine is executed. Values stored in an array may be lost between the time SaveToolbars is executed and RestoreToolbars is executed.

```
Sub SaveToolbars()
    ThisWorkbook.Sheets("Sheet1").Range("A:A").Clear
    Set SaveRange = _
        ThisWorkbook.Sheets("Sheet1").Range("A1")
    BarCount = 0
    For Each Bar In Toolbars
        If Bar.Visible Then
            BarCount = BarCount + 1
            SaveRange.Offset(BarCount - 1, 0).Value = _
               Bar.Name
            Bar.Visible = False
        End If
    Next Bar
End Sub
```

RestoreToolbars displays the toolbars that were saved by SaveToolbars:

```
Sub RestoreToolbars()
    Set SaveRange = _
       ThisWorkbook.Sheets("Sheet1").Range("A1")
    Set ColumnA = ThisWorkbook.Sheets("Sheet1").Range("A:A")
    For i = 1 To Application.CountA(ColumnA)
        Toolbars(SaveRange.Offset(i - 1, 0).Value).Visible = _
            True
    Next i
End Sub
```

Renaming toolbars

Although the on-line help for my version of Excel says otherwise, a Toolbar object's Name property is read-only. This "name protection" applies to both built-in and custom toolbars.

My guess is that the designers eliminated the capability to rename toolbars because of possible conflicts when a toolbar is stored in a workbook. As I discuss elsewhere, if a toolbar of the same name already exists, the toolbar in the workbook is not displayed. If a user could change the name of a toolbar, a new (identical) one could be added to the workspace.

Without this renaming capability, you're stuck if you create a toolbar and misspell its name. Your only alternative is to create a new toolbar and move the buttons to it — unless, of course, you have access to the VBA subroutine listed in this section.

NOTE: The following procedure, RenameToolbar, changes the name of a toolbar by adding a new toolbar with the desired name, copying all the toolbar buttons and gaps to the new toolbar, and then deleting the original toolbar. If you use this routine, make sure that you enter the appropriate names for OldName and NewName.

DISK: This routine is part of a more extensive utility which is available on the disk that accompanies this book. The filename is TBARTOOL.XLS. Besides renaming toolbars, TBARTOOLS.XLS lets you copy and delete toolbars, and easily change the tooltips for any toolbar button.

```
Sub RenameToolbar()
'   Renames a toolbar by copying it and
'   deleting the original

'   Array holds position of gaps in original
    Dim Gaps() As Integer

    OldName = "My Toolbar"
    NewName = "Budgeting Toolbars"

'   Check for duplicate name, or nonexistent
'   source toolbar
    Exists = False
    For Each Bar In Toolbars
        If Bar.Name = NewName Then
            MsgBox NewName & " already exists."
            Exit Sub
```

```
        End If
        If Bar.Name = OldName Then Exists = True
    Next Bar
    If Exists = False Then
        MsgBox OldName & " does not exist."
         Exit Sub
    End If

'   Add an empty toolbar and name it
    Toolbars.Add Name:=NewName

'   Determine gap positions in original toolbar
    GapCount = 0
    i = 0
    For Each Button In Toolbars(OldName).ToolbarButtons
        i = i + 1
        If Button.IsGap Then
            GapCount = GapCount + 1
            ReDim Preserve Gaps(GapCount)
            Gaps(GapCount) = i
        End If
    Next Button

'   Copy all the buttons
    For Each Button In Toolbars(OldName).ToolbarButtons
        Button.Copy _
            Toolbar:=Toolbars(NewName), _
             Before:=Toolbars(NewName).ToolbarButtons.Count + 1
    Next Button

'   Add matching gaps
    For i = 1 To GapCount
        Toolbars(NewName).ToolbarButtons.Add _
            Button:=0, _
            Before:=Gaps(i)
    Next i

'   Make it visible and the same dimensions
    Toolbars(NewName).Visible = True
    Toolbars(OldName).Visible = True
    Toolbars(NewName).Width = Toolbars(OldName).Width
    Toolbars(NewName).Left = Toolbars(OldName).Left
    Toolbars(NewName).Top = Toolbars(OldName).Top
```

```
'   Delete the old toolbar
    If Toolbars(OldName).ToolbarButtons.Count = _
       Toolbars(NewName).ToolbarButtons.Count Then _
            Toolbars(OldName).Delete Else _
                MsgBox ("Error - Original toolbar not _
                    deleted")
End Sub
```

The subroutine does some simple error checking to make sure that the old toolbar actually exists and that a toolbar with the new name does not exist. It then cycles though all the toolbar buttons, determines the position of the gaps, and stores this information in the Gaps array. Next, it copies each button by using the Copy method (gaps cannot be copied after the last toolbar button), and then it inserts the gaps. The new toolbar is then displayed in the same position and in the same size as the original. Finally, the old toolbar is deleted — but only if the button count matches (otherwise an error may have occurred).

Summary

- In this chapter, I described how to use Excel's built-in toolbars and customize toolbars for your applications.
- The next chapter discusses how to provide user help for your applications, including custom help files and other methods.

Chapter 16

Providing Help for Your Applications

In This Chapter

- How to provide on-line help to end users
- How to provide help by using only the tools supplied with Excel
- How to create Help files by using the Windows Help Compiler
- How to display a specific topic from a Help file by using VBA

Computer users have become rather spoiled over the years. Not too long ago, it was rare for software programs to provide on-line help. And the "help" provided often proved less than helpful.

Now just about all commercial software features on-line help. In fact, some vendors are substituting on-line help as the primary documentation; thick software manuals are an endangered species (good riddance!).

Help for Your Applications?

If you develop an application, it's a good idea to build in some sort of help for end users. Doing so makes the users feel more comfortable with the application and may eliminate those timewasting phone calls from users with basic questions. On-line help is always available (the instructions can't be misplaced or buried under a pile of books).

You can add user help to your applications in a number of ways, ranging from simple to complex. The method you choose should depend on your application's scope and complexity. Some applications may require only a brief set of instructions on how to start the application. Others may benefit from a full-blown searchable hypertext HLP file that uses the Windows WINHELP.EXE program. Most often, applications need something in between.

This chapter classifies help into two categories:

- Help systems that don't use WinHelp
- Help systems that use WinHelp

Non-WinHelp Methods of Providing Help

In this section, I provide an overview of some help techniques that don't use WinHelp. I discuss the following methods (and provide examples):

- *Use a worksheet.* A simple way to add help is to insert a worksheet, enter your help information, and name its tab Help. When the user clicks the tab, the worksheet is activated.
- *Use a separate workbook.* You can create a separate workbook that contains your help information and then display it when the user needs help.
- *Use Write or Notepad.* You can store your help information in a separate file (for Windows Write or Notepad) and then display the file upon command.
- *Create a dialog box with labels.* You can write a simple macro that modifies the text in a label object, allowing you to show multiple messages in a single dialog box.
- *Create a dialog box with a linked picture.* This approach, similar to the dialog-box-with-labels technique, uses a picture object linked to a worksheet range with help text in the cell.
- *Create a dialog box with scrolling text.* A more sophisticated version of the dialog-box-with-linked-picture technique, this method lets the user scroll forward or backward in the help text.
- *Create a slide show.* This method takes quite a bit of work to do well, but you can create some very attractive presentations.

The disk that accompanies this book contains a file named HLPDEMO1.XLS, which demonstrates each of the techniques in this section. The sheets in the workbook are coded with numbers so that you can see which sheets are used by each example. For example, the first demo uses Module1 and HelpSheet1, the second uses Module2, and so on. Figure 16-1 shows the opening screen for this workbook.

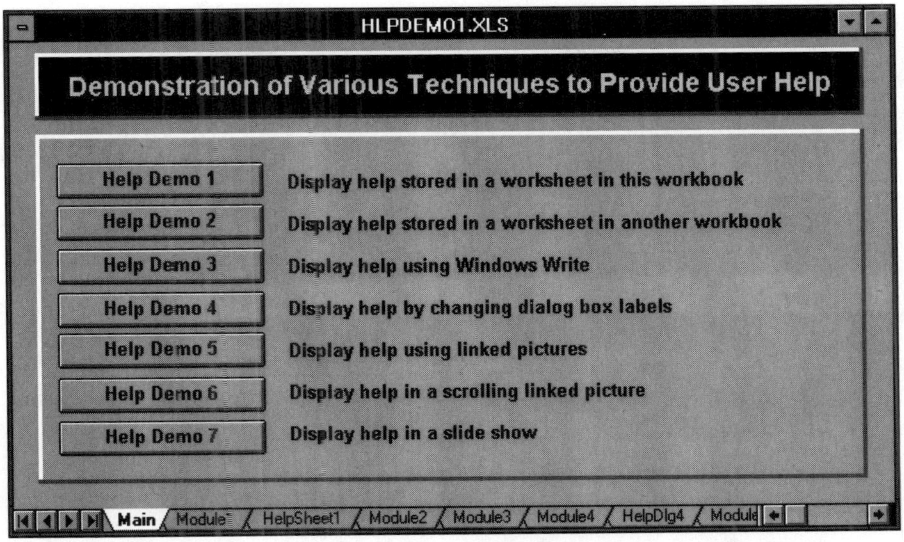

Figure 16-1: HLPDEMO1.XLS demonstrates seven ways to display user help without using WinHelp.

Using a worksheet for help text

The easiest way to add help to your application is to create a macro that activates a separate worksheet holding the help information. Just attach the macro to a button, toolbar button, or menu item, and voilà! — quick-and-dirty help.

Figure 16-2 shows a sample help worksheet. I designed the range that contains the help text to simulate a page from a yellow notebook pad — a fancy touch that you may or may not like.

To keep the user from scrolling around the worksheet, I hid all rows and columns that did not contain text. I also protected the worksheet to prevent the user from changing the text. In addition, I "froze" the rows so that the Return button is always visible, regardless of how far down the sheet the user has scrolled.

The following routine from the HLPDEMO1.XLS file displays help text in a worksheet in the same workbook. Notice that this routine places the cell pointer in cell A1, which is hidden (along with the rest of row 1); this routine thus hides the cell pointer, which could distract some users.

```
Sub ShowHelp1()
'   Activate help sheet
    Application.Goto _
        reference:=ThisWorkbook.Sheets("Help").Range("A1"), _
        scroll:=True
End Sub
```

The worksheet that contains the help text has a button that returns to the Main worksheet. This routine is

```
Sub ReturnFromHelp()
'   Return to application sheet
    Application.Goto _
        reference:=ThisWorkbook.Sheets("Main").Range("A1")
End Sub
```

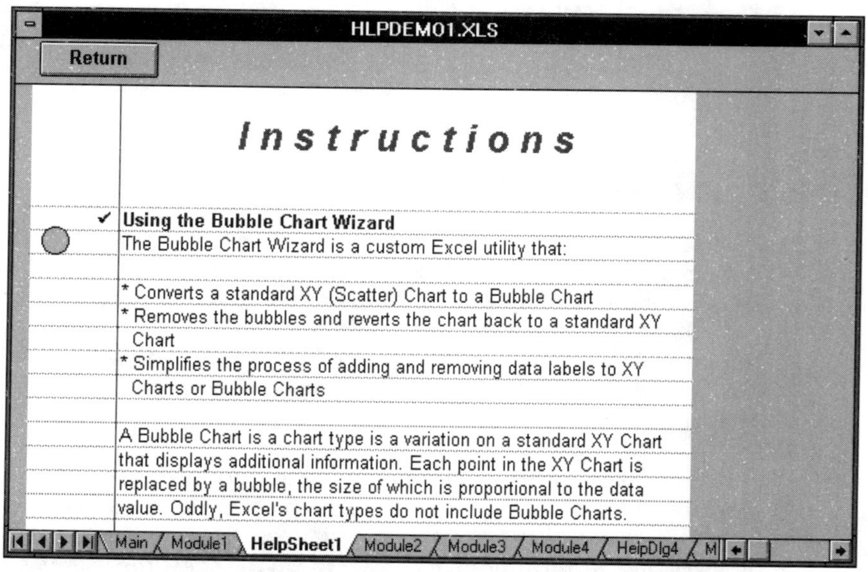

Figure 16-2: Putting user help in a separate worksheet is the easiest way to go.

Using a separate workbook for help text

Another method of providing help involves using a separate workbook to store help text. This method offers several advantages:

- The workbook is not opened if help is not needed — reducing the memory used.

- The user can view the help text and the application at the same time.
- The help file is easier to maintain because the developer can update the help workbook separate from the application workbook.
- The workbook with the help information can be made to look like the help displayed by WinHelp.

The sample help workbook

Figure 16-3 shows a sample help workbook. Note the following:

- The workbook has one worksheet (which holds the text) and one macro sheet.
- In the worksheet, all rows and columns that do not contain text are hidden to prevent the user from scrolling outside the text area.
- Rows 1 and 2 are frozen, so the buttons remain visible when the user scrolls down.
- The cell pointer is stored in cell A1, which is hidden (along with the rest of row 1). Therefore, the cell pointer won't be visible.
- The horizontal scroll bar, tab display, and row and column borders are all hidden.
- The worksheet is protected to prevent the user from changing the text.
- The VBA module is hidden.

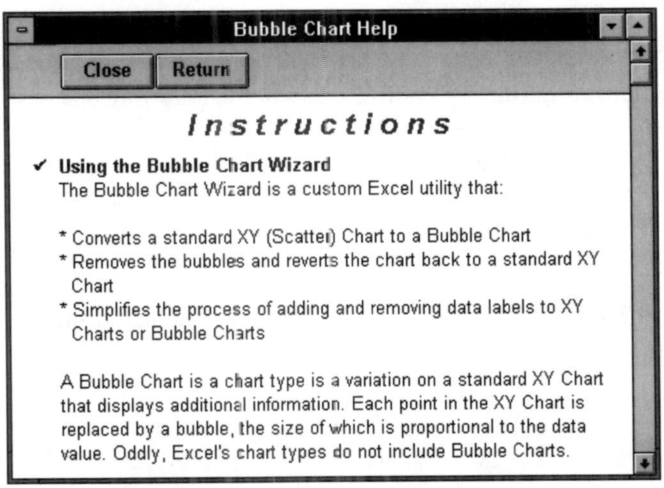

Figure 16-3: If you prefer to provide help in a separate window, putting the help in another workbook is an easy solution.

The net result of these effects is a window that looks unlike a spreadsheet — in fact, it sort of resembles a standard WinHelp window.

The following routine in Listing 16-1, the Auto_Open procedure found in HELPBOOK.XLS, ensures that the workbook window is not maximized. Then it changes the window caption to a more descriptive name and makes sure that the window is the proper size. Finally, it activates cell A1 (placing the cell pointer in a hidden row).

Listing 16-1 **Auto_Open Procedure**

```
Sub Auto_Open()
'   Make sure window is not maximized
    If ActiveWorkbook.Windows(1).WindowState = xlMaximized _
       Then _
        ActiveWorkbook.Windows(1).WindowState = xlNormal

'   Change caption, adjust height and width
    With ActiveWindow
        .Caption = "Bubble Chart Help"
        .Width = 350
        .Height = 250
    End With

'   Put cell pointer in A1
    Application.Goto _
        reference:=ThisWorkbook.Sheets("Help").Range("A1")
End Sub
```

The two buttons in HELPBOOK.XLS execute the following macros:

- CloseHelp closes the workbook without saving changes.

```
Sub CloseHelp()
    ThisWorkbook.Close savechanges:=False
End Sub
```

- ReturnToApp activates the next window — which is the application's window.

```
Sub ReturnToApp()
    Windows(1).ActivateNext
End Sub
```

The HELPBOOK.XLS file is a very simple example. You can, of course, make your help workbook as complex as you like. For example, you can add more worksheets, each detailing a separate topic. And perhaps the first worksheet can contain buttons to activate topics.

The workbook that opens the help workbook

The following subroutine in Listing 16-2 summons the help workbook described in the preceding section. (This subroutine should be stored in a VBA module in the application's workbook.) First, the procedure sets up an On Error label so that the user gets a message describing what file is missing and where it should be located if the file is not found. Next, the routine determines whether the help window is already open. If so, the workbook is activated. If not, the file is opened; notice that the file is expected to be in the same directory as the application. The final statement executes the Auto_Open macro in HELPBOOK.XLS (Auto_Open procedures are not executed when a workbook is opened by VBA).

Listing 16-2 ShowHelp2 Subroutine

```
Sub ShowHelp2()
'   Open the help workbook

    On Error GoTo NoFind

    Helpfile = "HELPBOOK.XLS"

    For Each Win In Windows
        If Win.Caption = "Bubble Chart Help" Then
            Windows("Bubble Chart Help").Activate
            Exit Sub
        End If
    Next Win
    Workbooks.Open _
        FileName:=ThisWorkbook.Path & "\" & Helpfile
    Workbooks(Helpfile).RunAutoMacros (xlAutoOpen)
    Exit Sub

NoFind:
    Msg = Helpfile & " cannot be located in "
    Msg = Msg & ThisWorkbook.Path
    MsgBox Msg, vbInformation
End Sub
```

Using Write or Notepad for help text

Every Windows package ships with copies of Windows Write and Notepad. Write is a simple word processor, and Notepad is a plain text editor. Using either, you can create a file that contains your help information and then write a macro to display the file upon command.

Figure 16-4 shows an example of help information contained in a Write file named BUBLWIZ.WRI.

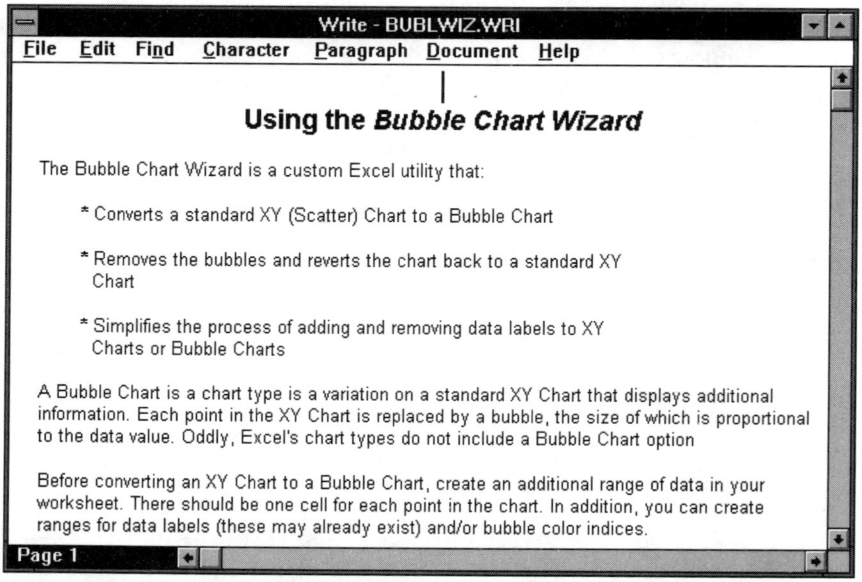

Figure 16-4: You also can use Windows Write or Notepad to display help information.

The routine that displays the Write file is

```
Sub ShowHelp3()
'   Open the Write file
    HelpFile = ThisWorkbook.Path & "\" & "BUBLWIZ.WRI"
    AppName = "Write"
    AppFile = "WRITE.EXE"

    On Error GoTo NotRunning
    AppActivate (AppName)
    Exit Sub

NotRunning:
'   Executed if Write is not already running
    Shell(AppFile & " " & HelpFile, 1)
End Sub
```

It's easy to use an external application, such as Write or Notepad, to hold your help text. But this method can be difficult to control. For example, you cannot control the size of the Write or Notepad window. Worse, if the file cannot be located, the user sees an error message from Write or Notepad.

Creating a dialog box with dynamic labels

One way to provide custom help is to create a huge dialog box and insert the help text as Label objects. But few people really want to read a large dialog box filled with text. A better approach is to break the information into bite-sized chunks and let the user control the display of the information. To do so, you can create multiple dialog boxes, but a better approach is to use a single dialog box and change the text displayed in it dynamically.

The example in this section uses a dialog box with three buttons (see Figure 16-5). Clicking the Next button displays the next set of text and clicking the Previous button displays the preceding set; these buttons call macros that change the text in the label object. Clicking the Done button closes the dialog box.

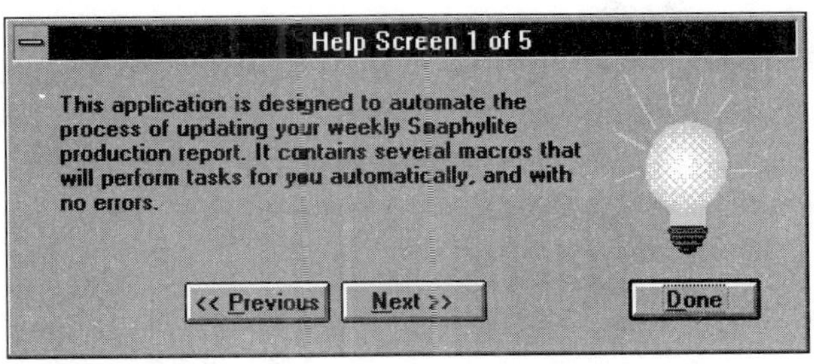

Figure 16-5: The buttons in this dialog box execute macros that change the text in the label.

The following routine sets up the messages that you want displayed and loads the first message into the label object. It also changes the dialog's caption to display the sequence number.

```
Sub ShowHelp4()
    MaxScreens = 5
    ReDim Msg(MaxScreens) As String
```

```
'   Assign the text displayed in each of the five "steps"
    Msg(1) = "This application is designed to automate "
    Msg(1) = Msg(1) & "the process of updating your weekly _
        Snaphylite "
    Msg(1) = Msg(1) & "production report. It contains _
        several macros "
    Msg(1) = Msg(1) & "that will perform tasks for you _
        automatically, "
    Msg(1) = Msg(1) & "and with no errors."

    Msg(2) = "Click the Begin button, and you will be asked "
    Msg(2) = Msg(2) & "to enter the beginning date of the
        week you "
    Msg(2) = Msg(2) & "are working on. " & Chr(13) & Chr(13)
    Msg(2) = Msg(2) & "This should be the date for a Monday."

    Msg(3) = "Next, a new workbook will be opened. You need _
        to enter "
    Msg(3) = Msg(3) & "the daily Snaphylite sales data, by _
        region."
    Msg(3) = Msg(3) & Chr(13) & Chr(13)
    Msg(3) = Msg(3) & "After you've entered the data, click _
        the button "
    Msg(3) = Msg(3) & "labeled Process."

    Msg(4) = "Processing the file will take a few minutes, _
        since several "
    Msg(4) = Msg(4) & "charts and summary reports are being _
        created."

    Msg(5) = "When processing is completed, click the Print _
        button "
    Msg(5) = Msg(5) & "to print the charts and reports. "
    Msg(5) = Msg(5) & Chr(13) & Chr(13)
    Msg(5) = Msg(5) & "If you have any additional questions _
        about this, "
    Msg(5) = Msg(5) & "call your supervisor."

'   Always start with the first step
    ScreenNum = 1
    DialogSheets("HelpDlg4").Labels("HelpText").Text = _
Msg(ScreenNum)

'   Display progress in the dialog's caption
    DialogSheets("HelpDlg4").DialogFrame.Caption = _
        "Help Screen " & ScreenNum & " of " & MaxScreens
```

```
'   Display the dialog box
    DialogSheets("HelpDlg4").Show
End Sub
```

Clicking the Next button executes the following subroutine, which changes the label's text to the next message in the sequence and updates the caption:

```
Sub Forward1()
'   Procedure will execute when Next⇨ button is clicked.

'   Beep and exit if we can't go forward any further
    If ScreenNum = MaxScreens Then
        Beep
        Exit Sub
    End If
    ScreenNum = ScreenNum + 1

'   Change the dialog's caption
    DialogSheets("HelpDlg4").DialogFrame.Caption = _
        "Help Screen " & ScreenNum & " of " & MaxScreens
    DialogSheets("HelpDlg4").Labels("HelpText").Text = _
      Msg(ScreenNum)
End Sub
```

The following procedure, which executes when the Previous button is clicked, is very similar:

```
Sub Backward1()
'   Procedure will execute when <<Previous button is
clicked.

'   Beep and exit if we can't go back any further
    If ScreenNum = 1 Then
        Beep
        Exit Sub
     End If
    ScreenNum = ScreenNum - 1

'   Change the dialog's caption
    DialogSheets("HelpDlg4").DialogFrame.Caption = _
        "Help Screen " & ScreenNum & " of " & MaxScreens
    DialogSheets("HelpDlg4").Labels("HelpText").Text = _
       Msg(ScreenNum)
End Sub
```

Creating a dialog box with a linked picture

The example in this section, which is similar to the preceding example, uses a linked picture object rather than a label. The advantage to using a linked picture object is the freedom to apply standard text formatting. Any formatting that you do in the worksheet range appears in the dialog box. Labels, on the other hand, cannot be formatted.

To get a linked picture, use the Camera tool or issue the Edit⇨Paste Picture Link command after copying a range (this command is available only when you hold down Shift as you select the Edit menu).

Figure 16-6 shows a dialog box with a linked picture object. A separate worksheet has five ranges named *Screen1*, *Screen2*, and so on. A linked picture object has a Formula property, which controls what's displayed in the picture (which is named HelpPicture). The formula is a string that refers to a range on a worksheet. Therefore, setting the picture object's formula to Screen2 displays the contents of the Screen2 range.

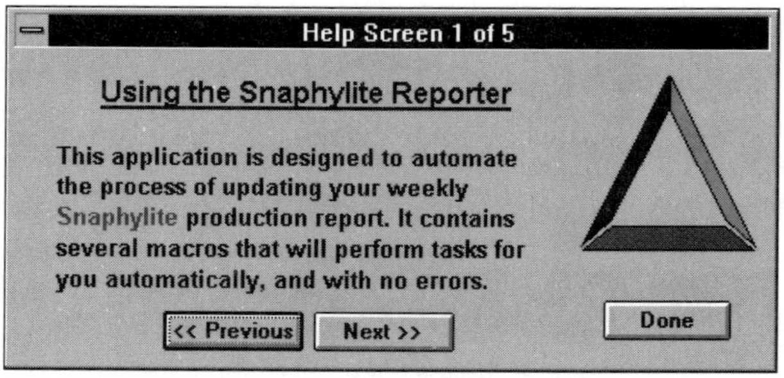

Figure 16-6: Using a linked picture object in a dialog box lets you display formatted text in a worksheet.

```
Sub ShowHelp5()
    ReDim HelpScreens(MaxScreens) As String
    Set HlpDlg = DialogSheets("HelpDlg5")

    MaxScreens = 5
    ScreenNum = 1

'   Build a formula
'   The ranges on HelpDlg5 are in the form Screen1, Screen2, etc.
    CurrentScreen = "Screen" & ScreenNum
    HlpDlg.DrawingObjects("HelpPicture").Formula = _
      CurrentScreen
```

```
'   Update the caption
    BoxCaption = "Help Screen " & ScreenNum & " of " & _
       MaxScreens
    HlpDlg.DialogFrame.Caption = BoxCaption

'   Show the dialog
    HlpDlg.Show
End Sub
```

As in the example from the preceding section, the dialog box has Previous and Next buttons that execute subroutines. In this case, the subroutines modify the formula for the linked picture object:

```
Sub Forward2()
'   Procedure will execute when Next⇨ button is clicked.
    If ScreenNum = MaxScreens Then
        Beep
        Exit Sub
    End If
    ScreenNum = ScreenNum + 1
    BoxCaption = "Help Screen " & ScreenNum & " of " & _
      MaxScreens
    HlpDlg.DialogFrame.Caption = BoxCaption

'   Build formula and update the picture
    CurrentScreen = "Screen" & ScreenNum
    HlpDlg.DrawingObjects("HelpPicture").Formula = _
      CurrentScreen
End Sub


Sub Backward2()
'   Procedure will execute when <<Previous button is
'   clicked.
    If ScreenNum = 1 Then
        Beep
        Exit Sub
    End If
    ScreenNum = ScreenNum - 1

    BoxCaption = "Help Screen " & ScreenNum & " of " & _
       MaxScreens
    HlpDlg.DialogFrame.Caption = BoxCaption

'   Build formula and update the picture
    CurrentScreen = "Screen" & ScreenNum
    HlpDlg.DrawingObjects("HelpPicture").Formula = _
      CurrentScreen
End Sub
```

Creating a dialog box with scrolling text

If you want to display help text in a custom dialog box, your best option may be to use a linked picture object but also provide a scroll bar (allowing the user to scroll the text forward or backward line by line or frame by frame).

Figure 16-7 shows an example. Again, a worksheet contains the help text in a single column. Clicking the scroll bar executes a macro that changes the formula for the linked picture object to refer to a different part of the worksheet.

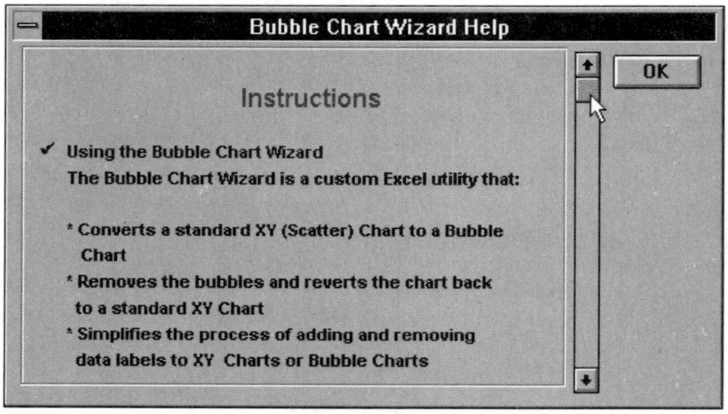

Figure 16-7: Scrolling through help that's set up as a linked picture.

The procedures are listed following. The ChangeViewPort subroutine is executed whenever the scroll bar is clicked. The value of the scroll bar determines the formula for the picture object, named *ViewPort*.

```
Sub ShowHelp6()
    Set ScrollText = ThisWorkbook.DialogSheets("HelpDlg6")
    Set ViewPort = ScrollText.Pictures("Viewport")
    Set TextScroller = ScrollText.ScrollBars("TextScroller")

    TextScroller.Value = 1
    Call ChangeViewPort
    ScrollText.Show
End Sub


Sub ChangeViewPort()
    First = TextScroller.Value
    Last = First + 11
    ViewPort.Formula = "HelpSheet6!$B$" & First & ":$C$" & _
       Last
End Sub
```

Creating a slide show

Help in the form of an on-screen slide show is most appropriate to introduce an application or provide an overview. For standard (read: practical) types of help, use one of the other techniques.

Although Excel has built-in slide show capability, for even better results you can embed an entire PowerPoint presentation in your workbook. Of course, you then need PowerPoint on the system to run the presentation. (Figure 16-8 shows a screen from a slide show developed with Excel.)

This example takes some explaining. I started by using Excel's Slide template to create a slide show; I then copied the Slide Show workbook to the HLPDEM1.XLS workbook.

The Slide Show template normally has buttons that are used to edit the slide show. These buttons execute macros in SLIDES.XLA, and the path to this file is hard-coded into the macro references, creating a link in the file. Consequently, every time HLPDEM1.XLS was loaded, a message appeared asking whether I wanted to update the links. Normally, this situation poses no problem. But I didn't want all the readers of this book to have to contend with such a message.

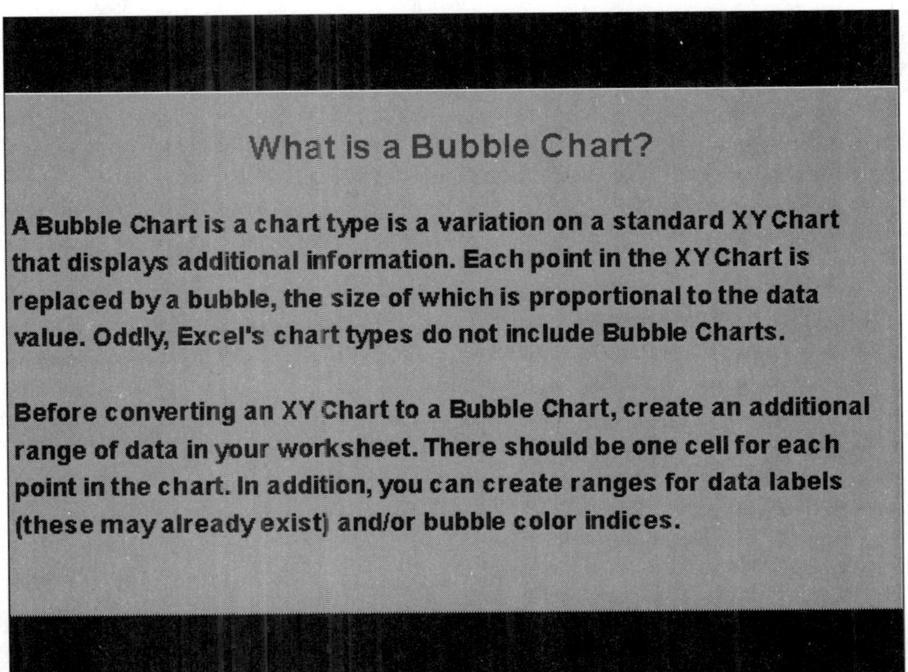

Figure 16-8: Sometimes a slide presentation is a good way to introduce a user to your application.

I realized, however, that I could remove the links simply by removing the buttons from the Slide Show sheet. But then I discovered that the slide show wouldn't execute unless SLIDES.XLA was in memory. So I wrote some code to ensure that this file was loaded. The net result is a file that contains a slide show but has no links (according to the Excel docs, this is impossible).

The code that executes the slide show is

```
Sub ShowHelp6()
'   Displays the slide show

'   See if Slide show add-in is open
    On Error Resume Next
    x = Workbooks("SLIDES.XLA").Sheets.Count
    If Err = 1004 Then
'       Not open, so try to open it
        SlideShow = Application.LibraryPath & _
           "\SLIDES\SLIDES.XLA"
        On Error Resume Next
        Workbooks.Open SlideShow
    End If

    If Err <> 1004 Then
'       Slide show add-in is open, so show the slides
        Application.ScreenUpdating = False
        ThisWorkbook.Sheets("Slide Show").Activate
        Application.ExecuteExcel4Macro _
            String:="SLIDE.SHOW(1,FALSE)"
        ThisWorkbook.Sheets("Main").Activate
        Exit Sub
    End If

'   An error occurred
    ThisWorkbook.Sheets("Main").Activate
    Msg = "Cannot open the Slide Show add-in in "
    Msg = Msg & Application.LibraryPath & "\SLIDES"
    Msg = Msg & Chr(13) & "The slide show add-in must be on _
        your "
    Msg = Msg & "system to use this feature."
    MsgBox Msg, vbExclamation
End Sub
```

The procedure starts by checking to see whether SLIDES.XLA is open. (It does so by referencing it — that is, accessing the Count property of its Sheets collection.) If the file is not loaded, Error 1004 is generated. If Err equals 1004, the routine tries to open the file, looking for it in its normal directory. If it can't be opened, another Error 1004 is generated. This time an error message appears; the slide show feature probably is not installed. If no errors occur, the slide show is displayed by an XLM macro (no VBA procedure can do so).

Come to think of it, this example may be more appropriate in a discussion of error handling than on-line help.

Creating WinHelp Files

The remainder of this chapter deals with standard Windows *help files* — specially formatted files that are loaded by WINHELP.EXE.

About WinHelp

WinHelp is best described as a hypertext reader; in other words, you need not access the information in the file sequentially. Most HLP files include *jumps* that let you quickly read another topic.

Figure 16-9, for example, shows a typical help topic. Some words, jump words, are displayed in a second color (probably green, but not necessarily so). Clicking a jump word that has a dotted underline displays another window with more explanation (often a definition). Clicking a jump word that has a solid underline either jumps to a new topic or displays a secondary help window.

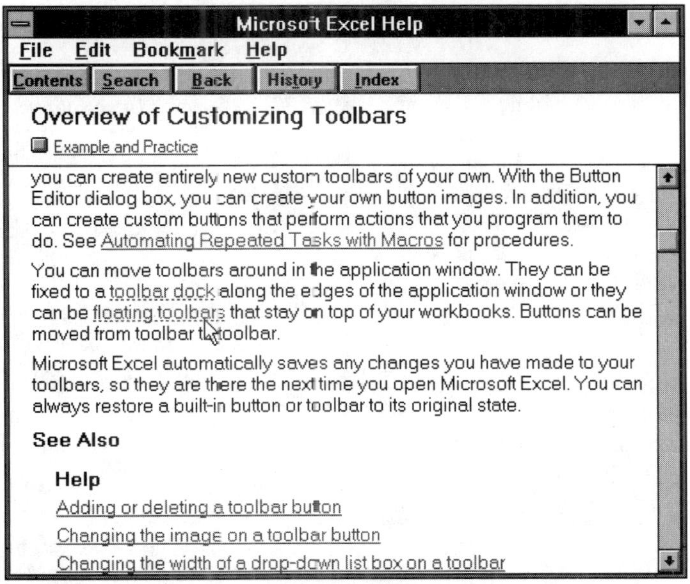

Figure 16-9: A typical topic in an Excel help file; jump words are underlined.

Creating WinHelp files is an art. An entire Usenet newsgroup is devoted to this topic (comp.os.ms-windows.programmer.winhelp), and I'm constantly amazed at the level of discussions in this group. It's clear that creating a good WinHelp file requires lots of experience and some good programming skills to boot.

What you need to create WinHelp files

To create an HLP file, you need a copy of Microsoft's Help Compiler. This program is widely available; it is distributed with many programming languages, including Microsoft Visual Basic Professional Edition. In addition, you can download it from the major on-line services, including CompuServe and America Online. If you have access to the Internet, you can also get it via anonymous ftp from ftp.microsoft.com (look for HC505.ZIP in the SOFTLIB/ MSLFILES directory).

To create an HLP file, you also need a word processing program that can read and write RTF (Rich Text Format) files. Most major word processors can do so, including the Big Three — Word for Windows, WordPerfect for Windows, and Ami Pro. In addition, I recommend getting a help authoring tool. Many such products are available, including shareware and commercial offerings. Some products work hand in hand with your word processor, and others include their own editors so that you don't even need a word processor.

Excel's Help system

Windows applications produced by major software manufacturers tend to have excellent help systems. Virtually all Windows applications ship with on-line help in the HLP format — a file format that can be read by WINHELP.EXE. (Although you may not realize it, you are undoubtedly familiar with WinHelp.)

Accessing Excel's on-line help system runs WinHelp and displays an appropriate topic from an HLP file. Excel's WinHelp file are quite sophisticated and well constructed. Excel includes more than six megabytes of on-line help, scattered across five files. The accompanying table lists and describes the help files included with Excel.

Help File	*Description*
MACROFUN.HLP	Help on XL4 macro functions
MAINXL.HLP	Excel's main help system
VBA_XL.HLP	Help for VBA
XLPSS.HLP	Help describing Microsoft's Product Support Services
XLREADME.HLP	General information (to be read after installing Excel)

By the way, you can write a VBA procedure to display a specific help topic from any of these files — as long as you know the Context ID of the topic. Unfortunately, this information is not easy to obtain.

Creating a simple WinHelp file

If your application's help requirements are on the simple side, you may be surprised to discover how easy it is to create a nonhypertext HLP file.

1. Create your help document in a word processor.
2. Save it in RTF format.
3. At the DOS prompt, enter the following, where *xxx.RTF* is the name of your file:

   ```
   HC31  xxx.RTF
   ```

4. Get back into Windows, execute WINHELP.EXE, and choose the File⇨Open command to load your new help file. (The new help file has the same filename as the original but with an HLP extension tacked on).

It may take you a few attempts before you're satisfied with the result. For example, you'll find that the formatting that you apply in your word processor doesn't translate precisely.

A simple help file created in this manner does not have any context IDs assigned. Therefore you are limited in how you can display the help file. One method that works is to use the Help method of the Application object (I cover this information later).

Several versions of the Microsoft Help Compiler exist, and the executable filename may vary. For example, the compiler may be named HC.EXE or HC30.EXE (the version for Windows 3.0). If you have HC30.EXE, you need to upgrade to the Windows 3.1 version.

Creating more complex WinHelp files

A complete discussion of creating help files is well beyond the scope of this book. Instead, I present enough information to enable you to develop some reasonably sophisticated help files. Keep in mind that developing help files is not easy. Fortunately, there are several tools available that can significantly simplify the task.

The example in this section produces a small help file that describes how to create a help file. The finished result is shown in Figure 16-10.

The example in this section can be found on the disk that accompanies this book. You may want to consult these files while reading through this section. The example consists of three files:

- SAMPLE.RTF contains the formatted help text. I used Word for Windows 6.0 to create this file.

- SAMPLE.HPJ is the (ASCII) project file.
- SAMPLE.HLP is the end result. You can open this file from WINHELP.EXE.

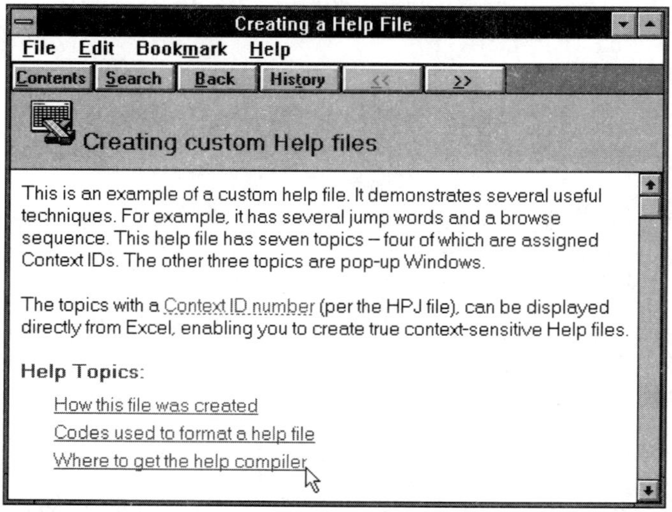

Figure 16-10: An example of a help file compiled with the Windows Help Compiler.

Determining the structure

When developing a help file, the first step is to determine its structure. I often find that it's helpful to organize a help file around an outline.

The help file in this example consists of four main topics (which need context IDs):

- An introductory description of the file; includes jumps to the other topics
- A description of how the help file was created
- Codes used to create a help file
- Where to get a copy of the Windows Help Compiler

In addition, the file should include three other topics that appear in pop-up windows:

- A description of CompuServe
- A description of America Online
- A listing of the file's context IDs

Writing the help text

I like to separate each topic with a page break. Typically, each topic starts with a heading and is followed by the help text.

TIP: You can easily produce consistent-looking help topics by taking advantage of your word processor's styles feature.

As you examine SAMPLE.RTF, note that I inserted a small picture at the beginning of each main topic (a touch that makes the file look more professional). Also notice that the "Codes used to format a help file" topic includes a three-column table, which I created by using Word's normal table features.

Adding the codes

Now for the fun part. You provide instructions to the Help Compiler by inserting footnotes into the RTF file. The footnotes are actually codes that describe certain aspects of the topic.

For example, the first topic in the example file has four footnotes:

Contents

$ Contents

K contents;overview

+ Browse:010

The number sign defines the topic's context string. The dollar sign defines the topic's title. The letter *K* defines searchable keywords. The plus sign defines a browse sequence that lets the user move sequentially through topics.

Table 16-1 summarizes the footnote codes that you can insert into your RTF file.

Table 16-1	Codes Inserted into a Help File	
Code Code	***Name***	***Purpose***
Number sign (#) footnote	Context string	Defines a context string that uniquely identifies a topic.
Dollar sign ($) footnote	Title	Defines the topic title. Titles appear in a list box when you use the Search button. Optional.
Letter K footnote	Keyword	Defines a keyword with which the user searches for a topic. Optional.
Plus sign (+) footnote	Browse sequence number	Defines a sequence that determines the order in which the user can browse through topics. Optional.
Asterisk (*) footnote	Build tag	Defines a tag that specifies topics that the Help Compiler builds into the system conditionally.
Strikethrough or double-underlined text	Jump text	Indicates the text that the user can choose to jump to another topic.
Underlined text	Definition	Specifies that a pop-up window appears when the user clicks the mouse button or presses Enter.
Hidden text	Context string	Specifies the context string for the topic that is displayed when the user selects the text immediately preceding it.
"Keep with next" paragraph beginning a topic	Unscrollable text	Determines the text that remains fixed at the top of a topic. Optional.

Adding additional information

This sample help file allows a user to jump to other topics and to pop up windows. You program in these features by using codes. You can examine the RTF file for the example file to see how I accomplished these jumps.

To jump to another topic, make the clickable text double-underlined. Follow it immediately with the context string of the topic to jump to and format the context string as hidden. When you load the RTF file, make sure that the option to display hidden text is turned on.

To specify a pop-up window, make the clickable text underlined (single underline) and follow it immediately with the context string formatted as hidden text.

Creating the HPJ file

After you set up the RTF file, it's time to create a *project file* — a plain text file with an HPJ extension.

The contents of the SAMPLE.HPJ:

```
[FILES]
sample.rtf

[MAP]
Contents 0
How_Created 5
Codes_Used 10
Where_to_get 15

[CONFIG]
BrowseButtons()

[WINDOWS]
Main = "Creating a Help File",,,, (192,192,192 )
```

An HPJ file is set up like an INI file; it consists of sections, enclosed in square brackets, followed by settings.

In this case, the [FILES] section lists the (single) RTF file used in the project. The [MAP] section specifies the context IDs for the help topics (these are the numbers that you need to program context-sensitive help in Excel). The [CONFIG] section includes a reference to a macro that displays browse buttons in WINHELP.EXE. These buttons appear as << and >>. Finally, the [WINDOWS] section specifies the text displayed in the title bar, as well as window color information.

Compiling the HLP file

When the RTF file and the HPJ file are completed, it's time to compile it. The following statement, entered at the DOS prompt, does the trick:

```
HC31SAMPLE.HPJ
```

If there are any errors, the Help Compiler lets you know. Then you must change either the RTF file or the HPJ file.

Once the HLP file is created, you can display it by using the File⇨Open command when WINHELP.EXE is running. Or you can use one of the VBA techniques described in the next section.

This example barely scratches the surface of help files. If you are interested in mastering this topic — or at least learning more than I present here — I suggest that you buy *The Developer's Guide to WinHelp* by Jim Mitchell (John Wiley and Sons, 1994). This comprehensive book is filled with useful examples and tips.

Displaying WinHelp Files from Your Application

Knowing how to create WinHelp files (either simple or complex) doesn't do much good unless you know how to display the information when it's needed. VBA provides several different ways to display specific help topics. I discuss these methods in the rest of this chapter.

The disk that accompanies this book includes HLPDEMO2.XLS, which demonstrates all the methods described in this section. Figure 16-11 shows the opening screen from this workbook.

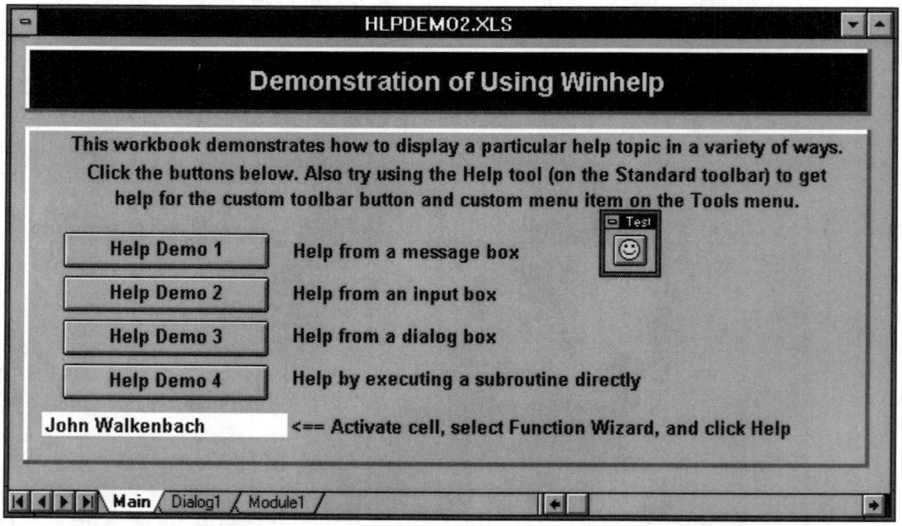

Figure 16-11: HLPDEMO2.XLS demonstrates the various ways to access a WinHelp file from VBA.

TIP

When the WinHelp application starts up, it reads WINHELP.INI, which can contain directory information for a specific help file. For example, if you store a custom help file called MYHELP.HLP in C:\EXCEL\MYAPP, you can include the following line in the [Files] section of WINHELP.INI to ensure that the help file is found:

```
MYHELP.HLP=C:\EXCEL\MYAPP
```

Assigning a help topic to a procedure

You can associate both a help file and a context ID with a VBA subroutine and function by using either the Object Browser or the MacroOptions method.

Figure 16-12 shows the standard Macro Options dialog box. At the bottom of the dialog box are boxes where you can enter the name of a help file and a context ID. Associating a particular help topic with a macro enables the user to get help in a few ways.

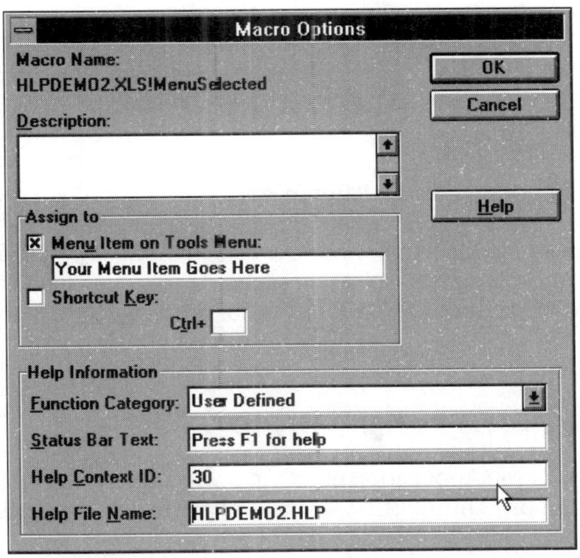

Figure 16-12: The Macro Options dialog box lets you assign a help file and context ID to each subroutine or function.

The following subroutine uses the MacroOptions method to set various options for a procedure named MyMacro. You can generate this macro by recording your actions while you set options in the Macro Options dialog box.

```
Sub SetOptions()
'   Set options for MyMacro
    Application.MacroOptions Macro:="MyMacro", _
        Description:="", _
        HasMenu:=True, _
        MenuText:="Generate Report...", _
        HasShortcutKey:=False, _
        Category:=14, _
        StatusBar:="Produces the report using current _
            settings", _
        HelpContextID:="30", _
        HelpFile:=ThisWorkbook.Path & "\RPTGEN.HLP"
End Sub
```

When a help file and context ID are assigned to a procedure, the help topic can be displayed in a number of ways. For example, if the macro is assigned to a menu item, the user can get help by

- Selecting the menu item and pressing F1
- Clicking the Help tool on the Standard toolbar and then selecting the command by using the mouse

TIP: The Help tool method also works if the macro is assigned to a custom toolbar button.

If the procedure is a custom function, the user can get help for the function by clicking the Help button in the Function Wizard.

NOTE: When you assign a help file to a procedure, you *must* specify a valid context ID as well as the name of the help file. As a result, HLP files produced by using the "simple" method that I described earlier cannot be assigned to a procedure.

Using the Application's Help method

The Help method of the Application object lets you display any help topic from any help file from VBA. This method works even if the help file doesn't have any context IDs defined.

The syntax for the Help method is

```
Application.Help(helpFile,helpContextID)
```

Both arguments are optional. If the name of the help file is omitted, Excel's help file is displayed. If the context ID argument is omitted, the help file is displayed from the beginning.

The following example displays the beginning of MYAPP.HLP, which is assumed to be in the same directory as the workbook that it's called from. Note that the second argument is omitted.

```
Sub ShowHelpContents()
    Application.Help ThisWorkbook.Path & "\HLPDEMO2.HLP"
End Sub
```

Displaying help from a custom dialog box

Every custom dialog box that you create can have one and only one Help button. You make a button a Help button by setting its Help property to True.

You can set a button's Help property to True by using VBA code or by right-clicking the button, selecting Format Object from the shortcut menu, and checking the Help check box in the Control tab of the Format Object dialog box (see Figure 16-13).

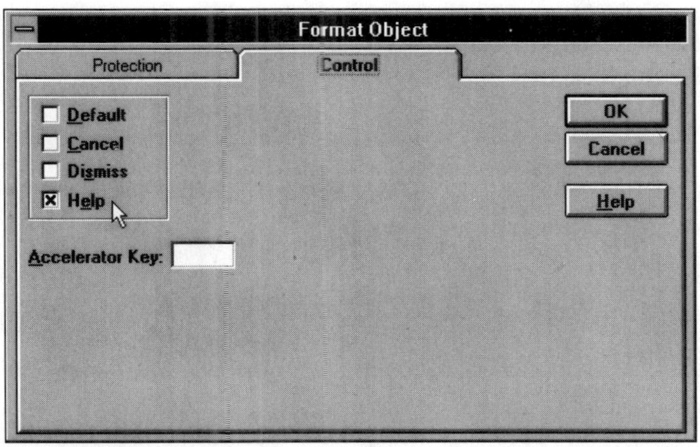

Figure 16-13: The Format Object dialog box enables you to set the Help property of a button on a custom dialog box.

You must assign a macro to a Help button. Usually, the macro displays a help file, but it can simply display a message box. For example, the following subroutine is a simple macro that's assigned to the Help button of a custom dialog box.

The macro uses the Help method of the Application object to bring up the help file named APPHELP.HLP and display the topic with a context ID of 50.

```
Sub DBoxHelp()
    Application.Help ThisWorkbook.Path & "\APPHELP.HLP", 50
End Sub
```

When a dialog box has a Help button, the user can get help by clicking the button or pressing F1. Either action executes the macro assigned to the Help button.

NOTE

I must qualify the preceding paragraph because of a bug in the current version of Excel. Pressing F1 does *not* execute the help macro if the dialog box's focus is an edit box, a list box, a drop-down list box, or a scroll bar. That doesn't leave a whole lot, does it?

Displaying help from a message box

When you display a message box, you can force the message box to display a Help button by including the optional Helpfile and Context arguments.

The following procedure displays the message box shown in Figure 16-14. Because the last two arguments are included, the message box includes a Help button. If the user clicks Help, the help topic in APPHELP.HLP with a context ID of 10 is brought up.

Figure 16-14: A message box with a Help button.

```
Sub MsgBoxHelp()
    HelpFile = ThisWorkbook.Path & "\APPHELP.HLP"
    MsgBox "Exit Now?", vbQuestion + vbYesNo, "Error", _
      HelpFile, 10
End Sub
```

Displaying help from an input box

The InputBox function works just like the MsgBox function described in the preceding section. If you include arguments for the help file and context ID, the input box displays a Help button that will display the specified help file.

Summary

- In this chapter, I presented many alternative methods of providing on-line help for end users. The two main options are

  Use any of several Excel-specific techniques to display help.

  Create a custom HLP file and display the help information by using the Windows WINHELP.EXE program.
- Chapter 17 discusses some ways in which your Excel applications can interact with other Windows applications.

Chapter 17

Interacting with Other Applications

In This Chapter

- Some of the ways you can automate the process of interacting with other applications
- How to activate another application from Excel
- Examples using Dynamic Data Exchange (DDE)
- Examples using OLE 2
- An example using the XLODBC add-in

In the early days of personal computing, interapplication interaction was rare. In the days before multitasking, users had no choice but to use one software program at a time. Any type of interaction between programs was limited to importing files.

Most software nowadays is designed to support at least some type of communication with other applications. At the very least, most Windows programs support the Clipboard for copy and paste operations between applications. Many Windows product support Dynamic Data Exchange (DDE), and leading-edge products such as Excel 5 and Word for Windows 6 support OLE 2. In this chapter, I outline the types of interactions that your Excel applications can perform. Of course, I provide several examples.

Starting Another Application

It's often useful to start up another application from Excel. For example, you may want to execute a communications program from Excel. Or as an application developer, you may want to make it easy for a user to access the Windows Control Panel.

VBA's Shell function makes launching other programs easy. The following example starts the Windows Control Panel application and displays the Date/ Time dialog box, which lets the user adjust the system's date and time. This example takes advantage of the fact that you can include the title of a control panel's icon on the command line to activate the icon.

The Shell function returns a task identification number of the application. You can use this number later to activate the task. The second argument for the Shell function determines how the application is displayed (1 is the code for normal size, with the focus).

If the Shell function is not successful, it generates an error. Therefore the routine uses an On Error statement to display a message if the file cannot be found or some other error occurs.

```
Sub ChangeDateandTime()
    On Error GoTo NotFound
    AppFile = "CONTROL.EXE Date/Time"
    x = Shell(AppFile, 1)
    Exit Sub

NotFound:
    MsgBox "Cannot start " & AppFile, vbCritical, "Error"
End Sub
```

You also can use the ChDir statement to change to a desired directory before starting the program.

NOTE

The Shell function runs the application *asynchronously* — that is, VBA does not pause while the application is running. If the routine has more statements after the Shell function is executed, these statements are executed while the new program is active. If any statement requires user intervention — for example, displaying a message box — Excel's title bar flashes while the other application is active. To avoid this scenario, it's usually best not to place other statements after the Shell function. Chapter 11 presents a workaround to this problem: you can pause VBA while the other application is running.

TIP

If the application that you want to start is one of several Microsoft applications, you can use the ActivateMicrosoftApp method of the Application object. For example, the following procedure starts Word for Windows:

```
Sub StartWord()
    Application.ActivateMicrosoftApp xlMicrosoftWord
End Sub
```

If Word is already running when the preceding procedure is executed, it is activated. Refer to the on-line help for details on the other constants available for this method.

Activating Another Application

A potential problem: If an application is already running, Shell starts another instance of it. In most cases, you'll want to activate the instance that's running, not start another instance of it.

The following routine demonstrates how to determine whether the application is running (if you call this routine, you won't open a second instance of an application that's already running). This routine uses the AppActivate statement to activate an application, Calculator, that's open. AppActivate uses the task identification number returned by the Shell function as its first argument. If the AppActivate statement generates an error, Calculator is not running. So the routine starts the application.

```
Public CalcTaskID

Sub StartCalculator()
    AppFile = "CALC.EXE"
    On Error GoTo NotRunning
    AppActivate (CalcTaskID)
    Exit Sub
NotRunning:
    CalcTaskID = Shell(AppFile, 1)
End Sub
```

The AppActivate statement also can use the title bar text as its argument. Because CALC.EXE displays *Calculator* in its title bar, the following statement also activates the Calculator program if it's already running:

```
AppActivate ("Calculator")
```

Dynamic Data Exchange

Dynamic Data Exchange, or DDE, is a Windows protocol that is supported by a large number of Windows applications. Unfortunately, programs vary widely in how they implement DDE, so using it often requires quite a bit of trial and error.

DDE involves establishing a link between two documents and updating the links — on demand or automatically. Usually, the documents involved are created by different applications. For example, you can set up a DDE link between a Word document and an Excel worksheet. In other words, you can link a range of cells from an Excel worksheet into a Word document. When the data in the range is changed in Excel, the changes are mirrored in the Word document.

You can think of a DDE link as a channel through which data flows. The Windows Clipboard is the mechanism used for this channel.

Creating DDE links manually

You can create DDE links manually by copying the information to be linked to the Clipboard and then choosing the Edit➪Paste Special command, which displays the Paste Special dialog box (see Figure 17-1). Choose the Paste Link option and then select from the As list box. If you're linking from Word to Excel, for example, choose the Text option.

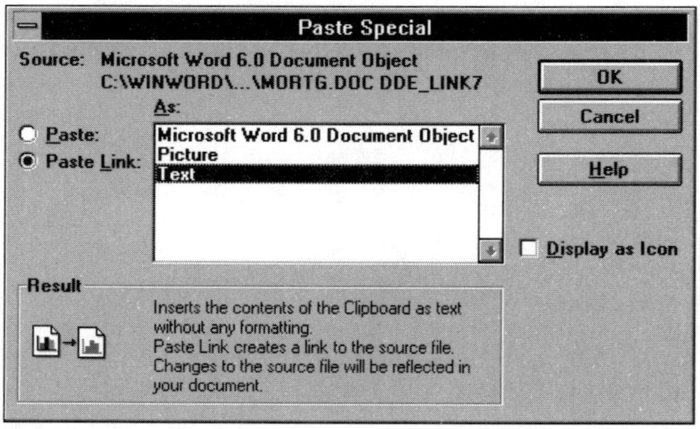

Figure 17-1: The Paste Special dialog box lets you create a DDE link manually.

The application that provides the data is the *server* application (also known as the *source* application). The *client* application (or *destination* application) receives the information from the server. You can have multiple DDE links between two documents, and you can even arrange things so that each document is both a server and a client.

NOTE: When the link is automatic, updates are triggered by changes made in the server application.

Figure 17-2 shows an example of a two-way link. The first three cells in the second column of the Word table are linked to cells in Excel. The last cell in the table is a link from an Excel cell that holds a formula. If the user changes any of the first three values in the Word table, the edits are sent to the Excel worksheet, which in turn updates the formula. The change in the formula cell then triggers a message that sends the new payment amount back to the Word document. In effect, Word is using Excel as a calculation engine. ***Note:*** This technique requires that the server application be running and the server document is open.

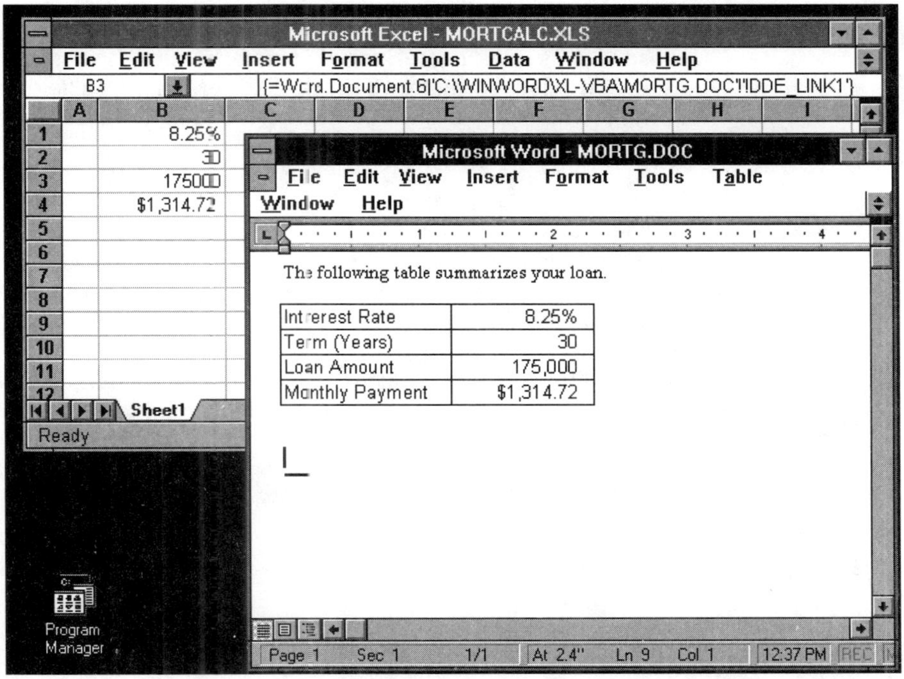

Figure 17-2: An example of a two-way link between a Word document and an Excel worksheet.

To create this two-way link,

1. Create the Word document, including the 4 x 2 table. Leave the lower-right cell in the table blank and save the file as MORTG.DOC.
2. Select the first three cells in the second column of the table and copy them to the Clipboard.
3. Activate Excel, open a new workbook, save it as MORTCALC.XLS, and move the cell pointer to B1.
4. Choose Excel's Edit⇨Paste Special command, select the Paste Link option button, and then highlight the Text option from the As list box. Excel inserts an array formula like the following into cells B1:B3:

   ```
   =Word.Document.6|'C:\WINWORD\MORTG.DOC'!'!DDE_LINK1'
   ```

5. Insert the following formula into cell B4 and then copy the cell to the Clipboard:

   ```
   =PMT(B1/12,B2*12,-B3)
   ```

6. Activate Word for Windows and select the lower-right cell of the table.
7. Choose Word's Edit⇨Paste Special command, click the Paste Link option button, and select Formatted Text (RTF). Word inserts a field code like the following (which displays the value in cell C4 of the worksheet):

```
{LINK  Excel.Sheet.5  C:\\EXCEL5\\MORTCALC.XLS Sheet1!R4C2 \a  _
      \r  \*  MERGEFORMAT}
```

After these DDE links are created, changing any of the values for Interest Rate, Term, or Loan Amount in the Word table causes Excel to recalculate and Word to redisplay the monthly payment.

NOTE

For automatic link updating to occur, make sure that the Ignore Other Applications check box in Excel's Options dialog box (General tab) is not checked. Also make sure that the link is set to automatic rather than manual (choose the Edit⇨Links command to double-check).

More about DDE

The connection between the client application and the server application is defined by three elements:

- The DDE application name is a unique identifier for the application; it is usually (but not always) the same as the program's executable filename without the extension. For example, Excel's application name is Excel.
- The *DDE topic* refers to an element of the application that is being dealt with. Often, the topic is a filename, such as C:\WINWORD\MEMO.DOC. However, special topics such as *System* can return a list of all topics supported by the server.
- The *DDE item* is the part of the DDE link that actually sends or receives information. In Excel, it can be a cell or range. In Word, it can be a defined bookmark name. In a database, it can be a record or a field within a record.

When you create DDE links manually by using the Edit⇨Paste Special command, all these details are handled for you, behind the scenes. The DDE link that you paste into an Excel cell actually inserts an array formula that has this information in it.

For example, when I pasted a DDE link from a Word for Windows document to an Excel worksheet, the following formula appeared:

```
=Word.Document.6|'C:\WINWORD\MORTG.DOC'!'!DDE_LINK1'
```

The application name is Word.Document.6, the DDE topic is 'C:\WINWORD\MORTG.DOC', and the DDE item is '!DDE_LINK1' (a default name). If the data link is named, the actual name is used for the topic name.

When you choose the Edit⇨Links command, Excel displays all the links in a more readable format — and Excel even lets you modify them. Figure 17-3 shows an example of the Links dialog box.

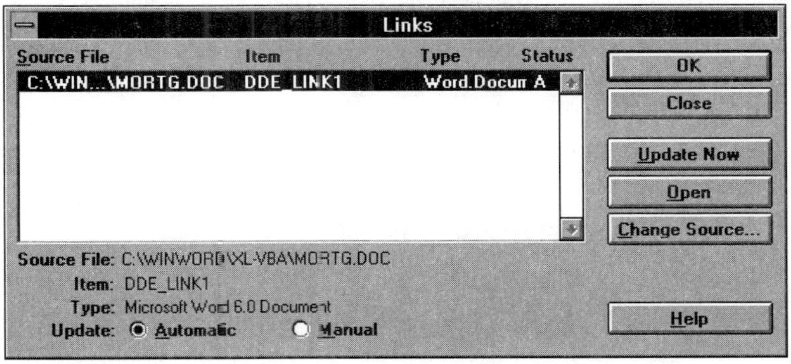

Figure 17-3: The Links dialog box displays all the links in the workbook.

In theory, DDE links may sound like the perfect solution to many problems. In practice, however, this technique requires lots of memory (don't even think about using DDE links on a system with only 4 megabytes of RAM). And if the links are updated automatically, you may find that an otherwise fast application slows to a crawl. Finally, the links are rather fragile, and you may find that moving a linked file or changing its name severs the link.

Using DDE with VBA

VBA has a number of Application object methods that let you create and work with DDE links. Typically, you need to initiate a link (also called a *channel*), do whatever it is you want to do using the link, and then terminate the link (close the channel).

Table 17-1 lists the DDE methods available in VBA.

Table 17-1	VBA's DDE Functions
Function	***What It Does***
DDEInitiate(*App, Topic*)	Opens a DDE channel to an application
DDEExecute(*Channel, String*)	Runs a command or performs an operation in an application by using the specified DDE channel
DDETerminate *Channel*	Closes a DDE channel that was opened by DDEInitiate
DDERequest(*Channel, Item*)	Requests information from an application using the specified DDE channel; the result is an array
DDEPoke(*Channel, Item, Data*)	Sends data to an application by using the specified DDE channel

Poking Excel data into a Word document

The example in this section updates a Word sales report document with new information that is contained in an Excel worksheet.

DISK

This example uses two files, both included on the disk that accompanies this book. WORD_DDE.XLS is an Excel file, and SALESREP.DOC is a Word for Windows 6.0 document. Word for Windows 6.0 must be installed on your system to use this example.

I used Word's Edit⇨Bookmark command to define four bookmarks — these are the locations that get *poked* to. The application is designed to be executed from the worksheet in WORD_DDE.XLS (see Figure 17-4). Clicking the worksheet's button updates the sales report with the data in the row of the active cell. To generate a report for July, move the cell pointer to any cell in row 8 and click the button. Figure 17-5 shows an example report.

The following procedure starts by making sure that a range is selected and that the active cell is in a row between 2 and 13. Then it creates object variables for the four data cells in the active row. The DDE channel is opened with the document name as the topic. Next, the data from the four cells are poked into the document (the DDEPoke method); the items are the predefined bookmarks in the document. Finally, the DDE channel is closed and Word is activated so that the user can see the report.

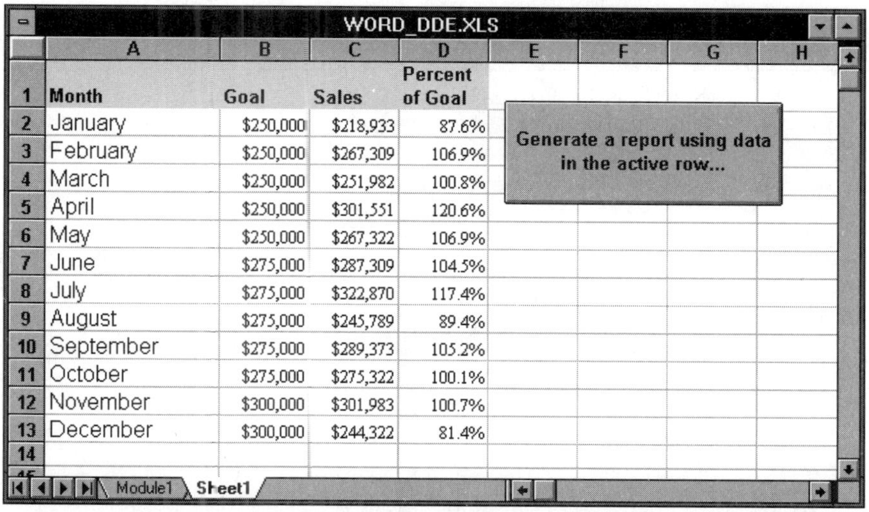

Figure 17-4: Clicking the button generates a report by using data in the active row.

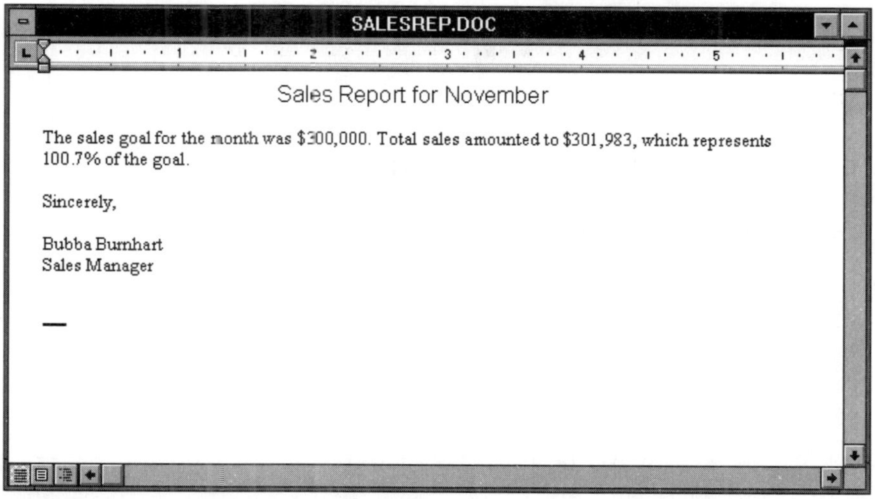

Figure 17-5: A report in Word, generated by Excel.

Listing 17-1 DDE_Demo Subroutine

```
Sub DDE_Demo()
'   Updates a sales report in Word using
'   data on Sheet1

'   Exit if a range is not selected
    If TypeName(Selection) <> "Range" Then Exit Sub

'   Exit if cell pointer is not in appropriate row
    If ActiveCell.Row = 1 Or ActiveCell.Row > 13 Then
        MsgBox "Select a cell in Rows 2 through 13."
        Exit Sub
    End If

'   Define data based on the active row
    Set CurrentRow = ActiveCell.EntireRow
    Set CurrMonth = CurrentRow.Cells(1)
    Set CurrGoal = CurrentRow.Cells(2)
    Set CurrSales = CurrentRow.Cells(3)
    Set CurrPercent = CurrentRow.Cells(4)

'   Note: The Word file has four bookmarks defined
    WordFile = ThisWorkbook.Path & "\SALESREP.DOC"

'   Open the DDE channel
    Channel = DDEInitiate("WinWord", WordFile)

'   Insert the current data into bookmarks
    DDEPoke Channel, "CurrentMonth", CurrMonth
    DDEPoke Channel, "Goal", CurrGoal
    DDEPoke Channel, "TotalSales", CurrSales
    DDEPoke Channel, "Percentage", CurrPercent

'   Close the DDE channel
    DDETerminate Channel
    Application.ActivateMicrosoftApp xlMicrosoftWord
End Sub
```

Controlling Program Manager with DDE using VBA

In this section, I show how to control an application by using DDE.

In this example, the application is the Windows Program Manager. The example adds a new program item to a program group of the user's choice; specifically, the new program item starts Excel and loads the SLIDES.XLT template. You can easily modify this code to add an icon for any other workbook.

Only a few statements in this procedure actually deal with DDE. The following block of statements gets a list of program groups to be displayed in a dialog box; Figure 17-6 shows the dialog box that lists the program groups. The first statement opens a DDE channel to Program Manager and assigns the channel number to the Channel variable. The DDERequest function requests a list of all program groups. The returned list is stored in GroupList, which is a variant array. The DDETerminate function closes the DDE channel that was opened by the DDEInitiate function.

```
Channel = DDEInitiate("Progman", "Progman")
GroupList = DDERequest(Channel, "Groups")
DDETerminate Channel
```

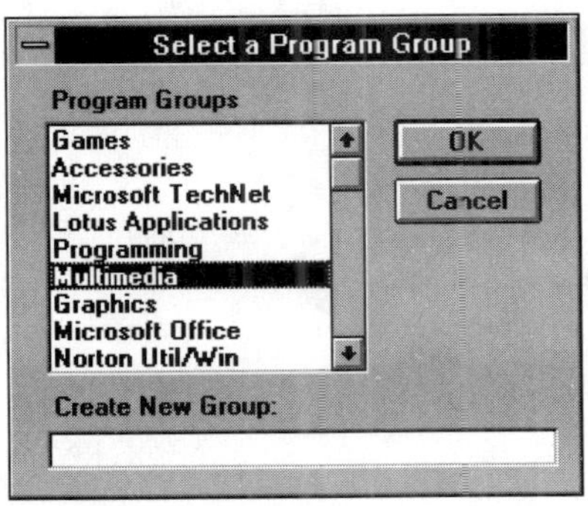

Figure 17-6: DDE was used to get a list of all program groups from Program Manager.

When the program group is selected, a new DDE channel is opened and the following function, DDEExecute, sends a command to create a new group. If the group already exists, it is activated.

```
Channel = DDEInitiate("Progman", "Progman")
DDEExecute Channel, "[CreateGroup(" & GroupName & ")]"
```

The following statement executes a command to add an item to the active program group. The AddItem command takes a single string for an argument. This string is built and assigned to the ItemString variable.

```
DDEExecute Channel, "[AddItem(" & ItemString & ")]"
```

The complete example, shown in Listing 17-2, , is on the disk that accompanies this book. The filename is DDE_DEMO.XLS. If SLIDES.XLT is not located in your EXCEL\LIBRARY\SLIDES directory, however, this example will not work.

Listing 17-2 **DDE_DEMO.XLS**

```
Sub AddIconToProgMan()
'   Adds an icon to a program group

''''''''''''''''''''''''''''''''''''''''''''''''''''''''''''''
'   Substitute your actual workbook path and icon
'   caption below. SLIDES.XLT is for demo purposes.
'
    Fullpath = Application.LibraryPath & _
       "\SLIDES\SLIDES.XLT"
    IconCaption = "XL Slide Template"
'
''''''''''''''''''''''''''''''''''''''''''''''''''''''''''''''

    Set DBox = ThisWorkbook.DialogSheets("Dialog1")
    Set GroupBox = DBox.ListBoxes("GroupBox")
    Set GroupName = DBox.EditBoxes("GroupName")

'   Get the group name
    Channel = DDEInitiate("Progman", "Progman")
    GroupList = DDERequest(Channel, "Groups")
    DDETerminate Channel

'   Clear the list boxes
    If GroupBox.ListCount <> 0 Then GroupBox.RemoveItem _
        Index:=1, _
        Count:=GroupBox.ListCount

'   Fill list box with group names
    For i = LBound(GroupList) To UBound(GroupList)
        GroupBox.AddItem Text:=GroupList(i, 1)
    Next i
    GroupBox.ListIndex = 1
    GroupName.Text = ""

'   Display the dialog
    DBoxOK = ThisWorkbook.DialogSheets("Dialog1").Show
    If Not DBoxOK Then Exit Sub

'   Determine selected group name
    If GroupName.Text <> "" Then _
        GroupName = GroupName.Text Else _
            GroupName = GroupBox.List(GroupBox.ListIndex)
```

```
'   Create (or activate) the group
    Channel = DDEInitiate("Progman", "Progman")
    DDEExecute Channel, "[CreateGroup(" & GroupName & ")]"

'   Build the string for AddItem
    ItemString = Fullpath & ","
    ItemString = ItemString & IconCaption & ","
    ItemString = ItemString & Application.Path & _
       "\EXCEL.EXE"

'   Add the item
    DDEExecute Channel, "[AddItem(" & ItemString & ")]"

'   Close the channel
    DDETerminate Channel
End Sub
```

The DDE_DEMO.XLS file includes a module that creates a worksheet database from all the information stored in Program Manager's icons.

OLE Automation

Excel, one of the few applications that currently supports OLE Automation, exposes objects that can be manipulated by other programs that support OLE Automation.

Before you read this section, you should be familiar with Excel's object model: you need to know, for example, that workbooks, ranges, charts, and so on are programmable objects that are exposed for other applications to use.

The concept behind OLE Automation is quite appealing. In theory, a developer who needs to generate a chart, for example, can just reach into another application's grab bag of objects and fetch a chart object to display. In fact, this situation does not pose a problem — as long as the objects are exposed. Excel exposes 128 objects that can be used by other applications. Of course, many are completely useless in other contexts. How many applications would need to manipulate one of Excel's MenuItem objects?

Other applications that currently support OLE Automation are Word for Windows 6.0, Access 2.0, Project 4.0, Visual Basic 3.0, and Shapeware's Visio 2.0 (a drawing application).

In this section, I demonstrate how to use VBA to access and manipulate the objects exposed by these applications.

Not all applications support both sides of OLE Automation. For example, Word for Windows can be controlled by other applications, but it cannot control other applications. Visual Basic, on the other hand, can control other applications, but it doesn't expose any objects to other applications.

If you understand how to use VBA with Excel's objects, you will have no problems working with objects in other programs. Basically, you repeat the same three-step process:

1. Establish a reference to the application by using the CreateObject or GetObject method. If the application's objects are in an object library (for example, Project), you can use the Tools⇨References command.
2. Write VBA code that manipulates the object's properties and uses their methods.
3. When you finish with the objects, close the reference and free up the memory used.

The example in this section uses Word for Windows 6.0. Word doesn't support VBA yet, so its objects are not exposed. However, Word *does* expose its entire WordBasic language — almost as good. Interestingly, WordBasic has built-in support for many functions that require calls to Windows API functions using VBA.

About OLE 2

OLE 2 is the general term for an interapplication communications protocol developed by Microsoft and supported by a fair number of applications. OLE 2 has many new features that make it easier for users to seamlessly create compound documents that use multiple applications. These features include

- *In-place editing* — the ability to edit an object within the context of its container. For example, when you activate an Excel object that has been inserted into Word, Excel's menus and toolbars replace Word's.
- *Faster execution* compared to OLE 1.
- *Drag-and-drop* across applications. For example, you can drag a range of cells from Excel to a Word document.
- *OLE Automation* — the ability to send messages, set properties, and execute methods on an OLE 2-defined object.

Working with foreign objects

As you know, you can use Excel's Insert⇨Object command to embed an OLE object in a worksheet. In addition, you can create an object and manipulate it with VBA. (This action is the heart of OLE automation.) When you do so, you have full access to the object's menus and commands. For example, you can use VBA to access the menus in Word. For developers, this course of action is more beneficial than embedding the object in a worksheet: When an object is embedded, the user must know how to use the server application. But when you work with the object by using VBA, you can program the object so that the user can manipulate it by an action as simple as a button click.

You already know how to manipulate Excel's objects with VBA. Manipulating objects from other applications is not much different. To access an object from another application, you must know about the objects.

Some applications, such as Excel and Project, provide object library files. You can establish a reference to the object library and then use its objects directly. For example, choose the Tools⇨References command to attach a reference to Project's object library (see Figure 17-7).

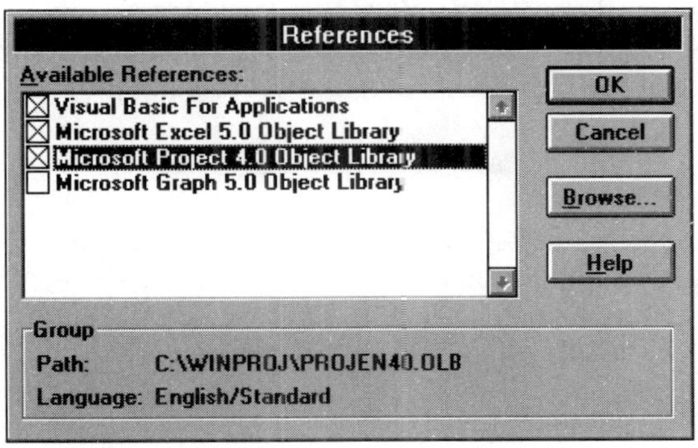

Figure 17-7: Attaching a reference to Project's object library file.

Once the reference to the object library is established, you can use the Object Browser to view the object names, methods, and properties (see Figure 17-8).

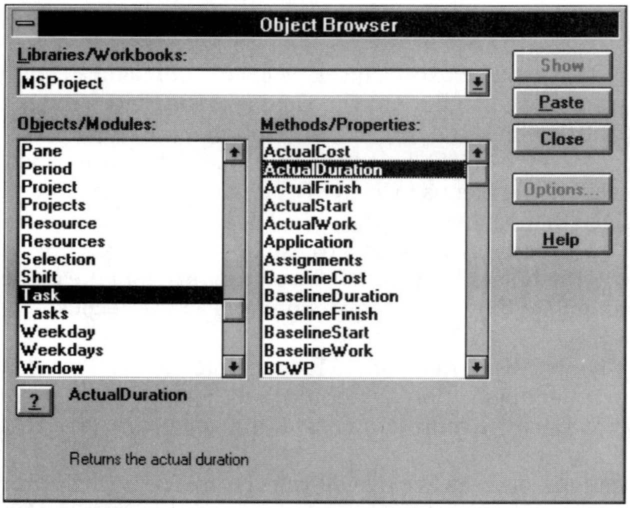

Figure 17-8: Using the Object Browser to learn about the objects in a referenced object library.

Other applications support OLE Automation but don't have an object library file. To use OLE Automation with Word for Windows, for example, you must first create an object by using the CreateObject method. (With Word, the object that you manipulate is the WordBasic language.) For example,

```
Set WinWord = CreateObject("Word.Basic")
```

After creating this object, you can execute its WordBasic commands directly from Excel, treating them as methods. In WordBasic, for example, FileNewDefault is the command to create a new document. Therefore you can open a new Word document with the following VBA statement:

```
WinWord.FileNewDefault
```

Automating a Word session

The example in this section is a simple OLE Automation demonstration. The MakeMemos procedure creates three customized memos in Word and then saves each to a file. The information for the memos is stored in a worksheet.

OLEAUTO.XLS is on the disk that accompanies this book. You must have Word for Windows 6.0 installed to execute the procedure.

The following routine, MakeMemos, starts by creating an object called Word. The routine cycles through the three rows of data in Sheet1 and uses WordBasic commands to create each memo and save it to disk.

Listing 17-3 MakeMemos Routine

```
Sub MakeMemos()
'   Creates memos in word using OLE Automation

'   Start Word and create an object
    Set Word = CreateObject("Word.Basic")

'   Information from worksheet
    Set Data = Sheets("Sheet1").Range("A1")
    Message = Sheets("Sheet1").Range("Message")

'   Cycle through all records in Sheet1
    Records = _
      Application.CountA(Sheets("Sheet1").Range("A:A"))
    For i = 1 To Records
'       Update status bar progress message
        Application.StatusBar = "Processing Record " & i

'       Assign current data to variables
        Region = Data.Offset(i - 1, 0).Value
        SalesAmt = Format(Data.Offset(i - 1, 2).Value, _
          "#,000")
        SalesNum = Data.Offset(i - 1, 1).Value

'       Send commands to Word
        With Word
            .FileNewDefault
            .Insert "M E M O R A N D U M"
            .InsertPara
            .InsertPara
            .Insert "Date:" & Chr(9) & Format(Date, "mmmm d, _
              yyyy")
            .InsertPara
            .Insert "To:" & Chr(9) & Region & " Manager"
            .InsertPara
            .InsertPara
            .Insert Message
             InsertPara
            .InsertPara
            .Insert "Units Sold:" & Chr(9) & SalesNum
```

(continued)

Listing 17-3 *(continued)*

```
                .InsertPara
                .Insert "Total Amount:" & Chr(9) & SalesAmt
                .InsertPara
                .InsertPara
                .Insert "Joe Manager"
                .StartOfDocument
                .EndOfLine 1
                .Bold
                .CenterPara
                .FileSaveAs Region & ".DOC"
                .DocClose
            End With
        Next i

'   Reset status bar
    Application.StatusBar = ""

    MsgBox "The memos were created and saved.",
vbInformation
End Sub
```

Using SendKeys

It's possible to control some applications even if they don't support DDE or OLE. The Application object's SendKeys method simply sends keystrokes to an application, simulating actions that a user might perform.

SendKeys can be quite tricky to use because the keystrokes are not actually sent until VBA is finished. For best results, your procedures should not perform any other actions after sending keystrokes to another applications.

SendKeys is documented in the on-line help system, which details how to send nonstandard keystrokes, such as Alt key combinations.

The following example is available in SNDKEYS.XLS. The CellToCardFile macro is assigned to a key combination (Ctrl+Shift+C). When executed from a worksheet, it uses SendKeys to transfer the contents of the active cell to the Windows CardFile application. If CardFile is not running, it starts it. Before transferring the text, the routine inserts a new card — by sending the F7 key. When the information has been transferred, the procedure sends Alt+Tab, which switches back to Excel.

Listing 17-4 CellToCardFile( ) Subfunction

```
Sub CellToCardFile()
'   Transfers active cell contents to cardfile
'   Ctrl+Shift+C executes this

    CellContents = ActiveCell.Value

'   Pause for 1 second
    Application.Wait Now + TimeValue("00:00:01")

'   Activate (or start) Cardfile
    On Error Resume Next
    AppActivate ("CardFile")
    If Err = 5 Then x = Shell("CardFile.exe", 1)

'   New card
    SendKeys "{F7}", True

'   Transfer cell contents to card title
    Application.SendKeys CellContents, True
    Application.SendKeys "{Enter}", True

'   Alt+Tab back to Excel
    Application.SendKeys "%{Tab}"
End Sub
```

Notice that I inserted a one-second pause. Without this pause, the application cannot keep up with the keystrokes.

Using the XLODBC Add-In

The final topic in this chapter involves working with an external database.

Excel can work with external databases in a number of ways:

- If the database table is not too large and is in a format supported by Excel, you can simply open the database as a worksheet in a workbook.
- You can use the MS Query add-in to return the results from a database.
- You can use the ODBC add-in to automate queries. Installing this add-in makes some new VBA functions available.

ODBC (Open Database Connectivity) is a standard development by Microsoft that uses drivers to access databases in different formats. Drivers are available for Microsoft Access, Microsoft SQL, ORACLE, DB2, dBASE, and other ODBC-compliant databases.

The ODBC Administrator (ODBCADM.EXE) is a separate program that lets you add, modify, or delete ODBC drivers and data sources. Before you can perform queries in VBA, the database that you're using must be set up as a data source.

The ODBC add-in gives you access to a number of new functions that you can use in VBA. Before you can use these functions, however, you must establish a reference to the XLODBC.XLA file by choosing the Tools⇨References command and selecting XLODBC.XLA.

The new functions, which are documented in the on-line help (they all begin with the letters *SQL*), let you connect to a database, perform queries by using the SQL language, and output the results. You also can add or delete records in the database, but you cannot create new database tables or modify the structure of the database in any way.

The disk that accompanies this book has a simple XLODBC demonstration. The file, ODBCDEMO.XLS, reads a small dBASE file (PRESDNTS.DBF) — also included on the disk — that holds information about the presidents of the U.S. The sample file demonstrates a few basic techniques, described next.

Connecting to an ODBC database

Before you can use an ODBC database in your routines, you must make sure that the proper driver is installed and that you can connect to the database. To do so, you use the ODBC Administrator program (see Figure 17-9).

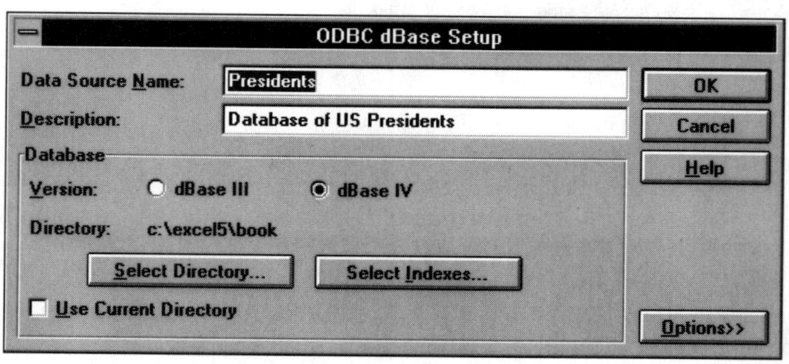

Figure 17-9: The ODBC Administrator program lets you specify an ODBC database.

The SQLOpen function is used to connect to a database. This function requires an argument that's a rather complex string containing information about the database name, its location, and the driver it uses. The sample file includes a procedure that lets you find out the connection string for the sample database (it varies by system) and stores the string in cell A1 on the sheet named *Read Me*.

The following statements open a connection to the sample database:

```
'   Connect to the database
    ConnectString = Sheets("Read Me").Range("A1")
    ConnectID = SQLOpen(ConnectString)
```

The variable ConnectID variable holds the connection ID returned by the SQLOpen function.

Performing a query

The SQLExecQuery function, which performs the query on the database, has two arguments: the connection ID returned by SQLOpen and a string that holds the query. The query is written in SQL and varies depending on the type of database.

CAUTION: The string that holds the SQL query cannot exceed 255 characters; if it does, Excel may crash. However, there's any easy workaround, which I explain later in this chapter.

The following code defines a simple query (stored in the string variable Q) and then performs the query on the database. The query displays the NAME and STATE_BORN fields for the presidents who were born in February.

```
'   Define the Query
    Q = "SELECT presdent.NAME, presdent.STATE_BORN "
    Q = Q & "FROM PRESDENT "
    Q = Q & "WHERE (presdent.BIRTH_MONT=2)"

'   Perform the query
    Result = SQLExecQuery(ConnectID, Q)
```

Retrieving the results of a query

The results of the query aren't actually stored in the variable Result. To retrieve the results, you use the SQLRetrieve function. The code used in the example is

```
'   Store the result in the worksheet
    Set Output = Sheets("Results").Range("A2")
    Result = SQLRetrieve(ConnectID, Output, , , True)

'   Display count and show results
    MsgBox Result & " records retrieved."
    Sheets("Results").Activate
```

This example dumps the results of the query in a worksheet range. The SQLRetrieve function has several options that let you control the type of output. If you want to store the query results in a file, use the SQLRetrievetoFile function.

Performing a long query

One of the problems encountered most frequently when using the ODBC functions involves lengthy queries. By their very nature, SQL queries tend to be long. And the 255-character limit doesn't quite cut it.

The solution is to break the lengthy query string into shorter strings and store them in an array. Then you can pass the array to the SQLExecQuery function.

This workaround is demonstrated in the XLODBC.XLS sample file. The following query exceeds the 255-character limit:

```
'   Define a long query
    Q = "SELECT presdent.NAME, presdent.YRS_SERV, "
    Q = Q & "presdent.BIRTH_YEAR, presdent.BIRTH_MONT, "
    Q = Q & "presdent.BIRTH_DAY, presdent.DEATH_AGE, "
    Q = Q & "presdent.PARTY, presdent.STATE_BORN "
    Q = Q & "FROM presdent "
    Q = Q & "WHERE (presdent.STATE_BORN='California') "
    Q = Q & "OR (presdent.STATE_BORN='Missouri') "
    Q = Q & "OR (presdent.STATE_BORN='Texas')"
```

The following custom function, SplitSQL, accepts a string as input and returns a variant array made up of 127-character strings:

```
Function SplitSQL(SQLString As String) As Variant
'   Splits a long sting into an array of strings * 127

'   Determine number of elements
    Parts = (Len(SQLString) + 127) \ 127
    ReDim SQLpart(1 To Parts) As String

'   Break the string apart
    For i = 1 To Parts
        SQLpart(i) = Mid(SQLString, 1 + ((i - 1) * 127), _
          127)
    Next i

    SplitSQL = SQLpart
End Function
```

This function is called directly within the second argument for the SQLExecQuery function, as in

```
'   Perform the query
    Result = SQLExecQuery(ConnectID, SplitSQL(Q))
```

NOTE

In some cases, using the ODBC add-in may cause your global variables to lose their values. If the add-in is not loaded when an ODBC function is encountered, the add-in will be loaded and the global variables will be zapped. So make sure that XLODBC.XLA is open before you call one of its functions.

Summary

- In this chapter, I touched on some of the ways you can automate the process of working with other applications.
- The next chapter describes a user-oriented application that demonstrates many of the techniques covered in previous chapters.

Chapter 18

Developing User-Oriented Applications

In This Chapter

- A description of a user-oriented application
- An analysis of a user-oriented application
- A checklist for application development

In this chapter, I attempt to pull together much of the information presented in the previous chapters.

This discussion centers around Quiz Master, an application that I developed. Useful in its own right, this application demonstrates several important application development techniques.

DISK

The application discussed in this chapter is available on the disk that accompanies this book. If you want to try out the sample application, open QUIZSAMP.XLS, which is set up with quizzes that address topics from the first five chapters of this book. The Quiz Master application (with no quizzes) is stored in QUIZMSTR.XLS. Use this file to create custom quiz applications.

Quiz Master: A Sample Application

I designed Quiz Master to simplify the work involved in designing and administering quizzes on-line.

An overview

Before I discuss how the application works, you may want to take a few minutes to become familiar with it. Follow these steps:

1. Open the QUIZSAMP.XLS workbook. Notice that a new menu, QuizMaster, appears.
2. Choose the QuizMaster⇨Test the Application command.
3. Follow the instructions on-screen. If you get stuck, on-line help is available.

Spend some time working through a few of the quizzes. Doing so will not only give you a good feel for how the application works, it will also test your comprehension of the first five chapters in this book.

Preparing quizzes with Quiz Master

A Quiz Master workbook can store any number of quizzes. Each quiz resides in its own worksheet and can have any number of items (questions). Each item can have as few as two response options (for example, a True/False item) to as many as five (a multiple-choice item).

Figure 18-1 shows a sample quiz sheet.

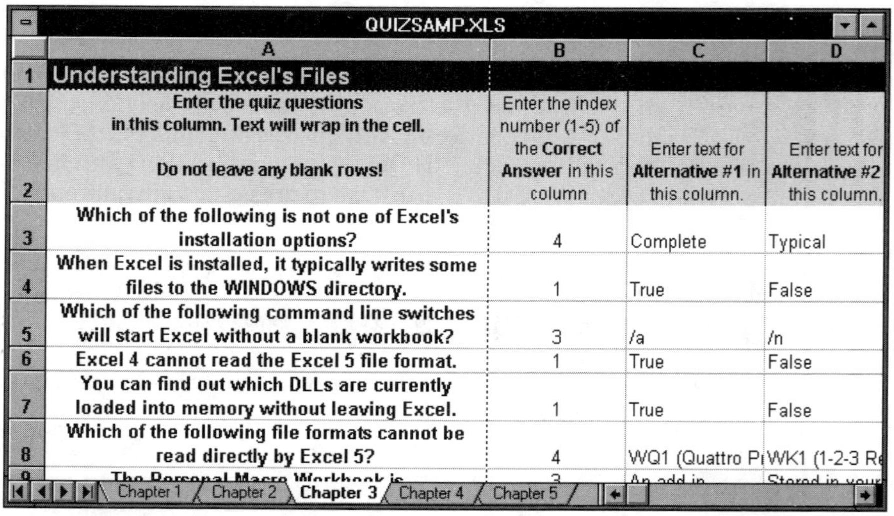

Figure 18-1: A Quiz Master quiz sheet.

Each quiz sheet is set up as follows:

- The sheet name is the name of the quiz.
- Cell A1 holds a description of the quiz.
- Row 2 contains descriptive information for the fields in the sheet.
- Column A holds the quiz item text.
- Column B holds the index number of the correct response.
- Columns C through G hold the responses. An item can have as few as two response options or as many as five.

NOTE

Columns C through G are formatted as text to allow the insertion of *True* and *False* as text strings rather than logical values.

Quiz Master recognizes the number of quiz sheets in a workbook and adjusts automatically. The application also makes it easy to insert new quiz sheet templates — empty quiz sheets that contain only the first two rows.

Administering quizzes with Quiz Master

After a quiz workbook is developed and tested, the workbook should be converted to an add-in. Although this step isn't absolutely necessary, because quizzes can be executed from the XLS file, creating an add-in makes the workbook more secure (it prevents quiz takers from tampering).

The add-in can be opened by choosing the File➪Open or Tools➪Add-Ins commands. When the add-in is opened, a QuizMaster menu is created. Choosing the Start Quiz Master menu item displays a dialog box (see Figure 18-2). The following options are available:

- *Allow backtracking of quiz items.* If this option is enabled, quiz takers can review and change responses to previous quiz items.
- *Display score after the quiz.* If this option is enabled, the score is displayed to the quiz taker upon completion of the quiz. The score consists of the number of correct items, the total number of items, and the percent correct. (In addition, the score is shown graphically, with a thermometer-style gauge.)
- *Display total time after the quiz.* If this option is enabled, the elapsed time is displayed to the quiz taker upon completion of the quiz.
- *Allow review of incorrect items after the quiz.* If this option is enabled, the quiz taker can see a list of the items answered incorrectly (along with the correct responses).
- *Store quiz results in a file.* If this option is enabled, the results of each quiz are stored in a comma-delimited text file. The information consists of the date, time, quiz-taker's name, time required to complete the quiz, quiz name, number of items answered correctly, total number of items on the quiz, and responses for each item. This file can be loaded directly into Excel.

- *Hide toolbars and menus.* If this option is enabled, Excel's menus and toolbars are hidden while the quiz taker is taking the quiz.
- *"No Exit" mode.* If this option is enabled, the quiz taker cannot exit the quiz without specifying the proper password. This option can be useful if the quizzes are being administered unattended.

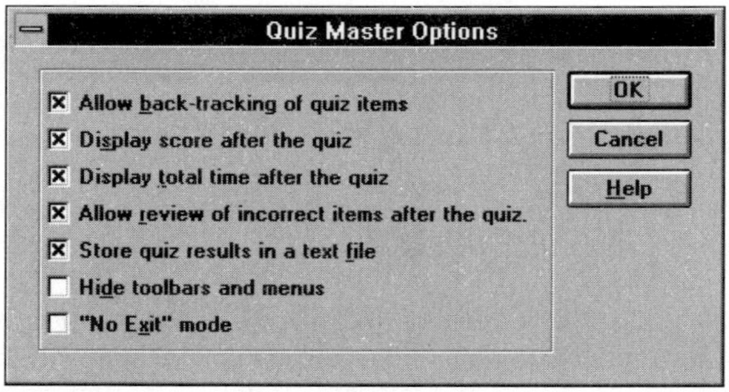

Figure 18-2: Quiz Master options.

After the options are selected, a dialog box like the one in Figure 18-3 appears. The quiz names in the list box correspond to the quiz sheet names. When a quiz is selected, the labels below the list box display:

- The number of items in the quiz
- A description of the quiz (this text comes from cell A1 of the quiz sheet)

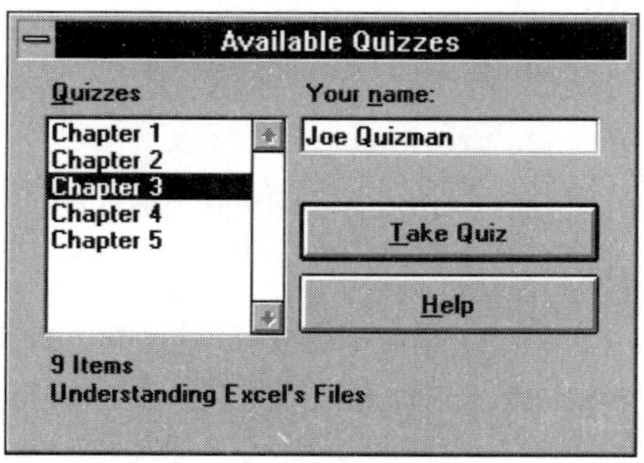

Figure 18-3: The Quiz Master quiz menu.

After a quiz is selected, the items are presented one at a time (as in Figure 18-4). Each item's options appear in the form of option buttons. A status box displays the number of items in the quiz, the number answered, and the number remaining (unanswered). If the Allow backtracking of quiz items option has been checked, the dialog box has two navigation buttons, Previous and Next. Otherwise, only the Next button is visible.

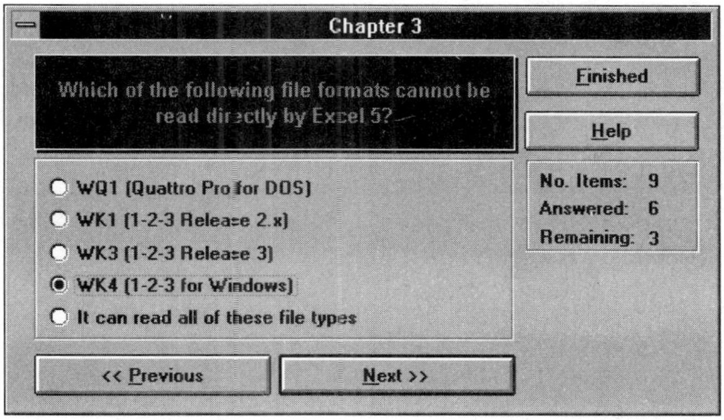

Figure 18-4: A quiz item.

More about Quiz Master

Quiz Master is designed with two audiences in mind:

- *Quiz administrators*. With Quiz Master, quiz developers need not know much about Excel. The application is designed so that creating quizzes and generating a Quiz Master add-in is a very easy task.
- *Quiz takers*. After the Quiz Master add-in is running, it can be left unattended. In fact, the quiz takers don't need to know anything about Excel; they need to know only how to click. In Quiz mode, the application is controlled by macros.

Administrator mode

When a Quiz Master file is opened, the Auto_Open subroutine determines whether the file is an XLS file or an add-in file, and responds accordingly. If it's an XLS file, the application assumes that the administrator is preparing a quiz and hides all irrelevant sheets (only the quiz sheets remain visible). Quiz Master also displays a QuizMaster menu, as shown in Figure 18-5:

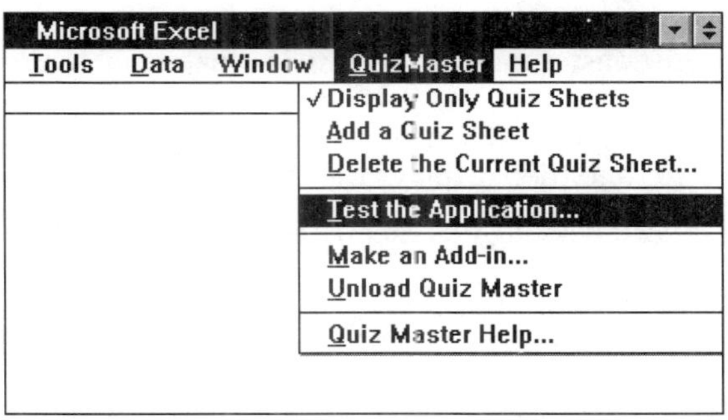

Figure 18-5: The QuizMaster menu in Administrator mode.

The Quiz Master menu has the following menu items:

- *Display Only Quiz Sheets.* A check mark next to this menu item indicates that only the quiz sheets are visible. Otherwise, all sheets in the workbook are visible. Selecting this item toggles the feature.
- *Add a Quiz Sheet.* Selecting this menu item adds a new quiz sheet to the workbook and prompts the user for a quiz name. The new sheet is a copy of the Template worksheet.
- *Delete the Current Quiz Sheet.* Selecting this menu item deletes the current quiz sheet.
- *Test the Application.* This menu item allows the administrator to test the quizzes without creating an add-in.
- *Make an Add-in.* Selecting this menu item creates an XLA add-in from the current Quiz Master workbook. The XLA add-in has the same name as the current worksheet but with an XLA extension.
- *Unload Quiz Master.* Selecting this menu item removes Quiz Master from memory.
- *Quiz Master Help.* Selecting this menu item displays the QUIZADM.HLP file.

Quiz mode

If the Quiz Master file is an add-in, the file opens in Quiz mode. The Auto_Open procedure calls a subroutine to create a different QuizMaster menu, shown in Figure 18-6:

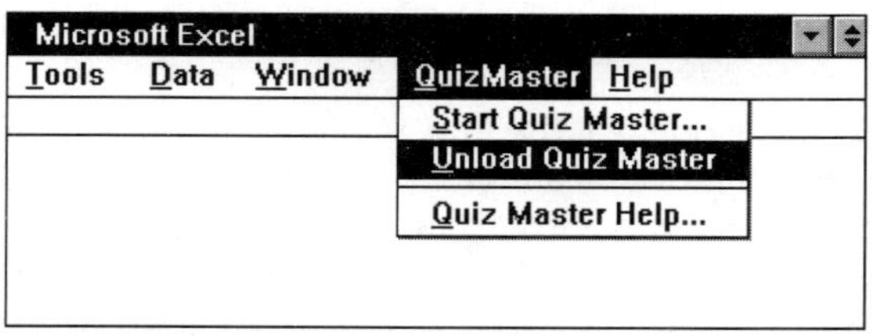

Figure 18-6: The QuizMaster menu in Quiz mode.

In Quiz mode, the QuizMaster menu has the following menu items:

- *Start Quiz Master.* Selecting this menu item displays the Quiz Master Options dialog box and then displays the menu of available quizzes.
- *Unload Quiz Master.* Selecting this menu item removes Quiz Master from memory.
- *Quiz Master Help.* Selecting this menu item displays the QUIZADM.HLP file.

The Quiz Master workbook structure

A Quiz Master workbook consists of the following sheets:

- *Admin.* A worksheet that holds the options specified in the Quiz Master Option dialog box. It also stores a list of all toolbars displayed when the workbook was opened.
- *Template.* A worksheet that's copied when a new quiz sheet is inserted. This sheet contains a text box that warns against it being used as a quiz sheet. It's also protected to prevent any data entry.
- *OptionsDlg.* A dialog sheet that contains the custom dialog box to set the Quiz Master options.
- *AdminMod.* A VBA module that contains the procedures used in Administrator mode.
- *QuizMod.* A VBA module that contains the procedures used in Quiz mode.
- *ContentsDlg.* A dialog sheet that contains the custom dialog box that displays the available quizzes in the workbook.
- *QuizDlg.* A dialog sheet that contains the custom dialog box that displays the quiz items and responses.
- *ShowScoreDlg.* A dialog sheet that contains the custom dialog box that displays the score following a quiz.
- *Quiz sheets.* These (the number will vary) sheets are copies of the Template worksheet that contains the items for each quiz.

Creating Quiz Master

The Quiz Master application evolved into a relatively complex project. I would like to say that I clearly envisioned the final product before I began developing it. But I'd be lying.

My basic idea was much simpler. I wanted to use worksheets to store quiz information, and I wanted to administer the quizzes by using a dialog box. But once I got started, I started thinking of ways to enhance my simple program. I eventually stumbled down several blind alleys; I had no clear idea of where I was heading. Some may consider my wanderings timewasting, but those false starts became a vital part of the development process.

As usual, my best insights came when I wasn't even working on the project. In fact, I was thinking about an alternative approach to this chapter (I was just about to scrap the entire Quiz Master idea) when I realized something pivotal: my end users would fall into two groups, those who develop quizzes and those who take them. After I happened upon this realization, the application came together quickly.

The entire project took two days, and I spent about 15 hours on it. I wound up deleting twice as much code as I kept. I designed five or six dialog boxes that didn't make the final cut.

Inside Quiz Master

In this section, I present the code to Quiz Master and describe how it works.

The Auto_Open procedure

The Auto_Open procedure, listed in Listing 18-1, is executed when the file is opened. First, the procedure saves a list of the current toolbars (the SaveToolBars subroutine). Then the procedure checks the FileFormat property of the Workbook object to determine whether the file is an add-in; the Select Case structure takes different actions depending on the file type.

If the workbook is not an add-in, the administrator is working on quizzes. So MakeXLSMenu is called, setting up the menu, and ToggleQuizzesOnly is called, hiding all sheets except the quiz sheet. From this point on, the users are free to do whatever they want — macro control ceases.

Listing 18-1 Auto_Open( ) subroutine.

```
Sub Auto_Open()
'   Executed when the file is opened

'   Save names of the current toolbars
    SaveToolbars

'   Different startup for XLS vs. XLA version...
    Select Case ThisWorkbook.FileFormat
        Case xlAddIn 'File is an add-in
            MakeXLAMenu
        Case Else 'File is not an add-in
           MakeXLSMenu
           ToggleQuizzesOnly
           ThisWorkbook.Worksheets(2).Activate
           Exit Sub
    End Select
End Sub
```

The SaveToolbars subroutine, listed in Listing 18-2, saves the names of all visible toolbars in a range (OldToolbars) in the Admin worksheet. This step is necessary if the Hide toolbars and menus option is set (the old toolbar configuration is restored when the quizzes are finished).

Listing 18-2 SaveToolbars subroutine.

```
Sub SaveToolbars()
    Dim i As Integer
    Dim SaveRange As Object
    Set SaveRange =
ThisWorkbook.Worksheets("Admin").Range("OldToolbars")

'   Clear out old names
    ThisWorkbook.Worksheets("Admin").Range(SaveRange, _
        SaveRange.End(xlDown)).ClearContents

'   Loop through the Toolbars collection
    i = 0
    For Each Bar In Application.Toolbars
        If Bar.Visible Then
            i = i + 1
            SaveRange.Offset(i - 1, 0).Value = Bar.Name
        End If
    Next Bar
End Sub
```

The MakeXLSMenu subroutine, listed in Listing 18-3, creates a new menu item QuizMaster, on the Worksheet and Module menus. Before creating the menus the procedure calls RemoveMenu to ensure that the menu doesn't already exist.

I created an array to hold the two constants (xlWorksheet and xlModule) and then used a For...Next loop to create the two menus and their menu items. As a result, I didn't have to duplicate the code for both menus.

Listing 18-3 MakeXLSMenu subroutine.

```
Sub MakeXLSMenu()
'   Adds QuizMaster menu
    Dim i As Integer
    Dim MenuNames(2) As Integer

    MenuNames(1) = xlWorksheet
    MenuNames(2) = xlModule

'   Delete old QuizMaster menu, if any
    RemoveMenu

'   Add QuizMaster menu
    For i = 1 To 2
        Application.MenuBars(MenuNames(i)).Menus.Add _
```

(continued)

Listing 18-3 *(continued)*

```
before:="&Help", Caption:="&QuizMaster"

'       Add the menu items
With Application.MenuBars(MenuNames(i)). _
            Menus("&QuizMaster").MenuItems
            .Add Caption:="Display Only Quiz Sheets", _
                 OnAction:="ToggleQuizzesOnly"
            .Add Caption:="&Add a Quiz Sheet", _
                 OnAction:="InsertNewQuiz"
            .Add Caption:="&Delete the Current Quiz Sheet...", _
                 OnAction:="DeleteQuiz"
            .Add Caption:="-"
            .Add Caption:="&Test the Application...", _
                 OnAction:="StartQuizzes"
            .Add Caption:="-"
            .Add Caption:="&Make an Add-in...", _
                 OnAction:="MakeAddIn"
            .Add Caption:="&Unload Quiz Master", _
                 OnAction:="UnloadQuizMaster"
            .Add Caption:="-"
            .Add Caption:="&Quiz Master Help...", _
                 OnAction:="ShowAdminHelp10"
        End With
    Next i
End Sub
```

Notice that the first new menu item, Display Only Quiz Sheets, has its OnAction property set to call the ToggleQuizzesOnly subroutine. This routine toggles the sheets that are displayed in the workbook (either all sheets or just the quiz sheets). The routine is shown in Listing 18-4.

Listing 18-4 ToggleQuizzesOnly( ) subroutine.

```
Sub ToggleQuizzesOnly()
    Dim MenuMod As Object, sheet As Object

    Set MenuMod = Application.MenuBars(xlWorksheet).Menus _
        ("&QuizMaster").MenuItems(1)

'   Toggle the check mark
    MenuMod.Checked = Not MenuMod.Checked

    Select Case MenuMod.Checked
        Case True ' Show only quiz sheets
            Application.ScreenUpdating = False
            On Error Resume Next
```

```
                ThisWorkbook.Modules.Visible = False
                ThisWorkbook.DialogSheets.Visible = False
                ThisWorkbook.Worksheets("Admin").Visible = False
                ThisWorkbook.Worksheets("Template").Visible = False
                ThisWorkbook.Worksheets(3).Activate
            Case False 'Show all sheets
                Application.ScreenUpdating = False
                On Error Resume Next
                For Each sheet In ThisWorkbook.Sheets
                    sheet.Visible = True
                Next sheet
        End Select
    End Sub
```

ToggleQuizzesOnly toggles the check mark on the menu item and then displays either all sheets or just the quiz sheets. The procedure uses a Select Case construct to handle the two alternatives. To hide all but the quiz sheets, I hid all modules and all dialog sheets and then the two non-quiz sheet worksheets (Admin and Template): only the quiz sheets remain. Then I activated the third worksheet, which is the first quiz sheet. To unhide all sheets, I just looped through all sheets in the Sheets collection and changed their Visible property.

The RemoveMenu routine, which is called by the MakeXLSMenu routine, simply cycles through all the menus and deletes the &QuizMaster menu if it's found. See Listing 18-5.

Listing 18-5 RemoveMenu( ) subroutine.

```
Sub RemoveMenu()
'   Removes the QuizMaster menu, if it exists

    Dim MenuNames(3) As Integer
    MenuNames(1) = xlWorksheet
    MenuNames(2) = xlModule
    MenuNames(3) = xlNoDocuments
    Dim item As Object

    On Error Resume Next
    For i = 1 To 3
        For Each item In _
            Application.MenuBars(MenuNames(i)).Menus
            If item.Caption = "&QuizMaster" Then
                item.Delete
            End If
        Next item
Next i
End Sub
```

Administrator mode

When the Quiz Master file is an XLS file and Auto_Open finishes, the workbook displays only the quiz sheets (the other sheets are hidden). The workbook is *not* under macro control, and the administrator is free to edit the quiz sheets, use Excel's normal commands, or use the newly created QuizMaster menu to

- Toggle between showing all sheets and just the quiz sheets (the ToggleQuizzesOnly routine)
- Add a new quiz sheet (the InsertNewQuiz routine)
- Delete the current quiz sheet (the DeleteQuiz routine)
- Create an add-in from the XLS file (the MakeAddIn routine)
- Get help (the ShowAdminHelp routine)
- Test the workbook (the StartQuizzes routine)

The Template worksheet (see Figure 18-7) is used to create other quiz sheets. It is protected and includes a text box that reminds the user not to use the sheet for a quiz.

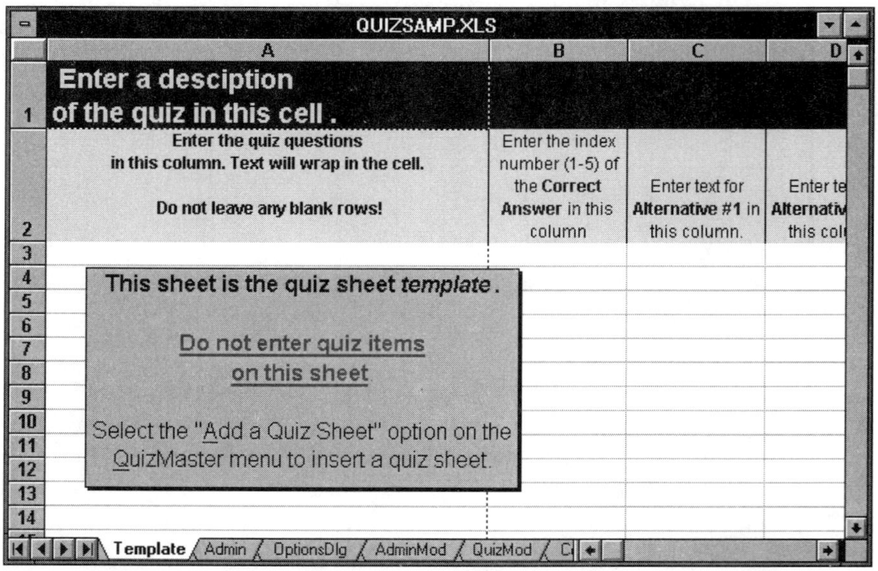

Figure 18-7: The Template worksheet is used to create new quiz sheets.

The InsertNewQuiz subroutine, shown in Listing 18-6, makes a copy of the Template worksheet and inserts it at the end of the workbook. I used the TemplateHidden variable to track whether the Template sheet was hidden — the Template sheet must be visible to be copied. After the copy is made, protection is turned off and the text box is deleted.

Listing 18-6 InsertNewQuiz( ) subroutine.

```
Sub InsertNewQuiz()
    Dim TemplateHidden As Boolean
'   Executed when Add a Quiz Sheet Template
'   menu choice is made

'   Copy the template, then remove protection
    Application.ScreenUpdating = False
    TemplateHidden = False
    If Not ThisWorkbook.Worksheets("Template").Visible Then
        TemplateHidden = True
        ThisWorkbook.Worksheets("Template").Visible = True
    End If
    ThisWorkbook.Worksheets("Template").Activate
    ActiveSheet.Copy after:=Sheets(Sheets.Count)
    ActiveSheet.Unprotect
    ActiveSheet.DrawingObjects.Delete
    ThisWorkbook.Worksheets("Template"). _
       Visible = Not TemplateHidden
    Application.ScreenUpdating = True
'   Prompt for new name
    Application.Dialogs(xlDialogWorkbookName).Show
End Sub
```

The final statement in InsertNewQuiz allows the user to change the name of the sheet. Figure 18-8 shows the dialog box that appears after the user chooses the QuizMaster⇨Add a New Quiz Sheet command.

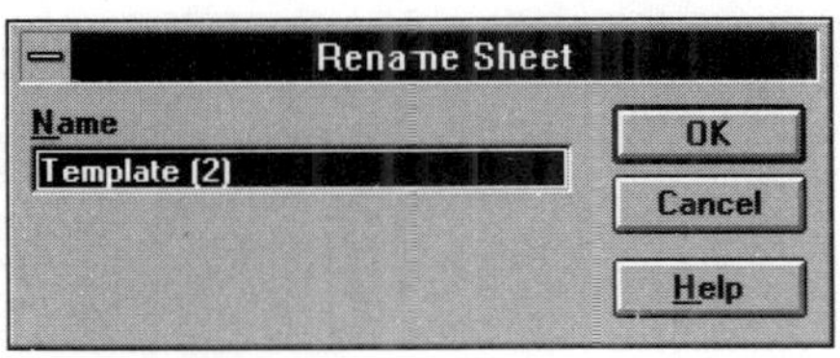

Figure 18-8: Naming a new quiz sheet.

The DeleteQuiz subroutine, shown in Listing 18-7, makes sure that the active sheet is a worksheet and that it's not the Template sheet or the Admin sheet. If any of these conditions are true, the routine is exited. Otherwise, the routine executes ActiveSheet.Delete.

Listing 18-7 DeleteQuiz( ) subroutine.

```
Sub DeleteQuiz()
'   Deletes the current sheet

'   Make sure a worksheet is active
    If TypeName(ActiveSheet) <> "Worksheet" Then
          MsgBox "The active sheet is not a quiz sheet.", _
          vbInformation, AppName
        Exit Sub
    End If

'   Make sure it's not the Template or Admin sheet
    If ActiveSheet.Name = "Template" Or ActiveSheet.Name = _
       "Admin" Then
        MsgBox "You cannot delete the Template or Admin _
        sheet.",
             vbInformation, AppName
        Exit Sub
    End If

    ActiveSheet.Delete
End Sub
```

The MakeAddIn routine, shown in Listing 18-8, creates an add-in from the Quiz Master workbook and stores it in the same directory as the XLS file. To do so, it first calls a custom function (QuizCount) to check whether the worksheet has any quiz sheets. If it doesn't, the user is warned. Oddly, no VBA command can create an add-in file, so I had to use an XLM macro function (VBA.MAKE.ADDIN). The Chr function inserts an extra set of quotation marks to conform to the method for specifying an XLM macro.

Listing 18-8 MakeAddIn( ) subroutine.

```
Sub MakeAddIn()
'   Creates an add-in file for the current set of Quizzes

    Dim item As Object
Dim CurrPath As String, AddInName As String
    Dim ExecString As String, Msg As String
    Dim QuizCnt As Integer, Ans As Integer
```

```
'   Warn if not quizzes
    If QuizCount() = 0 Then
        Msg = "There are no Quizzes in " & ThisWorkbook.Name
        Msg = Msg & Chr(13) & " Make add-in anyway?"
        Ans = MsgBox(Msg, vbExclamation + vbYesNo, AppName)
        If Ans = vbNo Then Exit Sub
    End If

    CurrPath = ThisWorkbook.Path & "\"
    AddInName = Left(ThisWorkbook.Name, _
      Len(ThisWorkbook.Name) - 3) & "XLA"
    AddInName = CurrPath & AddInName

'   Execute XLM macro
    ExecuteExcel4Macro "VBA.MAKE.ADDIN(" & Chr(34) & _
      AddInName & Chr(34) & ")"
    MsgBox AddInName & " created.", vbInformation, AppName
End Sub
```

I created two custom help files for this application: one for Administrator mode (QUIZ_A.HLP) and one for Quiz mode (QUIZ_U.HLP). The help files are assumed to be in the same directory as the application.

The ShowAdminHelp10 routine displays the help file with context ID of 10 (the contents):

```
Sub ShowAdminHelp10()
 Application.Help ThisWorkbook.Path & "\" & "QUIZ_A.HLP", 10
End Sub
```

The administrator can choose the QuizMaster⇨Test the Application command to set the quiz options and test the quizzes. This menu item calls the StartQuizzes routine, which actually calls two other subroutines: SetOptions displays the Quiz Master Options dialog box and ShowTheQuizNames displays the dialog box with the list of quizzes.

```
Sub StartQuizzes()
'   Executed when Test the Application menu option selected
    SetOptions
    ShowTheQuizNames
End Sub
```

Quiz mode

When the Quiz Master workbook is an add-in, the Auto_Open subroutine calls the MakeXLAMenu routine to create a new menu item on the Worksheet, Module, and No Document Open menu bars, as shown in Listing 18-9.

Listing 18-9 MakeXLAMenu( ) subroutine.

```
Sub MakeXLAMenu()
'   Adds QuizMaster menu
    Dim MenuNames(3) As Integer
    MenuNames(1) = xlWorksheet
    MenuNames(2) = xlModule
    MenuNames(3) = xlNoDocuments

'   Delete old QuizMaster menu, if any
    RemoveMenu

'   Add QuizMaster menu
    For i = 1 To 3
        Application.MenuBars(MenuNames(i)).Menus.Add _
            before:="&Help", Caption:="&QuizMaster"

'       Add the menu items
        With
Application.MenuBars(MenuNames(i)).Menus("&QuizMaster").MenuItems
            .Add Caption:="&Start Quiz Master...",
OnAction:="StartQuizzes"
            .Add Caption:="&Unload Quiz Master",
OnAction:="UnloadQuizMaster"
            .Add Caption:="-"
            .Add Caption:="&Quiz Master Help...",
OnAction:="ShowAdminHelp"
        End With
    Next i
End Sub
```

When a Quiz Master add-in is opened, the QuizMaster menu has three options:

- The *Quiz Master Help* menu item calls the ShowAdminHelp10 routine.
- The *Start Quiz Master* menu item calls the StartQuizzes routine.
- The *Unload Quiz Master* menu item calls the UnloadQuizMaster subroutine.

The StartQuizzes routine calls two subroutines: SetOptions and ShowTheQuizNames.

The SetOptions routine, shown in Listing 18-9, displays the Quiz Master Options dialog box (see Figure 18-9). The procedure starts by calling the custom QuizCount function to ensure that the workbook has at least one quiz sheet (not including the Template worksheet). If there are no quiz sheets or if the dialog box is canceled, the routine ends with no action. Note that the procedure uses the End statement, which stops Visual Basic, not just the current procedure.

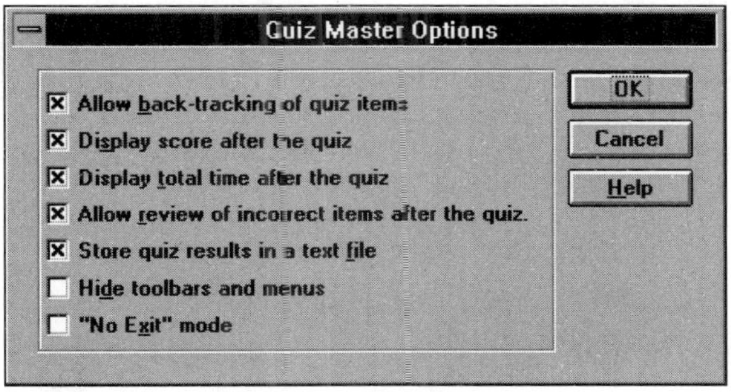

Figure 18-9: The Quiz Master Options dialog box appears before the quizzes begin.

The option settings are stored in named ranges on the Admin worksheet. The SetOptions routine reads the current settings and sets the check boxes accordingly. When the dialog box is closed, the new check box settings are translated as new values in the Admin worksheet.

If the Hide toolbars and menus option is set, the routine executes the QuizMode routine to hide the toolbars, menus, status bar, and formula bar. Otherwise, it executes the AdminMode routine, which displays these items. If the No Exit option is set, the routine prompts for a password, which will be required for Quiz mode to end.

Listing 18-10 **SetOptions( ) subroutine.**

```
Sub SetOptions()
'   Set the options for the Quizzes
    Dim OptionsDlg As Object
    Dim Admin As Object
    Dim item As Object
    Dim OptionsOK As Integer

    Set OptionsDlg = ThisWorkbook.DialogSheets("OptionsDlg")
    Set Admin = ThisWorkbook.Worksheets("Admin")

'   Make sure there is at least one quiz sheet
```

(continued)

Listing 18-10 *(continued)*

```
    If QuizCount() = 0 Then
        MsgBox "There are no Quizzes in " & _
             ThisWorkbook.Name, _
            vbExclamation, AppName
        End
    End If

'   Get current settings stored in Admin worksheet
    OptionsDlg.CheckBoxes.Value = xlOff
    If Admin.Range("BackTrack") = True Then _
        OptionsDlg.CheckBoxes("cbBacktrack") = xlOn
    If Admin.Range("DisplayScores") = True Then _
        OptionsDlg.CheckBoxes("cbDisplayScores") = xlOn
    If Admin.Range("DisplayTime") = True Then _
        OptionsDlg.CheckBoxes("cbDisplayTime") = xlOn
    If Admin.Range("AllowReview") = True Then _
        OptionsDlg.CheckBoxes("cbAllowReview") = xlOn
    If Admin.Range("SaveResults") = True Then _
        OptionsDlg.CheckBoxes("cbSaveResults") = xlOn
    If Admin.Range("HideStuff") = True Then _
        OptionsDlg.CheckBoxes("cbHideStuff") = xlOn
    If Admin.Range("NoExit") = True Then _
        OptionsDlg.CheckBoxes ("cbNoExit")

'   Show the dialog
    OptionsOK = OptionsDlg.Show
    If Not OptionsOK Then End

'   Transfer dialog box info to Admin worksheet
    If OptionsDlg.CheckBoxes("cbBacktrack") = xlOn Then _
        Admin.Range("BackTrack") = True _
        Else Admin.Range("BackTrack") = False
    If OptionsDlg.CheckBoxes("cbDisplayScores") = xlOn Then _
        Admin.Range("DisplayScores") = True _
        Else Admin.Range("DisplayScores") = False
    If OptionsDlg.CheckBoxes("cbDisplayTime") = xlOn Then _
        Admin.Range("DisplayTime") = True _
        Else Admin.Range("DisplayTime") = False
    If OptionsDlg.CheckBoxes("cbAllowReview") = xlOn Then _
        Admin.Range("AllowReview") = True _
        Else Admin.Range("AllowReview") = False
    If OptionsDlg.CheckBoxes("cbSaveResults") = xlOn Then _
        Admin.Range("SaveResults") = True _
        Else Admin.Range("SaveResults") = False
```

```
    If OptionsDlg.CheckBoxes("cbHideStuff") = xlOn Then _
        Admin.Range("HideStuff") = True
        QuizMode
    End If

    If OptionsDlg.CheckBoxes("cbHideStuff") = xlOff Then _
         Admin.Range("HideStuff") = False
         AdminMode
    End If

    If OptionsDlg.CheckBoxes("cbNoExit") = xlOn Then _
        Admin.Range("NoExit") = True
        PreventExit
        PW = InputBox("Enter a password that will allow _
                       exiting the program:", _
            AppName,
ThisWorkbook.Worksheets("Admin").Range("Password").Value)
        ThisWorkbook.Worksheets("Admin").Range("Password"). _
          Value = PW
    End If

    If OptionsDlg.CheckBoxes("cbNoExit") = xlOff Then
        Admin.Range("NoExit") = False
        AllowExit
    End If
End Sub
```

StartQuizzes also calls the ShowTheQuizNames subroutine, which is a loop that displays the Available Quizzes dialog box (see Figure 18-10) and then administers the selected quiz. The ShowTheQuizNames subroutine, shown in Listing 18-11, is in the QuizMod module. (It is rather complicated, so you may want to open the file and step through it.)

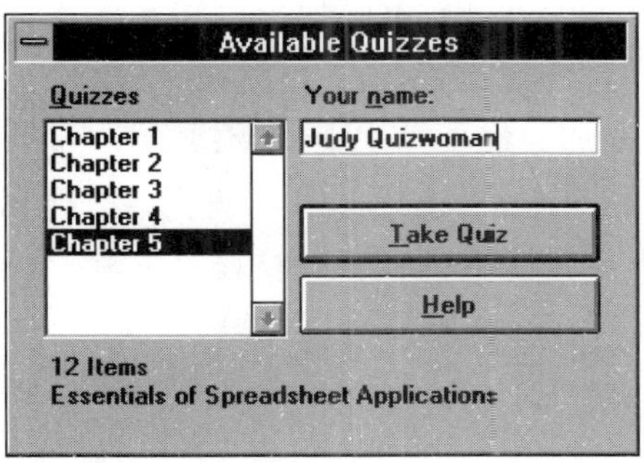

Figure 18-10: The Available Quizzes dialog box displays the names of all quizzes in the workbook.

Listing 18-11 ShowTheQuizNames( ) subroutine.

```
Sub ShowTheQuizNames()
    Dim DBoxOK As Boolean
    Dim Ans
    Dim Win As Object
    Dim WindowStates() As WinSpecs
    Dim PW As Object
    Dim Msg As String

    Set ContentsDlg =
ThisWorkbook.DialogSheets("ContentsDlg")
    Set NameEdit = ContentsDlg.EditBoxes("NameEdit")
    Set QuizList = ContentsDlg.ListBoxes("QuizList")
    Set PW =
ThisWorkbook.Worksheets("Admin").Range("Password")

'   Exit if no quizzes
    If QuizCount() = 0 Then
        MsgBox "There are no Quizzes in this workbook.", _
            vbInformation, AppName
        Exit Sub
    End If

'   Get list of quizzes
    FillQuizlist
    NameEdit.Text = ""

'   Minimize all windows, but save their states
    On Error Resume Next
    i = 0
    For Each Win In Application.Windows
        If Win.Visible Then
            i = i + 1
            ReDim Preserve WindowStates(i)
            WindowStates(i).Cap = Win.Caption
            WindowStates(i).State = Win.WindowState
            Win.WindowState = xlMinimized
        End If
    Next Win
    Windows.Arrange ArrangeStyle:=xlTiled

    Application.ScreenUpdating = True

    On Error GoTo 0
```

```
'   Show the list of quizzes
    DBoxOK = True
    Do Until True = False
        DBoxOK = ContentsDlg.Show
        Select Case DBoxOK
            Case False 'Canceled
                Select Case
ThisWorkbook.Worksheets("Admin").Range("NoExit")
                    Case True
                        Ans = InputBox("Enter the _
                          password...", AppName)
                        If Ans = PW.Value Then
                            AdminMode
                            Exit Do
                        End If
                    Case False
                        Msg = "Do you really want to exit _
                              QuizMaster?"
                        Ans = MsgBox(Msg, vbQuestion + _
                              vbYesNo, AppName)
                        If Ans = vbYes Then
                            AdminMode
                            Exit Do
                        End If
                End Select
            Case True 'Not Canceled
                    Do Until NameEdit.Text <> ""
                        NameEdit.Text = InputBox("What is _
                                                your name?")
                    Loop
                    StartAQuiz
                    ReportScore
            End Select
        End Select
    Loop

'   Restore the window states
    For i = 1 To UBound(WindowStates)
        Windows(WindowStates(i).Cap).WindowState = _
         WindowStates(i).State
    Next i

'   Restore QuizMaster menu
    If ThisWorkbook.FileFormat = xlAddIn Then MakeXLAMenu
Else MakeXLSMenu
End Sub
```

The ShowTheQuizNames routine starts by calling the custom QuizCount function to count the number of quizzes. If there are none, it exits. If there is at least one quiz sheet, the routine calls FillQuizlist to fill the list box in the Available Quizzes dialog with the names of the quiz sheets. Next, it minimizes all workbook windows but saves their WindowsState (minimized, maximized, or normal) so that they can be restored later; this information is stored in a user-defined data type.

The main loop is established with the Do Until True = False statement. Of course, this condition will never be true, so the code within the loop has other ways to exit. If the Available Quizzes dialog box is canceled, the routine checks to see whether No Exit mode is in effect. If so, it prompts for the password and exits only if the correct password is entered. If No Exit mode is not in effect, it verifies the user's intentions (the user could have canceled the dialog box accidentally).

If the dialog box is not canceled (that is, a quiz is selected), the code makes sure that the edit box that holds the name is not blank. Then it calls the StartAQuiz routine and the ReportScore routine.

The last part of ShowTheQuizNames, which is executed only when the Available Quizzes dialog box is closed, restores the windows and makes sure that the proper QuizMaster menu is displayed.

The FillQuizList subroutine, shown in Listing 18-12, loops through each worksheet to see whether it qualifies as a quiz. To qualify, it can't be named *Admin* or *Template*, and it must have at least one quiz item. It uses Excel's COUNTA function to count the number of nonblank cells in column A of each sheet. Because the first two rows have descriptive information, the count must be greater than two to indicate at least one quiz item.

Listing 18-12 FillQuizList( ) subroutine.

```
Sub FillQuizList()
'   Fills the quiz list

    Dim sheet As Object

'   Empty it first
    If QuizList.ListCount <> 0 Then _
        QuizList.RemoveItem Index:=1,
Count:=QuizList.ListCount

'   List all worksheets except Admin
    For Each sheet In ThisWorkbook.Worksheets
        If sheet.Name <> "Admin" Then _
            If sheet.Name <> "Template" Then
```

```
            If Application.CountA(sheet.Range("A:A")) _
               > 2 Then _
                       QuizList.AddItem Text:=sheet.Name
                End If
            End If
        Next sheet

        QuizList.Selected = 1
        QuizListChange
    End Sub
```

When the list box is clicked, it executes the QuizListChange routine. This subroutine, shown in Listing 18-13, sets an object variable (CurrentQuiz) to the selected quiz sheet. It also makes sure that the description isn't empty; if so, it inserts a space characters into cell A1. It uses Excel's COUNTA function to determine the number of quiz items, and it updates the labels in the dialog box to show the item count and the description.

Listing 18-13 QuizListChange( ) subroutine.

```
    Sub QuizListChange()
    '   Executed when user selects a quiz in the list

        Dim NumCorrect As Integer
        Set CurrentQuiz = _
        ThisWorkbook.Worksheets(QuizList.List(QuizList.ListIndex))

    '   Make sure description isn't empty
        If CurrentQuiz.Range("A1").Value = Empty Then _
            CurrentQuiz.Range("A1").Value = " "

        TotalItems = _
         Application.CountA(CurrentQuiz.Range("A:A")) - 2
        ContentsDlg.Labels("ItemsLabel").Text = TotalItems _
          & " Items"
        ContentsDlg.Labels("DescriptionLabel").Text = _
            CurrentQuiz.Range("A1").Value
    End Sub
```

The StartAQuiz routine, which is executed when the Available Quizzes dialog box is closed normally (not canceled), displays the Quiz dialog box (see Figure 18-11). The CurrentQuiz object variable is set to the selected quiz sheet.

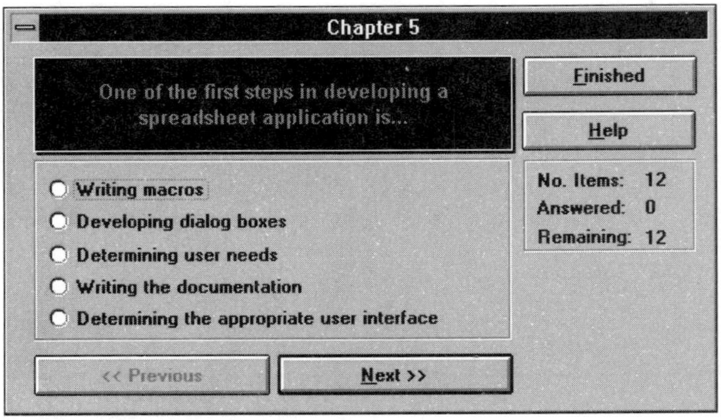

Figure 18-11: The Quiz dialog box.

The StartAQuiz routine, shown in Listing 18-14, starts by preparing the dialog box's controls and calls NewItem to get the quiz item. The Do Until…Loop structure contains the statement to display the dialog box and is exited only when all items are answered items (or the user ends the quiz early).

Listing 18-15 StartAQuiz( ) subroutine.

```
Sub StartAQuiz()
    Dim Ans As Integer
    Dim GoBack As Integer
    Set QuizDlg = ThisWorkbook.DialogSheets("QuizDlg")
    Set Answers(1) = QuizDlg.OptionButtons("Answer1")
    Set Answers(2) = QuizDlg.OptionButtons("Answer2")
    Set Answers(3) = QuizDlg.OptionButtons("Answer3")
    Set Answers(4) = QuizDlg.OptionButtons("Answer4")
    Set Answers(5) = QuizDlg.OptionButtons("Answer5")
    Set NextBtn = QuizDlg.Buttons("NextBtn")
    Set PreviousBtn = QuizDlg.Buttons("PreviousBtn")
    Set TheQuestion =
ThisWorkbook.Sheets("Admin").Range("TheQuestion")

'   Prepare dialog box
    CurrentItem = 1
    PreviousBtn.Enabled = False
    If TotalItems = 1 Then NextBtn.Enabled = False Else
NextBtn.Enabled = True
    CurrentQuiz.Range("H:H").Clear
    QuizDlg.DialogFrame.Caption = CurrentQuiz.Name
    QuizDlg.Labels("Items").Text = TotalItems
    QuizDlg.Labels("Answered").Text = "0"
```

```
    QuizDlg.Labels("Remaining").Text = TotalItems
    Call NewItem
    StartTime = Time

'   Display Previous button if option is set
    PreviousBtn.Visible = _
       ThisWorkbook.Sheets("Admin").Range("BackTrack").Value

'   Start the quiz
    GoBack = vbYes
    Do Until (GoBack = vbNo) Or _
         (QuizDlg.Labels("Remaining").Text = "0")
        QuizDlg.Show
        If QuizDlg.Labels("Remaining").Text <> "0" Then
            GoBack = MsgBox("There are " & _
            QuizDlg.Labels("Remaining").Text _
                    & " unanswered items." & Chr(13) & _
                    Chr(13) & _
                    "Return to the quiz?", vbQuestion + _
                    vbYesNo, AppName)
        End If
    Loop
End Sub
```

The NewItem subroutine (shown in Listing 18-15) loads a quiz item and its response alternatives into the dialog box by reading the information from the quiz sheet. The last part of the routine ensures that keyboard users can access the dialog box easily (for example, pressing Enter moves to the next item).

Listing 18-15 NewItem( ) subroutine.

```
Sub NewItem()
'   Loads a quiz item and its answers into dialog

    Dim i As Integer
    Dim PossibleAnswers As Integer
    Dim CurrAns As Object

'   Get the question
    TheQuestion.Value = _
          CurrentQuiz.Range("A1").Offset(CurrentItem + 1, _
            0).Value

'   Get the answers
    PossibleAnswers = 0
    For i = 1 To 5
        Set CurrAns = _
```

(continues)

Listing 18-15 *(continued)*

```
                CurrentQuiz.Range("A1").Offset(CurrentItem + 1, _
                  i + 1)
            Select Case CurrAns.Value
                Case Empty
                    Answers(i).Visible = False
                Case Else
                    PossibleAnswers = PossibleAnswers + 1
                    With Answers(i)
                        .Visible = True
                        .Text = CurrAns.Value
                    End With
                    If CurrentQuiz.Range("A1"). _
                    Offset(CurrentItem + 1, 7) = i _
                        Then Answers(i).Value = xlOn Else _
                        Answers(i).Value = xlOff
            End Select
        Next i

'   Set up dialog box for keyboard users
    On Error Resume Next
    QuizDlg.Focus = Answers(1).Name
    QuizDlg.Buttons("NextBtn").Default = True
End Sub
```

Both the Previous and Next buttons in the dialog box that shows the quiz items execute the GetAnotherItem procedure. This routine, shown in Listing 18-16, uses the Caller property of the Application object to get the name of the button that was clicked and then takes the appropriate action. CurrentItem is a global variable that stores the item number of the current quiz. Notice that the Previous button is disabled when the first quiz item is displayed, whereas the Next button is disabled when the last quiz item is displayed. The final statement calls NewItem to display the new quiz item. Also, if the Allow backtracking option is not set, the routine does not let the quiz taker leave an item blank.

Listing 18-16 GetAnotherItem() subroutine.

```
Sub GetAnotherItem()
    Dim NoAnswer As Boolean
    Dim i As Integer
'   Executed when Previous or Next button is clicked

'   Take action, depending on button
    Select Case Application.Caller
        Case "PreviousBtn"
            CurrentItem = CurrentItem - 1
```

```
                If CurrentItem = 1 Then
                    PreviousBtn.Enabled = False
                    NextBtn.Enabled = True
                End If
            If CurrentItem <> 1 Then
                PreviousBtn.Enabled = True
                NextBtn.Enabled = True
            End If

        Case "NextBtn"
'           No blanks allowed if backtracking is disabled
            If ThisWorkbook.Sheets("Admin"). _
            Range("BackTrack") = False Then
                NoAnswer = True
                For i = 1 To 5
                     If QuizDlg.OptionButtons(i).Value = xlOn _
                       Then NoAnswer = False
                Next i
                If NoAnswer Then
                    MsgBox "You didn't answer the
                           question.",vbInformation, AppName
                    Exit Sub
                End If
            End If
            CurrentItem = CurrentItem + 1
            If CurrentItem = TotalItems Then
                NextBtn.Enabled = False
                PreviousBtn.Enabled = True
            End If
            If CurrentItem <> TotalItems Then
                NextBtn.Enabled = True
                PreviousBtn.Enabled = True
            End If
    End Select
    NewItem
End Sub
```

When the quiz taker chooses an answer (by clicking an option button), the AnswerClick subroutine is executed. This routine, shown in Listing 18-17, enters the response number into column H of the current quiz sheet. It also updates the labels display in the dialog box to show the number of items answered and the number remaining.

Listing 18-17 AnswerClick( ) subroutine.

```
Sub AnswerClick()
'   Executed when user answers a quiz item

    Dim NumDone As Integer
    Dim i As Integer

'   Put the answer in the worksheet
    For i = 1 To 5
        If Answers(i) = xlOn Then
            CurrentQuiz.Range("A1").Offset(CurrentItem + 1, _
              7) = i
            Exit For
        End If
    Next i

'   Update status display
    NumDone = Application.CountA(CurrentQuiz.Range("H:H"))
    QuizDlg.Labels("Answered").Text = NumDone
    QuizDlg.Labels("Remaining").Text = TotalItems - NumDone
End Sub
```

When the quiz is ended (the users clicks the Finish button), the ReportScore subroutine is executed from the ShowTheQuizNames routine. This subroutine, shown in Listing 18-18, displays the quiz results. The information displayed is determined by the options set in the Quiz Master Options dialog box.

Listing 18-18 ReportScore( ) subroutine.

```
Sub ReportScore()
'   Report score when dialog is closed

    Dim DBoxOK As Boolean
    Dim Msg1 As String, Msg2 As String
    Dim ShowScoreDlg As Object
    Set ShowScoreDlg =
ThisWorkbook.DialogSheets("ShowScoreDlg")

'   Count correct items
    NumCorrect = 0
    For i = 1 To TotalItems
        If CurrentQuiz.Range("A1").Offset(i + 1, 1).Value = _
            CurrentQuiz.Range("A1").Offset(i + 1, 7).Value _
            Then NumCorrect = NumCorrect + 1
```

```
    Next i

'   Calculate time
    QuizTime = StartTime - Time

'   Action depending on DisplayScores setting
    Select Case
ThisWorkbook.Sheets("Admin").Range("DisplayScores")
        Case False
            Msg1 = "End of Quiz."
            ShowScoreDlg.DialogFrame.Caption = "Finished"
            ShowScoreDlg.DrawingObjects("Guage").Visible = _
             False
            ShowScoreDlg.DrawingObjects("GuageBack").Visible _
             = False
        Case True
            Msg1 = NumCorrect & " correct out of " & _
            TotalItems
            ShowScoreDlg.DialogFrame.Caption = _
                "Quiz Results for " & _
                ContentsDlg.EditBoxes("NameEdit").Text
            ShowScoreDlg.DrawingObjects("Guage").Visible = _
            True
            ShowScoreDlg.DrawingObjects("GuageBack").Visible _
            = True
            ShowScoreDlg.DrawingObjects("Guage").Text = _
                Format(NumCorrect / TotalItems, "##.0%") & " "
            ShowScoreDlg.DrawingObjects("Guage").Width = _
              ShowScoreDlg.DrawingObjects("GuageBack").Width * _
(NumCorrect / TotalItems)
    End Select

'   Action depending on DisplayTime setting
    If ThisWorkbook.Sheets("Admin").Range("DisplayTime") = _
    False Then _
        Msg2 = "" Else Msg2 = "Total Time: " & _
        Format(QuizTime, "hh:mm:ss")

'   Action depending on Allow Review setting
    Select Case
ThisWorkbook.Sheets("Admin").Range("AllowReview")
        Case True
```

(continued)

Listing 18-18 *(continued)*

```
                ShowScoreDlg.Buttons("ReviewButton").Visible = True
                If NumCorrect = TotalItems Then
                    ShowScoreDlg.Buttons("ReviewButton").Enabled _
                    = False
                        Else ShowScoreDlg.Buttons.Enabled = True
                End If
            Case False
                ShowScoreDlg.Buttons("ReviewButton").Visible = _
                False
        End Select

'       Save to file if Save Results setting is true
        If ThisWorkbook.Sheets("Admin")
        .Range("SaveResults").Value = _ True _
            Then Call WriteResults

'       Set up dialog and show it
        ShowScoreDlg.Labels("Msg1").Text = Msg1
        ShowScoreDlg.Labels("Msg2").Text = Msg2
        DBoxOK = ShowScoreDlg.Show

        If Not DBoxOK Then Exit Sub
        If DBoxOK And
    ThisWorkbook.Sheets("Admin").Range("AllowReview") = True _
            Then ReviewMisses
    End Sub
```

If the Allow review of incorrect items after the quiz option is set, the Results dialog box displays a button (the default button) that lets the user see the correct answers to the incorrect items. The ReviewMisses routine uses the MsgBox function to display the questions answered incorrectly and their correct answers (see Listing 18-19).

Listing 18-19 ReviewMisses( ) subroutine.

```
    Sub ReviewMisses()
        Dim Misses As Integer
        Dim UserIndex As Integer
        Dim CorrIndex As Integer
        Dim CorrectAns As String
        Dim Msg As String
        Dim MsgOK As Integer
```

```
    Misses = TotalItems - NumCorrect
    For i = 1 To TotalItems
        CorrIndex = CurrentQuiz.Range("A1").Offset(i + 1, _
        1).Value
        UserIndex = CurrentQuiz.Range("A1").Offset(i + 1, _
        7).Value
        CorrectAns = _
            CurrentQuiz.Range("A1").Offset(i + 1, CorrIndex _
            + 1).Value
        If CorrIndex <> UserIndex Then
            Msg = "Q: " & CurrentQuiz.Range("A1").Offset(i + _
            1, 0).Value
            Msg = Msg & Chr(13) & Chr(13) & "A: " & _
            CorrectAns
            MsgOK = MsgBox(Msg, vbOKCancel, CurrentQuiz.Name _
            & " (Item " & i & ")")
            If MsgOK = vbCancel Then Exit For
        End If
    Next i
End Sub
```

If the Store quiz results in a text file option is set, the quiz results are written to a text file. The WriteResults subroutine (Listing 18-20) stores the following information in a comma-delimited file:

- Date
- Time
- Quiz taker's name
- Time it took to complete the quiz
- Number of correct answers
- Number of items on the quiz
- List of the index numbers (1-5) of the quiz-taker's responses

The filename is the same as the workbook name but has a CSV extension. The file is stored in the same directory as the workbook. If the file doesn't exist, the Append keyword creates it. If it does exist, the new record is added to the file.

Figure 18-12 shows a sample text file created by Quiz Master; this file can be imported into Excel.

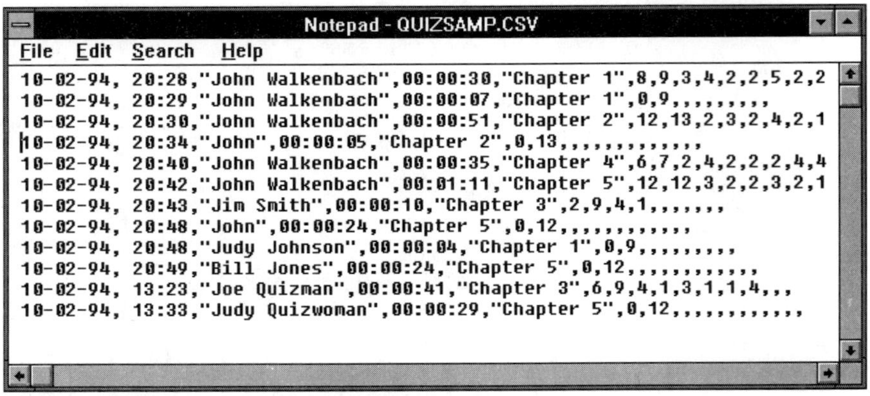
Notepad - QUIZSAMP.CSV

File Edit Search Help

```
10-02-94, 20:28,"John Walkenbach",00:00:30,"Chapter 1",8,9,3,4,2,2,5,2,2
10-02-94, 20:29,"John Walkenbach",00:00:07,"Chapter 1",0,9,,,,,,,,
10-02-94, 20:30,"John Walkenbach",00:00:51,"Chapter 2",12,13,2,3,2,4,2,1
10-02-94, 20:34,"John",00:00:05,"Chapter 2",0,13,,,,,,,,,,,,
10-02-94, 20:40,"John Walkenbach",00:00:35,"Chapter 4",6,7,2,4,2,2,2,4,4
10-02-94, 20:42,"John Walkenbach",00:01:11,"Chapter 5",12,12,3,2,2,3,2,1
10-02-94, 20:43,"Jim Smith",00:00:10,"Chapter 3",2,9,4,1,,,,,,
10-02-94, 20:48,"John",00:00:24,"Chapter 5",0,12,,,,,,,,,,,
10-02-94, 20:48,"Judy Johnson",00:00:04,"Chapter 1",0,9,,,,,,,,
10-02-94, 20:49,"Bill Jones",00:00:24,"Chapter 5",0,12,,,,,,,,,,,
10-02-94, 13:23,"Joe Quizman",00:00:41,"Chapter 3",6,9,4,1,3,1,1,4,,,
10-02-94, 13:33,"Judy Quizwoman",00:00:29,"Chapter 5",0,12,,,,,,,,,,,
```

Figure 18-12: A text file created by Quiz Master.

Listing 18-20 **WriteResults( ) subroutine.**

```
Sub WriteResults()
'   Write quiz results to a text file

    Dim ResultsFile As String
    Dim Rec As String
    Dim i As Integer

'   Create file name based on workbook name
    ResultsFile = ThisWorkbook.Path & "\" & _
        Left(ThisWorkbook.Name, Len(ThisWorkbook.Name) - 3) _
        & "CSV"
'   Build the Record to write
    Rec = Format(Date, "mm-dd-yy) & ","
    Rec = Format(Time, "hh:mm") & ","
    Rec = Rec & Chr(34) &
ContentsDlg.EditBoxes("NameEdit").Text & Chr(34) & ","
    Rec = Rec & Format(QuizTime, "hh:mm:ss") & ","
    Rec = Rec & Chr(34) & CurrentQuiz.Name & Chr(34) & ","
    Rec = Rec & NumCorrect & ","
    Rec = Rec & TotalItems & ","
    For i = 1 To TotalItems
        Rec = Rec & CurrentQuiz.Range("A1").Offset(i + 1, _
        7).Value
        If i <> TotalItems Then Rec = Rec & ","
    Next i

'   Open the file, write the Rec, an close it
    Open ResultsFile For Append As #1
    Print #1, Rec
    Close
End Sub
```

The ShowTheQuizNames routine loops until the Available Quizzes dialog box is canceled. Notice that there is no Cancel button, so the only way to cancel the dialog box is to press Esc. Before the subroutine ends, the windows are restored to their original states and the appropriate QuizMaster menu is created. The user then can use the QuizMaster menu to perform other actions.

If the QuizMaster➪Unload Quiz Master menu item is selected, the UnloadQuizMaster routine is executed:

```
Sub UnloadQuizMaster()
   On Error Resume Next
   If AddIns(AppName).Installed Then
       AddIns(AppName).Installed = False
       MsgBox AppName & " Uninstalled", vbInformation, _
       AppName
       Exit Sub
    End If
   ThisWorkbook.Close
End Sub
```

This routine is designed to handle two conditions:

- Quiz Master is an add-in and was opened when the user chose the Tools➪Add-Ins command. In this case, it will be a member of the Add-Ins collection and will be installed. The routine checks this and uninstalls it if necessary.
- Quiz Master was opened when the user chose the File➪Open command. This is the case when it's an XLS file or when it's an add-in that was not opened with the Tools➪Add-Ins command. The ThisWorkbook.Close statement closes it.

Before closing the file, the Auto_Close routine is executed. Note that this procedure is executed whether the workbook is either a normal workbook or an add-in.

```
Sub Auto_Close()
    RemoveMenu
    AdminMode
    AllowExit
End Sub
```

Before closing the file, Auto_Close calls three routines: the RemoveMenu, AdminMode, and AllowExit. The AdminMode routine, shown in Listing 18-21, restores the toolbars to their original state, resets all the menus, and makes sure that the formula bar and status bar are visible. It also resets Excel's caption to Microsoft Excel.

Listing 18-21 AdminMode subroutine.

```
Sub AdminMode()
'   Allows editing (if XLS version) and shows menus and
'   toolbars

    Dim Bar As Object
    Dim SaveRange As Object
    Set SaveRange =
ThisWorkbook.Worksheets("Admin").Range("OldToolbars")
    Set SaveRange =
ThisWorkbook.Worksheets("Admin").Range(SaveRange, _
        SaveRange.End(xlDown))

'   Restore Toolbars
    If SaveRange.Cells(1, 1) <> "" Then
        For Each Bar In SaveRange
            Application.Toolbars(Bar.Value).Visible = True
        Next Bar
    End If

'   Reset all menus
    For Each Bar In Application.MenuBars
        Bar.Reset
    Next Bar
    MakeXLSMenu

'   Restore formula bar and status bar
    With Application
        .DisplayFormulaBar = True
        .DisplayStatusBar = True
        .Caption = "Microsoft Excel"
    End With

    AllowExit
End Sub
```

The help files

I created two help files: one for Administrator mode (QUIZ_A.HLP), and one for the users in Quiz mode (QUIZ_U.HLP). QUIZ_A.HLP is accessible from the QuizMaster⇨Quiz Master Help command and from the Quiz Master Options dialog box. QUIZ_U.HLP is accessible from the Available Quizzes dialog box and from the dialog box that shows the quiz items.

DISK

Both help files, along with the RTF source files, are on the disk that accompanies this book.

Application development concepts

I know that it's often difficult to follow the logic in applications developed by others. To help you understand my work, I included lots of comments in the code. And I attempted to describe the program flow in the previous sections. But if you really want to understand this application, I suggest that you use the Debugger to step through the code.

At the very least, the Quiz Master demonstrates some useful techniques and concepts:

- Recognizing the file type (add-in or regular workbook)
- Using custom menus (including the Checked property)
- Selectively hiding sheets of a certain type
- Copying a worksheet
- Using a dialog box to retrieve and save a series of options
- Creating an add-in from VBA (I used an XLM macro function)
- Controlling the entire application with macros (Quiz mode only)
- Renaming TASKMAN.EXE to prevent the user from exiting Excel
- Removing the toolbars, menus, status bar, and formula bar — and restoring them later
- Changing Excel's title bar caption
- Using a custom help file (and displaying a particular topic)
- Using a user-defined data type (to save and restore the state of all windows)
- Using an infinite Do Until...Loop structure to avoid using GoTo statements
- Identifying which button was clicked in a dialog box (important because the Previous and Next buttons both execute the same macro)
- Changing labels in a dialog box dynamically, based on the selection in a list box control
- Setting the Enabled property of dialog box button controls dynamically
- Determining the elapsed time of a process
- Displaying a thermometer-style gauge to graphically depict a score

- Determining the contents of a dialog box dynamically, based on user options (that is, showing the quiz results)
- Using a text file to store information
- Using a linked picture object in a dialog box to allow more attractive text display
- Writing and retrieving and information selectively to and from worksheets

Some Final Words

Developing user-oriented applications in Excel is not easy. You have to keep many things in mind when developing the code. Although I tried to make this application bulletproof, I wouldn't be surprised if it fails under some conditions.

Application development checklist

When developing user-oriented applications, you need to keep in mind many things. Let the following checklist serve as a reminder.

- *Did you clean up after yourself?* Make sure that you restore toolbars and menus to their original state when the application ends.
- *Do the dialog boxes all work from the keyboard?* Don't forget to add hot keys and check the tab order carefully.
- *Did you make any assumptions about directories?* If your application reads or writes files, you can't assume that a particular directory exists or that it's the current directory.
- *Did you account for canceling all dialog boxes?* You can't assume that the user will end a dialog box by clicking the OK button.
- *Did you assume that no other worksheet are open?* If your application is the only workbook open during testing, you may overlook something that happens when other workbooks are open.
- *Did you test your application in monochrome VGA mode?* Doing so ensures that your dialog boxes and input screens are legible when running on minimal hardware.
- *Did you attempt to optimize the speed of your application?* For example, you often can speed up your application by declaring variable types and defining object variables.
- *Are your procedures adequately documented?* Will you understand your code if you revisit it in six months?
- *Did you include appropriate end user documentation?* Doing so often eliminates (or at least reduces) the number of follow-up questions.
- *Did you allow time to revise your application?* Chances are, the application won't be perfect the first time out. So build in some time to fix it.

Summary

- In this chapter, I described a relatively complex user-oriented application that was designed for two audiences.
- The next chapter discusses some additional resources that may help you master Excel.

Chapter 19

Other Resources

In This Chapter

- A list of other resources that you may find helpful

The information provided in this book is useful, but is by no means comprehensive. Therefore, I've compiled a list of additional resources that may help you become more proficient in Excel application development.

I've classified these resources into four categories:

- Microsoft technical support
- Microsoft Knowledge Base
- Excel discussion
- Periodicals and newsletters

Microsoft technical support

Technical support is the common term for personalized assistance provided by a software vendor. In this case, I'm talking about Microsoft assistance. Microsoft's technical support is available in several different forms, discussed here.

Telephone support

This is probably the most commonly used form of technical support — but it is by no means the most efficient. Telephone technical support representatives are trained to answer the most basic questions about the product. If you start getting into intermediate or advanced areas, you'll likely draw a blank and end up wasting your time and the support rep's time — and probably have only a hefty telephone bill to show for your efforts. In other words, telephone support is really for beginning users who don't mind spending money on phone calls.

For the record, here's how to contact Microsoft for technical support regarding Excel (for the U.S. only)

Recorded or fax information

This service is called FastTips, and it provides answers to common questions by fax or by a recorded message. It's free — including the phone call.

Telephone number:	(800) 936-4100
Hours:	24-hours a day, seven days a week

Standard support

Standard support is available weekdays and is free.

Telephone number:	(206) 635-7070
Hours:	6:00 am through 6:00 pm Pacific time

900 number priority support

This form of priority support is billed on your telephone bill.

Telephone number:	(900) 555-2100
Hours:	24-hours a day, seven days a week (except holidays)
Cost:	$2.00 per minute, $25.00 maximum

800 number priority support

This form of priority support is billed to your credit card.

Telephone number:	(800) 936-5700
Hours:	24-hours a day, seven days a week (except holidays)
Cost:	$25.00 per call

CompuServe support

Based on my experiences, I recommend CompuServe as the best route for Excel technical support. You'll need a CompuServe account, of course, but it's well worth the expense. The Excel Forum on CompuServe is divided into several areas, one of which deals exclusively with VBA. I've found that questions are answered quickly, and if the Microsoft reps can't come up with a solution, chances are another user will.

For an introductory CompuServe membership kit, call (800) 848-8199.

Microsoft Knowledge Base

This is the primary Microsoft product information source — a database of more than 25,000 detailed articles containing technical information, bug lists, fix lists and more. As I write this, the Knowledge Base contains 525 topics that deal with Excel 5 or VBA — and it's growing every month.

The knowledge base is available from several sources, including:

- *CompuServe*. The entire Knowledge Base is available on CompuServe. Access is free but normal CompuServe on-line charges apply.
- *Internet*. You can also access the Knowledge Base by anonymous ftp to ftp.microsoft.com (the IP address is 198.105.232.1).
- *Microsoft TechNet*. This is a subscription service that provides CD-ROMS on a monthly basis. Each month, you'll get the latest update of the entire Microsoft Knowledge Base in an easy-to-use searchable format. Figure 19-1 shows the TechNet software in action.

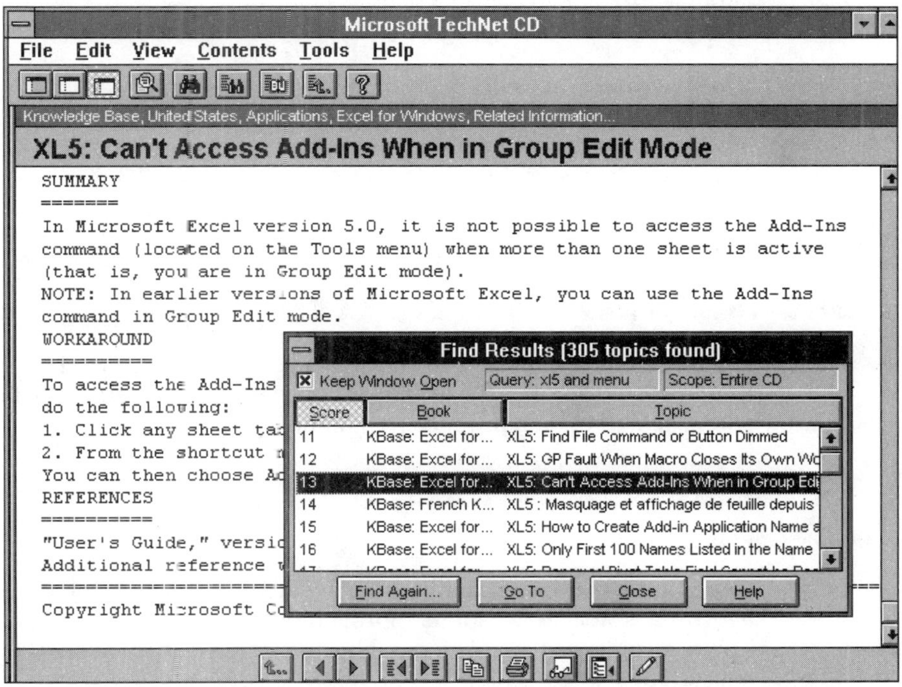

Figure 19-1: Microsoft's TechNet CD-ROM contains hundreds of useful articles about Excel and VBA — updated monthly.

Excel Discussion

There are two on-line resources that you can use to carry on discussion with other Excel users and developers.

CompuServe's Excel/VBA forum

If you're a CompuServe member, you should definitely check out the Excel/VBA forum. Besides providing technical support, as described above, this forum is an excellent place to meet other Excel developers and exchange ideas.

comp.apps.spreadsheets

USENET is an Internet service that provides access to several thousand different special interest groups that let you communicate with others who share common interests. One of the newsgroups is called comp.apps.spreadsheets. Although it's not one of the more popular newsgroups (it typically receives about a dozen or so new messages each day from users around the world), it is interesting to see what kinds of problems others are having.

Excel questions, answers, and comments account for roughly half of the messages. If you post a question to this newsgroup, chances are you'll see the answer within the next day or two — or it may show up in your e-mail box. And the answer may even be from me.

Periodicals and Newsletters

Personal computer users have no shortage of periodicals to choose from. Here's a list of some of the leading magazines and newsletters that cover spreadsheets, add-on products, and industry news.

InfoWorld

This is a weekly periodical published by IDG and designed for managers. *InfoWorld* is well-known for its thorough reviews and product comparisons. This is a controlled-circulation publication, and you may qualify for a free subscription.

Subscription information: (708) 647-7925

Inside Microsoft Excel

This is a monthly newsletter produced by the Cobb Group. Dig out your Excel packaging — it may include a coupon for a free three-month trial subscription.

Subscription information: (800) 223-8720

PC Magazine

PC Magazine, from Ziff-Davis, is thick, full of useful articles and ads, and comes out every two weeks! *PC Magazine* is the most technical of all the magazines listed here. Every issue has a column about spreadsheets.

Subscription information: (800) 289-0429

PC World

PC World is a monthly magazine from IDG that that covers all aspects of personal computing. Every issue has a column on spreadsheets, as well as lots of useful tips.

Subscription information: (800) 234-3498

PC/Computing

PC/Computing is another monthly magazine from Ziff-Davis that covers general computing topics, including spreadsheets.

Subscription information: (800) 365-2770

Visual Basic Programmer's Journal

This magazine, from Fawcette Technical Publications, is published bimonthly. Although it deals primarily with Visual Basic, it also covers VBA.

Subscription information: (303) 541-0610

Windows Magazine

Windows Magazine is a monthly from CMP Publications. As the name implies, it deals exclusively with Windows software — including spreadsheets.

Subscription information: (800) 829-9150

Windows Sources

Another monthly from Ziff-Davis, Windows Sources deals exclusively with Windows software.

Subscription information: (800) 365-3414

Chapter 20

Frequently Asked Questions About Excel and VBA

In This Chapter

- Lists of frequently asked questions about Excel and VBA
- Answers to those questions

If you like to cruise the Internet, you're undoubtedly familiar with FAQs — text files available for download that contain lists of *frequently asked questions* (and their answers) about a particular topic. These files are prevalent in the Usenet discussion groups, and are posted in an attempt to reduce the number of messages that ask the same questions over and over again. (But they rarely serve their intended purpose because the same questions keep appearing despite the FAQs.)

I've found that people tend to ask the same questions about Excel and VBA, so I put together a list of FAQs about Excel/VBA. Although this certainly won't answer *all* of your questions, it covers many common questions and may set you straight about a thing or two. I started collecting these questions when Excel 5 was first released. These questions (and many of the answers) came from the following sources:

- The Excel/VBA Forum on CompuServe
- The comp.apps.spreadsheets Usenet group on the Internet
- Microsoft's Knowledge Base
- Actual questions posed to me by clients and other Excel users

I organized this list of questions by classifying each question into one of eight categories:

- General VBA questions
- VBA modules

- Subroutines and functions
- Objects, properties, and methods
- VBA commands and statements
- Dialog boxes
- Add-ins
- Toolbars

In some cases, my classifications are rather arbitrary because the question could justifiably be in one or more other category. Also, questions within each category are listed in no particular order.

By the way, most of the information in this chapter is discussed in other chapters.

General VBA Questions

Why does Excel contain two macro languages?

Excel's two macro languages are the Visual Basic Programming System Applications Edition (VBA) and the Excel version 4.0 macro language (XLM). Microsoft included both languages in Excel 5 to ease the transition from XLM to VBA. Both languages give you nearly complete control over Excel 5.

Do XLM macros written for previous versions of Excel work in Excel 5?

Yes.

Should I learn both macro languages?

No! If you're just starting with Excel, ignore XLM and focus on VBA. The VBA language is more flexible and much easier to learn and use than XLM. In addition, XLM is essentially a dead language and won't be enhanced to include new features in subsequent versions of Excel. VBA is destined to be Microsoft's common macro language and eventually will be included in most Microsoft applications.

How does the Microsoft Visual Basic 3.0 language compare to Visual Basic for Applications?

The two languages are very similar, yet very different. VBA is designed to work with Microsoft applications. (Excel is just the first of many applications that will support VBA.) It does not produce stand-alone applications. Visual Basic 3.0 lets you create stand-alone applications (EXE files). Visual Basic programmers who use VBA will notice that VBA has a limited set of object properties for dialog box controls. For example, you can't format or align text in dialog box controls, and the events that you can use for the controls are limited to OnClick, OnChange, and OnShow. Visual Basic 3.0 has other events that you can work with (such as Focus, Keydown, and Mousedown). Finally, the user interfaces for the two products are very different. By and large, however, VBA is an excellent macro language that is well-suited to controlling Excel and other applications.

I'm a Visual Basic 3.0 programmer, and have accumulated many VBX custom controls. Can I use these with VBA?

No. The current version of VBA does not support custom controls.

Does VBA offer any new programming concepts compared to Visual Basic 3.0?

Yes, two of them: With..End With and For Each...End For.

Included in Visual Basic 4.0!

Is VBA a compiled language?

Yes. Although it doesn't generate EXE files, the code is compiled into p-code before it is executed, making it faster than an interpreted language.

I often call special functions (including Windows API functions) in DLLs from Visual Basic 3.0. Can I do this in VBA?

Yes. You can often perform otherwise impossible tasks by calling DLL functions directly from VBA.

Does Microsoft Word for Windows 6.0 support VBA?

The macro language in Word for Windows is WordBasic. It seems to be similar to VBA, but it's not really. However, you can control Word for Windows with Excel VBA using OLE automation. Word for Windows provides other applications with an object called "Basic." Using this object, VBA can send WordBasic instructions to Word for Windows. But Word for Windows cannot use OLE Automation to access other applications. It's quite likely that a future version of Word for Windows will include VBA.

I need to distribute a workbook to someone who's still using Excel 4. Is there a way to have Excel 5 record my actions to an XLM macro?

Yes. Choose Tools⇨Record Macro⇨Record New Macro, and then click the Options button. In the expanded dialog box click the MS Excel 4.0 Macro option button. And don't forget to save the workbook in the Excel 4 format.

Is there a way to automatically convert Excel 4 macros to VBA macros?

No. Such conversions must be done manually.

I have lots of experience with Excel 4 (XLM) macros, but I'm trying to learn VBA. How can I find the equivalent VBA command for an XLM macro function?

Excel's on-line help system contains a cross-reference of VBA equivalents for XLM macro functions. Choose the Help⇨Contents command and select Reference Information. Under General Reference, select Microsoft Excel Macro Functions Contents. Select Visual Basic Equivalents for Macro Functions and Commands. To see the VBA statement that is equivalent to an XLM macro function, click the first letter of the macro function and scroll through the list to find the macro function you're interested in.

Is there a way to automatically convert 1-2-3 or Quattro Pro macros to VBA macros?

No way.

Do I really need to be concerned with data types?

For simple subroutines, no. If you don't explicitly declare your variables Excel handles all the details behind the scenes. But if speed and efficient memory use are important to you, you should really declare all of your variables to be of the proper data type.

What is a *variant* data type?

A variant data type is unique to VBA. Variables that aren't specifically declared are assigned as a variant type, and VBA automatically converts the data to the proper type when it's used. This is particularly useful when getting values from a worksheet cell when you don't know in advance what the cell contains. Generally, it's a good idea to specifically declare your variables (using the Dim statement) because using variants is quite a bit slower.

Sometimes when I attempt to name a cell or range using the Name Box, Excel gives me a "Type Mismatch" error. The name is perfectly valid. What gives?

Most likely, you're trying to use a name that corresponds to one of the VBA or Excel constants (such as XLYes or VBOK). Despite the error message, the name is assigned. If you use the Insert Name command, you won't get this erroneous message.

Where can I find examples of VBA code?

When you install Excel, it places a file called SAMPLES.XLS in your EXCEL\SAMPLES directory. This files has lots of VBA code to peruse. Also, VBA's on-line help contains many short segments of code to demonstrate the use of methods and properties. Look for the word "Example" directly below the help topic name and click it. You can even copy this code to a module to try it out yourself.

I like VBA's on-line help file. Is there an easy way to print the entire help file?

No. However, you can get a copy of the VBA help file in Windows Write (WRI) format, which you can then print from. This file is available from several sources, including CompuServe, Genie, Microsoft on-line, the Microsoft Download Service (MSDL), the Internet (ftp.microsoft.com), and Microsoft Product Support Services

VBA Modules

Can I use the VBA macro recorder to record all of my macros?

No. Recording is useful only for very simple macros. Macro that use looping or any other type of program flow changes cannot be recorded. However, you can often take advantage of the macro recorder to write some parts of your code. This is usually much easier than entering the code manually.

Can you record everything that you do in Excel to a VBA macro?

No. Although most of your actions will generate some VBA code, a few commands are not recorded. For example, actions performed in the Module General or Module Format tabs of the Options dialog box are not recorded.

Does recording a VBA macro always ensure that you'll get "runnable" code?

In most cases, yes. But to demonstrate a case where it doesn't, try using drag-and-drop to copy a range of cells to a destination that contains non-blank cells. The resulting VBA code contains an error.

Why is there no toolbar button that will start macro recording at the current cursor position in a VBA module?

Good question. It sure would be handy. When Excel doesn't provide the tool you need, create your own. Here's a simple VBA subroutine that will start the macro recorder and put the code at the current position:

```
Sub MarkAndRecord()
    SendKeys "%TRM"
    SendKeys "%TRE"
End Sub
```

I have some macros that are general purpose in nature. I would like to have these available all the time. What's the best way to do this?

Consider storing those general purpose macros on your Personal Macro Workbook. This is a (normally) hidden workbook that is loaded automatically by Excel. When you record a macro, you have the option of recording it to your Personal Macro Workbook. The file, PERSONAL.XLS, is stored in your EXCEL\XLSTART directory.

Can I copy a macro from one workbook to another?

Certainly. Select the text and use the normal Edit menu commands to copy and paste using the Windows Clipboard. To copy a complete module to a different workbook, just press Ctrl and drag the module's tab to the other workbook.

Is there a way to view a VBA module and a worksheet at the same time? These are both in the same workbook.

Yes. Use the Window⇨New Window command to create a new window into the current workbook. You can activate sheets in each window independently of the other. You can have as many windows for a single workbook as you like.

When I insert a new module, it always starts with an "Option Explicit" line. What does this mean?

If this line is included at the top of a module, it means that you must declare every variable before you use it. If you don't want this line to appear in new modules, select the Tools⇨Options command, click the Module General tab, and uncheck the Require Variable Declaration check box. Then you can either declare variables or let VBA handle the data typing automatically.

Why does my VBA code appear in different colors? Can I change these colors?

VBA uses color to differentiate various types of text — comments, keywords, identifiers, statements with a syntax error, and so on. You can adjust these colors using the Tools⇨Options command (Module Format tab).

I want to delete a VBA module using VBA code. Can I do this?

Yes, you can use the Delete method for the Modules collection — as long as the code that deletes the module isn't contained in the module that you want to delete.

I can't seem to get the VBA line continuation character (underscore) to work.

Make sure that you precede the underscore with a space character. Also, be careful: If you copy and paste lines of code that contain continuation characters, you may get a GPF that crashes Excel. A final warning: Don't use a line continuation character between square brackets (this also crashes Excel).

I like to print my VBA modules in landscape orientation. For some reason, this setting is not saved with the file and I have to manually adjust it each session. Why is this?

This is a known problem in Excel 5. The page setup settings are not saved for VBA modules and always revert to their default settings. An easy workaround it is to write a macro to adjust the settings before printing.

I assigned a key combination to a VBA macro and then I changed the name of the macro. Now the key combination doesn't work.

When you change the name of a VBA subroutine that's executed by a key combination, you get an error message the first time you attempt to invoke the macro. After the first time, it works correctly. This is a known problem in Excel 5.

The Module Format tab of the Options dialog box lets me change the font used in my VBA modules. The font list doesn't show all of the fonts displayed on my system. Why not?

The font list shows only your installed fixed-width fonts. Actually, you can type in any installed font and it will be used in your VBA modules. Most people find that it's much easier to work with fixed-width fonts when writing and editing code.

When I make a change — even a minor change — to my VBA code, there is a delay before it runs the first time. Why is this?

Excel detects when you make a change to your VBA code, and recompiles it before you can execute it again. The time delay should only be apparent the first time you execute the new code.

Are there any VBA code-entry tricks I should be aware of?

One trick that I find particularly useful is the undocumented multilevel undo (or Alt+Backspace) and redo (or F4). Unlike the undo in a worksheet, you can use these commands repeatedly. For example, if you delete 10 lines using 10 separate commands, you can get each line back in turn by press Alt+Backspace 10 times.

Is it possible to hide a VBA sheet? When a VBA module is active, there is no Format command on the menu.

Yes. In a VBA module the command to hide the current sheet is Edit⇨Sheet⇨Hide.

Why isn't the File⇨Print Preview command available in a VBA module?

The Excel designers apparently thought this command was not necessary because you can't really do any formatting on a VBA module sheet. If you really must preview a VBA module, copy the code to a worksheet and use the worksheet's print preview feature.

I'm having trouble with the concatenation operator (&) in VBA. When I try to concatenate two strings, I get an error message.

This is probably because VBA is interpreting the ampersand as a type declaration character. Make sure you insert a space before and after the concatenation operator.

I've noticed after deleting a major amount of VBA code that the XLS file size is not reduced accordingly. Why is this?

I'm not sure why this happens, but it does. Apparently, VBA keeps the old code around for some reason. This sometimes causes some subtle problems with variables that you no longer use. The only way I know of to fix it is to start with an empty workbook and use the Clipboard to copy the VBA code to a blank module.

I distributed an XLS application to many users. On some machines, my VBA error-handling procedures don't work. Why not?

The error-handling procedures won't work if the user has the Break on All Errors option set. This option is available in the Options dialog box under the Module General tab. Unfortunately, there is no easy way to change this setting using VBA. To avoid this problem, you can distribute your application as an XLA add-in.

Subroutines and Functions

What's the difference between a VBA subroutine and a macro?

Nothing really. With Excel 5, these terms can be used pretty much interchangeably.

How can I run a VBA subroutine macro?

You can choose from many methods:

- *From another subroutine,* just enter the subroutine name as a statement, or use the Call keyword.
- *Assign a shortcut key to the macro* using the Tools⇨Macro command.
- *Assign the macro to a command* on the Tools menu using the Tools⇨Macro command.
- *Assign the macro to an object* such as a button or rectangle. Select the object and use the Tools⇨Assign Macro command. This technique changes the OnAction property of the object.
- *Assign the macro to a toolbar button,* by using the View⇨Toolbars command, and then click the Customize button.

- *Give the subroutine any of four special names* to cause it to execute automatically. The special names are Auto_Open, Auto_Close, Auto_Activate, and Auto_Deactivate.
- *Change certain properties of certain objects* to cause the macro to execute when a particular event occurs. Example of such properties are OnTime, OnDoubleClick, OnEntry, OnKey. There are several others.

Can a custom worksheet function written in VBA perform the same types of actions as a subroutine?

No. Functions called from worksheets have some limitations. In general, they must be strictly "passive" — they can't change the active cell, open workbooks, change the active sheet, and so on. Functions can perform only calculations. An exception to this rule is the VBA MsgBox function. A custom function can display a MsgBox whenever it is recalculated. This is very handy for debugging a custom function.

I'm very familiar with creating formulas in Excel. Does VBA use the same mathematical and logical operators?

Yes. And it includes some additional operators that aren't valid in formulas. These new operators are

\	Division with an integer result
Eqv	Returns True if both expressions are true or both are false
Imp	Logical implication on two expressions
Is	Compares two object variables
Like	Compares two strings using wildcard characters
Xor	Returns True if only one expression is true

How can I execute a subroutine that's in a different workbook?

First, set up a reference to the workbook that contains the subroutine that you want to call (references are set up with the Tools⇨References command). Then, precede the subroutine name with the workbook name (in square brackets), a period, and the module name (in square brackets). The following example calls the SetUp procedure in Module1 of BUDGET.XLS:

```
[BUDGET.XLS].[Module1].SetUp
```

I've created several custom functions using VBA. I like to use these functions in my worksheet formulas, but I find it inconvenient to precede the function name with the workbook name. Is there any way around this?

Yes. Convert the workbook that holds the function definitions to an XLA add-in. When the add-in is open, you can use the functions in any other worksheet without referencing the function's filename.

I have a workbook with an Auto_Open subroutine. Is there a way to prevent this from executing when I open the workbook?

Yes. Hold down Shift when you issue the File⇨Open command. This technique also works with Auto_Close, Auto_Activate, and Auto_Deactivate.

I would like a particular workbook to be loaded every time I start Excel. I would also like a macro in this workbook to execute automatically. Am I asking too much?

Not at all. To open the workbook automatically, just store it in your EXCEL\XLSTART directory. To have the macro execute automatically, just name it Auto_Open.

Can I use the same Subroutine or Function name in multiple open workbooks?

Sure. If you call a subroutine from a VBA procedure, it first searches for the subroutine in the current workbook. If not found, it then searches in all workbooks to which the current workbook has references (references are set up with the Tools⇨References command). It runs the first subroutine it finds with the name you specified.

I created a custom worksheet function. When I access this function using the Function Wizard, it says "no help available." How can I get Function Wizard to display a description of this function?

In your VBA module, press F2 to access the Browser. Select the workbook that contains the function from the Libraries/Worksheets drop-down list, select the module in the Objects/Modules list box, and select your function from the Methods/Properties list box. Click the Options button and enter the descriptive text in the Description box.

Is it possible to write recursive functions in VBA?

A recursive function is a function that calls itself a number of times. Theoretically, it's possible. But in practice, you often run into stack limitations that cause the function to fail. In general, it's best to avoid using recursive functions in VBA.

Are variables in a VBA procedure available to other VBA procedures? What if the procedure is in a different module? Or in a different workbook?

You're talking about a variable's scope. There are three levels of scope: local, module-level, and public. Local variables have the narrowest scope and are declared within a procedure. A local variable is visible only to the procedure in which it was declared. Module-level variables are declared at the top of a module, prior to the first procedure. Module-level variables are visible to all procedures in the module. Public variables have the broadest scope, and they are declared using the Public keyword.

Is it possible to pass arguments to a VBA subroutine executed by a custom menu?

Yes. Assume you have a subroutine called MySub, and it's designed to accept one argument. Further assume that you would like to call the subroutine from a custom menu, and pass the value 10 as an argument. In the menu editor, specify the macro and its argument value separated by a spaced and enclosed in single quotes, like this:

```
'MySub 10'
```

To pass additional arguments, separate each argument with a comma.

I'm trying to write a VBA procedure that executes an SQL query on an external database. I'm having lots of problems with long queries. Am I missing something?

Before you can work with SQL databases, you need to load the XLODBC.XLA add-in. This gives you access to several new functions. The SQLExecQuery and SQLRequest functions are used to perform a query, but they have some problems. The most notable problem is that the query cannot exceed 255 characters. A common workaround is to convert a long query string into an array, and then pass the array. However, if you do this, each array element cannot exceed 127 characters. Another approach is to store your query in a worksheet range, and then use a statement such as:

```
Res = _
SQLExecQuery(Connection,Worksheets("Sheet1").Range("D1:D4"))
```

In this case, the query is stored in four cells on Sheet1. If you use this method, each cell can contain no more than 127 characters.

Can you use Excel's built-in worksheet functions in your VBA code?

Yes. The trick is to precede the function name with the Application object. For example, you could access the POWER worksheet functions with a statement such as:

```
Ans = Application.Power(5, 3)
```

This example raises 5 to the third power. Generally, if VBA includes an equivalent function you cannot use Excel's worksheet version. For example, because VBA has a function to compute square roots (Sqr) you cannot use the SQRT worksheet function in your VBA code.

Is it possible to create your own DLLs (dynamic link libraries) that can be called from Excel VBA code?

Yes. The procedure is described in the Microsoft Excel Developer's Kit, which is available directly from Microsoft or at many retail stores. You do, however, need to know how to program in C or Pascal to create DLLs.

Objects, Properties, and Methods

I don't understand the concept of objects. Is there a listing of all of the Excel objects I can use?

Yes. Appendix A of this book presents the complete Excel object model. This shows you how the objects relate to each other, and which objects are contained within other objects.

I'm overwhelmed with all of the properties and methods available. How can I find out which methods and properties are available for a particular object?

There are several ways. Appendix B of this book lists the methods and properties available for each object. You can also use the Object Browser from a VBA module. Press F2 to access the Object Browser. Choose Excel from the Libraries/Workbooks drop-down list. The list on the left shows all of the Excel objects. When you select an object, its corresponding properties and methods appear in the list on the right (unfortunately, there's no indication as to whether the entry in the right list is an object or a property). The on-line help system for VBA is very extensive, and lists the properties and methods available for every object. The easiest way to access this is to enter the object in your VBA module and move the cursor anywhere within the object name. Press F1 and you'll get the help topic appropriate for the object.

What's the story with collections? Is a collection an object? What are collections?

A collection is an object that contains a group of related objects. A collection is designated by a plural noun. For example, the Worksheets collection is an object that contains all of the Worksheet objects in a workbook. You can think of this as an array. Worksheets(1), for example, refers to the first Worksheet object in the workbook. Rather than use index numbers, you can also use the actual worksheet name, such as Worksheets("Sheet1"). The concept of a collection makes it easy to work with all related objects at once, and to loop through all objects in a collection.

I've discovered that I can often use square brackets in place of a lengthy object reference in VBA. For example, I can use [Sheet1!A1] instead of Sheets("Sheet1").Range("A1"). Is this a good practice?

Although it may save you a few seconds when entering the code, code that uses square brackets takes slightly longer to execute. For some lengthy procedures, this may make a noticeable difference. Also, this method is less flexible because you can't use names within brackets. For example, if you have a range named summary, [Sheet1!summary] will not work.

Can a VBA procedure access a cell's value in a workbook that is not open?

No.

I want to use the OnDoubleClick property to execute a macro when I double-click a cell. But I also like the idea of editing cell contents directly in the cell (which occurs when I double-click). Does this mean that I have to turn off the Edit Directly in Cell setting in the Edit tab of the Options dialog box?

No. This setting is automatically disabled when the OnDoubleClick property of a worksheet contains a macro.

What's the difference between Application.Goto and Range.Select?

Use Application.Goto to select a named range in a workbook (range names are global in a workbook). Application.Goto may or may not make another sheet the active sheet. Range.Select will select a range on the *active* worksheet only.

Is there a VBA command to quit Excel? When I try to record the File⇨Exit command, Excel closes down before I can see what code it generates!

Use Application.Quit to end Excel.

How can I turn off the screen updating while a macro is running?

The following statement turns off screen updating and speeds up macros that modify the display:

```
Application.ScreenUpdating=False.
```

I recorded a VBA macro that copies a range and pastes it to another area. The macro uses the Select method. Is there a more efficient way to copy and paste?

Yes. Although the macro recorder selects cells before copying them, selecting is not necessary and slows down your macro. Recording a very simple copy and paste operation generates four lines of VBA code (two of which use the Select method). Here's an example:

```
Range("A1").Select
Selection.Copy
Range("B1").Select
ActiveSheet.Paste
```

These four lines can be replaced with a single statement, such as:

```
Range("A1").Copy(Range("B1"))
```

Notice that this statement does not use the Select method.

My VBA macro needs to count the number of rows selected by the user. Using Selection.Rows.Count doesn't work when nonadjacent rows are selected. Is this a bug?

Actually, this is the way it's supposed to work. The Count method returns the number of elements in only the *first* Area of the selection (a noncontiguous selection has multiple areas). To get an accurate row count your VBA code must first determine the number of areas in the selection and then count the number of rows in each area. Use Selection.Areas.Count to count the number of areas. By the way, this is also relevant to counting columns and cells.

Is there a workbook property that will force an Excel workbook to always remain visible — similar to the "Always on Top" option available in WinHelp?

No.

When I use the Data⇨Filter⇨AutoFilter command to filter a list of data, I can select the filtered list and copy it to another location. Only the visible cells are copied. But when I try to do this with VBA code, the hidden cells are also copied. Problem or feature?

Problem — but there's an easy workaround. Just use the following statement prior to copying the cells in your VBA code.

```
Selection.SpecialCells(xlVisible).Select
```

If you're recording a macro, you'll need to perform one additional step before copying the filtered data. Select the Edit⇨GoTo command, click Special, and then select the Visible Cells Only option.

Using the Time function in VBA gives me an OLE Automation 440 error. What's wrong?

This is a strange problem that occurs on a very small percentage of computers. Fortunately, there's an easy solution. Run the Windows Control Panel and access the International utility. Add leading zeros to the date format setting and your problem will be gone.

Is there a way to stop Excel from displaying messages while my macro is running?

The following statement turns off Excel's warning messages:

```
Application.DisplayAlerts = False
```

Does using Application.DisplayAlerts=False prevent the display of *all* warning messages?

Unfortunately, no. For example, it doesn't eliminate the "Selection is too large. Continue without undo?" message box. If this message always appears, you may be able to use Application.SendKeys("~") to send an Enter keystroke to dismiss the message box. It also doesn't eliminate the messages that come from add-ins (for example, Solver).

I can't find any VBA commands to automate Solver. Does this mean I can't create macros that use Solver?

Solver is an add-in, not part of Excel. Therefore, it's not part of Excel's object model and cannot be manipulated with VBA. However, you can control Solver using XLM macro code executed from a VBA module. To see how this works, try recording your actions to a VBA macro while setting up a problem for Solver.

VBA Commands and Statements

Is there a VBA command to select the last entry in a column or row. Normally, I can use Ctrl+↓ or Ctrl+→ to do this, but how can I do it with a macro?

The VBA equivalent for Ctrl+↓ is

```
Selection.End(XLDown).Select
```

The constants used for the other directions are XLToLeft, XLToRight, and XLUp.

Is it possible to call an Excel 5 VBA routine from an Excel 4.0 XLM macro?

Yes, by using the Run function. For example, the macro below runs the "Test" subroutine contained in Module1 in workbook BOOK1.XLS.

```
=RUN(BOOK1.XLS!Module1.Test)
```

Is there a way to disable the shortcut menus that appear when the user clicks the right mouse button?

Yes. There are actually 25 different shortcut menus, each of which can be selectively disabled using the ShortcutMenus method. For example, to disable the shortcut menu that appears when you right-click a cell, use the following:

```
ShortcutMenus(xlWorksheetCell).Enabled = False
```

How can I change the mouse pointer to something else, like an hourglass?

There is no way to do this using VBA. You may be able to use a Windows API call to do this, but it doesn't always work properly because Excel seems to reset the mouse pointer frequently.

VBA references can get very lengthy, especially when you need to fully qualify an object by referencing its sheet and workbook. Is there a way to reduce the length of these references?

Yes, create an object variable using the Set command. Here's an example:

```
Dim MyRange as Object
Set _
MyRange=Workbooks("MyBook").Worksheets("MySheet").Range("A1")
```

After the Set statement is executed, you can refer to the Range object simply as MyRange. For example, you can assign a value to the range with:

```
MyRange.Value=10
```

Besides making it easier to refer to objects, using object variables can also make your code execute faster.

Is there a way to dimension an array if you don't know how many elements it will have?

Yes. You can dimension the array with the Dim command using empty parentheses, and then redimension with the ReDim command when you know how many elements it has. Use ReDim Preserve if you don't want to lose the current array contents when redimensioning it.

Is there a way to initialize an array without looping through each element?

Yes, by using the Array function — which actually returns a variant that contains an array. Here's an example that initializes an array to hold abbreviations for the first six months of the year.

```
Months= Array("Jan", "Feb", "Mar", "Apr", "May", "Jun")
```

I tried the example in the previous question and found that Months(1) returns *Feb*, not *Jan*. Is this a bug?

No. Unless you tell it otherwise, VBA uses 0 as the first index number for an array. If you want your arrays to start with 1, insert the following statement at the top of your VBA module:

```
Option Base 1
```

What's the difference between variables declared using Global and variables declared using Public?

Nothing. Global is included with VBA for compatibility with other versions of Basic. Public is preferred, but using Global does exactly the same thing.

I'm confused over the Public keyword. According to the Visual Basic User's Guide: "Variables declared using the Public statement are available to all procedures in all modules in all applications unless Option Private Module is in effect; in which case, the variables are Public only within the project in which they reside." This does not seem to be the case. Why?

For this to work, you must use the Tools⇨References command (available only in VBA modules) to register the workbook that contains the reference you want to use.

I'm having trouble using SendKeys to send a right bracket (]). It tells me there's an invalid procedure call.

This is a known bug in Excel 5 with no known workaround.

I need to prompt a user for an answer and insert the answer into a cell. Is there a way to do this without developing a custom dialog box?

Sure, the InputBox function makes this a snap. The VBA statement that follows demonstrates. In this example, the input box displays a prompt ("Enter a number") and the number entered is entered into cell B1 on the active sheet of the active workbook.

```
Range("B1").Value = InputBox("Enter a number")
```

Is there any way to read or write information to INI files using VBA?

Although VBA does not support this directly, you can use a Windows API call to read and write information to INI files. Use the GetPrivateProfileString and WritePrivateProfileString API functions.

I use VBA's FileCopy command to copy files. But unlike every other copy utility I've used, this command changes the file's date and time to the time the copying occurred. Feature or bug?

This is a known bug. A workaround involves changing the system's date and time to the date and time of the file before performing the copy operation.

Dialog Boxes

Calling a custom dialog box worked fine, until I converted the XLS file to an XLA add-in. Now, I get an error message whenever I try to access the custom dialog box using the Show method. What's wrong?

You need to qualify the reference to the dialog sheet with a reference to its workbook. This makes the dialog box callable when any workbook is active. Using ThisWorkbook is the most general way to do this. Here's an example:

```
ThisWorkbook.Dialogsheets("Dialog1").Show.
```

How can you give the controls in a custom dialog box more meaningful names? Names like Option Button 1 and Button 12 are difficult to use.

Use the Name Box at the left side of the input line. This is the same tool used to provide names for cells and ranges.

My custom dialog box has several buttons that all call the same macro. How can I determine which button was clicked?

Use Application.Caller or ActiveDialog.Focus.

When I try to set the value of a check box to XLMixed, I get an error (even though the on-line help states that this is valid). Is the Help system wrong?

Yes, the Help system is wrong in this case.

I know you can link the value of a custom dialog box control to a worksheet cell, but I can't get this to work with some controls. Why?

Not all dialog box controls can be linked to cells. Right-click a control and then select the Control tab of the Format Object dialog box. If Cell Link does not appear as an option, that control cannot be linked to a cell. You'll have to write VBA code to transfer the information to a cell.

Some of my applications that use custom dialog boxes generate a error that tells me I'm out of stack space. What gives?

This error may occur if you try to display more than two dialog boxes at a time. Generally, you should close a dialog box before displaying another one. SQL queries also use this stack space, so it's often not possible to execute an SQL query while a dialog box is displayed.

I need to display a progress indicator (like those used during software installation) while a lengthy process is being executed. How can I do this?

Unfortunately, there is no way to do this. You can use the status bar or Excel's title bar to display progress reports (but these aren't very noticeable). Another option is to display the progress information in a small workbook window (but you have to make sure this window is always visible).

I have several 1-2-3 for Windows files and Quattro Pro for Windows files that contain custom dialog boxes. Is there a utility to convert these to Excel dialog boxes?

No.

The Help file says that it's not possible to create a list box that allows multiple selections. Is there any way around this?

Yes. The Help file is wrong. Set the Multiselect property to true.

I need to concatenate strings and display them in a list box. But when I do so, they aren't aligned properly. How can I get them to display equal spacing between strings?

Unfortunately, you can't. The font used to display text in a dialog box uses proportional spacing — which makes it impossible to line up text. Even using chr(9), the tab character, doesn't work.

What's the best way to display a built-in Excel dialog box from VBA?

Most (but not all) of Excel's dialog boxes can be displayed using the Application.Dialogs method. For example, the following statement displays the dialog box that normally appears when you issue the File⇨Open command:

```
Application.Dialogs(xlDialogOpen).Show
```

Use the Object Browser to display a list of the constants for the built-in dialog boxes (press F2 while in a VBA module, or select the View⇨Object Browser command). Then select the Excel library and then the Constants object. The Method/Properties list will display the constants for the built-in dialogs (they all begin with xlDialog).

How can I change the font or alignment of text in a label object in a custom dialog box?

You can't. One way to get around this is to use a linked picture. Create the text you want to display in a worksheet range and then copy the range to the Clipboard. Then activate your dialog sheet, hold down Shift, and choose the Edit⇨Paste Picture Link command. This creates a picture object that displays the current contents of the linked range — including formatting.

My dialog box has a Help button, which has the HelpButton property set to True. Pressing F1 usually calls up my custom Help file. However, if an edit box has the focus, F1 doesn't work. What's wrong?

This appears to be a bug in Excel 5 — and the bug is more extensive than this questions indicates. F1 will not work if an edit box, list box, drop down, or scroll bar has the focus.

Is it possible to create a custom dialog box without a title bar?

No, but you can make the dialog box's caption blank by deleting the text. You can also do this from VBA using a statement such as:

```
Dialogsheets("Dialog1").DialogFrame.Caption="".
```

When I double-click an item in a list box on a custom dialog box, the dialog box is dismissed (as if I clicked the OK button). Why does this happen?

In custom dialog boxes, double-clicking an option button or an item in a standard list box activates the default button if one has been set. If you don't want this to happen, turn off the Default attribute for all of the buttons in the dialog box.

Can I create a custom dialog box that displays in the same size, regardless of the video display resolution?

No. To make sure your custom dialog boxes display properly on all video displays, you should create the dialog boxes using standard VGA mode.

Is it possible to create a custom dialog box that lets the user select a range in a worksheet by pointing — like the method used in the built-in Goal Seek dialog box?

Yes. Add an edit box to your dialog, right-click it and choose Format Object from the shortcut menu. Then select the Reference option to make the edit box accept a cell or range (the user can enter the range reference directly, or point to it in the worksheet using standard methods).

I understand that you can place custom dialog box controls directly on a worksheet. I'm not able to place some of the controls on a worksheet. What's wrong?

Although you can insert most dialog box objects on a worksheet, the following objects cannot be inserted: edit boxes, combination list-edit boxes, and combination drop-down edit boxes.

Custom dialog boxes always appear in the position where the last dialog box appeared. Is there a way to change the position of a custom dialog box?

Yes. You can change the Left and Top properties of the DialogFrame object before you display the dialog box.

Excel sometimes crashes when I attempt to format a custom dialog box using the Format⇨Object command.

This is a known problem (bug), and occurs only when the dialog sheet is protected. To avoid this, don't protect your dialog sheet until after you've made all of your edits and changes.

How can I add another dialog box to a dialog sheet?

You can't. Each dialog sheet can hold only one dialog box.

When I try to copy a cell or range to a custom dialog box, I get an error message stating that locked cells cannot be changed. What does this mean?

This is an erroneous error message. To copy a cell or range to a dialog sheet, use the Edit⇨Paste Picture command or the Edit⇨Paste Picture Link command (you must hold down Shift to access these menu commands).

I'm not able to print anything when a custom dialog box is displayed. Is this right?

I'm not sure if it's right, but that's the way it is. You must dismiss your dialog box before using the PrintOut or PrintPreview method.

Is there a way to change the grid size in a custom dialog box?

No. If you need to position a control precisely turn the grid off.

Add-ins

Where can I get add-ins?

You can get Excel add-ins from a number of places:

- Excel includes several add-ins that you can attach if you need.
- Third-party developers sell add-ins for special purposes.
- Shareware developers distribute add-ins on bulletin boards and on-line services.
- You can create your own add-ins using the Tools⇨Add-Ins command from a VBA module.

When I add an add-in to the Add-Ins dialog box, it shows up without a name or description. How can I give my add-ins a description?

Before creating the add-in, use the File⇨Summary Info command to bring up the Summary Info dialog box. In the Title box, enter the text that you want to appear in the Add-Ins dialog box. In the Comments field enter the description for the add-in. Then create the add-in as usual.

How can I write a VBA macro to create an add-in? I've searched everywhere for a VBA command and can't find it.

There is no VBA command to create an add-in. You can, however, use an XLM macro to do so. The following VBA statement creates an add-in called MYADDIN.

```
ExecuteExcel4Macro  "VBA.MAKE.ADDIN(""MYADDIN.XLA"")"
```

I have several add-ins that I no longer use, yet I can't figure out how to remove them from the Add-Ins Available list in the Add-Ins dialog box. What's the story?

There is no way to remove unwanted add-ins from the list directly from Excel. Edit your EXCEL5.INI file (located in your WINDOWS directory) and remove the references to the add-in files you don't want listed.

What's the difference between an XLS file and an XLA file created from it? Is the XLA version compiled? Does it run faster?

There isn't a great deal of difference between the files, and you generally won't notice any speed differences. VBA code is always "compiled" before it is executed. This is true if it's in an XLS file or an XLA file. The compilation creates p-code, which is faster than simply interpreting each statement. However, XLA files contain the actual VBA code, not compiled code. The main difference is that the casual user can't view XLA files.

I used a file viewer to examine an XLA add-in that I created, and I can still see the comments I inserted into my VBA code. Doesn't Excel remove these comments before creating an XLA file?

No. The comments and spaces remain in the XLA file, making it larger than it need be. To make your XLA file as small as possible, you should remove all comments, extra spaces, and blank lines from your VBA code before creating the add-in.

Is there any way to automatically remove all comments, excess spaces, and blank lines from a VBA module?

No. However, you can use the Edit⇨ Replace command from a VBA module to help you. For example, to remove excess spaces, replace all occurrences of two spaces with one space. And if you've used apostrophes only for comments, you can replace '* (that's an apostrophe followed by an asterisk) with nothing — but make sure you check the Use Pattern Matching option. I know of no way to automatically remove blank lines from a VBA module.

Are my XLA add-ins safe? In other words, if I distribute an XLA file, can I be assured that no one else will be able to view my code?

Although the Excel manuals claim that there is no way to recover VBA code from an XLA file, this definitely is not true. A few simple VBA commands is all it takes to convert an XLA back to its original XLS. To make it more difficult, you should protect the sheets on your workbook with a password before creating an add-in. Even then, it's likely that the password can be broken by someone who knows the secret.

Doesn't protecting the add-in with a password help keep it secure?

You can password protect add-in files, but whoever uses the add-in must know the password in order to open the file. And if the XLA add-in file can be opened, someone who knows the secrets can probably convert it back to an XLS file.

What is the secret of recovering the XLS version of an XLA file?

If I told you it wouldn't be a secret.

Toolbars

I added a custom button to a toolbar, but the tool tip continues to display "Custom." How can I get it to show something more meaningful?

The tool tip for a toolbar button is actually the Name property of the button. The only way to change the Name property is by using VBA macro code. Here's an example that will display "Process Data" as a tool tip for the first button on a toolbar named MyBar:

```
Toolbars("MyBar").ToolbarButtons(1).Name = "Process Data"
```

When creating custom menus and toolbar buttons, how do you set the status bar line to display descriptive information about the selected item?

Use the Tools⇨Macro command, select the name of the macro assigned to the toolbar button or menu item, and then click the Options button. In the Macro Options dialog box, enter the text into the text box labeled Status Bar Text. To assign the status bar text with VBA code, use a statement such as:

```
Application.MacroOptions Macro:="myMacro", StatusBar:= _
    "My Text"
```

I have a macro attached to a toolbar button. Is it possible to have the macro perform a different action if the user presses Shift while the button is clicked?

Yes, but you have to use a Windows API call to do it. The GetKeyState API function lets you determine which keys are pressed. Your macro can then take appropriate action.

How can you change the name of a custom toolbar? Whenever I try to do so by using the Name property, I get an error stating that Name is not a writable property. (According to the Help file, it is a read-write property).

The Help file is wrong. Oddly (and unfortunately), there is no way to change the name of a custom toolbar.

Can a toolbar contain more than one row of buttons?

Yes and no. You can change the size and dimensions of free-floating toolbars and make them any number of rows and columns you want. But if you plan to dock the toolbar on an edge of the window it can have only one row or column of toolbar buttons.

I spent a lot of time creating custom toolbars in Excel 4. When I upgraded to Excel 5 they were gone. Tell me I don't have to do all of this work again.

You don't have to do all of that work again. Use the File⇨Open command to open EXCEL.XLB (stored in your WINDOWS directory). This brings your old toolbars back to life. When you exit Excel, they are saved automatically to EXCEL5.XLB.

I like to dock my toolbars to the left or right edge of the screen. Some toolbars just refuse to be docked there. What gives?

If the toolbar contains nonstandard toolbar buttons, they can't be docked on the right or left. Nonstandard toolbar buttons include Font, Font Size, Zoom Control, Color, and a few others.

I have a custom toolbar, but cannot reference a specific toolbar button (named MyButton) in VBA using the ToolbarButton method. For example, the following statement generates an error:

```
MsgBox _
Toolbars("MyToolbar").ToolbarButtons("MyButton").OnAction
```

The on-line help erroneously states that you can use a toolbar button's name to index toolbar buttons. This doesn't work. Rather, you must use a number: 1 for the first button, 2 for the second button, and so on. Also, be aware that a spacer in a toolbar counts as a button. So if your toolbar has two buttons with a space in between them, the index number for the second button is 3 (not 2).

I've noticed that some programs have "secret" commands that display a list of the people who developed the program. Is there such a command in Excel?

Yes. These hidden messages are sometimes known as "Easter Eggs." To see the list of Excel developers, you need to customize a toolbar by adding the Solitaire button. Then, hold down Shift, Ctrl, and Alt and click the Solitaire button. You'll be greeted with an interesting animation. To stop it, press Esc.

Part V

Appendixes

Appendix A

Excel 5.0 Object Model Reference

Excel contains 128 objects, each of which can be manipulated using VBA. This appendix contains a complete list of these objects arranged heirarchically. For example, the Application object can contain a MenuBar object, which can contain a Menu object, which can contain a MenuItem object. Objects marked with an asterisk can be part of a collections. For example, there is a MenuBars collection.

Application Object (Excel)

- **AddIn***
- **Debug**
- **Dialog***
- **MenuBar***
  - *Menu**
    - MenuItem*
- **Toolbar***
  - *ToolbarButton**
- **Window***
  - *PageSetup*
  - *Pane**
- **Workbook***
  - *Chart**
    - Axis
      - *AxisTitle*
      - *Gridlines*
      - *TickLabels*
    - ChartArea
    - ChartGroup*
      - *ChartTitle*
      - *DownBars*
      - *DropLines*
      - *HiLoLines*
      - *Series**
        - ErrorBars
        - DataLabel*
        - Point*
          - DataLabel
        - Trendline*
          - DataLabel

- *SeriesLines*
- *UpBars*

Corners

DrawingObjects*

- *Arc**
- *Button**
- *ChartObject**
  - Chart
- *CheckBox**
- *Drawing**
- *DropDown**
- *GroupBox**
- *GroupObject**
- *Label**
- *Line**
- *ListBox**
- *OLEObject**
  - Object
- *OptionButton**
- *Oval**
- *Picture**
- *Rectangle**
- *ScrollBar**
- *Spinner**
- *TextBox**

Floor

Legend

- *LegendEntry**
  - LegendKey

PageSetup

PlotArea

Walls

*DialogSheet**

DialogFrame

DrawingObjects*

- *Arc**
- *Button**
- *ChartObject**
  - Chart
- *CheckBox**
- *Drawing**
- *DropDown**
- *EditBox**
- *GroupBox**
- *GroupObject**
- *Label**
- *Line**
- *ListBox**

- *OLEObject**
    - Object
- *OptionButton**
- *Oval**
- *Picture**
- *Rectangle**
- *ScrollBar**
- *Spinner**
- *TextBox**

PageSetup

- *Module**
    - PageSetup
- *Name**
- *RoutingSlip*
- *Style**
    - Border
    - Font
    - Interior
- *Window**
    - Pane*
- *Worksheet**
    - DrawingObjects*
        - *Arc**
        - *Button**
        - *ChartObject**
            - Chart
        - *CheckBox**
        - *Drawing**
        - *DropDown**
        - *GroupBox**
        - *GroupObject**
        - *Label**
        - *Line**
        - *ListBox**
        - *OLEObject**
            - Object
        - *OptionButton**
        - *Oval**
        - *Picture**
        - *Rectangle**
        - *ScrollBar**
        - *Spinner**
        - *TextBox**
    - Outline
    - PageSetup
    - PivotTable*
        - *PivotField**
            - PivotItem*
    - Range

*Areas**
Border
Characters
Font
Font
Interior
Name
SoundNote
Style
Border
Font
Interior
Scenarios*

**** Collection***

Appendix B

Excel Object, Property, and Method Reference

This appendix contains a comprehensive listing of every object, property, and method available in Excel 5. The objects are listed in alphabetical order. For complete details consult Excel's on-line help.

AddIn Object

An add-in, either installed or not installed.

Methods

(None)

Properties

```
AddIn.Application
AddIn.Author
AddIn.Comments
AddIn.Creator
AddIn.FullName
AddIn.Installed
AddIn.Keywords
AddIn.Name
AddIn.Parent
AddIn.Path
AddIn.Subject
AddIn.Title
```

AddIns Object

A collection of AddIn objects.

Methods

```
AddIns.Add
AddIns.Item
```

Properties

```
AddIns.Application
AddIns.Count
AddIns.Creator
AddIns.Parent
```

Application Object

Excel itself; note that Excel's worksheet functions are actually methods of the application object.

Methods

```
Application.Acos
Application.Acosh
Application.ActivateMicrosoftApp
Application.AddChartAutoFormat
Application.AddCustomList
Application.AddIns
Application.And
Application.Asin
Application.Asinh
Application.Atan2
Application.Atanh
Application.AveDev
Application.Average
Application.BetaDist
Application.BetaInv
Application.BinomDist
Application.Calculate
Application.Ceiling
Application.Cells
Application.CentimetersToPoints
Application.Charts
Application.CheckSpelling
Application.ChiDist
Application.ChiInv
Application.ChiTest
Application.Choose
Application.Clean
Application.Columns
Application.Combin
Application.Confidence
Application.ConvertFormula
Application.Correl
Application.Cosh
Application.Count
Application.CountA
Application.CountBlank
Application.CountIf
Application.Covar
Application.CritBinom
Application.DAverage
Application.Days360
Application.Db
Application.DCount
Application.DCountA
Application.Ddb
Application.DDEExecute
Application.DDEInitiate
Application.DDEPoke
Application.DDERequest
Application.DDETerminate
Application.Degrees
Application.DeleteChartAutoFormat
Application.DeleteCustomList
Application.DevSq
Application.DGet
Application.Dialogs
Application.DialogSheets
Application.DMax
Application.DMin
Application.Dollar
Application.DoubleClick
Application.DProduct
Application.DStDev
Application.DStDevP
Application.DSum
Application.DVar
Application.DVarP
Application.Evaluate
Application.Even
Application.Excel4IntlMacroSheets
Application.Excel4MacroSheets
Application.ExecuteExcel4Macro
Application.ExponDist
Application.Fact
Application.FDist
Application.Find
Application.FindB
Application.FindFile
Application.FInv
Application.Fisher
Application.FisherInv
Application.Fixed
Application.Floor
```

Application.Forecast
Application.Frequency
Application.FTest
Application.Fv
Application.GammaDist
Application.GammaInv
Application.GammaLn
Application.GeoMean
Application.GetCustomListContents
Application.GetCustomListNum
Application.GetOpenFilename
Application.GetSaveAsFilename
Application.Goto
Application.Growth
Application.HarMean
Application.Help
Application.HLookup
Application.HypGeomDist
Application.InchesToPoints
Application.Index
Application.InputBox
Application.Intercept
Application.Intersect
Application.Ipmt
Application.Irr
Application.IsErr
Application.IsError
Application.IsLogical
Application.IsNA
Application.IsNonText
Application.IsNumber
Application.Ispmt
Application.IsText
Application.Kurt
Application.Large
Application.LinEst
Application.Ln
Application.Log
Application.Log10
Application.LogEst
Application.LogInv
Application.LogNormDist
Application.Lookup
Application.MacroOptions
Application.MailLogoff
Application.MailLogon
Application.Match
Application.Max
Application.MDeterm
Application.Median
Application.MenuBars
Application.Min
Application.MInverse
Application.MIrr
Application.MMult
Application.Mode
Application.Modules
Application.Names
Application.NegBinomDist
Application.NextLetter
Application.NormDist
Application.NormInv
Application.NormSDist
Application.NormSInv
Application.NPer
Application.Npv
Application.Odd
Application.OnKey
Application.OnRepeat
Application.OnTime
Application.OnUndo
Application.Or
Application.Pearson
Application.Percentile
Application.PercentRank
Application.Permut
Application.Pi
Application.Pmt
Application.Poisson
Application.Power
Application.Ppmt
Application.Prob
Application.Product
Application.Proper
Application.Pv
Application.Quartile
Application.Quit
Application.Radians
Application.Range
Application.Rank
Application.Rate
Application.RecordMacro
Application.RegisterXLL
Application.Repeat

```
Application.Replace
Application.ReplaceB
Application.Rept
Application.ResetTipWizard
Application.Roman
Application.Round
Application.RoundDown
Application.RoundUp
Application.Rows
Application.RSq
Application.Run
Application.Save
Application.Search
Application.SearchB
Application.SendKeys
Application.SetDefaultChart
Application.Sheets
Application.ShortcutMenus
Application.Sinh
Application.Skew
Application.Sln
Application.Slope
Application.Small
Application.Standardize
Application.StDev
Application.StDevP
Application.StEyx
Application.Substitute
Application.Subtotal
Application.Sum
Application.SumIf
Application.SumProduct
Application.SumSq
Application.SumX2MY2
Application.SumX2PY2
Application.SumXMY2
Application.Syd
Application.Tanh
Application.TDist
Application.Text
Application.TInv
Application.Toolbars
Application.Transpose
Application.Trend
Application.Trim
Application.TrimMean
Application.TTest
Application.Undo
Application.Union
Application.USDollar
Application.Var
Application.VarP
Application.Vdb
Application.VLookup
Application.Volatile
Application.Wait
Application.Weekday
Application.Weibull
Application.Windows
Application.Workbooks
Application.Worksheets
Application.ZTest
```

Properties

```
Application.ActiveCell
Application.ActiveChart
Application.ActiveDialog
Application.ActiveMenuBar
Application.ActivePrinter
Application.ActiveSheet
Application.ActiveWindow
Application.ActiveWorkbook
Application.AlertBeforeOverwriting
Application.AltStartupPath
Application.Application
Application.AskToUpdateLinks
Application.Build
Application.CalculateBeforeSave
Application.Calculation
Application.Caller
Application.CanPlaySounds
Application.CanRecordSounds
Application.Caption
Application.CellDragAndDrop
Application.ClipboardFormats
Application.ColorButtons
Application.CommandUnderlines
Application.ConstrainNumeric
Application.CopyObjectsWithCells
Application.Creator
Application.CustomListCount
Application.CutCopyMode
```

Application.DataEntryMode
Application.DDEAppReturnCode
Application.DefaultFilePath
Application.DisplayAlerts
Application.DisplayClipboardWindow
Application.DisplayExcel4Menus
Application.DisplayFormulaBar
Application.DisplayFullScreen
Application.DisplayInfoWindow
Application.DisplayNoteIndicator
Application.DisplayRecentFiles
Application.DisplayScrollBars
Application.DisplayStatusBar
Application.EditDirectlyInCell
Application.EnableCancelKey
Application.EnableTipWizard
Application.FileConverters
Application.FixedDecimal
Application.FixedDecimalPlaces
Application.Height
Application.IgnoreRemoteRequests
Application.Interactive
Application.International
Application.Iteration
Application.LargeButtons
Application.Left
Application.LibraryPath
Application.MailSession
Application.MailSystem
Application.MathCoprocessorAvailable
Application.MaxChange
Application.MaxIterations
Application.MemoryFree
Application.MemoryTotal
Application.MemoryUsed
Application.MouseAvailable
Application.MoveAfterReturn
Application.Name
Application.OnCalculate
Application.OnData
Application.OnDoubleClick
Application.OnEntry
Application.OnSheetActivate
Application.OnSheetDeactivate
Application.OnWindow
Application.OperatingSystem
Application.OrganizationName
Application.Parent
Application.Path
Application.PathSeparator
Application.PreviousSelections
Application.PromptForSummaryInfo
Application.RecordRelative
Application.ReferenceStyle
Application.RegisteredFunctions
Application.ScreenUpdating
Application.Selection
Application.SheetsInNewWorkbook
Application.ShowToolTips
Application.StandardFont
Application.StandardFontSize
Application.StartupPath
Application.StatusBar
Application.ThisWorkbook
Application.Top
Application.TransitionMenuKey
Application.TransitionMenuKeyAction
Application.TransitionNavigKeys
Application.UsableHeight
Application.UsableWidth
Application.UserName
Application.Value
Application.Version
Application.Visible
Application.Width
Application.WindowsForPens
Application.WindowState

Arc Object

An arc graphic object drawn on a chart or worksheet.

Methods

```
Arc.BringToFront
Arc.Copy
Arc.CopyPicture
Arc.Cut
Arc.Delete
Arc.Duplicate
Arc.Select
Arc.SendToBack
```

Properties

```
Arc.Application
Arc.Border
Arc.BottomRightCell
Arc.Creator
Arc.Enabled
Arc.Height
Arc.Index
Arc.Interior
Arc.Left
Arc.Locked
Arc.Name
Arc.OnAction
Arc.Parent
Arc.Placement
Arc.PrintObject
Arc.Top
Arc.TopLeftCell
Arc.Visible
Arc.Width
Arc.ZOrder
```

Arcs Object

A collection of Arc objects.

Methods

```
Arcs.Add
Arcs.BringToFront
Arcs.Copy
Arcs.CopyPicture
Arcs.Cut
Arcs.Delete
Arcs.Duplicate
Arcs.Group
Arcs.Item
Arcs.Select
Arcs.SendToBack
```

Properties

```
Arcs.Application
Arcs.Border
Arcs.Count
Arcs.Creator
Arcs.Enabled
Arcs.Height
Arcs.Interior
Arcs.Left
Arcs.Locked
Arcs.OnAction
Arcs.Parent
Arcs.Placement
Arcs.PrintObject
Arcs.Top
Arcs.Visible
Arcs.Width
Arcs.ZOrder
```

Areas Object

A collection of areas in a Range. Each area corresponds to the sections of a noncontiguous selection of cells.

Methods

```
Areas.Item
```

Properties

```
Areas.Application
Areas.Count
Areas.Creator
Areas.Parent
```

Axes Object

A collection of Axis objects.

Methods

```
Axes.Item
```

Properties

```
Axes.Application
Axes.Count
Axes.Creator
Axes.Parent
```

Axis Object

An axis on a chart.

Methods

```
Axis.Delete
Axis.Select
```

Properties

```
Axis.Application
Axis.AxisBetweenCategories
Axis.AxisGroup
Axis.AxisTitle
Axis.Border
Axis.CategoryNames
Axis.Creator
Axis.Crosses
Axis.CrossesAt
Axis.HasMajorGridlines
Axis.HasMinorGridlines
Axis.HasTitle
Axis.MajorGridlines
Axis.MajorTickMark
Axis.MajorUnit
Axis.MajorUnitIsAuto
Axis.MaximumScale
Axis.MaximumScaleIsAuto
Axis.MinimumScale
Axis.MinimumScaleIsAuto
Axis.MinorGridlines
Axis.MinorTickMark
Axis.MinorUnit
Axis.MinorUnitIsAuto
Axis.Parent
Axis.ReversePlotOrder
Axis.ScaleType
Axis.TickLabelPosition
Axis.TickLabels
Axis.TickLabelSpacing
Axis.TickMarkSpacing
Axis.Type
```

AxisTitle Object

An axis title on a chart.

Methods

```
AxisTitle.Characters
AxisTitle.Delete
AxisTitle.Select
```

Properties

```
AxisTitle.Application
AxisTitle.Border
AxisTitle.Caption
AxisTitle.Creator
AxisTitle.Font
AxisTitle.HorizontalAlignment
AxisTitle.Interior
AxisTitle.Left
AxisTitle.Name
AxisTitle.Orientation
AxisTitle.Parent
AxisTitle.Shadow
AxisTitle.Text
AxisTitle.Top
AxisTitle.VerticalAlignment
```

Border Object

The border of a cell or graphics object.

Methods

(None)

Properties

```
Border.Application
Border.Color
Border.ColorIndex
Border.Creator
Border.LineStyle
Border.Parent
Border.Weight
```

Borders Object

A collection of Border objects.

Methods

```
Borders.Item
```

Properties

```
Borders.Application
Borders.Color
Borders.ColorIndex
Borders.Creator
Borders.LineStyle
Borders.Parent
Borders.Value
Borders.Weight
```

Button Object

A custom button graphic object on a chart or worksheet (not a toolbar button).

Methods

```
Button.BringToFront
Button.Characters
Button.CheckSpelling
Button.Copy
Button.CopyPicture
Button.Cut
Button.Delete
Button.Duplicate
Button.Select
Button.SendToBack
```

Properties

```
Button.Accelerator
Button.AddIndent
Button.Application
Button.AutoSize
Button.BottomRightCell
Button.CancelButton
Button.Caption
Button.Creator
Button.DefaultButton
Button.DismissButton
Button.Enabled
Button.Font
Button.Formula
Button.Height
Button.HelpButton
Button.HorizontalAlignment
Button.Index
Button.Left
Button.Locked
Button.LockedText
Button.Name
Button.OnAction
Button.Orientation
Button.Parent
Button.PhoneticAccelerator
Button.Placement
Button.PrintObject
Button.Text
Button.Top
Button.TopLeftCell
Button.VerticalAlignment
Button.Visible
Button.Width
Button.ZOrder
```

Buttons Object

A collection of Button objects.

Methods

```
Buttons.Add
Buttons.BringToFront
Buttons.Characters
Buttons.CheckSpelling
Buttons.Copy
Buttons.CopyPicture
Buttons.Cut
Buttons.Delete
Buttons.Duplicate
Buttons.Group
Buttons.Item
Buttons.Select
Buttons.SendToBack
```

Properties

```
Buttons.Accelerator
Buttons.AddIndent
Buttons.Application
Buttons.AutoSize
Buttons.CancelButton
Buttons.Caption
```

```
Buttons.Count
Buttons.Creator
Buttons.DefaultButton
Buttons.DismissButton
Buttons.Enabled
Buttons.Font
Buttons.Formula
Buttons.Height
Buttons.HelpButton
Buttons.HorizontalAlignment
Buttons.Left
Buttons.Locked
Buttons.LockedText
Buttons.OnAction
Buttons.Orientation
Buttons.Parent
Buttons.PhoneticAccelerator
Buttons.Placement
Buttons.PrintObject
Buttons.Text
Buttons.Top
Buttons.VerticalAlignment
Buttons.Visible
Buttons.Width
Buttons.ZOrder
```

Characters Object

A collection of characters (text) in a cell, text box, or custom button graphic object.

Methods

```
Characters.Delete
Characters.Insert
```

Properties

```
Characters.Application
Characters.Caption
Characters.Count
Characters.Creator
Characters.Font
Characters.Parent
Characters.Text
```

Chart Object

A chart in a workbook.

Methods

```
Chart.Activate
Chart.ApplyDataLabels
Chart.Arcs
Chart.AreaGroups
Chart.AutoFormat
Chart.Axes
Chart.BarGroups
Chart.Buttons
Chart.ChartGroups
Chart.ChartObjects
Chart.ChartWizard
Chart.CheckBoxes
Chart.CheckSpelling
Chart.ColumnGroups
Chart.Copy
Chart.CopyPicture
Chart.CreatePublisher
Chart.Delete
```

```
Chart.Deselect
Chart.DoughnutGroups
Chart.DrawingObjects
Chart.Drawings
Chart.DropDowns
Chart.Evaluate
Chart.GroupBoxes
Chart.GroupObjects
Chart.Labels
Chart.LineGroups
Chart.Lines
Chart.ListBoxes
Chart.Move
Chart.OLEObjects
Chart.OptionButtons
Chart.Ovals
Chart.Paste
Chart.Pictures
Chart.PieGroups
Chart.PrintOut
Chart.PrintPreview
Chart.Protect
Chart.RadarGroups
Chart.Rectangles
Chart.SaveAs
Chart.ScrollBars
Chart.Select
Chart.SeriesCollection
Chart.Spinners
Chart.TextBoxes
Chart.Unprotect
Chart.XYGroups
```

Properties

```
Chart.Application
Chart.Area3DGroup
Chart.AutoScaling
Chart.Bar3DGroup
Chart.ChartArea
Chart.ChartTitle
Chart.Column3DGroup
Chart.Corners
Chart.Creator
Chart.DepthPercent
Chart.DisplayBlanksAs
Chart.Elevation
Chart.Floor
Chart.GapDepth
Chart.HasAxis
Chart.HasLegend
Chart.HasTitle
Chart.HeightPercent
Chart.Index
Chart.Legend
Chart.Line3DGroup
Chart.Name
Chart.Next
Chart.OnDoubleClick
Chart.OnSheetActivate
Chart.OnSheetDeactivate
Chart.PageSetup
Chart.Parent
Chart.Perspective
Chart.Pie3DGroup
Chart.PlotArea
Chart.PlotVisibleOnly
Chart.Previous
Chart.ProtectContents
Chart.ProtectDrawingObjects
Chart.RightAngleAxes
Chart.Rotation
Chart.SizeWithWindow
Chart.SubType
Chart.SurfaceGroup
Chart.Type
Chart.Visible
Chart.Walls
Chart.WallsAndGridlines2D
ChartArea Object
The chart area of a chart.
```

Methods

```
ChartArea.Clear
ChartArea.ClearContents
ChartArea.ClearFormats
ChartArea.Copy
ChartArea.Select
```

Properties

ChartArea.Application
ChartArea.Border
ChartArea.Creator
ChartArea.Font
ChartArea.Height
ChartArea.Interior
ChartArea.Left
ChartArea.Name
ChartArea.Parent
ChartArea.Shadow
ChartArea.Top
ChartArea.Width

ChartGroup Object

A chart group on a chart.

Methods

ChartGroup.SeriesCollection

Properties

ChartGroup.Application
ChartGroup.AxisGroup
ChartGroup.Creator
ChartGroup.DoughnutHoleSize
ChartGroup.DownBars
ChartGroup.DropLines
ChartGroup.FirstSliceAngle
ChartGroup.GapWidth
ChartGroup.HasDropLines
ChartGroup.HasHiLoLines
ChartGroup.HasRadarAxisLabels
ChartGroup.HasSeriesLines
ChartGroup.HasUpDownBars
ChartGroup.HiLoLines
ChartGroup.Overlap
ChartGroup.Parent
ChartGroup.RadarAxisLabels
ChartGroup.SeriesLines
ChartGroup.SubType
ChartGroup.Type
ChartGroup.UpBars
ChartGroup.VaryByCategories

ChartGroups Object

A collection of ChartGroup objects.

Methods

ChartGroups.Item

Properties

ChartGroups.Application
ChartGroups.Count
ChartGroups.Creator
ChartGroups.Parent

ChartObject Object

An embedded chart on a sheet (a container that provides the size of the chart).

Methods

```
ChartObject.Activate
ChartObject.BringToFront
ChartObject.Copy
ChartObject.CopyPicture
ChartObject.Cut
ChartObject.Delete
ChartObject.Duplicate
ChartObject.Select
ChartObject.SendToBack
```

Properties

```
ChartObject.Application
ChartObject.Border
ChartObject.BottomRightCell
ChartObject.Chart
ChartObject.Creator
ChartObject.Enabled
ChartObject.Height
ChartObject.Index
ChartObject.Interior
ChartObject.Left
ChartObject.Locked
ChartObject.Name
ChartObject.OnAction
ChartObject.Parent
ChartObject.Placement
ChartObject.PrintObject
ChartObject.RoundedCorners
ChartObject.Shadow
ChartObject.Top
ChartObject.TopLeftCell
ChartObject.Visible
ChartObject.Width
ChartObject.ZOrder
```

ChartObjects Object

A collection of ChartObject objects.

Methods

```
ChartObjects.Add
ChartObjects.BringToFront
ChartObjects.Copy
ChartObjects.CopyPicture
ChartObjects.Cut
ChartObjects.Delete
ChartObjects.Duplicate
ChartObjects.Group
ChartObjects.Item
ChartObjects.Select
ChartObjects.SendToBack
```

Properties

```
ChartObjects.Application
ChartObjects.Border
ChartObjects.Count
ChartObjects.Creator
ChartObjects.Enabled
ChartObjects.Height
ChartObjects.Interior
ChartObjects.Left
ChartObjects.Locked
ChartObjects.OnAction
ChartObjects.Parent
ChartObjects.Placement
ChartObjects.PrintObject
ChartObjects.RoundedCorners
ChartObjects.Shadow
ChartObjects.Top
ChartObjects.Visible
ChartObjects.Width
ChartObjects.ZOrder
```

Charts Object

A collection of charts in a workbook.

Methods

```
Charts.Add
Charts.Copy
Charts.Delete
Charts.Item
Charts.Move
Charts.PrintOut
Charts.PrintPreview
Charts.Select
```

Properties

```
Charts.Application
Charts.Count
Charts.Creator
Charts.Parent
Charts.Visible
```

ChartTitle Object

The title of a chart.

Methods

```
ChartTitle.Characters
ChartTitle.Delete
ChartTitle.Select
```

Properties

```
ChartTitle.Application
ChartTitle.Border
ChartTitle.Caption
ChartTitle.Creator
ChartTitle.Font
ChartTitle.HorizontalAlignment
ChartTitle.Interior
ChartTitle.Left
ChartTitle.Name
ChartTitle.Orientation
ChartTitle.Parent
ChartTitle.Shadow
ChartTitle.Text
ChartTitle.Top
ChartTitle.VerticalAlignment
```

CheckBox Object

A check box control on a dialog sheet or worksheet.

Methods

```
CheckBox.BringToFront
CheckBox.Characters
CheckBox.CheckSpelling
CheckBox.Copy
CheckBox.CopyPicture
CheckBox.Cut
CheckBox.Delete
CheckBox.Duplicate
CheckBox.Select
CheckBox.SendToBack
```

Properties

CheckBox.Accelerator
CheckBox.Application
CheckBox.Border
CheckBox.BottomRightCell
CheckBox.Caption
CheckBox.Creator
CheckBox.Display3DShading
CheckBox.Enabled
CheckBox.Height
CheckBox.Index
CheckBox.Interior
CheckBox.Left
CheckBox.LinkedCell
CheckBox.Locked
CheckBox.LockedText
CheckBox.Name
CheckBox.OnAction
CheckBox.Parent
CheckBox.PhoneticAccelerator
CheckBox.Placement
CheckBox.PrintObject
CheckBox.Text
CheckBox.Top
CheckBox.TopLeftCell
CheckBox.Value
CheckBox.Visible
CheckBox.Width
CheckBox.ZOrder

CheckBoxes Object

A collection of CheckBox objects.

Methods

CheckBoxes.Add
CheckBoxes.BringToFront
CheckBoxes.Characters
CheckBoxes.CheckSpelling
CheckBoxes.Copy
CheckBoxes.CopyPicture
CheckBoxes.Cut
CheckBoxes.Delete
CheckBoxes.Duplicate
CheckBoxes.Group
CheckBoxes.Item
CheckBoxes.Select
CheckBoxes.SendToBack

Properties

CheckBoxes.Accelerator
CheckBoxes.Application
CheckBoxes.Border
CheckBoxes.Caption
CheckBoxes.Count
CheckBoxes.Creator
CheckBoxes.Display3DShading
CheckBoxes.Enabled
CheckBoxes.Height
CheckBoxes.Interior
CheckBoxes.Left
CheckBoxes.LinkedCell
CheckBoxes.Locked
CheckBoxes.LockedText
CheckBoxes.OnAction
CheckBoxes.Parent
CheckBoxes.PhoneticAccelerator
CheckBoxes.Placement
CheckBoxes.PrintObject
CheckBoxes.Text
CheckBoxes.Top
CheckBoxes.Value
CheckBoxes.Visible
CheckBoxes.Width
CheckBoxes.ZOrder

Corners Object

The corners of a 3-D chart.

Methods

```
Corners.Select
```

Properties

```
Corners.Application
Corners.Creator
Corners.Name
Corners.Parent
```

DataLabel Object

A data label on a chart series, or on a single point of a chart series.

Methods

```
DataLabel.Characters
DataLabel.Delete
DataLabel.Select
```

Properties

```
DataLabel.Application
DataLabel.AutoText
DataLabel.Border
DataLabel.Caption
DataLabel.Creator
DataLabel.Font
DataLabel.HorizontalAlignment
DataLabel.Interior
DataLabel.Left
DataLabel.Name
DataLabel.NumberFormat
DataLabel.NumberFormatLinked
DataLabel.Orientation
DataLabel.Parent
DataLabel.Shadow
DataLabel.ShowLegendKey
DataLabel.Text
DataLabel.Top
DataLabel.Type
DataLabel.VerticalAlignment
```

DataLabels Object

A collection of DataLabel objects for the points on a series.

Methods

```
DataLabels.Delete
DataLabels.Item
DataLabels.Select
```

Properties

```
DataLabels.Application
DataLabels.AutoText
DataLabels.Border
DataLabels.Caption
DataLabels.Count
DataLabels.Creator
DataLabels.Font
DataLabels.HorizontalAlignment
DataLabels.Interior
DataLabels.Left
DataLabels.Name
DataLabels.NumberFormat
```

DataLabels.NumberFormatLinked
DataLabels.Orientation
DataLabels.Parent
DataLabels.Shadow
DataLabels.ShowLegendKey
DataLabels.Text
DataLabels.Top
DataLabels.Type
DataLabels.VerticalAlignment

Dialog Object

A builit-in Excel dialog box.

Methods

Dialog.Show

Properties

Dialog.Application
Dialog.Creator
Dialog.Parent

DialogFrame Object

The frame of a custom dialog box.

Methods

DialogFrame.Characters
DialogFrame.CheckSpelling
DialogFrame.CopyPicture
DialogFrame.Select

Properties

DialogFrame.Application
DialogFrame.Caption
DialogFrame.Creator
DialogFrame.Height
DialogFrame.Left
DialogFrame.Locked
DialogFrame.LockedText
DialogFrame.Name
DialogFrame.OnAction
DialogFrame.Parent
DialogFrame.Text
DialogFrame.Top
DialogFrame.Width

Dialogs Object

A collection of Dialog objects.

Methods

Dialogs.Item

Properties

Dialogs.Application
Dialogs.Count
Dialogs.Creator
Dialogs.Parent

DialogSheet Object

A dialog sheet in a workbook.

Methods

```
DialogSheet.Activate
DialogSheet.Arcs
DialogSheet.Buttons
DialogSheet.ChartObjects
DialogSheet.CheckBoxes
DialogSheet.CheckSpelling
DialogSheet.Copy
DialogSheet.Delete
DialogSheet.DialogFrame
DialogSheet.DrawingObjects
DialogSheet.Drawings
DialogSheet.DropDowns
DialogSheet.EditBoxes
DialogSheet.Evaluate
DialogSheet.GroupBoxes
DialogSheet.GroupObjects
DialogSheet.Hide
DialogSheet.Labels
DialogSheet.Lines
DialogSheet.ListBoxes
DialogSheet.Move
DialogSheet.OLEObjects
DialogSheet.OptionButtons
DialogSheet.Ovals
DialogSheet.Paste
DialogSheet.PasteSpecial
DialogSheet.Pictures
DialogSheet.PrintOut
DialogSheet.PrintPreview
DialogSheet.Protect
DialogSheet.Rectangles
DialogSheet.SaveAs
DialogSheet.ScrollBars
DialogSheet.Select
DialogSheet.Show
DialogSheet.Spinners
DialogSheet.TextBoxes
DialogSheet.Unprotect
```

Properties

```
DialogSheet.Application
DialogSheet.Creator
DialogSheet.DefaultButton
DialogSheet.DisplayAutomaticPageBreaks
DialogSheet.Focus
DialogSheet.Index
DialogSheet.Name
DialogSheet.Next
DialogSheet.OnDoubleClick
DialogSheet.OnSheetActivate
DialogSheet.OnSheetDeactivate
DialogSheet.PageSetup
DialogSheet.Parent
DialogSheet.Previous
DialogSheet.ProtectContents
DialogSheet.ProtectDrawingObjects
DialogSheet.Visible
```

DialogSheets Object

A collection of DialogSheet objects.

Methods

```
DialogSheets.Add
DialogSheets.Copy
DialogSheets.Delete
DialogSheets.Item
DialogSheets.Move
DialogSheets.PrintOut
DialogSheets.PrintPreview
DialogSheets.Select
```

Properties

DialogSheets.Application
DialogSheets.Count
DialogSheets.Creator
DialogSheets.Parent
DialogSheets.Visible

DownBars Object

A down bar on a chart.

Methods

DownBars.Delete
DownBars.Select

Properties

DownBars.Application
DownBars.Border
DownBars.Creator
DownBars.Interior
DownBars.Name
DownBars.Parent

Drawing Object

A graphic object created by the Freehand, Freeform, or Filled Freeform toolbar buttons.

Methods

Drawing.AddVertex
Drawing.BringToFront
Drawing.Copy
Drawing.CopyPicture
Drawing.Cut
Drawing.Delete
Drawing.Duplicate
Drawing.Reshape
Drawing.Select
Drawing.SendToBack

Properties

Drawing.Application
Drawing.Border
Drawing.BottomRightCell
Drawing.Creator
Drawing.Enabled
Drawing.Height
Drawing.Index
Drawing.Interior
Drawing.Left
Drawing.Locked
Drawing.Name
Drawing.OnAction
Drawing.Parent
Drawing.Placement
Drawing.PrintObject
Drawing.Shadow
Drawing.Top
Drawing.TopLeftCell
Drawing.Vertices
Drawing.Visible
Drawing.Width
Drawing.ZOrder

DrawingObjects Object

A collection of all graphic objects on a sheet.

Methods

```
DrawingObjects.AddItem
DrawingObjects.BringToFront
DrawingObjects.Characters
DrawingObjects.CheckSpelling
DrawingObjects.Copy
DrawingObjects.CopyPicture
DrawingObjects.Cut
DrawingObjects.Delete
DrawingObjects.Duplicate
DrawingObjects.Group
DrawingObjects.Item
DrawingObjects.LinkCombo
DrawingObjects.RemoveAllItems
DrawingObjects.RemoveItem
DrawingObjects.Reshape
DrawingObjects.Select
DrawingObjects.SendToBack
DrawingObjects.Ungroup
```

Properties

```
DrawingObjects.Accelerator
DrawingObjects.AddIndent
DrawingObjects.Application
DrawingObjects.ArrowHeadLength
DrawingObjects.ArrowHeadStyle
DrawingObjects.ArrowHeadWidth
DrawingObjects.AutoSize
DrawingObjects.Border
DrawingObjects.CancelButton
DrawingObjects.Caption
DrawingObjects.Count
DrawingObjects.Creator
DrawingObjects.DefaultButton
DrawingObjects.DismissButton
DrawingObjects.Display3D Shading
DrawingObjects.DisplayVertical
ScrollBar
DrawingObjects.DropDownLines
DrawingObjects.Enabled
DrawingObjects.Font
DrawingObjects.Height
DrawingObjects.HelpButton
DrawingObjects.HorizontalAlignment
DrawingObjects.InputType
DrawingObjects.Interior
DrawingObjects.LargeChange
DrawingObjects.Left
DrawingObjects.LinkedCell
DrawingObjects.List
DrawingObjects.ListFillRange
DrawingObjects.ListIndex
DrawingObjects.Locked
DrawingObjects.LockedText
DrawingObjects.Max
DrawingObjects.Min
DrawingObjects.MultiLine
DrawingObjects.MultiSelect
DrawingObjects.OnAction
DrawingObjects.Orientation
DrawingObjects.Parent
DrawingObjects.PhoneticAccelerator
DrawingObjects.Placement
DrawingObjects.PrintObject
DrawingObjects.RoundedCorners
DrawingObjects.Selected
DrawingObjects.Shadow
DrawingObjects.SmallChange
DrawingObjects.Text
DrawingObjects.Top
DrawingObjects.Value
DrawingObjects.VerticalAlignment
DrawingObjects.Vertices
DrawingObjects.Visible
DrawingObjects.Width
DrawingObjects.ZOrder
```

Drawings Object

A collection of Drawing objects.

Methods

```
Drawings.Add
Drawings.BringToFront
Drawings.Copy
Drawings.CopyPicture
Drawings.Cut
Drawings.Delete
Drawings.Duplicate
Drawings.Group
Drawings.Item
Drawings.Reshape
Drawings.Select
Drawings.SendToBack
```

Properties

```
Drawings.Application
Drawings.Border
Drawings.Count
Drawings.Creator
Drawings.Enabled
Drawings.Height
Drawings.Interior
Drawings.Left
Drawings.Locked
Drawings.OnAction
Drawings.Parent
Drawings.Placement
Drawings.PrintObject
Drawings.Shadow
Drawings.Top
Drawings.Visible
Drawings.Width
Drawings.ZOrder
```

DropDown Object

A drop-down list box.

Methods

```
DropDown.AddItem
DropDown.BringToFront
DropDown.Characters
DropDown.Copy
DropDown.CopyPicture
DropDown.Cut
DropDown.Delete
DropDown.Duplicate
DropDown.RemoveAllItems
DropDown.RemoveItem
DropDown.Select
DropDown.SendToBack
```

Properties

```
DropDown.Application
DropDown.BottomRightCell
DropDown.Caption
DropDown.Creator
DropDown.Display3DShading
DropDown.DropDownLines
DropDown.Enabled
DropDown.Height
DropDown.Index
DropDown.Left
DropDown.LinkedCell
DropDown.LinkedObject
DropDown.List
```

DropDown.ListCount
DropDown.ListFillRange
DropDown.ListIndex
DropDown.Locked
DropDown.Name
DropDown.OnAction
DropDown.Parent
DropDown.Placement
DropDown.PrintObject
DropDown.Selected
DropDown.Text
DropDown.Top
DropDown.TopLeftCell
DropDown.Value
DropDown.Visible
DropDown.Width
DropDown.ZOrder

DropDowns Object

A collection of DropDown objects.

Methods

DropDowns.Add
DropDowns.AddItem
DropDowns.BringToFront
DropDowns.Characters
DropDowns.Copy
DropDowns.CopyPicture
DropDowns.Cut
DropDowns.Delete
DropDowns.Duplicate
DropDowns.Group
DropDowns.Item
DropDowns.RemoveAllItems
DropDowns.RemoveItem
DropDowns.Select
DropDowns.SendToBack

Properties

DropDowns.Application
DropDowns.Caption
DropDowns.Count
DropDowns.Creator
DropDowns.Display3DShading
DropDowns.DropDownLines
DropDowns.Enabled
DropDowns.Height
DropDowns.Left
DropDowns.LinkedCell
DropDowns.List
DropDowns.ListFillRange
DropDowns.ListIndex
DropDowns.Locked
DropDowns.OnAction
DropDowns.Parent
DropDowns.Placement
DropDowns.PrintObject
DropDowns.Selected
DropDowns.Text
DropDowns.Top
DropDowns.Value
DropDowns.Visible
DropDowns.Width
DropDowns.ZOrder

DropLines Object

Drop lines on a chart.

Methods

```
DropLines.Delete
DropLines.Select
```

Properties

```
DropLines.Application
DropLines.Border
DropLines.Creator
DropLines.Name
DropLines.Parent
```

EditBox Object

An edit box on a dialog sheet.

Methods

```
EditBox.BringToFront
EditBox.Characters
EditBox.Copy
EditBox.CopyPicture
EditBox.Cut
EditBox.Delete
EditBox.Duplicate
EditBox.Select
EditBox.SendToBack
```

Properties

```
EditBox.Application
EditBox.BottomRightCell
EditBox.Caption
EditBox.Creator
EditBox.DisplayVerticalScrollBar
EditBox.Enabled
EditBox.Height
EditBox.Index
EditBox.InputType
EditBox.Left
EditBox.LinkedObject
EditBox.Locked
EditBox.MultiLine
EditBox.Name
EditBox.OnAction
EditBox.Parent
EditBox.Placement
EditBox.PrintObject
EditBox.Text
EditBox.Top
EditBox.TopLeftCell
EditBox.Visible
EditBox.Width
EditBox.ZOrder
```

EditBoxes Object

A collection of EditBox objects.

Methods

```
EditBoxes.Add
EditBoxes.BringToFront
EditBoxes.Characters
EditBoxes.Copy
EditBoxes.CopyPicture
EditBoxes.Cut
EditBoxes.Delete
EditBoxes.Duplicate
EditBoxes.Group
EditBoxes.Item
EditBoxes.Select
EditBoxes.SendToBack
```

Properties

```
EditBoxes.Application
EditBoxes.Caption
EditBoxes.Count
EditBoxes.Creator
EditBoxes.DisplayVerticalScrollBar
EditBoxes.Enabled
EditBoxes.Height
EditBoxes.InputType
EditBoxes.Left
EditBoxes.Locked
EditBoxes.MultiLine
EditBoxes.OnAction
EditBoxes.Parent
EditBoxes.Placement
EditBoxes.PrintObject
EditBoxes.Text
EditBoxes.Top
EditBoxes.Visible
EditBoxes.Width
EditBoxes.ZOrder
```

ErrorBars Object

Error bars on a chart.

Methods

```
ErrorBars.ClearFormats
ErrorBars.Delete
ErrorBars.Select
```

Properties

```
ErrorBars.Application
ErrorBars.Border
ErrorBars.Creator
ErrorBars.EndStyle
ErrorBars.Name
ErrorBars.Parent
```

Floor Object

The floor of a 3-D chart.

Methods

```
Floor.ClearFormats
Floor.Select
```

Properties

```
Floor.Application
Floor.Border
Floor.Creator
Floor.Interior
Floor.Name
Floor.Parent
```

Font Object

A font description.

Properties

```
Font.Application
Font.Background
Font.Bold
Font.Color
Font.ColorIndex
Font.Creator
Font.FontStyle
Font.Italic
Font.Name
Font.OutlineFont
Font.Parent
Font.Shadow
Font.Size
Font.Strikethrough
Font.Subscript
Font.Superscript
Font.Underline
```

Gridlines Object

Major or minor gridlines on a chart.

Methods

```
Gridlines.Delete
Gridlines.Select
```

Properties

```
Gridlines.Application
Gridlines.Border
Gridlines.Creator
Gridlines.Name
Gridlines.Parent
```

GroupBox Object

A frame used to label and group sets of dialog box controls (usually option buttons).

Methods

```
GroupBox.BringToFront
GroupBox.Characters
GroupBox.CheckSpelling
GroupBox.Copy
GroupBox.CopyPicture
GroupBox.Cut
GroupBox.Delete
GroupBox.Duplicate
GroupBox.Select
GroupBox.SendToBack
```

Properties

```
GroupBox.Accelerator
GroupBox.Application
GroupBox.BottomRightCell
GroupBox.Caption
GroupBox.Creator
GroupBox.Display3DShading
GroupBox.Enabled
GroupBox.Height
GroupBox.Index
GroupBox.Left
GroupBox.Locked
GroupBox.LockedText
GroupBox.Name
GroupBox.OnAction
GroupBox.Parent
GroupBox.PhoneticAccelerator
GroupBox.Placement
GroupBox.PrintObject
GroupBox.Text
GroupBox.Top
GroupBox.TopLeftCell
GroupBox.Visible
GroupBox.Width
GroupBox.ZOrder
```

GroupBoxes Object

A collection of GroupBox objects.

Methods

```
GroupBoxes.Add
GroupBoxes.BringToFront
GroupBoxes.Characters
GroupBoxes.CheckSpelling
GroupBoxes.Copy
GroupBoxes.CopyPicture
GroupBoxes.Cut
GroupBoxes.Delete
GroupBoxes.Duplicate
GroupBoxes.Group
GroupBoxes.Item
GroupBoxes.Select
GroupBoxes.SendToBack
```

Properties

```
GroupBoxes.Accelerator
GroupBoxes.Application
GroupBoxes.Caption
GroupBoxes.Count
GroupBoxes.Creator
GroupBoxes.Display3DShading
GroupBoxes.Enabled
GroupBoxes.Height
GroupBoxes.Left
GroupBoxes.Locked
GroupBoxes.LockedText
GroupBoxes.OnAction
GroupBoxes.Parent
```

GroupBoxes.PhoneticAccelerator
GroupBoxes.Placement
GroupBoxes.PrintObject
GroupBoxes.Text
GroupBoxes.Top
GroupBoxes.Visible
GroupBoxes.Width
GroupBoxes.ZOrder

GroupObject Object

A group of graphic objects.

Methods

GroupObject.BringToFront
GroupObject.CheckSpelling
GroupObject.Copy
GroupObject.CopyPicture
GroupObject.Cut
GroupObject.Delete
GroupObject.Duplicate
GroupObject.Select
GroupObject.SendToBack
GroupObject.Ungroup

Properties

GroupObject.AddIndent
GroupObject.Application
GroupObject.ArrowHeadLength
GroupObject.ArrowHeadStyle
GroupObject.ArrowHeadWidth
GroupObject.AutoSize
GroupObject.Border
GroupObject.BottomRightCell
GroupObject.Creator
GroupObject.Enabled
GroupObject.Font
GroupObject.Height
GroupObject.HorizontalAlignment
GroupObject.Index
GroupObject.Interior
GroupObject.Left
GroupObject.Locked
GroupObject.Name
GroupObject.OnAction
GroupObject.Orientation
GroupObject.Parent
GroupObject.Placement
GroupObject.PrintObject
GroupObject.RoundedCorners
GroupObject.Shadow
GroupObject.Top
GroupObject.TopLeftCell
GroupObject.VerticalAlignment
GroupObject.Visible
GroupObject.Width
GroupObject.ZOrder

GroupObjects Object

A collection of GroupObject objects.

Methods

GroupObjects.BringToFront
GroupObjects.CheckSpelling
GroupObjects.Copy
GroupObjects.CopyPicture
GroupObjects.Cut
GroupObjects.Delete
GroupObjects.Duplicate
GroupObjects.Group
GroupObjects.Item
GroupObjects.Select
GroupObjects.SendToBack
GroupObjects.Ungroup

Properties

```
GroupObjects.AddIndent
GroupObjects.Application
GroupObjects.ArrowHeadLength
GroupObjects.ArrowHeadStyle
GroupObjects.ArrowHeadWidth
GroupObjects.AutoSize
GroupObjects.Border
GroupObjects.Count
GroupObjects.Creator
GroupObjects.Enabled
GroupObjects.Font
GroupObjects.Height
GroupObjects.HorizontalAlignment
GroupObjects.Interior
GroupObjects.Left
GroupObjects.Locked
GroupObjects.OnAction
GroupObjects.Orientation
GroupObjects.Parent
GroupObjects.Placement
GroupObjects.PrintObject
GroupObjects.RoundedCorners
GroupObjects.Shadow
GroupObjects.Top
GroupObjects.VerticalAlignment
GroupObjects.Visible
GroupObjects.Width
GroupObjects.ZOrder
```

HiLoLines Object

High-low lines on a chart.

Methods

```
HiLoLines.Delete
HiLoLines.Select
```

Properties

```
HiLoLines.Application
HiLoLines.Border
HiLoLines.Creator
HiLoLines.Name
HiLoLines.Parent
```

Interior Object

The interior of a cell or graphic object.

Methods

(None)

Properties

```
Interior.Application
Interior.Color
Interior.ColorIndex
Interior.Creator
Interior.Parent
Interior.Pattern
Interior.PatternColor
Interior.PatternColorIndex
```

Label Object

A static text object on a dialog sheet.

Methods

Label.BringToFront
Label.Characters
Label.CheckSpelling
Label.Copy
Label.CopyPicture
Label.Cut
Label.Delete
Label.Duplicate
Label.Select
Label.SendToBack

Properties

Label.Accelerator
Label.Application
Label.BottomRightCell
Label.Caption
Label.Creator
Label.Enabled
Label.Height
Label.Index
Label.Left
Label.Locked
Label.LockedText
Label.Name
Label.OnAction
Label.Parent
Label.PhoneticAccelerator
Label.Placement
Label.PrintObject
Label.Text
Label.Top
Label.TopLeftCell
Label.Visible
Label.Width
Label.ZOrder

Labels Object

A collection of Label objects.

Methods

Labels.Add
Labels.BringToFront
Labels.Characters
Labels.CheckSpelling
Labels.Copy
Labels.CopyPicture
Labels.Cut
Labels.Delete
Labels.Duplicate
Labels.Group
Labels.Item
Labels.Select
Labels.SendToBack

Properties

Labels.Accelerator
Labels.Application
Labels.Caption
Labels.Count
Labels.Creator
Labels.Enabled
Labels.Height
Labels.Left
Labels.Locked
Labels.LockedText
Labels.OnAction
Labels.Parent
Labels.PhoneticAccelerator
Labels.Placement

```
Labels.PrintObject
Labels.Text
Labels.Top
Labels.Visible
Labels.Width
Labels.ZOrder
```

Legend Object

The legend of a chart.

Methods

```
Legend.Delete
Legend.LegendEntries
Legend.Select
```

Properties

```
Legend.Application
Legend.Border
Legend.Creator
Legend.Font
Legend.Height
Legend.Interior
Legend.Left
Legend.Name
Legend.Parent
Legend.Position
Legend.Shadow
Legend.Top
Legend.Width
```

LegendEntries Object

A collection of LegendEntry objects.

Methods

```
LegendEntries.Item
```

Properties

```
LegendEntries.Application
LegendEntries.Count
LegendEntries.Creator
LegendEntries.Parent
```

LegendEntry Object

Text and data marker labels contained within a chart legend (used for the text and marker).

Methods

```
LegendEntry.Delete
LegendEntry.Select
```

Properties

```
LegendEntry.Application
LegendEntry.Creator
LegendEntry.Font
LegendEntry.Index
LegendEntry.LegendKey
LegendEntry.Parent
```

LegendKey Object

Text and data marker labels contained within a chart legend (used for the formatting properties).

Methods

LegendKey.ClearFormats
LegendKey.Delete
LegendKey.Select

Properties

LegendKey.Application
LegendKey.Border
LegendKey.Creator
LegendKey.Interior
LegendKey.InvertIfNegative
LegendKey.MarkerBackgroundColor
LegendKey.MarkerBackgroundColorIndex
LegendKey.MarkerForegroundColor
LegendKey.MarkerForegroundColorIndex
LegendKey.MarkerStyle
LegendKey.Parent
LegendKey.Smooth

Line Object

A line graphic object.

Methods

Line.BringToFront
Line.Copy
Line.CopyPicture
Line.Cut
Line.Delete
Line.Duplicate
Line.Select
Line.SendToBack

Properties

Line.Application
Line.ArrowHeadLength
Line.ArrowHeadStyle
Line.ArrowHeadWidth
Line.Border
Line.BottomRightCell
Line.Creator
Line.Enabled
Line.Height
Line.Index
Line.Left
Line.Locked
Line.Name
Line.OnAction
Line.Parent
Line.Placement
Line.PrintObject
Line.Top
Line.TopLeftCell
Line.Visible
Line.Width
Line.ZOrder

Lines Object

A collection of Line objects.

Methods

```
Lines.Add
Lines.BringToFront
Lines.Copy
Lines.CopyPicture
Lines.Cut
Lines.Delete
Lines.Duplicate
Lines.Group
Lines.Item
Lines.Select
Lines.SendToBack
```

Properties

```
Lines.Application
Lines.ArrowHeadLength
Lines.ArrowHeadStyle
Lines.ArrowHeadWidth
Lines.Border
Lines.Count
Lines.Creator
Lines.Enabled
Lines.Height
Lines.Left
Lines.Locked
Lines.OnAction
Lines.Parent
Lines.Placement
Lines.PrintObject
Lines.Top
Lines.Visible
Lines.Width
Lines.ZOrder
```

ListBox Object

A scrollable list of items.

Methods

```
ListBox.AddItem
ListBox.BringToFront
ListBox.Copy
ListBox.CopyPicture
ListBox.Cut
ListBox.Delete
ListBox.Duplicate
ListBox.RemoveAllItems
ListBox.RemoveItem
ListBox.Select
ListBox.SendToBack
```

Properties

```
ListBox.Application
ListBox.BottomRightCell
ListBox.Creator
ListBox.Display3DShading
ListBox.Enabled
ListBox.Height
ListBox.Index
ListBox.Left
ListBox.LinkedCell
ListBox.LinkedObject
ListBox.List
ListBox.ListCount
ListBox.ListFillRange
```

ListBox.ListIndex
ListBox.Locked
ListBox.MultiSelect
ListBox.Name
ListBox.OnAction
ListBox.Parent
ListBox.Placement
ListBox.PrintObject
ListBox.Selected
ListBox.Top
ListBox.TopLeftCell
ListBox.Value
ListBox.Visible
ListBox.Width
ListBox.ZOrder

ListBoxes Object

A collection of ListBox objects.

Methods

ListBoxes.Add
ListBoxes.AddItem
ListBoxes.BringToFront
ListBoxes.Copy
ListBoxes.CopyPicture
ListBoxes.Cut
ListBoxes.Delete
ListBoxes.Duplicate
ListBoxes.Group
ListBoxes.Item
ListBoxes.RemoveAllItems
ListBoxes.RemoveItem
ListBoxes.Select
ListBoxes.SendToBack

Properties

ListBoxes.Application
ListBoxes.Count
ListBoxes.Creator
ListBoxes.Display3DShading
ListBoxes.Enabled
ListBoxes.Height
ListBoxes.Left
ListBoxes.LinkedCell
ListBoxes.List
ListBoxes.ListFillRange
ListBoxes.ListIndex
ListBoxes.Locked
ListBoxes.MultiSelect
ListBoxes.OnAction
ListBoxes.Parent
ListBoxes.Placement
ListBoxes.PrintObject
ListBoxes.Selected
ListBoxes.Top
ListBoxes.Value
ListBoxes.Visible
ListBoxes.Width
ListBoxes.ZOrder

Mailer Object

The PowerTalk Mailer for a workbook (available only in the Macintosh version of Excel).

Methods

(None)

Properties

```
Mailer.Application
Mailer.BCCRecipients
Mailer.CCRecipients
Mailer.Creator
Mailer.Enclosures
Mailer.Parent
Mailer.Received
Mailer.SendDateTime
Mailer.Sender
Mailer.Subject
Mailer.ToRecipients
```

Menu Object

A drop-down, shortcut, or cascading menu.

Methods

```
Menu.Delete
Menu.MenuItems
```

Properties

```
Menu.Application
Menu.Caption
Menu.Creator
Menu.Enabled
Menu.Index
Menu.Parent
```

MenuBar Object

A built-in or custom menu bar.

Methods

```
MenuBar.Activate
MenuBar.BuiltIn
MenuBar.Delete
MenuBar.Menus
MenuBar.Reset
```

Properties

```
MenuBar.Application
MenuBar.Caption
MenuBar.Creator
MenuBar.Index
MenuBar.Parent
```

MenuBars Object

A collection of MenuBar objects.

Methods

```
MenuBars.Add
MenuBars.Item
```

Properties

```
MenuBars.Application
MenuBars.Count
MenuBars.Creator
MenuBars.Parent
```

MenuItem Object

A menu item (command or separator bar).

Methods

```
MenuItem.Delete
```

Properties

```
MenuItem.Application
MenuItem.Caption
MenuItem.Checked
MenuItem.Creator
MenuItem.Enabled
MenuItem.Index
MenuItem.Parent
```

MenuItems Object

A collection of MenuItem objects.

Methods

```
MenuItems.Add
MenuItems.AddMenu
MenuItems.Item
```

Properties

```
MenuItems.Application
MenuItems.Count
MenuItems.Creator
MenuItems.Parent
```

Menus Object

A collection of Menu objects.

Methods

```
Menus.Add
Menus.Item
```

Properties

```
Menus.Application
Menus.Count
Menus.Creator
Menus.Parent
```

Module Object

A VBA module in a workbook.

Methods

```
Module.Activate
Module.Copy
Module.Delete
Module.InsertFile
Module.Move
Module.PrintOut
Module.Protect
Module.SaveAs
Module.Select
Module.Unprotect
```

Properties

```
Module.Application
Module.Creator
Module.Index
Module.Name
Module.Next
Module.OnDoubleClick
Module.OnSheetActivate
Module.OnSheetDeactivate
Module.PageSetup
Module.Parent
Module.Previous
Module.ProtectContents
Module.Visible
```

Modules Object

A collection of Module objects.

Methods

```
Modules.Add
Modules.Copy
Modules.Delete
Modules.Item
Modules.Move
Modules.PrintOut
Modules.Select
```

Properties

```
Modules.Application
Modules.Count
Modules.Creator
Modules.Parent
Modules.Visible
```

Name Object

A defined name (built-in or user-defined).

Methods

```
Name.Delete
```

Properties

```
Name.Application
Name.Category
Name.CategoryLocal
Name.Creator
```

```
Name.Index
Name.MacroType
Name.Name
Name.NameLocal
Name.Parent
Name.RefersTo
Name.RefersToLocal
Name.RefersToR1C1
Name.RefersToR1C1Local
Name.ShortcutKey
Name.Value
Name.Visible
```

Names Object

A collection of Name objects.

Methods

```
Names.Add
Names.Item
```

Properties

```
Names.Application
Names.Count
Names.Creator
Names.Parent
```

OLEObject Object

A chart embedded on a worksheet, or a linked or embedded OLE object.

Methods

```
OLEObject.Activate
OLEObject.BringToFront
OLEObject.Copy
OLEObject.CopyPicture
OLEObject.Cut
OLEObject.Delete
OLEObject.Duplicate
OLEObject.Select
OLEObject.SendToBack
OLEObject.Update
OLEObject.Verb
```

Properties

```
OLEObject.Application
OLEObject.AutoUpdate
OLEObject.Border
OLEObject.BottomRightCell
OLEObject.Creator
OLEObject.Enabled
OLEObject.Height
OLEObject.Index
OLEObject.Interior
OLEObject.Left
OLEObject.Locked
OLEObject.Name
OLEObject.Object
OLEObject.OLEType
OLEObject.OnAction
OLEObject.Parent
OLEObject.Placement
OLEObject.PrintObject
OLEObject.Shadow
OLEObject.Top
OLEObject.TopLeftCell
OLEObject.Visible
OLEObject.Width
OLEObject.ZOrder
```

OLEObjects Object

A collection of OLEObject objects.

Methods

OLEObjects.Add
OLEObjects.BringToFront
OLEObjects.Copy
OLEObjects.CopyPicture
OLEObjects.Cut
OLEObjects.Delete
OLEObjects.Duplicate
OLEObjects.Group
OLEObjects.Item
OLEObjects.Select
OLEObjects.SendToBack

Properties

OLEObjects.Application
OLEObjects.Border
OLEObjects.Count
OLEObjects.Creator
OLEObjects.Enabled
OLEObjects.Height
OLEObjects.Interior
OLEObjects.Left
OLEObjects.Locked
OLEObjects.OnAction
OLEObjects.Parent
OLEObjects.Placement
OLEObjects.PrintObject
OLEObjects.Shadow
OLEObjects.Top
OLEObjects.Visible
OLEObjects.Width
OLEObjects.ZOrder

OptionButton Object

An option button.

Methods

OptionButton.BringToFront
OptionButton.Characters
OptionButton.CheckSpelling
OptionButton.Copy
OptionButton.CopyPicture
OptionButton.Cut
OptionButton.Delete
OptionButton.Duplicate
OptionButton.Select
OptionButton.SendToBack

Properties

OptionButton.Accelerator
OptionButton.Application
OptionButton.Border
OptionButton.BottomRightCell
OptionButton.Caption
OptionButton.Creator
OptionButton.Display3DShading
OptionButton.Enabled
OptionButton.Height
OptionButton.Index
OptionButton.Interior
OptionButton.Left
OptionButton.LinkedCell
OptionButton.Locked

OptionButton.LockedText
OptionButton.Name
OptionButton.OnAction
OptionButton.Parent
OptionButton.PhoneticAccelerator
OptionButton.Placement
OptionButton.PrintObject
OptionButton.Text
OptionButton.Top
OptionButton.TopLeftCell
OptionButton.Value
OptionButton.Visible
OptionButton.Width
OptionButton.ZOrder

OptionButtons Object

A collection of OptionButton objects.

Methods

OptionButtons.Add
OptionButtons.BringToFront
OptionButtons.Characters
OptionButtons.CheckSpelling
OptionButtons.Copy
OptionButtons.CopyPicture
OptionButtons.Cut
OptionButtons.Delete
OptionButtons.Duplicate
OptionButtons.Group
OptionButtons.Item
OptionButtons.Select
OptionButtons.SendToBack

Properties

OptionButtons.Accelerator
OptionButtons.Application
OptionButtons.Border
OptionButtons.Caption
OptionButtons.Count
OptionButtons.Creator
OptionButtons.Display3DShading
OptionButtons.Enabled
OptionButtons.Height
OptionButtons.Interior
OptionButtons.Left
OptionButtons.LinkedCell
OptionButtons.Locked
OptionButtons.LockedText
OptionButtons.OnAction
OptionButtons.Parent
OptionButtons.PhoneticAccelerator
OptionButtons.Placement
OptionButtons.PrintObject
OptionButtons.Text
OptionButtons.Top
OptionButtons.Value
OptionButtons.Visible
OptionButtons.Width
OptionButtons.ZOrder

Outline Object

An outline on a worksheet.

Methods

Outline.ShowLevels

Properties

Outline.Application
Outline.AutomaticStyles
Outline.Creator
Outline.Parent
Outline.SummaryColumn
Outline.SummaryRow

Oval Object

An oval graphic object.

Methods

```
Oval.BringToFront
Oval.Copy
Oval.CopyPicture
Oval.Cut
Oval.Delete
Oval.Duplicate
Oval.Select
Oval.SendToBack
```

Properties

```
Oval.Application
Oval.Border
Oval.BottomRightCell
Oval.Creator
Oval.Enabled
Oval.Height
Oval.Index
Oval.Interior
Oval.Left
Oval.Locked
Oval.Name
Oval.OnAction
Oval.Parent
Oval.Placement
Oval.PrintObject
Oval.Shadow
Oval.Top
Oval.TopLeftCell
Oval.Visible
Oval.Width
Oval.ZOrder
```

Ovals Object

A collection of Oval objects.

Methods

```
Ovals.Add
Ovals.BringToFront
Ovals.Copy
Ovals.CopyPicture
Ovals.Cut
Ovals.Delete
Ovals.Duplicate
Ovals.Group
Ovals.Item
Ovals.Select
Ovals.SendToBack
```

Properties

```
Ovals.Application
Ovals.Border
Ovals.Count
Ovals.Creator
Ovals.Enabled
Ovals.Height
Ovals.Interior
Ovals.Left
Ovals.Locked
Ovals.OnAction
Ovals.Parent
Ovals.Placement
Ovals.PrintObject
Ovals.Shadow
Ovals.Top
Ovals.Visible
Ovals.Width
Ovals.ZOrder
```

PageSetup Object

A page setup description (page setup attributes are properties).

Methods

(None)

Properties

```
PageSetup.Application
PageSetup.BlackAndWhite
PageSetup.BottomMargin
PageSetup.CenterFooter
PageSetup.CenterHeader
PageSetup.CenterHorizontally
PageSetup.CenterVertically
PageSetup.ChartSize
PageSetup.Creator
PageSetup.Draft
PageSetup.FirstPageNumber
PageSetup.FitToPagesTall
PageSetup.FitToPagesWide
PageSetup.FooterMargin
PageSetup.HeaderMargin
PageSetup.LeftFooter
PageSetup.LeftHeader
PageSetup.LeftMargin
PageSetup.Order
PageSetup.Orientation
PageSetup.PaperSize
PageSetup.Parent
PageSetup.PrintArea
PageSetup.PrintGridlines
PageSetup.PrintHeadings
PageSetup.PrintNotes
PageSetup.PrintQuality
PageSetup.PrintTitleColumns
PageSetup.PrintTitleRows
PageSetup.RightFooter
PageSetup.RightHeader
PageSetup.RightMargin
PageSetup.TopMargin
PageSetup.Zoom
```

Pane Object

A pane of a workbook window.

Methods

```
Pane.Activate
Pane.LargeScroll
Pane.SmallScroll
```

Properties

```
Pane.Application
Pane.Creator
Pane.Index
Pane.Parent
Pane.ScrollColumn
Pane.ScrollRow
Pane.VisibleRange
```

Panes Object

A collection of Pane objects.

Methods

```
Panes.Item
```

Properties

```
Panes.Application
Panes.Count
Panes.Creator
Panes.Parent
```

Picture Object

A graphic object created by the Camera toolbar button, or a bitmap or metafile pasted on a sheet.

Methods

```
Picture.BringToFront
Picture.Copy
Picture.CopyPicture
Picture.Cut
Picture.Delete
Picture.Duplicate
Picture.Select
Picture.SendToBack
```

Properties

```
Picture.Application
Picture.Border
Picture.BottomRightCell
Picture.Creator
Picture.Enabled
Picture.Formula
Picture.Height
Picture.Index
Picture.Interior
Picture.Left
Picture.Locked
Picture.Name
Picture.OnAction
Picture.Parent
Picture.Placement
Picture.PrintObject
Picture.Shadow
Picture.Top
Picture.TopLeftCell
Picture.Visible
Picture.Width
Picture.ZOrder
```

Pictures Object

A collection of Picture objects.

Methods

```
Pictures.Add
Pictures.BringToFront
Pictures.Copy
Pictures.CopyPicture
Pictures.Cut
Pictures.Delete
Pictures.Duplicate
Pictures.Group
Pictures.Insert
Pictures.Item
Pictures.Paste
Pictures.Select
Pictures.SendToBack
```

Properties

```
Pictures.Application
Pictures.Border
Pictures.Count
Pictures.Creator
Pictures.Enabled
Pictures.Formula
Pictures.Height
Pictures.Interior
Pictures.Left
Pictures.Locked
Pictures.OnAction
Pictures.Parent
Pictures.Placement
Pictures.PrintObject
Pictures.Shadow
Pictures.Top
Pictures.Visible
Pictures.Width
Pictures.ZOrder
```

PivotField Object

A pivot field in a pivot table (contains PivotItem objects).

Methods

```
PivotField.PivotItems
```

Properties

```
PivotField.Application
PivotField.BaseField
PivotField.BaseItem
PivotField.Calculation
PivotField.ChildField
PivotField.ChildItems
PivotField.Creator
PivotField.CurrentPage
PivotField.DataRange
PivotField.DataType
PivotField.Function
PivotField.GroupLevel
PivotField.HiddenItems
PivotField.LabelRange
PivotField.Name
PivotField.NumberFormat
PivotField.Orientation
PivotField.Parent
PivotField.ParentField
PivotField.ParentItems
PivotField.Position
PivotField.SourceName
PivotField.Subtotals
PivotField.TotalLevels
PivotField.Value
PivotField.VisibleItems
```

PivotFields Object

A collection of PivotField objects.

Methods

```
PivotFields.Item
```

Properties

```
PivotFields.Application
PivotFields.Count
PivotFields.Creator
PivotFields.Parent
```

PivotItem Object

A pivot item in a pivot table.

Methods

(None)

Properties

PivotItem.Application
PivotItem.ChildItems
PivotItem.Creator
PivotItem.DataRange
PivotItem.LabelRange
PivotItem.Name
PivotItem.Parent
PivotItem.ParentItem
PivotItem.ParentShowDetail
PivotItem.Position
PivotItem.ShowDetail
PivotItem.SourceName
PivotItem.Value
PivotItem.Visible

PivotItems Object

A collection of PivotItem objects.

Methods

PivotItems.Item

Properties

PivotItems.Application
PivotItems.Count
PivotItems.Creator
PivotItems.Parent

PivotTable Object

A pivot table on a worksheet (contains PivotField objects).

Methods

PivotTable.AddFields
PivotTable.PivotFields
PivotTable.RefreshTable
PivotTable.ShowPages

Properties

PivotTable.Application
PivotTable.ColumnFields
PivotTable.ColumnGrand
PivotTable.ColumnRange
PivotTable.Creator
PivotTable.DataBodyRange
PivotTable.DataFields
PivotTable.DataLabelRange
PivotTable.HasAutoFormat
PivotTable.HiddenFields
PivotTable.InnerDetail
PivotTable.Name
PivotTable.PageFields
PivotTable.PageRange
PivotTable.Parent

PivotTable.RefreshDate
PivotTable.RefreshName
PivotTable.RowFields
PivotTable.RowGrand
PivotTable.RowRange
PivotTable.SaveData
PivotTable.SourceData
PivotTable.TableRange1
PivotTable.TableRange2
PivotTable.Value
PivotTable.VisibleFields

PivotTables Object

A collection of PivotTable objects.

Methods

PivotTables.Item

Properties

PivotTables.Application
PivotTables.Count
PivotTables.Creator
PivotTables.Parent

PlotArea Object

The plot area of a chart.

Methods

PlotArea.ClearFormats
PlotArea.Select

Properties

PlotArea.Application
PlotArea.Border
PlotArea.Creator
PlotArea.Font
PlotArea.Height
PlotArea.Interior
PlotArea.Left
PlotArea.Name
PlotArea.Parent
PlotArea.Top
PlotArea.Width

Point Object

A single point in a chart series.

Methods

Point.ApplyDataLabels
Point.ClearFormats
Point.Copy
Point.Delete
Point.Paste
Point.Select

Properties

Point.Application
Point.Border
Point.Creator
Point.DataLabel
Point.Explosion
Point.HasDataLabel

```
Point.Interior
Point.InvertIfNegative
Point.MarkerBackgroundColor
Point.MarkerBackgroundColorIndex
Point.MarkerForegroundColor
Point.MarkerForegroundColorIndex
Point.MarkerStyle
Point.Parent
Point.PictureType
Point.PictureUnit
```

Points Object

A collection of Point objects.

Methods

```
Points.Item
```

Properties

```
Points.Application
Points.Count
Points.Creator
Points.Parent
```

Range Object

A cell, row, column, selection of cells, multiple selection, or 3-D range.

Methods

```
Range.Activate
Range.Address
Range.AddressLocal
Range.AdvancedFilter
Range.ApplyNames
Range.ApplyOutlineStyles
Range.Areas
Range.AutoFill
Range.AutoFilter
Range.AutoFit
Range.AutoFormat
Range.AutoOutline
Range.BorderAround
Range.Borders
Range.Calculate
Range.Cells
Range.Characters
Range.CheckSpelling
Range.Clear
Range.ClearContents
Range.ClearFormats
Range.ClearNotes
Range.ClearOutline
Range.ColumnDifferences
Range.Columns
Range.Consolidate
Range.Copy
Range.CopyPicture
Range.CreateNames
Range.CreatePublisher
Range.CurrentArray
Range.CurrentRegion
Range.Cut
Range.DataSeries
Range.Delete
Range.Dependents
Range.DialogBox
Range.DirectDependents
Range.DirectPrecedents
Range.End
Range.EntireColumn
Range.EntireRow
Range.FillDown
Range.FillLeft
Range.FillRight
Range.FillUp
Range.Find
Range.FindNext
Range.FindPrevious
Range.FunctionWizard
```

Range.GoalSeek
Range.Group
Range.Insert
Range.Item
Range.Justify
Range.ListNames
Range.NavigateArrow
Range.Next
Range.NoteText
Range.Offset
Range.Parse
Range.PasteSpecial
Range.Precedents
Range.Previous
Range.PrintOut
Range.PrintPreview
Range.Range
Range.RemoveSubtotal
Range.Replace
Range.Resize
Range.RowDifferences
Range.Rows
Range.Run
Range.Select
Range.Show
Range.ShowDependents
Range.ShowErrors
Range.ShowPrecedents
Range.Sort
Range.SortSpecial
Range.SpecialCells
Range.SubscribeTo
Range.Subtotal
Range.Table
Range.TextToColumns
Range.Ungroup
Range.Worksheet

Properties

Range.AddIndent
Range.Application
Range.Column
Range.ColumnWidth
Range.Count
Range.Creator
Range.Font
Range.Formula
Range.FormulaArray
Range.FormulaHidden
Range.FormulaLocal
Range.FormulaR1C1
Range.FormulaR1C1Local
Range.HasArray
Range.HasFormula
Range.Height
Range.Hidden
Range.HorizontalAlignment
Range.Interior
Range.Left
Range.LocationInTable
Range.Locked
Range.Name
Range.NumberFormat
Range.NumberFormatLocal
Range.Orientation
Range.OutlineLevel
Range.PageBreak
Range.Parent
Range.PivotField
Range.PivotItem
Range.PivotTable
Range.PrefixCharacter
Range.Row
Range.RowHeight
Range.ShowDetail
Range.SoundNote
Range.Style
Range.Summary
Range.Text
Range.Top
Range.UseStandardHeight
Range.UseStandardWidth
Range.Value
Range.VerticalAlignment
Range.Width
Range.WrapText

Rectangle Object

A rectangle graphic object.

Methods

```
Rectangle.BringToFront
Rectangle.Copy
Rectangle.CopyPicture
Rectangle.Cut
Rectangle.Delete
Rectangle.Duplicate
Rectangle.Select
Rectangle.SendToBack
```

Properties

```
Rectangle.Application
Rectangle.Border
Rectangle.BottomRightCell
Rectangle.Creator
Rectangle.Enabled
Rectangle.Height
Rectangle.Index
Rectangle.Interior
Rectangle.Left
Rectangle.Locked
Rectangle.Name
Rectangle.OnAction
Rectangle.Parent
Rectangle.Placement
Rectangle.PrintObject
Rectangle.RoundedCorners
Rectangle.Shadow
Rectangle.Top
Rectangle.TopLeftCell
Rectangle.Visible
Rectangle.Width
Rectangle.ZOrder
```

Rectangles Object

A collection of Rectangle objects.

Methods

```
Rectangles.Add
Rectangles.BringToFront
Rectangles.Copy
Rectangles.CopyPicture
Rectangles.Cut
Rectangles.Delete
Rectangles.Duplicate
Rectangles.Group
Rectangles.Item
Rectangles.Select
Rectangles.SendToBack
```

Properties

```
Rectangles.Application
Rectangles.Border
Rectangles.Count
Rectangles.Creator
Rectangles.Enabled
Rectangles.Height
Rectangles.Interior
Rectangles.Left
Rectangles.Locked
Rectangles.OnAction
Rectangles.Parent
Rectangles.Placement
Rectangles.PrintObject
Rectangles.RoundedCorners
Rectangles.Shadow
Rectangles.Top
Rectangles.Visible
Rectangles.Width
Rectangles.ZOrder
```

RoutingSlip Object

The routing slip of a workbook.

Methods

RoutingSlip.Reset

Properties

RoutingSlip.Application
RoutingSlip.Creator
RoutingSlip.Delivery
RoutingSlip.Message
RoutingSlip.Parent
RoutingSlip.Recipients
RoutingSlip.ReturnWhenDone
RoutingSlip.Status
RoutingSlip.Subject
RoutingSlip.TrackStatus

Scenario Object

A scenario on a worksheet.

Methods

Scenario.ChangeScenario
Scenario.Delete
Scenario.Show

Properties

Scenario.Application
Scenario.ChangingCells
Scenario.Comment
Scenario.Creator
Scenario.Hidden
Scenario.Index
Scenario.Locked
Scenario.Name
Scenario.Parent
Scenario.Values

Scenarios Object

A collection of Scenario objects.

Methods

Scenarios.Add
Scenarios.CreateSummary
Scenarios.Item
Scenarios.Merge

Properties

Scenarios.Application
Scenarios.Count
Scenarios.Creator
Scenarios.Parent

ScrollBar Object

A scroll bar on a dialog sheet or worksheet.

Methods

```
ScrollBar.BringToFront
ScrollBar.Copy
ScrollBar.CopyPicture
ScrollBar.Cut
ScrollBar.Delete
ScrollBar.Duplicate
ScrollBar.Select
ScrollBar.SendToBack
```

Properties

```
ScrollBar.Application
ScrollBar.BottomRightCell
ScrollBar.Creator
ScrollBar.Display3DShading
ScrollBar.Enabled
ScrollBar.Height
ScrollBar.Index
ScrollBar.LargeChange
ScrollBar.Left
ScrollBar.LinkedCell
ScrollBar.Locked
ScrollBar.Max
ScrollBar.Min
ScrollBar.Name
ScrollBar.OnAction
ScrollBar.Parent
ScrollBar.Placement
ScrollBar.PrintObject
ScrollBar.SmallChange
ScrollBar.Top
ScrollBar.TopLeftCell
ScrollBar.Value
ScrollBar.Visible
ScrollBar.Width
ScrollBar.ZOrder
```

ScrollBars Object

A collection of ScrollBar objects.

Methods

```
ScrollBars.Add
ScrollBars.BringToFront
ScrollBars.Copy
ScrollBars.CopyPicture
ScrollBars.Cut
ScrollBars.Delete
ScrollBars.Duplicate
ScrollBars.Group
ScrollBars.Item
ScrollBars.Select
ScrollBars.SendToBack
```

Properties

```
ScrollBars.Application
ScrollBars.Count
ScrollBars.Creator
ScrollBars.Display3DShading
ScrollBars.Enabled
ScrollBars.Height
ScrollBars.LargeChange
ScrollBars.Left
ScrollBars.LinkedCell
ScrollBars.Locked
ScrollBars.Max
ScrollBars.Min
ScrollBars.OnAction
```

ScrollBars.Parent
ScrollBars.Placement
ScrollBars.PrintObject
ScrollBars.SmallChange
ScrollBars.Top
ScrollBars.Value
ScrollBars.Visible
ScrollBars.Width
ScrollBars.ZOrder

Series Object

A series on a chart.

Methods

Series.ApplyDataLabels
Series.ClearFormats
Series.Copy
Series.DataLabels
Series.Delete
Series.ErrorBar
Series.Paste
Series.Points
Series.Select
Series.Trendlines

Properties

Series.Application
Series.AxisGroup
Series.Border
Series.Creator
Series.ErrorBars
Series.Explosion
Series.Formula
Series.FormulaLocal
Series.FormulaR1C1
Series.FormulaR1C1Local
Series.HasDataLabels
Series.HasErrorBars
Series.Interior
Series.InvertIfNegative
Series.MarkerBackgroundColor
Series.MarkerBackgroundColorIndex
Series.MarkerForegroundColor
Series.MarkerForegroundColorIndex
Series.MarkerStyle
Series.Name
Series.Parent
Series.PictureType
Series.PictureUnit
Series.PlotOrder
Series.Smooth
Series.Type
Series.Values
Series.XValues

SeriesCollection Object

A collection of Series objects.

Methods

SeriesCollection.Add
SeriesCollection.Extend
SeriesCollection.Item
SeriesCollection.Paste

Properties

SeriesCollection.Application
SeriesCollection.Count
SeriesCollection.Creator
SeriesCollection.Parent

SeriesLines Object

Series lines on a bar or column chart.

Methods

```
SeriesLines.Delete
SeriesLines.Select
```

Properties

```
SeriesLines.Application
SeriesLines.Border
SeriesLines.Creator
SeriesLines.Name
SeriesLines.Parent
```

Sheets Object

A collection of sheets in a workbook.

Methods

```
Sheets.Add
Sheets.Copy
Sheets.Delete
Sheets.FillAcrossSheets
Sheets.Item
Sheets.Move
Sheets.PrintOut
Sheets.PrintPreview
Sheets.Select
```

Properties

```
Sheets.Application
Sheets.Count
Sheets.Creator
Sheets.Parent
Sheets.Visible
```

SoundNote Object

A sound note in a cell.

Methods

```
SoundNote.Delete
SoundNote.Import
SoundNote.Play
SoundNote.Record
```

Properties

```
SoundNote.Application
SoundNote.Creator
SoundNote.Parent
```

Spinner Object

A spinner control on a dialog sheet or worksheet.

Methods

Spinner.BringToFront
Spinner.Copy
Spinner.CopyPicture
Spinner.Cut
Spinner.Delete
Spinner.Duplicate
Spinner.Select
Spinner.SendToBack

Properties

Spinner.Application
Spinner.BottomRightCell
Spinner.Creator
Spinner.Display3DShading
Spinner.Enabled
Spinner.Height
Spinner.Index
Spinner.Left
Spinner.LinkedCell
Spinner.Locked
Spinner.Max
Spinner.Min
Spinner.Name
Spinner.OnAction
Spinner.Parent
Spinner.Placement
Spinner.PrintObject
Spinner.SmallChange
Spinner.Top
Spinner.TopLeftCell
Spinner.Value
Spinner.Visible
Spinner.Width
Spinner.ZOrder

Spinners Object

A collection of Spinner objects.

Methods

Spinners.Add
Spinners.BringToFront
Spinners.Copy
Spinners.CopyPicture
Spinners.Cut
Spinners.Delete
Spinners.Duplicate
Spinners.Group
Spinners.Item
Spinners.Select
Spinners.SendToBack

Properties

Spinners.Application
Spinners.Count
Spinners.Creator
Spinners.Display3DShading
Spinners.Enabled
Spinners.Height
Spinners.Left
Spinners.LinkedCell
Spinners.Locked
Spinners.Max
Spinners.Min
Spinners.OnAction
Spinners.Parent
Spinners.Placement
Spinners.PrintObject
Spinners.SmallChange
Spinners.Top
Spinners.Value
Spinners.Visible
Spinners.Width
Spinners.ZOrder

Style Object

A style description (style attributes are properties).

Methods

Style.Borders
Style.Delete

Properties

Style.AddIndent
Style.Application
Style.Creator
Style.Font
Style.FormulaHidden
Style.HorizontalAlignment
Style.IncludeAlignment
Style.IncludeBorder
Style.IncludeFont
Style.IncludeNumber
Style.IncludePatterns
Style.IncludeProtection
Style.Interior
Style.Locked
Style.Name
Style.NameLocal
Style.NumberFormat
Style.NumberFormatLocal
Style.Orientation
Style.Parent
Style.Value
Style.VerticalAlignment
Style.WrapText

Styles Object

A collection of Style objects.

Methods

Styles.Add
Styles.Item
Styles.Merge

Properties

Styles.Application
Styles.Count
Styles.Creator
Styles.Parent

TextBox Object

A text box graphic object on a sheet.

Methods

TextBox.BringToFront
TextBox.Characters
TextBox.CheckSpelling
TextBox.Copy
TextBox.CopyPicture
TextBox.Cut
TextBox.Delete
TextBox.Duplicate
TextBox.Select
TextBox.SendToBack

Properties

TextBox.AddIndent
TextBox.Application
TextBox.AutoSize
TextBox.Border
TextBox.BottomRightCell
TextBox.Caption
TextBox.Creator
TextBox.Enabled
TextBox.Font
TextBox.Formula
TextBox.Height
TextBox.HorizontalAlignment
TextBox.Index
TextBox.Interior
TextBox.Left
TextBox.Locked
TextBox.LockedText
TextBox.Name
TextBox.OnAction
TextBox.Orientation
TextBox.Parent
TextBox.Placement
TextBox.PrintObject
TextBox.RoundedCorners
TextBox.Shadow
TextBox.Text
TextBox.Top
TextBox.TopLeftCell
TextBox.VerticalAlignment
TextBox.Visible
TextBox.Width
TextBox.ZOrder

TextBoxes Object

A collection of TextBox objects.

Methods

TextBoxes.Add
TextBoxes.BringToFront
TextBoxes.Characters
TextBoxes.CheckSpelling
TextBoxes.Copy
TextBoxes.CopyPicture
TextBoxes.Cut
TextBoxes.Delete
TextBoxes.Duplicate
TextBoxes.Group
TextBoxes.Item
TextBoxes.Select
TextBoxes.SendToBack

Properties

TextBoxes.AddIndent
TextBoxes.Application
TextBoxes.AutoSize
TextBoxes.Border
TextBoxes.Caption
TextBoxes.Count
TextBoxes.Creator
TextBoxes.Enabled
TextBoxes.Font
TextBoxes.Formula
TextBoxes.Height
TextBoxes.HorizontalAlignment
TextBoxes.Interior
TextBoxes.Left
TextBoxes.Locked
TextBoxes.LockedText
TextBoxes.OnAction
TextBoxes.Orientation
TextBoxes.Parent
TextBoxes.Placement
TextBoxes.PrintObject
TextBoxes.RoundedCorners
TextBoxes.Shadow
TextBoxes.Text
TextBoxes.Top
TextBoxes.VerticalAlignment
TextBoxes.Visible
TextBoxes.Width
TextBoxes.ZOrder

TickLabels Object

The text associated with tick marks on a chart axis.

Methods

```
TickLabels.Delete
TickLabels.Select
```

Properties

```
TickLabels.Application
TickLabels.Creator
TickLabels.Font
TickLabels.Name
TickLabels.NumberFormat
TickLabels.NumberFormatLinked
TickLabels.Orientation
TickLabels.Parent
```

Toolbar Object

A toolbar (built-in or custom).

Methods

```
Toolbar.Delete
Toolbar.Reset
Toolbar.ToolbarButtons
```

Properties

```
Toolbar.Application
Toolbar.BuiltIn
Toolbar.Creator
Toolbar.Height
Toolbar.Left
Toolbar.Name
Toolbar.Parent
Toolbar.Position
Toolbar.Top
Toolbar.Visible
Toolbar.Width
```

ToolbarButton Object

A button on a toolbar.

Methods

```
ToolbarButton.Copy
ToolbarButton.CopyFace
ToolbarButton.Delete
ToolbarButton.Edit
ToolbarButton.Move
ToolbarButton.PasteFace
ToolbarButton.Reset
```

Properties

```
ToolbarButton.Application
ToolbarButton.BuiltIn
ToolbarButton.BuiltInFace
ToolbarButton.Creator
ToolbarButton.Enabled
ToolbarButton.Id
ToolbarButton.IsGap
ToolbarButton.Name
ToolbarButton.OnAction
ToolbarButton.Parent
ToolbarButton.Pushed
ToolbarButton.Width
```

ToolbarButtons Object

A collection of ToolbarButton objects.

Methods

ToolbarButtons.Add
ToolbarButtons.Item

Properties

ToolbarButtons.Application
ToolbarButtons.Count
ToolbarButtons.Creator
ToolbarButtons.Parent

Toolbars Object

A collection of Toolbar objects.

Methods

Toolbars.Add
Toolbars.Item

Properties

Toolbars.Application
Toolbars.Count
Toolbars.Creator
Toolbars.Parent

Trendline Object

A trend line on a chart.

Methods

Trendline.ClearFormats
Trendline.Delete
Trendline.Select

Properties

Trendline.Application
Trendline.Backward
Trendline.Border
Trendline.Creator
Trendline.DataLabel
Trendline.DisplayEquation
Trendline.DisplayRSquared
Trendline.Forward
Trendline.Index
Trendline.Intercept
Trendline.InterceptIsAuto
Trendline.Name
Trendline.NameIsAuto
Trendline.Order
Trendline.Parent
Trendline.Period
Trendline.Type

Trendlines Object

A collection of Trendline objects.

Methods

```
Trendlines.Add
Trendlines.Item
```

Properties

```
Trendlines.Application
Trendlines.Count
Trendlines.Creator
Trendlines.Parent
```

UpBars Object

An Up bar on a chart.

Methods

```
UpBars.Delete
UpBars.Select
```

Properties

```
UpBars.Application
UpBars.Border
UpBars.Creator
UpBars.Interior
UpBars.Name
UpBars.Parent
```

Walls Object

The walls of a 3-D chart.

Methods

```
Walls.ClearFormats
Walls.Select
```

Properties

```
Walls.Application
Walls.Border
Walls.Creator
Walls.Interior
Walls.Name
Walls.Parent
```

Window Object

Any window in Excel.

Methods

```
Window.Activate
Window.ActivateNext
Window.ActivatePrevious
Window.Close
Window.LargeScroll
Window.NewWindow
Window.Panes
Window.PrintOut
Window.PrintPreview
Window.ScrollWorkbookTabs
Window.SelectedSheets
Window.SetInfoDisplay
Window.SmallScroll
```

Properties

```
Window.ActiveCell
Window.ActiveChart
Window.ActivePane
Window.ActiveSheet
Window.Application
Window.Caption
Window.Creator
Window.DisplayFormulas
Window.DisplayGridlines
Window.DisplayHeadings
Window.DisplayHorizontalScrollBar
Window.DisplayOutline
Window.DisplayRightToLeft
Window.DisplayVerticalScrollBar
Window.DisplayWorkbookTabs
Window.DisplayZeros
Window.FreezePanes
Window.GridlineColor
Window.GridlineColorIndex
Window.Height
Window.Index
Window.Left
Window.OnWindow
Window.PageSetup
Window.Parent
Window.ScrollColumn
Window.ScrollRow
Window.Selection
Window.Split
Window.SplitColumn
Window.SplitHorizontal
Window.SplitRow
Window.SplitVertical
Window.TabRatio
Window.Top
Window.Type
Window.UsableHeight
Window.UsableWidth
Window.Visible
Window.VisibleRange
Window.Width
Window.WindowNumber
Window.WindowState
Window.Zoom
```

Windows Object

A collection of Window objects.

Methods

```
Windows.Arrange
Windows.Item
```

Properties

```
Windows.Application
Windows.Count
Windows.Creator
Windows.Parent
```

Workbook Object

An Excel workbook.

Methods

```
Workbook.Activate
Workbook.ChangeFileAccess
Workbook.ChangeLink
Workbook.Charts
Workbook.Close
Workbook.DeleteNumberFormat
Workbook.DialogSheets
Workbook.Excel4IntlMacroSheets
Workbook.Excel4MacroSheets
Workbook.ForwardMailer
Workbook.LinkInfo
Workbook.LinkSources
Workbook.Modules
Workbook.Names
Workbook.NewWindow
Workbook.OpenLinks
Workbook.PrintOut
Workbook.PrintPreview
Workbook.Protect
Workbook.Reply
Workbook.ReplyAll
Workbook.Route
Workbook.RunAutoMacros
Workbook.Save
Workbook.SaveAs
Workbook.SaveCopyAs
Workbook.SendMail
Workbook.SendMailer
Workbook.SetLinkOnData
Workbook.Sheets
Workbook.Styles
Workbook.Unprotect
Workbook.UpdateFromFile
Workbook.UpdateLink
Workbook.Windows
Workbook.Worksheets
```

Properties

```
Workbook.ActiveChart
Workbook.ActiveSheet
Workbook.Application
Workbook.Author
Workbook.Colors
Workbook.Comments
Workbook.CreateBackup
Workbook.Creator
Workbook.Date1904
Workbook.DisplayDrawingObjects
Workbook.FileFormat
Workbook.FullName
Workbook.HasMailer
Workbook.HasPassword
Workbook.HasRoutingSlip
```

Workbook.Keywords
Workbook.Mailer
Workbook.Name
Workbook.OnSheetActivate
Workbook.OnSheetDeactivate
Workbook.Parent
Workbook.Path
Workbook.PrecisionAsDisplayed
Workbook.ProtectStructure
Workbook.ProtectWindows
Workbook.ReadOnly
Workbook.ReadOnlyRecommended
Workbook.Routed
Workbook.RoutingSlip
Workbook.Saved
Workbook.SaveLinkValues
Workbook.Subject
Workbook.Title
Workbook.UpdateRemoteReferences
Workbook.WriteReserved
Workbook.WriteReservedBy

Workbooks Object

A collection of Workbook objects.

Methods

Workbooks.Add
Workbooks.Close
Workbooks.Item
Workbooks.Open
Workbooks.OpenText

Properties

Workbooks.Application
Workbooks.Count
Workbooks.Creator
Workbooks.Parent

Worksheet Object

A worksheet in a workbook (includes XLM macro sheets).

Methods

Worksheet.Activate
Worksheet.Arcs
Worksheet.Buttons
Worksheet.Calculate
Worksheet.Cells
Worksheet.ChartObjects
Worksheet.CheckBoxes
Worksheet.CheckSpelling
Worksheet.ClearArrows
Worksheet.Columns
Worksheet.Copy
Worksheet.Delete
Worksheet.DrawingObjects
Worksheet.Drawings
Worksheet.DropDowns
Worksheet.Evaluate
Worksheet.GroupBoxes
Worksheet.GroupObjects
Worksheet.Labels
Worksheet.Lines
Worksheet.ListBoxes
Worksheet.Move
Worksheet.OLEObjects
Worksheet.OptionButtons
Worksheet.Ovals
Worksheet.Paste
Worksheet.PasteSpecial
Worksheet.Pictures

Worksheet.PivotTables
Worksheet.PivotTableWizard
Worksheet.PrintOut
Worksheet.PrintPreview
Worksheet.Protect
Worksheet.Range
Worksheet.Rectangles
Worksheet.Rows
Worksheet.SaveAs
Worksheet.Scenarios
Worksheet.ScrollBars
Worksheet.Select
Worksheet.ShowAllData
Worksheet.ShowDataForm
Worksheet.Spinners
Worksheet.TextBoxes
Worksheet.Unprotect

Properties

Worksheet.Application
Worksheet.AutoFilterMode
Worksheet.CircularReference
Worksheet.ConsolidationFunction
Worksheet.ConsolidationOptions
Worksheet.ConsolidationSources
Worksheet.Creator
Worksheet.DisplayAutomaticPageBreaks
Worksheet.FilterMode
Worksheet.Index
Worksheet.Name
Worksheet.Next
Worksheet.OnCalculate
Worksheet.OnData
Worksheet.OnDoubleClick
Worksheet.OnEntry
Worksheet.OnSheetActivate
Worksheet.OnSheetDeactivate
Worksheet.Outline
Worksheet.PageSetup
Worksheet.Parent
Worksheet.Previous
Worksheet.ProtectContents
Worksheet.ProtectDrawingObjects
Worksheet.ProtectScenarios
Worksheet.StandardHeight
Worksheet.StandardWidth
Worksheet.TransitionExpEval
Worksheet.TransitionFormEntry
Worksheet.Type
Worksheet.UsedRange
Worksheet.Visible

Worksheets Object

A collection of Worksheet objects.

Methods

Worksheets.Add
Worksheets.Copy
Worksheets.Delete
Worksheets.FillAcrossSheets
Worksheets.Item
Worksheets.Move
Worksheets.PrintOut
Worksheets.PrintPreview
Worksheets.Select

Properties

Worksheets.Application
Worksheets.Count
Worksheets.Creator
Worksheets.Parent
Worksheets.Visible

Appendix C

Excel and VBA Constants Reference

This appendix is a complete listing of constants and their values as defined in Excel and VBA.

Excel Constants

Constant	*Value*	*Constant*	*Value*
xl24HourClock	33	xlAbsRowRelColumn	2
xl3DArea	-4098	xlAccounting1	4
xl3DBar	-4099	xlAccounting2	5
xl3DColumn	-4100	xlAccounting3	6
xl3DEffects1	13	xlAccounting4	17
xl3DEffects2	14	xlAdd	2
xl3DLine	-4101	xlAddIn	18
xl3DPie	-4102	xlAll	-4104
xl3DSurface	-4103	xlAllAtOnce	2
xl4DigitYears	43	xlAlternateArraySeparator	16
xlA1	1	xlAnd	1
xlAbove	0	xlArea	1
xlAbsolute	1	xlAscending	1

Constant	*Value*	*Constant*	*Value*
xlAutoActivate	3	xlCascade	7
xlAutoClose	2	xlCategory	1
xlAutoDeactivate	4	xlCenter	-4108
xlAutoFill	4	xlCenterAcrossSelection	7
xlAutomatic	-4105	xlCGM	7
xlAutomaticUpdate	4	xlChangeAttributes	6
xlAutoOpen	1	xlChart	-4109
xlAverage	-4106	xlChart4	2
xlAxis	21	xlChartAsWindow	5
xlBar	2	xlChartInPlace	4
xlBelow	1	xlChartSeries	17
xlBIFF	2	xlChartShort	6
xlBitmap	2	xlChartTitles	18
xlBlanks	4	xlChecker	9
xlBMP	1	xlChronological	3
xlBoth	1	xlCircle	8
xlBottom	-4107	xlClassic1	1
xlBuiltIn	0	xlClassic2	2
xlButton	15	xlClassic3	3
xlByColumns	2	xlClipboard	3
xlByRows	1	xlClipboardFormatBIFF	8
xlCancel	1	xlClipboardFormatBIFF2	18
xlCap	1	xlClipboardFormatBIFF3	20

Constant	Value	Constant	Value
xlClipboardFormatBIFF4	30	xlClipboardFormatSYLK	6
xlClipboardFormatBinary	15	xlClipboardFormatTable	16
xlClipboardFormatBitmap	9	xlClipboardFormatText	0
xlClipboardFormatCGM	13	xlClipboardFormatToolFace	25
xlClipboardFormatCSV	5	xlClipboardFormatToolFacePICT	26
xlClipboardFormatDIF	4	xlClipboardFormatVALU	1
xlClipboardFormatDspText	12	xlClipboardFormatWK1	10
xlClipboardFormatEmbeddedObject	21	xlClosed	3
xlClipboardFormatEmbedSource	22	xlCodePage	2
xlClipboardFormatLink	11	xlColor1	7
xlClipboardFormatLinkSource	23	xlColor2	8
xlClipboardFormatLinkSourceDesc	32	xlColor3	9
xlClipboardFormatMovie	24	xlColumn	3
xlClipboardFormatNative	14	xlColumnField	2
xlClipboardFormatObjectDesc	31	xlColumnHeader	-4110
xlClipboardFormatObjectLink	19	xlColumnItem	5
xlClipboardFormatOwnerLink	17	xlColumns	2
xlClipboardFormatPICT	2	xlColumnSeparator	14
xlClipboardFormatPrintPICT	3	xlColumnThenRow	2
xlClipboardFormatRTF	7	xlCombination	-4111
xlClipboardFormatScreenPICT	29	xlCommand	2
xlClipboardFormatStandardFont	28	xlConsolidation	3
xlClipboardFormatStandardScale	27	xlConstants	2

Constant	Value	Constant	Value
xlContents	2	xlCut	2
xlContinuous	1	xlDash	-4115
xlCopy	1	xlDashDot	4
xlCorner	2	xlDashDotDot	5
xlCount	-4112	xlDatabase	1
xlCountNums	-4113	xlDataField	4
xlCountryCode	1	xlDataHeader	3
xlCountrySetting	2	xlDataItem	7
xlCrissCross	16	xlDate	2
xlCross	4	xlDateOrder	32
xlCSV	6	xlDateSeparator	17
xlCSVMac	22	xlDay	1
xlCSVMSDOS	24	xlDayCode	21
xlCSVWindows	23	xlDayLeadingZero	42
xlCurrencyBefore	37	xlDBF2	7
xlCurrencyCode	25	xlDBF3	8
xlCurrencyDigits	27	xlDBF4	11
xlCurrencyLeadingZeros	40	xlDebugCodePane	13
xlCurrencyMinusSign	38	xlDecimalSeparator	3
xlCurrencyNegative	28	xlDefaultAutoFormat	-1
xlCurrencySpaceBefore	36	xlDelimited	1
xlCurrencyTrailingZeros	39	xlDescending	2
xlCustom	-4114	xlDesktop	9

Constant	*Value*	*Constant*	*Value*
xlDialogActivate	103	xlDialogCheckboxProperties	435
xlDialogActiveCellFont	476	xlDialogClear	52
xlDialogAddChartAutoformat	390	xlDialogColorPalette	161
xlDialogAddinManager	321	xlDialogColumnWidth	47
xlDialogAlignment	43	xlDialogCombination	73
xlDialogApplyNames	133	xlDialogConsolidate	191
xlDialogApplyStyle	212	xlDialogCopyChart	147
xlDialogAppMove	170	xlDialogCopyPicture	108
xlDialogAppSize	171	xlDialogCreateNames	62
xlDialogArrangeAll	12	xlDialogCreatePublisher	217
xlDialogAssignToObject	213	xlDialogCustomizeToolbar	276
xlDialogAssignToTool	293	xlDialogDataDelete	36
xlDialogAttachText	80	xlDialogDataLabel	379
xlDialogAttachToolbars	323	xlDialogDataSeries	40
xlDialogAttributes	219	xlDialogDefineName	61
xlDialogAxes	78	xlDialogDefineStyle	229
xlDialogBorder	45	xlDialogDeleteFormat	111
xlDialogCalculation	32	xlDialogDeleteName	110
xlDialogCellProtection	46	xlDialogDemote	203
xlDialogChangeLink	166	xlDialogDisplay	27
xlDialogChartAddData	392	xlDialogEditboxProperties	438
xlDialogChartTrend	350	xlDialogEditColor	223
xlDialogChartWizard	288	xlDialogEditDelete	54

Constant	*Value*	*Constant*	*Value*
xlDialogEditionOptions	251	xlDialogFormulaFind	64
xlDialogEditSeries	228	xlDialogFormulaGoto	63
xlDialogErrorbarX	463	xlDialogFormulaReplace	130
xlDialogErrorbarY	464	xlDialogFunctionWizard	450
xlDialogExtract	35	xlDialogGallery3dArea	193
xlDialogFileDelete	6	xlDialogGallery3dBar	272
xlDialogFillGroup	200	xlDialogGallery3dColumn	194
xlDialogFillWorkgroup	301	xlDialogGallery3dLine	195
xlDialogFilterAdvanced	370	xlDialogGallery3dPie	196
xlDialogFindFile	475	xlDialogGallery3dSurface	273
xlDialogFont	26	xlDialogGalleryArea	67
xlDialogFontProperties	381	xlDialogGalleryBar	68
xlDialogFormatAuto	269	xlDialogGalleryColumn	69
xlDialogFormatChart	465	xlDialogGalleryCustom	388
xlDialogFormatCharttype	423	xlDialogGalleryDoughnut	344
xlDialogFormatFont	150	xlDialogGalleryLine	70
xlDialogFormatLegend	88	xlDialogGalleryPie	71
xlDialogFormatMain	225	xlDialogGalleryRadar	249
xlDialogFormatMove	128	xlDialogGalleryScatter	72
xlDialogFormatNumber	42	xlDialogGoalSeek	198
xlDialogFormatOverlay	226	xlDialogGridlines	76
xlDialogFormatSize	129	xlDialogInsert	55
xlDialogFormatText	89	xlDialogInsertObject	259

Constant	Value	Constant	Value
xlDialogInsertPicture	342	xlDialogOptionsListsAdd	458
xlDialogInsertTitle	380	xlDialogOptionsTransition	355
xlDialogLabelProperties	436	xlDialogOptionsView	320
xlDialogListboxProperties	437	xlDialogOutline	142
xlDialogMacroOptions	382	xlDialogOverlay	86
xlDialogMailLogon	339	xlDialogOverlayChartType	186
xlDialogMailNextLetter	378	xlDialogPageSetup	7
xlDialogMainChart	85	xlDialogParse	91
xlDialogMainChartType	185	xlDialogPasteSpecial	53
xlDialogMenuEditor	322	xlDialogPatterns	84
xlDialogMove	262	xlDialogPivotFieldGroup	433
xlDialogNew	119	xlDialogPivotFieldProperties	313
xlDialogNote	154	xlDialogPivotFieldUngroup	434
xlDialogObjectProperties	207	xlDialogPivotShowPages	421
xlDialogObjectProtection	214	xlDialogPivotTableWizard	312
xlDialogOpen	1	xlDialogPlacement	300
xlDialogOpenLinks	2	xlDialogPrint	8
xlDialogOpenMail	188	xlDialogPrinterSetup	9
xlDialogOpenText	441	xlDialogPrintPreview	222
xlDialogOptionsCalculation	318	xlDialogPromote	202
xlDialogOptionsChart	325	xlDialogProtectDocument	28
xlDialogOptionsEdit	319	xlDialogPushbuttonProperties	445
xlDialogOptionsGeneral	356	xlDialogReplaceFont	134

Constant	Value	Constant	Value
xlDialogRoutingSlip	336	xlDialogSetUpdateStatus	159
xlDialogRowHeight	127	xlDialogSheet	-4116
xlDialogRun	17	xlDialogShowDetail	204
xlDialogSaveAs	5	xlDialogShowToolbar	220
xlDialogSaveCopyAs	456	xlDialogSize	261
xlDialogSaveNewObject	208	xlDialogSort	39
xlDialogSaveWorkbook	145	xlDialogSortSpecial	192
xlDialogSaveWorkspace	285	xlDialogSplit	137
xlDialogScale	87	xlDialogStandardFont	190
xlDialogScenarioAdd	307	xlDialogStandardWidth	472
xlDialogScenarioCells	305	xlDialogStyle	44
xlDialogScenarioEdit	308	xlDialogSubscribeTo	218
xlDialogScenarioMerge	473	xlDialogSubtotalCreate	398
xlDialogScenarioSummary	311	xlDialogSummaryInfo	474
xlDialogScrollbarProperties	420	xlDialogTable	41
xlDialogSelectSpecial	132	xlDialogTabOrder	394
xlDialogSendMail	189	xlDialogTextToColumns	422
xlDialogSeriesAxes	460	xlDialogUnhide	94
xlDialogSeriesOrder	466	xlDialogUpdateLink	201
xlDialogSeriesX	461	xlDialogVbaInsertFile	328
xlDialogSeriesY	462	xlDialogVbaMakeAddin	478
xlDialogSetControlValue	455	xlDialogVbaProcedureDefinition	330
xlDialogSetPrintTitles	23	xlDialogView3d	197

Constant	Value	Constant	Value
xlDialogWindowMove	14	xlDouble	-4119
xlDialogWindowSize	13	xlDoubleAccounting	5
xlDialogWorkbookAdd	281	xlDoubleClosed	5
xlDialogWorkbookCopy	283	xlDoubleOpen	4
xlDialogWorkbookInsert	354	xlDoubleQuote	1
xlDialogWorkbookMove	282	xlDoughnut	-4120
xlDialogWorkbookName	386	xlDown	-4121
xlDialogWorkbookNew	302	xlDownThenOver	1
xlDialogWorkbookOptions	284	xlDownward	-4170
xlDialogWorkbookProtect	417	xlDrawingObject	14
xlDialogWorkbookTabSplit	415	xlDRW	4
xlDialogWorkbookUnhide	384	xlDXF	5
xlDialogWorkgroup	199	xlEditionDate	2
xlDialogWorkspace	95	xlEntireChart	20
xlDialogZoom	256	xlEPS	8
xlDiamond	2	xlErrDiv0	2007
xlDIF	9	xlErrNA	2042
xlDifferenceFrom	2	xlErrName	2029
xlDirect	1	xlErrNull	2000
xlDisabled	0	xlErrNum	2036
xlDistributed	-4117	xlErrorHandler	2
xlDivide	5	xlErrors	16
xlDot	-4118	xlErrRef	2023

Constant	*Value*	*Constant*	*Value*
xlErrValue	2015	xlFillYears	8
xlExcel2	16	xlFilterCopy	2
xlExcel2FarEast	27	xlFilterInPlace	1
xlExcel3	29	xlFirst	0
xlExcel4	33	xlFitToPage	2
xlExcel4IntlMacroSheet	4	xlFixedValue	1
xlExcel4MacroSheet	3	xlFixedWidth	2
xlExcel4Workbook	35	xlFloating	5
xlExcelLinks	1	xlFloor	23
xlExcelMenus	1	xlFormats	-4122
xlExponential	5	xlFormula	5
xlExtended	2	xlFormulas	-4123
xlExternal	2	xlFreeFloating	3
xlFill	5	xlFullPage	3
xlFillCopy	1	xlFunction	1
xlFillDays	5	xlGeneral	1
xlFillDefault	0	xlGeneralFormatName	26
xlFillFormats	3	xlGray16	17
xlFillMonths	7	xlGray25	-4124
xlFillSeries	2	xlGray50	-4125
xlFillValues	4	xlGray75	-4126
xlFillWeekdays	6	xlGray8	18

Constant	*Value*	*Constant*	*Value*
xlGrid	15	xlLandscape	2
xlGridline	22	xlLast	1
xlGrowth	2	xlLastCell	11
xlGrowthTrend	10	xlLeft	-4131
xlGuess	0	xlLeftBrace	12
xlHairline	1	xlLeftBracket	10
xlHGL	6	xlLeftToRight	2
xlHidden	0	xlLegend	24
xlHide	3	xlLightDown	13
xlHigh	-4127	xlLightHorizontal	11
xlHorizontal	-4128	xlLightUp	14
xlHourCode	22	xlLightVertical	12
xlIcons	1	xlLine	4
xlImmediatePane	12	xlLinear	-4132
xlIndex	9	xlLinearTrend	9
xlInfo	-4129	xlList1	10
xlInside	2	xlList2	11
xlInteger	2	xlList3	12
xlInterpolated	3	xlListSeparator	5
xlInterrupt	1	xlLocalFormat1	15
xlIntlAddIn	26	xlLocalFormat2	16
xlIntlMacro	25	xlLogarithmic	-4133
xlJustify	-4130	xlLogical	4

Constant	*Value*	*Constant*	*Value*
xlLong	3	xlMicrosoftWord	1
xlLotusHelp	2	xlMin	-4139
xlLow	-4134	xlMinimized	-4140
xlLowerCaseColumnLetter	9	xlMinimum	2
xlLowerCaseRowLetter	8	xlMinusValues	3
xlMacintosh	1	xlMinuteCode	23
xlMacrosheetCell	7	xlMixed	2
xlManual	-4135	xlModule	-4141
xlManualUpdate	5	xlMonth	3
xlMAPI	1	xlMonthCode	20
xlMax	-4136	xlMonthLeadingZero	41
xlMaximized	-4137	xlMonthNameChars	30
xlMaximum	2	xlMove	2
xlMDY	44	xlMoveAndSize	1
xlMedium	-4138	xlMovingAvg	6
xlMetric	35	xlMSDOS	3
xlMicrosoftAccess	4	xlMultiply	4
xlMicrosoftFoxPro	5	xlNarrow	1
xlMicrosoftMail	3	xlNext	1
xlMicrosoftPowerPoint	2	xlNextToAxis	4
xlMicrosoftProject	6	xlNo	2
xlMicrosoftSchedulePlus	7	xlNoCap	2

Constant	*Value*	*Constant*	*Value*
xlNoDocuments	3	xlOverThenDown	2
xlNoMailSystem	0	xlPageField	3
xlNoncurrencyDigits	29	xlPageHeader	2
xlNone	-4142	xlPageItem	6
xlNonEnglishFunctions	34	xlPaper10x14	16
xlNormal	-4143	xlPaper11x17	17
xlNotes	-4144	xlPaperA3	8
xlNotPlotted	1	xlPaperA4	9
xlNotYetRouted	0	xlPaperA4Small	10
xlNumber	-4145	xlPaperA5	11
xlNumbers	1	xlPaperB4	12
xlOff	-4146	xlPaperB5	13
xlOLEEmbed	1	xlPaperCsheet	24
xlOLELink	0	xlPaperDsheet	25
xlOLELinks	2	xlPaperEnvelope10	20
xlOn	1	xlPaperEnvelope11	21
xlOneAfterAnother	1	xlPaperEnvelope12	22
xlOpaque	3	xlPaperEnvelope14	23
xlOpen	2	xlPaperEnvelope9	19
xlOpenSource	3	xlPaperEnvelopeB4	33
xlOr	2	xlPaperEnvelopeB5	34
xlOutside	3	xlPaperEnvelopeB6	35

Constant	*Value*	*Constant*	*Value*
xlPaperEnvelopeC3	29	xlPaperTabloid	3
xlPaperEnvelopeC4	30	xlPaperUser	256
xlPaperEnvelopeC5	28	xlPart	2
xlPaperEnvelopeC6	31	xlPCT	13
xlPaperEnvelopeC65	32	xlPCX	10
xlPaperEnvelopeDL	27	xlPercent	2
xlPaperEnvelopeItaly	36	xlPercentDifferenceFrom	4
xlPaperEnvelopeMonarch	37	xlPercentOf	3
xlPaperEnvelopePersonal	38	xlPercentOfColumn	7
xlPaperEsheet	26	xlPercentOfRow	6
xlPaperExecutive	7	xlPercentOfTotal	8
xlPaperFanfoldLegalGerman	41	xlPIC	11
xlPaperFanfoldStdGerman	40	xlPICT	1
xlPaperFanfoldUS	39	xlPicture	-4147
xlPaperFolio	14	xlPie	5
xlPaperLedger	4	xlPivotTable	-4148
xlPaperLegal	5	xlPlaceholders	2
xlPaperLetter	1	xlPlotArea	19
xlPaperLetterSmall	2	xlPLT	12
xlPaperNote	18	xlPlus	9
xlPaperQuarto	15	xlPlusValues	2
xlPaperStatement	6	xlPolynomial	3

Constant	*Value*	*Constant*	*Value*
xlPortrait	1	xlRowItem	4
xlPower	4	xlRows	1
xlPowerTalk	2	xlRowSeparator	15
xlPrevious	2	xlRowThenColumn	1
xlPrimary	1	xlRTF	4
xlPrinter	2	xlRunningTotal	5
xlProduct	-4149	xlScale	3
xlPublisher	1	xlScreen	1
xlPublishers	5	xlScreenSize	1
xlR1C1	-4150	xlSecondary	2
xlRadar	-4151	xlSecondCode	24
xlReadOnly	3	xlSelect	3
xlReadWrite	2	xlSemiautomatic	2
xlReference	4	xlSemiGray75	10
xlRelative	4	xlSendPublisher	2
xlRelRowAbsColumn	3	xlSeries	3
xlRight	-4152	xlShort	1
xlRightBrace	13	xlShowLabel	4
xlRightBracket	11	xlShowLabelAndPercent	5
xlRoutingComplete	2	xlShowPercent	3
xlRoutingInProgress	1	xlShowValue	2
xlRowField	1	xlSimple	-4154
xlRowHeader	-4153	xlSingle	2

Constant	Value	Constant	Value
xlSingleAccounting	4	xlTextBox	16
xlSingleQuote	2	xlTextMac	19
xlSolid	1	xlTextMSDOS	21
xlSortLabels	2	xlTextPrinter	36
xlSortValues	1	xlTextValues	2
xlSquare	1	xlTextWindows	20
xlStack	2	xlThick	4
xlStandardSummary	1	xlThin	2
xlStar	5	xlThousandsSeparator	4
xlStDev	-4155	xlTIF	9
xlStDevP	-4156	xlTiled	1
xlStError	4	xlTimeLeadingZero	45
xlStretch	1	xlTimeSeparator	18
xlStrict	2	xlTitleBar	8
xlSubscriber	2	xlToLeft	-4159
xlSubscribers	6	xlToolbar	1
xlSubtract	3	xlToolbarButton	2
xlSum	-4157	xlTop	-4160
xlSYLK	2	xlTopToBottom	1
xlSyllabary	1	xlToRight	-4161
xlTableBody	8	xlTransparent	2
xlTemplate	17	xlTriangle	3
xlText	-4158	xlUp	-4162

Constant	*Value*	*Constant*	*Value*
xlUpdateState	1	xlWK1FMT	30
xlUpdateSubscriber	2	xlWK3	15
xlUpperCaseColumnLetter	7	xlWK3FM3	32
xlUpperCaseRowLetter	6	xlWKS	4
xlUpward	-4171	xlWMF	2
xlVALU	8	xlWorkbook	1
xlValue	2	xlWorkbookTab	6
xlValues	-4163	xlWorks2FarEast	28
xlVar	-4164	xlWorksheet	-4167
xlVarP	-4165	xlWorksheet4	1
xlVertical	-4166	xlWorksheetCell	3
xlVeryHidden	2	xlWorksheetShort	5
xlVisible	12	xlWPG	3
xlWatchPane	11	xlWQ1	34
xlWeekday	2	xlX	-4168
xlWeekdayNameChars	31	xlXYScatter	-4169
xlWhole	1	xlY	1
xlWide	3	xlYear	4
xlWindows	2	xlYearCode	19
xlWJ2WD1	14	xlYes	1
xlWK1	5	xlZero	2
xlWK1ALL	31		

VBA Constants

Constant	*Value*	*Constant*	*Value*
vbAbort	3	vbIgnore	5
vbAbortRetryIgnore	2	vbInformation	64
vbApplicationModal	0	vbInteger	2
vbArchive	32	vbKatakana	16
vbArray	8192	vbLong	3
vbBoolean	11	vbLowerCase	2
vbCancel	2	vbNarrow	8
vbCritical	16	vbNo	7
vbCurrency	6	vbNormal	0
vbDataObject	13	vbNull	1
vbDate	7	vbObject	9
vbDefaultButton1	0	vbOK	1
vbDefaultButton2	256	vbOKCancel	1
vbDefaultButton3	512	vbOKOnly	0
vbDirectory	16	vbProperCase	3
vbDouble	5	vbQuestion	32
vbEmpty	0	vbReadOnly	1
vbError	10	vbRetry	4
vbExclamation	48	vbRetryCancel	5
vbHidden	2	vbSingle	4
vbHiragana	32	vbString	8

Constant	***Value***
vbSystem	4
vbSystemModal	4096
vbUpperCase	1
vbVariant	12
vbVolume	8
vbWide	4
vbYes	6
vbYesNo	4
vbYesNoCancel	3

Appendix D

VBA Statements and Functions Reference

This appendix contains a complete listing of all VBA statements and built-in functions. For complete details, consult the on-line help.

Summary of VBA Statements

Statement	*Action*
Array	Create an array
Beep	Sounds a tone using the computer's speaker
Call	Transfers control to another procedure
ChDir	Changes the current directory
ChDrive	Changes the current drive
Close	Closes a text file
Const	Declares a constant value
Date	Sets the current sytem date
Declare	Declares a reference to an external procedure in a DLL
Dim	Declare an array locally
Do...Loop	Loop
DoEvents	Lets operating system process events
End	Exits the program
Erase	Reinitialize an array
Err	Sets Err to a specified value

Statement	***Action***
Error	Simulates a specific error condition
Exit Do	Exits a block of Do...Loop code
Exit For	Exits a block of Do...For code
Exit Function	Exits a function procedure
Exit Property	Exits a property procedure
Exit Sub	Exits a subroutine procedure
FileCopy	Copies a file
For Each...Next	Loop
For...Next	Loop
Function	Declares the name and arguments for a Function procedure
Get	Reads data from a text file
GoSub...Return	Branch
GoTo	Branch
If...Then...Else	Processes statements conditionally
Input #	Reads data from a sequential text file
Kill	Deletes a file from disk
Let	Assigns the value of an expression to a variable or property
Line Input #	Reads a line of data from a sequential text file
Lock...Unlock	Controls access to a text file
LSet	Left-aligns a string within a string variable
Mid	Replaces characters in a string with other characters
MkDir	Creates a new directory
Name	Renames a file or directory
On Error	Branch on an error
On...GoSub	Branch on a condition
On...GoTo	Branch on a condition
Open	Opens a text file
Option Base	Changes default lower limit
Option Compare	Declares the default comparison mode when comparing strings
Option Explicit	Forces declaration of all variables in a module

Statement	Action
Option Private	Indicates that an entire module is Private
Print #	Writes data to a sequential file
Private	Declares a local array
Property Get	Declares the name and arguments of a Property Get procedure
Property Let	Declares the name and arguments of a Property Let procedure
Property Set	Declares the name and arguments of a Property Set procedure
Public	Declare a public array
Put	Writes a variable to a text file
Randomize	Initializes the random number generator
ReDim	Changes the dimensions of an array
Rem	Specifies a line of comments (same as an apostrophe)
Reset	Closes all open text files
Resume	Resumes execution when an error-handling routine finishes
RmDir	Removes an empty directory
RSet	Right-aligns a string within a string variable
Seek	Sets the position for the next access in a text file
Select Case	Processes statements conditionally
SendKeys	Sends keystrokes to the active window
Set	Assigns an object reference to a variable or property
SetAttr	Changes attribute information for a file
Static	Change the dimensions of an array, keeping the data intact
Stop	Pauses the program
Sub	Declares the name and arguments of a Sub procedure
Time	Sets the system time
Type	Defines a custom data type
While...Wend	Loop
Width #	Sets the output line width of a text file
With	Sets a series of properties for an object
Write #	Writes data to a sequential text file

Summary of VBA Functions

If an equivalent VBA function is not available, you can use Excel's worksheet functions in your VBA code. Just precede the function with the Application object. For example, VBA does not have a function to convert radians to degrees. Because Excel has a worksheet function for this, however, you can use a VBA statement such as the following:

```
Deg = Application.Degrees(3.14)
```

Function	*Action*
Abs	Returns the absolute value of a number
Array	Returns a variant containing an array
Asc	Converts the first character of string to its ASCII value
Atn	Returns the arctangent of a number
CBool	Converts an expression to boolean
CCur	Converts an expression to currency data type
CDate	Converts an expression to date data type
CDbl	Converts an expression to double data type
Chr	Converts an ANSI value to a string
CInt	Converts an expression to integer data type
CLng	Converts an expression to long data type
Cos	Returns the cosine of a number
CreateObject	Creates an OLE Automation object
CSng	Converts an xpression to single data type
CStr	Converts an expression to string data type
CurDir	Returns the current path
CVar	Converts an expression to variant data type
CVErr	Returns a user-defined error number
Date	Returns the current system date
DateSerial	Converts a date to a serial number
DateValue	Converts a string to date
Day	Returns the day of the month of a date
Dir	Returns the name of a file or directory that matches a pattern
EOF	Returns True if the end of a text file has been reached
Erl	Returns the line number that caused an error
Err	Returns the error number of an error condition

Function	*Action*
Error	Returns the error message the corresponds to an error number
Exp	Returns the base of the natural logarithms (*e*) raised to a power
FileAttr	Returns the file mode for a text file
FileDateTime	Returns the date and time when a file was last modified
FileLen	Returns the number of bytes in a file
Fix	Returns the integer portion of a number
Format	Displays an expression in a particular format
FreeFile	Returns the next available file number when working with text files
GetAttr	Returns a code representing a file attribute
GetObject	Retrieves an OLE Automation object from a file
Hex	Converts from decimal to hexadecimal
Hour	Returns the hour of a time
Input	Returns characters from a sequential text file
InputBox	Displays a box to prompt a user for input
InStr	Returns the position of a string within another string
Int	Returns the integer portion of a number
IsArray	Returns True if a variable is an array
IsDate	Returns True if a variable is a date
IsEmpty	Returns True if a variable has been initialized
IsError	Returns True if an expression is an error value
IsMissing	Returns True if an optional argument was not passed to a procedure
IsNull	Returns True if an expression contains no valid data
IsNumeric	Returns True if an expression can be evaluated as a number
IsObject	Returns True if an expression references an OLE Automation object
LBound	Returns the smallest subscript for a dimension of an array
LCase	Returns a string converted to lower case
Left	Returns a specified number of characters from the left of a string
Len	Returns the number of characters in a string
Loc	Returns the current read or write position of a text file
LOF	Returns the number of bytes in an open text file
Log	Returns the natural logarithm of a number

Function	*Action*
LTrim	Returns a copy of a string with no leading spaces
Mid	Returns a specified number of characters from a string
Minute	Returns the minute of a time
Month	Returns the month of a date
MsgBox	Displays a modal message box
Now	Returns the current system date and time
Oct	Converts from decimal to octal
RGB	Returns a number representing an RGB color value
Right	Returns a specified number of characters from the right of a string
Rnd	Returns a random number between 0 and 1
RTrim	Returns a copy of a string with no trailing spaces
Second	Returns the second of a time
Seek	Returns the current position in a text file
Sgn	Returns an integer that indicates the sign of a number
Shell	Runs an executable program
Sin	Returns the sin of a number
Space	Returns a string with a specified number of spaces
Spc	Positions ouput when printing to a file
SQLBind	Specifies location for results when using the SQLRetrieve function
SQLClose	Closes a connection to an external data source
SQLExecQuery	Executes a query on a data source
SQLGetSchema	Returns information about the structure of a data source
SQLOpen	Establishes a connection to a data source
SQLRequest	Connects to an externa data source and runs a query
SQLRetrieve	Retrieves results from a previously executed query
SQLRetrieveToFile	Places the results from a previously executed query into a file
Sqr	Returns the square root of a number
Str	Returns a string representation of a number
StrComp	Returns a value indicating the result of a string comparison

Function	*Action*
String	Returns a repeating character or string
Tab	Positions ouput when printing to a file
Tan	Returns the tangent of a number
Time	Returns the current system time
Timer	Returns the number of seconds since midnight
TimeSerial	Returns the time for a specified hour, minute and second
TimeValue	Converts a string to a time serial number
TypeName	Returns a string that describes the data type of a variable
UBound	Returns the largest available subscript for a dimension of an array
UCase	Converts a string to upper case
Val	Returns the numbers contained in a string
VarType	Returns a value indicating the subtype of a variable
Weekday	Returns a number representing a day of the week
Year	Returns the year of a date

Appendix E: VBA Error Code Reference

This appendix contains a complete listing of the VBA error codes, along with the error message and an explanation.

Error Code	*Error message*
3	**Return without GoSub** A Return statement was encountered without using a GoSub statement to branch.
5	**Invalid procedure call** This error most often means that an argument exceeded the range of permitted values.
6	**Overflow** A number is too large to be represented within the range allowed for the data type of the variable.
7	**Out of memory** The program needs more memory than is currently available. You may be able to solve this problem by closing any unnecessary applications or documents.
9	**Subscript out of range** You attempted to access an element of an array outside of its current dimensions.
10	**Duplicate definition** You declared a variable twice, or you attempted to use ReDim to change the number of elements in a fixed-size array.

11	**Division by zero** Division by zero is not allowed on this planet.
13	**Type mismatch** VBA encountered the wrong data type for the operation it was attempting to perform. This message also appears if you pass an object to a procedure that expects a single value.
14	**Out of string space** A string cannot exceed 65,535 characters, minus 50 characters used for overhead. Also, this error appears when your system runs out of memory.
16	**String formula too complex** The string expression is too complicated. You can often solve this problem by assigning strings to variables and using the variables in your expression.
17	**Can't perform requested operation** This message most often occurs in Break mode when you attempt to do something that would make the current state of the project invalid.
18	**User interrupt occurred** You pressed Ctrl+Break while VBA was executing.
20	**Resume without error** VBA encountered a Resume statement when an error has not been trapped, or the Resume statement is outside of the error handler code.
28	**Out of stack space** This error can be caused by using too many nested routines (including recursive routines) or too many global variables.

35	**Sub or Function not defined**
	VBA encountered a statement that it didn't recognize. Most likely, it's a spelling mistake or you're trying to call a procedure in another module that was declared Private. This error also occurs if you try to call a procedure in another project without adding a reference to that project in the References dialog.
48	**Error in loading DLL**
	A Dynamic Link Library file can't be loaded. There is either a problem with the DLL, or it can't be located.
49	**Bad DLL calling convention**
	You probably used an incorrect argument when calling a DLL function. The function may expect arguments by value and you omitted the ByVal keyword in the DLL function's declaration.
51	**Internal error**
	This indicates an internal error with VBA. If this error persists, contact Microsoft.
52	**Bad file name or number**
	You specified an invalid filename or tried to use a file number that was not specified in an Open statement (or the file has been closed).
53	**File not found**
	You referred to a file that does not exist or is in a different directory.
54	**Bad file mode**
	You attempted to use a statement that's invalid for the type of text file you're reading or writing. Or, you may be attempting to write to a read-only file.
55	**File already open**
	You tried to open a text file that's already open.

57	**Device I/O error**
	Some type of error occurred with a printer, disk drive, or other I/O device. Correct the problem and try again.
58	**File already exists**
	You attempted to create a new file, but a file with that name already exists. This error also occurs if you use SaveAs and specify the name of an open file.
59	**Bad record length**
	You used a record length in a Get or Put statement that doesn't correspond to the record length specified in the Open statement.
61	**Disk full**
	This error message is fairly self-explanatory.
62	**Input past end of file**
	An Input or Line Input # statement is trying to read past the end of a file.
63	**Bad record number**
	The record number used in a Put or Get statement is less than or equal to zero, which is not allowed.
67	**Too many files**
	You have too many files open at once. The maximum varies and is specified in your CONFIG.SYS file.
68	**Device unavailable**
	You tried to access a device that does not exist or is not currently available.
70	**Permission denied**
	You tried to write to a write-protected disk or to access a locked file.

71	**Disk not ready**
	This occurs with floppy disk drives. Either there is no disk in the drive or the drive door is open.
74	**Can't rename with different drive**
	You tried to rename a file with a new drive designation. Use the FileCopy command to copy the file, then use the Kill command to delete the old file.
75	**Path/File access error**
	You specified an incorrect path in a file specification.
76	**Path not found**
	You specified an incorrect path in a file specification.
91	**Object variable not set**
	You attempted to use an object variable that hasn't been defined, references an invalid object, or has been set to Nothing.
92	**For loop not initialized**
	VBA encountered a Next statement without a corresponding For statement.
93	**Invalid pattern string**
	You used the Like operator and specified an invalid comparison string.
94	**Invalid use of Null**
	You tried to get the value of a Variant variable that is Null (that is, a subtype that indicates the item contains no valid data).
95	**User-defined error**
	This is the message that appears when VBA traps a user-defined error (one with an error code that is not used by VBA).

323	**Can't load module; invalid format** VBA encountered a problem when loading a module.
423	**Property or method not found** An object you referred to does not have the property or method you specified.
424	**Object required** You referred to an object property or method, but did not include a valid object qualifier. This is a fairly common error, so check your reference carefully.
430	**Class does not support OLE Automation** The object you're referring to doesn't expose any objects or doesn't support OLE Automation.
438	**Object doesn't support this property or method** You specified a property or method that doesn't exist for the object. This is often due to a spelling error.
440	**OLE Automation error** You performed an OLE Automation command and it generated an error. The error is reported from the application that created the object.
445	**Object doesn't support this action** You specified an operation that doesn't exist for the object. This is often due to a spelling error.
446	**Object doesn't support named arguments** You used arguments for an object that doesn't take arguments.
447	**Object doesn't support current locale setting** The language setting for the object doesn't match the language you're using.

448	**Named argument not found** You specified an incorrect named argument, or the procedure does not accept arguments.
449	**Argument not optional** You omitted an argument that's required.
450	**Wrong number of arguments** You specified the wrong number of arguments.
451	**Object not a collection** You specified a property for a noncollection object that works only with collections.
452	**Invalid ordinal** This occurs when using an invalid argument to a DLL function.
453	**Specified DLL function not found** The DLL function you specified was not found in the DLL.
1000	**[Object] does not have [property name] property** The property you specified does not exist for this object.
1001	**[Object] does not have [method name] method** The method you specified does not exist for this object.
1002	**Missing required argument [argument]** You omitted a required argument for a method.
1003	**Invalid number of arguments** You called a procedure with the wrong number of arguments.

1004	**[Method name] method of [object] class failed** The method you specified cannot be used on the object. You may be trying to access an object that doesn't exist or using the method in the wrong context.
1005	**Unable to set the [property name] property of the [object] class** VBA cannot change the object's property. You may be using an invalid property value or the property may be read-only.
1006	**Unable to get the [property name] property of the [object] class** VBA cannot get an object's property. You may have selected a nonexistent item in a collection.

Appendix F
ANSI Code Reference

This appendix contains the ANSI codes, the character (if any) they produce, their hex value, binary value, and the keystroke (if any) that generates the code.

ANSI Code	*Character*	*Hex Code*	*Binary Code*	*Keystroke**
1	<None>	&H01	0000 0001	<None>
2	<None>	&H02	0000 0010	<None>
3	<None>	&H03	0000 0011	<None>
4	<None>	&H04	0000 0100	<None>
5	<None>	&H05	0000 0101	<None>
6	<None>	&H06	0000 0110	<None>
7	<None>	&H07	0000 0111	<None>
8	<Backspace>	&H08	0000 1000	Backspace
9	<Tab>	&H09	0000 1001	Tab
10	<Line feed>	&H0A	0000 1010	<None>
11	<None>	&H0B	0000 1011	<None>
12	<None>	&H0C	0000 1100	<None>
13	<Carriage Return>	&H0D	0000 1101	Return
14	<None>	&H0E	0000 1110	<None>
15	<None>	&H0F	0000 1111	<None>
16	<None>	&H10	0001 0000	<None>
17	<None>	&H11	0001 0001	<None>
18	<None>	&H12	0001 0010	<None>

ANSI Code	Character	Hex Code	Binary Code	Keystroke*
19	<None>	&H13	0001 0011	<None>
20	<None>	&H14	0001 0100	<None>
21	<None>	&H15	0001 0101	<None>
22	<None>	&H16	0001 0110	<None>
23	<None>	&H17	0001 0111	<None>
24	<None>	&H18	0001 1000	<None>
25	<None>	&H19	0001 1001	<None>
26	<None>	&H1A	0001 1010	<None>
27	<None>	&H1B	0001 1011	<None>
28	<None>	&H1C	0001 1100	<None>
29	<None>	&H1D	0001 1101	<None>
30	<None>	&H1E	0001 1110	<None>
31	<None>	&H1F	0001 1111	<None>
32	<Space>	&H20	1000 0000	Space
33	!	&H21	1000 0001	!
34	“	&H22	1000 0010	“
35	#	&H23	1000 0011	#
36	$	&H24	1001 0100	$
37	%	&H25	1001 0101	%
38	&	&H26	1001 0110	&
39	'	&H27	1001 0111	'
40	(	&H28	1010 1000	(
41	)	&H29	1010 1001	)
42	*	&H2A	1010 1010	*

ANSI Code	Character	Hex Code	Binary Code	Keystroke*
43	+	&H2B	1010 1011	+
44	,	&H2C	1011 1100	,
45	-	&H2D	1011 1101	-
46	.	&H2E	1011 1110	.
47	/	&H2F	1011 1111	/
48	0	&H30	1100 0000	0
49	1	&H31	1100 0001	1
50	2	&H32	1100 0010	2
51	3	&H33	1100 0011	3
52	4	&H34	1101 0100	4
53	5	&H35	1101 0101	5
54	6	&H36	1101 0110	6
55	7	&H37	1101 0111	7
56	8	&H38	1110 1000	8
57	9	&H39	1110 1001	9
58	:	&H3A	1110 1010	:
59	;	&H3B	1110 1011	;
60	<	&H3C	1111 1100	<
61	=	&H3D	1111 1101	=
62	>	&H3E	1111 1110	>
63	?	&H3F	1111 1111	?
64	@	&H40	1000 0000	@
65	A	&H41	1000 0001	A
66	B	&H42	1000 0010	B

ANSI Code	Character	Hex Code	Binary Code	Keystroke*
67	C	&H43	1000 0011	C
68	D	&H44	1000 0100	D
69	E	&H45	1000 0101	E
70	F	&H46	1000 0110	F
71	G	&H47	1000 0111	G
72	H	&H48	1001 1000	H
73	I	&H49	1001 1001	I
74	J	&H4A	1001 1010	J
75	K	&H4B	1001 1011	K
76	L	&H4C	1001 1100	L
77	M	&H4D	1001 1101	M
78	N	&H4E	1001 1110	N
79	O	&H4F	1001 1111	O
80	P	&H50	1010 0000	P
81	Q	&H51	1010 0001	Q
82	R	&H52	1010 0010	R
83	S	&H53	1010 0011	S
84	T	&H54	1010 0100	T
85	U	&H55	1010 0101	U
86	V	&H56	1010 0110	V
87	W	&H57	1010 0111	W
88	X	&H58	1011 1000	X
89	Y	&H59	1011 1001	Y
90	Z	&H5A	1011 1010	Z

ANSI Code	Character	Hex Code	Binary Code	Keystroke*
91	[	&H5B	1011 1011	[
92	\	&H5C	1011 1100	\
93	]	&H5D	1011 1101	]
94	^	&H5E	1011 1110	^
95	_	&H5F	1011 1111	_
96	‘	&H60	1100 0000	‘
97	a	&H61	1100 0001	a
98	b	&H62	1100 0010	b
99	c	&H63	1100 0011	c
100	d	&H64	1100 0100	d
101	e	&H65	1100 0101	e
102	f	&H66	1100 0110	f
103	g	&H67	1100 0111	g
104	h	&H68	1101 1000	h
105	i	&H69	1101 1001	i
106	j	&H6A	1101 1010	j
107	k	&H6B	1101 1011	k
108	l	&H6C	1101 1100	l
109	m	&H6D	1101 1101	m
110	n	&H6E	1101 1110	n
111	o	&H6F	1101 1111	o
112	p	&H70	1110 0000	p
113	q	&H71	1110 0001	q
114	r	&H72	1110 0010	r

ANSI Code	Character	Hex Code	Binary Code	Keystroke*
115	s	&H73	1110 0011	s
116	t	&H74	1110 0100	t
117	u	&H75	1110 0101	u
118	v	&H76	1110 0110	v
119	w	&H77	1110 0111	w
120	x	&H78	1111 1000	x
121	y	&H79	1111 1001	y
122	z	&H7A	1111 1010	z
123	{	&H7B	1111 1011	{
124	|	&H7C	1111 1100	|
125	}	&H7D	1111 1101	}
126	~	&H7E	1111 1110	~
127		&H7F	1111 1111	Del
128	_	&H80	1000 0000	Alt+0128
129	_	&H81	1000 0001	Alt+0129
130	,	&H82	1000 0010	Alt+0130
131	*f*	&H83	1000 0011	Alt+0131
132	„	&H84	1000 0100	Alt+0132
133	…	&H85	1000 0101	Alt+0133
134	†	&H86	1000 0110	Alt+0134
135	‡	&H87	1000 0111	Alt+0135
136	ˆ	&H88	1000 1000	Alt+0136
137	‰	&H89	1000 1001	Alt+0137
138	_	&H8A	1000 1010	Alt+0138

ANSI Code	Character	Hex Code	Binary Code	Keystroke*
139	‹	&H8B	1000 1011	Alt+0139
140	Œ	&H8C	1000 1100	Alt+0140
141	_	&H8D	1000 1101	Alt+0141
142	_	&H8E	1000 1110	Alt+0142
143	_	&H8F	1000 1111	Alt+0143
144	_	&H90	1001 0000	Alt+0144
145	‘	&H91	1001 0001	Alt+0145
146	’	&H92	1001 0010	Alt+0146
147	“	&H93	1001 0011	Alt+0147
148	”	&H94	1001 0100	Alt+0148
149	•	&H95	1001 0101	Alt+0149
150	–	&H96	1001 0110	Alt+0150
151	—	&H97	1001 0111	Alt+0151
152	˜	&H98	1001 1000	Alt+0152
153	™	&H99	1001 1001	Alt+0153
154	_	&H9A	1001 1010	Alt+0154
155	›	&H9B	1001 1011	Alt+0155
156	œ	&H9C	1001 1100	Alt+0156
157	_	&H9D	1001 1101	Alt+0157
158	_	&H9E	1001 1110	Alt+0158
159	Ÿ	&H9F	1001 1111	Alt+0159
160		&HA0	1010 0000	Alt+0160
161	¡	&HA1	1010 0001	Alt+0161
162	¢	&HA2	1010 0010	Alt+0162

ANSI Code	Character	Hex Code	Binary Code	Keystroke*
163	£	&HA3	1010 0011	Alt+0163
164	¤	&HA4	1010 0100	Alt+0164
165	¥	&HA5	1010 0101	Alt+0165
166	¦	&HA6	1010 0110	Alt+0166
167	§	&HA7	1010 0111	Alt+0167
168	¨	&HA8	1010 1000	Alt+0168
169	©	&HA9	1010 1001	Alt+0169
170	ª	&HAA	1010 1010	Alt+0170
171	«	&HAB	1010 1011	Alt+0171
172	¬	&HAC	1010 1100	Alt+0172
173	–	&HAD	1010 1101	Alt+0173
174	®	&HAE	1010 1110	Alt+0174
175	¯	&HAF	1010 1111	Alt+0175
176	°	&HB0	1011 0000	Alt+0176
177	±	&HB1	1011 0001	Alt+0177
178	2	&HB2	1011 0010	Alt+0178
179	3	&HB3	1011 0011	Alt+0179
180	´	&HB4	1011 0100	Alt+0180
181	µ	&HB5	1011 0101	Alt+0181
182	¶	&HB6	1011 0110	Alt+0182
183	·	&HB7	1011 0111	Alt+0183
184	¸	&HB8	1011 1000	Alt+0184
185	1	&HB9	1011 1001	Alt+0185
186	º	&HBA	1011 1010	Alt+0186

ANSI Code	Character	Hex Code	Binary Code	Keystroke*
187	»	&HBB	1011 1011	Alt+0187
188	_	&HBC	1011 1100	Alt+0188
189	_	&HBD	1011 1101	Alt+0189
190	_	&HBE	1011 1110	Alt+0190
191	¿	&HBF	1011 1111	Alt+0191
192	À	&HC0	1100 0000	Alt+0192
193	Á	&HC1	1100 0001	Alt+0193
194	Â	&HC2	1100 0010	Alt+0194
195	Ã	&HC3	1100 0011	Alt+0195
196	Ä	&HC4	1100 0100	Alt+0196
197	Å	&HC5	1100 0101	Alt+0197
198	Æ	&HC6	1100 0110	Alt+0198
199	Ç	&HC7	1100 0111	Alt+0199
200	È	&HC8	1100 1000	Alt+0200
201	É	&HC9	1100 1001	Alt+0201
202	Ê	&HCA	1100 1010	Alt+0202
203	Ë	&HCB	1100 1011	Alt+0203
204	Ì	&HCC	1100 1100	Alt+0204
205	Í	&HCD	1100 1101	Alt+0205
206	Î	&HCE	1100 1110	Alt+0206
207	Ï	&HCF	1100 1111	Alt+0207
208	_	&HD0	1101 0000	Alt+0208
209	Ñ	&HD1	1101 0001	Alt+0209
210	Ò	&HD2	1101 0010	Alt+0210

ANSI Code	Character	Hex Code	Binary Code	Keystroke*
211	Ó	&HD3	1101 0011	Alt+0211
212	Ô	&HD4	1101 0100	Alt+0212
213	Õ	&HD5	1101 0101	Alt+0213
214	Ö	&HD6	1101 0110	Alt+0214
215	x	&HD7	1101 0111	Alt+0215
216	Ø	&HD8	1101 1000	Alt+0216
217	Ù	&HD9	1101 1001	Alt+0217
218	Ú	&HDA	1101 1010	Alt+0218
219	Û	&HDB	1101 1011	Alt+0219
220	Ü	&HDC	1101 1100	Alt+0220
221	Y	&HDD	1101 1101	Alt+0221
222	_	&HDE	1101 1110	Alt+0222
223	ß	&HDF	1101 1111	Alt+0223
224	à	&HE0	1110 0000	Alt+0224
225	á	&HE1	1110 0001	Alt+0225
226	â	&HE2	1110 0010	Alt+0226
227	ã	&HE3	1110 0011	Alt+0227
228	ä	&HE4	1110 0100	Alt+0228
229	å	&HE5	1110 0101	Alt+0229
230	æ	&HE6	1110 0110	Alt+0230
231	ç	&HE7	1110 0111	Alt+0231
232	è	&HE8	1110 1000	Alt+0232
233	é	&HE9	1110 1001	Alt+0233
234	ê	&HEA	1110 1010	Alt+0234

ANSI Code	Character	Hex Code	Binary Code	Keystroke*
235	ë	&HEB	1110 1011	Alt+0235
236	ì	&HEC	1110 1100	Alt+0236
237	í	&HED	1110 1101	Alt+0237
238	î	&HEE	1110 1110	Alt+0238
239	ï	&HEF	1110 1111	Alt+0239
240		&HF0	1111 0000	Alt+0240
241	ñ	&HF1	1111 0001	Alt+0241
242	ò	&HF2	1111 0010	Alt+0242
243	ó	&HF3	1111 0011	Alt+0243
244	ô	&HF4	1111 0100	Alt+0244
245	õ	&HF5	1111 0101	Alt+0245
246	ö	&HF6	1111 0110	Alt+0246
247	÷	&HF7	1111 0111	Alt+0247
248	ø	&HF8	1111 1000	Alt+0248
249	ù	&HF9	1111 1001	Alt+0249
250	ú	&HFA	1111 1010	Alt+0250
251	û	&HFB	1111 1011	Alt+0251
252	ü	&HFC	1111 1100	Alt+0252
253	y	&HFD	1111 1101	Alt+0253
254	_	&HFE	1111 1110	Alt+0254
255	ÿ	&HFF	1111 1111	Alt+0255

* For keystrokes that use the Alt key, use the numeric keypad with NumLock on.

Index

Symbols

A

B

E

F

I

J

K

L

M

N

Q

R

S

U

Y

Z

IDG BOOKS

Order Form

Order Center: (800) 762-2974 (8 a.m.-5 p.m., PST, weekdays) or (415) 312-0650

For Fastest Service: Photocopy This Order Form and FAX it to: (415) 358-1260

Quantity	ISBN	Title	Price	Total

Shipping & Handling Charges

Subtotal	U.S.	Canada & International	International Air Mail
Up to $20.00	Add $3.00	Add $4.00	Add $10.00
$20.01-40.00	$4.00	$5.00	$20.00
$40.01-60.00	$5.00	$6.00	$25.00
$60.01-80.00	$6.00	$8.00	$35.00
Over $80.00	$7.00	$10.00	$50.00

In U.S. and Canada, shipping is UPS ground or equivalent.
For Rush shipping call (800) 762-2974.

Subtotal __________

CA residents add applicable sales tax __________

IN and MA residents add 5% sales tax __________

IL residents add 6.25% sales tax __________

RI residents add 7% sales tax __________

Shipping __________

Total __________

Ship to:

Name ____________________

Company ____________________

Address ____________________

City/State/Zip ____________________

Daytime Phone ____________________

Payment: ❑ Check to IDG Books (US Funds Only) ❑ Visa ❑ Mastercard ❑ American Express

Card# ________________ Exp.________ Signature________________

Please send this order form to: IDG Books, 155 Bovet Road, Suite 310, San Mateo, CA 94402.

Allow up to 3 weeks for delivery. Thank you!

IDG BOOKS WORLDWIDE LICENSE AGREEMENT

Important — read carefully before opening the software packet. This is a legal agreement between you (either an individual or an entity) and IDG Books Worldwide, Inc. (IDG). By opening the accompanying sealed packet containing the software disk, you acknowledge that you have read and accept the following IDG License Agreement. If you do not agree and do not want to be bound by the terms of this Agreement, promptly return the book and the unopened software packet to the place you obtained them for a full refund.

1. License. This License Agreement (Agreement) permits you to use one copy of the enclosed Software program(s) on a single computer. The Software is in "use" on a computer when it is loaded into temporary memory (i.e., RAM) or installed into permanent memory (e.g., hard disk, CD ROM, or other storage device) of that computer.

2. Copyright. The entire contents of this disk and the compilation of the Software are copyrighted and protected by both United States copyright laws and international treaty provisions. The individual programs on the disk are copyrighted by the authors of each program respectively. Each program has its own use permissions and limitations. You may only (a) make one copy of the Software for backup or archival purposes, or (b) transfer the Software to a single hard disk, provided that you keep the original for backup or archival purposes. To use each program, you must follow the individual requirements and restrictions detailed for each throughout this Book. Do not use a program if you do not want to follow its Licensing Agreement. None of the material on this disk(s) or listed in this Book may ever be distributed, in original or modified form, for commercial purposes.

3. Other Restrictions. You may not rent or lease the Software. You may transfer the Software and user documentation on a permanent basis provided you retain no copies and the recipient agrees to the terms of this Agreement. You may not reverse engineer, decompile, or disassemble the Software except to the extent that the foregoing restriction is expressly prohibited by applicable law. If the Software is an update or has been updated, any transfer must include the most recent update and all prior versions.

4. Limited Warranty. IDG Warrants that the Software and disk are free from defects in materials and workmanship for a period of sixty (60) days from the date of purchase of this Book. If IDG receives notification within the warranty period of defects in material or workmanship, IDG will replace the defective disk. IDG's entire liability and your exclusive remedy shall be limited to replacement of the Software, which is returned to IDG with a copy of your receipt. This Limited Warranty is void if failure of the Software has resulted from accident, abuse, or misapplication. Any replacement Software will be warranted for the remainder of the original warranty period or thirty (30) days, whichever is longer.

5. No Other Warranties. To the maximum extent permitted by applicable law, IDG and the author disclaim all other warranties, express or implied, including but not limited to implied warranties of merchantability and fitness for a particular purpose, with respect to the Software, the programs, the source code contained therein and/or the techniques described in this Book. This limited warranty gives you specific legal rights. You may have others which vary from state/jurisdiction to state/jurisdiction.

6. No Liability For Consequential Damages. To the extent permitted by applicable law, in no event shall IDG or the author be liable for any damages whatsoever (including without limitation, damages for loss of business profits, business interruption, loss of business information, or any other pecuniary loss) arising out of the use of or inability to use the Book or the Software, even if IDG has been advised of the possibility of such damages. Because some states/jurisdictions do not allow the exclusion or limitation of liability for consequential or incidental damages, the above limitation may not apply to you.

5 1/4", 1.2MB Disk Format Available.

The enclosed disks are in 3 1/2" 1.44MB, high-density format. If you have a different size drive, or a low-density drive, and you cannot arrange to transfer the data to the disk size you need, you can obtain the programs on 5 1/4" 1.2MB high-density disks by writing: IDG Books Worldwide, Attn: *Title of Book,* IDG Books Worldwide, 155 Bovet Rd., Suite 310, San Mateo, CA 94402, or call 800-762-2974. Please specify the size of disk you need, and please allow 3 to 4 weeks for delivery.

About the Companion Disk

The companion disk has more than two megabytes of sample files. The files on the disk are compressed, and must be expanded before you can use them. The files are installed *directly from Excel,* using an add-in (SETUP.XLA).

To install the files:

1. Start Windows.
2. Start Excel 5.
3. Insert the disk in drive A or B, whichever is appropriate for your machine.
4. Choose the File⇨Open command from Excel's menu.
5. Enter **A:SETUP** or **B:SETUP** and press Enter.
6. Follow the instructions on the screen.

By default, SETUP creates a directory named XL5PPT (a subdirectory of your EXCEL directory), plus several subdirectories that correspond to the chapters in the book (\CH06, \CH08, etc.). The files are described next.

Directory	*File*	*Description*
CH06	RECTANGL.XLS	Demonstrates various properties of Rectangle objects
CH08	SHTSORT.XLS	A procedure that sorts the sheets in a workbook
CH09	KEYBOARD.XLS	An object library to read and change keyboard states
CH09	MYSUM.XLS	A custom function that mimics Excel's SUM function
CH09	SYSCOLOR.XLS	An object library that lets you change system colors
CH10	DBOXDEMO.XLS	Various dialog box techniques
CH10	NAMESEX.XLS	Transferring information from a dialog box to a worksheet
CH11	DEMO_01.XLS	Demonstrates how to select to the end of a range
CH11	DEMO_02.XLS	Enters an AVERAGE formula (similar to AutoSum)
CH11	DEMO_03.XLS	Manipulates cells in a selection selectively
CH11	DEMO_04.XLS	Deletes all empty rows in the selection
CH11	DEMO_05.XLS	Two methods to fill a range with values
CH11	DEMO_06.XLS	Displays details about the selected range
CH11	DEMO_07.XLS	Toggles the wrap text property for selected cells
CH11	DEMO_08.XLS	Displays the date and time
CH11	DEMO_09.XLS	Demonstrates three array sorting techniques
CH11	DEMO_10.XLS	Displays information about the selection
CH11	DEMO_11.XLS	Processes a group of files
CH11	DEMO_12.XLS	Creates a dialog box on the fly
CH11	DEMO_13.XLS	Determines the Windows directory
CH11	DEMO_14.XLS	Determines the version of Windows and DOS
CH11	DEMO_15.XLS	Displays all of the directories in the DOS path
CH11	DEMO_16.XLS	Displays information about the active printer
CH11	DEMO_17.XLS	Displays the video resolution
CH11	DEMO_18.XLS	Displays free system resources
CH11	DEMO_19.XLS	Determines if Alt, Ctrl, or Shift is pressed
CH11	DEMO_20.XLS	Reads and writes to an INI file
CH11	DEMO_21.XLS	Plays WAV files
CH11	DEMO_22.XLS	Prevents the user from exiting Excel
CH11	DEMO_23.XLS	Opens a DOS window
CH11	DEMO_24.XLS	Starts Solitaire and sends keystrokes
CH11	DEMO_25.XLS	Starts or activates Minesweeper
CH11	TEXT01.TXT	Text file used with DEMO_11.XLS
CH11	TEXT02.TXT	Text file used with DEMO_11.XLS
CH11	TEXT03.TXT	Text file used with DEMO_11.XLS
CH12	TEXTOOLS.HLP	Windows Help file for TEXTOOLS.XLS
CH12	TEXTOOLS.HPJ	Project file for TEXTOOLS.HLP
CH12	TEXTOOLS.RTF	Source document for TEXTOOLS.HLP
CH12	TEXTOOLS.XLS	Custom utility to manipulate text incells
CH13	AIPROMPT.XLA	Add-in version of AIPROMPT.XLS

Directory	File	Description
CH13	AIPROMPT.XLS	Prompts to unload add-ins before exiting (add-in)
CH14	GRIDTOGL.XLS	Toggles grid display using custom menu item
CH14	MENUDEMO.XLS	Demonstrates how to access Excel's menus
CH14	MENUSHEN.XLS	Modifies worksheet menus in some strange ways
CH15	TBARTOOL.XLS	A custom utility to work with toolbars
CH15	TOOLFACE.XLS	Contains 100 custom toolbutton faces
CH16	BUBLWIZ.HLP	Help for the bubble chart utility in Windows HLP format
CH16	BUBLWIZ.WRI	Help for the bubble chart utility in Windows Write format
CH16	BUBLWIZ.XLS	A custom utliity to create bubble charts
CH16	HELPBOOK.XLS	A workbook that displays help information
CH16	HLPDEMO1.XLS	Demonstrates methods to display user help
CH16	HLPDEMO2.HLP	Windows Help file displayed by HLPDEMO2.XLS
CH16	HLPDEMO2.HPJ	Project file for HLPDEMO2.HLP
CH16	HLPDEMO2.RTF	Source document for HLPDEMO2.HLP
CH16	HLPDEMO2.XLS	Workbook that displays HLPDEMO2.HLP
CH16	SAMPLE.HLP	A sample Windows help file
CH16	SAMPLE.HPJ	Project file for SAMPLE.HLP
CH16	SAMPLE.RTF	Source document for SAMPLE.HLP
CH17	DDE_DEMO.XLS	Demonstrates DDE using Program Manager
CH17	ODBCDEMO.XLS	Contains ODBC database queries
CH17	OLEAUTO.XLS	Demonstrates OLE Automation with Word for Windows
CH17	PRESDENT.DBF	Simple databsae used by ODBCDEMO.XLS
CH17	SALESREP.DOC	Word for Windows document used by WORD_DDE.XLS
CH17	SNDKEYS.XLS	Demonstrates SendKeys using Cardfile
CH17	WORD_DDE.XLS	DDE example that uses SALESREP.DOC
CH18	QUIZADM.HLP	Help for Administrator mode of QuizMaster
CH18	QUIZADM.HPJ	Project file for QUIZADM.HLP
CH18	QUIZADM.RTF	Source document for QUIZADM.HLP
CH18	QUIZMSTR.XLS	Sample application that creates on-line quizzes
CH18	QUIZSAMP.XLS	Sample quizzes created with QUIZMSTR.XLS
CH18	QUIZUSR.HLP	Help for User mode of QuizMaster
CH18	QUIZUSR.HPJ	Project file for QUIZUSR.HLP
CH18	QUIZUSR.RTF	Source document for QUIZUSR.HLP
CH18	SETUP.XLS	Source document for SETUP.XLA